Our Common Denominator

Our Common Denominator
Human Universals Revisited

Christoph Antweiler

Translated by Diane Kerns

Published by
Berghahn Books
www.berghahnbooks.com

English-language edition
@ 2016, 2018 Berghahn Books
First paperback edition published in 2018

German-language edition
© 2009 Wissenschaftliche Buchgesellschaft
Was ist den Menschen gemeinsam? Über Kultur und Kulturen, 2nd edition,
by WBG (Wissenschaftliche Buchgesellschaft), Darmstadt, Germany.

All rights reserved. Except for the quotation of short passages
for the purposes of criticism and review, no part of this book
may be reproduced in any form or by any means, electronic or
mechanical, including photocopying, recording, or any information
storage and retrieval system now known or to be invented,
without written permission of the publisher.

Library of Congress Cataloging-in-Publication Data

Names: Antweiler, Christoph, author.
Title: Our common denominator : human universals revisited / Christoph Antweiler ; translated by Diane Kerns.
Other titles: Was ist den Menschen gemeinsam? English
Description: New York : Berghahn Books, 2016. | Includes bibliographical references and index.
Identifiers: LCCN 2015041496 (print) | LCCN 2016005009 (ebook) | ISBN 9781785330933 (hardback : alk. paper) | ISBN 9781785338243 (paperback : alk. paper) | ISBN 9781785330940 (ebook)
Subjects: LCSH: Universals (Philosophy) | Anthropology—Philosophy. | Civilization—History.
Classification: LCC B105.U5 A5813 2016 (print) | LCC B105.U5 (ebook) | DDC 301.01—dc23
LC record available at hkp://lccn.loc.gov/2015041496

British Library Cataloguing in Publication Data

A catalogue record for this book is available from the British Library

ISBN 978-1-78533-093-3 (hardback)
ISBN 978-1-78533-824-3 (paperback)
ISBN 978-1-78533-094-0 (ebook)

for Maria, Dario, and Craig

Contents

List of Figures	viii
List of Tables	ix
Preface	xi
Introduction	1
Chapter 1. Humankind: Current Societal Debates	11
Chapter 2. A World of Cultures: Their Differences and Likenesses	27
Chapter 3. Cultures and Human Nature: Human Beings Are Biologically Cultural	65
Chapter 4. Universals: Examples from Several Realms	97
Chapter 5. Methods: Deduction, Case Studies, and Comparison	157
Chapter 6. Taxonomy: The Forms, Levels, and Depth of Universals	193
Chapter 7. Toward Explanation: Why Do Universals Exist?	211
Chapter 8. Critical Positions: Arguments against Universalism	243
Chapter 9. Synthesis: Human Universals and the Human Sciences	253
Bibliography	265
Index	338

List of Figures

Figure 0. Garbage collectors in Mumbai, India.
Photo by Maria Blechmann-Antweiler. xiv

Figure 1. Rickshaw puller in Makassar, Indonesia.
Photo by Maria Blechmann-Antweiler. 10

Figure 2. A pharmacy in Yangon, Myanmar.
Photo by Maria Blechmann-Antweiler. 26

Figure 3. Vegetable vendor in Kuala Lumpur, Malaysia.
Photo by Maria Blechmann-Antweiler. 64

Figure 4. Young German in Queens, New York, US.
Photo by Maria Blechmann-Antweiler. 96

Figure 5. Graffiti artist in New York, US.
Photo by Maria Blechmann-Antweiler. 156

Figure 6. Banana transport in Kottayam, India.
Photo by Maria Blechmann-Antweiler. 192

Figure 7. Electrical engineer in Hong Kong, China.
Photo by Maria Blechmann-Antweiler. 210

Figure 8. Building worker in Madurai, India.
Photo by Maria Blechmann-Antweiler. 242

Figure 9. Traveling in South Asia.
Photo by Maria Blechmann-Antweiler. 252

Figure 10. A German woman selects postcards.
Photo by Maria Blechmann-Antweiler. 264

List of Tables

Table 2.1. Terms containing the word "universals" found in well-established dictionaries and textbooks for anthropology and cultural anthropology as well as further selected works 40

Table 2.2. Prevalence of the topic "universals" on the Internet in 2002 and 2014 43

Table 2.3. Deficit models from the nineteenth century: Non-Western societies characterized by traits or features that they are supposedly lacking 49

Table 3.1. Relationship between universality and diversity as seen from antiquity, and the early to late modern era 69

Table 3.2. "Human nature": Examples of different conceptual interpretations 83

Table 3.3. Organic basis of specific human characteristics 90

Table 3.4. The relative nature of human uniqueness, based on empirical traits of individuals and populations 92

Table 3.5. Shared traits among individuals and societies, with great intercultural and/or interpersonal variability 94

Table 3.6. Specific human characteristics 94

Table 4.1. Features of local knowledge as universal mode of knowledge 136

Table 5.1. Extrapolating cross-cultural definitions through the example of marriage 168

Table 5.2. Features (traits) that, contrary to Western notions, are not universal	172
Table 5.3. Universals according to findings from social psychology	173
Table 5.4. Two fundamental dimensions of cultural variation	184
Table 5.5. Synchronic and diachronic cultural comparison in relation to universal concepts of varying breadth	186
Table 6.1. Critique of isomorphism 1: Missing parallels between ontics and epistemics, i.e., methodology	205
Table 6.2. Critique of isomorphism 2: Missing parallels between ontic and political positions	206
Table 6.3. Critique of isomorphism 3: Missing parallels between ontics and perspectives relating to diversity	206
Table 6.4. Independent dimensions that are inaccurately discussed as isomorphic in cultural analysis (simplified polarized representation of continua)	208
Table 6.5. Locating universal research with regard to constructivist approaches among cultural theorists and (in parentheses) anthropologists	208
Table 7.1. Faulty assumptions and causal reasoning found in research on universals	212
Table 7.2. A look at more immediate and distant explanations, using incest as an example	224
Table 9.1. Factors limiting the potential diversity in "ethnographic hyperspace" to realized or actual diversity	254
Table 9.2. Basic orientations found in the human sciences: Universal approach vs. absolutism and relativism	262

Preface

This book is something of a deviance. Cultural anthropologists are, in general, extremely reluctant to acknowledge universal features in cultures, and with good reason. Most anthropologists are cultural anthropologists, and cultural anthropology is about diversity. In no way do I dismiss the reality of human diversity. However, I support re-examining anthropological theory in favor of looking at pancultural similarities.

Fundamental propositions on what it is to be human are examined in work coming out of the life sciences today. And yet at the same time we hear broad criticism of any focus that derives solely from the standpoint of human biology alone. We need contributions that offer a thorough and authentically conceived biocultural understanding of human culture. As far as academic or general nonfiction is concerned, little work is being done on such a broad level, apart from contributions characterized by ideological viewpoints. Even though this book aims to offer a scientific contribution to the topic, political questions and concerns nevertheless arise. Figuratively speaking, the question presented here is how we can discuss or approach the human world in its entirety less as a globe, with an emphasis on differences, and more as a planet, from a vantage point open to commonalities.

This book had a long gestation period as its ideas developed out of my background as a cultural anthropologist with an interest in evolutionary sciences. The book was originally written for German readers; this text is a severely revised, shortened version of the second German edition. This version contains recent discussions up to 2015. The two German editions generated a good deal of interest from both the academic world and the media. More and more people appear dissatisfied with the notion that culture should be seen primarily as representing differences among people, with identities only spelled out in the plural form. The public debate on globalization is another site of general demand for scientific contributions that empirically explore the unity of humankind.

I would like to offer general thanks to the anonymous reviewers for Berghahn Books and several reviewers of the two German editions of this book. Among the numerous colleagues with whom I enjoyed long discussions on the topic of universals, I want especially to thank Elmar Holenstein (Yokohama) and Peter Hejl (Bonn). I am grateful also to several research groups and collaborative research projects financed by the German Research Society (Deutsche Forschungsgemeinschaft), which gave me the opportunity to present my research. Thanks also go to the Apfelbaum Foundation in Cologne, which funded feedback questionnaires on the German editions. This translation by Diane Kerns was made possible by the financial support of the Volkswagen Foundation within the framework of the initiative Deutsch plus—Wissenschaft ist mehrsprachig (German Plus: Science Is Multilingual) and its goal of "translating outstanding German-language scientific work in another international language" (Volkswagenstiftung 2014). I was honored to have my work thus recognized and am grateful to the Volkswagen Foundation for making the publication of this English-language version possible. The topics discussed here are and have been intensely discussed in the English-speaking world, as the bibliography – covering literature up to 2016 – clearly indicates. German and French quotations have been translated.

Cologne, Germany
January 2016

Christoph Antweiler

Figure 0. Garbage collectors in Mumbai, India. Photo by Maria Blechmann-Antweiler.

Introduction

> *Whether it admits it or not, anthropology aims to be a universal science.*
> —Maurice Godelier, "'Mirror, Mirror on the Wall ...'"

In a Nutshell

Journalists often ask writers to summarize their books in a sentence or two. Considering the broad scope of this book, I will allow myself three: Despite the incredible diversity existing among and within human cultures, there are many phenomena that occur regularly in all known societies. These commonalities, or universals, while deriving in part from human nature, may also have specific social, cultural, and systemic sources. We need to develop a working understanding of these universals so that we might advance legitimate, empirically based human science set on creating knowledge that is politically relevant to fostering real solutions to the problems that complicate human coexistence in the Age of the Anthropocene.

Universals in a World of Diversity and the "Ethnographic Dazzle"

Human universals (hereafter referred as simply "universals") should not be understood as the counterpart to diversity in human societies. Throughout the twentieth century and up to (though somewhat less) today, the emphasis has been on difference. Our respect for pluralism, our celebration of difference, and our concern for identity politics are all hallmarks of a progressive, modern democracy (Malik 2014). In an increasingly globalized world of melding and interacting cultures, the need to respect difference is of course fully legitimate. From the viewpoint of an anthropologist, the strength of ethnography lies in showing the richness and variations of cultures. Universals become truly interesting when we see them as a pattern set in the context of the diversity of human existence in biocultural terms (see Sobo 2013 for an overview). Godelier's observation that anthropology is universal is to be understood in two ways: one, it is a science; and two, no society is excluded from analysis, since anthropology aims to discover phenomena and mechanisms present in all societies (Godelier 1994: 97). Anthropology can help reduce the problem of focusing on Western, educated, industrial, rich, democratic (i.e., WEIRD) people, a severe problem that has pervaded fields such as psychology and economic research all along (Henrich, Heine, and Norenzayan 2010; Norenzayan 2013: 52–54, 166–68).

Research on universals offers an especially dynamic and useful tool for understanding our so-called human nature. It enables us to find a middle ground between speculative approaches and wishful thinking, on the one hand, and the nontheoretical collecting and sorting of assumed similarities, on the other. What interests me is finding a nonmetaphysical approach to the question of what is human. "The grand theory of universals is that in combination they constitute building blocks or armature of the human condition; subsets of them are equally building blocks and armature of human nature" (D. Brown 2013: 411). My basic credo here is that what is human is not simply a matter of nature or of culture, and that culture, or the definition of culture, cannot be limited to an intellectual or mental construct but must also be based on an inherent social component. This book is meant to contribute to an anthropology that identifies the smallest common working denominator in the dialogue between all the fields that explore or study human beings. Anthropology is here formulated as the "question concerning the possibilities within being human, and the limitations of the humanly possible" (Hauschild 2005: 61). Thus conceived, research into universals can contribute to an all-encompassing human science, and yet more fully to an empirically based but theory-driven anthropology understood as the science or the study of the human being in his or her entirety.

My belief is that our fascination with the complexity of cultural variants has overshadowed our ability to see the commonalities between cultures. I speak from my own experience. I am interested in exploring human universals, but at the same time am impressed as always by the diversity and complexity among and between individuals within the kaleidoscope of human cultures. This book calls on scholars to be more explicit in our images of human beings, to create these images based on empirical research and to employ the approaches used in the many fields of study that explore universals. This does not mean simply casting ourselves or other human beings or cultures in the role of what could be the general or average type among us. My point here is rather that the social sciences and humanities of today have become too focused on the specific particularities of individual cultures or subcultures. Cultural differences, which are often easy to establish, tend to blind us to less obvious similarities. Fox (2014: 7, 17, 176) properly described our fascination with differences as "ethnographic dazzle." Those who maintain an ultra-relativistic focus on cultural differences distance themselves all too easily from the universals that do in fact exist for all human cultures.

Universals, Humanism, and Anthropology

Scientists carry out research on certain phenomena not only for the sake of knowledge, but also with much broader intellectual interests in mind. They are motivated to explore nonscientific impulses as well, which could eventually lead them to draw certain problematic conclusions—and the topic of universals is already filled with such conclusions. Upon finding likenesses or common features among cultures, we might then purposely extrapolate further commonalities out of these original likenesses (Welsch 2006: 122; 2012). Herein lies the danger of hoping we see certain universals without taking the time to prove their existence. For political purposes, the notion of humanity as a cosmopolitan community can be an enticing concept. An example of this involves the current interest in German politics for development strategies invoking the belief of "one world," an idea that proves effective as a base of action grounded in humanistic ethics and global responsibility. In light of the concern about cultural fragmentation and the problem of rapid globalization, the search for universals in constructing arguments against xenophobia and racism is perfectly understandable. In a globally changing ideological climate dominated by individualism and competition, critics of globalization are often driven by a strong desire to prove that contrary norms or motives are in fact universal. Accordingly, what we end up hoping to find in the search for universals are the human attitudes or characteristics deemed more positive for people and for cultures, such as sociality or altruism.

Cultural anthropology became a field of study in the mid-nineteenth century. In the scientific-historical perspective, the field is rooted in the Enlightenment and the essential question of a nontheological explanation for the diversity found in cultures. Cultural anthropology today also focuses on the complexity of human cultures. As always, work in cultural anthropology concentrates primarily on the unique characteristics of cultures and cultural diversity. In view of the wide speculation on universals found today in many fields of study and in the popular media, cultural anthropology is able to offer a critical and empirical perspective on the topic and examine assumptions made about universals by researchers schooled in methods of cross-cultural comparison.

In the German-speaking world from the nineteenth century up to World War II, certain prominent figures in cultural anthropology, such as Adolf Bastian (1881, 1895; also see Chevron 2004) and Wilhelm E. Mühlmann (e.g.,

1962, 1966), were dedicated to the study of universals. Today only a few anthropologists deal with universals in their work. They include Andreas Bruck, Thomas Hauschild, Hans-Jürgen Hildebrandt, Jürgen Jensen, Klaus E. Müller, Joachim W. Raum, Wolfgang Rudolph, Justin Stagl, and Peter Tschohl. The few more current studies on the topic touch upon universals in large part as a critique on the extreme forms of cultural relativism. I know of only one large cultural anthropology research project concerning universals in continental Europe: an Austrian project entitled "Human Universals and Cultural History," directed by Karl R. Wernhart and Marie-France Chevron (Chevron and Wernhart 2000–2001; Chevron 2004: esp. 398–422).

The characterizing aspects of classical anthropology are a focus on cultural specifics and a methodological approach based on case studies, with an essentializing of differences. The focus not only characterizes cultural anthropology in the German-speaking world; it also shapes the image of the field worldwide, a fact complicating a broadly based study like the one presented here. Ethnographers have often demonstrated an interest in universals and cultural comparison, which is well suited for the pursuit of identifying universals and has always been a pillar of the discipline. In day-to-day operations, though, researchers in the field concentrate on particularized research questions that are examined according to a "microscopic" methodological approach. The particularized view includes—though some do not freely admit to it—the search for general patterns as well, since anthropologists are primarily interested in patterns and regularities, even at the level of individual societies (K. Fox 2014: 9–10). The descriptions of specific cultures are implicitly comparative, indirectly addressing universals in that they explain the ways of life of certain "other" (foreign) cultures to the members of another, mostly Western, culture (Peacock 2001: 96).

The focus on particulars and on cultural differences shapes how the field is perceived in general. The media and popular culture portray cultural anthropology as chiefly concerned with the foreign, the strange and the exotic (Antweiler 2005a: 46–52; Schönhuth 2005: 83–88). This is also how other cultural and social sciences perceive the field. Business, the media, and politics borrow theories and research from cultural anthropology but do so almost exclusively to emphasize differences among cultures. This perception results from the general acceptance of cultures as representing separate entities or clearly delimited 'containers'. Although differences are not the entire focus of the cultural sciences, they are at present the leading global 'currency' in the thinking on culture. Fearing the homogenizing power of global society and the steady disappearance of cultural diversity, academics, politicians, and media personalities have directed their searching gaze toward boundaries and differences within cultures. The now prevalent term 'intercultural', with its implicit assumption of a relationship between clearly separate units, signals the re-emergence of problematic thinking that sees cultures as separate spheres, units, or containers. This way of thinking has been partially overcome in cultural studies, but only partially, as these fields also thrive on presenting extreme points of view (for a critical response, see van der Walt 2006; Welsch 2006: 123, 2012; but also see Griese 2008, 2014).

Universals and Interdisciplinary Cooperation

Interdisciplinary work is not a mere hopeful stab at universality but rather a platform based on pure necessity. Anthropology alone cannot sufficiently tackle the topic of universals. Case in point: to address the topic, I needed to explore various fields of scientific study and ways of thinking, an undertaking that of course takes some time. I also needed to acquaint myself with older and even remote published sources. Apart from my other ongoing projects, preparation of this book took ten years. I turned to contributions from the humanities, the cultural and social sciences, and the natural sciences—hence the long reference section included at the end of this book. For me, many of the more important or inspiring authors are not cultural anthropologists. These include Scott Atran (psychology), Pascal Boyer (philosophy of religion), Wolfgang Welsch (philosophy), Carl Degler and Jörn Rüsen (history), Ellen Dissanayake (prehistory), Elmar Holenstein (linguistics, philosophy), Bruno Latour (sociology), Peter J. Richerson (ecology) and Frans de Waal (primatology). Considering the scope of the topic, I found it difficult not to end up feeling like somewhat of a dabbler. I was trained as a cultural anthropologist, but I also have a background in natural history. Based on my own experience, and with respect to a broad spectrum of disciplines, I chose to focus on knowledge and findings from the social and cultural sciences, as well as on diverse approaches originating from those human sciences inspired by the work of Charles Darwin.

Goals and Limitations

I assume that universals cannot simply be deciphered by way of some kind of public opinion poll of the world's peoples (Geertz 1965: 102). My work here is a general synthesis of empirical data drawn from within a consistent theoretical framework. With this book, I want to provide a systematic overview of the topic of cultural universals. Apart from work coming out of the field of linguistics, very few monographs are available on the topic. Relevant here is a book by the anthropologist Donald Edward Brown, the most recent monograph on the subject (D. Brown 1991; see Lehmann 1994). Internationally a few collected volumes have appeared, while in the German-speaking world, a few papers and the edited volumes of Neil Roughley (2000), Peter Hejl (2001) and Beat Sitter-Liver (2009) represent the sum of the work dedicated to the topic.

I believe that cultural anthropology can offer a special contribution to the topic through its essentially cautious approach to universals. Having been schooled in cultural relativism, anthropologists have a fundamentally contextualist and comparative perspective. They will almost always regard universal claims with a skeptical eye. In a book on universals, this approach helps me keep a critical distance from any hastily formed postulates on universals. I am bringing universality and diversity together instead of playing them off each other. For this purpose, I am using, among other materials, the results of research on universals that was carried out in the field of linguistics in the 1960s and only marginally appreciated in cultural anthropology and the other cultural sciences at that time. A rather radical but discussion-worthy argument arising from this research claims that differences within societies and diversity between societies are in type, degree, function, and effect the same (Holenstein 1998d: 326; Cappai 2007: 96). The intracultural complexity within a culture is therefore analogous to the intercultural variability within humanity (Holenstein 2013). With this in mind, the research into universals will make a contribution to the question of the boundaries between cultures and to models concerning cultural diversity (Antweiler 2012c).

With regard to cultural studies and especially anthropology, I would like to rehabilitate research into universals. Universals are both constraining and generative (D. Brown 2013: 411). With this in mind, the work presented here should do three things. First, it should complement and update Brown's monograph and his systematic presentation. Furthermore, my discussion on the factors that cause universals should amend Brown's slant toward evolutionary psychology by pointing out other possible causes of pancultural phenomena or patterns. For these purposes I turn to German and English sources and, to a lesser extent, older works and some contributions from the French-speaking world. Second, it addresses the criticism of research into universals. Fundamental criticism, or rather the critical stances that deny the existence of universals, claim they are trivial, or assume they would be constructed merely by equalization will all be part of the discussion that follows. Authors who strictly reject generalized science and especially any talk of human nature will be considered as well. These critical voices have arisen from a postmodern, post-structuralist or postcolonialist worldview. And third, this book summarizes the new and unfortunately far-flung results of research into universals since the 1990s.

Even a broad approach faces certain limitations. I decided to refrain from outlining the complicated trajectories in the historical development of scientific interest in universals within the Western history of ideas (on this Antweiler 2012a: ch. 3 and 4; 2012b: ch. 2). This decision means the book does not discuss universal concepts within great non-Western traditions like those of Confucius, Mencius, Lao-tse, Chuang-tse, or the Vedas, Upanishads, and Shankar. In these traditions it is common to find universal ideas presented logically, tied to economic notions and framed within political concepts (Jullien 2014). The history of universal thinking is an important yet complicated research topic, as it involves many scientific disciplines and philosophical schools of thought. To explore the topic fully would require another book. The book in your hands follows a systematic approach. I am not only interested in posing difficult questions and issues, but in answering them as well:

- How do we understand the sentence "All cultures are alike" without facing logical and empirical inconsistencies?
- How do we identify universals more precisely without falling (even unintentionally) into the Eurocentric or ethnocentric trap?
- Which universals can be postulated without producing trivial similarities?
- How do pancultural patterns become empirically established, and which of the postulated universals bear up to empirical evidence?
- How do we explain universals? Of all possible explanations available, which tend to be contradictory or complementary of each other?
- Why do some phenomena, such as vegetarianism, polygamy, or public sexual intercourse, remain rare as cultural behavior while others, such as food taboos and animal sacrifice, are surprisingly common?
- What is the relationship between universality and cultural diversity?
- Do universals have methodical value in explaining intracultural and intercultural change?
- How are universals relevant to the humanities and social sciences?
- What specific research contribution can a theoretically driven, empirical anthropology make to the many disciplines in which studying universals would be relevant?

The Intended Reader and Chapter Outline

The book addresses, first off, researchers and academics from all fields interested in developing an interdisciplinary perspective on the topic of universals. It is also intended for people involved in making decisions or setting policy in the public domain, or anyone else who would like to gain a general overview of the topic. I am interested in establishing a tie between diverse fields of study that need an understanding of universals but rely on their own separate forms of technical jargon to communicate about the topic. With a broad readership in mind, I have avoided using copious footnotes and have instead created an extensive reference section of cited works cutting across a broad range of topics and including original works as well as general summaries.

With the historical discourse and current debates in mind, Chapter 1 discusses why the likenesses that occur between cultures are at once fascinating and controversial. Since the universal statements being made in the world today are never in short supply, there is an increased premium on developing techniques that give greater empirical confidence to claims of universality. Chapter 2 presents the key terms of the discussion on universals while demonstrating how polysemous the word "universal" is. I expand the discussion by introducing central concepts and elucidating the topic's importance for cultural studies and social sciences. One of the main points here is that the search for commonalities in human cultures and the study of particular societies are interdependent. Chapter 3 includes, as a theoretical basis, a basic portrayal of the relationship between cultures and so-called human nature. It also describes the question of human beings' unique status using the most current theoretical insights and empirical findings. A central point in this chapter is that universals, contrary to broadly held assumptions, are not the same as natural or inherent human attributes. Whereas human nature is reflected within every individual, universals refer to the level of cultures as collective units. Chapter 4 provides an overview of a selection of specific universals within the context of chosen topic areas. Here the importance of ethnographic reporting becomes quite clear, as do the limitations involved in verifying the existence of universals. Chapter 5 elaborates on the methodological approaches used when universals are postulated, recognized, and examined on a cross-cultural comparative level. It also discusses the possibility of culturally independent concepts and the problems that accompany the presentation of lists of universals, a classical approach to their study. Alternative ways of describing commonalities, such as involving narrative and more holistic approaches, are presented here.

Turning the general idea of universals into working propositions for empirical comparative research requires that we describe them precisely, classify them, and expand the very notion of universals. Chapter 6 clarifies the diversity in types and variants of universals, and Chapter 7 presents possibilities for explaining universals. It is made clear that there exist only a few explanations of why universals occur, and that the biological nature of human beings, though important, is only one such explanation. Chapter 8 provides an overview of moderate to fundamental criticisms of the study of universals. Moderate critics see the search for common patterns as futile or misguided and are critical of comparative approaches. These critiques most often refer to Clifford Geertz's detracting remarks. A more vehement criticism sees the search for universals as an outcome of Eurocentrism, Western arrogance, or imperialism. The chapter demonstrates that radical critiques most often take severe misrepresentations of twentieth-century anthropology as their point of departure. Chapter 9 summarizes the important points made throughout the discussion to show that the problem of cross-cultural similarities and a comparative approach are at the core of the anthropological enterprise. The extensive bibliography that follows mainly includes titles from English- and German-speaking academia going back to the mid-twentieth century and extending to recent research till 2016.

Figure 1. Rickshaw puller in Makassar, Indonesia. Photo by Maria Blechmann-Antweiler.

CHAPTER 1

Humankind
Current Societal Debates

> *Universals and norms are not the same things.*
> —Karl Eibl, *Animal Poeta*

My initial approach to the topic of universals will consider certain sociopolitical debates and the varying realms in which cultural universals may function. We are all aware of universal statements in daily conversation or in the mass media, starting with phrases such as "in every human culture there is …" or "people in all cultures want …" or people all over the world feel that …" or "people everywhere are x, y and z" or "we're just one big family." Such generalizing views are common in both radio reports in newspaper articles. A book on the cultural history of noodles is entitled *Universal Food* (Serventi and Sabban 2002). Politicians well versed in universal rhetoric refer to fundamental or age-old human characteristics. Kofi Annan, in his Nobel Lecture of 10 December 2001, described people the world over within the context of a common humanity as well as in terms of individual suffering (Annan 2002: 21).

Universal Postulates Everywhere!

Universal statements are supposedly all-encompassing truths about individuals as well as entire societies or cultures. Often we talk of human beings with reference to all humans, or to all of humanity or humankind without differentiating between individuals and cultures. Generalizing claims have been made throughout the last 2,000 years of history. Plato claimed that all of humanity, Greeks and non-Greeks alike, believe in the existence of gods. A blurb appearing on a book published by the Wissenschaftliche Buchgesellschaft contained the following remark: "Rituals allow us to cope with critical and social situations alike. They occur in the most elaborate of ways in all cultures and time periods" (Ambos et al. 2005).

It appears that being interested in human nature, and particularly in the tension between universal notions and cultural specifics, is in fact itself a universal. Interest in the topic tends to grow in periods marked by cultural contact, or hybridity. When interviewed, social or cultural scientists are often asked questions such as "What is more pronounced, the differences among people or the common denominator that ties people together despite all the different cultural influences?" (Wiegand 1999: 42). We find the expression of universal statements especially common in mass media interviews of prominent figures or academics, for example, a psychologist discussing the topic of casting shows: "Question: Is the desire to become famous a basic human need? Answer: No. We shouldn't forget that there are millions of young people who would rather cut off their hand than make a fool out of themselves for one second. The desire for care and attention is, though, an anthropological constant" (Ernst and Ottenschläger 2003: 142).

Academic texts rarely hold such explicit universal statements as the one in the following quote from Pinker's bestseller on universals at the individual level: "The evidence suggests that humans everywhere on the planet see, talk, and think about objects and people in the same basic way" (Pinker 1997: 34). Assumptions about cultural universals, though not always so striking, are found throughout academic texts in and outside the field of cultural anthropology. Wolfgang Marschall comments relatively clearly that "the search for identity is an important part of human activity" (Marschall 1990a: 8). More often we find universal statements made implicitly in textbooks on cultural anthropology, psychology, or economics as to the essence, nature, or defining attributes of human beings. Universal statements about anthropological topics are found quite often in popularized forms of cultural anthropology, such as ethnographic museums or television shows. In a brochure of the new Rautenstrauch-Joest Museum for Ethnography in Cologne (from 2005), we read the following: "The human issues that move people across the globe, though dealt with in different ways based on regional and cultural influences, are the basic foundations for the new facility at Neumarkt in the heart of the city" (Gesellschaft für Völkerkunde zur Förderung des Rautenstrauch-Joest-Museums n.y.: 3).

Universals can be very general or very specific. The more general they are, the more obvious, trivial, or banal they appear. More specific universals may be surprising but are often deemed too speculative or even dubious. We see this in the incest taboo and the Oedipus complex, two of the more broadly known examples of possible universals. Sigmund Freud described a concept of the male child as caught between father and mother in universal terms. Malinowski questioned this idea in cultural anthropology, pointing out that among the matrilineal Tobrianders, the biological father is neither a person of authority for the male children nor a sexual rival in the fight for the mother

(Malinowski 1924: 256–58). The Oedipus complex appears, according to more current findings, to be practically universal. However, very different phenomena are understood here with respect to both terms. Contrary definitions often play a decisive role in whether or not we categorize a phenomenon as universal. Vague or implicitly understood definitions are a notorious problem for research into universals.

Universals become more interesting the farther removed they are from elementary physiological facts, such as metabolism or simple sensory functions. But even a shared biology does not make the situation simple (Schiefenhövel 1999: 1). Almost everyone would agree with the statement that human beings want to survive and that they have sexual impulses. But in many cultures it is "normal" that certain persons or groups of people practice celibacy. Also, there have been and still are people who consciously and willingly accept death by starvation. Universals that appear obvious in effect lead to the long-term survival of human beings, a species that depends on organized social ties for that survival. Universals tied to social networks include those associated with tools, physical or bodily protection, communication systems, and cooperation in the search for food and in methods for rearing children. Less obvious are those universals not associated with individuals' immediate survival. These include division of labor, restrictions on sexual relations between certain categories of family members, organized ways of sharing food resources and exchanging goods, belief in supernatural forces, rites of passage, and the existence of sport (Peoples and Bailey 2015: 43; Herzog-Schröder 2001).

When human beings see themselves as separate individuals going about their daily lives, then they are quick to notice, especially in their own faces, the incredible differences—but not the similarities—in and among human beings. Even when entire cultures are compared, the differences between them are what we end up seeing, as is currently communicated worldwide in public debate on the topic of cultural comparisons. Commonalities between cultures are emphasized only after their differences are cited as central in the comparison, or when similarities are initially denied. The perception of relative differences depends strongly on the level of comparison. When people do not place themselves or their cultures in comparison with other people or cultures, but rather with animals or animal populations, then the perceived differences between human groups disappear almost completely from view. Likenesses pertaining to the biological factors of the human condition take precedence, and the emphasis is on separating humans from their closest biological relatives among the higher primates (Lewontin 1986: 1–2). The human condition (*Conditio Humana*) can also easily turn into a kind of naturalistic mysticism. The desire for positive universals, as mentioned earlier in the preface, appears almost harmless. But such a desire includes certain problems seen in the world of visual popular culture.

Popular Universality in Visual Media: "The Family of Man"

In recent years, the number of works focusing on visual documentation of human diversity has risen steadily (e.g., Ommer 2000; Lonely Planet 2005; Winston 2004; Komatsu and Komatsu 2006). At first glance these books present all the different varieties of people with their diverse ways of life. But they also refer indirectly to universal themes occurring among human beings and common problems facing all cultures. Similar projects with an educational bent have been initiated (Cleveland, Craven, and Danfelser 1979) and can currently be found via the Internet (Payne and Gray 1997). Over ten years ago, the Geosphere Project supported by UNESCO put together a CD-ROM presenting data taken from questionnaires answered by thirty "randomly selected" families from across the entire world (see Wenker 2001; Menzel and Aluisio 2004, 2005).

The classic forerunner to these initiatives remains the extremely successful photo exhibition entitled *The Family of Man*, conceived by the curator Edward Steichen for the Museum of Modern Art in New York. Presented in connection with the Universal Declaration of Human Rights in 1948, the exhibit held 503 black-and-white images by 273 amateur and professional photographers from 68 countries around the world. Using photography as a universal language, the show was divided into twenty-four image categories representing universal human themes and problems such as play, work, birth, disease, aging, and death. Steichen wanted to create a mirror into the world of the human species (Steichen 1955). Complementing the pictures were selected quotations with a timeless quality about them, for example proverbs or sayings from the Old Testament. Each image category was placed in its own room (for details, see Philipp 1987; J. Schmidt 1996). From 1955 to 1961 *The Family of Man* toured sixty-seven countries as a traveling exhibition in the form of "travelling editions." It was an amazing success, presenting humanity as a unifying concept in the midst of the Cold War. The things that divide human beings appeared as a superficial layer over a common substance. The combination of diversity and unity among human beings in their behaviour and emotions fascinated a public of millions. That was still the case when the restored exhibition was shown again in many countries around the world, including Japan. In a time of cultural upheaval, this same fascination, combined with a humanistic form of Utopia, is present in more recent exhibitions and books.

Wishful thinking, sentimentality, an implicit political agenda, or a hidden religious ideal might be found lurking within such presentations of humanity. The exhibit was entitled "All of Us" (Wir alle) in Berlin and "The Large Family of Man" (La Grande Familie des Hommes) in Paris. In his *Mythologies*, Roland Barthes (2013: 101) criticized the exhibit during its time in Paris as moralizing, sentimentalizing, and pseudo-religious. He claimed that the images first dramatized the differences among people through skin color and customs in a form of "babelising," only to then extract human unity out of this plurality by way of magic. In 1994 the exhibition, which the U.S. government had already given to Luxembourg as a present in 1964, found a permanent home in Luxembourg's Palace Clerveaux in a restored form. Most of the contributions for an anniversary publication (Back and Bauret 1994) in honor of the exhibit paid homage to Steichen (though with a few exceptions; see Segalen 1994). Meanwhile, the work and the exhibition led to intense discussion that expanded on themes introduced by Barthes (J. Schmidt 1996; Back and Schmidt-Linsenhoff 2004; see Kissler 2000). Both the unintentional emphasis on physical differences and the universalizing texts accompanying the images were criticized. The monumental expression of brotherhood was seen as adamantly denying every possible type of social difference. Finally, it was seen as an instrument of U.S. imperialism at the time of the Cold War. The exhibition not only masked social inequality and related problems but also avoided the topic of the Jewish Shoah. Many people criticized the patriarchal undercurrents of the "human family" and the so-called typical American family as a indirectly implied ideal representation of family in the exhibit. Others accused it of presenting a not-so-subtle didactic. The exhibition was also criticized for its form, which was considered a precursor to consumer-oriented depictions, similar to Benetton's United Colours advertising campaign.

The exhibition drew on the so-called "we are one" feeling (During 2005: 86) presented, for example, in the framework of the Olympic games, the soccer World Cup, global charity events, and companies such as Benetton. But a closer look at the Benetton advertisement campaign reveals completely different concepts of what we might mean by cultural diversity. On seeing the Family of Man exhibit, one may notice that many of the critics' concerns were justified but at times exaggerated. The term "family of man" is a good example here, being both problematic and full of potential, as Gernot Böhme has claimed. Family as metaphor does not necessarily imply something Christian, Jewish or patriarchal; nor does it have to be simply comforting or sentimental. This metaphor can also be understood within its historical or phylogenetic context. Seeing the individual as belonging within humanity in general in terms of family or kinship produces a particular form of solidarity and unity. "Man is a human being, because he descends from humans" (Böhme 1999: 26). As such, humanity could be defined through relationships or from within contexts, conceived by extension with allowances for diversity. In contrast, defining humanity by localizing specific human features would not likely permit room for diversity. An understanding of humanity through the metaphor of family could also be useful in the debate on the universal dimensions of worldwide cultural diversity. This implies that we are dealing with one aspect of many universal statements, or simply the pursuit of the universal.

Normative Universalism

Human Rights and Civil Society

Universals are often postulated in political and religious contexts with an emphasis on furthering intercultural understanding. Commonalities could help forge ties between cultures (for possibilities and limitations, see Pohl 1999: 28–29). The problems associated with the public treatment of universality are readily seen in current discussions on human rights, ecology, democracy, and political and medical ethics. With increasing regularity since the mid-1990s, general statements on human beings or human societies have been made with reference to the goal of forging a new world culture in the sense of global solidarity for peace or sustained development (Brieskorn 1997; Müller and Reder 2003; Argyrou 2005; Jörke 2005: 99–108), or have concerned democracy and the ideals imbedded in human rights (Berg-Schlosser 1997; Derichs 1998). These discussions often reflect an image of humanity as the cosmopolitan community of interests described in the anthropology of the Greek Stoics or the work of Cicero (Gladigow 2004: 74). Dieter Weiss (2000: 133), in a journal for development politics, wrote: "An increasingly interdependent global society could be barely functional without the creation of an elementary, worldwide consensual basis that calls for respecting the vast richness of cultural diversity."

Through intensive debate, and despite numerous differences, human rights are now understood within a certain pragmatic consensus, and with specific normative tendencies. A constant but as yet unanswered question in the discussions on the topic concerns if and when the goals of these rights can be based on the existence of empirically substantiated universals. The human rights charter of the United Nations (UN) from 1948 contains explicit wording on universal human rights: every single individual is worthy of human dignity. Accordingly, these rights fulfill the fundamental characteristics of universality, as Tönnies (2001: 15) explains: "Universality follows the rule 'quod semper, quod ubique, quod omnibus,' which means forever valid, for everyone everywhere, and therefore rests on the assumption that human beings, from a certain vantage point, are all 'equal.'" According to one argument, human rights arise from the assumption of a universal human form for both suffering and happiness. The philosopher Johannes Müller (2002: 51–52) offers a clear example of this when describing human suffering and the capability of human sympathy as the basis for societal development: the experience of human suffering is direct and immediate, closely connected with the physical state of being human. All people share in this in some way. The feelings produced by suffering are projected in much the same form everywhere, such as in our facial expressions when we experience physical pain.

Meanwhile, others vehemently oppose the idea of allowing assumed universal human characteristics to be incorporated into the debate on human rights. Many authors view universal human rights as something diffuse. They find the thesis of a supposedly universal ideal concerning human rights to lack a solid empirical basis in data. According to François Lyotard (1987), points of reference to universality are absent in non-Western cultures. Lyotard's contention is that the values associated with universality exist only in Western or Western-oriented societies. Critically understood, the universal postulate of human rights is seen by many as something tending toward the idealistic, ideological, progressive, Western, Eurocentric, or ethnocentric. This criticism is based on a general suspicion that all forms of universality arise out of particular interests, and therefore out of a form of particularism. Such universality, then, is a questionable form of hegemony. The supposed universal is in fact a particularistic bourgeois ideal stemming from the European eighteenth century or Western individualism or the so-called American way of life (Wallerstein 2007: xiii, 1–35). Supporting this position is the fact that certain humanistic movements under the "Universal" banner have often excluded certain categories of people from "universal rights," such as those with darker skin or women (Davies 2007: 26, 167). Even the progressively understood term "tolerant universality," coined by the abolitionist Abbot Grégoire during the French Revolution, was used to uphold the ideas behind conquest and colonialism (Goldstein-Sepinwall 2005).

The critique of universal human rights also has a tradition in the field of cultural anthropology. After the initial euphoria in support of human rights and the UN, leading anthropologists of the time, such as Claude Lévi-Strauss, abandoned the human rights movement (American Anthropological Association 1947) because they understood human rights as related to cultural communities and not to universally based individual rights of protection and self-defense (Hauschild 2004: 124–25). The moral horizons of many non-European cultures are radically particularistic and self-focused, something ignored in the concept of human rights. Examples like the caste system in India, marriages of young girls in the Arab world, or extreme forms of punishment among Australian Aborigines would demonstrate that the values incorporated in the notion of human rights are not, in the strict sense, universal. They do not comply with the concepts of justice found in different cultures, let alone among most people on the planet (Wimmer 1997: 124). However, these opposing viewpoints—like the arguments in favor of human rights—are rarely backed by empirical data (see Renteln 1988, 1990; Wuketits 2003).

The thinking behind human rights is in fact the brainchild of Western intellectual history, which projects the idea of human equality before God and the guiding notion of the universal Christian mission. Both ideas were taken up in the European and American Enlightenment, secularized by political liberalism, and radicalized in the nineteenth century (Wimmer 1997: 124). Western theories understanding human rights as rights of the individual before the state were deeply influenced by the Judeo-Christian value system. The inalienable freedom of the individual rests solidly at the core of the Declaration of Universal Human Rights from 1948 (Graf 2004: 211–13). With the Cold War and the period of decolonization, consensus on human rights began to erode. The first objections came from the then communist countries, where social rights and individual responsibility with respect to the community received more legal emphasis. The new countries in the developing world also understood human rights beyond the level of the individual, focusing more on "community," "the people," or "the nation" as the primary platforms for human rights. Community ties, social responsibility, and the well-being of the "people" in both Islamic and Chinese thought represent a concept different from the individualism and human rights in Western societies. The universality of human rights is open for debate. A general uncertainty reigns over the status of occidental rationalism. In Jürgen Habermas's (2005) recent characterization, "the image of the norm for the future is the exception for all other cultures". As Terkessidis (1998: 229) concludes, "it no longer is the case, as in the time of colonial expansion, of the universalizing of particular European cultures, but rather the particularizing of Western universality."

Relative Universalism, Negotiated Universals, and Multiple Modernities

Cultural differences, typically presented as intercultural contrasts in the discussion on human rights, are in fact intracultural as well (Holenstein 1985b: 142). Failure to acknowledge this represents a general methodological mistake, for example in Roland Barthes's (2013) orientalizing representation of the differences between the Japanese and Europeans. The human rights debate is often described as a conflict between cultures or "clash of civilizations." Yet there is neither a unified Islamic nor a universal Western, let alone simple Christian, position here. Only in the 1960s did the Catholic and the Protestant churches go from rejecting to accepting human rights. Now as before, there is great opposition to the classical liberal understanding of human rights and individual rights of self-defense. Christianity does not share a particularly historical or political affinity for the modern notion of human rights based on individualism. Therefore, the discussion cannot be described simply as a conflict between cultures (Graf 2004: 216–17). In general, Western philosophy and legal theory have both been marked by bitter disputes as to the nature of individual rights. This is also the case for other cultures. Formally declared rights stand in direct conflict with traditions and pure injustice. According to Elmar Holenstein, the differences in legal ideals and philosophical ideas can lead to the following assumption: "What varies from culture to culture are not rights per se, or at least not the most fundamental of rights, but rather the weight placed on specific rights within specific conflicts" (Holenstein 1985b: 117).

The general agreement concerning the universal quality of certain basic values stands in constant contrast to the many justifications or grounds on which these values are interpreted (Maier 1997; Hoppe 1998: 32–34). Accordingly, the current consensus at the level of the UN is mostly pragmatic: universal human rights should be demanded (from governments and societies), but the reasoning behind these rights should not be narrowly defined. Instead of searching for specific universal values as the smallest common denominator, the most current discussions stand more for the universalizing of human rights, that is, rights that originated in Northwestern Europe but should be spread throughout the world in such a way as to make them more attractive (Bracht 1994: 109–10). A "relative universalism," in the sense of what Jack Donnelly (2005) described, ties basic consensus over human rights to plurality in the societal conception of these rights. "What should hold true for everyone can be justified by each person in his own way and thus made acceptable within the group as a whole" (Graf 2004: 222). This position fits well within the debate on alternative modernities, or multiple modernities (Eisenstadt 2006), in which universal values on the one hand, and different stages of development as well as plurality on the other, are equally valued. Universals are not conceived as universalized Western values based on a universal rationale but rather as negotiated universals that can be accepted in varying cultures for various reasons, based on different levels of reasoning (Kocka 2002: 124; Riedel 2002: 277; Lepenies 2003).

A "deliberative universalism" offers us the possibility of saying that in multicultural societies, resolution of some conflicts—for example, those concerning human genetics—cannot happen through trust in reason or in decisions made by the majority but occurs rather through the tolerance or respect we show for other positions (Gutmann 1995: 296–304). General ideas on values and rights, such as those expressed in Christian social ethics, might make intercultural dialogue possible as a kind of communication interface (Hoppe 1998: 29–31). Particularized religious or ethical frameworks and different metaphorical perceptions could be seen in an interactive relationship with the prospect of universal claims. This means leaving already existing cultural norms in place. Universalizing refers to the act of accepting of human rights as conventions rather than as universals (Bracht 1994: 111). A somewhat similar position, represented in the work of the political philosopher Seyla Benhabib, refers back to Kant. She ties individual human rights to the national right of self-determination and argues that cosmopolitan norms in democratic systems are finding their way into law all over the world. Moral universalism could well be joined to the principle of a federal institutionalized (or legal) cosmopolitanism (Benhabib 2008). This alleviates any suspicion that a new kind of Western imperialism has developed, an imperialism packaging "human rights" with cultural values. Specific cultural explanations and metaphors used to legitimize human rights would thus contribute to the goal of fostering human rights throughout the world. The perimeters of such compromises are set through a normative core of suprapositive (transcendental) rights derived from the nature of human beings for the sake of the individual in relation to the general good and general well-being of all human beings.

The Expanding Scope of Universalization and the Problematic Limits of Humanity

The expansion of human rights has meant that the "anthropocentric universalizing radius" has extended to new frontiers. First off, the individual rights spelled out in the human rights convention of 1948 have broadened into the so-called human rights of the second and third generation, expanding into new categories and collectives, such as those regarding women, children, and indigenous groups. This has led to discussion of the relationship between human rights and the rights of minorities (Bielefeldt 2004: 32). Do universal (or general) human rights stand in structural conflict to (more specifically) minority rights? Alain Finkielkraut, for example, objects to a multicultural focus on the special needs of very specific groups. What he sees at work here is the problematic legacy of Johann Gottfried Herder: endless circling levels of experience, a pageant of narcissism and provincialism with no commonality possible, and humankind in danger of falling into the trap of pluralism. He therefore calls for human rights to be based on a universalism of human rights (Finkielkraut 1989: 19). The opposing cultural position focuses on the idea of individual uniqueness. Charles Taylor believes in recognizing not only our humanness but also our individuality in interpreting universals. The right to be different, according to Taylor, cannot be limited to individuals, since their security or well-being is in many ways dependent upon collective entities (Taylor 1997; see Honneth 1992; Honneth and Joas 1980; Schiffauer 1997: 144). This position on human rights as the right to be different is problematic in that it is practically impossible to combine it with a rationale for universal norms (Apel 1995: 15–16).

Even more complicated questions arise from the varied and vast expansion of rights currently under debate in the fields of moral and legal philosophy as well as ecology and environmental ethics. With the expansion of the universalizing radius, the anthropocentric boundary has been crossed (see v. d. Pfordten 1996: 16; Rolston 1999), and the legal obligations and equal status of non-human beings are subjects of intense discussion. The higher primates, such as the chimpanzee and the orangutan, are a case in point due to their cognitive abilities and capacity to endure suffering. This stance in opposition to a human-oriented speciesism is a problematic position. First, it appears impossible to place humans and nonhumans in the same moral category without at the same time excluding certain human beings, such as the unborn or extremely mentally challenged persons, who might, in theory but not de facto, be able to speak (Hull 1998). Secondly, the universality, or the indivisibility, of human rights would be lifted, transforming rights into privileges (Fernández-Armesto 2005: 137). Within these debates, the basic question arises of whether *Homo sapiens* represents a coherent moral category, a point that has been denied at times by many cultures throughout history.

The debate on human rights is only one area in which questions of universality are of practical and political concern. Claims of universality are often the expression of a universal, generally idealistic way of thinking. This is seen quite clearly in the work of the International Society for Universalism, founded in 1989 in Warsaw (see contributions in Claessens and Mackensen 1992). The debate on universalism further occurs in the area of biopolitics (Fukuyama 2002: 184–251). The twentieth century will best be described as a time in which the human being became a living creature capable of becoming optimized. There were many attempts at an "anthropology in the gerund" (Bröckling 2004: 188). As the twenty-first century proceeds, the possibilities offered by biopolitics and especially by anthropolitics will become increasingly more real. The civilizing process re-addresses old questions through new possibilities and new global dangers: "What is a human being, and above all who is a human being, can now be newly debated thanks to cloning, cyborgs and supposedly intelligent computers" (Bröckling 2004: 174). New technologies force us to re-examine certain uncomfortable questions regarding what it means to be human. Fernández-Armesto (2005: 155) comes to the uneasy conclusion that "… we do not know what humankind means; we do not know what it is that makes us human; so naturally, we will not be aware [of losing it]."

Arguments that search for universals with anti-relativistic and prescriptive intentions are found today in the current debate in medical ethics (Macklin 1999), in environmental ethics, and in the discussion concerning the communitarian social model (Matjan 1995). A central point here is that human beings as organisms are simply part of the living world, and that the biosphere is the basis of all human life. One established consensus in this debate is that human beings need to be protected from the abuses that can occur in medical practice (Kather 2008: 56). Universalistic assumptions are used in debates as a positive kind of anthropocentrism in order to establish what is proper and responsible in ecological practice. Anthropocentrism represents not dominating but acting responsibility for and in the natural world. Nature includes also human groups that are facing increasing changes through the rise of biotechnology.

Universal Religion, Utopias, and a New Cosmopolitanism

As social and personal fragmentation and instability characterize the shape of the modern world, so do universalism and the search for a unified image of humanity belong to the idea of the modern, at least according to current cultural theory. Tension between these two poles marks the literary works that fit the modern archetype. In *Ulysses,* James Joyce describes the fragmented conscious self in a nonrealistic narrative form, but he does so within the myth of Ulysses, a story that characterizes a universalistic image of human beings (Barker 2012: 190-1, 318-9). Images of humanity are often discussed not only as representations of the essence of what it is to be human in social contexts, but also as normative models of human existence—"models of humanity." Many universalistic theories from the fields of sociology and psychology, which are presented as purely scientific, include not only descriptive and interpretive features but also unspoken or unexpressed normative touches. The use of insufficiently examined and ideologically tainted concepts is a continually lurking danger in description or discussion of human beings (Kapp 1983: 144; Rippe 1999: 11–14). Only a few authors explicitly state that they follow the developments of research into universals with the goal of conveying particular values. An example of this would be Raoul Naroll and his concept of "sociometrics." Within his cultural comparative approach, he speaks in favor of the universal right of individual and cultural autonomy and diversity (Naroll 1983: 27–33, 48; see also Corning 2011).

The inherent danger of mixing ideals and realistic descriptions in certain images or ideas of humanity is clear in Johan Georg Adam Forster's (1754–1794) idea of progress leading to a "universal knowledge of the human race" (Heintze 1990: 77–78). We find more recent examples of normative and utopian elements in the otherwise scientifically based theories of Piaget, Kohlberg, Parsons, and Inkeles, as they express implicit goals or objectives (Schöfthaler 1983: 338; see also Sieferle 1989). Normative universal ideas are also apparent in models for ritual constitutionalism or for intercultural interpretative communities, as in Apel's "transcendental universal grammar" and Habermas's "communicative competence" (see Masson 1980: 135–36; Jörke 2005: 73–87, 127–31). Pinker concludes that surprising similarities exist even in languages with the least in common. He does so with a statement that demonstrates nicely, in the choice of words and examples, how aesthetic as well as normative aspects come into play in the research on universals: "To see these deep parallels in the languages of the French and the Germans, the Arabs and the Israelis, the East and the West, people living in the Age of the Internet and people living in the Stone Age, is to catch a glimpse of the psychic unity of mankind" (Pinker 1999: 239).

A normative and universalistic focus has often been a matter of concern outside of science and law, for instance in fields associated with art, language, and religion. It is especially pronounced within theology and the study of religion, and mainly with regard to hierophany, and how the appearance of the "holy" or how the objects considered "holy" might be perceived. Earlier generations of experts in the field of religious studies, under the influence of

Rudolf Otto's a priori theory, had considered it self-evident that the idea or existence of things "holy" is universal (Colpe 1997: 1). Today people in the field tend to be more careful about how they speak of religion, limiting their discussion to religions from the Mediterranean area (Colpe 1997: 12). Currently discussed issues involve globally shared religious experiences and a possible transcendental pragmatism. Attempts to create an interfaith dialogue have included discussions about the possibility of simply bearing witness to religious experiences between religions (Schaeffler 2005: 212–18). In religion, art, and language, the topic of universals often has an especially intense normative aspect to it, with a practical, programmatic, or even utopian direction. An example would be Joseph Campbell's book comparing mythologies throughout (mostly the Western) world, which even today remains popular with writers and screenwriters alike. Campbell specifically expressed his nonscientific motivation in searching for shared truths among all belief systems as a way of building cross-cultural understanding (Campbell 1953: 8).

The fundamental problems and questions pertaining to our identity as both cultural beings and creatures controlled by nature seem relevant in all societies. Religious traditions often point to a mystical unity between human beings and the natural world (e.g., Tooten 2002). The more important beliefs are ubiquitous throughout history. The great world religions only seem to systematize the same questions that arise in all forms of belief, for example, via monism and monotheism (Ohlig 2012: 229–30, 256–57; see Voland and Schiefenhövel 2009). The idea of transcultural norms has existed for some time within the Islamic concept of the *umma* (Bennison 2002: 61). Since the nineteenth century, explicitly universal religious movements have aimed to find common ground in all religions. The point here is that despite differences in religious persuasion, common unity can be found, for example, in making mysticism or transcendental experiences between all people somehow accessible under certain conditions (Figl 1993: 146–48). One area through which a common identity is sought or even artificially created is language. Examples would be in the ecstasy of the Kabbulah, in the grammar of Dante, the use of Esperanto (Eco 2002), or attempts since the seventeenth century to overcome the scattered babel of languages by establishing communication through gestures or signs that represents an international body language.

Even the work of anthropologists often holds a normative understanding of universals, sometimes explicitly laid out. In a contribution entitled "Universals in Cultures" (not *of* cultures!), written for an encyclopedia of anthropology, Xanthopoulos defines universals as the cumulative artistic and intellectual achievements of humanity. He considers the topic of universals to be especially significant at the beginning of the twenty-first century, a time when the concept of human may need redefining, and he emphasizes that such universals do not emerge simply through the sum of great works of art but rather through the "global experience" of appreciating these works of art (Xanthopoulos 2006: 2244). With this in mind, he mixes and combines descriptive aspects of the human community with regard to myths, or visions of what should or could be, for example in our ideas concerning love.

Recently, universal ideas have penetrated revived discussions on the concept of the "world citizen," newly contrived under the term cosmopolitanism (e.g., Appiah 2007: 122–27). Cosmopolitan ideas are found, as mentioned above, in various schools of thought and traditions, such as among the Stoics, Rabindranath Tagore, Sri Aurobindo, Martha Nussbaum, Amartya Sen, and Ananta Kumar Giri. Their work is united under the common theme that all human beings belong to one world (see Antweiler 2012b: 61–83). After the experience of global warfare and environmental crises, one fact stands out: that all human beings are "citizens" of an endangered planet (see the "World Ethos" project of Küng 2008; Küng and Kuschel 2000). Humanity appears as a global interest group (see Ryn 2003). This probably explains why the notion of "the global," physical globes and expressions like "we're all in one boat" are so popular these days. Ulrich Beck remarks that human beings and political structures are not only understood within local contexts but are increasingly being rethought or restructured beyond local to even global networks. This helps create a "cosmopolitan view," often characterized as mostly skeptical, self-critical, and without illusions (Beck 2004: 7–25, 152–54).

A modest variant of cosmopolitanism, taken from Kwame Anthony Appiah, searches for universal norms and values but emphasizes that, at least in daily life, very few are needed. The cosmopolitan interest or curiosity in other peoples or cultures does not necessarily imply the search for commonality, since common ground already exists. When two people meet, they often have a lot more in common than the things that might be common to all people (Appiah 2007: 125). Such a path to world citizenry is probably more realistic. It does not require production of universals and is therefore protected from the trap of wishful thinking. Postcolonial proponents of cosmopolitanism critically point out that the concepts of Western cosmopolitanism ignore both the colonial context from which many of these ideas developed and the varying forms of cultural experience in the world (Giri 2006). It is worth remembering that cosmopolitan culture, according to Beck, is a transnational, pluralistic, and open culture in which diversity does not succumb to forced integration for the sake of unity.

In political philosophy, universality is a contentious issue. Judith Butler's writing exemplifies a currently widespread point of view: "the exclusion of certain contents from any given version of universality is itself responsible for the production of universality in its empty and formal vein" (Butler 2000: 137). Meanwhile, many voices on the political left support developing a concept of universality even as others strictly object to the notion, as demonstrated in current debates (see Laclau 2000 vs. Butler 2000; Assiter 2003: 32–52). Altogether we find that the assumptions that universals exist are as widespread as they are disputed, and that relativistic and universalistic perspectives exist in a complicated relationship to each other: "Relativism and Universalism are not so easy to combine, as we are sometimes led to believe when we listen to professed political opinions or basic assertions on enlightened, liberal or progressive thinking" (Hauschild 2005: 66).

Figure 2. A pharmacy in Yangon, Myanmar. Photo by Maria Blechmann-Antweiler.

CHAPTER 2

A World of Cultures
Their Differences and Likenesses

> *Universals help delineate the nature of the human species as such.*
> *To do this, has been the principal scientific aim of anthropology.*
> —Ward Hunt Goodenough, *Description and*
> *Comparison in Cultural Anthropology*

In this chapter, I demonstrate that we cannot simply do away with difference in order to decipher universals. A focus on cultural diversity must not necessarily stand in the way of developing an interest in universals. I am arguing here from the stance that both vantage points are necessary and even essential for our purposes. My basic position assumes that universal as well as relativistic research approaches may complement each other. Decisive here is the comparative study of variation under the maxim that variants are not exceptions or deviations but rather part of a larger spectrum within the framework of universal phenomena. Universality is not to be confused with uniformity. When clear tendencies, similarities, patterns, and regularities begin to appear from within a broader and empirically documented world of variation and fluctuation, things can get interesting. Generalizations concerning people and cultures might begin to seem useful. I cite below two researchers who emphasize cultural differences and peculiarities in the fields of a language-oriented cultural philosophy and cognitive anthropology:

> The new universalism does not argue against the diversity in languages and cultures. (How could it?) What it challenges is the randomness of variation. Its primary interest is in the limits of inter- as well as intra-cultural variation. (Holenstein 1998a: 245; also see Lemke 2006: 27).

Even some colleagues stressing a particularist stance and emphasizing historical change see this point:

The range of variation is turning out to be a good deal less wide than we thought it might be. The same domains [of thought] are turning up in different cultures and the diversity in semantic categories in at least some domains is turning out to be a good deal less extreme than one might have expected. (Keesing and Keesing 1971: 122)

Finding Patterns in Diversity: George Peter Murdock and Donald Edward Brown

From the mid twentieth century on, the field of anthropology became more open to questions about universals. In the postwar period, interest grew in comparative studies, that is, in discerning the regularities in cultural development, which was partially due to the hundredth anniversary of the publication of Darwin's "On the Origin of the Species" and the subsequent renewed openness to evolutionary questions (Stocking 1987: 291). Important steps were taken in the direction of explicit research into universals from the schools of thought known as neo-evolutionism and cultural ecology, or ecological anthropology, through the work of Alexander Lesser, Leslie Alvin White, Alfred V. Kidder, Julian Haynes Steward, Elman Rogers Service, and the early Marshall Sahlins (Lesser 1985; L. White 1949; Kidder 1940; Steward 1950, 1955). Kidder examined the correlation between likenesses and identities. Julian Steward argued against the unilinear evolutionary model and examined partial and parallel similarities between cultures in terms of multilinear evolution instead. He was looking for "real and meaningful" similarities through their form, function, and movement between cultural areas (Steward 1955: 18–20; see also 1950). These similarities were not the result of human nature or diffusion but rather developed through specific environmental necessities. His long-term goal was to look for the origin of certain features (1955: 18–19). Steward created the concept of the *culture core*, through which he explained functional parallels from within specific environments. From the viewpoint of Darwinian ecology and variation, Steward's concept is somewhat limited (Alland 1970: 169); he examined only regional and not global similarities. But he was nevertheless an important researcher of universals methodologically, in his explicitly empirical comparative approach, and theoretically, in his search for causes and cultural uniformities.

The most important step toward modern universal research in anthropology was taken by the cross-cultural anthropologist George Peter Murdock (1897–1985). Murdock was part of the comparative tradition associated with Herbert Spencer. He was a student of Albert Galloway Keller (1874–1956), whose predecessor at Yale University as of 1872 had been William Graham Sumner (1840–1910). Sumner, who founded comparative studies at the Department for Science and Society, combining sociology and cultural anthropology (Ember and Ember 2009: 11, Peregrine 2013: 408), had been a student of Herbert Spencer. Keller and Sumner were impressed by Spencer's *Descriptive Sociology* (1879–1934), a work in thirteen volumes in which Spencer set down a comprehensive compilation of anthropological data. The uniqueness of the work lay in the comparative quality of how data were indexed according to categories. Sumner shared the same interest and worked until the end of his life on a project to publish a comparative representation of the whole range of human cultures. The last volume of his four-volume work was completed by Keller (Sumner and Keller 1927) and included ethnographic case study examples that, through an index, referenced the other three volumes. This index served as the model for Murdock's comparative study on kinship and family structures from 250 societies (his *Social Structure* of 1949) and for the categories in his *Outline of Cultural Materials*, first published in 1938 (Murdock et al. 2008; see Harris 2001a: 607–8).

Revising his earlier relativism from the 1938 publication mentioned above, Murdock began focusing on a comparative approach to culture through a rigorous systematic method. In 1937 he founded the Cross-Cultural Survey, a collection of data that in 1947 became the *Human Relations Area Files* (Levinson and Malone 1980; Peregrine 2013; Ember, Ember, and Peregrine 2015: 565, 574–76). This collection of data was originally designed to document the diversity in cultures. Within this context of systematic quantitative cultural comparison, Murdock produced "The Common Denominator of Cultures" in 1945, which for the first time shone the spotlight on the topic of universals in anthropology (1945; also see 1949, 1955). Here, based on a comparison of around one hundred societies, Murdock presented an inventory of human universals in the form of a list of seventy-three, which I will discuss only briefly here. A more detailed discussion of these universals appears later in Chapter 5, where Murdock's list is compared to other lists of this kind.

Murdock organized these universals alphabetically, that is, without theoretical considerations, in order to emphasize the diversity among universals. He probably also wanted to avoid anyone interpreting a system behind his data (Eibl 2004: 355). He did not want to imply that the list was by any means complete or meant to be complete; in fact he described it explicitly as a "partial list" (Murdock 1945: 124). He also did not specifically describe the method by which his data were produced, but claimed that the regularities and consistencies spring forth when societies are systematically compared. The universals permeate all significant areas of culture, such as child rearing, body language, language, music, and the manufacture of tools, and are recorded in varying detail:

> Age-grading, athletic sports, bodily adornment, calendar, cleanliness training, community organization, cooking, cooperative labor, cosmology, courtship, danc-

ing, decorative art, divination, division of labor, dream interpretation, education, eschatology, ethics, ethnobotany, etiquette, faith healing, family, feasting, fire making, folklore, food taboos, funeral rites, games, gestures, gift giving, government, greetings, hair styles, hospitality, housing, hygiene, incest taboos, inheritance rules, joking, kin-groups, kinship nomenclature, language, law, luck superstitions, magic, marriage, mealtimes, medicine, modesty concerning natural functions, mourning, music, mythology, numerals, obstetrics, penal sanctions, personal names, population policy, postnatal care, pregnancy usages, property rights, propitiation of supernatural beings, puberty customs, religious ritual, residence rules, sexual restrictions, soul concepts, status differentiation, surgery, tool making, trade, visiting, weaning, and weather control. (Murdock 1945: 89)

A look at this list reveals a way to organize the universals according to subject matter. Wendell Oswalt (1972: 5) uses a variant of Clark Wissler's categories, originally published in 1923 (Wissler 1965), to divide Murdock's seventy-three universals into the following groups, emphasizing that this ordering is also somewhat arbitrary:

1. Language
2. Subsistence (economic self-sufficiency)
3. Material culture
4. Knowledge (scientific, traditional, and mythic)
5. The Supernatural
6. Society
7. Property
8. Political structure
9. Violence

Murdock does not interpret all the phenomena he names as universals, strictly-speaking; rather, they are "empty frames" or blanket categories" (Murdock 1945: 124; 1965: 89). Mourning, for example, may be a universal, but the specific forms that mourning may take are exceedingly different (Oswalt 1972: 6). He emphasizes the task of looking for real or substantive universals, or the way in which human beings classify or categorize. He also qualifies cultural commonalities as the factors involved in creating habitual behavior. Murdock's universals may be further subdivided into components (see Eibl 2004: 355). An example would be Brown's more recent study of over twenty universals within sociocentric attitudes and behavior, or as Sumner astutely put it, the universal syndrome of ethnocentrism (D. Brown 2012).

In 1953, a paper by Clyde Kay Mayben Kluckhohn helped advance anthropological research into universals. Influenced by the 1952 publication of Roman Jakobson's discovery of universal patterns in language phonology, Kluckhohn argued against the classic dogma, represented by Murdock and

Wissler, that universals were general categories void of content. He opposed Alfred Louis Kroeber's biological reductionism and argued in favor of a phenomenological approach to determining universals (Kluckhohn 1953: 516, 520–21). After distancing himself from the relativism of the culture-and-personality school, Kluckhohn introduced the concept of "universal categories of culture"—the universal factors that operate or appear in different places and can lead to parallel transformations. Kluckhohn concluded that certain aspects of culture develop purely by historical accident while others are formed through universal forces (see Geertz 1965: 100–102 for a critical response). He called attention to the possibility of completely different causes for universal cultural patterns, presenting a contrast with Malinowski's biotic needs. After biotic and psychic commonalities, Kluckhohn considered other factors, such as parallels in social interactive patterns, and the relationship humans have to the material world.

Kluckhohn's often reprinted publication and Murdock's catalog were the most specific contributions to the topic of universals up until the 1960s: "There is a generalized framework that underlies the apparent and striking facts of cultural relativity. All cultures constitute so many somewhat distinct responses to essentially the same questions posed by human biology *and by the generalities of the human situation*" (Kluckhohn 1951: 105; italics mine; see also Kluckhohn 1959). Kluckhohn had expressed similar ideas in an essay in which he responded to the inescapable problems of human existence by characterizing culture as an adaptive measure for making the world we live in a safer, more stable place. He claimed that universals are not reducible to biological factors and argued that there is a general and common framework underlying all examples of cultural relativity (Kluckhohn 1951: 78).

After a long break in research on universals, Donald Edward Brown published a monograph under the title *Human Universals* (Brown 1991) in 1991. Brown was trained in the academic mainstream of anthropology with a concentration on cultural diversity and cultural relativism. During fieldwork in Brunei, he became suddenly aware of a universal basis that was often overlooked in the focus on cultural particulars. He demonstrated this in his introduction by describing the behavior patterns tied to greetings and the interaction he had had with informants in the field who had first appeared to him just as typical Malay behavior. He found, however, that behind what appeared to be culturally specific behavior lay general levels of universals hidden from view, universals such as politeness, humor, and high value placed on social rank and status. This led Brown to comb the literature in pursuit of references to universals, a search that proved enlightening.

In his book Brown presents a theoretically based summary of the results of his research on universals, including some relevant relativist arguments that he discusses using six examples: adolescence in Samoa, emotion conveyed in facial expressions, the Oedipus complex, concepts of time among the Hopi, gender roles among the Chambuli, and the classification of color. Brown demonstrates that quite a few universals are theoretically important. A major section of his book is dedicated to controversial statements that have been made on the topic of universals. Brown ends his work with a fascinating, elegantly written chapter that reads something like a novel, in which he sketches the contours of an imaginary "universal people." In the world of international anthropology and other social and cultural sciences, Brown's monograph was for the most part well received and even highly praised (e.g., Boehm 1992; Lonner 1994). His work has also been mentioned in books covering political and economic issues. Francis Fukuyama, who described globalization as the realization of universals in the special sense of that which is everywhere and always true, refers to Brown's book in his work on biopolitics (Fukuyama 2002: 198, 318).

Brown's ideas found particular resonance in works pertaining to intercultural contact and management (e.g., Sherry 1995: 286–90; Payer 2000). While some researchers have proclaimed that Brown opened their eyes to the subject (e.g., Quant 1992, Cronk 1993, 1999: 24), others have reacted critically (e.g., Sussman 1999; Roughley 2000). Sadly, Brown's masterpiece is now out of print. In European cultural studies and even in anthropology, Brown's book has received hardly any attention and is rarely cited. In the German-speaking world, his arguments have gained little notice in debate (Roughley 2000); instead they have become known through the popular works of Steven Pinker (1994; 2002). In 1977, Greenwood and Stini could still assert, with regard to Murdock's catalog of universals and to the emphasis on the unity of humanity, that "the job has been pursued vigorously, especially in the earlier part of this century, and the universality of all the traits on Murdock's list is generally accepted by anthropologists" (Greenwood and Stini 1977: 314). From the mid 1980s to the end of the twentieth century, however, this approving attitude was less clearly represented .

Universals as Subject Matter: Concepts, Terms, and Metaphors

Definitions and Concepts

In this section I discuss definitions and their conceptual content before turning to the many terms found in the literature. Universals, as simply put as possible, are characteristics shared by all of humanity. More specifically, universal characteristics or phenomena are those found in all *societies* on our planet. The classic and most clearly known examples concern kinship, family, and marriage (Greenwood and Stini 1977: 314). I have already mentioned incest as one such example and will often refer to it here. The incest taboo is, simply put, the avoidance of sexual intercourse, marriage, or reproduction between persons who are considered related. The latest research shows that this tendency to avoid what is deemed incestuous is universal, though the rules governing its prohibition can vary widely (Munroe and Munroe 2001: 227). Prohibition often extends beyond the immediate family: "In all societies, people extend the incest taboo to some persons outside the primary or nuclear family" (Ember and Ember 1997: 127). Incest avoidance, meanwhile, can vary strongly in terms of what persons' sex is viewed as incestuous and how and how strongly people react to incest (J. Fox 1984; Héritier 1994, 1999; Turner and Maryanski 2005: 27–52). What is truly universal is the prohibition or ban on reproduction between mother and son, while incest prohibition in other constellations (brother-sister, father-daughter) is nearly universal as well.

While something might occur as a phenomenon in all cultures, its occurrence does not necessarily imply that it must be a phenomenon for all individuals in all societies (Opolka 1999: 2). This key point is significant here because universals are often erroneously thought of as referring to or relating to individuals. For example, we find that although dance exists in all cultures, it is most often reserved for only certain groups or categories of persons, such as men or members of a given priesthood. The problematic assumption that all people dance is known as a typical fallacy of division that I can illustrate with another example (after Lett 1997: 65):

- Religion is a cultural universal.
- Every person in the world belongs to a culture.
- Every person in the world has religious beliefs.

This syllogism is obviously not correct, as societies have emergent features that are not shared in all their component parts. For example, to say that culture is "acquired by man as a member of society" (according to Tylor's famous definition from 1871) is not the same as saying that people accept culture as members of *a* society (or a specific society) (Klass 2003: 24). Another important difference exists between the sentences "all human beings can speak, that is, have a language" and the statement "languages are spoken in all cultures." No person speaks simply language; rather, people speak specific languages. The first statement refers to the cultural capability of human beings as individuals (culture in the singular); the second is a statement on universals at the level of compared cultures (culture in the plural).

Universals are in this sense not to be confused with attributes marking a certain species (an understanding of universals often used in biology; e.g., Kappeler and Silk 2010). Such attributes are valid for all individuals of a certain species, at least within a certain phase of life. Universals are not, then, the same as describing the nature of human beings, or human nature, even in the implied sense (Schiefenhövel 1997, 1999: 1; Bargatzky 2000: 266). A simple example would be homosexuality, which is more or less manifest in all known societies, but not in all individuals.

Distinguishing between universality on a societal level and on an individual level through the ubiquitous occurrence of something found among individuals is important in that many authors use terms in the sense of "… all human beings from all cultures with the same inherent commonalities …" (Salat 2003: 133), or in the sense of an "… anatomically based system of cultural and individual thoughts …" (Pope 2000: 40). When universals are spoken of in terms of individuals, these universals do not necessarily have to occur in all phases of life (Konner 2003: 440). Compared to adults, children in all cultures learn languages without much effort, because this is a characteristic of being human. Some authors restrict cultural universals thematically, either to only those associated with social institutions (König 1975: 52) or to those referring to behavior (Barash 1979: 42). The latter concern cultural universals as "fundamental behavioral characteristics … of societies" (Scupin and DeCorse 2016: 213; similarly, Sidky 2004: 422; see also Sidky 2003). This is also true of a working definition used within a research group on "transcultural universals" at the Hanse-Wissenschaftskolleg (Hanse Institute for Advanced Study): "A human behavior (e.g., shame) or an institution (e.g., family) should be considered universal or transcultural when it occurs *regularly* in all (or in almost all) societies *that have become thus far known*" (Opolka 1999: 2; see also Schiefenhövel 1999: 1).

Universals can even occur beyond the realm of conspicuous behavior. The holistic cultural concept of cultural anthropology proposes a search for such universals. Cultural universals can exist in living conditions; in behavior, thought, and feelings; and in institutions and objects. These could include (1) complex social institutions, such as marriage and the division of labor, (2) behavioral conduct, as in the use of fire, drug use, and reciprocal exchange, (3) cognitions, or (4) material culture such as tools and housing structures. The expression "in all … societies known to date" refers to all societies ("ethnic groups," "cultures") that have so far been studied by, for example, anthropologists, ethnographers, or historians. According to anthropologists, such societies are those that currently exist or that existed up until the recent past and were documented. The term "regular," as in "regularly occurring," refers to a phenomenon that occurs not just once or on rare occasions in a culture that has been studied, but rather often and across generations. Since it is difficult to define the exact boundaries between societies and ethnic groups, one can include subgroups in defining universals more carefully as "elements of culture that exist in all human *groups* or societies" (Peoples and Bailey 2015: 43; italics mine). The central point is that groups need to be referred to as collective units of identity with clear continuity and coherence:

As this [culture as system of meaning] shapes the shared elements of all groups with a stable sense of identity, it offers as well the groundwork for the development of a *core system* of *transcultural universals* from which all uniqueness, individualisation and select occurrences appear as the result of local adaptations, historical interactions and internal societal differentiating processes, all of which can then be deductively *explained*. (K. Müller 2003a: 9; italics in the original)

According to another understanding of the term, universal phenomena are those that occur not just in all living cultures but in all known human communities. That is, these universals occur in all cultures and in all time periods. Such an understanding corresponds to universals as stringently maintained commonalities over time (Hultkrantz 1960: 283; During 2005: 87). However, ethnographic knowledge is far from complete when it comes to living human cultures, let alone prehistoric ones. It is therefore difficult to categorically accept such a definition of universals. Yet this does not restrict us from investigating diachronic universals, since incomplete or insufficient empirical data can be supplemented through other methods, such as deduction and retrodiction. Identifying universals as such reminds us of Kroeber's well-known definition of cultural anthropology as both a synchronic and a diachronic field of study. Accordingly, Brown defines human universals as trans-cultural as well as trans-historical: Human universals comprise those "features of culture, society, language, behavior, and psyche that, so far as the record is clear, are found in all ethnographically *or* historically recorded human societies" (D. Brown 2013: 410, italics mine; also see D. Brown 1999a: 382; 2004). There should be no known exception to their existence. This, then, is the definition of absolute universals. Later on we will discuss more limited forms of universals, such as near universals.

Cultural universals always consist of particular features from within collectives or societies, and not the sum of all these features. The claim that there are similarities in societies in relation to feature A does not exclude that differences exist in further characteristics B, C, and so on, or even in all other features. Universals, once established, do not ignore the fact that peculiarities are still inherent in specific objects, conditions, people, or societies. They simply imply that an object in question may not be entirely unique in every aspect. Put differently, we could say that each person is in many ways like every other person, or like some people, or like no one else before (Kluckhohn and Murray 1953: 15). Modern studies on human physical diversity show that all people are basically the same, and that each person is different (Lewontin 1986; also see Grossmann and Grossmann 2007: 249–54).

The definition of universals as characteristics occurring throughout all human societies does not expressly presume that these characteristics are not found in other primate populations. This point must be emphasized here, since some authors assume that human beings as individuals share universal features that animals do not (Staal 1988: 1; after Saler 2000: 155; similar to Pope 2000: 291; in contrast, see Kohl 2008: 549). These features, termed "species specific" in this book, are set apart from universals and discussed in a separate chapter on human nature. "Hidden copulation" is an example of a feature that fulfills this additional criterion: not only is ovulation hidden among human beings; copulation is as well. In all human cultures, sexual intercourse commonly does not take place in public but in private (and is therefore associated with secrecy and shame; Duerr 1988). This is not the case for any other primates (Schröder 2000: 59; Ehrlich 2002: 187–88).

Ethological Universals and the Problem of Definition

Cultural universals can be distinguished from genetic or biological universals (Eriksen 2015: 54). Here, the distinction is made only for the sake of analysis. In most instances, we do not know how situation, environment and culture affect the formation or development of universals, which is why "universals" are more explained than defined in this book. The following quotes, taken from a critic of the biological conception of human nature, will show, especially through the emphasis I place on certain words, the problems involved in distinguishing universals. Dupré writes: "With regard to ... causal factors biologically common to all nondefective humans, the interaction of these with innumerable contextual factors makes it unlikely that such factors will in any *interesting* ways determine the *details* of human behaviour." Furthermore, he says, "there is no reason to think that there are universal biological features of humans directed at the production of *specific* modes of behaviour. Rather, such universal features must be seen as *more or less constant* inputs into the *complexly interactive processes* by which human minds develop" (Dupré 2003: 100; italics mine).

The example of mental structures can illustrate this complicated biocultural dynamic. The common explanation concerns genetics (e.g., the proximate explanations given in evolutionary psychology), and the common alternative explanations are based on environment or socialization (e.g., the brain as formed with enormous inborn capabilities without specific content, as in the blank slate form of social constructivism), there are other possible explanations. It is plausible that pervasive and persistent brain or thought structures are not only biologically determined, but rather are also influenced by persistent cultural input: "a brain constructed by a variety of more or less stable and reliable resources *including* resources that are *reliably produced by human cultures*" (Dupré 2003: 31; italics mine). If humans, based on biology, are culturally dependent beings, this is not to say that all humans currently alive are simply the product of biotically successful reproduction and natural selection. We are also dependent on culture or socialization for the sake of survival. Cultural inputs that determine survival today might have been around since the Stone Age, while other inputs today could be radically different from anything known in the distant past (Dupré 2003: 31).

Contrary to a commonly held opinion, universality is not necessarily biotically determined and diversity culturally determined. The prevalence of a feature or attribute in people or cultures cannot be understood simply from a biotic basis (Dennett 1995: 486–87), a point I will discuss in more detail below. It is therefore necessary to make clear that the following definition, which is used in the fields of research on behavior (human ethology, e.g., Medicus 2012) or social biology, does not apply to universals as I am describing them in this book: "Universals … within the most varying of cultural conditions in the same form and/or in the succession of emerging behavioural patterns, *are genetically determined, and interpreted as species-specific behaviour*" (Lethmate 1992: 72; italics mine; the same practically word for word found also in Sütterlin 1992: 53; Simon 1990b; but see Spindler 1984: 14, 18). A connection between reducing the conceptual scope to behavior, on the one hand, and linking behavior with causal assumptions—in this case genetic—on the other, is also found in Heymer's dictionary for behavioral biology:

> In ethology, universals describe behaviors that in all human beings, independent of race or culture, occur within a similar context, produce similar reactions, have the same meaning, and are similarly understood. Crying, laughing, smiling, the expression of distrust, of grief, the grimaces of pain, or threatening glances are all examples of such behavior and are most certainly inborn in humans and not culturally dependent (Heymer 1977: 177).

Similarly, Eibl-Eibesfeldt describes universals as inborn "programming" that can also be replaced or repressed (Eibl-Eibesfeldt 2004: 198, 725; 1993a, 1993b; Eibl-Eibesfeldt and Sütterlin 2007). Such narrowly determined concepts are also found in the definition described below, which is less genetically based than Heymer's definition but still includes specific causal assumptions. The sociobiologist Edward O. Wilson argues that cultural universals could be explained by the effects of epigenetic rules (whereas cultural diversity arises out of wider norms of reaction). He characterizes cultural universals as initiated from culture and from epigenetic rules (E. Wilson 1998: 167).

In the analysis below, the concept of universals will remain broadly defined as concerns causation. I will neither limit my understanding of universals simply to matters of behavior (such as, e.g. Supin & De Corse 2015: 437), nor incorporate causal meaning into a definition of universals. I am explicitly interested in finding causes for pancultural phenomena (see Chapter 7). Though simple, the definition given above encompasses some of the fundamental problems in cultural anthropology that will be addressed throughout this book. The main problem pertains to the concept of culture and the assumptions regarding the nature of human beings that are implicitly, or explicitly, implied when discussing culture. The second problem consists in the enormous difficulty of establishing perimeters between cultural units (cultures), something that does not have to remain unresolved. Based on the considerations presented in this chapter, I will use a slightly modified version of the definition from the project on transcultural universals mentioned above: A feature, or phenomenon, is universal when it appears regularly in all or nearly all known societies, or in many societies. I call such a feature a universal.

Setting Perimeters: What Universals Are Not

What should not fall under the heading of universal? What I do not include here are philosophically understood universals in the sense of general terms. The discussion (see Stegmüller 1974) concerning the relationship of universal (Latin: *universale*) to particular things (*res*) will not be dealt with here, even at times when I use the insights from this discussion for my own purposes, for example, in the chapter on methods and the question of culturally independent concepts. Furthermore, more banal or obvious universals will not be dealt with here. These would include the fact that people need to eat in order to survive, that most people walk on two legs, that healthy people can speak or that every society needs to raise a future generation. The pure existence of basic institutions or functional establishments for the satisfying of needs in societies, such as food preparation and child rearing, will also remain outside the discussion, though the similarities in their form or structure will not. The term "universal" will not include phenomena that are

1. directly functional and necessary for short-term or long-term survival (see Peoples and Bailey 2003: 38),
2. limited to low brain function, or
3. obviously tied to the anatomy or physiology of the individual.

The first two types of phenomena are not always so obvious, and the last type will prove difficult to identify, as many points described in this book will show. The boundaries between obvious physical attributes and indirect, theoretical universals based on the particular traits observed in the organisms known as *Homo sapiens* are often nebulous. (see, e.g., the list of *species universals in man* in Crook 1985: 156–86). The boundary between culture and bios is well known to be a fundamental theoretical problem. What is problematic regarding universals is setting perimeters within "the dual structure of similar needs but varying solutions" (on "need universals," see Welsch 2006: 143). Biological demands and fundamental needs cannot be completely neglected on a long-term basis for a society as a whole. But these needs are related to individual requirements and do not always apply to all members of a society. Biological fitness is more a perimeter for human behavior than a specific behavioral guideline (Markl 1986: 76). Excluded from the discussion therefore are also phenomena that arise out of a direct response to basic needs from people as organisms (for basic needs, see Malinowski 1944: 39–41; for precultural needs or universal species realities, see Dissanayake 1992: 215). To satisfy such needs, every society must fulfill fundamental requirements. Every society must, according to the language of Malinowski, find its respective variant, or type, of "universal institution," or more simply put, must meet needs with systemic solutions such as

- system of food supply
- system of kinship
- system of social control
- system of communication
- systems of imagined supernatural powers that explain the unexplainable. (Ferraro 2001a: 33)

Not to be excluded here are the respective manifestations and specific traits of these systems, or "the ways in which diverse human cultural practices are the means of satisfying universal human needs" (Dissanayake 1992: 75). The ways in which needs are satisfied are especially likely to indicate universal patterns. Meanwhile, a borderline case is formed by universal needs that are established as biotic needs and are manifested in all societies but are primarily concerned with the needs of the individual, though not every individual or in every situation. An example would be Larry Arnhart's conservative and politically oriented concept of twenty "natural needs," such as family ties and property (Arnhart 1998: 31–36; 2005: 33).

Also not prefigured in our discussion of universals is Marvin Harris's understanding of a "universal pattern" as the inventory of components that, from a material-culture perspective, reoccur in all cultural systems. He distinguishes three levels: infrastructure (modes of production and reproduction), structure (domestic and political economy), and superstructure (behavior and thought). Harris understands these levels as a heuristic device that allows him to compare cultures and systematize data (1980: 17–19). In his later work, Harris incorporates etic behavioral and emic mental dimensions into his three levels (Harris 1999: 141–52, see also Sanderson 2001). A specific causal assumption emerges from Harris's three-part system. From his techno-deterministic perspective, the infrastructure and the etic aspects of the structure and superstructure are primary causal forces, indicating an infrastructural determinism. In cultural materialism, universal patterns are more incorporated in universal levels than is the concept of universals itself. Harris's definition of universal patterns includes an assertion that, compared to what will be presented in this book, is more in line with the definitions expounded by Wilson and Eibl-Eibesfeldt, although in terms of content that is decidedly different.

Terms and Concepts: A Broad Spectrum

In the literature, universals are studied under a wide variety of designations. Only some of the terms are expressed explicitly as "universal" (Table 2.1). In German publications on the topic, we most often find terms such as "Universalien" (universals) or "Kulturuniversalien" (universals of culture) or "kulturelle Universalien" (cultural universals). The term "cultural universals" indicates the level at which universals are observed, meaning that they are observed in all societies, or cultures. Accordingly, one could misunderstand this to mean these universals are attributes occurring in all individuals. The word "culture" could easily be understood as indicating a cause, namely a cultural cause, for the existence of universals. As mentioned above, I prefer the term "universals" to "cultural universals" in the present context due to my interest in a working definition of universals that does not imply causal assumptions at the outset.

Universals have been studied under terms such as "universal pattern" (P. Meyer 1990: 133, 1998), "pancultural factors," "pancultural cultural patterns," or "pancultural truths" (Osgood, May, and Miron 1975: 160–61; Geertz 1984).

Table 2.1. Terms containing the word "universal" found in well-established dictionaries and textbooks for anthropology and cultural anthropology as well as further selected works

Term	Definition	Reference
Universals	Objects, cultural elements, institutions or cultural areas that occur in all known human cultures	Beer 1999: 391
Universal	Something that exists in every culture	Kottak 2008: 59
Cultural universal	Common features (shared by) all cultures of the world; those general cultural traits found in all societies of the world	Ferraro & Andreatta 2014: 36-38, 419
Cultural universals	Elements found in all cultures; elements of culture that exist in all known human groups or societies	Peoples and Bailey 2003: 397; 2015: 43
Cultural universal	Features of culture, society, language, behavior, and psyche that exist in all ethnographically or historically recorded human societies, with no known exceptions	D. Brown 1996a
Universals	Fundamental behavioral characteristics ... of societies	Scupin and DeCorse 2015: 213
Cultural universals	Phenomena one can expect to find in any and every culture	Berry et al. 2011: 233

More seldom, we find the terms "cultural universals" (Marschall 1990a: 8), "anthropological universals" (Kohl 2008: 849; Jullien 2014: 77–78, 111), "sociocultural universals" (Chapais 2014), and "transcultural universals" (Leininger 1991; Hanse Wissenschaftskollege Delmenhorst 1993; Bargatzky 2000: 266; K. Müller 2003a; 2003b: 27; Chevron and Wernhart 2000–2001; Wernhart 2004: 154; D. Brown 2012: 1). There are also isolated examples of terms such as "universality" (Wernhart 1986: 648), "intercultural universality" (W. Meyer 2002: 26), "transcultural universality" (Rüsen 1998: 21), "transcultural commonalities" and "fundamental commonalities" (both in Gingrich 1999: 276, 277), "cultural commonalities" (Chasiotis 2007: 204), "intercultural commonalities" (Holenstein 1997: 61), "universal cultural characteristics" (P. Meyer 1990: 133) or "supercultural elements" (Ekman 1970). Rarely used terms include "species-specific facts and circumstances" and "species-specific" (Cramer and Mollenhauer 1998: 120; Hansen 2003: 280), "constant basic experiences" (Opolka 1999: 2), and "elementary species experiences" (Renn 2002: 57). The latter terms present a transition to the topic of human nature that will be discussed further below.

Apart from social scientists, the academics in the German-speaking world who are interested in the topic tend to be phenomenological philosophers or philosophers who represent an intercultural philosophy. Here universals fall under the name of "cultural invariant" phenomena (Holenstein 1981: 198). They could be more specifically defined as "intercultural equivalents" or as cultural appearances that are typologically similar, independent of the divisions between cultures or civilizations. It is important to remember that internal cultural differences are not the same as intercultural differences. Examples of typological similarities can be seen in particular groupings of people who share the same values or worldview as people from other cultures but not with other groups of people from the same culture, such as country folks (vs. city folks) in East Asia and Western Europe (Holenstein 1997: 51; see 64).

Anglo-American scholars usually refer to "universals" or "human universals." One can also speak of cultural universals, or *universeaux culturels* in the French-speaking world. Use of the term universality is rarer but occurs, for example, in cultural comparative psychology ("an essential universality," Lonner 1980; also Triandis 1978: 1; Smith and Bond 1993: 55; Smith, Bond, and Kagitcibasi 2006: 25), environmental psychology (Gardner and Stern 1995: 188), or philosophy (Roughley 2000, 2011; Stagl 2000). Some authors emphasize those aspects that span borders, as in the use of such terms as cross-cultural patterns and cross-cultural universals (K. Fox 2014: 17). In rare instances we might read the following terms: cross-cultural uniformity (Tooby and Cosmides 1992: 88), the cross-cultural (Klass 1995: 27), panhuman patterns (Alverson 1994), the panhuman (Klass 1995: 27), general pancultural principles (Dissanayake 1992: 68), universal cultural predisposition (Dissanayake 1992: 16), universal human tendency or commonality (Adams 1998: 184; Dupré 2003: 101; Sterelny 2003:

192), common design (Keesing and Keesing 1971: 119), consistencies across cultures (Hauser 2007: 300), or simply cultural elements (Peoples and Bailey 2015: 44).

In addition, in both the German- and the English-speaking world, we find terms that emphasize spatial frequency or temporal stability. Here the talk is of "constants" or "invariants" (cultural constant, cultural invariants; transcultural invariants or intercultural invariants; see Simon 1990a; Morin and Piatelli-Palmarini 1974: 8; Schiefenhövel 1999: 14; Opolka 1999: 2; Messelken 2002b; K. Müller 2003b: 28), "universal constants" (Mühlmann 1966: 19–20) or "universally constant antecedent conditions" (K. Müller 2003b: 34). The expression "the universal given" (Lautmann 2002: 474) refers as well to an understanding of universals as constant values. A few authors combine intercultural likenesses and cultural content, which is something shared by all individuals in a society. This pertains, for example, to Ralph Linton and his use of the term universals of culture (Linton 1936; also see S. Wilk 2007: 396).

One unusual use of terms is Paul Spindler's (1984) and Karl Wernhart's (1987) *Universalia humana*, which they understand to include universal physical features, or biotic human predispositions, such as the structure of our brains, which is the same worldwide (similar to Fox's "biological universals"; J. Fox 1971: 281–82). Wernhart differentiates between this and his conception of the double nature of human beings with the term *universalia cultura* (*universalium culturicum* in the singular). These *universalia*—products of the process of learning through the passing on of traditions since the beginning of human history—influence our inherent developmental potential (Wernhart 1986, 1987, 2001: 47; 2004: 24–25, 38; Chevron and Wernhart 2000–2001: 21). Wernhart assumes that in today's world the two *universalia* are empirically inseparable or no longer separable (see also Plachetka 1997: 116–18). Similarly, Crook uses the term "species universals in man" to describe species-specific constraints, especially those regarding social behavior (Crook 1985: 156). Keesing and Strathern claim that "the range of cultures that are thinkable and learnable by members of a species is probably—in terms of formal organization and logic—quite narrow. But on the other hand, the variation in content and substance (as opposed to structure and organization) of culturally constructed worlds is striking" (Keesing and Strathern 1998: 242).

Some researchers reformulate terms to avoid being too abstract, too general, or too specific. Examples of this would be the understated universal categories of culture (Kluckhohn 1953) and the stronger genuine cultural uniformities (Leach 1982: 111), as well as uniformities, or generic human traits (Brown 1996: 3). Cohen recoins terms into contents and structures that are shared by different cultures (shared content and space; Cohen 1998: 74). Eriksen reformulates universals as "shared cultivated, social dimensions of humanity" and purposely leaves open the distinction between genetic and cultural universals (Eriksen 2015: 54). Psychologists and philosophers also speak at times of universal humanity, panculturalism (Rolston 1999: 156; 220), pancultural human psychological characteristics (Hinde 1999: 14), pancultural patterns, and metaculture (Sperber 1989; Tooby and Cosmides 1992: 53) as well as metacultural universals (Runciman 2000: 213; Hinde 2003: 15). Many of the terms used in the literature are also found on the Internet, though in varying degrees of frequency (Table 2.2).

Table 2.2. Prevalence of the topic "universals" on the Internet in 2002 and 2014 (NR = not researched; research for 2014: Dario Antweiler).

	Hits, Google 9.9.2002, exact wording	Hits, Google 1.1.2014, exact wording	Hits, Google 1.1.2014, unlimited
Anglophone Search words			
universal	10,500,000	256,000,000	256,000,000
human universal	1,910,000	49,600	104,000,000
cultural universals	20,200	50,200	458,000,000
universals	82,000	172,000,000	172,000,000
cultural universal	1,150,000	42,900,000	46,000,000
universal category of culture	259,000	6	759,000,000
cross-cultural universal	58,900	435	102,000,000
cross-cultural universals	NR	469	11,000,000
culture-universal	1,060	10,400	13,100
cross cultural pattern	51	261	115,000,000
cross-cultural pattern	NR	261	113,000,000
cross-cultural uniformity	26	113	154,000
human invariant	94,000	16,600	108,000,000
generic human trait	11,100	34	989,000
Metaculture	1,640	19,500	19,500
cultural invariant	1,330	976	946,000
pan-human	747	21,000	34,300
pan-human pattern	131	5	16,600
cross-cultural similarity	82	408	786
inter-cultural invariant	77	2	25,900
transcultural invariant	NR	2	858
basic similarity	NR	66,100	457,000,000
anthropological constant	NR	660	1,130,000
cultural constant	716,000	1,300	16,000,000
pancultural	NR	0	22,800
pan-cultural	NR	39,400	60,600
global culture	NR	879,000	277,000,000
world culture	NR	11,000,000	627,000,000

Unclear or metaphorical concepts or terms are often used, especially the widely used expression "anthropological constants" (e.g., Wehler 1990: 232; Straub 2003: 139; Mittelstraß 2004: 23–24; R. Groh 2005: 213). This term—which, when used, sounds more like "anthropic constants"—is often understood to represent the constituent parts or characteristics of deep-seated structures of or within humanity. These supposed constants, which cannot be circumvented, are universal conditions influenced by historic diversity or diversity specific to a local setting (Mittelstraß 2004: 24), for example, aspects of culture or capacity for culture. We also hear, though more rarely, of "transcultural constants" (e.g., in Mühlmann 1962, 1966: 19; also see "constants across culture" in Ekman and Friesen 1971: 124–25). Formulations such as "common heritage" are also used, though often in a way that leaves their meaning vague or unclear (Eibl-Eibesfeldt 1976: 241–43; 1993a, 1993b), which is also the case for "universal system of controls" or "deeply imbedded structure" (Eibl-Eibesfeldt 1986: 89–90). The expression "binding heritage" (Eibl-Eibesfeldt and Sütterlin 2007: 491) emphasizes a link between human beings from different cultures.

Walter Burkert, a scholar in classics and religious studies, offers examples of a more colorful use of terms in his examination of cultural similarities that span the boundaries of culture, from an ethological basis. He names these similarities "worldwide similarities," "recurrences in time and space," or "widely distributed recurrences" (Burkert 1996: 42) or describes them as existing "beyond individual civilisations" and as "a general class transcending single cultural systems" (Burkert 1996: 4). He characterizes these transcultural patterns as "striking similarities" (Burkert 1996: 2), and some as "intercultural and undeniable family resemblances" (Burkert 1996: 4, 17). And in some cases Burkert speaks also of "anthropological universals" (1996: 1, 4), which, in the use of the term, tends more in the direction of anthropological constants.

The concept of human nature (*conditio humana*) has been so widely interpreted that I devote a separate, more extensive discussion to it later in this book. The difficulty of analytically isolating general features of human beings that are found in every individual human being, on the one hand, from universals that reoccur regularly in different societies on the other, is illustrated in the following: "one set of the universals that unify our *species* namely that set of capacities that allows us to create cultural diversity" (Carrithers 1992: 5, italics mine).

The academic literature features many examples of authors describing universal characteristics, clearly or otherwise, without actually using the word "universal" or defining what the concept might mean. A few examples include the following: "practically proven to be found in all cultures" (Mühlmann 1966: 19), "in all known societies" (König 1975: 52), "shared by all people and all societies" (Bruck 1985: 128), "universally salient" (Dissanayake 1992: 231), "found in every human society" (Dissanayake 1992: 48), "for almost all cultures" (Dissanayake 1992: 71), "believed to exist in all human societies" (R. Wilk 1996: 396), "common major features" (E. Wilson 1998: 116; Runciman 2002: 11), "universally given" (Lautmann 2002: 474), "underlying commonalities between all human cultures" (Dupré 2003: 101), "the large stable core" (vs. variation in frequency and context; Konner 2003: 440), "existing everywhere but in varying degrees" (Haller & Shore 2005: 29).

Similarities and Family Resemblances

When discussing transcultural patterns, many authors are more careful with the topic of universal characteristics, preferring the phrase "universal human tendencies" (Peacock 2001: 97). Some authors prefer to speak of "similarities" (as in cultural similarities, cross-cultural similarities or similarities across cultures, basic similarities, or widespread similarities; see Boas 1938: 165; Kluckhohn 1953: 512; Moghaddam 1998: 11, 274; Myers: 2002: 173; Ehrlich 2002: 12; Ellen 2003: 47; Ochs 2004: 86). These terms are chosen more carefully than Murdock's concept of "uniformities and consistencies" which suggests the lesser or weaker forms of commonalities. Here Murdock is considering commonalities that occur between certain specific cultures that stand out within a sea of cultural diversity (1945: 123). Narrowly defined similarities are not to be compared to universals but are important in the search for universals, as will be discussed in the chapter on methods.

Anthropologists study similarities between some or even many cultures less often than they do individual cultures, but much more often than they study universals, strictly speaking. The more relevant work on the subject has come out of systematic research in intercultural comparisons, known in the international literature as cross-cultural comparison, intercultural comparison, or more rarely as holocultural, transcultural, or sampled/complete-universe statistical comparison. By using the term "similarities" we run into the problem found in the work of some authors who describe universals as "structural similarities in behavior" (e.g., P. Meyer 1990: 133; 1998; see also Alland 1970: 152). Benson Saler characterizes cultural universals as "resemblances in form that are claimed to be found in every culture" (Saler 2000: 150; also see 156). According to this definition, universals then are, first, limited to entities of pure form, and second, explicitly understood as postulates. Third, by using the word resemblances, Saler associates universals more with "family resemblances" as understood by Vygotsky and Wittgenstein than with monolithic universals.

Regarding content, certain terms are closely related to the concept of universals. Ruth Groh prefers the term "anthropological fundamentals" to "anthropological constants" (Groh 2004: 321–22; SFB 511 2005: 45–46). This distinction will be discussed in more detail below. Basic human faculties like speech, sexuality, and imaginative capabilities are the focus here. The ability to experience joy or grief, for example, is not an observable construct, according to Groh, and therefore must be understood through actualization, such as laughter signaling joy and crying signaling grief. As pointed out in the chapter on universals in current societal debate, the assumptions, associations, and research involving universals are relevant not only in an academic but also in a practical sense, and are of no little importance.

Universals Do Matter: The Relevance of Universals in General and for Cultural Studies

Universals shape our general view of humanity, whether in daily life experiences or within a political or an academic framework (Kuper 1994; Wolters 1999: 96; Fahrenberg 2004). In cultural anthropology, universals are important in more specific frameworks, above all with regard to cultural theory. They are also significant in many other fields within the humanities and social and cultural sciences, in the same way that they are important as the basis for a scientific cultural anthropology. Universals can be a powerful instrument in negotiating the complicated interactions between biological and cultural systems. They help to answer questions concerning the factors influencing human character and personality that are found in every society (Schiefenhövel 1999: 2). Universals are also relevant to how we see ourselves and how this self-perception influences how we form our future (Welsch 2004: 64).

Presumptions Both Implicit and Widespread

Presumptions concerning universal characteristics of human culture are widespread in daily life. These presumptions themselves may very well be called universal. Taking a closer look, we come across a constant flow of universal statements involving, for instance, the behavior of superiors to subordinates, the wealthy to the poor, parents to their children, or women to men. In the academic world we often find universals in the form of implicit assumptions hidden within theory. In psychoanalysis, universal statements are made according to very specific regional or historic material. In economics, universal postulates are put forward in models on individual behavior, for example in rational choice theory and in the critical responses to models (Antweiler 2000: chap. 2). A great many of the claims made in works of social psychology are based on studies carried out in Western cultures that feature the attributes of individualism and low power distance (Smith and Bond 1993: 46). Books on sociology present supposedly valid intercultural concepts on the structure and function of human societies in social theory that are drawn from universal assumptions on humans and human groups. In general, these assumptions lurking behind social theories receive little or no notice. Only in rare cases do we come across clear statements by anthropologists who say that studies and findings about universals are helpful or useful for the field (e.g., Berry et al. 2011: 5). Research on universals could help do away with basic anthropological assumptions found in other fields that are unrealistically rigid or far too abstract (Opolka 1999: 1). An example would be the idea of human beings' limitless potential for learning as the tabula rasa in educational philosophy; the idea, held by many economists, of the perpetual maximizing of profit; or the notion that rational behavior is the driving force of *Homo oeconomicus*. The latest research in empirical economics (e.g., Voland 2001; Henrich 2002: 260–75; Gächter and Thöni 2004; Fehr and Renninger 2004) demonstrates how unrealistic these ideas may be when expressed in their extreme form.

Universal statements on human beings have a practical purpose, as becomes clear in the fields of psychotherapy, intercultural consulting, and intercultural mediation and especially in political attempts at intercultural understanding. At the same time, very few practically oriented or politically motivated authors attempt to clarify their overall view of humanity for their readers. A rare example of an author being explicit on the subject is Andreas Bruck's *Lebensfragen* (Life's Questions), a guidebook on life's important questions with an explicit anthropological fundament. The author uses the subtitle of his book to explain where the answers will come from, namely, from a "practical anthropology" (Bruck 1997). He describes his cultural anthropological and functionalistic assumptions about human beings in detail. In some of the more recent guides for intercultural mediation, the search for cultural commonalities between conflicting parties or for common goals is spelled out as an explicit strategy (Busch 2007: 170–71). Franz König, the Roman Catholic cardinal of Vienna, once answered the question of how dialogue is possible between religions by stating that "that is simple. I begin with what we have in common" (quoted in Salat 2003: 133). Individuals active in intercultural communication and conflict management should approach their work in a way that exposes universal norms, values, and concepts of justice. By appreciating and recognizing these universal concepts, participants in dialogue would then have the chance to form new commonalities for the purposes of better understanding (Schramkowski 2001: 92, 113–15).

An anthropology that focuses on the entire person, or complete human being (Rossner 1986; see also Wernhart 1987, 2004: 21–25, Markl 2002: 15), whether for purely scientific or practical purposes, needs an empirical base. Universals that are determined through deliberate, methodically based cultural comparison prevent the field from falling for utopian notions in sociological theory. If empirical work reveals certain anthropological constants, then we can better understand the limits of our capabilities for change (Messelken

2002b: 287). Those who would like to form an empirically based image of humanity beyond a self-understanding of what it is to be "human" will need empirical data on cultural universals. Otherwise, any statements articulated on humanity as a whole remain simple formulations on the nature of humanity. "A secular prohibition of image-making will not protect us from images of humanity. What is not done explicitly will be, by implicit assumption, done anyway" (Bröckling 2004: 172).

For the most part, ideas or images of what it is to be human remain implicitly understood due to their inherent or supposedly obvious quality. As obvious and therefore self-evident, these unexpressed notions of humanity are left unexamined and empirically unsubstantiated (see Sieferle 1989). Since the time of the earliest evolutionists, people have postulated a "psychophysical human unity" (Mühlmann 1984: chap. 9; Stagl 1985: 104; Shore 1996: 15–41). This humanistic principle, which in Western countries developed out of a stoic and Christian tradition, has counterparts in other traditions as well. Unity, as mentioned above, is based on the fundamental possibility of intercultural understanding and existential transcultural experiences, as found in anthropological fieldwork (Stagl 1985: 104; Aleksandrowicz 2011). To become more than simply a postulate, such an idea must be qualified by more than just mere speculation on universals.

Universals are also obviously relevant to the debate on whether something is inborn or learned. The antithetical relationship of nature versus nurture has been discussed since the work of Francis Galton (1822–1911), though over time the debate has given way to the idea of "acquisition" of capacities (Pinker 1997: 32; 2002). In recent years, theories on competition and proportions of nature and nurture have been replaced in favor of the idea of a nature-nurture nexus, for example, in an interdisciplinary science of human evolution (Voland 2000; Keller, Poortinga, and Schölmerich 2002; Rogoff 2003; Petermann, Niebank, Herbert Scheitauer 2004: 64, 240, 255–61; Chasiotis 2007: 180–81, 203–7). The results of research on universals could contribute here, especially when universals are openly defined instead of equivocated with genetic features or anthropological constants.

Appreciating Cultural Comparison and Explaining Ethnocentrism

Cultural universals are important in making cultural comparisons, especially when these comparisons are expressly made with the desire to avoid an ethnocentric or Eurocentric bias (Kluckhohn 1951: 101; Jensen 1999: 60). We cannot fail to remember that cultural anthropology grew out of a time when foreign cultures were defined within deficit models. In the past, anthropologists developed theories on cultural differences by making lists of features not present in other cultures (see Greenwood and Stini 1977: 313; Kuper 2005). These types of assumptions exist in a modified form today, even in the academic literature. Table 2.3 presents some of the most common claims, especially those broadly used in the imaginative ethnography of the nineteenth century—some of which are still in use today.

The authors of deficit models and those who employed such models compared other cultures with cultures of specific Western countries—typically England, France, or the United States—during the industrialization of the mid nineteenth century. These lists were Eurocentric or Occidentalist in that features that clearly existed in Western cultures were the basis of comparison with non-Western cultures. How these features—such as "government" and "family"—were defined generally remained implicitly understood, but they were of course oriented de facto to specific European forms, such as parliament as a political institution or the bourgeois concept of the family. Thus the emphasis on the otherness of cultures contained in itself a critique of Eurocentrism and its universalistic assumptions, though in actuality this internal critique was rarely perceived as such.

A consequence of the comparison of cultural features was that certain cultures were then defined by negation, the absence of features, defects, or handicaps. Though one could claim that these features were in effect simply being described, in fact they were often being evaluated or judged. Defining other cultures by way of marginalization, negation, exclusion, and abasement is the central characteristic of ethnocentrism, as historical (Rüsen 1998: 16–17) and anthropological findings (K. Müller 2003b; Antweiler 2004a) have demonstrated. The definitions or method of defining described above can be seen as having a Eurocentric way of making comparisons and an ethnocentric way

Table 2.3. Deficit models from the nineteenth century: Non-Western societies characterized by traits or features that they are supposedly lacking

- Societies without writing
- Societies without religion
- Societies without technology
- Societies without science
- Societies without limitations on sexuality
- Societies without authority, power, hierarchy
- Societies without social inequality, or social differentiation
- Societies without a state, without government
- Societies without law
- Societies without monogamous matrimony
- Societies without exploitation
- Societies without patriarchy
- Societies without aggression, without war
- Societies without history 1: cultures without change, static cultures
- Societies without history 2: cultures without historical consciousness
- Societies without history 3: cultures without historical writing

of devaluing cultures. The term "primitive peoples" (*Naturvölker* in German), though at times marked by positive connotations, has a negative or degrading meaning as well. In popular anthropology, terms like these are often used without hesitation or replaced by new terms such as "ethnic conflicts" (see Antweiler 2005a).

However, underlying this tallying of deficits in non-Western cultures is the implicit idea that there are commonalities in all cultures. This becomes especially clear when the features that supposedly occur only in Western societies are counted and listed, often under binary specifications. The listing of features such as industrial technology, monotheistic religion, experimental science, monogamous marriage, and government based on law can also be read as a statement that technology, religion, science, marriage, and government as such appear everywhere. Anthropology can help to reduce the severely problematic focus on Western, educated, industrial, rich, and developed (WEIRD) people that pervades current psychology and economic research (Henrich et al. 2010; Norenzayan 2013: 52–54, 166–68), among other fields. One of cultural anthropology's core contributions is thus to define a broad means for comparison that becomes useful in creating ideal types:

> In defining the basic concept, cultural anthropology has here the most to offer since it possesses the broadest analytical latitude concerning elementary social and cultural types. Accordingly, the field could provide a scientific basis, though at times in a limited manner, for all the human sciences with regard to tendencies toward universal behavior. (K. Müller 2003a: 9; also see K. Müller 2003b: 31)

Comparisons do not a priori equate two or more entities, but rather aid in determining likenesses, similarities, and dissimilarities. Research into universals not only exposes commonalities between and among cultures but can also reveal how supposedly universal characteristics are indeed not universals (so-called negative universals). To expose these supposed negative universals for what they are would be a major contribution that could have political implications as well. For example, cultural comparative studies could demonstrate that despite widespread opinion, homosexuality is *not* deemed "unnatural" in all known societies (Ehrlich 2002: 199).

Within the framework of modern politics, where cultural difference and culturalization or ethnicization are part of the working agenda and history is invented many times over, the problem of ethnocentrism becomes a problem of intercultural communication. As such, it represents an enormous barrier separating cultural differences and particularities on the one hand from universal discourse on the other (Rüsen 1998: 21). Accordingly, creation of a better understanding of universal commonalities would contribute both to international development and to a positive humanism in a period of globalization (Bielefeldt 1994; Kulturwissenschaftliches Institut Essen 2006: 83). Based on his analysis of the third, most intensive wave of globalization—which we now face—Robbie Robertson has called for an "inclusive reading of history" in order to facilitate attempts at a universal consciousness (Robertson 2003).

The Ethnicization of Cultural Discourse since the Early Twentieth Century and What It Means for Intercultural Exchange

An anthropological perspective on universality is not just important for making empirically based comparisons covering a wide spectrum of peoples and cultures. More significantly, the insights of the field can powerfully influence how we think about and discuss culture and cultures worldwide. Since the early decades of the twentieth century, a kind of ethnicization has changed how we think in the modern Western world and, more recently, how people think globally. Beginning in the 1920s, talk of "the other" and cultural diversity replaced a discourse on civilization, evolution, temporary primacy, and emancipation. In parallel with the change from nineteenth-century evolutionary concepts to twentieth-century alterity, a different approach developed toward the relationship between individuality and universality.

As a result, the way we order phenomena has also changed, from the distinction between unity and diversity to biology and culture. The nineteenth century and the first part of the twentieth century saw the emergence of the idea that humans could overcome their cultural boundaries in order to forge a universal society. Since World War II, the dominant attitude has become that universals are only to be found in our common biology. Culture, alternatively, is an expression of diversity. This dichotomy unifies universalists and culturalists, who differ only in how much weight they place on the role of biology. Relativists believe human nature is homogeneous, for the sake of making human empathy possible, but also changeable or fluctuating. A biology that unifies us then appears lacking in substance. What is missing in both these positions is the possibility that human beings could form a culturally created unity through consciousness and agency (Malik 2008: 254–55; Stagl 2000: 28).

An increasing focus on cultural differences and diversity has influence not only academic fields and science but also a broad part of our public lives, as the same notions of culture, diversity, alterity, and identity are expressed by colonial rulers, orientalists, indigenous artists, and anticolonialist and nationalist intellectuals alike. Joel Kahn describes this in detail with reference to the early twentieth-century debates on expressionism, on *peasants* (farmers integrated in statal systems) in poorer countries, and on multiculturalism in the cities of the United States (Kahn 1995: 48–50, 109–22). Instead of observing or identifying the relationship between universality and individuality within the context of individual behavior, we look toward a broader context of behavior defined in terms of "worlds," "realms of experience," "cultures," or common worldviews. Fuchs describes this candidly in his remark that "the twentieth century took up the problem of universality and turned it into the problem of the relationship between cultures" (Fuchs 1997: 142). Only in recent years have some people begun to rethink the notion of multiculturalism and consider the diversity of individuals as the key point without focusing on culturalization. Multiculturalism without culture might make commonalities more apparent or accessible to the observer (Phillips 2007: 11–41, esp. 33–34, 67–69). However, this position is far from being mainstream.

The problem of culturalization, or ethnicization, plays a part in normative operations within cultures, for example in intercultural education, especially considering the educational ideas that have long been associated with universalism. These ideas are tied to the notion that we need to overcome culturally held prejudices. In the educational context, understanding relativism and universalism as complementary points of view is a guiding principle of humanistic cultural studies (Schöfthaler 1983: 342–44; U. Schmidt 1987; Nieke 2000).

When we consider what conditions are necessary on an intercultural level for establishing meaning, we cannot avoid dealing with the problem of cultural relativism versus universalism. We can see divisions between socially accepted patterns of interpretation only after we have analyzed what they have in common (Masson 1980: 133). Universalism and cultural relativism are therefore in an interdependent relationship. Relativism lacks external criteria and therefore tends toward a sense of randomness, so that in politics or pragmatism we are unable to be truly critical and end up facing contradiction and even irrelevance (Kolakowski 1980: 275–77). Universalism lacks internal criteria and therefore tends to evaluate specific aspects of culture too quickly, for example by devaluing something as atavistic or dysfunctional. Only when taken together do both ways of thinking have the chance to offer lasting possibilities for intercultural communication and relevance: "They can, as two approaches in a humanistic cultural science, advance concepts that allow both the acceptance and the resistance to change and diversity" (Schöfthaler 1983: 345).

The postcolonial period of global communication and interconnectedness, which is also marked by an emphasis on cultural differences and boundaries, shows the practical importance of universals and their mediating role between human beings who come from differing cultures. When universals are simply capable of revealing general response patterns, behavioral tendencies, or basic emotional sensitivities that are common to us all, then there is a good chance that people will find common ground, for "the human being is at home in many cultures" (Nordenstam 2001: 11–12). Cultural translations are at least possible in theory. We do not need to regard culture as a divisive element separating human beings due to differences in lifeways and perspectives. Mutual recognition of diversity is possible within a context of overlapping living situations and attitudes as well as shared problems.

Universals in Cultural Anthropology Today: The Forgotten Half in the Science of Humanity

Why is there so little explicit interest in universals in anthropology? Anthropologists have been and still are principally skeptical when it comes to assumptions or claims of universal patterns between societies. Since around the mid twentieth century, they have shared the almost unanimous opinion, current in both Anglo-American and continental European philosophy, that cultures differ in such a way as to rule out the validity of transcultural assertions (Holenstein 1985b: 104; D. Brown 2013: 210). This is even more the case in the postmodern period. The logic of modernism looks for relevance or meaning in unity, whether from a capitalist-critical or ecosophical point of view (Argyrou 2005: 78, 84). Studies on universals are viewed with suspicion as representing prejudices or the dreams of the authors more than basic science (Rossi 1978: 201).

Anti-universalism: Geertz and Co.

The particular skepticism found in cultural anthropology is not surprising, since the field places prime value on looking at the complexity and diversity among cultures. The history of the anthropological concept of culture has been associated with a departure from the Enlightenment and its idea of the unified nature of human beings. We cannot understand human beings by looking behind or beyond diversity; rather, we must directly examine differences in historical and local influences, as Clifford Geertz so vividly put it: "what man is may be so entangled with where he is, who he is, and what he believes that it is inseparable from them. It is precisely the consideration of such a possibility that led to the rise of the concept of culture and the decline of the uniformitarian view of man" (1965: 96).

Anthropologists are traditionally understood as specialists in the uniqueness of specific societies and the diversity among cultures. In general relativism is a leading force in the field, but it tends to be a force that is atheoretical, arising from the quasi-instinctive attitude fostered among anthropologists. Critics among them see this as an "on the job sickness" (Boyer 1994: 6, 111). The English anthropologist Edmund Ronald Leach criticized the inclination to study specific or singular ethnicities with the marvelous term "amongitis" (Leach 1982). Up to the present day, cultural anthropology remains essentially more productive in documenting particularities in societies, differences between them, and cultural diversity on a worldwide scale rather than in recording cultural similarities or commonalities. Horace Miner's famous "Nacirema" description of the American way of life in the form of a foreigner looking at something exotic from the outside reveals how effective such representations can be. The daily routine of Americans in their bathrooms, for instance, looks like strange and disconcerting ritualized physical fixations (Miner 1974).

Geertz and other leading anthropologists have explicitly recommended that colleagues see themselves as "traders in diversity" (Geertz 1986; for the moral problems associated with this, see Köpping 1993: 121–25). In some of his publications Geertz described himself as a "merchant of astonishment" (Kramer 2000). One reason for this attitude, which still influences the popular forms of the field today, developed in cultural anthropology before the beginning of the twentieth century: the valid skepticism of speculative, idealized, or normative generalizations concerning "human nature." In light of fundamental differences, similarities between cultures are made to seem like superficial phenomena. This, and not the search for fundamental commonalities under the surface of differences and diversity, has become standard practice. As an indication of this mainstream focus on difference, I quote the first sentence of an article on universal patterns of child rearing. Naomi Quinn asserts: "This may be a singularly unpropitious time, given a climate of ethnographic particularism and anti-psychologism in American cultural anthropology, to propose cultural universals rooted in human psychology" (Quinn 2005: 477). An alternative would be to turn away from this either-or concept—this need to see things as fundamental versus superficial attributes—as in Geertz's critique of the notion of stratified development, in which human beings and a layer cake are seen as evolving in a similar way. This is a point of view that I will develop further.

The schism between biological anthropology and cultural anthropology is due in part to the basic anti-universalistic attitude, and not only in Germany. Within the anti-biological or evolutionary critical perspective, idealists find themselves united with the leading cultural materialist, Marvin Harris. Other cultural materialists are a little more open to evolutionary models (e.g., Sanderson 2001: 147–48; 2014). However, this general attitude is also found in ambivalent, program-oriented statements such as that in a well-known resolution put forth by the American Anthropological Association. The association's president, James Peacock, stated that the "participants affirmed the strength of abiding commitments to biological and cultural variation *and* to the refusal to biologize or otherwise essentialize diversity" (Peacock 1995: 3, emphasis mine; also see Degler 1991; Somit 1992). Peacock does not state how both directions in the field are to be brought together, nor does he communicate how biology could do something other than emphasize differences, for example by pointing out how it might contribute to the view of commonalities between humans and human groups.

Particularism and the Unacknowledged Search for Universals

Despite all the particularism in the field, most ethnographers do strive toward pragmatic means of presenting information. They want to present examples of how people live, and they want to tell stories that go beyond the specific cultures being described. In an essay on political clientelism and patronage published for a popular audience, Thomas Hauschild writes, "Whether in New Guinea, Italy or in the Christian Democratic Party [in Germany], anthropologists discover the same rituals everywhere" (2000: 42). This is a classic form of anthropological writing: through the description of a specific society, we are given a representation of typical human ways of life or problems, or universal phenomena. This generalizing conclusion is not overtly expressed but implied, and therefore not necessarily apparent. The work of Malinowski offers a classic example of this.

Many unacknowledged universal-leaning tendencies are those that occur in culturally specific, personally written monographs, "such that they are believed to be true of all selves in all societies" (Pocock 1994: 133, after D. Williams 2004: 13; see D. Groh 1992b). This holds true for a large portion of the literature on indigenous medical systems and culturally specific or *culture-bound* syndromes in medical cultural anthropology. Generally, cultural features or peculiarities are excluded here. A rare exception is the explicit naming of universals in medical systems (Foster and Anderson 1978: 38–42). Another example of implicit universals occurs in current popularly marketed studies with titles such as "The Politics of Gender" or "The Politics of Belief." They arise in general out of ultra-relativistic intentions, but the titles alone, and the use of the trope "the politics of," hold implicit universal assumptions in that they pertain to what is political (Hauschild 2005: 68).

In monographs on non-Western cultures, descriptions of specific scenes of life are almost always written so as to be understandable to the lay reader. Carrithers demonstrates this using a passage from Raymond Firth's (1901–2002) description of an event that took place during fieldwork in Tikopia. The episode, as Firth tells it, becomes directly plausible, and the event and the participants appear intelligible to the reader, even without knowledge of the local vocabulary or the complexity of the cultural context. The episode as described generates an immediate feeling of naturalness that, though not true for all ethnographic descriptions, makes it independent of the specific function of Firth's text (Carrithers 1992: 159–60, 170). This is evidence of the general notion that stories and storytelling can be understood beyond specific cultural borders. Within our capacity for intersubjective (and intercultural) understanding lies a central and profound human universal.

The Plural Form of Culture, the Particularizing of Comparison, and the Concept of Constructivism

With regard to cultural anthropology as a discipline, a book on universals is particularly challenging to write in today's world, when in terms of culture the field itself can speak only in the plural form. Cultural anthropology has oscillated from representing a scientific push toward the generalized view to a position shaped by a humanistic, interpretative, relativistic understanding of itself (see Bloch 2005: 1–2). Whereas behavior and action were more often the sources of study in the past, in the present we find the focus is on symbols and meaning. One exception is the so-called political economy or cultural materialism of Marvin Harris, whose approach can be understood as a reaction against ultra-relativistic attitudes and positions.

Cultural anthropology, over the course of its history, has produced many great comparative traditions (see Nader 1994 for the situation in American anthropology). For evolutionists, the comparative development took the form of a diffusionist search for comparative historical roots and cultural ties. In functionalism, anthropologists were looking at society in terms of functional relationships on a large scale. In reflexive cultural anthropology today, comparative approaches are more specialized. Like generalization, empirical and broad cultural comparison have lost favor to a more reflexive, self-critical orientation. This is in part the result of radical inferences based on the limitation of intercultural understanding (for a critical perspective, see Stagl 1992; Carneiro 1995; Saalmann 2005: 127–92).

Dan Sperber described this as relativistic replacement of a prerelativistic hierarchy, or a kind of cognitive apartheid: "If we cannot be superior in the same world, let each of us live in his or her own world" (Sperber 1989: 107; similarly, see Weber-Schäfer 1997: 243–44; 1998). An exception would be comparisons, often implicitly drawn, between the societies under study and those to which the ethnologists belong. Opponents of comparative studies like to make such comparisons, though often presenting their own cultures as supposedly a neutral baseline and thus creating the risks of unconscious ethnocentrism and cultural contamination (Hunt 2007: 19, 40–41). Such a comparison leads quickly to dichotomous thinking and the subsequent "othering" of cultures and solidifying of differences in power or strength (J. Goody 1977: 36–51, 146–62; Munroe and Munroe 2001: 223; Weber 2001: 93; Latour 2015: 18–21; Antweiler 2004a). Ross summarizes the point as follows: "Our studies are inherently comparative, if only because the reader compares the presented data to his or her own culture. Making this comparison explicit prevents the creation of the 'other' taking away the perspective of the Western middle class as being the gold standard" (N. Ross 2004: 61).

Colleagues who do explicit work in cultural comparisons form a very small minority in all national anthropological traditions. "Cross-cultural similarities are often treated as relatively unimportant, or outside the scope of anthropology" (Boyer 1994: 4). Apart from Mary Douglas and her well-known concept of "Bongo-Bongoism" (1970: 5), this certainly also has something to do with anthropologists' desire to avoid methods employing statistics and probability (Boyer 1994: 8). In training as well, comparative perspectives play a very limited role in educating future anthropologists. At first glance, a comeback of cultural comparative studies might be discernible from the number of collected volumes now appearing with the word "comparative" in the title. But if cultural comparative work is being carried out in cultural anthropology today, then is it more often done only in an implicit way or within a relativistic framework. As mentioned above, implicit comparisons based on categories in case studies are the core feature of ethnographies. This is more apparent when fieldwork reports refer to other case studies. Otherwise, comparisons are almost always made as individualizing comparisons—a means for offering contrast in the analysis of unique cultural features (e.g., Holy 1987). Generalizing or even universalizing comparisons are mostly rejected in order to avoid the traps of seeing the world in strictly and sharply separated cultures, as in the ideas of Johann Gottfried Herder, and of creating forced comparisons through a blurring of differences (Kaschuba 2003: 342–44, 349). But even comparisons on a more restricted or controlled level (Eggan 1954) are still rare. Broad, cross-cultural studies in the tradition of Murdock are rarely undertaken (de Munck 2000b: 282–85). Avoiding explicitly formed comparisons is especially prevalent in the German-speaking anthropological world (in contrast to French cultural anthropology). Even the operation of comparison is hardly ever discussed, whereas in sociology we find substantial debate on the subject in quite a number of collected works (Matthes 1992a; Kaelble and Schriewer 2003; Srubar, Renn, and Wenzel 2005).

A sign of the skepticism involved in considering the topic of comparison appears in an edited volume that reactivates cultural comparative research, but on the basis of reflexive or constructivist approaches (Gingrich and Fox 2002). The authors distance their work from broadly produced and empirically based cross-cultural approaches. While Murdock and Harold Driver (1907–1992) are mentioned—critically, for the most part—the discussion does not mention the work of anthropologists working actively in a systematic, holocultural comparative method, such as Carol Ember, Melvin Ember, and Douglas White. Due to the particularist interest of the authors, comparative work in psychological anthropology and cultural anthropology like that of the Munroes is not even mentioned. Even in North America, where textbooks propagate cultural comparative methods, along with fieldwork, as the pillars of anthropological methodology, only a few introductory books even focus on cultural comparison (with the exception of Ember and Ember 2009; Eriksen 2015).

Constructivist approaches do not, however, fundamentally exclude comparative methods and universalistic arguments (Hejl 2001a: 7–8)—a fact that is often overlooked due to the polarized discussion in the current "science wars" between social constructivism and biological theories. The antagonists take pleasure in describing their opponents in negative terms. The evolutionary theorists counter the old and nebulous term "biologism" by applying the polemic terms "culturism" and "standard social science model" to all social science approaches (Tooby and Cosmides 1992: 23–42; Workman and Reader 2004: 12–14). When represented in more moderate forms, the two positions are absolutely compatible. A careful reconstruction of the argument reveals that the roots of the conflict lie in differing semantic conceptions of meaning and reference. Philosophers of science have demonstrated this using the example of the compatibility of cultural relativistic and evolutionary psychological theories on emotion (Mallon and Stich 2000: 144–50). The task here is to define the basis for social construction (Ochs 2004: 86). To be able to explain the varying forms of constructed realities, all forms of constructivism require a theory on universals (Hejl 2001a: 8; Barkow 2001: 131; see Barkow, Cosmides, and Tooby 2001; H. Keller 2007). Even a cognitive ethnologist exploring primarily a culturally specific rationality and local knowledge will realize that "finding cultural differences in cross-cultural studies should constitute the starting point and not the endpoint of our research endeavour" (N. Ross 2004: 15).

Atheoretical Relativism

The reserve shown toward explicit comparisons or universal questions in general is hardly surprising, given the broadly held attitude in cultural anthropology today that regards even the most carefully formulated generalizations as somehow suspicious. Generalizing is strictly avoided, to the extent that it amounts almost to a rejection of science. In his criticism of this position, Kuper describes the current notion, widespread in many circles, of an extremely exaggerated culturalist attitude: "Knowledge is culturally constructed, and culturally relative. There are no absolutes, *no universals*. Science itself should be treated as a cultural discourse, with an ideological purpose.... Invocations of science are disguised popular powerplays, strategies for the *imposition of one set of values on the whole world*" (Kuper 2000: 221; italics mine).

Besides the search for generalizations and comparative methods, there are other, more popular trends. The relativism generated via an overall pre-theoretical bias in cultural anthropology has today given way to development of, simply put, a more specialized, more radical form of relativism in the form of a global humanism (Stagl 1992: 146, 150), with a theoretical basis emphasizing social constructedness, postmodernism, and postcolonialism of various shapes and sizes. As mentioned above, in a particularly sarcastic essay Geertz called on anthropologists to stand up against anti-relativism: "We hawk the anomalous, peddle the strange" (Geertz 1984: 275, similar 2000: 64). Pinker was correct in saying this relativist attitude clearly leads us to blur every possible universal pattern in the lives of human beings (Pinker 1994: 462). And Thomas Hauschild, who can hardly be suspected of supporting biologism, has over the years come ever closer to the conclusion that universal approaches are needed for the sake of intercultural understanding beyond the confines of Eurocentrism: "If European knowledge wants to find its way subtly into the realm of foreign discourse, then it will evoke universal theories on human development and the shared physiological and cultural inheritance of *Homo sapiens*" (Hauschild 2005: 76; also 2004; similarly, Bloch 2005: x–xii, 12–14).

Most relativistic positions since Boas (1938) and Herskovits (1966) share the same claim that cultures are to be studied "on their own terms," meaning studied from within their own categories *and* by their own values (Berry et al. 2011: 325). The tendency toward relativism does not characterize cultural anthropology alone or pertain only to contemporary cultures. Relativism is more current than ever in historical works as well. The following sentence appears in the foreword to the first German-language handbook of historical anthropology: "It is no longer possible to speak of the human being" (Wulf 1997; see also Wulf 2013: 113–61). Unlike earlier and similar works, the volume no longer bears the title *Der Mensch*, (The Human Being) but is called "Vom Menschen" (On the human being). Despite the title and intent, the authors do not stick to the agenda; several articles in the book discuss topics that suggest universal content, such as the "body," "space," "institution," or "generation." In many other publications, human beings are discussed in a general way (Cramer and Mollenhauer 1998: 121–21).

Today in the cultural sciences and especially in cultural anthropology, the leading academic texts or references are for the most part the work—and I deliberately mean this across the board—of more or less committed relativists, social constructivists, culturalists and scientific skeptics, and especially of those representing an anti-biological point of view. This we see in current or popular readers in theory by members of the so-called "culture club," Geertz being the sole anthropologist who is an established member (see, e.g., Hofmann, Korta, and Niekisch 2004, 2006). Texts from other disciplines that are taken seriously by anthropologists were authored by, among others, Michel Foucault, Stuart Hall, Jacques Derrida, Edward Wadie Said, Gayatri Chakravorti Spivak, Stephen Greenblatt, Slavoj Žižek, and Judith P. Butler. This corresponds with the situation found today in the humanities and cultural sciences in general (see Müller-Funk 2006).

In contrast, anthropologists absorb very little of the work done in other fields that is universally oriented and internationally discussed, such as that of the philosophers Daniel Clement Dennett and Jürgen Habermas, the sociologist Ernest Gellner, the historian Immanuel Maurice Wallerstein, the linguist Steven Pinker, or the primatologist Sarah Blaffer Hrdy. There is very little in the way of a response to the work coming out of cultural studies, work that is more moderate than the mainstream and shows a regard for such facts as that humans are evolved beings and this might influence their cultures (e.g.,

Barker 2004: 122–51). In terms of what is well received among colleagues within cultural anthropology itself, the work of Geertz, Sahlins, Strathern, and Abu-Lughod tends to dominate. Publications that take a materialist point of view or are written by cross-cultural anthropologists like Murdock, Adam Kuper, Roy A. Rappaport, Douglas White, William Durham, or Pascal Boyer are rarely cited.

Anthropologists are skeptical of any universal statement because of their fundamental relativism with regard to values. They do not want to evaluate culture for its truth or value, but rather present, explain, and understand it. If anthropologists, as cultural relativists, really want to evaluate, they do so only from the vantage point that each culture be recognized on its own terms and supported in its inviolable sovereignty. That does not sit well with the discussion on universals, which are subtly or subliminally normative. Universals that constitute de facto normative postulates are often presented as declarations of supposed facts. Seldom do researchers speak from an intermediate position in which they directly look for universal patterns but at the same time represent a contextualized universalism, a "soft" form of cultural relativism (Gingrich 1999: 34, 117, 120, 199). Geertz (1965: 100) aptly summarized the challenge of universal research in his argument against the dualism of supposed universality vs. "cultural" variability. He claimed that a universal must

- possess a substantive core instead of representing the mere naming of empty categories;
- be understandable and explainable by noncultural processes (biotic, psychic, social) instead of being vaguely connected to "underlying realities";
- stand as a the core element in defining what it is to be human, while reducing the many cultural peculiarities to a more subordinate role.

In any case, proving the existence of specific and absolute universals is not the key substantive challenge regarding universals. Simply put, 100 percent probability that certain phenomena occur is not the goal. The approach should rather be to recognize that certain cultural features do occur on a widespread basis throughout many different societies (Hogan 1997: 228). It is often true that the frequency or distribution pattern of these features is not random or arbitrary. The causal implication is that cultural characteristics are not completely local or historically specific, and not entirely incidental. Rather than showing arbitrary variations, diversity itself reveals obvious limits: "contrary to the widespread belief that cultures can vary arbitrarily and without limit, surveys of the ethnographic literature show that the peoples of the world share an astonishingly detailed universal psychology" (Pinker 1997: 32; see Boyer 1994: 5; Cronk 1999). The scientific challenge here will be discussed systematically in later sections of this book. At this point, however, I would like to discuss my view of the topic in terms of the political challenge from within the field of cultural anthropology itself.

Writing a book on cultural universals is risky, and not only in terms of the generally existing skepticism of cross-cultural comparison and generalization. The first difficulty is that publications that explicitly take on the topic of universals are comparatively few and scattered. Yet if we were to expand the search for universals to include human nature, then we would find ourselves overwhelmed by the number of titles existing on that topic. Cronk responds coyly to the number of sources on the topic of human nature by concluding that "this is a tricky business, to be sure" (Cronk 1999: 24–25). Meanwhile, within specific academic fields themselves, very few researchers explicitly study or consider universals. No single discipline displays a focused interest on universals, and cross-disciplinary discussion on the topic of universals in fields such as sociology, psychology, and anthropology is rare. As a topic of research, universals tend to founder between disciplines marked by a strong relativism that do not address universals at all, and universalizing disciplines that assume, often implicitly, that their findings are universal, like psychology and economics.

Moreover, the subject matter is deeply complex in more than one respect, encompassing multiple disciplines found on both sides of the conventional divide between "two cultures" (Snow 1967), that is, the so-called natural sciences and the humanities. Some anthropologists have explicitly supported any efforts to bridge the gap between the scientific "cultural divide." Many consider it a reasonable endeavor without actively participating in the process. Others are of the opinion that such bridge building is not only too difficult but maybe not even worth the effort (e.g., Geertz 2000: chap. 9; but in contrast, see the early Geertz 1965: 106). Even when approaching the topic as an anthropologist above all else, I need a working knowledge of other fields' theories and findings concerning human nature or the subject of human beings as part of the natural world as well as members of a culture (on the nature vs. culture antinomy; see Vogel 2000 and Mittelstraß 2004: 26).

Particularism and Universality

Cultural anthropology as a scientific study of human culture oscillates between two poles: universality and particularity. Culture can be studied in a particularistic way, in terms of its specific forms within separate societies and global cultural diversity; or in a universalistic way, with regard to global unifying patterns of culture. This range of methods is often thought of as inhabiting a spectrum between cultures in the plural (particularistic cultural concept) and culture in the singular (generic cultural concept). Since the work of Radcliffe-Brown, cultural anthropology has often described as the "science of culture," though de facto mostly as a "science of cultures," as Stocking properly remarked (Stocking 1987: 302). According to my understanding, the strength of cultural anthropology lies in its consideration of both the particularistic and the universalistic approach (see Vivelo 1995; Scupin and DeCorse 2016). Its dialectic coherence and most especially its methodological combination of particularism and universalism via comparison (Adams 1998: 5–6) are part of the core foundation of cultural anthropology. According Kroeber in *Anthropology Today*, cultural differences and likenesses are both at the heart of his definition of anthropology as "science devoted to the study of man, the study of differences *and similarities* of all aspects of life of man without limitation in time and space" (Kroeber 1948b:12; italics mine; similarly Redfield 1957: 159; 1962: 442–43).

Consideration of all three perspectives—particularism, universalism, and comparativism—is the contribution of cultural anthropology within the current proliferation of fields such as cultural studies, European ethnography, cultural sociology, cultural geography, and cultural psychology. This contribution on the part of cultural anthropology is largely a non-trivial response to the question of unity in diversity or universals in diversity (Adams 1998: 183) in certain cultural phenomena. Only under such terms can cultural anthropology, through cooperation and collaboration with other fields of study, make a legitimate contribution to science. "Thus the fundamental challenge facing anthropology is how to deal with the fact that all cultures exhibit the same basic features yet are inherently different. All cultures are the same … all cultures are different" (Greenwood and Stini 1977: 317). Gregor and Tuzin (2001: 7) argue that universals are "i inherent in the act of classification, by which we identify unfamiliar behaviors, describe institutions, and communicate the results of our work to others. We cannot describe one society without having others in mind, for comparison is the recurring element of our basic analytical tools."

A good rule of thumb comes from Kenneth Lee Pike (Pike 1954, 1993): something that is highly pronounced in one culture will be most likely found in all other cultures as well (see Holenstein 1979; 1985b: 133; 1997: 53, 2013). This tension between the two poles of universalism and particularism is exactly what makes the search for universals even more fascinating, given the great diversity offered worldwide in culture and cultures that appears at first specifically local in form and content. A perfect example of this can be drawn from cultural expression in the form of music, which on an immediate level may seem to exemplify diversity but might rather be understood, according to a leading and globally oriented ethnomusicologist, as follows: "In the heart of the ethnomusicologist there are two strings: one that attests to the universal character of music, to the fact that music is indeed something that all cultures have or appear to have … and one responsive to the enormous variety of existing cultures" (Nettl 1980: 3, quoted in Ferraro 2001a: 337).

Like the authors quoted above, I regard specific case studies, cross-cultural studies, and the issue of universals all as part of the overall anthropological project known as cultural anthropology. Universals and culturally specific phenomena are the two poles of a continuum filled with many intermediate elements. This broad range is easily forgotten, resulting in a focus on either the universal or the culturally specific. The universalistic and particularistic viewpoints do vary. Universal insights are developed by blurring peculiarities: "who ever focuses on the universal anthropological cannot keep an eye on the historically specific and culturally unique at the same time" (Assmann 2004b: 104). Yet each depends on the other. Jerome Bruner (1981: 262) said it right when he wrote: "Universals found their way back into studies of culture as an antidote to cultural relativism. The emphasis upon them has surely served a useful function. But one need not live on a diet of antidote alone." Still, instead of the possibilities of a dualist approach being appreciated, the question of "relativity vs. universality" is often seen as dueling between factions—as antithetical and dichotomous. The two poles are woven together in binary opposition, becoming then a cultural paradigm, as when universal humanity is described as the "self" defending itself against the "other" (for a critique see Lossau 2002: 47–59). The study of the individual psyche provides us with a far richer, more complex image than the one we receive through dichotomous categories: "Far from being wholly culturally constructed, individual psychological predispositions and mental states are also shaped by universal biological attributes and developmental stages" (Mathews and Moore 2001: 15). Furthermore, Mathews and Moore (2001: 15) go on to say that common human activities result from shared material adaptations, and that culturally specific intrapsychic conflicts stem from "disjunctions between shared cultural values and the realities of everyday experiences."

Anthropology is about human similarities and differences. Thus, in theory, universals make up half of our concerns as anthropologists. Cross-cultural similarities—together with differences—have been at the core of anthropology all along, as Donald Brown (2013) recently demonstrated again by using methodological arguments in the study of universals. In view of the history of cultural anthropology, this was brought home by Herbert Lewis by carefully revisiting the storehouse of knowledge in twentieth-century U.S. and British anthropology (Lewis 2014). I will return to this in Chapter 8's discussion of criticism of the search for universals.

Figure 3. Vegetable vendor in Kuala Lumpur, Malaysia. Photo by Maria Blechmann-Antweiler.

CHAPTER 3

Cultures and Human Nature
Human Beings Are Biologically Cultural

> *Answering the question of what is a human being is a dangerous undertaking that we can hardly avoid.*
> —Ulrich Bröckling, "Um Leib und Leben"

The question of universals is closely tied to the question of human nature, though the two are not identical. This is an important point in this book, producing many important questions to follow, such as whether universals represent a unique or specific source from which a unified form of human nature can be empirically inferred. A further question would be whether pancultural patterns are the proper level from which to answer the classic question of what a human being is or whether the answer must be determined at another level that has more to do with human biology, such as in the biotic basis of cognitive, motivational, and affective capacities (Schiefenhövel 1999: 4).

In this chapter I will discuss attempts made to approach the subject of universals through an integrated analytical framework. This consists above all in an empirically based determination of the general features characterizing human beings. We will be working within a conceptual framework of "common denominators" (Kapp 1983: 136, 133–48). I want to reveal the tightly bound relationship of natural and cultural characteristics within human beings. "Human" is a proper word for both points of view, as the word corresponds to both *humus,* indicating the natural in human nature, and to *humanitas* and *humanus,* which refer to culture (Rappaport 1999: 406; cf. Morris 2014).

The Nexus of Intracultural Diversity and Universals

It is impossible here to discuss the basic concept of culture with a proper degree of thoroughness. Instead, I will outline my basic assumptions so far as they are relevant to the topic of universals. To reveal the link between the modern, nonessentialist concept of culture (Hauck 2006: 178–88) and the topic of universals, I turn to the findings uncovered in linguistic research into universals, especially with regard to the cultural theoretical work of Elmar Holenstein (1985a, 1985b, 1998a–d).

Despite all the differences associated with specific approaches, the currently dominant position among anthropologists and other cultural scientists assumes that cultures are not clearly separate entities. They are not static or homogenous. They are not even, in any agreed upon form, coherent from within. I share, then, in the implicit criticism of a static and monadic concept of culture, but believe the baby is being thrown out with the bathwater when it comes to contemporary cultural theory. Cultures are not containers, but neither are they pure assemblages of elements that together remain formless, without limits or contours. As ethnicity research has shown, specific and separate cultures are viewed both emically, that is, from within, and generally as strictly distinct from other cultures. From the scientific or etic viewpoint, they operate beyond a cognitively emotional and self-identifying limit, even as a part of social reality, and can be separated from one another only imperfectly. Cultures are not, according to current knowledge, incommensurable Herderian spheres (Wiredu 1995, 2001: 76, 81).

Cultures are not discrete and closed systems or independent units, but rather overlapping entities (Holenstein 1998a: 239). They also are not logically consistent and coherent forms, as an exaggerated holistic understanding of cultures would have it. All the elements existing within cultures must not be understood from the standpoint of a total concept (as in systems "où tout se tient", "where everything stands"), as presented in the hermeneutic principle of a correlation between parts and wholes, or as presented in holism as well as in the metaphor of "culture as text." Rather, cultures correspond more to the metaphorical model of bricolage, a term Lévi-Strauss suggested for "simple" cultures that exist in specific environments and scrape by with very limited resources (Lévi-Strauss 1962), an image expanded upon by the biologist François Jacob, who adapted it to his own field with the term *tinkering* (Jacob 1977: 1161; J. Marks 2004). The diverging tendencies in individuals speak against a closed cultural perspective. According to an ex negativo argument, day-to-day human action would hardly be possible within closed cultural orientations. Later I will discuss positive rationales through empirical observations such as are found in intuitive models (Holenstein 1998a: 243–44).

Cultures are heterogenic, which means they display intracultural diversity (Boster 1996, 1999; Boster and D'Andrade 1989). This is often overlooked due to the ecological fallacy, as in some psychologically based cultural comparisons in which individuals in one culture, seen as homogenous, are compared with individuals from another culture, likewise viewed as homogenous (Choi, Han, and Kim 2007: 319). Apart from positive lawmaking, hardly anything to be found (a) occurs only in one culture, (b) occurs in all members of one culture and (c) occurs in no members of another culture. Two cultures do not differentiate themselves through a bundle of features in culture A that are completely absent in culture B, which contains its own bundle of exclusive features. Attributes of culture A will be found, at least to some degree, in most if not all other cultures (Pike 1967, cited in Holenstein 1985b: 133, 198; fn. 49). Cultures do not differ due to specific characteristics that they possess or collections of features that are exclusively their own; rather, they differ based on the value or importance they place on certain characteristics. What distinguishes one culture from another is the difference in hierarchies or the varying emphasis placed on what are, for the most part, shared attributes, a condition backed by relatively recent findings of research on individualistic (and analytically separate) versus collectivist (and holistic) styles of thought, or mentalities (Nisbett et al. 2001; Nisbett 2003). This has immediate relevance for an understanding of universals in the general sense and for the methods used in cultural comparison in the more particular sense: "the assumption of discontinuous and mutually exclusive types of cultures [requires] some revision through the understanding of continuously merging types" (Holenstein 1985b: 104; addition mine). "What distinguishes two cultures from one another is less the presence or absence of certain characteristics but more the varying dominance of the more or less pre-existing *universally given* characteristics" (Holenstein 1998a: 240; emphasis mine; see also Holenstein 1985b: 137–39).

The variations that occur within a single culture (e.g., with reference to aging, profession, class, region, and time period) are as significant as those occurring between cultures (intercultural diversity), and sometimes even greater (Antweiler 2003, 2007). Subcultures and nonconformity are something normal, and inter-individual differences are quite often substantial, like age differences between people. Holenstein goes so far as to say that differences in type, degree, function, and effect are similar. The intracultural diversity in one culture is analogous to the intercultural variability among human beings (Holenstein 1985b: 149; 1998a: 240; 1998b: 279, 285; 1998d: 326). This amounts to a neutralization of intra- and intercultural differences that, in my opinion, goes too far. Yet Holenstein's position is worth considering, especially when contrasted with statements made by the younger Habermas, as it expresses the currently dominant attitude in the cultural sciences: "It is easier to make assertions concerning human beings as a species, that is, assertions that are true for all human beings and not for other living creatures, than it is concerning specific cultures, or populations, that is, assertions that are true for all members of one culture and not for those of another culture" (Holenstein 1998d: 326; also see 1998a: 265, and for more detail 1998b: 265). "We cannot say human beings exist in the same way we cannot say that language exists. Because human beings make themselves to be what they are, according to this or that circumstance, there are societies and cultures that, as with plant or animal species, can be defined through general or broad statements; but this is not the case for human beings themselves" (Habermas 1973: 106).

As already stated, cultures are by no means simple accumulations or bundles of elements heaped together that outwardly are fully penetrable. This is my objection to too strongly conceived versions of transculturality, as found in the early work of the cultural philosopher Wolfgang Welsch. Cultures do form compact units of lifeways ((Welsch 1992; Hepp 2006: 63–64), or in consumer patterns and professional lifestyles, but at the same time these compact units cannot be broken apart into easily understandable parts. They have relations with the outside world and are dynamic in form, but they are not easily integrated. Cultures are systematically organized but not uniform. Specific subsystems can enjoy relative autonomy in a modular sense.

Looking at universals over time in an anthropological synthesis (Table 3.1) offers us a better understanding of possible universality. The relative autonomy of structures from within cultures is necessary to compare cultures over time and space. Universalism and pluralism are not only compatible but also mutually beneficial: "intra-cultural non-uniformity (incoherence or plurality) makes inter-cultural uniformity (invariance, universality) possible" (Holenstein 1998a: 244).

Just as universals are difficult to comprehend without a serious consideration of cultural diversity, so too are cultural differences difficult to understand without an appreciation for similarities or, eventually, universals. An example will make this clear (after N. Ross 2004: 13). In a study by López et al. (1997), knowledge concerning mammals and categorical thinking was studied by comparing Itza Maya from Pétén, Guatemala, and students from Michigan in the United States. Obvious likenesses were revealed in how both groups classify animals, showing similarities to Carl von Linné's (1707–78) classifying system. The general means of reasoning through induction were similar. Both groups used taxonomic assumptions about species. Clear differences were revealed in the reasoning behind the categories: the Maya often used ecological knowledge, whereas the Michigan students proposed taxonomic arguments. The question now remains as to whether these disparities arose simply out of specific cultural differences and whether the similarities indicate universals. Other studies have shown that the logic behind reasoning is more dependent on personal experience. The differences could be explained less by culturally specific conditions than by goal- and task-specific factors. Nonprofessional experts from various cultures share more similarities than do laypeople from different cultures, although both follow cultural models (Medin et al. 2002). This then raises the question of whether similarities found among these groups could be construed as universals.

Table 3.1. Relationship between universality and diversity as seen from antiquity, and the early to late modern era

	Basic understanding of the relationship between universality and diversity		
	Platonic	Romantic	Synthetic
1. Type of universality	Universals that are profound and necessary to being	No universals, or they are trivial or abstract	Contingent universals that are both profound and superficial, e.g., universals of expression (form)
2. Scope of variability	Essential component of being human and the contingent heterogeneity of culture	Outer heterogeneity of humanity; internal homogeneity of cultures	Contingent homogeneity of humanity and internal homogeneity of cultures, modular and limited
3. Relationship of inner to outer form	Mutually independent	Within its totality, mutually dependent	In meaning and expression mutually dependent, but not completely within every context
4. Concept of the world	Invariant in its ontic existence, appearance is arbitrary	Without structure, chaotic or random and changeable ("anything goes")	Naturally limited variability (constraints)
5. Value system	Hierarchical, harmonious, stable	Labile and relative in an unlimited way (value relativism)	Heterarchical network of values with hierarchy and conflict (polytheism of values)
6. Structure of languages	Alterable, particular, arbitrary, varying on the surface	Determined by history, radically different	Phylogenetically determined on all levels
7. Determining factor in worldview	Structure of the world à language structure, universal	Language structure à Experience, worldview, more particular	Brain à Possibilities of experience and language, universal
8. Possibility of intercultural understanding	Return to ideas	Hardly possible, at best through assimilation	Possible through change of perspective

Source: severely modified after Holenstein 1998b: 265–74

Human Nature and the Proper Image of Who We Are

A current and widespread image of human beings as essentially existing beyond nature has emerged from the concept propagated by the United Nations. The "UNESCO Man" (Degler 1991: 204–5; Malik 2001: 115–47, 250, 2008: 158; Eriksen 2001) is considered a cultural being, as opposed to the natural "Übermensch" associated with racism. Thus humanity appears in biological uniformity and in cultural plurality. The founders of UNESCO believed they were speaking the language of the Enlightenment. Their concept—embodying the hopes of a generation that had witnessed and experienced bestial forms of racism—was produced by moral considerations rather than scientific arguments, and it prepared the way for today's multiculturalism (Malik 2008: 158, 167).

As demonstrated above, the debate on universalism vs. relativism includes assumptions about the world and epistemic assumptions about its perceptibility. According to Ernest Gellner, two decisive questions arise here: "Is there but one kind of man, or are there many? Is there but one world, or are there many?" (Gellner 1985: 83). The first question refers to biotic human uniformity, the second to the possibility of uniformity in scientific knowledge. In multiculturalism, the differences between people—as opposed to differences defined by a racist or social Darwinist (or social-Spencerist)—originate on the cultural rather than the physical level. But given the focus on differences, the problem of racism still remains (Malik 2008: 159–65; 2014). Where the racist sees different races in a world that is uniform and rational (physically different people living differently in one world), advocates of the UNESCO human being see a uniform image of human beings living in cultures with very different living and cognitive realities (living culturally in different worlds).

This concept of a unified and unique humanity is a bit strange when we consider intercultural comparisons. First, many cultures do not separate themselves so clearly from the animal world, and second, they tend to exclude certain categories of human beings along ethnocentric and racial lines. In view of the current uncertainty about the concept of humanity in relation to genetic technology and artificial intelligence, the historian Felipe Fernández-Armesto has described the historical development of the images of humankind, demonstrating that the widespread image of human beings in historical and diachronic comparison is far from clear. In many cultures, human beings and primates were and are considered very similar. An extremely widespread idea is that human beings could, for example, in violation of certain rules or norms, transform into apes, that apes are the offspring of outcasts, and that there are crossbreeds or hybrids. Common or prevalent zoomorphological thinking and totemic understanding see strong, close relationships between human beings or kinship groups and animals (Fernández-Armesto 2005: 39–40, 63–64). Briefly put, the current and dominant concept of human beings has only been accepted after long, contentious debate and conflict in Eurasian culture and elsewhere, "yet our present concept is a recent contrivance: most people in most societies for most of history would have been astonished by such an all-encompassing category" (Fernández-Armesto 2005: 7). The idea of human superiority over nature, or a human responsibility toward or for nature, can be traced back historically only to Karl Jasper's "axial age" in the first millennium BC, more specifically between 800 and 200 BC, which is marked by an intellectual and historical departure from the periods preceding it (Jaspers 1955: 37; see Holenstein 2004: 50-62; Eisenstadt 2006: 53-65; for a summary, see K. Armstrong 2006). This concept of superiority is also found in the Indian Upanishads (Fernández-Armesto 2005: 37, 44).

Especially problematic is the commonly held and established separation of humans from the natural world and the related contrast between materiality and culture. Culture as the result or effect of nongenetic knowledge or information transfer is found in individuals on a mental level and throughout the body . Beyond that, culture exists in the out-of-body form of artifacts. Accordingly, culture as a group feature is in part superorganic (see de Munck 2000a, 2000b; Handwerker 2015: 23-33). It is important to understand that the assumption that human beings are not a form of specialized ape but rather a completely unique species does not mean we make a clear separation between biological anthropology and cultural anthropology. The unique qualities of human beings could originate through biotic rather than cultural conditions, such as those concerning our specific genome (Leach 1982: 120).

Nature and Culture: Beyond the UNESCO Man and Lara Croft

Culture is manifested in phenomena that are made, manufactured, or produced, as works or facts, by human beings (Konersmann 2006: 14-15). These made quantities can be intellectual or can occur as artifacts. The latter could be objects, anthropogenetically modified landscapes, or artificially modified human bodies. Culture is therefore not in any way reducible simply to the material as cognitive or material objects, but rather reaches through and beyond many material forms (Tschohl 2004). Separating the body from the mind is not a solution. Culture is not an entity that stands outside of the natural world. Meanwhile, the concept of a natural human being ignorant of culture is just as problematic. Culture, in the sense of factors beyond those that are genetic, is a biotic given and a necessity for human existence. Therefore, there is no empirical concept of human beings as nature without, or independent of, culture. What empirically manifests itself as nonvariant nature "is nowhere pure nature, but rather nature modified or defined by that which is known as society" (Maiers 1993: 68). This is true for individuals as well as for all of humankind. As Geertz aptly put it, "culture, rather than being added on, so to speak, to a finished or virtually finished animal, was ingredient, and centrally ingredient, in the production of that animal itself" (1965: 110). The problem with Geertz's argument, as will be argued here, is that he reduces culture to particular forms of culture (1965: 113, 117).

Human nature cannot be simply biotic when culture is fundamentally biocultural (Greenwood and Stini 1977: 317; Kapp 1983: 64–66). However, notions of a culturally free human nature are widespread. Robin Fox, who in many ways has contributed to universal research, claimed in an earlier work that "if Adam and Eve could survive and breed—still in total isolation from any cultural influences—they would produce a society which would have …" (quoted in Malik 2001: 250–51). This kind of thinking, which Kenan Malik appropriately dubs Lara Croft theories of history, is based on the idea that culture is something encoded in our genes. The problem here is assuming that culture is something pre-given in the minds of individuals, something that must simply be then realized. Human beings, or human beings in a pure natural state, do not exist. We should abandon any "layer-cake concepts of reality in which culture is an autonomous level of reality lying over biology" (D. Brown 2013: 410). The broadly shared uncritical acceptance of such an assumption in twentieth-century anthropology has limited the theoretical significance of universals. Humans live in physical environments that they to some degree create by using their own innovations (Latour 2015: 241). They necessarily live with artifacts and in anthropogenically modified landscapes. Culture in the form of learning, innovation, and behavioral flexibility is, according to the bio-anthropological view, an existential requirement for human beings (Henke and Rothe 2003: 15; Medicus 2012). To imagine humans without culture is, according to Kenan Malik, "a bit like imagining that a leopard could exist without its spots or an elephant without its trunk. Such denuded creatures would not be leopards or elephants" (Malik 2001: 247).

We can assume that nonhuman animals' "nature" is equated with species-specific corporeal features or species-specific behavior, and that these develop, in the Darwinian sense, above all as a product of natural selection. This cannot be so easily said when it comes to human beings (Malik 2001: 252) because nongenetic variables play a part in the necessarily existential and biological forms associated with human beings. Gehlen expressed this well in 1940 with his idea of culture as a "second nature" in which human beings by their nature are cultural beings (Gehlen 2004: 37–40; similarly, see Landmann 1969: 183), even when this is also associated with the idea of human beings as defective creatures (*Mängelwesen*). Newborns cannot survive without the help of others. This care has much to do with capacities and knowledge that are passed on nongenetically. As Ellen Dissanayake describes it, "being cultural and acculturable is part of human biological nature" (Dissanayake 1992: 76). For human beings, culture is not a crust, shell, or veneer that simply complements human nature. It is an integral part of that nature. An example would be the forming of social contracts that involve not only kin. As Wilson correctly ascertained, the creation of social contracts or agreements is more than a cultural universal; it is also a characteristic feature of *Homo sapiens* like language and abstract thinking (E. Wilson 1998: 171).

Indeed, some human lifeways resemble an earlier phase in human evolution more than others. For instance, hunter-gatherer societies could be described as more "natural" or their cultures as closer to nature. But such cultures do not produce a kind of "original or pristine human" or a "natural folk" in an original state, in the sense of people who do not as yet have culture. Biologically understood, culture is an indispensable adaptive necessity, and the fundamental capabilities associated with this capacity for culture are of central importance in the complex set of biotically given features specific to the human species, something I will explore in in more detail below.

Concepts and Critics of a "Human Nature"

Studies concerning present-day societies and historical cultures are not just conceived as a way of examining the fundamental human condition; rather, they are an attempt to address human nature itself (Ingham 1996: 21; Davies 2007: 127). Explicit mention of human nature or human essence is popular, especially in discussing an inherently fundamental concept in anthropology, philosophy, politics, or ethics. A current example of this is the project known as The Human Condition. In this long-term, well-financed undertaking, scientists and activists are working together to advance a notion of humankind within a moral framework. Under the direction of Jeremy Griffith, brochures and CDs are distributed worldwide (Griffith 2004). This publication includes normative statements and selected scientific findings on human beings as well as many statements from famous scientists and researchers in various fields, giving the project a quasi-religious feel.

Human beings generally and historically do not see themselves in solidarity with the world around them and with other living creatures. They see more difference than similarity, meaning there might not be a great "mortal cord" binding all creatures of the world together. But although difference is a fundamental part of human co-existence, philosophy and especially philosophical anthropology still deal with human nature in various ways. Regardless of the field or the perspective, all ideas on the topic share basic themes. Human nature almost always assumed to have the following characteristics: it is universal, appearing in all members of the species, and is not cultural; it creates the natural existential basis; it places restrictions on how humans act or behave due to its invariability. However, precise definitions are lacking, and "every attempt at reconstructing a definition is confronted with many competing definitions" (Bayertz 1987: 97). The use of the term as practically a given produces the impression that the concept is basically unproblematic for many authors. Only in a few cases do authors explicitly touch upon the vagueness of the term: "The concept of human nature is a leading and useful idea in behavioral research, but it is too early to produce an exact definition for human nature" (Wehler 1990: 243).

Human nature is a central topic in philosophical anthropology. It can be understood as either biotic dispositions and behavioral uniformities, or the living world of common experiences. Some authors limit the conceptual structure to pancultural psychic potentials, or the characteristics shared by all adult human beings or all members of a particular age group or sexual category (e.g., Hinde 1994: 15). Meanwhile, many philosophers flatly reject the concept of human nature, as do, above all, many outside of philosophy and theology. This is even more the case when biotic or organism-related factors are addressed (see O'Hear 2001; in contrast, see Richards 2000).

Many believe the concept to be simply a reactionary doctrine tied to a lack of freedom, ineptness, right-wing ideology, sexism, and colonial thinking, or even social Darwinism. When human nature is mentioned on an individual level, critics often assume the term is being used automatically to explain differences among people, when in fact it could just as likely be explaining similarities as well (Harris 2001a: 155). The general rejection of the term human nature is quite strong and most often based on the suspicion that universal statements are attempts to codify human characteristics. José Ortega y Gasset, for example, has said in a simple dictum that "the human being, in one word, does not have a nature; what he has is history" (Ortega y Gasset 1961: 21, also 1943: 68). Voices in existential philosophy similarly emphasize human freedom: Sartre, for example, talks of "unhindered self-creation." Tsvetan Todorov regards the fact that human beings are constantly reassessing or revising their lives as in itself human. The more important species-specific feature would be the freedom to alter the emphasis on aspects of culture and to reject more narrowly constructed definitions (Todorov 1993). Paul Drechsel's thought moves in a similar direction when he states that there is a universal capacity to consider the givens in one's own culture as only one of many reasonable possibilities (Drechsel 1984: 47). Classic thinkers in historical materialism, such as Vladimir Ilyich Lenin, Lucien Sève, and Louis Althusser, refrained from using the term human nature, even though Marx, for one, had clear ideas on what it is to be a human being (Ottomeyer 1976; Rückriem 1978a: 9; Tomberg 1978: 42). A minority of Marxist writers refer explicitly to human nature because they assume that already existing assumptions would otherwise remain unspoken (e.g., Tomberg 1978; similarly, see Kamper 1973: 11).

Philosophical anthropologists emphasize historicity and flexibility—the plasticity of human beings and the contingent character of culture. Plessner and Scheler also underline the openness human beings have to the world. Hellmuth Plessner, more so than Scheler, supported integrative thinking, so his work was oriented more along the lines of biological and social scientific research, and characterized humans by their nature as able to construct themselves artificially, that is, not naturally (1981: 360–65, 383). His famous formulation of "eccentric positionality" stressed the possibility and necessity of conscious behavior arising from the inner self in (1981: 362). What is most important is the ability to accept an eccentric middle ground, that is, to adopt a reflexive, detached perspective of staying in the middle, between our internal and external worlds (Bialas 2004: 104–5). In all contexts human beings can take a step back to allow themselves to see the world and themselves from a distance (Thies 2004: 54). One might agree with such arguments insofar as they suppose that cultural change is not determined by nature. Ortega y Gasset's assertions are fundamentally problematic in that he maintains that humans develop away from nature yet remain a part of it. Kant thought human beings could not be defined simply as natural organisms due to deficiencies in their physical makeup. He argued dualistically but connected the dual spheres of the human world by saying that human beings' inadequate physical form made it necessary for them to alter themselves, a fact that rests at the core of any definition of what it means to be human.

Still other criticisms concerning the concept of human nature issue from those who guard the realms of philosophical and cultural anthropology. Some critics of the established positions in philosophical anthropology are interested in "anthropological difference" as a research model. They say that the central goal of constructive and historically informed anthropological criticism is to establish a concept of human beings that, through critical analysis, allows for the impossibility of such a concept (Kamper 1973: 11, 23, 38–47, 152–71). Geertz has criticized the "'stratigraphic' conception of the relations between biological, psychological, social, and cultural factors in human life" (1965: 98), which expresses a global image of man as a composite of levels that may be peeled away layer by layer. Here he is criticizing the notion of human beings as made up of autonomous layers that are in themselves complete and irreducible (cf. Geertz 1965: 103, 106).

Tim Ingold argues in a similar fashion when describing the constant change associated with the capacity for culture that is transformed into myth when the topic turns to origins. He concludes that "the entire project of searching for the genesis of some essential humanity is seriously misguided" (Ingold 2002: 64). This critique is noteworthy, in light of biocultural coevolution. Through its harsh formulations, it equates nature with determination and ahistoricity. There is tradition behind this parallel notion: various thinkers from Giambattista Vico (*mondo naturale* vs. *mondo civile*) to Voltaire considered nature to be uniform and timeless and culture to represent diversity and change (Konersmann 2003: 142). This shapes the Manichaean dichotomy of the humanities versus the natural sciences to the present day. Yet critics have too easily overlooked the notion that nature—as conceived at least since Lyell and substantiated by Darwin—is not static but rather historical (see Degler 1991: 5; Gould 1986; Maiers 1993; Rolston 1999: 157).

Equating nature with determination contradicts recent insights in the philosophy of biology. Furthermore, when the all-too-feared biological determinism is replaced by a logocentric or symbolic cultural reductionism or cultural determinism, there promptly emerges a danger of contradicting well-established findings in neurobiology, developmental psychology, primatology, and palaeoanthropology—for example, those proving the enormous consequence of emotions and nonverbal capabilities in the formation of thought (Spiro 1994; Ingham 1996: 21; Wahl 2000; Sedmak 2004: 14; Schmidinger and Sedmak 2004). In anthropological research, assumptions concerning human nature are basically unavoidable, though they remain often implicit. Biologist George Gaylord Simpson argued from a paleontological perspective that fields such as metaphysics, theology, and art offer an important contribution to our image of human beings, but "unless they accept, by specification or by implication, the nature of man as a biological organism, they are fictional fancies or falsities, however interesting they may be in those nonfactual categories" (Simpson 1969: 80). Anthropologist Robert Murphy has characterized the vacuum created by cultural anthropology's refusal to address the topic of human nature as follows:

> Social science has ... departed from the popular and persistent belief that some of our most cherished values and entrenched patterns of behavior are part of "human nature." ... The social sciences, especially anthropology, have effectively refuted this folklore and sometimes scientism, of imalleable human nature and instinct, but they have provided no substitute view, except by omission, of an irreducible and common humanity. It is as if, having rejected the biological specificity of panhuman instincts, we were left with neither a view of existential problems universal in mankind nor a curiosity about the general propensities and structures of the mind. (Murphy 1971: 8–9)

Even the clear rejection of the existence of human nature by those arguing from symbolic, postmodern, and constructivist points of view (e.g., Judith P. Butler), depends necessarily on certain assumptions about the nature of humans. An argument that dismisses the concept of human nature needs in itself some structural image of human beings. Forming images of what human beings are is an unavoidable part of the cultural and human sciences, even when these images remain only tentative (Ricken 2004: 164–70). As a way of representing an image of human nature, Geertz's contention that the essence of human beings lies in their diversity resembles the statement that the unchangeable in human beings is their changeability (Böhme, Matussek, and Müller 2000: 131–32). Geertz is strictly opposed to speaking of a human nature and critical of universal research. His definition of religion (extremely well known among anthropologists) as a system of symbols rests on the assumption that human beings, by their very nature, have a creative need or impulse. Such general assumptions, which are mostly functionalist, pervade Geertz's anthropological work on religion (Saler 2000: 95; see Whitehead 2000: 4–5). Only universal assumptions and findings can make the nonrandom distribution of cultural diversity comprehensible. Only those who hold these assumptions can explain what is made possible in the spectrum of diversity and can determine the limits of these variations. The symbolic anthropologist Carrithers says it best: "An explanation of variability ... must show what all humans must share in order to be able to create diversity, and therefore it concerns human nature explicitly. ... To ask about humans and human nature is, in this context, to ask about what makes that, or any, variation possible" (Carrithers 1992: 5).

The view of human nature as something inborn is shared by authors who have no problem with the idea of human nature itself as well as by many critics of the concept. Human nature is often associated with inborn behavioral tendencies, though these are understood differently. Wehler, for example, writes that "in the current form, the concept of human nature has returned to the question concerning inborn behavioral tendencies" (Wehler 1990: 241; see also Boehm 1989: 922). However, this is only one abbreviated form of the issue, as culture belongs to the species-specific adaptive potential of human beings—a point that encompasses not only the biotically-based ability to have culture but also our need for room to maneuver.

The concept of "nature" is already somewhat problematic, especially when the implicitly understood converse of nature is that which is artificial or stems from culture. It is especially limiting to think of nature as something uniform and constant, and history as altering, as shown by the example of eye color, an inborn trait that can also vary (Holenstein 1998a: 248). There are no general, clear criteria for establishing whether the current features of an object or a phenomenon are natural or artificial (Monod 1975: 23–25). We need knowledge ofr the genesis, the historic origins of the phenomenon. Since every human feature is somehow influenced by human action, we can only speak of a certain degree of naturalness or artificiality (Bayertz 1987: 139). Any behavior is the final result of a "multi-level reduction process" (Markl 1986: 67; also see Antweiler 1988; Dupré 2003: 99) in which potential behavior is maneuvered, formed, and limited by various natural and cultural processes of selection, such as randomness in the genome, the prenatal environment, the epigenesis of fetal development, and personal decision. What is problematic is to equate human nature per se with permanence: "The natures of Americans today are very different from their natures in 1940. Indeed, today's human *natures* everywhere are diverse products of change, of long genetic and, especially, cultural evolutionary processes" (Ehrlich 2002: 13; italics mine; cf. Roughley 2011). Beyond the uniformity in the genome, Ehrlich argues (2002: 12–13, 231, 330), there is no human nature but rather human natures.

Genus proximum *and* differentia specifica: *Human Beings as One-Dimensional*

A conventional notion defining human beings, or rather distinguishing humans from other living creatures, is the use of the descriptive and evaluative word *Homo* or *Animale*. A famous example of this in the social sciences is in Lord Dahrendorf's 1958 coining of the term *Homo sociologicus* (Dahrendorf 2006), a term that is only a prominent one of many sociological concepts for human beings (Endruweit 1999: 9–15; Wahl 2000; Huinink 2001: 86–96). The paradigm model for such formulations—*Homo sapiens* (*sapiens*)—comes from Linné's binary classification system. In terms of content, these characterizations do not always follow the biological goal of determining the distinctions between species (Gladigow 2004: 77). And just as the word "anthropology" did not originally refer to the human organism but rather to the anthropomorphic expression of God (Rust 1999: 155), ideas of what makes a human being, or statements on the nature of humans, do not refer per se to the biological nature of human beings (see Meinberg 1988; Reichardt and Kubli 1999).

Most of these definitions posit a key variable that rests in the unmistakable and reductionist characterization of human beings. In general, one feature such as tool making, rationality or language, is singled out and expounded as if wholly determining and universal. This attribute is often treated normatively, as either positive or negative. A survey of the many attributes used (Table 3.2) should indicate two things. At one level, a strong tendency to define human beings based on a single dimension emerges from the desire to distinguish human beings from other living creatures. This parallels attempts to unlock the key element of human beings through monistic assertions. As such, specific activities that occur under certain circumstances are given universal meaning, such as the "will to power" or the "principle of desire" (Kapp 1983: 168). Among the few exceptions that still emphasize diversity despite a binary terminology (*Genus proximum* and *differentia specifica*) are Emil Durkheim's classic formulation *Homo duplex*, Eckard Meinberg's *Homo mundanus*, and the human being as a multilevel creature acting through meta-symbols in Hans Lenk's (1995, 2010: 7–58) term *Homo symboliciter performans*. This plurality or multidimensionality has become an assumed part of other conceptions of human beings that more often are understood under the heading *Lebensformen*, or lifeways (Gladigow 2004: 77; examples found in Meinberg 1988 and Barsch and Hejl 2000). At another level, the broad spectrum of supposed human attributes is more discernible if all proposed versions of *Homo sapiens* are listed according to the "genus proximum et differentia specifica" concept. The most detailed list of this kind that I know of was created by Hans Lenk in a table including around 400 "anthropika" (after Scheler) that adequately characterize human beings (Lenk 2008: 129–67; 2010: 87–123). The number and broad range of specific features clearly indicate how useless it is to define human beings by naming features.

The Escape into Negative and Deductive Anthropology

Images of human beings, or anthropological notions as to the nature of human beings, entail one or more of the following dangers: (1) they homogenize diversity into monistic, species-like determinations; (2) they tie heterogenic features together as additions to a string of beads; (3) they bind historical change and cultural contingency to the *Condition humaine*; (4) they make attributes universal that are in fact particular, or (5) they put forth ideals for how human beings should be. Despite this, forming concepts of what it is to be human is inescapable. Any attempt at theory without a formulated concept of what a human being is—such as in Foucault's "void of the vanished human being" (1997: 388)—ultimately includes an anthropological basis: "Avoiding positive-constructed definitions does not free us from the problem; even speaking in terms of non-determined essence or being remains a statement regarding essence or being" (Bröckling 2004: 172).

The range of empirical or supposedly empirically based definitions of human beings is diverse and sometimes contradictory. Three conclusions drawn from this are briefly described below but will not be explored further, due to my fundamental materialist orientation. A common result of the extreme variation generated by so many definitions is the opinion that human beings are not definable. An exact form of such "negative anthropology" is found in the principal rejection of ever being able to determine or define human beings (R. Groh 2004: 318), a position analogous to "negative theology" with its more tempered definition of human nature based on its artificiality and inconsistency. Many philosophers, philosophical anthropologists, and literary figures have drawn similar conclusions, as in the cases of Plato, Islamic mysticism, and modern authors like Berthold Brecht and Jean-Paul Sartre (examples taken from Assmann 2004b: 90–95). In a historically reconstructed "anthropology of in-determinancy," the task of defining human beings should be abandoned—not because it is in itself predetermined but because of the lack of a concrete basis. Consequently, an anthropology that does not know what constitutes human nature should avoid delimiting human beings in general. Such an anthropology could, in its role as reflexive "borderline science" with critical intentions—or as practical anthropology—show that every response is adjustable (Bröckling 2004: 194). A second form of "negative anthropology" does not argue formally but materially, believing that human beings have a nature in the ontological sense. This kind of anthropology approaches the topic epistemologically, in that the being in human is not determinable due to its uniqueness. It is the nature of human beings to have a hidden nature; Hellmuth Plessner therefore referred to them as *Homo absconditus* (Plessner 1976: 138–40). Both forms of negative anthropology can be contrasted with a third form that is negative in the sense of value, such as in Theodor Adorno's pessimistic description of human beings (example from R. Groh 2004: 323–24).

Another response to the problem is to define human beings without relying on evidence, that is, through deductive anthropology (Assmann 2004b: 104–6). The skeptic Kenneth Burke offers one example. In an essay entitled "The Definition of Man," Burke names five descriptive features that he draws from all the concrete practices and attachments of human beings: the use of symbols, the invention of the negative, the separation from nature through the use of instruments, the tendency toward perfection, and the tendency toward hierarchy (Burke 1966: 2–24, quoted in Assmann 2004b: 106–9). By contrast, the literary anthropologist Wolfgang Iser avoids characterizations via the naming of features. Instead, based on assumptions concerning human freedom and opposition to restraint, he deduces one single imperative: self-transformation. His approach is less descriptive and more prescriptive: human beings must liberate, transform, and fabricate themselves. They must break through all limitations, even those from within, and are able to do so especially through the work of imagination and literature (Iser 2001: 151; 2004: 35).

A third, more moderate approach arises from a new, interdisciplinary anthropology that at its core is more oriented toward literary studies. In Germany this happens most often in cultural anthropology (SFB 511 2005: 31). Explicitly distancing itself from its classical form, this anthropological approach examines conceptions of human beings rather than searching for the essence of being human. It distinguishes between a descriptive anthropological discourse aimed at describing human beings, and a humanist approach that develops a discourse focused on the delimitations and values of human beings (*Anthropologon* vs. *Humanum*; see Assmann 2004a: 12–14, 16–18; R. Groh 2004: 323). Advocates of this approach want to consider fundamental structures and capacities of human beings. They do so under the above-mentioned concept of "anthropological fundamentals" or "basal anthropologica." In cultural anthropology, this approach not only moves away from concentrating on anthropological constants, as is done in the classical form of philosophical anthropology, but also rejects radical social constructivism and the extreme forms of historicizing: "What the human being makes of himself is not a simple construct, not a *creatio ex nihilo*, or more exactly *constructo ex nihilo*, but rather a construct built upon a solid basis" (R. Groh 2004: 320). Fundamentals such as sexuality and the ability to invent are considered "formal conditions in the possibility of cultural construction" (R. Groh 2004: 321; SFB 2005: 44-45). They form a conceptual opposition to social construction, since they are comprehended as basic states and abilities that cannot be observed. Fundamentals thus understood are basically universals, but not necessarily (SFB 2005: 47). A conception of human beings, though weaker in form, could be developed in contrast with one that is more self-evident (R. Groh 2004: 322; see Jörke 2005: 107, 121). This rather sparing approach has my sympathy due to its more moderate form. What proves problematic for me here, though, is the emancipating gesture, along with the implicit value judgments. We take a stance against universals by minimizing a super-societal need for meaning in order to escape never-ending sameness (Bargatzy 2000: 268, 273). To say that if we cannot observe fundamental structures or capacities, then we choose simply to abandon the search for universals altogether is to court dangers.

Good and Evil: Polarity versus Ambivalence

Universals include polar opposites that present contrasting views of human nature. Optimism and pessimism would be examples here, along with notions of good and evil (R. Groh 2004: 319, 323-25; Thies 2004: 124-37). Accordingly, one thinks in terms of "tragic" vs. "utopian" views of humanity (Pinker 2002: 203-18). These views characterize human beings either in the Hobbesian sense, as individualistic, egoistic, and aggressive, and in relationships as unequal and competitive (in cultural anthropology we find this in the work of Napoleon Chagnon, for example); or in the tradition of Kropotkin, as social, communal, collective, and cooperative, or mutualistic, and therefore egalitarian (e.g., Erdal and Whiten 1996). Polarized political positions can be understood in the same context. Liberal and conservative thinkers more often recognize self-interest, whereas socialist and anarchist thinkers emphasize sociality (for the latter, see Dickens 2002: 82-86). The current dominating lines of argument among primatologists, palaeoanthropologists and anthropologists, in contrast to earlier time periods, focus on sociality and egality. Many primatologists who work in cognitive ethology and ecological behavior research assume that social intelligence and cooperation are the means by which individuals accomplishing goals (Machiavellian intelligence; see Byrne 1995;; Rothe and Henke 2005: 163).

Other researchers, who tend to be a minority of evolutionarily oriented social scientists, argue in favor of individualistic tendencies in human behavior. Maryansky and Turner (1992: 84) do not characterize hunter-gatherer societies as simply egalitarian. Contrary to the Durkheimian tradition, they stress that these societies are oriented to individual interests because, for example, they place high value on self-reliance (for a critical perspective on this, see

Dickens 2002: 87). Modern societies suppress this tendency through, for example, rules governing marriage and structures shaped by bureaucracies. According to these authors, complex societies apply limitations and constraints on sociality as "social cages" that confine individuals (Maryanski and Turner 1992), leading to stress, territoriality, and aggression that cannot all be blamed on human nature alone.

Some authors, though not many, expressly assume that fundamental and varying behavioral tendencies are found within all human beings. One such author is Karl Marx, whose work contains varying remarks on human beings in general. On the one hand, he emphasizes the essential sociality as a species-characteristic of human beings (humans as "species-being": see Dickens 2002: 81–82, 95–97). Elsewhere, Marx stressed that human beings have the unique capability to reflect and abstract upon their experiences in a detached manner and to consider and communicate about their own actions and the actions of others ("species-life"). For most individuals in the majority of societal structures, however, this ability is hardly ever realized. At other times, he goes further, arguing that human beings do not have an essential nature; rather, it is the ensemble of social relationships that determines their being and activity. In *Kapital*, Marx combines the position of an invariant human nature (human nature in general) with the variety of ways in which this nature is realized in different social structures and situations, a human nature which is modified in every historical period. Various leftist and Marxist anthropologists, such as Alice Rossi and Fred Willhoite, recognize a partial genetic component in human nature (see Heyer 1982). Peter Dickens, a Marxist-leaning evolutionist who opposes all essentializing definitions, even in the political realm, has said of human beings that "they have inherited a number of alternative potentials as regards their behaviour and it is difficult to predict in advance which of these will be predominant" (Dickens 2002: 82).

More recent approaches bind the two poles together, emphasizing that human beings are contradictory and social relationships are always ambivalent. These are often more differentiated and empirically supported. After many years of fieldwork on political behavior among human beings and chimpanzees, Christopher Boehm has concluded that political behavior is always a compromise between egalitarian controls from below and hierarchical or despotic controls from above (Boehm 1997). Recent studies have moreover distinguished more precisely between a short-term basis for action and long-term effect. Behavioral tendencies not only diverge but can also come into conflict with societal systems of norms laid out by human beings. Humans can consciously form their own societies and thereby expand a society that contradicts the very nature of human beings, at least partially and for certain time periods.

The positions described above suggest the general argument that currently dominant social structures and human nature do not harmonize well with each other. But at the same time, these positions generate completely different and opposing points of view. Either we human beings are fundamentally social beings who live in an egoistical, hierarchical society (in line with Erdal and Whiten's rationale), or we are individualistic and made to live in "social cages." Accordingly, authors from these two approaches take quite different views of democracy and economics in modern complex societies. Whereas Maryansky and Turner consider them concessions to latent individualism, Boehm regards democracy as an authority controlling the tensions between human beings—who are by nature fundamentally ambivalent—and as an instrument of the elite to reduce rather than enhance the individualism of human beings.

In the discussion on so-called human nature, there always emerges the technical problem that we use terms as if they express similar meanings, though upon scrutiny they turn out to have different conceptual perimeters. This is not only true of philosophical handlings of the subject, but of empirical studies as well—in biology or psychology, for example (Table 3.2). Often, what is conceptually meant is limited to certain accepted causes, for example, arising from the biotic sphere (vs. the cultural sphere), or confined to certain general areas such as behavior (vs. the psyche or physical body), social behavior (vs. non-social behavior), or norm-controlled social behavior (vs. non-norm-controlled social behavior).

Table 3.2. "Human nature": Examples of different conceptual interpretations

Citation	Conceptual dimensions	Reference/author
Species-wide biological uniformity	Biotic, entire species	Leach 1982: 123
Shared inheritance	Cross-cultural; genetic causes	Eibl-Eibesfeldt 1976: 241–43
Universal regulating system; universal grammar of human social behavior	Universal, overriding culture; principles of social interaction	Eibl-Eibesfeldt 1986: 89, 90; Eibl-Eibesfeldt and Sütterlin 2007: 150–54
Biological constitution, (determined) features of physical organization and behavior	General, phenotypic, non-alterable	Bayertz 1987: 97
For us humans … difficult to imagine	Species, inborn tendencies	Eibl-Eibesfeldt 2004: 469
Universal biological attributes and developmental stages	Universal, biotic, ontogenetic	Mathews and Moore 2001: 15
Biogenetic potential	Phylogenetic inheritance, but contra determination	Vogel 1986: 65

(continued)

Citation	Conceptual dimensions	Reference/author
Fundamental attributes of every human being	Functional significance; related to the organism	Markl 1986: 84
Basic biological makeup	Biotic; implicit: fundamental	Markl 1986: 87
Bio-psychological frames	Purely biotic, limiting culture	Boas 1938
Universal human nature	Universal, species-related	Pinker 1994: 461–62
Universal species-wide; our species nature; species universals in man	Species-wide	Dissanayake 1992: 211, 235; Crook 1985
Common human nature universal traits of humans, fundamentally social and interactive … human nature	Sociality and creativity as potential for creative diversity; species-related	Carrithers 1992: 146, 161, 169
Unified human nature	Unifying, against racism	Degler 1991: 25
Psychobiological propensities	Psyche, biotic	Hollan 1992: 285–86.
Regularity and similarity across cultures, … robust bio-psychological point of reference	Psyche; biotic; secured through empirical comparison	Munroe and Munroe 2001: 226
Fundamental human nature, basic biological structure of behavior, biologically determined social structural principles, natural basis of norm-related behavior	Fundamental; species *Homo sapiens* behavior, biotic, sociality biotic norms, behavior; biotic	Markl 1986: 84, 86, 87
Fundamental tendencies, "natural" readiness, channeled areas of behavioral development	Opposed to determination vs. inevitable paths	Markl 1986: 86
Universal cultural predisposition, universal human predisposition	Universal, opposed to determination	Dissanayake 1992: 16, 42, 229
Core behavioral tendency	Observable behavior	Dissanayake 1992: 229
Innate human behavioral tendency	Inborn, tendency only	Dissanayake 1992: 68
How all humans are alike		Dissanayake 1992: 73
Bio-psychological constants	Psyche	Harris 1980: 63; Sanderson 2001: 146–47
What is inside the organism	Traits of people	Sanderson 2014: 11–12
Unity of mankind, unity of man	Cultural idea instead of objective reality	Leach 1982: 49, 78

Homo sapiens: Uniqueness versus Special Status

Forming a concept of human nature is possible only if we temporarily put aside particularist forms of historical or regional and societal phenomena without completely forgetting them. A purely theoretical approach leads all too easily to definitions that are highly abstract, creating metaphysical super-subjects. There is also always the hidden danger of forming unspoken normative terms. Some think that an empirical approach is not helpful, since in the end it offers nothing more than commonplace platitudes about human beings (see, e.g., Bayertz 1987: 106). Then again, even relativists need a concept for human nature. Ludwig Wittgenstein and Peter Winch were thus able to anchor their arguments in assumptions on the biotic infrastructure of human beings (Scholte 1984: 964).

With Darwin's theory of evolution, a response developed as of the mid-nineteenth century as to the "question of all questions" concerning "man's place in nature," as Thomas Huxley (1825–95) formulated it in 1863 (Huxley 2003: 57). If all life forms are part of one greater evolutionary context in which only gradual change occurs, then can we say that the differences between humans and other animals develop only gradually—though substantially (Lenk 1974: 12)—and are therefore nonessential? This characterizes the position known as assimilationism in the philosophical discussion about whether animals have mind or consciousness and debates on the so-called naturalization of the mind (for a summary, see Perler and Wild 2005). This position contrasts with differentialism, which addresses the principal differences between human beings, starting with commonalities, and attempts to work out differences step by step (Brandom 2004: 11–12). An assimilationist perspective does not as yet name specific human characteristics; instead it suggests a current view represented in the work of the philosopher Welsch: "Human uniqueness can only be determined in a gradual manner as we are speaking of capabilities that alone correspond only to humans" (Welsch 2004: 64; similar to Fernández-Armesto 2005: 13).

Empirically, human nature can be determined by listing the species-specific biotic features of *Homo sapiens* that place them in the subfamily Homininae and among primates (van Schaik and van Duijnhoven 2004: 168; Strachan and Read 2005: 405–57; Lecointre and Guyader 2006: 649–51). This genetic or primatologic approach goes against the main current in Western philosophy, which since the time of antiquity has explicitly regarded human nature as based on more than characteristics associated with the human organism. It has been dualistically assumed that human nature goes beyond biotic or natural attributes, deriving from characteristics that extend outside of nature (Bayertz 1987: 99).

There are, though, monistic approaches that are careful to acknowledge the danger in reductionism. The anthropologist Edmund Leach, for example, rejects the notion of human beings as a special kind of primate, emphasizing that humans are a unique species. At the same time he opposes the antithetical separation of culture and nature currently so well established in his field (similar to Mühlmann 1966: 20). Leach asserts that many unique, specifically human behavior patterns can be traced to our biotic features, but it is difficult to determine exactly which features these might be (Leach 1982: 120). Conceptually defining culture as purely human also defers the question of what specifically is a human being (McGrew 2001: 233; 2003). Today there is more concrete information on the uniqueness of human beings than there was in Gehlen's time. The point is that biotic features cannot be reduced simply to matters of anatomy, as Simpson (1969: 88) has determined: "human anatomy reflects truly essential man-ness or human nature only to the extent that it is related to human activities and psychology."

Homo sapiens: *Comparisons Showing Continuity and Uniqueness*

Determining human nature by considering species-specific features is anything but easy. Biology in the second half of the twentieth century has shown with increasing clarity that it is difficult to distinguish among species according to features that are (1) true for all individuals of the species and (2) exclusive to the members of one species only (Fernández-Armesto 2005: 4, 169). This is true both generally and in the special case of human beings (see Arnhart 1998: 31–36; Cartmill 1990; Fukuyama 2002: 197).

The traits that make modern humans very different from other Hominoidea (see Henke and Rothe 2003: 19; 2005) include their reduced body hair, facial morphology, non-differentiated and therefore omnivore dentition, and descended larynx. At first glance, human beings have only a few purely anatomic, morphologic or physiologic features that surpass or outweigh those of other primates. They can throw with aim, something important for the development of weapons, and they have a unique ability to perspire, which can be important for maintaining stamina when hunting in groups. From a biological point of view, the special human features are:

(a) erect posture and walking on two legs, which influences many other unique aspects of human anatomy and physiology, such as pelvis shape and the non-specialized hand;
(b) highly developed brain, especially the cerebrum with its prefrontal cortex that determines such things as behavioral control and language ability;
(c) specific parameters in reproduction, sexuality, early ontogenesis, and further aspects of life history;
(d) hypercomplex form of sociality with diverse forms of social organization that indicate not one and only species-typical form of sociality.

When humans are compared with other higher primates, humans' unique attributes in terms of sexuality and life history are obvious. Both the developmental phase, with its elaborate teaching and learning, and the postmenopausal phase are significantly longer than they are in other primates. A perennial sexuality associated with strong bonds and a long child and adolescent phase characterize humans even more distinctly. In spite of the lack of maturity in newborns (secondary altriciality; on the "early extra-uterine year" see Portmann 1956: 68–80), they clearly are comparatively large and heavy (van Schaik 2004: 180–81). These features can be explained as the outcome of humans' erect posture and hypertrophic brains (Wills 1996; Schröder 2000; Grupe, Schröder, and Wittwer-Backofen 2012: 16–19; Read 2012). Systematic correlations exist between species-specific life histories and evolutionary cognitive capabilities (Chasiotis 2007: 205–6; H. Keller 2007). Features concerning life history could be understood as a kind of filter: organisms of species with a long life history will very likely have cognitive adaptive abilities that refer to social or environmental features. Various forms of cognitive adaptations accumulate in species with longer life histories (van Schaik and Deaner 2003: 18–20).

Specific capabilities arise out of these characteristics, such as the planned manufacture of tools or the use of tools ("organs according to need" or extracorporal organs; Osche 1983). They exist as an extension of physical organs or as organ projections (K. Müller 2003b: 19), which enable human beings to create cultural artifacts like physical tools or mental/cognitive tools like words that not only require intelligence but also lend intelligence to their users. Tools make living creatures intelligent by opening up new possibilities in action and behavior and providing new thinking challenges. As such they form what Dennett (2001: 123–25) called "Gregorian creatures." Human ideas are embodied in the tools that were created or invented, improved, and discarded by other humans. Some "cultural tools for thinking" (Rogoff 2003: 258–70) are especially significant: writing, mathematics, and further thinking tools like cognitive cards, classifications, schemas, and computer games, for example. These tools are particularly efficient for creating distributed knowledge that groups can use for communal problem-solving, such as to steer an oil tanker for instance, or travel long-distances without a compass as the people of Polynesia do (Hutchins 1995, 2006: 380–82; Rogoff 2003: 270–81).

These possibilities are augmented by humans' ability to be aware of time and capacity to interpret from interpretations (metasymbolization; Lenk 1995: 14; also see Deacon 1998; Schmidinger and Sedmak 2007). Human beings can imagine the entire axis of time, grasp the makings of the past and the outlines of future time periods, or "let themselves drift over the axis of time" (Bischof-Köhler 1991: 178). This makes it possible to strive for improvement or even perfection, pointing to the "utopian potential" of human beings (Stagl 200: 26–27).

Another outcome of human organic features, especially with reference to points (b) and (c), is the capacity for language—a capability that is unique in comparison to all other animal languages due to the use of real arbitrary symbols in the sense of those described by Charles Sanders Peirce, the high degree of symbolization, and the syntax, grammar, and intent to communicate. The existence of a verbal repository of words with shared meaning allows humans to leave their private world of thought and enter into conversation (shared cognitive artifacts; E. Goody 1997: 391). Human brains have the capacity for "cognitive fluidity," as Stephen Mithen (1996, 2006) described the transferring capabilities between different parts of the brain. As such, language mediates a great amount of meta-information, that is, knowledge over information. Information can be turned over quasi off-line to its own management, in the form of meta-information sorting (Eibl 2007: 9–10). In animal languages, the three communication functions described by Karl Bühler—representation, expression, and appeal—are melded together, becoming simultaneously tri-functional. Humans can isolate the relevance of a thing through language expression. The representational function can be separated from the expressive and appeal functions and used in isolation.

The cooperative use of language allows social cooperation to become a social tool. With such a tool, humans can form "cognitive communities," which are closely tied to the development of language capabilities in the evolutionary process (for "communities of mind" see Donald 2008: 221–23; also see James 2003: 30–31). This allows groups to form as cooperative "cultural survival vehicles" (Pagel 2012: 12, 45–46, 73–77, 133–34). This language capability is the most diagnostic single trait of human beings (Simpson 1969: 91). It is probably directly related to the complexity and size of the human brain, and especially in the further development of the prefrontal cortex (G. Roth 2003: 546; Henke and Rothe 2003: 115). It does not, however, consist of multiple parts that can be partly controlled by nonhuman primates (Bischof-Köhler 1991: 183–84; Jackendorff 2003: 94–95). Emphasizing the unique aspects of human language does not mean forgetting that the lion's share of human communication is done without language (Fernández-Armésto 2005: 18), since nonverbal communication can flow from many more channels than its verbal counterpart. The more recent discussions on the subject tend to differentiate between a broadly understood language capability that animals partially possess and language capability in more restricted terms. Species-comparative studies show that the phenomena of metarepresentation and recursion are mainly what make human language so unique. In systems of counting, for instance, a very limited number of syntactic elements enable us to form a potentially unlimited number of discrete means of expression. Recursion in human language probably developed phylogenetically through noncommunicative and cognitive problem-solving in the navigation of space, the counting of objects, and social relationships (Hauser, Chomsky, and Fitch 2002: 1572–73).

Altogether, we could say that human beings are unique, but this uniqueness is neither constant throughout many features nor based on one single characteristic. Only in combining knowledge from several disciplines—palaeoanthropology, comparative human biology (anthropology), human ethology, and comparative primatology in particular—are we able today to formulate more precise assertions, or even one sentence, on the uniqueness of the human organism. Evolution-oriented behavioral ecology has produced especially challenging results (for a summary, see Smith and Winterhalder 2003), as have the newer fields within cognitive ethology and so-called cultural primatology, or primate ethnography (de Waal and Tyack 2003, de Waal 2005: 114–15, 222, 251–52).

In the overall picture, however, human biotic characteristics—with the possible exception of language—appear in many ways in a modified form among primates (Grupe et al. 2005: 19). A summary of primate research points to the latest trend in empirical research today: "Humans do occupy a special place among the primates, but this place increasingly has to be defined against a backdrop of substantial similarity" (de Waal 2005: 56). *Homo sapiens*, together with chimpanzees, form a monophyletic unit. Their ways separated only 7 to 8 million years ago. With the exception of Broca's area, the human brain has been found to be markedly similar to the brains of large apes. Even the cerebral cortex and frontal lobe are found in mammals and especially primates, following the same evolutionary trends discovered in the human brain (G. Roth 2003: 545). The complex of features found in primates is itself a continuation of trends found in mammals that reveal the older evolutionary patterns found in reptiles (Ingham 1996: 25). Darwin's goal was to prove that the observed characteristics that make humans unique are found in other animals as well: "It is true that, in many ways, we are very like our near cousins, the social primates. It is also true that we differ from them. The similarity makes the comparison relevant; the differences make it illuminating" (Carrithers 1992: 7).

Additionally, today we can make a detailed list of specific human characteristics that does prove to be empirically sound. The organic basis can be determined, more or less, and joined with specific human capabilities. A systematic approach furthers a discriminating view of the particularities characterizing human beings (for more detail, see Henke and Rothe 2005: 91; Langdon 2005). These characteristics are presented in Table 3.3 in order to show that it is not the particulars themselves but their eventual combination that creates human uniqueness.

Crossing the Rubicon

We know today with certainty that complex sociality, learning, the passing on of traditions (transmission), and the manufacture and use of tools are not limited to human beings, at least when we consider these capabilities more

Table 3.3. Organic basis of specific human characteristics

- Larger brain with higher forebrain (cerebralization and encephalization)
- Exclusively bipedal
- Hand with opposable thumb
- Larynx, language-related cerebral specialization
- Early birth, less development in newborns (secondary altriciality)
- Dependency on parental care (by natural or social parents)
- Longer postnatal period, longer growth and maturity phases (childhood and adolescence)
- Greater generation overlapping
- Retention of juvenile traits (neoteny)
- Permanent sexual readiness (entire menstruation cycle)
- Post-reproductive female longevity (greater role of grandmothers)
- Less sexual dimorphism
- Concealed ovulation

broadly (see McGrew's 1992: 77 list of eight conditions for recognizing behavior as cultural; Segall et al. 1999: 11; see also Enfield and Levinson 2006). However, apes today lack certain features that are not associated with transmission in the broad sense but with more specific forms of transmission, such as active instruction. Nonhuman primates do not (1) understand pointing gestures (unlike dogs); (2) use gestures, even to show members of their own species something; or (3) instruct their children. Michael Tomasello (2006) sees this as indicating that nonhuman primates lack an understanding of causality, a concept of intentionality, the capability of common focus or joint attention, and the ability to identify with members of their own species.

Interaction between nonhuman primates generally remains an immediate relationship between two individuals, one the transmitter, the other the receiver, with communication being mostly dyadic and imperative. Apes live, to exaggerate a bit, in a kind of solipsistic world (Tomasello 1999, 2004: 6–8, 2006: 516–18; see Avital and Jabonkla 2000; Welzer 2004; Sterelny 2012). On the other hand, according to current findings, primates show many behavioral forms that were once considered solely human. Frans de Waal therefore argues cautiously in terms of anthropomorphism (de Waal 2001: 57–78; also see Kennedy 1992). In other words, "it is by no means a given that a chimpanzee behaving as we know humans to behave does so for the same reasons" (Lenzen 2003: 108). One reason these debates can take on a virulent tone is that similar forms of behavior, even among related species, are not necessarily due to similar causes.

The gradual development of shared features is a further point in the debate. From an evolutionary perspective, specifies-specific characteristics apparently do not arise all at once but develop over a lengthy step-by-step process. However, an overall continual development cannot be ruled out, given that specific capabilities, once established, might have had sudden powerful effects on, for example, the emergence of social behavior (Sawyer 2005). In terms of specifics, however, it remains unclear how this plays out in the decisive but empirically abstruse human features of causal understanding and awareness of the intentions of social partners in human interaction (as in theory of mind; see Premack and Woodruff 1978). Wulf Schiefenhövel recommends the use of the term "enphronesis" to describe the human capability of emotional empathy (Schiefenhövel 2003: 241–42, 2004: 283–85). "Truth lies in the details" then applies accurately to the discussion on tool use and manufacture vs. the intention behind tool manufacture.

In terms of results, the debates remain open on (1) learning through experience, such as by registering change that has come about through a social partner without at the same time understanding the strategies behind this change (emulative learning), as opposed to (2) learning through imitation, with explicit reference to the intentions of a social partner, or (3) learning through instruction (Segall et al. 1999: 10–12; Tomasello 1999, 2004: 7–8, 2006; Welzer 2004: 367; de Waal 2001; Rossano 2010; Distin 2011; Mesoudi 2011; Mesoudi, Whiten, and Laland 2006). Altogether, the features do not turn out to offer humans a real "special position" in the natural world (Darwin 2005: 160; Osche 1987; Bischof-Köhler 1991: 143; Wills 1996; Vogel 2000; G. Roth 2003: 545). In comparison with their nearest relatives in the animal world, human beings appear more like "another unique species" (Foley 1987: 1–14). Evidence pointing to a perspective of continuities between humans and other primates and to the differential evolution of the specifics in the capacity for culture has grown in recent years (e.g., Blute 2010, Grupe et al. 2012: 13–15, 21, Sterelny 2012, Whiten et al. 2012). A few colleagues in the humanities also emphasize this view today, like the historian Fernández-Armesto (2005: 13, 16, 37, 169–70) and the philosopher Welsch (2004: 59, 70; 2012). And the continuity between human beings and other organisms can be demonstrated quite accurately, with precise indicators showing the level and degree of similarities found among different organisms. Some of the common features presented in Table 3.4 illustrate that earlier claims that many characteristics were exclusively human do not stand up to empirical examination.

Human beings' particularities and similarities give them the appearance of being unique but at the same time do not establish a "special position" for them in the world. This is the dominant position today in human biology, and it clearly contradicts the various theological positions (see the contributions in Cyran 1990; see also, e.g., Splett 1990). Karl Eibl has aptly remarked that "the question is whether human uniqueness really is something truly unique, or something completely different" (Eibl 2007: 1). There is a difference between an assumed gradual "uniqueness" and the more intrinsic or categorical idea of a "special position" for human beings in the natural and animal world.

Table 3.4. The relative nature of human uniqueness, based on empirical traits of individuals and populations (author's own summary, following the work of various authors)

Traits shared with higher primates (esp. chimpanzees and bonobos):   • Long pregnancies, small-sized litters, longer period between births   • Greater parental effort, longer child dependency   • Well-planned and well-executed toolmaking   • Multiple-use tools   • Manufacture of tools from alternative materials   • Innovations, inventions   • Transmission (intragenerational and intergenerational), "tradigenetic heredity," transmission, cultural transmission (to some extent disputed)   • Recognition of social partners as individuals   • Intentional influence over the behavior of social partners (first-order intentionality)   • Modulation of social interaction through nonverbal symbols   • Order of dominance, gerontocracy, status inheritance   • Machiavellian intelligence, deception   • Coordinating the behaviors of multiple individuals   • Formation of coalitions and alliances (only *Pan troglodytes*)   • Cultural differences between species populations (esp. *Pan troglodytes*)   • Female orgasm potential (at least for bonobos)   • Masturbation   • Modularity of thought, multiple intelligence; domain specificity (disputed)

Traits shared among nearly all primates:
   • Long life expectancy
   • Later maturity, long period of maternal care
   • Greater learning potential, intelligence
   • Varying social relationships in a population
   • Tool use
   • Individual behavioral strategies
   • Aggression and systems of dominance
   • Greater male investment in child rearing

Traits shared with many mammals:
     • Social relationships and social learning necessary for survival, postnatal care, breeding; care for offspring (parentalism and familialism)
     • Feeding of offspring, mostly through female members

Shared traits with all mammals:
       • Internal fertilization
       • Warm blooded
       • Nepotism
       • Emotional expression as social signal

Shared traits with almost all reproductive organisms:
         • Sexual dimorphism, inclusive behavioral preferences
         • Sexual selection
         • More investment by female members in individual offspring

Shared traits with all organisms: • Tendency to maximize genetic representation in future generations (*inclusive fitness*)

Human uniqueness has had far-reaching, cumulative effects, first among them being the enormous diversity of many human features, such as in the development of almost 7,000 languages in approximately thirty language families. Cultural differences have also been documented in various chimpanzee populations, as well as among gorillas (Tylor and Goldsmith 2003), an important discovery as it reveals that there is no absolutely solid species-specific behavioral inventory (ethogram). But what is often overlooked is that these types of cultural differences are, in comparison to those found among humans, extremely limited (Sussman 1999). A second effect of human uniqueness, apart from diversity, is the sheer size of human societies. The range is in fact enormous, but the fundamental fact remains that human cultural units, such as ethnic groups, are in general much larger than any primate group. Nonhuman primate communities do not extend past a local setting, mostly because of their all-too-limited means of symbolic communication (Goldschmidt 2006: 16). A third effect is the geographic dispersal of human beings to all climatic zones. Human beings are a species found everywhere. A fourth effect is the sheer number of human beings in the world. Today, for example, humans on the earth are more than 100 times more numerous than any other individuals of a species similar in body size (Rolston 1999: 152).

The question of which attributes were decisive in producing what effects within biocultural hominization remains thoroughly open. Even with such a list, no matter how fascinating it may be, we still would not know which attributes in the evolutionary process were decisive in making *Homo sapiens* unique and which were of lesser importance—for example, what were apomorphic features and what represent evolutionary traces. Michael Tomasello has argued, on the basis of comparative research on infants and higher primates, that human beings are clearly distinct from other primates. According to him, nonhuman primates' lack of understanding of causality and intentionality hinders their capacity for the cross-generational, cumulative learning that leads to inventing something new from what was built or created in the past. In other words, they are missing the ratchet effect known in humans. This effect arises as invention combines with later, more diverse modifications or improvements to innovations, resulting in an irreversible development. Decisive here is the reliable social transmission of information to later generations, which produces a stabilizing effect on the learning process. The ratchet effect allows for social learning in a cumulative form of cultural evolution (Tomasello 1999, 2006; Sterelny 2003: 116–21; in contrast, see de Waal 2001: 35). Huxley has argued in a similar manner, talking about a ("Noesphere", in distinction from the biosphere (J. Huxley 1941; see Welzer 2004: 364).

A minority position on the subject, though an important position nevertheless, can be found in the field of biology. More recent interdisciplinary findings correspond with philosophical conclusions culminating from discussions on two research fronts: the debates on (1) genetic research and (2) inorganic thinking, intelligence, and rationality, or artificial intelligence and machines. Interdisciplinary debates converge in the view that not only are humans unique beings that exhibit a clear break from other animals, but their biotic nature is also to some extent changeable (Habermas 2005; see the contributions in Bolz and Münkel 2003; Müller and Reder 2003; Schmidinger and Sedmak 2004). On the other hand, one should not hypostatize the particular biotic nature of human beings to a universal human nature (Kleeberg and Walter 2001: 40). From a sociological perspective, the uniqueness of human beings cannot be defined exclusively in terms of "animal rationale" (Wahl 2000; Lopreato and Crippen 2002; Schmidinger and Sedmak 2004). Any such definition must be made on a more gradual level, determined by a wide range of capabilities from which only a few belong solely to human beings. The philosopher Wolfgang Welsch has concluded that not only are the attributes proposed as being the privileged domain of humans empirically questionable, but also the assumption of specifically exclusive human attributes is in general mistaken: "the entire direction of the search is false" (Welsch 2004: 63). In Table 3.5, I have listed the features that are considered quasi-examples of human nature in all cultures but vary dramatically between cultures and between individuals. Table 3.6 presents uniqueness as a complex of many features, mostly in the form of capabilities.

Table 3.5. Shared traits among individuals and societies, with great intercultural and/or interpersonal variability

- Values, norms, goals, concept of duty
- Personality
- Preferences for choice of partner
- Concept of kinship and the form of a family
- Disposition toward illnesses or diseases
- Intelligence
- Knowledge
- Curiosity and capability of innovation
- Extensive transformation of the natural environment (esp. regarding artificially structured environments)

Table 3.6. Specific Human Characteristics (after various authors; see text)

1. Capability of speaking aloud with grammar and syntax; the function of communicating
2. Capability of forming sustainable communities extending beyond the family
3. Capability of forming sustainable personal relationships with relations and nonrelations
4. Capability of, strictly speaking, cultural and nongenetic transmission
5. Capability of manufacturing tools or implements using previously manufactured tools or implements (*intentional affordances, artifacts*)

6. Capability of reification from facts or circumstances (creating concepts for the attributes of objects)
7. Capability of realizing time, → anticipation, anticipation of needs, → controlling of needs, → future-oriented cultural variation (*constructed virtual future reality*); planning for the future
8. Capability of, and dependency on, learning from real instruction and imitation (rather than learning by emulation)
9. Capability of nonphysical transmission of knowledge (writing, constructing monuments)
10. Capability of modifying innovations and cross-generational accumulation through reliable transference (*cumulative cultural evolution, ratchet effect*)
11. Capability of spontaneous (non-induced) communication with arbitrary symbols
12. Capability of communicating with the conscious assumption that one is in possession of information that others are not (*truly communicative, intentional teaching*)
13. Capability of controlling behavior and of processing psychic uncertainties
14. Capability, after the age of nine months, of joint attentional activities (activities done with divided attention)
15. Understanding of other persons as intentional actors (social cognition, understanding conspecifics; enphronesis), unemotional (social cognition) or emotional (empathy), → intersubjectivity/adoption of alternative perspectives, → instruction
16. Capability, starting at three or four years of age, of shared intentionality and collectively shared intentionality, → collaboration
17. Capability of planned instruction, i.e., influencing the intention or the psyche (not only the behavior) of social partners (*second-order intentionality*, narrative thought)
18. Linguistic representation of previous, noncurrent, and/or future circumstances and concepts; consciousness of history
19. Mediation between intelligence modules (*cognitive fluidity, metarepresentation*)
20. Complex technology, → possibility of excess or surplus, → division of labor, → hierarchy
21. Division of labor
22. Capability of forming large societies (with much larger populations than among the higher primates)
23. Possibility of drastically changing the environment, → altering selection pressure
24. Capability of using artificial means to influence the longevity of certain living beings: domestication
25. Expressive culture in the form of art, music, and performance (e.g. dance)
26. Socially constructed concepts of gender ideals and roles
27. Hidden sexual intercourse
28. Often lifelong (and often polygynous) ties to a partner; tendency toward bringing the male into the family and male paternal investment
29. Capability of birth control, conscious nonreproduction, → the potential to act against the tendency to maximize genetic representation in future generations
30. Capability of self-murder, → the potential to act against the tendency to maximize genetic representation in future generations
31. Capability of imagination, complex game playing, and self-deception,

→ = important implications of individual capabilities

Figure 4. Young German in Queens, New York, US. Photo by Maria Blechmann-Antweiler.

CHAPTER 4

Universals
Examples from Several Realms

> *If one takes seriously the comparative mission of anthropology,
> one cannot fail to discern seeming cross-cultural universals.*
> —Naomi Quinn, "Universals of Child Rearing"

This chapter is meant not only to present a more concrete picture of universals but also to substantiate their importance in concrete topics and issues. In the sense of a holistic cultural concept, I would like to show where universals are found in biotic, psychic, and social contexts. It is essential to emphasize the selective nature of the material presented below, which is based on my limited knowledge of the entire spectrum of possible universals available. I am not attempting an exhaustive approach but rather a view expounded through examples that will clearly present the complexity of the material. With regard to the subject matter in the last chapter and the search for an empirically based concept of human nature, universals are relevant in both the general and the particular sense. As Donald Brown (pers. comm., 2005) has emphasized: "I do think it is possible to state the scientific utility of universals as an approach to human nature.... It is however, largely a matter of the inferences that can be drawn from the existence of universals.... Given this inference, it follows that particular universals each suggest some particular aspect of human nature. Whether the inference is correct, is always an empirical matter."

Qualifying Remarks

Below I present a selection of postulated universals for which there is at least some empirical evidence. We often claim that specific universals exist without providing further proof or a theoretical basis for such claims. For example, an anthropological monograph states: "The impulse that created tourism is universal and found in all cultures. It is the impulse to leave the structures of daily life and to step within those of others. The change from the known to the unknown is more or less institutionalized in all forms of everyday life in the world" (Binder 2005: 39; see Hennig 1999: 89).

One problem in how we define universals is that many authors do not even attempt to define them, or else they assume that universals by definition stem from biotic causes. In this book I have consciously avoided defining universals by way of causal assumptions. In contrast, definitions arising from more recent research often characterize universals as inborn features. This is especially the case in studies on universals from the fields of music, performance, art, and to a limited degree in research on psychic and language universals. Dissanayake describes a feature as universal when it is not learned but rather is latent in all normal persons, appearing spontaneously (Dissanayake 2001). Similarly, universals appear as a keyword under universals of music perception in Wikipedia and are defined as inborn and therefore independent of culture ("Universalien der Musikwahrnehmung" 2008). In this chapter, I discuss the results of my research into universals at the level of culture and cultures. I have found that in the literature, these cultural universals are not clearly distinguished from findings or claims concerning species-specific human features.

In the following I demonstrate the over-simplification entailed by using such expressions as "in all cultures there exist …" or "in all societies we find …" or "societies everywhere reveal …" instead of formulations chosen more carefully (though admittedly more tediously). The word "everywhere" is, as Lechner and Boli (2005: 21) have pointed out, an exceedingly slippery concept. The statements provided below should therefore be read with appreciation of the fact that almost all of them are not absolute but rather assumed:

1. Universals named in this book were found in publications from diverse fields of study. As mentioned above, most disciplines do not generally provide much information on universals since there is no particular field of study that considers the subject matter a primary focus.
2. The basis for claims about specific universals is varied. Some claims arise inductively from empirical comparative studies, others are derived from single or specific case studies, still others are deduced from theoretical assumptions, and others remain pure, albeit interesting, speculation. To date, many aspects of universal claims lack a clear empirical basis in the sense of systematic culturally comparative research, even in cultural anthropology.
3. The relevance of postulated or discussed universals has been assessed variously. The views on the subject matter depend heavily on fundamental theoretical assumptions about human nature.
4. As explanations for universals vary, so too is there extreme variation in different researchers' interpretations of specific universals, a topic I will approach systematically below (see Chapter 7).

5. Due to the problematic lack of a distinction between universals on the comparative level of cultures on the one hand, and the level of species-specific features on the other, many of the universals described below are considered rooted in the form of the individual. This relates to the fact that universals that are based on interaction, are social, or above all are macrosocial are more difficult to determine and have been less studied as well.
6. In general, it is important to remark that such a whirlwind tour of specific universals raises questions more than it offers clear answers.

In explicating the examples that follow, I demonstrate how universals may "have particular meaning when stated in the negative: in no society does x occur (D. Brown 2013: 412). As in my analysis on taxonomy, presented in Chapter 6, we will see that universals can be organized in a variety of ways and presented in altering sequences or varying orders, such as from well known universals like the incest taboo to lesser known examples, from important to trivial commonalities, from well-established to purely speculative, or from biotic to social. I present the selection of universals in thematic blocks and begin with some astonishing evidence of universals in narrative expression in literature and in art.

Narration and Expressive Culture

Narrated History and Narrative Structures

In a methodically innovative urban anthropological study on biographies of inhabitants of the planned city of Milton Keynes, England, Finnegan (1998) comes to some interesting conclusions on the role of storytelling in the development of urban experience. Even in the most particularized tales she discovered general or universal elements that go far beyond the cases of specific persons and events. A core element of any narrative or story is its generalizing potential. The understanding of types of causes of events is shared in such a way as to make a story a prototype for a general or universal pattern ("universal in particular": Finnegan 1998: 9–11, 120–21). Furthermore, these aspects of social exchange by means of storytelling appear to be universal: "the striking thing is our capacity not only to enact stories but to recognise the due conventions of appropriate genres. Without being overtly instructed, as it were, people already have the creative narrative resources to tell and hear stories in recognised ways" (Finnegan 1998: 178).

Historiography, understood as historical storytelling in its function as self-understanding and self-confirmation, is also found in every culture. Narratives form the widespread response to the question of identity. They help in the search for a response to the individual and collective questions of who I am and who we are: "Narrative is a universal cultural practice of bringing the remembered past into the present, with the purpose of providing orientation to life in the circumstances shaping the present and of providing perspective for the future.... The role of narrative is found in all cultures" (Rüsen 1998: 22, 23).

Universal structures, then, exist on the one hand from within different and varying life history narratives (see the debate in Rosaldo 1976 vs. Spiro), and on the other as general features in greater histories. We can also expect biographic and historical narratives to reveal similarities due to their common identity-forming function. Such narrated histories most often universalize their own uniqueness, whether concerning an individual person or a group of persons. Other people, living creatures, and cultures have little or no substance in these stories. Identity gained through exclusion is found throughout time and in all cultural spheres, but that does not exclude the possibility of creating collective identity through inclusion as well (Rüsen 1998: 30).

Brown was able to reveal many commonalities through a culturally comparative study of narrative history in twenty-five complex societies (D. Brown 1988). Cultures characterized by inherited caste systems—despite their societal complexity—are missing qualified biographies, realistic portraits, and a uniform educational system, as well as political science, sociology, and natural science. In their narrative history, caste societies favor legends and myths over more exact and accurate descriptions. In India, for example, historiography has played hardly any role in the past, whereas in China detailed genealogies have been recorded for a long time. These are examples of implied universals, that is, characteristics that occur as universals only through the existence of another feature.

Literature and Visual Culture

Literature, and especially belles lettres, represents a case where, as with religion, only diversity seems apparent. In view of culturally specific uniqueness in all its diverse forms, the search for universals here is anything but easy. This frames the classical anthropological view formulated by Laura Bohannan in her essay "Shakespeare in the Bush" (Bohannan 1966). During her fieldwork among the Tiv of West Africa, she read Hamlet out loud and discussed the story with informants. She found that the Tiv's interpretation of the text differed greatly from that of Western readers. Bohannan was surprised, as before doing the fieldwork she had assumed that "the general plot and motivation of the greater tragedies would always be clear" (Bohannan 1966: 44).

The findings of research on media impact reveal a similar turn regarding culturally specific interpretations of television shows such as American soap operas like *Dallas* or *Dynasty* in China and Mexico. These media products are perceived often in culturally specific ways. A "localization" of global media thus occurs (Kottak 1990; Lull 1991, 2000). Bohannan's observation and the research on media reception challenge the thesis that "great literature speaks deeply to all and expresses universally held beliefs about the human condition" (Bazerman 1989: 44, cited in Scalise Sugiyama 2003: 384). Other researchers, based on Bohannan's implicit assumptions, have concluded that such cultural variation rules out any kind of cognitive universality (examples in Scalise Sugiyama 2003: 384). According to this line of argument, Bohannan's essay represents a relativistic view that opposes the notion of human nature. But to draw such a broad conclusion from Bohannan's observations is a bit too hasty. The main difference between the Tiv and English readers is namely their natural environment.

Folklore or oral literature (*orature*) holds many indicators of approximate forms of universal motives and themes. Examples here would be the Cinderella theme of conflict between stepparents and stepchildren, and the Little Red Riding Hood theme of attacking predators. Both refer to important questions on a broad evolutionary level. We can assume that such stories are used to identify conflicts of interest and problems of survival, and to help people learn and live with these issues (Daly and Wilson 1988; Scalise Sugiyama 2006: 319–21; Mecklenburg 2009). Dangerous animals as subject matter are at least found on a broad scale, though in completely varied forms of storytelling and literary traditions (Scalise Sugiyama 2006: 326–29). An evolutionary and ecological line of argument would expect to find universal features in the listener's or the reader's interpretation of stories with subject matter like marriage, but differences on the micro level, such as local solutions to the general topic of the story. From an evolutionary standpoint, we could immediately assume that literature (and visual art as well) must resemble life in order for human beings to find it interesting (Storey 1996). More recent work coming out of evolutionary psychology has pointed out that fictional texts could have an adaptive function instead of being simply a by-product of human thinking (see Tooby and Cosmides 1992, Boyd 2005: 168). A reanalysis of Bohannan's essay reveals many universal aspects in the supposedly culturally specific comments of the Tiv (Storey 1996: 131–35; Scalise Sugiyama 2003: 390).

Indications of possible literary universals are suggested by the parallels found in myths. There is a "striking recurrence of similar motives in various religions" (Wright 1994: 365). Many prominent scholars of myths and religion, such as James G. Frazer, Carl Gustav Jung, Karl Kerényi, Erich Neumann, Robert von Ranke-Graves, Mircea Eliade, and above all Joseph Campbell, have emphasized the repeated topoi and themes found in myths despite their amazing diversity (see Meier-Seethaler 1997: 287). Campbell, who did comparative research on mythologies throughout the world, especially those from the Western world, and found striking similarities within the diverse forms and variants. One group of archetypes constitutes the *monomyth*, which describes a hero's journey, incorporating many stages (departure, initiation, and return), tests (J. Campbell 1953: 93–103), and final rescue (1953: 193–213). The hero is a human prototype who is set apart from other people due to extraordinary abilities. Notions of magical numbers and concepts of cyclical development (1953: 247) occur in the most varied of origin myths and ideas on the creation of the cosmos. Campbell's findings have been used by other authors, especially Christopher Vogler in his guide to writing screenplays. Vogler identifies the equal combination of originality and universality as the best means of attaining success with an audience (Vogler 1998). Campbell's book (1953) are therefore especially popular among writers and scriptwriters even today.

Early on, in a study on dreams among the North American Navajo, Kluckhohn and Morgan (1951, cited in Kahle 1981: 310) postulated the existence of universally motivational types in stories and myths as well as dreams. Attempt to predict the future in stories are widespread, as the ongoing popularity of astrology and horoscopes attests (Ganten, Deichmann, and Spahl 2005: 541). Literary analysts have demonstrated the existence of fundamental motives in works of world literature through comparative examinations of motives and themes and structural analysis of parallels, mostly using examples from Western literature (e.g., Frenzel 1999, 2005). But similarities are not detected only in European literature. According to the work of Georges Polti, 80 percent of the themes in dramas and novels in world literature revolve around conflicts involving sexuality, love, and kinship (Polti 1977). This is interesting in that Polti's findings mirror assumptions found in evolutionarily oriented literary analysis, though not necessarily through the theoretical impulses of the author himself.

Many indications of universals with evolutionary relevance in world literature are found in Barash and Barash's (2005) wonderfully entitled volume *Madame Bovary's Ovaries*. The book is a work of "Bio-Lit-Crit," a more recent trend in literary analysis that looks at works of literature from an evolutionary point of view. Another example here would be a study on the Japanese *Ballad of Genji*, written in the year 1000 by Murasaki Shikibo. This book contains universal themes and motives, not only in the text but also in 233 woodcuts (Thiessen and Umezawa 1998: 300–307, 314, Table 3). These adaptationist approaches from evolutionary psychology function together with adaption-oriented examinations in the visual arts as "Biopoetics" (Cooke and Turner 1999), an approach emphasized in the work of Gottschall, Carroll, and Hogan (Carroll 1995, 2001, 2005; Hogan 1997, 2003a, 2003b; Gottschall and Wilson 2005). Carroll's quantitative content analysis presents a selectionist argument but provides indications of themes that are in some ways explainable on an evolutionary level. Carroll poses the question of why the characters from the Victorian novellas he is studying are so interested, for example, in education (Carroll

2005). A variant of this type of analysis, found in the German-speaking world, applies evolutionary theory and behavioral research, along with ontogenetic factors, to the study of texts, as in the work of Karl Eibl (Eibl 2004, 2009).

In visual media, universal motives and structures are apparent but rarely studied on a culturally comparative level. Projects currently under way at the University of Siegen study such phenomena, directed by media sociologists Hejl and Uhl in cooperation with Indian colleagues. They compare blockbuster films produced in Hollywood and successful "Bollywood" films from India, seeking similarities in quantitative studies. The results thus far appear to reveal universals that probably suggest an adaptational explanation. Themes and motives such as violence, sexuality, and material resources are foci of all these entertainment media (Uhl and Kumar 2004; Uhl 2009; Barkow 2005; Hejl 2005).

Art: Aesthetic Universals and "Making Special"

Are there commonalities in the area of expressive culture where we first register only diversity? The idea that art in some form is found in every known culture has circulated ever since Franz Boas (Rothfuchs-Schulz 1980: 39; Ehrlich 2002: 221). Moreover, we know that artworks have fascinated people on a transcultural level: they have a magnetic effect on people who know nothing of the culture from which the works originated or how the works were produced (Welsch 2006: 123–26). Though at the same time people still vehemently argue against the existence of aesthetic universals (Reck 1992). Whether the concept "aesthetics" is useful in cultural comparative research is even a contested point (for a pro and contra discussion, see Weiner et al. 1996; van Damme 1996: 39–57). We do find that in all material cultures, some objects are understood as having purely aesthetic meaning. That objects can be created with a higher meaning—intentionally produced to express beauty beyond a specific place and time—is a widespread concept (Szalay 1999: 129; Ehrlich 2002: 225; Florence 2004; G. Paul 2008a: 80–101). An anthropological textbook summarized this as follows: "Art, anthropologists recognize, is a cultural universal. But beyond this the artistic impulse is seen in the everyday lives in individual human beings, for we are all both producers and consumers of art" (Peoples and Bailey 2015: 347). Peoples and Bailey (2015: 347) also write that all cultures have artistic objects, designs, songs, dances, and other ways of expressing their appreciation for the aesthetic, and that the "aesthetic impulse is universal, although cultures vary in their ways of expressing it and the social functions and cultural meanings they attach to it."

Art in all cultures and from all time periods reveals certain similarities (Dutton 2000, 2005: 286–88, 2009: 51–59). Two decisive cross-cultural features found in art include the intrinsic joy felt in the manufacture of art and a certain separation that occurs from the daily routines of life (Dissanayake 2008: 251). The means and methods attached to the performance of taking the mundane and producing something unusual or special are highly valued in all cultures ("making special": Dissanayake 1992: 54, 1995, 1999: 31, 2008: 252). The capability of elevating something to the status of "extraordinary" or "exceptional" has already been described above with regard to ritualization. It shapes the connection between ritual behavior and universal forms of performance, or in other words, of artistic (or plastic) representation. The key factor here is the aesthetic motive to make something special by transforming it from the common to the unusual. The feeling of wanting to express uniqueness or the "faculty for making and expressing specialness" characterizes and shapes the realms of art, ritual, and play (Dissanayake 1992: 46, 71, 95–101). This "making something special" corresponds with the capability of self-transformation that is felt by the agent involved in a merging or self-transcendence (Dissanayake 1992: 48). Dissanayake refers to a possible connection to ethnocentrism, a universal that I will explore later. The experience, the quality of being able to make something "special," or being able to differentiate not only between the common and the surprising—which animals can do—but also between oneself and other animals and all of nature, contributes to the attitude that one or one's group is "truly special" or even better than others and other groups (Dissanayake 1992: 49, 71–72).

Though psychologists have determined certain concepts of beauty that influence how partners are chosen, we know very little about specific similarities and likenesses between aesthetic concepts from different societies (see here Dutton 2000, 2005; Seel 2005; Scharfstein 2008). One of the very few examples of explicitly comparative work on the subject is Richard Anderson's (2004) *Calliope's Sisters: A Comparative Study of Philosophies of Art*. The title refers to the relationship between Calliope, who as daughter of the goddess Mnemosyne brought art to human beings, and the nine muses who according to Hesiod represent specific forms of art. Does Calliope lead the other muses, or are all ten muses governed by Apollo, the god of light? Anderson examines concepts of aesthetics and philosophies of art in nine non-Western societies and compares them to several Western traditions. He considers differences and similarities with regard to meaning, style, capabilities, and emotions evoked by art while emphasizing that many supposed differences either exist only on the surface or relate to the complexity of the societies in question. Art in simple societies reveals a clear similarity in that the inner or *emic* view of the artist becomes transported everywhere, or to others, as significant in meaning (Anderson 2004: 236; chap. 13).

In all representational media, all known cultures value contrasts involving light or dark, small or large, light or heavy, loud or quiet. They represent elemental structures of perception and are reflected in language as well (Dissanayake 1992: 81–82, 173; Mithen 1996). Art everywhere responds in a similar way to a great number of perceptual and experience preferences (see Scharfstein 2008: 344–46). Alongside natural phenomena like the setting sun, art holds a special place in human societies for evoking widespread emotions. This reflects universal psychic responses to certain forms and associations evoked in the perception of art and the recognition of art's originality (Aiken 1998: 16–17).

When considering universal aesthetics, it is reasonable not to reduce aesthetics to a feeling arising from visual beauty or from static material objects. The topic invokes other senses or concepts that define aesthetics as well, such as a sense for what is ugly or strange, and for the experiences these concepts occasion. Also, universal forms or the features of forms—for example in qualities of allure or appeal—which are valued beyond cultural borders (and therefore are transcultural forms), on the one hand, need to be distinguished from formal principles of aesthetic evaluation (pluricultural or pancultural principles; van Damme 1996: 56, 60–61, 2000: 258, 263) on the other. Possibly universal aesthetic principles include skill or artistry, symmetry and balance, clarity, smoothness and light, youthfulness or newness, and refinement (van Damme 1996: 73–91). An example of the combination of concrete forms and principles of evaluation is represented in the "golden ratio" so often postulated as universal in its invocation of beauty, a claim that is rarely if ever examined in any experimental form (van Damme 1996: 66, 102).

Proposed explanations for the occurrence of universal aesthetic patterns include preferences in human perception, as well as experiences had everywhere by human beings independent of one another. Supposedly a general need for order and rhythm exists among human beings. Evolutionary reasons for universal patterns in art have been debated for some time (see Rensch 1991: 186–93). We can explain universal concepts of beauty in the natural world in many different ways as (a) as product of adaptation, (b) a functional by-product, (c) in its original form, an arbitrary by-product that gained some secondary function (*spandrels*, Gould and Lewontin 1979: 582), or (d) as the result of signal evolution (Dissanayake 1995: 105–6; Voland 2003: 253–57; Seel 2005: 326–28). The latter must not necessarily indicate efforts toward beauty but more the *costly signal* of fitness in the sphere of sexual selection (the so-called handicap principle; Zahavi 1975; Zahavi and Zahavi 1997; see Tooby and Cosmides 2001 and Voland 2003, as well as contributions in Voland and Grammer 2003). "Making something special" would therefore mean, in concrete form, making something that is complex or requires effort, or making something of higher value (Voland 2003: 243–44). In more recent times, people have speculated on the ultimate reasons for the universality in art. An anthropological argument states that artistic products could foster societal adaptation or could at least understood as a shift in the function of a trait (exaptation). Societies can better transport, record, and store beliefs by way of art, a process I call the *thesaurization* of art, which in the visual arts functions much like texts, as a pulling together of beliefs in a supercoherent way (Eibl 2004).

Music and Performance Arts

As with representational art, there is evidence that music is universal. This position is held by many musicians, such as Leonard Bernstein (Bernstein 1991; Schenker 1980), as well as anthropologists of music such as Alan Lomax and Bruno Nettl (Lomax 1994; Nettl 1983; Ferraro 2001a: 337) and psychologists (Harré 2006). In all cultures we find singing and the production of specific rhythms by drumming and hand clapping. Many universals regarding tones, melodies, and rhythms are of a very specific type ("Universalien der Musikwahrnehmung" 2008). Tonal or musical scales in all cultures contain only a few ranges, mostly of five or six tones. Tonal intervals almost always differ in size from culture to culture. Tonal hierarchies exist everywhere, even when they are in themselves quite variable. The grouping of tones into perceptual units is also universal. Rhythms are everywhere organized in hierarchies and allow for emphases, such as regularly occurring pulses that are divided through asymmetrically arranged sounds. Many of these universals embedded within the structure of music correspond to species-specific features of perception and cognitive as well as emotional processing of information (Sloboda 2003). Recently, the search for musical universals has been connected to biological and ecological concepts of function in the realm of an "evolutionary biomusicology" (Wallin, Merker and Brown 2000; Welker 2007). Here ethnological findings are linked to archaeological and psychological results and understood on evolutionary terms. It has been speculated whether words that are expressed through song have a mediating function between an ephemeral life and cross-generational collective memory (Dissanayake 1992: 71). An open question today in universal research in the area of music asks whether music is in fact a phenomenon from a transcultural point of view, or whether one can speak here only of music in the plural form (on *Musiken* see Welker 2007: 273–74).

There also appear to be universally widespread criteria for quality in performance art. Agility, stamina, and elegance are highly rated in the field of dance (Hanna 1987). Liveliness is appreciated everywhere, as are rhythmic or tonal echoes in language, and resonance and energy in percussion. We find games and game playing in all cultures that are characterized first by rules defining strategy, success, and failure; and second by the fact that they have no further meaning beyond their own intended purposes, as Johan Huizinga has pointed out (Huizinga 1956; Weber-Schäfer 1998: 38). That does not necessarily exclude the fact that game playing maintains a (universal) function as a way to practice behavior in a relaxed, unburdened setting (Eibl 2004: 370), similar to the function of storytelling (Scalise Sugiyama 2006: 321; Tooby and Cosmides 2006). These general characteristics make it possible to transport games, which are easily established easily from one culture to the next, and to find so many games spread out throughout the world (Weber-Schäfer 1998: 45).

If there are universal patterns in art and music, then we can venture toward a concept of aesthetics that has at its core the notion that certain things are perceived as especially attractive (Stout 1971; Seel 2005: 328; also see Menninghaus 2003: 138–97). We can then empirically explain what on average is found to be pleasing. This does not imply normative or absolute claims of a biological aesthetic with biological causes. However, it leaves wide open the possibility of determining universal aesthetic patterns and of considering what "on average" is understood as attractive.

Sociality

Social Structure and Basic Norms

One of the most common universals not even explicitly mentioned in most lists of universals is the fact that all societies have rules governing human action. Cultural perimeters on nourishment or eating would be an example. Most items in an inventory of universals, when not already clearly expressed as rules, would be introduced as follows: "Rules exist concerning …" Katie Fox expressed it precisely when she said that the human species is addicted to rule making (Fox 2014: 19). A large portion of these rules concern interaction between human beings in their own respective society. We are reminded of Radcliffe-Brown's core idea of human beings living not simply as individuals, or organisms, in social groups, but rather as persons in complex social relationships within clearly formed social structures (Radcliffe-Brown 1952: 189, 193–94). The existence of a specific social structure is, in this sense, a universal within cultures.

The social psychologist Moghaddam (2002: 9–10) has pinpointed three norms for human interaction that he describes as strong candidates for universals. He argues deductively by stating that social life would be hardly imaginable without these norms, which he describes as expectations for correct behavior in human interaction. The first is the basic norm of reciprocal trust. The second is the norm of truth, whereby people generally assume their social partners are telling the truth. The first norm places responsibility on the receiver of information, the second on the deliverer of information. The third basic norm is that of turn-taking dialogue, in which both partners in conversation speak, listen, and respond to what the other has said. This norm implies the universal norm of reciprocal respect. In all the great traditions, and probably in all cultures, we find conceptual equivalents of the "golden rule" in the sense of "do unto others as you would want them to do unto you" (example in Hauser 2007: 357). This rule is at times formulated as explicit doctrine, at times as implicit value—as negative or positive, for example. The idea of cooperation and especially of reciprocity is a core universal. What becomes obvious in a comparison of the great religions is that in the face of an ethical dilemma, moral judgments strongly coincide in the degree of their internal limitations and their own innate contradictions despite the differences in religious orientation. An unconscious moral system proves to be relatively immune to religious doctrine. This could indicate a core area of morality that has an evolutionary background, understood in terms of a *moral grammar* (Hauser 2007: 419–25).

Kinship and Family

Like other higher primates, human beings live principally in groups (Coon 1946). They spend most of their lives as persons in some kind of social group. Primary groups are truly universal; secondary groups and reference groups are at least very widespread (Moghaddam 1998: 449–50). Contrary to certain assertions, human beings in traditional societies are not the only ones attached socially to families, partnerships, other cooperative relationships, and friendships. Psychological studies in modern societies have demonstrated that kinship and partnership in behavior and in experience are universally meaningful and the most strongly desired and realized forms in life (Neyer and Lang 2007: 45; Hruschka 2010).

Kinship plays a central role in all cultures (Holy 1987: 151–53; Eriksen 2001: 118–19; Rogoff 2003) and is a central theme of everyday discourse in the prevailing number of known human societies. Sociological network analyses reveal how kinship relationships are, in comparison to other relationships, clearly over-represented in the active network of a person, even in more recent modern societies (J. F. K. Schmidt 2007: 25). As mentioned earlier, kin maintains precedence in all societies, even in contradiction to other clear cultural norms (on favoring kin, see Midgley 1996: 148). Non-kinship friendships are often expressed in terms of family, as fictive or metaphorical kinship relationships. The ubiquity of pseudo-kinship systems, such as the "old boy" networks and sisterhood leagues, is ultimately understood through who is allowed to pass on whose genes to whom (Ehrlich 2002: 193, 238).

Considering both ethological and anthropological findings together, it would be oversimplifying to claim that concepts of kinship simply imitate biotic kinship everywhere in the world. What we are more likely to find are semantic representations of kinship in all societies that prove influential in a vast array of societal contexts. According to Schmidt, kinship semantics operate on a level that is autonomous of biology but take on proximate bio-kinship mechanisms. The feeling of proximity or closeness is ultimately based on genetic kinship, due to its correlation, as a rule, with related persons living together. Feelings of belonging are expressed, and empathy is in fact generated—even when no biotic kinship exists, such as in the case of adoption. Individuals consider emotional closeness a proximate indicator of genetic and biotic kinship. Kinship semantics reflect this proximate mechanism in the constructing of a unique form of social relationship (J. F. K. Schmidt 2007: 29, 33–36). Kinship is therefore more than a broad molding of biotic ancestry. Contrary to David Schneider's (1972) culturalist argument against the concept of universal kinship, kinship is also more than a simple cultural idea on relationships and belonging, completely independent of blood ties. This explains why kinship remains incredibly influential and counts, therefore, as a broad and widespread universal concept in many different kinds of relationships.

The core family, in the specific sense of a unit composed of a mother and child or children, is universal. A family in the sense of a unit with parents and child or children is merely widespread (Kottak 2008: 54, Georgas 2011). Men, as already mentioned, tend to be less permanently present as members of a family but are expected in almost all societies to offer some contribution to child rearing in even a limited way. Based on a broad cultural comparison, Murdock (1949) named four functions of the family: economic, social, sexual, and reproductive. Families are also typically the unit for both biotic procreation and social reproduction, although this is not by nature an absolute. A more recent cultural comparative study of thirty countries showed that all four functions still occur on a worldwide scale and across all socioeconomic backgrounds. This study examined twenty-two family roles in detail, based on personal accounts. It uncovered potential universals with regard to family, described below, though they still need to be more fully examined. The emotional ties occurring within core families are, across all societies, stronger than the ties that develop between more extended family relations. Mothers form the core substance of families, followed by siblings and fathers (Poortinga and Georgas 2006: 96–97; Georgas et al. 2006: 233). These relationships' expressive and emotional functions are independent of their instrumental and material functions. The instrumental, or financial, role of the family is more variable than the emotional function. Whereas hierarchies within families vary more than any other aspect of the family unit, the emotional bond in the core family is the least vulnerable cultural variable (Georgas et al. 2006: 195–96, 222–24). The study shows trends as well. The position and influence of the mother increases according to the increase in her economic role. Today the economic function of families is decreasing, and the sexual function has less to do with marriage and reproduction (Poortinga and Georgas 2006: 97–98).

In species comparison with other higher primates, human families are unique in that they (1) are multigenerational, (2) are formed by ties between partners who have produced children and raised children, and (3) include adult members of both sexes, such as older unmarried children, siblings of parents, and parents of parents. This complex constellation can, despite all forms of variation, be seen as an "elementary structure of human society" (Schlegel 2007: 227). An example of this that occurs in many traditional societies is *stem families*, composed of two pairs and several other adults in their reproductive years, making obvious the meaning of incest avoidance (Schlegel 2007: 228). This elementary structure can explain several cross-cultural behavioral differences between adolescents of both sexes, such as contact avoidance between opposite-sex siblings and differences in competitive and antisocial behavior (Schlegel 2007: 234–36).

Marriage is institutionalized in all known societies, and is not in any culture exclusively an individual decision. The restrictions refer to limits placed on appropriate sex partners and proper marriage partners. All societies have rules that govern which partners are favored and which are to be avoided (Ember and Ember 1997: 103). Despite all the supposed evidence for the universality of marriage, it is in fact difficult to prove, something I have already discussed in light of the problems arising in the construction of a useful and culturally comparative definition of marriage. The institutionalized form of marriage as regulation of access to women capable of reproduction is, with a few exceptions (e.g., the Nayar of South India in the nineteenth century), universal. A woman's marriage partner is generally a male individual, but not always (e.g., the Nuer); nor is it always just one person. Some anthropologists therefore do not consider marriage to be a universal and concede only that similarities as regards families occur, as presented by Edmund Leach (1982: 226, 235) and his description of affinal ties (Leach 1982: 226). In view of the number of marriage partners, it appears that there has never been a strict form of monogamy in human society. Most societies allow polygamy, though nowhere is it the dominant form. Most marriage in all cultures is in fact monogamous. Out of 1,154 former or current societies, 980 allow polygamy; of these, 972 allow polygyny but only 6 allow polyandry. In 43 percent of those 980 societies, polygamy occurs only in isolated forms (Wright 1994: 90, 401n71; Ehrlich 2002: 388).

Social exchange in some form is universally widespread (see the communal sharing described by Fiske 1991: 41). Everywhere we find ideals guiding etiquette and friendliness. According to Marcel Mauss (1872–1950), the exchange of goods and services exists in all human societies (Mauss 1990: 136–38). Exchanging food, goods, and persons as well is a universally broad means of creating social relationships. Giving, presenting, sharing, and exchanging gifts are also universal. If interaction with strangers proves positive, the strangers are not only welcomed but also honored with words, service, food, and festivity. The common meal, or commensality, is found in all societies as the internal expression of community (Kohl 2006: 107). We find reciprocity or reciprocal altruism in all societies (Wright 1994: 202; Fetchenhauer and Bierhoff 2004). The reciprocal exchange of work, goods, service, and wares is widespread (Moebius and Papilloud 2006). The highest form of mutual giving comes in matrimonial exchange (Lévi-Strauss 1958). In all cultures we find alliances in and between subgroups (Greenwood and Stini 1977: 314). Emotions as well, such as empathy, thankfulness, affection and the feeling of a duty to return services are all universal (Wright 1994: 203). Altruistic action or behavior is focused on genetically related kin. Everywhere we find that difference and preference are upheld for one's own children and close kin, in contrast to more distant kin. Contractual agreements in the form of long-term contracts between nonrelated persons are universal. The specific human capacity for altruism extends not only to nonrelatives but *all* people we might expect to meet over and over (Pagel 2012: 191, 230; Read 2012: 145). Thus, extended trust and mutual dependency in extended and durable interactions allow for the building of symmetric social relationships and emergence of institutions.

Enculturation of Norms

Enculturation practices usually convey social norms specific to the society in question. Anthropological research into childhood and child care is almost always particularistic, as readers and textbooks show (Rogoff 2003; LeVine and New 2008; Lancy 2015; see also De Loache and Garland 2000). However, there are universal patterns in the ways cultures instill norms in children.

The few existing comparative studies on child rearing are a rich source for understanding universal patterns in the learning of norms. Some studies, instead of making broad cross-cultural comparisons, compare a limited set of geographically separated, historically (almost) unrelated societies (Newman 1976; Whiting and Edwards 1988; Munroe and Munroe 2001; Röttger-Rössler et al. 2013; Whiting and Whiting 2014). In a recent secondary analysis of published field reports done by anthropologists and psychologists, Quinn (2005) compared child rearing practices. The reports were empirical studies based on fieldwork in individual non-Western societies. Quinn carried out a fine-grained reanalysis of the studies through a careful reading and systematic comparison. It should be noted that the anthropologists who conducted the original studies were particularists concerned with meaning rather than explanation, so the studies were aimed at describing culturally specific models (ethnotheories, folk theories) and conducted without universal claims whatsoever. The leading question for Quinn was to determine what it is about child rearing that makes it so crucial in forming adult behavior and personality (selfhood). Are there universal ways to raise children? If so, how is it that child rearing is so effective everywhere in transforming children into "culturally valued adults" (2005: 478, 507), that is, persons who know social norms and conform to these norms willingly? Quinn employed the concept of cultural models from cognitive anthropology. Cultural models are shared cognitive representations (schemas, scripts). Such default models function to make meaning of the world, interpret sensory input, and shape behavior. Rarely articulated, they are linked to the shared acts and artifacts produced in a community. They are "automatic pilots" allowing us to conduct our daily business without employing too much mental energy (Bennardo and DeMunck 2014: 3–6, Antweiler forthcoming).

Cultural solutions to the daily task of living that the individual brain cannot work out alone provide us with a particular kind of cultural model. Here other people are needed because the individual faces a task that is complex, recurrent, and vital. Furthermore, the given task is widespread enough within the population to make a common solution attractive. Instilling social norms in the process of raising children is such a critical, recurrent, widespread, complex task in societies. A cultural model of child rearing specifies (1) the desired kind of adults that children should become and (2) a set of practices to socialize children toward becoming these adults. The ideal concepts of adults vary from society to society, as the ideal must correspond with local ecological and economic conditions. With respect to cultural models, Quinn links norm socialization to a perspective that understands norms as endogenous products of an individual's interactions with others in a group. This is a perspective that is often dismissed in the social science literature. Common forms of sanctioning poor behavior in children include beating, teasing, shaming, intensive staring at the child, gaze avoidance, invoking the threat of danger, isolating the child from others, or leaving the child alone (Lancy 2015: 178–80).

According to Quinn, the methods of instilling social norms vary in their combination and practice among the societies she compares, but they share some traits: (1) experiential constancy, (2) emotional arousal, (3) general evaluation of the child, and (4) predispositional emotional priming (Quinn 2005: 480). Taken together, this limited set of child-rearing practices seems to be the main requirement for effective norm socialization. First, learning norms must incorporate practices that maximize the constancy of a child's experience. This develops through regularity and repetition. Child rearing means avoiding contradictory, extraneous, and diverting experiences for the sake of facilitating habitual behavior. Body language, such as averting one's gaze or not smiling as a sign of disapproval, offers an explicitly understood form for correcting the behavior of a child. These measures are embedded in the usual cultural patterns of behavior that children experience on a day-to-day level.

Second, child rearing also includes practices that produce strong emotions. This occurs through teasing, frightening, shaming, and beating, or in a more positive sense, through generous forms of praise. Physical punishment is a common practice in sanctioning a child's behavior. Another practice is to frighten a child with claims that poor behavior will cause attacks by animals or spirits.

Other common ways of frightening children that are found throughout the world is having an adult dress up like a ghost or using foreigners (sometimes the anthropologist!) to frighten children: "Here comes the foreigner (bronyi); she's going to take you away," as Quinn experienced in Ghana (Quinn 2005: 492).

These methods might appear harsh to some Western readers, but they often are used in a loving, stable environment. They are applied in a repeated manner and are frequently incorporated into a co-narrated story in which the adult tells a story that includes the child. Children are thus motivated to learn and remember these normative lessons. Briggs reports, for example, the detailed ways in which Inuit adults instill values and a sense of belonging in children through role-playing in which grandparents show mock hostility toward the parents (Briggs 1998: 94, 127, 134). A related practice is to show mock hostility by alternating the sounds of one's voice, abruptly changing between a soft, seductive timbre and a throaty tone .

Third, teaching norms is often linked to global evaluation of a child's behavior. Approval or disapproval is emotionally arousing, as it is linked to expectations of security and care given by parents or other members of the society (Quinn 2005: 491). These global evaluations entail explicit labeling, such as saying "Yes, you are a good girl." Beatings are accompanied by exclamations such as "This is a bad child" or by comments expressing withdrawal of affection or love, like "We don't want you." Learning norms involves generally nongratifying experiences that are abstract, complex, or other otherwise demanding. Thus, and fourth, child-rearing practices involving the teaching of norms help to train children toward emotional predispositions in order to prime them for subsequent learning (Quinn 2005: 502). Goals in child rearing always include norms that regulate the adequate expression of emotional behavior. Moreover, emotions are often explicitly given a socializing function. Children are trained not only to adjust their behavior to norms, but also to manage their repertoire of emotions such as anger and embarrassment. Quinn's notion of "predispositional priming" could be substituted by the idea of "socializing emotions" (Röttger-Rössler et al. 2013: 3–6).

One example of enculturation includes raising children to become sensitive to the feeling of a specific form of shame (*malu*) if, for example, the Malay norm of respect is violated (Goddard 1996; Collins and Bahar 2000; Fessler 2004). The use of dramatic forms of narrative can create a sense of fear and vulnerability in children, making them sensitive to specific sanctions applied as they grow older. Thus, visceral dramatization *primes* the child for verbal sanctions that come later in life. In Minangkabau society in Indonesia and elsewhere in the Malay cultural realm, it is common to hear people speak positively of children who can suppress anger (*marah*) and "already know how to feel ashamed" (*suda tahu malu*). If someone's transgression of a norm becomes public, then anyone related to the offender is also expected to feel shame ("vicarious shame"). Thus, *malu* should be regarded as a blend of social fear and virtue (Röttger-Rössler et al. 2013: 19, 27).

On a didactic level, all these techniques function both to make norm socialization effective in general and to motivate members of a society to learn norms in such a way that they never forget them. Quinn's four universal features for effective norm socialization focus on instilling norms by evoking emotions within the human psyche. The four features, or methods, are built upon different human psychological mechanisms that are used within cultures. We can say that culture makes use of the human brain and its capacity for learning in order to solve universal problems in norm socialization (Quinn 2005: 480).

Though teaching is rare in traditional societies, we do find it in the instruction in good social manners, especially appropriate behavior vis-á-vis kin (Lancy 2015: 172–73). The methods described above are often specifically planned, controlled, and explicitly related to myths in instructive folktales. This may be astonishing, since even crucial parts of enculturation do not depend on deliberate adult instruction, as reflected in the widespread (and realistic) expectation in most cultures that children will learn to talk without needing explicit teaching (Ochs and Shieffelin 1984). But as humans differ, and as the problem of norms everywhere is related to specific traditions and environments, every childrearing community has to develop a solution to the universal problem of norm socialization (Quinn 2005: 479–80, 506). Whereas the substance of what we teach is immensely variable, we can expect similarly designed mechanisms for effective child rearing to be reinvented by any human community.

Inequality, Rank, Status, and Power

All cultures display indications of the pursuit of power (Boehm 1989; de Waal 2001: 352). Anthropologists worldwide have observed the manipulation of social relationships for the purpose of individual gain. The universality of "triangular consciousness" plays a part here: knowledge of one's own relationship to others (A-B, A-C) and knowledge of the relationship between others and oneself (B+C to A). While conformity is universal (Moghaddam 1998: 11), social scientists do not altogether agree about whether people play particular roles in all societies. While a social psychologist has written in a textbook that "all cultures assign people to certain roles" (Myers 2002: 178) and cross-cultural psychologists have determined that examples of role diversity and role obligations are found everywhere (Berry et al. 2011: 54), a dictionary of sociology states that it is an open question whether role-playing is a universal category or only an analytical cognitive model (Griese 2002: 461). The concept of roles is a good example of the way many basic works in the empirical sciences implicitly refer to universally accepted phenomena as only supposedly universal. Certain subject matter could turn out to be universalized Eurocentric or Asian-centric concepts. Addressing the problems that arise from such issues is a central contribution of research into universals.

In all societies there are forms that go beyond the social structures of sex, age, and kinship categories. Socioeconomic inequality is observed everywhere, as is interest in inequality with regard to general status, rank, and prestige. Acquired status and rules governing succession carry significant weight almost everywhere. All known human cultures feature a system of dominance. They share this trait with primate societies, a fact that says nothing about homologous causes. Despite certain contradictory reports, status differentiation can be found in Murdock's "common denominator" (Murdock 1945) as a universal. In all known cultures, most individuals strive for prestige or higher self-esteem. Thinking in categories of status is universal: "People in all cultures, whether they fully realize it or not, want to wow their neighbors, to rise in local esteem" (Wright 1994: 265). From an evolutionary perspective, this continuity among primates in terms of social rank and dominance probably signifies homology rather than analogy. Jerome Barkow emphasizes, however, that when it comes to human beings and dominance, abstraction and cognitive value come into play (Barkow 1975: 553–55). Universal though status might be, its basis can be highly diverse: "to finish a string a pearls, to make music, to hoard money or to collect scalps" (Wright 1994: 260). The universal interest in status corresponds with the motive of promoting one's own reputation (Wright 1994: 202, 213), something Lawrence Kohlberg describes as the third step in moral development, associated with the wish to be known as a nice or upstanding person.

Forms of address are universal, revealing both horizontal social distance and vertical social status (D. Brown 1991). The offer to establish acquaintance is usually made by the person of higher rank. This pertains not only to the form of address but also to invitations, borrowing of pens, and body language such as touching someone on the shoulder (Brown, cited in Myers 2002: 174). In studies done on twenty-seven languages, Roger Brown was able to demonstrate that human beings who live in societies shaped by status hierarchies use more formal address when speaking to people of higher standing but more familiar address to communicate with lower-ranking individuals like friends, women, children, or even dogs. The manner of speaking used with persons of higher rank is similar to that used to express politeness to strangers (Kroger and Wood 1992; see Myers 2002: 173).

Regulating Conflict, Political Leadership, and Values

The twentieth-century anthropology of law was heavily oriented to case studies, expressing little interest in the question of natural law but more in the transferability of Western concepts of law to non-Western societies (Adams 1998: 186). Laura Nader, a sage in the field, did list two of eight fundamental research topics in the anthropology of law as follows: "Is law present in all societies?" and "What are the universal characteristics of law wherever it is found?" (Nader 1994: 2–4). According to Leopold Pospísil, another luminary in the field, the following universals are observed to be the "basic patterns of law" (Pospísil 1986): all cultures impose sanctions on those who step outside of established norms; all cultures recognize authority; and in all societies disputes are settled through regulated generalizations. Fikentscher generally supports this, while noting the following: "One negative result should be mentioned: there is as yet no indication that certain *modes* of legal thought are universal" (Fikentscher 1995: 64).

All cultures impose certain regulations to prohibit murder, violence, and rape, whereby exceptions also occur, e.g. usually in times of war. Punishments commonly take the form of isolating individuals found guilty of an offense from the rest of the community. Widespread forms of social exclusion include expulsion, ostracization, incarceration, and execution. Behavior that is deemed damaging to the group is severely punished all over the world. All cultures have certain rules defining membership in permanent social units with accompanying rights and duties. In almost all cultures we find not only established forms of conflict regulation and specialists who administer this regulation, but also specialists who make decisions involving public matters. Murdock describes this universal as "government." People everywhere take on leadership roles, even when these roles are only temporary or dependent on certain situations. Munificence is normally expected of those with leading roles. Political leadership becomes in general a de facto oligarchy: neither completely democratic nor completely autocratic.

As early as the 1950s, researchers, and above all Kluckhohn, raised questions about distinctly cultural values and the concept of universal values. Kluckhohn referred to both: "There is a personal selection of limited cultural possibilities, which are, in turn, a selection from a limited number of universal possibilities" (Kluckhohn 1951: 417). To date, however, anthropologists and social psychologists studying values have more often concentrated on differences between cultures. Among the few exceptions are Shalom H. Schwartz and his colleagues, who have been studying culturally specific values from a perspective that considers similarities as well. In a series of comprehensive studies, they examined individual values in sixty countries at a parallel level and according to an emic approach. Values were defined as concepts covering the pursuit of trans-situational goals that govern action and behavior. Functionally they refer back to biotic needs and demands to facilitate the welfare of the group (Schwartz and Bilsky 1987: 550; 1990). In terms of methods, the few initially suggested categories of values were then expanded through the work with case studies. Finally, values were compared, making it possible to distinguish a list of ten value types according to motivational content (Schwartz 1994: 22–24) and fifty-six single values. It became apparent that many values in many (national) cultures converge, and that at least four higher-ranking value types are universal. More recent studies have pointed out cross-cultural similarities in conflicting values and suggested the existence of a pancultural hierarchy of values (Schwartz 1994: 42; Schwartz and Bardi 2001). The results correspond to findings of completely independent studies using other methods and sometimes having other goals, such as the pursuit of a classification of cultures (e.g., Fiske 1991; Hofstede and Hofstede 2005; also see P. Smith et al. 2006: 35–44).

Ethnicity and Ethnocentrism

Universals under this heading follow the logic of a collective identity defined by one group separating itself from another. The historian Jörn Rüsen describes this as a "cultural fact of human socialization" or a "universal phenomenon" (Rüsen 1998: 15, 30). In contrast, human beings also possess a universal ability to see beyond their own cultural norms (Drechsel 1984: 47). As mentioned earlier, the capability of self-transformation, experienced as a transcendence into others or as the opening up to others, is found throughout the world (Dissanayake 1992: 70; also see V. Turner 1974). In all cultures there is willingness or openness, at least on the part of some persons, for cross-cultural dialogue (Busch 2007: 108).

Every culture also has the concept of a collective or individual identity and the concept of the "we-group" as a means of separating one's own from another group by clearly demarcating "we" from "they" or "the others." This is the core phenomenon in what anthropologists describe as "ethnicity." From the perspective of human ethology, the logic here refers to a self-centered organization of categories relevant to actions and behaviors of others. Three concentric circles are involved here: (1) kinship, (2) cultural affiliation, and (3) cultural others—those outside our own cultural affiliation (Markl 1986: 85–86). This logic depicts the structure of important conflicts according to in-group and out-group, as well as the structure of internal disputes and of conflict occurring with those outside a group (Leach 1982: 118; Pinker 2002: 39, 319).

The doyen of ethnocentric research, William G.(1959; first published in 1906), describes this specific phenomenon as members of one ethnic group looking at members of other collectives through their own cultural lenses. Ellen Dissanayake characterizes this attitude as a "universal cultural disposition" (1992: 16). An simple indicator of it is the widespread use of ethnonyms that describe the members of one's own group as "humans" while defining people from another group as animal-like, nonhuman, bad, imperfect, or somewhat unusual. These ethnonyms in themselves reveal only a limited kind of universality, since they are possibly connected to linguistic markings (Greenberg 1963, 1975). In the most general terms, ethnocentrism confirms the tendencies that are already anchored in the phenomenon of ethnicity (Le Vine and Campbell 1971; Pagel 2012: 88–95). The unifying and restricting elements of a social entity are viewed rigidly, and its people's affiliation is tied to criteria considered coherent and natural. The two forms of stereotypes, the hetero-stereotype and the auto-stereotype, are universal in the way they reflectively complement each other, whereby the hetero-stereotype is more often associated with a negative image of other persons, groups, or cultures (D. Campbell 1967; K. Müller 2003b; Antweiler 2004a). Rüsen, from the historical standpoint, characterizes ethnocentrism as universal. One's own social realm or time period is seen as substantially different from all others in space and time. What is known or inherent for one person is judged positively in comparison to the unknown or foreign spheres of being inhabited by others. In the words of the historian, we are dealing with "a cultural strategy for creating identity … (with a) … 'logic' derived from affiliation and dissociation" (Rüsen 1998: 30). Ethnocentrism is revealed in a diversity of forms, and within this diversity we find, on careful analysis, specific universals. In a detailed study, Brown distinguished twenty-three specific features in the context of ethnocentrism that are either widespread or practically universal (D. Brown 2012).

In the restricted sense, ethnocentrism occurs only when ethnicity and the "we vs. they" construct are combined with a positive form of self-awareness and a devalued view of others, as ethnicity alone does not necessarily indicate a devaluing of others. It is therefore empirically left open whether the combination of both aspects is in any way present. Similarly, Marschall has characterized ethnocentrism as universal in the combination of inner reinforcement through ritual and outer reinforcement through the creation of negative images of the other (Marschall 1990a: 8). A feature often associated with ethnicity is a dual morality, or an "ethical dualism" (Pinker 2002: 269). Some assume that the differentiation of three moral spheres, corresponding to the division of three social spheres discussed earlier, occurs universally. It has also been claimed that human beings basically assume there are such things as universal moral rules (Pinker 2002: 272). According to the social philosopher Michael Walzer, each type of moral system includes two types of morality: a concrete morality based on clear and positive maxims that are maximalist and specific to a certain culture or locality, and a loose morality based on moral standards that can be chosen by consensus and are mostly negative decrees that are minimalist but, unlike the maximalist type, universal (Walzer 1996: 24). A sense of justice as a "broad universal" is widespread in the form of moral aggression against those who go against group norms (Masters 1996: 382; for a general view, see de Waal 1996, 2005).

Worldview and Images of Humanity

Views of the world, its formation, and its function reveal cross-cultural similarities. The cosmology based on a unified world, with its structuring cosmogony, is widespread. What unites varying worldviews is the desire to express order (Servier 1991: 1424–26; Stagl 1992: 156–57; Bischof 1996). In established myths from different parts of the globe, the particulars of the beginning of the world and its development reveal many commonalities concerning not only worldviews in general but images of humanity too.

Dichotomies, Nature, Culture, and the Individual Person

A universal feature of human societies appears to be the dichotomous separation of things that are deemed similar and different in the subject matter of the world, society, and the individual person. Almost all societies either expressly or implicitly acknowledge the following fundamental differences between humans and animals: only humans have fire, not only for warmth but also for cooking; only humans have exclusively structured sexual relations with other humans; and only humans change their bodies through body painting, mutilation, or clothing (Leach 1982: 118).

It also appears that the tendency to anthropomorphize and reify nature is universal (E. Wilson 1998: 153; Kennedy 1992). Nonhuman living creatures almost everywhere are not only regarded as having human attributes but imagined with a human form as well (Kohl 2006: 104–5). The dichotomization of nature versus culture is probably also universal (Dissanayake 1992: 72–73; see Freud 1956), though this has not yet been empirically examined. Some anthropologists strongly doubt that the clear distinction of nature as a reality completely independent of culture is in fact a cultural universal; rather, such a distinction could represent the projection of Cartesian and therefore Western dualism on nature and culture. "Nature" would then be a cultural category denied its cultural association. Josephus Platenkamp discussed this topic: "[The] idea of nature being a universal reality, not influenced by our social and moral actions or behaviours, is a relatively recent notion in Western thought … [and is] … at best a concept … specific to only a limited number of societies and … to a relatively short period of time" (Platenkamp 1999: 6).

Conceptions of the world develop out of images on a macro-, meso-, and micro-level. Conceptual views of individuals as acting persons are drawn foremost from the individual's reactions to, experiences of, and reflections on the surrounding world. Some higher primates appear to have the cognitive capacity for self-reflection, at least according to several studies on second-order intentionality, although the extent of this capacity is contested (see Tomasello 2004; Schiefenhövel 2004; de Waal 2005). The concept of the self-reflective actor is found in all human cultures: "It appears a basic need of each human being to form a concept of his own personal identity and to protect his own autonomy, that is, to maintain a certain level of self-control in order to defend himself against outside forces" (Markl 1986: 84–85).

Geertz has emphasized the universality, in the distinction of "self" and "other," of persons as objects and subjects, not just as reactive agents (Geertz 1965). The concept of intentionality is universal in the assumption that interactive partners usually want something; and that they can plan and can make decisions. The universal concept of the actor is a related concept that holds the actor at least partially responsible for his or her own actions. Another widespread view is the distinction between actions that can be influenced by humans and actions that cannot. People from all cultures regard decision making and responsibility as the expression of the ambivalence of human action. Therefore the idea that human action is always ambivalent—especially with regard to decision making—is found everywhere (see Boehm 1989). Concepts of the self-reflective actor also determine the use of metaphor or imagery, found everywhere in the ascription of personal attributes to social constructs.

Most anthropologists are of the opinion that the specific concept of the person—as opposed to the actor—as an individual with autonomy and lasting identity is universal (Carrithers 2000; Mathews and Moore 2001: 1; Wierzbicka 2005: 265–66; pace Shweder and Bourne 1984: 162). With regard to language, surprisingly many similarities pertain to how persons are described in cultures that are otherwise very different, even in terms of interpersonal diversity. This could indicate universal conceptions that correspond to solidarity versus conflict and dominance versus subordination (G. White 1980: 765). Studies claiming that probably not all cultures recognize the concept of the autonomous person are therefore especially worth considering. Ethnographies on societies from the Pacific realm have increasingly presented evidence of such a phenomenon (Loizos and Heady 1999; Strathern and Stewart 2000; Gregor and Tuzin 2001; see also Köpping, Welker, and Wiehl 2002). Several Western theories that otherwise argue in terms of universals do not present blanket assumptions on the concept of the person as a universal phenomenon. According to Marxism, the specific historical formation of the means of production constitutes the subject, thereby negating the possibility of a universal person (Barker 2004: 225).

What universal worldviews are shaped by the meso- and macro-level? Michael Kearney, from the perspective of cultural materialism, has developed a general model for worldviews based on cross-cultural studies and deductive arguments (Kearney 1984, 1996). He has thus taken up the old question of psychic human unity. Kearney's generalized form of "world-view universals" (Kearney 1984: 65–107; 1996: 1380; also see Wrightsman 1975) can be equated in many ways to Redfield's (1953) older universal model (see Kearney's Table 1 in 1984: 39 and Table 6 in 1984: 106). According to both models, the most fundamental universal distinction is that between "self" and "other." With more emphasis than Redfield, Kearney presents the logical connections between this and other dichotomous distinctions. Further distinctions are, for the most part, dependent on a more fundamental dichotomy. The conceptions of time and space correspond more to the concept of causality than to each other.

Whereas Redfield describes worldview universals from within an idealist tradition, Kearney is more interested in their genesis and function. In terms of historical materialism, he refers to them as a practical and social phenomenon (Kearney 1984: 66, 119–21, Table 7). According to Kearney, worldview universals reflect general human experiences with the practical circumstances of life. The concept of space and time, for example, is therefore pre-Einstein in that time and space are seen as distinct categories. Kearney's categories correspond to many findings emerging from Piaget's genetic psychology on the development of logical thinking in children (Kearney 1984: 84–91, 208). Few studies to date have been explicitly designed to explore universals in the personal development of worldviews in children and their corresponding psychic capabilities. The studies done so far refer to increasing complexity in conceptions of the world and the displacement of autonomic identity by reciprocally oriented identity in young adulthood (Oerter 1999a: 192–97; 2007: 508–22).

A universal that is strongly associated with worldviews occurs in the ideas people the world over have about the existence of natural law and their conceptions of behavioral norms or ideals. There are of course various notions of natural law, whose basis is found in forms such as God, reason, human nature, or societal necessity. In nonliterate societies, natural law often takes an implicit form, understood in contrast to man-made laws (Adams 1998: 121). Within the otherwise diverse conceptions of natural law, we are able to discern the central and broadly held theme of an "essential unity" between law and the highest expression of nature. Ubiquity and constancy determine what law may be. Universality indicates a naturalness, and this naturalness refers then to what is right, proper, or true (Adams 1998: 115–17).

Several authors have postulated many specific universals in worldviews or speculated on their existence. I will name here only a few examples—to begin with, theories concerning the weather, good and bad fortune, and health and sickness. The view of a causal connection between sickness and death is found everywhere, and diagnosis based on little evidence, regarding animals or illnesses, is pervasive. Magic occurs in all cultures with regard to general protection or gaining attention from the opposite sex. Furthermore, some have speculated on the universal occurrence of positive magic and the belief that, through the manipulation of symbols or images, people can influence the things being symbolized or represented. Even extremely specific ideas have been considered universal. According to Edmund Leach, the symbolic associations of hair, particularly with genitalia, are an example of a universal (Leach 1958: 147–49). Many questions concerning commonalities and differences in worldviews or in ways of thinking are still left unanswered. Keesing and Strathern (1998: 241) put it well: "The gulfs between cultural models of reality of different peoples cannot be aptly characterized as either superficial or deep. The processes of thought, perception, and memory by a *Homo sapiens* brain that are the same in Amazonia or Nigeria or New York or the Trobriand islands."

Concepts of Time and Space

Concepts of time are often used as examples to explain cultural diversity and argue against universality. The supposed proof is taken from Whorf's work on the language of the Hopi, in which he deduces that they have completely different concepts of time as compared to other cultures. Less known is Malotki's critique of this. In a detailed empirical analysis, Malotki was able to show dozens of forms used by the Hopi to describe time in daily life (Whorf 1956; Malotki 1983). The diversity claimed for conceptions of time is and was, however, nearly always exaggerated. All languages are able to communicate time units, sometimes implicitly, when referring to lengths of time. Wiezbicka has named eight concepts of time that are found in all known languages: "when," "now," "after," "before," "a long time," "a short time," "for some time," and "one moment" (Wierzbicka 2005: 261). The difference between concepts of time in day-to-day life, in which length of time is the focus, and especially in those ideas concerning history, ritual, myth, or cosmology, is critical in matters of comparison (Keesing 1994b: 5–7). All known cultures consider time in day-to-day behavior and activities as an arrow, even when cyclical or other concepts are also available. It is possible that both the linear and the cyclical concepts are universal conceptions of time. There are standards or terms of reference for both in the day-to-day experiences of the world (Keesing 1994b: 6).

This also shows that as a rule, time-related phenomena take shape through the expression of spatial relations, as in the examples "in March" or "before we eat" or "after the war." In contrast to Whorf's theses, all known languages use spatial concepts metaphorically to express time. A study concerning adverbs of time in fifty languages taken from a worldwide sample was able to demonstrate this. Therefore the thesis asserting fundamental differences in how people the world over conceive and express time could be explicitly rejected—even when the sample is somewhat Europe-oriented, when not all concepts of time in all languages can be expressed through spatial markers, and when the temporal markers have a tendency of becoming autonomous (Haspelmath 1997).

This also holds true for spatial concepts and the way they are reflected in language. Despite the enormous grammatical and lexical variation with regard to spatial relations and forms, some spatial concepts do not empirically reveal variation, such as "where" as in place, "here," "over," "under," "near," "far," "in," and "on" (Goddard 2003: 427). In connection to ethnicity and ethnocentrism, the significance of measuring or delineating space is practically universal. Concepts concerning locality or regarding territory are found everywhere (Lopreato and Crippen 2002: 252–53), even for transient or nomadic groups and sea nomads. Securing, defending, and expanding territory are basic motivations in the history of human actions, and may in fact be conditional strategies (E. Wilson 1998: 171).

Spatial references are one of many currently extensively studied topics that are filled with contradicting tendencies. In the literature it is often assumed that the spatial domains expressed in language are structured universally by reference to the body or the geographical environment (e.g., left, right, in front, behind). All known cultures make maps. Small two- or three-dimensional models of places or landscapes in an overhead perspective that include iconic or noniconic symbols carrying certain meaning are produced everywhere. This aligns with the fact that representations uncovered in prehistoric contexts since the Late Paleolithic often resemble maps, and with findings that even children at an early age draw maps, and that children older than five can quickly recognize spatial views or areal images as maps (Stea, Blaut, and Stephens 1996: 348–52, 356).

More recent studies, however, indicate that orientation-related systems developing from spatial relations can hardly be considered universals of natural perception but rather represent cultural constructs. As far as we know, there are "where" questions in all cultures that are normally answered by spatial descriptions. But the form of such questions can vary significantly from culture to culture (Levinson 1996: 359). Danziger has demonstrated that the Mopan Maya of Belize and Guatemala describe objects in terms of their spatial nearness from one object to part of another (Danziger 2001: 205–10). Arguments concerning the universal symbolism connected to the right hand versus the left, considered universal since Robert Hertz's work on the topic in 1909 (Hertz 2006), appear less clearly universal in the most recent studies. Around one-third of all languages seem to have no words for "right" and "left" and their speakers often do not use the hand for orientation in space (Levinson 1996: 376; 2003; Holenstein 1985a: 14–58; see Pinker 2008: 141–48 for a critical analysis). These results indicate a relativistic viewpoint. The culturally varying contextualization of domains does not, however, rule out the possibility of comparison or the existence of universals per se. It could very well be the case that whereas various forms for conceptualizing and communicating space do occur, they exist according to a universal set of limitations. The number of variants for every domain is therefore limited. With regard to the example of preference for left- or right-handedness, we are able to state a universal implication: when a culture shows preference for one, it is always for the right hand (D. Brown 2005a: 2).

Rituals and Beliefs

Problems of Definition and Universal Religiosity

When considering the forms of belief found on earth, what becomes immediately apparent to the observer is their enormous diversity. Religious diversity is a matter of different religions, confessions, sects, and denominations, but much more so of assumptions concerning higher beings, their powers and authority, and the morality and rituals generated by belief. This multilayered diversity in belief is not properly expressed in the well-known statistics on the subject and in atlas maps, which strongly reflect the perceptions of the great world religions. And yet, one could expect to find a universal religion, since all human beings can envision the future and have existential experiences, and these two capabilities raise questions about why we are the way we are. These experiences are above all those associated with life's finitude—with birth, illness, and death. Human beings from all cultures are searching for a deeper understanding; they ask whether life's discontinuation is unavoidable or whether there is something that exists beyond life as we know it (Kather 2008: 48–49).

Many supposedly religiously based universals are, according to cross-cultural examination, anything but universal (Boyer 2001: 6–10). Supernatural beings can be extremely various, with some gods being mortal and some spirits being dumb. Salvation is not the central point of many religions. Many human beings do not have religion in terms of a separate sphere of life, and quite a few are religious but do not have a word for "religion" or would not say that they "believe," but rather that they "know." Despite this, the diversity in the concepts of religion is not unlimited, which raises the question of whether this limitation is predicated on general human psychic structures (Boyer 1994: viii; 2001; Eichinger Ferro-Luzzi 1996: 581).

The question of universality in religion is closely associated with the problem of defining religion, or defining belief. Research in this direction has remained statically based on the work of leading religious experts, namely Evans-Pritchard and Geertz (see Wax 1984: 5–6; Straub and Shimada 1999). Social scientists continue to debate whether religion is an absolute and universal phenomenon, though most of them maintain that it is. Talcott Parsons drew mainly from the work of Malinowski in describing the universality of religion, saying that human beings everywhere differentiate between rational and magical acts or practices. In his introduction to the American edition of Max Weber's *Sociology of Religion*, he briskly claimed that "this view that belief in the supernatural is universal has been completely confirmed by modern anthropology" (Parsons 1963, quoted in Klass 1995: 25). Other writers proclaim a little more cautiously that some form of belief in spiritual things is universal on the societal level (D. Brown 1991: 139; Ehrlich 2002: 213; also see McCauley and Lawson 2002; Light and Wilson 2004), while others ask whether specific religious forms are universal, such as the mystical concept of a journey of the soul (Schimmel 1996).

Religious anthropologists and scholars of comparative religion, while maintaining highly varied positions on the question of the definability of religion, tend toward the assumption that religion is practically or nearly universal. Brian Morris, for example, with reference to Plato, has determined that all known societies make reference to holiness or to spiritual beings and therefore declared that "few would deny that some form of religion is universal among mankind" (Morris 1987: 1). Quite similar to this is the cautiously formulated position of Roy A. Rappaport, who has emphasized that what the careful observer would call religion has been found in all the societies known to anthropology. He has even spoken in terms of an "absolute ubiquity of religion" (Rappaport 1999: 1), adding that among the many points of empirical evidence, there are functional reasons too for the occurrence of religion. Human beings are not only ensnared in their own webs of meaning, as Geertz has said, but also live in a material world that provides no intrinsic meaning and demands adaptation. Human beings are subordinate to natural conditions that they never fully understand. Creation of meaning that adequately refers to the environment is therefore an adaptive necessity among human beings (Rappaport 1999: 21, 406).

Some researchers do not consider religion a universal phenomenon, but instead support defining it explicitly. In contrast, some doubt universality; a few of these researchers consider finding an exact definition of religion to be a hopeless endeavor (see Saler 2000: 27–69). Robin Horton (1960: 211) and Melford Spiro have argued that there are such things as universal aspects of religion. Unlike Horton, Spiro (1966: 94) warns against universalizing parts of comparative definitions but considers belief in superhuman beings to be nevertheless practically or nearly universal: "the belief in superhuman beings … approaches universal distribution." This must therefore be a core variable in every definition of religion.

This debate touches upon the philosophical problem of universals. In the intercultural comparison of concepts of belief, the use of the term "supernatural" (as opposed to "natural") and other such terms is highly problematic as it unavoidably involves Eurocentrism, as Klass has convincingly demonstrated (Klass 1995: 25–33). The problem here is finding a precise definition for religion that can be used in intercultural comparison (Klass 1995: 17–24, 34–40; Saler 2000). Only if we avoid "supernatural" constructs, defining religion as, say, an institutionalized interaction between human beings as well as between human beings and a conceptualized universe—that is, as a belief system that offers order and a feeling of control (Klass 1995: 22, 38, 170)—can we then regard religion as universal. This corresponds with the thesis that religion is universal because it fulfills the human need for orientation and meaning, which is why it has not become repressed through modern science (Bargatzky 2000: 273; see Burkert 2000: 105–9).

Unnatural Agents

Many researchers consider religion to be universal only in the restricted sense that conceptions of nonobservable and unnatural agents and processes are at work everywhere (Boyer 1994: 5). Universal is then the distinction between worldly, ordinary, or natural spheres on the one hand, and unusual or supernatural realms on the other (Dissanayake 1992: 49). Others, though, classify specific religiously oriented phenomena as universal. Until recently theologians and scholars of religion tended toward the assumption that religion is above all universal in the sense of a universal conception of "holiness" (Colpe 1997; Schaeffler 2005). Classical theories of religion are heavily based on the assumption that there are not only formal but also *rich universals* (Boyer 1994: 12–13). Examples of this are, according to Edward Burnett Tylor, universal conceptions of "spirits" and, according to Emil Durkheim, the universal distinction between profane and holy things (rather than the separation of natural and supernatural; Wax 1984: 13). For Durkheim, holiness implies a remote, forbidden aura, and actions and behavior associated with it create a moral community, or "church." These rich universals have often been explained through specific mechanisms in a "generative model" that does not recognize other possible explanations (Boyer 1994: 13, 191). Durkheim interpreted religion as a metaphysical representation of the social order, while Tylor and Sir James George Frazer (1854–1941) understood religion as the result of cognitive needs for explanation or control (see similarly Horton 1982).

The belief in the existence of a nonvisible or nonpalpable realm within the world is fundamentally universal (Peoples and Bailey 2015: 292). Certain specific universals, and especially near universals within religion, have also been postulated (Ehrlich 2002: 408). The Viennese anthropologist Karl Wernhart has described universal features in religions with reference to his work on "ethnic religions." In all religions he sees not only the longing for religious spirituality but ecstasy as well, even when these do not represent a particular manifestation of belief (Wernhart 2004: 39). According to Wernhart (2004: 39–40), asceticism is both synchronically and historically universal: "In all religions there are many types of long-term or temporary forms in the renouncement of wealth, eating, drinking, sleeping, pleasures of all types, sexual activity, social relationships, etc. … In the history of religion, asceticism is known in all cultures."

Many religious anthropologists are of the opinion that belief in existence after death is universal (Eichinger Ferro-Luzzi 1996: 582). Boyer more specifically notes a generally widespread belief that a nonphysical human component will exist beyond death and remain an intentional person, that is, a person with beliefs and intentions (Boyer 1994: 5). Boyer has named further universals pertaining to beliefs that certain humans have attained direct inspiration or information from supernatural agents like gods or spirits. Such beliefs are based on the concept of gods as existing at a great distance from humans, and as such requiring the use of special means, or "channels," to reach them (Boyer 1994: 5-6).

It is widely accepted among religious anthropologists that all cultures have a concept of the immortality of ancestors, though ancestor worship is not universal. According to Swanson (1964), ancestral cults always appear when kinship groups composed of a number of small families form autonomous social units. This would make ancestral worship only a universal of implication. However, more recent cultural comparative studies have suggested otherwise, pointing out that ancestral belief, in the sense of belief in communication between forebears and their progeny, is universal. A reanalysis of cultures that supposedly, according to Swanson (1964: 97-108), had no ancestral worship indicates they apparently do, though this universality is valid only if these cultures are not required to have an explicit vocabulary for ancestors (Steadman, Palmer, and Tilley 1996: 63-65, 72-74).

Further universal beliefs have been postulated but are not yet backed by empirically based studies. The myth of the virgin birth, for example, is a universal and structural theme appearing in complex religions in correlation with the known lack of interest in biological fatherhood in more simple forms of belief (Leach 1967: 46). Wernhart considers intrinsic religious pluralism to be a "*transkulturelle Universalie*" (2004: 154). According to some scholars, a concept of affective evil, exemplified in massacres and *Amok*, exists in all religions (Girard 2011, Thies 2004: 127). Another universal feature is the concept of taboo, manifested in the ritualized prohibition of touching, eating, or using certain things, humans, or other living creatures or when performing certain actions in certain places or at certain times (Leach 1982: 118; Douglas 1970, 2002; Stagl 2002: 592; Steiner 1999). In all cultures there are taboo topics, objects and persons, and almost everywhere these taboos are seen as key elements in the respective social order. It is arguable whether specific taboo concepts relating to physical characteristics such as blood are universal (see, e.g., Knight 1991; Watts 2005).

Pascal Boyer, as an empiricist and evolutionarily oriented philosopher of religion, has characterized not only the concept of the virgin birth but also other, very specific concepts of belief as universal, for example, ideas concerning the existence of angels and of personality after death. Strikingly, these concepts go against basic intuition (see Ecok 2002: 409). Maintaining assumptions that are not intuitively plausible is a consistent feature of religions. Things that become possible in the realm of the supernatural remain impossible in daily life and are often characterized as unnatural or supernatural. Gods normally maintain a combination of intuitively understood attributes and capabilities that run counter to any type of daily experience (Eichinger Ferro-Luzzi 1996: 582). Boyer has examined this in empirically detailed studies of memory performance regarding religious ideas in two cultures (the Fang in Gabon and the monks of Tibet), comparing them with each other and with the ideas of Western people. This demonstrated that in both these very different cultures, human beings could most often remember violations of their intuitive expectations. The cognitive effects of these violations were independent of the accustomed religious beliefs, no matter how different they were, how seriously they were taken, or whether they came from written or oral traditions (Boyer 2001: 83–84). Boyer's thesis argues that human beings, in explicitly forming culturally specific conceptions of nonvisible phenomena (e.g., life after death), tend to use principles that are counterintuitive: "when people develop nonintuitive, culturally transmitted explicit conceptions of some nonobservable domain of reality, they tend to create principles that go against their own intuitive principles" (Boyer 1994: 113).

Rituals and Ritualizing

In the debate on the definition of religion, one may ask whether the core of religion is based less on conceptions of belief than on ritual behavior and action. Rituals can act as communication between human beings and nonhuman beings (Kohl 2006: 103). Accordingly, universals are found more often in rituals than in the substantive nature of faith. In his comprehensive analysis of religious practices, Roy A. Rappaport came to the conclusion that the forms of religious rituals and the concepts associated with them are universal. In detail, he describes the conception of the sacred, the numinous, and the divine, and their fusion in the holy (Rappaport 1999: 1–3, 407). The function of rituals in creating public norms and values, unifying members of the group, and "explaining" the unexplainable—birth, death, natural catastrophes—appears to be pervasive. The idea that following ritual precisely can lead to changes in the material world is universal, according to Boyer (1994: 5), who has described a behavioral scheme of stereotyped, highly repetitive actions performed in sequence as occurring in ritual and as universal, though not in the intellectual comprehension of ritual (Boyer 1994: 189–91; similarly, see Burkert 2000: 105). Ritual practice or behavior and ritualizing, which also occur in the nonreligious realm and are often decoded by cultural anthropologists and human ethologists (Koenig 1970; Eibl-Eibesfeldt 1976, 2004), could be more universal than the substantive nature of belief.

Ellen Dissanayake (1992: 71; 1999: 31) has emphasized the connection between rituals and the fundamental universal desire to behave or act ritually, a drive often associated with art (*Dromena*). Religious behavior and artistic behavior are connected by the use of symbols. Some symbols that are not universal are nevertheless very widespread, such as light, water, and mountains, as well as the snake, the Swastika, the tree of life, the *omphalos*, or the association of the left hand with disorder or with that which is "false" and the right hand with order or that which is "right" (examples in Lurker 1992; Durand 1993; also see Job 2006: 1253). Art and religion manifest common features: separation from the day-to-day, stylization or conscious performing, formalization (e.g., in movement), and the function of fostering social cohesion. Dissanayake draws broad conclusions here about the selective functionality of rituals in human evolution: "Ritual ceremonies are universal, found in every human society" (Dissanayake 1992: 48), and "ceremonial ritual is a universal behavioural characteristic to the human animal, one that allowed individuals (and groups) that performed ceremonies to survive better than those who did not" (1992: 68).

Cognition and Knowledge

Logic, Classifying and Essentialism

In arguing for basic cultural differences, one of the most important ventures is to portray non-Western logics as irreconcilable with Aristotelian logic. But the widespread relativistic claims of incompatibility of logical principles between the great traditions in thought are not tenable. Human beings have, as part of their basic configuration, the capacity to reach logical conclusions, to solve simple mathematical problems, and to work with probabilities (Ganten et al. 2005: 514). The forms of logical conclusions are for the most part independent of differences occurring in languages or cultures. Thus the claim that a specific type of "Eastern logic" exists does not stand up to careful examination (G. Paul 2008a: 29, 49–73, 2008b). Detailed studies of non-western logic systems demonstrate many similarities, for example in Chinese and Japanese traditions (Lenk and Paul 2014: 21–30, chaps. 16–18). Especially through empirical analysis, it is possible to show that logical operations are determinant and universal, but also capable of producing a variety of specific forms. The ability to form logical conclusions is one of the phenomena in which the psychic unity of human beings is manifested (Silverberg 1978: 293). Logical judgments, logical forms, and logical principles like the law of the excluded middle (*tertium non datur*) are especially universal. Accordingly, the mathematical traditions of many cultures contain many significant parallels that indicate similarities in thought patterns (Lakoff and Núnez 2000; Lenk and Paul 2014: 253–62, 453–60).

One indication of a universal logic is found within the semantic relationships occurring in all languages. An example would be type-semantics, such as "S is a type of R." Those studying ethnosemantics have been able to record almost twenty more semantic universals, such as cause and effect, or contingency ("X is dependent on Y"), attribution ("X is a characteristic of Y") and rationality ("X is a reason to do Y") (Hamill 1990: 20, 42, Table 2-2; Spradley 1997: 93). In a synopsis of cognitive anthropological studies, Werner and Schoepfle (1987a: 111–15, 1987b: 205) have claimed that there are three semantic universals—modification, taxonomy, and implication—each with its own respective logic. These universals are the building blocks of semantic relationships, such as the part-whole relationship.

In general, human beings can spontaneously form categories of "medium resolution" (Ganten et al. 2005: 511). Recognizing prototypes is a universal capability (Dissanayake 1992: 159). Everyone can differentiate between the general and the specific, and between the part and the whole. In all cultures we find classifications of body parts, internal circumstances, types of behavior, flora, fauna, weather conditions, tools or equipment, and geographic space. This is only the case from an outside perspective, though, and is not always so for the actors involved, that is, from the inner perspective. People everywhere make a dichotomous differentiation between "normal," "healthy," or "appropriate" behavior and "abnormal," "sick" and "inappropriate" behavior. Regarding consciousness, a distinction between normal and abnormal, particularly sickness-related, states of consciousness is found everywhere. Beyond these binary distinctions there are also total binary taxonomies that create contrasting meanings, such as left and right, nature and culture, black and white, man and woman, good and bad (for binarism, see Dissanayake 1992: 159–60, 190–92; for structural binarity, see Leach 1982: 113; Schiefenhövel 2004: 277, 281–83). Some of these classification universals are often criticized as trivial. Every living creature needs to be able to simplify complex information through binary thought. But at the same time, interesting details become apparent. Taxonomies, for example, are seen for the most part as continua with degrees and a center between polar opposites. With respect to vision, the difference between light and dark is not only a universal attribute but also the fundamental form of perception and thereby of establishing meaning (Sahlins 1976). The tendency to form categories is related to the universal tendency to compare, which has been documented in many ethnographies (e.g., De Coppet 1992).

Dichotomic sexual terms are universal or nearly universal. Even in cases in which quite a few terms may occur, the third or fourth term is formed by combining the other two, as in "hermaphrodite," or by creating a crossover, as in "a man behaves like a woman." If four terms are used, then two usually characterize what are considered the "normal" sexes and the other two are the "crossovers." Kinship terminology is everywhere found to have specifications for sex and age or generation. The terms mother and father can always be differentiated and are not necessarily blended into the term parent. All such terms can be connected others by reference to reproduction. All cultures have an apparent terminology for age that moves linearly by degrees: child, adolescent, adult. This is not something "natural" as in inevitable, since terms can vary. Children and older people could be seen together as being "dependent." Even very specific terms, such as those for members of the first generation, reveal universal structures. This can be explained by deeper structures independent of experience (Hamill 1998: 46–48). Meanwhile, Munroe and Munroe have postulated that kinship terminology within an ethnic group is predictable 99 percent of the time by way of implication through an understanding of the social organization (Munroe and Munroe 2001: 227).

Furthermore, representational essentialism is found the world over (Astuti, Solomon, and Carey 2004; Gelman 2005: 281; Atran and Medin 2008). Even children clearly believe certain categories are real and natural, and that words used in daily life reflect the structures of the real world. Essentialist thinking differs from categorical thinking in that it concerns causal assumptions, and because artificial categories cannot be considered essentialist. The core of essentialist thinking is the intuitive belief that an inner, nonobservable or deeper attribute (such as part, substance, or quality) determines the category of an observable thing. This unchangeable essence determines the identity of members of a category and their shared similarities (Gelman 2005: 7–8, 323–25). Psychic essentialism may be less a specific disposition than a side effect of the way human beings organize their knowledge of the world. Here the capacities for thought converge, for instance in the distinction between appearance and unseen realities, induction from the accumulation of attributes, causal thinking, and the concept of enduring identity. The way essentialism works depends upon whether the subject matter pertains to animals or groups of people, and it is influenced by culture and language.

Individual Development of Thinking

A vast array of often implicitly understood universal assumptions are tied to the topic of individual human development, but few cross-cultural studies can back these assumptions. I agree with Lancy, who states that "ethnographic studies in non-Western societies could be used to 'de-universalize' claims made in the mainstream development psychology literature" (Lancy 2015: 1). This would lead to a more refined image of, for example, thinking and how it develops. Piaget postulated a universal development process with four steps to explain the individual development of thinking. With regard to the first, prelanguage sensomotoric phase, the majority of findings from non-Western cultures indicate intense universality. The proposed order of phases is also found everywhere, though the tempo associated with each phase can alter depending on the culture. The significant environmental factors that shape early development are similar in even the most diverse cultures. These include the primary caregiver's (often the mother's) attention and attachment to the infant and the availability of objects that can be manipulated (Wenzel 2005: 58, Van Ijzendoorn and Sagi 2002). Despite the many specifics, cross-cultural patterns are evident (see cases in Rothbum and Morelli 2005 and Quinn and Mageo 2013). Regarding the transition from the second, preoperational phase to the phase involving concrete operations, the scope of culturally invariant structures appears to shrink (Dasen 1977: 166–78; see Cole and Cole 1993; Ohler and Nieding 1997: 28–29; Helfrich 2003, 2013). The third phase of concrete operations and above all the fourth phase of formal operations tend to be "weak" universals (Dasen 1981: 144–46). Operational capabilities that shape the majority of the population are found only in complex or urban societies. Their actual use appears above all to require formal educational institutions tied to complex learning. The universality here exists by way of capability, but only under certain conditions by way of performance (for competence universals vs. performance differences, see Bruner 1981: 259). Developmental psychology has determined that cultural variance is lowest in perception and cognition and highest in social behavior (Trommsdorff 2007: 447–49).

Domain-Specific Intuitive Thought

Experimental studies on thought development in children have shown principles in intuitive thought, or heuristics, especially with regard to intuitive ontologies and the forming of categories (natural kinds). Children from vastly different societies are able to form concepts of things, for example, through separate or single characteristic attributes, but they develop definitions for these concepts only later. This delay takes place in various domains of thought in different time phases. The studies demonstrate that these heuristics appear spontaneously and are similar across cultures, even as far as the detail involved (Keil 1981: 204–5, 1986; Boyer 1994: 100–102, 111). In addition to his ideas mentioned above, Boyer (1994: 113) adheres to the position that if human beings develop culturally specific and explicit concepts about nonintuitive phenomena (such as life after death), they do so using principles that counter their own intuition. Intuitive theories are understood as quasi-"natural" thought. As studies in experimental psychology have shown, infants already have at their disposal, in terms of a priori knowledge, the following intuitive assumptions about physical reality (Ganten et al. 2005: 513–14): (1) objects move according to a cohesive or coherent vs. fragmentary path or trajectory; (2) objects form a complete entity that is coherent; (3) only through contact can objects move. Domain-specific ways of thinking have been demonstrated especially vividly in the field of folk biology, but also as regards social categorization and conceptions of the supernatural, something I will explore in more detail below (see Sperber and Hirschfeld 2004 for a summary).

Ethnobiology and Local Knowledge

In all cultures, human beings are open to new things because they are curious. They share this trait with other animals as they spread across borders, existing in many different eco-niches (Kohl 2008: 849). Furthermore, there is a fundamental empirical orientation not only in Western cultures but in all cultures. In the general sense of a sought-out intersubjectivity, science itself is universal, in the same way that rationality has been claimed as the basis for an "epistemic unity in human kind" (Hollis 1974: 218). Science can be understood as a systematization of a universal human "empirical-objective orientation" (Rudolph 1968: 126f., 1973: 164) centered around experience and self-objectification. This orientation is necessary in life, generated through evolution for the sake of existence (Rudolph and Tschohl 1977: 219–20; Jensen 1999: 57; Fischer 1998, 2006; Hunn 2006: 177).

The universal elements of knowledge found thus far relate especially to the diversity of animals and plants, ecosystems, and general principles of organic life (for more on folk biology, see Berlin, Breedlove, and Raven 1973; C. Brown 1984; Atran 1990, 1998). A major focus of ethnobiological research concerns classifications, especially of plants. Taxonomic and exclusive ranking order appears to be universal in the preference for generic categories, or types, and the essentialization of life forms. Apart from local and culturally specific variations, a high degree of conformity or consistency is found in the widest variety of cultures (Schiefenhövel 2004: 281; for an overview see Ellen 2003: 51–60). These concepts from folk biology are easily learned, resistant to experience, and very difficult to unlearn. They are also similar between individuals from within societies and reveal historical continuity. Even when folk taxonomies tend to place more importance on size and visible features, they show similarities, according to the most recent findings, to Linnaean scientific taxonomies (Atran and Medin 2008: 18–20, 116–19, 166–67). If these findings were confirmed, which is beyond the scope of studies focused only on specific cultures, then they would be highly interesting. After critiquing certain methodological weaknesses in cross-cultural cognition research and universalist studies in ethnosemantics, Roy Ellen concluded: "However, one lasting impact of this body of work has been the irrefutable conclusion that all cultures encode a concept of basic category, and that they repeatedly divide up the natural world in particular and similar ways" (Ellen 2006a: 10).

The similarities could indicate that these divisions correspond to basic experiences occurring long ago in the evolutionary past of human beings, as in human beings' interaction with plants and animals (Boster 1996; Atran and

Medin 2008: 118). This would correspond with findings that indicate there is no universal classification in folk biology in the area of material culture, which is a great deal younger than material nature (Field 2004: 19). As stated above, a main concern of ethnobiological research is classification, of plants in particular. The classifications of the living world (1) are often very diverse or complex, (2) refer to more than utilitarian use, (3) are often quite similar between ethnic groups that have no relationship to each other, and (4) also reveal similarities to Linnaean taxonomy. A cross-cultural determination of organisms is not based on intuitively understood characteristics such as color, size, and availability, but rather on inherent and typical configurations and morphological features that are only recognized with some effort. All "traditional societies" studied so far classify the living world hierarchically, independent of possible culture-specific divisions, in the following categories, which Kenan Malik (2001: 239) appropriately termed "default taxonomy": "kingdoms" (plants, animals), "living forms" (fish, bird, tree, bush, grass), "generic type" (i.e., species, such as shark or dog), "specific type" (poodle, white oak), and these types' "varieties" (toy poodle, swamp white oak [Berlin 1992]).

Almost all societies assign the greatest importance to the category of species and assume that species are characterized by essential attributes that secure the continuity of the category despite the diversity of forms and the change in forms through growth. Dividing living things in categories allows those active in science or in local taxonomies to not only organize information coherently but also draw conclusions on the probable attributes of living things (Atran 1998; Ellen 2003, 2006). At the level of species, great similarities are evident between classifications by cultures that at first appear to be very different. For example, the bioclassification used by the society from Groote Eyland on the northern coast of Australia includes 86 percent of the species classified within the biological taxonomy of mammals and reptiles, 79 percent of the birds and insects, and even 50 percent of life forms from the sea. Even among plant species, their classification corresponds to 75 percent of modern species (Worsley 1997: 66–73). Atran has explained this with reference to the universal human mental ability to (1) distinguish between plants and animals on the one hand and nonliving things on the other, and (2) think of living beings in a special way, that is, form special categories for them. Atran considers this universal folk biology an inborn feature of our species that has its basis in the modular organization of our brains (for the folk biology module, see Atran 1998; Carruthers 2005; Sperber 2005).

Biophilia is generally understood as a human need for a close relationship with the natural environment, especially with plants and animals. Wilson introduces the concept in terms of personal experience, defining it as "the inner tendency to focus on life and lifelike processes" (E. Wilson 1984: 1; also see Dubos 1968: 39–42; Iltis, Louks, and Andrews 1970; Gardner and Stern 1995:

183–92; Kellert 2003). Those representing this position assume that biophilia represents a genetically conditioned "inclination to be affiliated with life" (Kellert 1993: 21). A disposition toward environmental protection has thereby been deduced, with biophilia seen as an aid in demanding deliberate action to protect biodiversity.

Critics of the biophilia hypothesis initiate their arguments especially on this point. The metaphorical association of biophilia and biodiversity implicitly projects moral beliefs or ideas. The concept contains a faulty naturalistic conclusion (see G. Moore 1993), confusing genesis and application, and arrives at a faulty normative conclusion through direct deduction from instructive guidelines out of a universal biophilia. Some consider the concept a secularized form of consolation for nonreligious people who want to redeem Creation (Potthast 1999: 163–64). What should actually be criticized is the near total lack of empirical findings to support biophilia. The biophilia thesis is more a hermeneutic construct of the human being–nature relationship than hardcore evolutionary biology. The environmental preferences that have thus far been demonstrated are much more specific: fondness for open landscapes and close proximity to rivers or water sources, neither of which is dependent on the biophilia thesis (Potthast 1999: 165).

In the border zone between worldview and local knowledge, universals have yet to be explicitly studied. As the name "local knowledge" or indigenous knowledge" demonstrates, all research has been directed at culture-specific cognition. This kind of knowledge is only available through its local manifestations, so the investigation of more widespread or universal patterns becomes difficult (Ellen 2003: 47). If, however, one were to read the hundreds of empirical studies on local knowledge and then scrutinize the few examples of theoretically based literature on local knowledge, one would find similarities or continual patterns. I have tried elsewhere to present universal or general patterns in local knowledge, demonstrating that local knowledge is a multi-part entity of practically based performance knowledge that is adapted to irregular and variable environments (Antweiler 1998, 2004b). We then face the question of whether local knowledge might not represent a particular orientation arising from day-to-day living and universally occurring forms of thinking (Table 4.1).

Languages and Speaking

Universals in Language versus Universals of Languages

Our first reaction to human languages is to immediately recognize their diversity and variety. This central point in comparative language studies is represented in the history of thought on language by Mithridates, King of the Black

Table 4.1. Features of local knowledge as universal mode of knowledge

1. Combining specific knowledge with daily and practical rules of thumb (*knowing*)
2. Empirically based in local observations and in small trials
3. Determining quality in terms of practical efficiency
4. Mostly implicit, less verbalized, hardly ever formalized (*performance knowledge*)
5, Tested over time in the "laboratory of life"
6. Adapted to local and common but not quite similar environmental parameters
7. Represented in parallel forms in quite a few cultural areas, and therefore redundant
8. Learned through practice; oral and informal
9. Originating and transferable in local social products
10. High in intracultural diffusion, but not homogenous
11. Imprecise but necessary for practical purposes (*optimal ignorance*)

Source: Antweiler 2004b: 20, revised

Sea, who according to legend spoke all twenty-two languages of the people living under his rule (Trabant 2003). However, language is also an area of study in which universals are sought with especial intensity (Aitchison 1996: 175–86). In view of the about 7,000 living languages in the world (6,912, according to Gordon 2005, 7,102 to Lewis et al. 2015; see also Frühwald 2004: 234–42), I should start off by saying we should be very much impressed that research on language universals is at all possible in the first place. Below I summarize the findings on empirically substantiated language universals and on formal linguistic universals, which are deduced from linguistic theory on the essence of language. Critics find fault with the circular form of many generalizing universal statements on language, taken simply out of the definition of language. Such trivial generalizations would be something like: "All languages consist of units with symbolic character" or "all languages consist at least of verbs and nouns" (*Universalien der Musikwahrnehmung* 2008).

Notwithstanding the diversity found among languages, similarities do occur between them on various levels concerning, for instance, vocabulary, tonal structure, and patterns in sentence structure (Goddard 2001: 1–65; Maddieson 2006: 89–99; Mairal and Gil 2006a: 9–18, 26; Bybee 2006). These are universal to varying degrees (Kephart 2005: 2247–48). Absolutely universal are the dual pattern (phoneme > morpheme), the existence of yes and no, the question why, and pronouns for the first and second person. Nearly universal are the occurrence of five vowels (though Aymara has only three), nasal consonants such as *m* and *n* (which are missing, for example, in the language of the Wichita), and the existence of personal pronouns in the third person (missing in Latin). These near universals are traceable back to common historical roots, as in the example of similarities between languages in one language family. But commonalities in languages can have other causes too, such as diffusion. This is represented in a new world atlas that cartographically depicts tonal structures and patterns in sentence structure for 2,560 languages (Haspelmath et al. 2005: CD-ROM, or see http://wals.info/). A surprising observation gleaned from the 142 distribution maps is that structural attributes in languages are geographically homogenous. In general, languages share many commonalities with neighboring languages, even when these languages are unrelated or from a different language family. Finnish, for example, shares surprisingly more similarities with its neighboring languages Swedish and Russian than it does with related Finno-Ugric languages, taking all language features into consideration.

Furthermore, language universals could refer to inborn features. It is important here to differentiate between directly and indirectly inborn or inherent universals. The fact that we communicate with the vocal-auditory channel is directly inborn, a part of our human genetic makeup. By contrast, the fact that all languages have nouns could simply mean that the world in which human beings live consists for the most part of separate objects (Aitchison 1996; R. Keller 2003: 153). If this were understood as an indirectly inborn universal, it would then indicate a genetic basis for thinking in nouns, or it could be a simple deduction from general and specific nonlinguistic principles or circumstances.

Several language universals refer to aspects of universal thought processes (Ohler and Nieding 1997) and therefore do not strictly represent linguistic universals. The fundamental thing here is the human capacity for true symbolization by way of connecting words and content together in an arbitrary way and speaking abstractly about things that are not physically present. Accordingly, a good command of the language is highly valued in all societies. Human beings everywhere are conscious of the fact that linguistic capability permits social manipulation. Rumors and gossip are as universal as deliberate lying and the awareness of lying.

Word Order, Vocabulary, and Other Linguistic Universals

Everyday language evinces a great disparity between often used words and rarely used words. Some words are used thousands of times more than others. A mere twenty-five words make up around 25 percent of our daily speech (Pagel 2012: 293). With regard to the universal meaning of words, Goddard (2001: 8–10, 57–58) has shown that semantic primes as defined by Wierzbicka 1992 or the more abstract or conceptual universals are clearer candidates for precise lexical universals than are universal terms, which refer to experience or environment. Approximately forty words have been found to be almost certainly universal, and they are, for the most part, semantically simpler than terms for natural phenomena, body parts, and other concrete objects, or terms that have been suggested by others or found in bilingual dictionaries (e.g., Brown and Witkowski 1981).

In all known languages, the most frequently used words are quite often shorter than rarely used words. Grammar in all languages is at least in some respects redundant. In English, both subject and verb show number; in Spanish, both nouns and adjectives show gender. Phonemes in all languages reveal a contrast between vowels and nonvowels as well as between stops and nonstops. The number of phonemes is never less than ten or more than seventy. The above-mentioned mental contrasts of good and bad, deep and shallow, wide and narrow are expressed directly, not through marked forms, though that might be plausible.

All languages distinguish between the verb, object, and prepositions or postpositions. They all form sentences through a dominating lexical unit, or head—as in a verb or a preposition and a complement, such as a noun or nominal expression—and all dictate an obligatory order of the two. Of 128 possible combinations of the most important heads, 95 percent of all languages use only two of them. These include the ordering of verb before object, as in English, and object before verb, as in Japanese. About a dozen fundamental parameters explain many of the differences between the grammars of the world's languages (Baker 2001; see Pinker 2002: 37), even if not all linguists accept the concept of "language atoms." In generative phonology, rules have been discovered that involve not vowels or consonants but their parts, or their so-called "features." Rules that govern features and not phonemes make it possible to use fewer rules, as these can be combined in different ways with each other (Pinker 1999: 94–95). A counterexample to Pinker's words and rules theory is found in Mandarin Chinese, which has no inflection, since each word has a sound or tone independent of its use (Pinker 1999: 237).

Noam Chomsky is well known for his universalistic theory. He maintains that behind all the diversity in languages and their specific generative grammars, there lies a basic pattern, or universal grammar. Those supporting the idea of a universal grammar presume that we have inherent or inborn universal grammar and associated capabilities. This is demonstrated by the fact that even within the limited time frame for language learning, every language can be learned. It appears that we have a language drive, preparedness, or instinct (Pinker 1994; Jackendorff 2003: 95–97). Children therefore have at their disposal a priori knowledge concerning probable communication content (Tooby and Cosmides 1992: 92–93; Imai and Gentner 1997).

With regard to a universal grammar, and alongside the information produced by research on language structures, nonlinguistic evidence is especially important when it comes to universals. I will name four areas that, though independent of one another, suggest a general or universal biotic ability to learn grammar (Jackendorff 2003: 94–101). First, the use of symbols and the combination of symbols extending beyond simple symbolic *strings* appear to be unique to human beings. Second, the capacity to learn language is very age-specific, meaning that *every* organically normal child who is brought at an early age to *any* society and raised there has the ability to learn the common language of that society. The brains of small children treat every language available as a mother tongue. Findings showing that ability to learn language decreases with age also show how deaf people are able to learn sign language. Third, research on aphasia has demonstrated that in affected persons, a specific disconnection separates abilities with regard to grammar from other dimensions of language capacity. Also relevant here is the proven break between language capability and general intelligence seen in many forms, such as linguistic savants, Williams Syndrome, and specific language impairment (SPI). Fourth, children can invent completely new grammatically structured languages. Interesting cases include deaf children who invent their own sign language ("home sign") while their parents have no practice of it; and the change from pidgin speech to Creole languages, wherein children growing up in communities where pidgin is spoken take the pidgin as raw material and develop it into a Creole language, which includes grammar. There is one well-documented case of both phenomena occurring in a combined form (Bickerton 2014: 218–57).

In all known cultures, inflection or intonation and timing are used for the modeling of spoken expression. Onomatopoeia, or the vocal imitation of a thing or sound, is found everywhere (Dissanayake 1992: 173), as is poetry. Throughout the world, poems are recited in units with repetitions and pauses. The length of a verse amounts to three seconds. All societies have ideas about the appropriate standards in poetry and rhetoric. In all human languages, specific forms exist for special occasions, and it is everywhere common to find examples of code switching or code mixing, depending on speaker, addressee, and situation. It holds true for all languages thus far studied that the longer a speech becomes, the more polite it is meant to be (Haiman 1983: 800–801).

Many language universals are implicational universals (if-then), as mostly typological studies on grammar have revealed. Every language with a future tense has a simple past as well, though the reverse is not the case. If a language has rounded front vowels, such as the *u* in French word *tu*, then it also has a correspondingly nonrounded vowel, like the *i* in *dire*. If the word order is object-verb, as in Japanese, then the language has in all likelihood post- and prepositions as well (Kephart 2006: 2246). If a language has the word order rule of adjective-noun (AN), then it has the rule of number-noun (NumN). Accordingly, the combinations AN/NumN, NA/NumN and NA/NNum are then possible, though never AN/NNum (Croft 2003b: 435).

In all languages, all speakers make reference to movement, place, tempo, and other basic dimensions. In all the languages studied thus far in the world, two-thirds to three-fourths of all words in descriptions of sensory impressions refer to hearing and seeing, reflecting the audio-visual tendency of human beings. The one-fourth to one-third of remaining words, when used to convey other senses, refer then to smell, taste, touching, temperature, air moisture (humidity), and electric fields (E. Wilson 1998: 152). All languages have words for objects with greater meaning in daily life, such as black, white, face, hand. Likewise, color categories exist everywhere. Between two and eleven concepts exist for basic or primary colors, and if there are only two, then they are words for black and white. With an increasing number of color terms, the respectively next concepts are given in an evolutionary order (Berlin and Kay 1969; E. Heider 1972; Hardin and Maffi 1997; Kay and Regier 1997; Saunders 2000). One should keep in mind here that many of these universals are very controversial among linguists, especially those who work with single or specific languages (P. Brown 2002: 177; see also Roberson, Davies, and Davidoff 2000). A prime example of a cultural relativistic position that has been re-studied and found to be, at the least, grossly exaggerated is the supposed extreme number of terms the Inuit have for snow (Pullum 1991; Pinker 1996: 462–63). Similar claims, such as the 240 words for horse among the Argentinian Gouchos (Steiner 1975: 87, cited in C. Berry 1986: 70), have never been empirically examined.

The Use of Metaphor and Basic Concepts

The use of linguistic images or figurative speech is a universal phenomenon. We all live with metaphors, as Lakoff and Johnson aptly put it in the title of their book, *Metaphors We Live By* (Lakoff and Johnson 2003). They present a theory integrating both universal and culturally relative elements. The universal process of the metaphorical extension represents the core of the psychic "making of the world." Thought processes are structured in a kind of projection through metaphors, which originate from preconceptual, cultural, and physical images, or *kinesthetic image schemata* that arise through human beings' invariant experiences with objects and events.

Lakoff's approach posits a universalism of experience (Lakoff 1987: 265–67) rather than with an internal realism, which assumes all people have a similar material world. Pancultural physical and emotional experiences produce pancultural conceptual metaphors. Examples of this are "progress is advancing" and "causes are forces." Which image schemata relay structure varies according to environment and culture. The use of words that express psychic attributes with physical or bodily metaphors, such as "she is really hot," is widespread. The metaphorical relationship to physical things has identical connotations in otherwise completely different languages (Ash 1955, cited in Dissanayake 1992: 174). Linguistic and cognitive psychological studies of nonrelated languages indicate that all human societies use not only metaphors but also metonyms ("pars pro toto"), polysemy, and antonyms and synonyms (Brown and Witkowski 1981; Kövecses 2010: 35–64, 292–94). Another line of research involves common structures in narratives and storytelling, and the question of narrative universals (Boyd 2005, 2009).

A further, specific research area is the intersection of linguistic and cognitive universals. Anna Wierzbicka and colleagues (Wierzbicka 1992, 1999, 2002; Goddard and Wierzbicka 1994; Goddard 2001, 2003; see Kronenfeld 1996: 20–21) have spent years searching languages for fundamental semantic expressions that could point the way to a cognitive metalanguage, or *lingua mentalis*. By means of a descriptive linguistics for certain languages and for varying thematic domains (values, emotions, ethnobiology, artifacts, religion, speech acts), they have so far found about sixty universal concepts, called *semantic primitives* or *universal conceptual primes* (Wierzbicka 1992, 2002: 21), such as "thing," "because," "existing," "up," or "down." On a lexical level, these primes take the shape of specific words or word elements in every language and are grouped in fifteen thematic clusters. Together they form a *natural semantic metalanguage*. Considering that almost all words are polysemic, the proof of universal primes is not trivial (Goddard 2001). The syntax of these primes is also universal in the sense that there are certain combinations in all languages. Wierzbicka and coauthors assume that all fundamental ideas are expressed through these primes, making them relevant on a practical level as they help to create semantic bridges between members of different cultures. These semantic primes must then be linked to a universal grammar, though this approach is problematic in that these basic semantic forms refer again and again to a natural language, like English (Werlen 2002: 85). In general, these semantic universals offer a good example of how postulated universals need not necessarily ignore cultural diversity. It is particularly surprising here that in many years of research, only sixty prime words have been found, which implies that the overwhelming proportion of words and of syntax in all languages is not universal but specific to local culture. The discovery of semantic universals reinforces the assertion that all languages, apart from containing universally independent concepts, possess a specific "ethnosyntax," a point much like the one Humboldt made (Goddard 2003: 409–10, 427).

A new area of research involves comparison of natural languages with sign languages. There are many indications of universal features shared in both language types despite their many variants (Sandler and Lillo-Martin 2006). Evidence of language universals is mounting in research areas that are primarily interested in examining cultural differences. An example of this is the linguistic structuring of social action or behavior. Ochs has named an entire list of universal or near-universal candidates in the context of the linguistic construction of social identity (Ochs 2004: 86–87). Examples include the use of pronouns as well as greater intonation in questions seeking information, and the use of tags in looking for acknowledgement or recognition, and the form for showing agreement. There are also universal forms in the area of the qualification used to show the degree of understanding and in emotional condition or status. Thus the methods for indicating certainty or uncertainty in statements or for marking the direct or indirect sources of knowledge (evidentiality) are similar in many languages.

Behavior and Experience

Emotions and Expressing Emotion

Do human beings everywhere have similar emotions when confronting dangerous situations or showing empathy for people in trouble? Does a feeling of guilt occur in all cultures when aid or assistance is not given? Do we find murder arising everywhere from "arguments"? Do people everywhere fear noise or snakes? Are snakes universal images in dreams (for the latter, see Wright 1994: 161; E. Wilson 1998: 71–72, 78–81)? Researchers of emotion in a cross-cultural focus pose these types of questions, and the majority respond to them with a cautious yes. It appears that at least core universal emotions, such as fear or menace, exist and may very well be alluded to in relativist positions: "General cultural comparative studies indicate that emotions do not exclusively reveal cross-cultural commonalities" (Friedlmeier 2005: 148). Indeed, universality versus relativism in feelings, such as with regard to romantic love, is endlessly debated (Jankowiak and Fischer 1992; Jankowiak 1995 vs. Hockett 1973: 278–79; Leavitt 1996: 516; see contributions in Röttger-Rössler and Engelen 2006). I elaborate on this below. The question of change vs. continuity in feelings of shame and affect control is also controversial, as seen in the work of Hans-Peter Duerr, a critic of the work of Norbert Elias (1897–1990; see Duerr 1999–2003). New studies question whether emotions that have been considered specific to culture could also contain universal components. The Japanese *amae* and the Korean *shimcheong* could very well be locally specific only in terms of their semantic core (Choi et al. 2007: 334–35).

Empirical studies on the universality of emotions go back to Charles Darwin. He sent out questionnaires to missionaries all over the world and, through their responses, was able to determine universal expressions of feelings (Darwin 2000). The number of basic emotions postulated varies among authors, such as Carol Izard and Paul Ekman. As an example, the following especially refined list distinguishes nine types of "universal affect": interest-excitement, enjoyment-joy, surprise-startle, distress-anguish, disgust, contempt, anger-rage, shame-humiliation, and fear-terror (Tomkins, cited in Dissanayake 1992: 179). An important finding is that emotional limits are similarly stored according to independent features, namely, physiological symptoms, subjective feelings, and emotional expression (Wallbott and Scherer 1986; Izard 1994; Ekman 1994; J. Russell 1995). I need to emphasize that the empirical studies conducted so far mostly focus only on emotional reactions, or the output-side of affect, not on the causes of emotions. The classic studies on this subject conducted by Paul Ekman and Wallace V. Friesen and co-authors show that human beings in all cultures react similarly to triggers of fear. These studies do not, however, show that the things that trigger fear are similar in all cultures (Griffiths 1997: 55). Meanwhile, things that produce fear—for example, social rejection and rivalry—do display universal similarities. These have to be seen within the particularities of specific contexts (Mesquita and Frijda 1993: 197–98).

Recognizing Emotion

Around a hundred years after Darwin's main publications, Ekman and Friesen systematized his approach. In a series of studies, they examined ten cultures little influenced by mass media, or "non-TV cultures" (Ekman 1970, 1992, 1993, 2004; Ekman and Friesen 1971; Ekman and Rosenberg 1997; Ekman, Sorensen, and Friesen 1969). The studies showed that the mimic expression of such fundamental emotions as joy, grief, fear, anger, surprise, disgust, and contentment is, even in detail, cross-culturally similar and understandable. Emotions depicted in photographs can be properly described. They can also be properly recognized based on vocal pitch (Scherer, Banse, and Wallbott 2001). Differences in how various emotions are recognized turn up as well: boredom and anger, for instance, are more recognizable through paralanguage than through mimic. Emotional expression is in part willingly suppressed; cultural norms may dictate when a person may show emotion (Ekman 1992, 1993). Despite the enormous scope of this research, the intercultural recognition of emotion and universal expression of emotion are not beyond dispute. Differences in methodology may play a role here, as a meta-analysis of almost a hundred studies has demonstrated (Elfenbein and Ambady 2002: 229–32). Emotions and the display of emotions are recognized beyond the confines of culture, but they lose their comprehensibility between one culture and another, indicating something equivalent to "emotional dialects."

The neurocultural theory that Ekman and Friesen have developed from their studies on mimic expression is particularly fascinating with regard to universals, as it integrates evolutionary and culture-specific factors. The showing of basic emotions is considered inherent, or "neuro," activating involuntary and universal forms of response. This involuntary expression is modified by cultural or so-called representational norms. Expressing emotion has a social function: Ekman and Friesen claim that, along with many culturally specific emotional expressions, certain affect signals also occur in all societies, such as expressions of joy, grief, rage or anger, disgust, surprise, fear, and contempt. These so-called basic emotions, also known as "primary affects," are universal and correspond to the emotions felt or displayed by the great apes. Various primates display a similar form of mimicry and use mimic as a form of signaling, whether to indicate a threatening posture or to show a game face (for lip-smacking, see Merten 2003).

In contrast to other emotions, basic emotions reveal the following characteristics: they produce physiological symptoms that lead to common results, begin quickly and have a short duration, and occur in an uncontrolled manner (Ekman 1992; Merten 2003). A deep, constant psychic structure that is part of a universal human nature interacts with culturally specific and relative norms (Kahle 1981: 307; Eckensberger 1996). Ekman has speculated that a quick, quasi-automatic evaluating process and a subsequent longer, conscious evaluating process work together in human beings. The latter is defined by cultural norms that include certain display rules depending on the social situation (Ekman 1992). It is worth mentioning here that, other than in the case of mimic, physical distance, such as in greetings, varies remarkably from culture to culture, as findings in kinesics and proxemics have shown (e.g., Birdwhistell 1963). Furthermore, certain behaviors are correlated with specific emotions in all cultures and are therefore seen by the actors involved as the expression of those respective emotions. These associations are, however, specific to culture, time, and social class. An example is the current association in Germany of packing a child's school lunch with parental love (Röttger-Rössler 2004: 98).

Research on facial expressions relative to feelings or emotions is in general divided into the relativist or interpretive and constructivist school (represented by the work of Catherine Lutz 1988), and the experimental or universalistic and biological school (e.g., the Ekman school of thought). As in emotion research altogether, this can be variously understood as the reflexive dichotomous response of representing the world by nature or by culture, or by body or mind (Mallon and Stich 2000; Röttger-Rössler 2004: 7–9, 95–96). The lack of intermediate positions, as in the classic example of Margaret Mead or currently in the work of David Matsumoto, has characterized the research as somewhat repetitive (see Barrett and Katsikis 2003: 4–6 and Röttger-Rössler 2004: 69–101). The harsher critics on the side of the relativists, through their fundamental approach and the details of their experimental cross-cultural studies, have had the positive effect of fostering better methodological replication studies in current research. Anger, revulsion, fear, joy, grief, and surprise are seen today as universal emotions that at the same time reveal distinctive and varying physiological profiles (Frank 2003: 262).

In recent years, an increasing number of studies conducted by psychologists (Boucher 1979: 175; Hinton 1999; Moghaddam 2002: 274–76) and anthropologists (Moore et al. 1999; Fessler 1999) provide evidence of universal emotions while representing independent voices in support of the Ekman theory. Some of these studies refer in part to specific emotions and specific terminology for emotions. Casimir and Schnegg (1999), for example, have examined the negative or poor self-esteem that arises in persons who are observed violating societal norms. In a large, comprehensive sample taken from 135 cultures in all cultural regions of the world, they found strong evidence of pancultural patterns in the emotional expression of shame, embarrassment, and shyness. Color metaphors reveal such patterns in their relationship to observable emotion and local expressions describing shameful blushing. They have concluded that due to evolutionary prehistory, certain pancultural types of occurrences bring about certain universal "families of emotions," moderated at the same time by culturally specific, or emic, concepts (1999: 290).

One would expect to find universals more at the level of basic emotions, rather than in terms of more complex emotions such as shame and jealousy (Oatley and Jenkins 2013: 71). But they are found in the latter emotions across a broad spectrum of cultures, as I will describe below. In this active, vibrant area of research, we might say that while some basic emotional categories are pancultural, some core areas of emotion are truly universal and some possibly universal, and that the emotional life of all human beings is strongly influenced by their respective cultures (J. Russell 1991: 444, 1995; Ellsworth 1994: 23; Röttger-Rössler 2004: 69–101; Röttger-Rössler and Markowitsch 2006).

Smiling and Nonverbal Behavior

Psychologists and human ethologists who use comparative methods to study human behavior have, over the last thirty years, come up with a large number of behavioral patterns that appear to be likely universals (for a summary see Segerstråle and Molnár 1997a; Ekman 2004; Eibl-Eibesfeldt 2004; also see Adams 1998: 184). The work is in large part based on studies of individual behavior. The units of study refer to individuals or, less often, to small groups, which makes the studies themselves important in describing the nature of *Homo sapiens* (see Chapter 3) in the form of a human ethogram. Comparatively little is known about the universal aspects of interpersonal relationships, though this is itself an active area of study (Schiefenhövel 1997; Goodwin 1999).

In broad terms, the results produced by behavioral specialists are highly relevant for research into universals. The findings of Irenäus Eibl-Eibesfeldt and colleagues have documented situation-specific behavioral patterns unknown half a century ago that occur among all healthy human beings or human groups. These patterns had previously been considered completely relative to culture or that were judged as occurring only among persons of other cultures, as described in Chapter 1. These studies are also cross-cultural in design and performed in a natural setting, that is, the natural environment as opposed to a laboratory. Finally, they use original rather than secondary data. In general, they analyze only a few (5–10) societies that lie great distances apart and therefore are historically almost certainly independent of one another. If nontrivial likenesses turn up in such a sample, then it is highly likely that they are evidence of universality. These studies, though, do not offer definitive evidence (pace Eibl-Eibesfeldt) that inborn or inherent factors lie behind these behavioral patterns (Antweiler 1989 vs. Eibl-Eibesfeldt 1990; see Plachetka 1997).

I will present here a small selection of the findings uncovered by these studies (Eibl-Eibesfeldt 1976, 1986, 1993a, 1993b, 2004). In all the societies that were examined, human beings showed affection for children by kissing them. Children everywhere showed wariness of strangers by around one year of age. In all known cultures, parents greet their children with a certain facial expression, or "greeting face," and talk to small children in a baby language (motherese) at a higher pitch with greater tonal variation. Shyness (for coyness display see Eibl-Eibesfeldt 1976) is found everywhere, as are special forms of mimic, such as the open-mouth face and the sulking face (Eibl-Eibesfeldt 1976: 61). All cultures use smiling as a form of communication in similar ways. In all cultures, body language—especially in the form of gestures—is widespread and produced unconsciously, though received consciously, as in the response of screaming, crying, or blushing. In all societies, people use a nonverbal no (Eibl-Eibesfeldt 1976). Human beings everywhere touch each other on the shoulder (Brown, cited in Myers 2002: 174). Not only do behavioral forms for greeting, expressing embarrassment, and flirting exist in all cultures, but they also reveal similarities, even in matters of detail (Grammer 2005; Grammer and Oberzaucher 2006; see McNeill 2007). In terms of universal categories of body language, Wierzbicka (1995) names three categories of nonverbal behavioral: (1) universal forms of meaningful behavior, such as laughing and crying; (2) universally available natural forms, such as hugging and holding hands, and (3) culturally dependent and more or less geographically determined or limited forms. Many behavioral universals are also found in the area of political communication, something that is studied in the field of biopolitics (Salter 2001; also see Flohr 1989). Some linguists and social psychologists have claimed that politeness is a universal (Brown and Levinson 1978; Weinrich 1986). However, there is a great difference between saying the existence of forms of politeness is universal and saying specific forms of behavior, such as forms of greeting, are universal. Here, competing voices are found in studies that examine the same universal on a very specific level, such as a "positive or negative face" in interpersonal contact, but offer very different explanations for its occurrence (Brown and Levinson 1987: 61; Kasper 2004: 61–64).

Personality and Violence

In the psychological literature, such as that used in teaching and textbooks, an implied universality attaches to certain statements concerning experience and behavior. An example would be Sigmund Freud's 1917 claim of the "tendency to keep unpleasant things away from memory" (Freud 1969: 72). Based on personal experience, most of us would consider this claim to be plausible. However, this statement has never been examined on an intercultural and comparative level. Textbooks also explicitly describe attributes and mechanisms as universal, though not in the sense of cultural features. Here, "universal" means that which is granted to any "healthy" individual. Still, these statements are relevant to the general topic of universals presented in this book. It has often been a matter of dispute whether assumptions in the field of psychology on psychic mechanisms and functions are valid on a cross-cultural level. Due to the dominance of laboratory studies, mechanisms that, in a methodically critical perspective, appear as "decontextualized universals" are often categorized as universal (Marsella et al. 2000, cited in Fahrenberg 2004: 196). Ohler and Nieding (1993: 23) point out that the cultural invariance of psychic phenomena is more a metatheoretical bias of psychology than an empirical fact.

Cross-cultural personality studies are most often directed at examining specific mentalities that could indicate more concrete constellations of universals. Here, five universal dimensions of personality, or basic personality attributes, have been determined: neuroticism, extraversion, openness, agreeableness, and conscientiousness (for the five-factor model or the Big Five, see McCrae and Costa 1997: 513–14; Nettle 2006: 625–27). These types, though repeatedly determined on an empirical basis, are marked as well by multiple problems, above all in the effects of the study situation on the results. Procedural problems in self-reporting in subjective Lickert scales are a particular concern (Marsella et al. 2000; Poortinga and Van Hemert 2001; Heine et al. 2002; Norenzayan and Heine 2005; Norenzayan, Schaller, and Heine 2006). A new direction in study based on the single individual in person-centered ethnography emphasizes the need to combine data based on personal experience and intracultural diversity, on the one hand, with intercultural comparisons on the other (Hollan 1992; Mathews and Moore 2001: 15).

A further area of study related to the human psyche looks into physical violence and murder. Both are found in all known cultures, as are the associated mechanisms intended to prevent violence and murder. One absolute universal appears to be murder as an act of revenge; blood vengeance in particular is a widespread response to the baseless killing of one's kin. This proves to be synchronic and occurring throughout history. Based on a comprehensive review of historical and recent empirical data, Martin Daly and Margo Wilson (1988: 226) have come to the conclusion that "lethal retribution is an ancient and cross-culturally universal recourse of those subjected to abuse." Similar patterns exist worldwide with regard to violence, aggression, and gender. The stronger impulse of male aggression is one of the best-documented universals coming out of emotion research (Whiting and Whiting 2014). Here, results from cultural comparisons correspond with those from interspecies comparisons.

In all cultures, men commit more acts of violence, including murder, than do women (Wright 1994: 100). Violence happens most often to and among men. In all cultures men are involved in aggression more than women are, whether as perpetrators or victims. This is true of both human beings and other primates. In all cultures, murder and manslaughter are commited far more often by men than by women. Among nonhuman primates, intraspecies killing is almost without exception committed by males (G. Roth 2003: 89). Rape and its condemnation and sanction are universal. A reanalysis of supposed exceptions could show this (C. Palmer 1989: 1–3, 16; Fry 2006: 262). In all known societies, boasting, duals, aggression-related competition, and sport are found mostly among men. And almost everywhere we find male aggression valued as something positive (Murdock 1967a; Lopreato and Crippen 2002: 153). The most violent age is early childhood, and "boys in all cultures spontaneously engage in rough-and-tumble play, which is obviously practice for fighting. They also divide themselves into coalitions that compete aggressively" (Pinker 2002: 316)

Stepchildren, more often than other children, are in danger of experiencing violence and psychic humiliation at the hands of their parents (Daly and Wilson 1988), a phenomenon that corresponds to genetic interests in kinship. The status of stepchildren, though, is by no means constant. Varying kinship systems lead to very different kinds of situational frameworks that do not all conform to a Cinderella structure. In a monogamous dowry system in strictly stratified societies such as are found in Europe or India, sisters—whether stepsisters or not—have conflicting interests. In an African polygamous system based on bride price, in which girls are considered a source of future wealth, this does not occur to the same degree (James 2003: 24). Human violence against non-kin children, though comparable to the violence against non-kin offspring among animals—and in some ways revealing similar causes—is not to be understood on the same level. Ultimate explanations for such occurrences must be understood within the context of culturally specific and proximate factors (see J. F. K. Schmidt 2007).

Egoism, Nepotism, and Rationality

In all cultures human beings try to seek personal advantages for themselves at the cost of others or of their general communities (Pinker 2002: 258). Everywhere, there appear to be conflicts of interests between people of different ages, different sexes, and different social standing, and all groups must periodically deal with the conflicts between private interests and public duties, just as individuals must try to find compromise between the two. The preferential treatment given to biological kin, that is, the existence of nepotism, appears to be extremely widespread (Turke 1996; Irons and Cronk 2000: 10; Pinker 2002: 245–47). Something similar occurs as a structural phenomenon in terms of corruption (Haller and Shore 2005). Gannanath Obeyasekere (1990, quoted in Carrithers 1992: 161) thinks that attitudes and relationships that play out around desire and dominance are universal. In a hypothetical dilemma, moral philosophers ask the following: Is there any number of non-kin children who could, in an emergency, get a human being to save them rather than their own kin when forced to choose? Generally speaking, parents leave their wealth to their own children, representing a problem for any egalitarian society. Solutions to this problem have been attempted by transferring inheritance to eunuchs, celibate persons, slaves, or other people whose homes are far away (Masters 1989: 207–8).

Most people appear to see children as extensions of themselves (Pinker 2002: 245). "Family values" or family loyalty is often in conflict with individual moral attitudes on the one hand, and state institutions' duty to uphold equal rights for everyone on the other (Holenstein 1997: 55). In many countries, all people are treated the same under the law, though consideration is given to family circumstances, such as in the right to refuse to testify against one's next of kin, or even against one's in-laws or those connected to an individual by betrothal (Holenstein 1997: 55). Pinker has thus concluded that "Family love indeed subverts the ideal of what we should feel for every soul in the world" (Pinker 2002: 245). For these reasons, each society must organize social relationships above or beyond the level of kin, thus producing the well-known dilemma described by Hobbes (Field 2004: 20).

The dominant economic theories assume that individuals follow their own interests with the limited means they have available. Meanwhile, empirical findings from economic studies have recently indicated that the assumption of rational economic behavior in the sense of ego-maximizing activity has its limits. More recent studies in experimental economics have been able to show that in proximate reality situations, reciprocity and genuine altruistic behavior, or psychic altruism, appears regularly (Gächter and Thöni 2004: 268–70; also see Gächter and Thöni 2004 for the so-called *ultimatum game* experiments). Sober and Wilson (1998) have shown that selfless behavior can have a functional component and is clearly widespread, even when we do not necessarily have to follow or agree with the authors' group-selective interpretation (Field 2004: 98–119). Norms of fairness are not just Western concepts (or English concepts, according to Wierzbicka 2005: 281–85) but are very widespread, at least as a behavioral concept (Simon 1990a; Wilson and Sober 1998; see Batson, Lishner, and Stocks 2003: 376; Fehr and Renninger 2004). Also in terms of long-term planning, human beings often do not behave in an economically rational way: "Economists are often finding that human beings give out their money like drunken sailors" (Pinker 2002: 269). They do not save, but behave as if the future were fully unforeseeable, or as if they were to die tomorrow. This relates more to the reality of our forefathers, as measured against the reality of the present day, that is, according to the assumption of the *Homo oeconomicus*. Societies curb this tendency through social insurance systems and obligatory contributions to retirement pensions.

Gender, Sexuality, and Social Reproduction

Gender Concepts and Sexual Differences

The assumption that concepts related to gender could be universal appears at first contradictory, as the term gender refers to cultural and culturally specific constructions of sex. Opinions about universals diverge considerably when the focus is on gender and sex. The differing approaches become clear in two recent, diametrically opposed assertions by sociologists. Rüdiger Lautmann has written that "little can be termed universal when referring to sexual culture" (Lautmann 2002: 474). Sex occurs everywhere in a similar fashion, but with the exception of incest, the only things shared "are alone the outward behavioural features, not the meaning, regulation and conflicts" (Lautmann 2002: 474). In contrast, two sociologists with a Darwinian orientation and an interest in universals have argued that there are cross-cultural gender differences in the following areas: the potential for aggression, the engagement shown in the care of children, techniques used in finding a partner, partner relationships, parental behavior, and division of labor in both the household and gainful employment (Lopreato and Crippen 2002: 136, 150).

Differences among the sexes of course vary in the areas mentioned above, but taken together they are in fact found everywhere. Some of these differences are especially drastic, historically consistent, and found at certain levels among some primates (Murdock 1967; Maryansky and Turner 1992; A. Campbell 2013; Rogoff 2003: 71–77, 180–93; Bischof-Köhler 2006; Low 2015). For example, women do the majority of work in the household the world over. In contrast, men everywhere are more active in the productive sector of society and in more public activities (Lopreato and Crippen 2002: 195). Some of the most widespread gender stereotypes do at times (!) reflect real circumstances, of which I will provide just one example. Lueptow et al. (1995; quoted in Lopreato and Crippen 2002: 201–2) analyzed students at a Midwestern U.S. university in a long-term study spanning almost twenty years (1974–91) at a time marked by transformation in gender roles and ideals found throughout American society. Gender-specific features of personality remained remarkably stable, even in the face of the great changes taking place during this time period. One must keep in mind, though, that stereotypes as preconceived expectations can affect behavior.

Values and the Cultural Embeddedness of Sex

Everywhere in the world, sexuality is embedded in our ethical values. Sexual activity is regulated or restricted in different ways in all societies. From the research done on incest, we can say generally that sexual intercourse is regarded as not only an individual activity but a societal one as well (Vivelo 1994: 214–30). "Human beings have never been seen as pure biological creatures who, at specific times, are simply involved in following their basic instincts" (Kather 2008: 62). Sexuality and sexual fantasy are regulated by taboos affecting the private and intimate worlds of human beings. Only in very specific and unique situations do human beings copulate in public. Nowhere is sexual intercourse coram populo regarded as "normal" (Brown 1991: 39, 150; Friedl 1994; Schiefenhövel 1999; Ehrlich 2002: 1187). "In all societies, sex is at least somewhat 'dirty'" (Pinker 2002: 253), and "among all peoples it is primarily men who court, woo, proposition, seduce, employ love charms and love magic, give gifts in exchange for sex, and use the services of prostitutes" (Symons 1979, quoted in Pinker 2002: 252).

Some gender ideals and sexual stereotypes have been empirically found to exist in very different types of societies. To illustrate this point by way of example, I will list some findings as they appear in sociology and social psychology textbooks or works in evolutionary psychology. Women are considered to be more agreeable, according to a study of twenty-seven countries conducted by John Williams (Williams, Satterwhite and Best 1999; see also Lueptow 1995, quoted in Myers 2002: 37). Women are sexually more reserved than men from the same culture (Wright 1994: 45–46). Women everywhere who display unconstrained sexual desire are considered abnormal as compared with libidinous men (Wright 1994: 45). It is universal, or practically universal, to say that men and women are naturally different. Everywhere it is assumed that sexual differences result from the different roles the sexes play in reproduction, for example in assuming men are by their nature more physically aggressive. Similar ideas on "natural" differences between adults and children are very widespread. In light of cultural diversity, this specific uniformity creates a challenge for those seeking to explain its occurrence, something I will explore later. A few empirical findings worth mentioning here come from cross-cultural studies showing that girls and boys are in many ways socialized in a similar fashion. Societies in which aggression or subjugation plays a part in child rearing tend to socialize both sexes in both these elements. This is true not only in modern societies (Schlegel 2007: 237).

Partner Preferences

Alongside the individual and culturally specific ideas or concepts regarding sexual or potential marriage partners, many preferences and ideals exist uniformly on a worldwide basis (Lopreato and Crippen 2002: 163, Table 6.2). Men prefer younger partners, women older (for all thirty-seven cultural units studied by Buss; see Buss 1989, 1997, 2003). Women prefer partners who are hardworking and ambitious, and who offer potentially good financial prospects. They also place more value on gifts of flowers or other such conventional displays of affection than do men (Wright 1994: 61). Physical attractiveness in a lover or sexual partner is anything but random or a mere cultural construct. This is revealed in studies on pornographic literature and fictional erotic literature produced for women (Salmon and Symons 2001: 59–80). There are certain cross-cultural features of sexual attractiveness and beauty. Human beings of both sexes consider a symmetrical and average face more attractive and prefer particular body proportions (Cunningham et al. 1995; Etcoff 1999; Pinker 1997: 480–88; Rhodes 2006: 201–11). Men should be larger than their female partners, as found in a study in which only one of 720 pairs went against this norm (Gillis and Avis, quoted in Myers 2002: 197). Quite a few studies concerning these concepts or norms have been published in recent years. The literature on the universality of preferred body proportions, such as the waist-to-hip ratio, is extensive (Streeter and McBurney 2003). Clear patterns emerge pertaining to many aspects of beauty, shown in more recent studies and meta-analyses on already existing studies (Henss 1998; Langlois et al. 2000).

Cross-cultural features of physical beauty include smooth skin, symmetry (or no extreme deviations from bilateral symmetry), prominent cheekbones and slender facial features, and certain childlike features in women (Cunningham Factors), such as smaller lower facial form (Renz 2006: 69). Human beings who are considered physically attractive are on average more socially and economically successful, and at times more outgoing, self-confident, and physically healthier, while attractive children are more intelligent than unattractive children (Renz 2006: 238). In many cases, though, the findings in these areas are not always uniform or consistent, leading to interpretations that are less than clear or emphatic (Gangestad and Scheyd 2005: 531–39). An example would be the ideal physical body size. In certain societies relatively heavy or corpulent people, especially women, are judged attractive, unlike in contemporary Western societies. It could be that a universal pattern rests behind this contrast, in that each type represents a sign of well-being in the respective society: corpulence is a sign of wealth and health in societies with problems in food supply or a lack of proper food resources, whereas in industrial countries slenderness is a sign of health and a higher standard of living (van Damme 2000: 273).

Many claims and assumptions pertain to sexual differences, sexual frequency, and diversity in sexual partners, but only recently have global comparative studies been carried out on the topic. Even today psychologists and human biologists dispute whether human beings are naturally monogamous or naturally promiscuous, or whether they follow a mixture of short and long-term strategies, varying their choices according to situation and time of life. More recent findings show that women, like men, look for short-term sexual relations in all cultures, but in varying degrees as well as for different reasons. A rigorously methodological study that collected personal statements from over 16,000 people (mainly college students) from all the large cultural areas of the world (Schmitt et al. 2005) substantiated earlier assumptions about motivations: men are more motivated by a desire for diversity in sexual relations, women more by a desire for a partner with higher status or a higher degree of reproductive health. Analyses of personal statements and studies using other methods all show that, in the case of short-term sexual relations, gender differences in the search for diversity are culturally universal. In all societies, including gender-egalitarian cultures, both sexes look for short-term sex partners, but men desire more sexual diversity, are more willing to engage in sexual intercourse, and more actively look for short-term sex partners. This sexual difference is independent of standards or norms, or of the situation involving current relationships, in sexual orientation or in the active search for short-term partners (Schmitt et al. 2005: 85, 98–101). This difference, which is more a sign of biotic behavioral tendencies, is strengthened in many cultures by the creation of similarly oriented cultural role models, a point that demonstrates the importance of conducting studies among noneducated persons.

Sexual Jealousy and Romantic Love

Sexual jealousy is universally widespread (D. Brown 1991; Pinker 1997: 488). It also appears universal that jealousy among men is more tied to violence than it is among women (Bruck 1985; Daly and Wilson 1988; D. Brown 1991: 109; Ehrlich 2002: 193). The psychic form of emotions and the cultural response to these emotions reveal very real differences. For example, the acceptance of multiple (partible) paternity in many societies in the interior of South America calls the supposed universality of jealousy arising from the uncertainty of paternity into question (Beckermann and Valentine 2002). Like so much else presented in this book, it must be noted that these findings have yet to be tested rigorously in broad cross-cultural studies.

Whereas love is considered in general to be a universal, romantic love has until recently been regarded as a unique characteristic of European and Euro-American cultures, Western-oriented societies, or smaller, more mobile and fragmented societies. Even researchers who explicitly examine the universality of romantic or passionate love expressly deny that romantic love occurs everywhere (e.g., Hockett 1973: 278–79; see his list, presented here in Table 5.2). Only recently has an increase in contrasting evidence produced more animated discussion and empirical research in the area of love (contributions in Jankowiak 1995, 2008b; Röttger-Rössler and Engelen 2006). Romantic love is defined as intense attraction in an erotic context that is tied to the idealization of one's partner and the expectation of a certain duration of feeling. In the *Standard Cross-Cultural Sample* of 186 cultures, 88.5 percent of these cultures defined romantic love in similar terms (Jankowiak and Fischer 1992: 150). Since these findings were published, other cultures have been documented and can be included here; indeed, the list of cultures revealing ethnographic evidence of romantic love has recently become quite extensive (Jankowiak 2008: 267–79; see Jankowiak and Paladino 2008: 7–9). The evidence now indicates that romantic love is found on a pancultural level and represents a "near" universal. It would be interesting to systematically and comparatively determine the extent of variation in emic concepts of romantic love, something rarely studied to date.

Life Stages and Socialization

Ever since Philippe Ariès conducted his now extremely influential and historical studies, the dominant opinion in the social and cultural sciences has been that childhood as a phase of life is not a universal stadium. According to this opinion, childhood represents a specific Western concept that first appeared after the twelfth century and is falsely and Eurocentrically construed as universal. The work of Ariès is based on studies involving the visual arts and points out that instead of childhood, there are two pre-adult phases: that of the baby as undeveloped human, and that of the incompetent pre-adult. His criticism of Eurocentrism has since triggered many historical studies, producing contrary results (Lancy 2015: 5). Seen historically, the concept of childhood has existed at least since the time of the ancient Egyptians. Childhood in human beings is ontogenetic and particularly pronounced in comparison to other primates. Childhood as a phase of life is clearly delimited in many societies, even though its duration can differ markedly depending on the culture. This corresponds with the widespread assumptions in many cultures that children do not need long to learn what is necessary for their own survival (Lancy 2015: 7). The question of whether there are in fact universal patterns in child rearing and socialization has long been a point of contention. Margaret Mead (1928) claimed that the period we call adolescence occurs only in modern societies. This has been refuted (D. Brown 1999a, 1999b), and today we also know from long-term cross-cultural studies covering a selection of 186 societies that young people are treated in a unique or special way from around the time of puberty and through their late teens. In many traditional and almost all modern societies, a special stage of life we know as "youth" is separated from other phases of life. The background for this rests within the formation of the family as the basic structure of human societies (Schlegel 2007: 227).

Figure 5. Graffiti artist in New York, US. Photo by Maria Blechmann-Antweiler.

CHAPTER 5

Methods
Deduction, Case Studies, and Comparison

> *Check-lists ... are never intellectually satisfying:*
> *the mind craves an overall characterization.*
> Felipe Fernández-Armesto, *So You Think You're Human?*

> *Every claim of universality is just that: a claim.*
> Donald E. Brown, "Human Universals"

Is it possible to find universals by simply extracting the commonalities from cultures in order to produce the "consensual human being," as Geertz (1965: 98–101) remarked? In the introduction I stated that universals are not to be reached simply by transcultural consensus through a kind of opinion poll of all peoples of the world. Only through a synthesis of empirical data within a consistent theoretical framework is the search for universals at all relevant. One of the first leading assumptions behind the following remarks is that in order to establish and verify the existence of universals, we need to be ready to combine multiple methodological strategies. A second leading assumption is that comparisons between cultures and between species are key to gaining understanding of the unity and diversity of human cultures. The goal must be to question or look into the existence of universals in our study of cultures, and not to project universality into cultures or simply recognize or infer the legitimacy of other cultures by comparing them with our own. The choice of research methods is for me what the physicist Murray Gell-Mann has said about scientific work in general: "People must ... get away from the idea that serious work is restricted to beating to death a well-defined problem in a narrow discipline, while broadly integrative thinking is relegated to cocktail parties. In academic life, in bureaucracies, and elsewhere, the task of integration is insufficiently respected" (Gell-Mann 1994).

In this chapter I will introduce a process for determining potential or probable universals and for formulating an empirical investigation. I will present the ways in which potential candidates for universal phenomena can be found and the process for establishing proof of their existence. The possibilities and limitations found in the comparative process are central to the following discussion. The problems of comparison lie first of all in the ambiguity in such things as naming phenomena in order to make likenesses more empirical, and second, in the ever-present threat of contamination through the use of our own cultural concepts (Hunt 2007: 27, 40–42, 156–58). A fundamental danger lies in finding regularities and then interpreting them as universals when they are actually the result of certain constants stemming from our approach to research (Pollnac 1978: 229). The basic questions are whether culturally independent concepts are even possible and whether it is possible or even desirable to compare cultures through these concepts. I conclude by discussing the advantages and disadvantages found in the different means for presenting universals, such as in lists or through narrative.

Finding Potential Candidates and Deducing from Theory

How do researchers go about postulating universals? In various works on universals, the basis of certain claims is not often made clear. It remains then uncertain as to whether universals are extracted through speculation or theoretical conjecture, through generalizations arising from single observed cases, or from explicitly comparative studies. Theoretically based universals are often found in philosophical anthropology or the work of social philosophers. An example includes species ethics (*Gattungsethik*) in the more recent work of Habermas. In his critique of genetic engineering, he assumes a cross-cultural ethical position arising from an ethical self-conception or identity of human beings as human beings with a strong reference to the physical body (Habermas 2005: 72–74). Habermas does not, however, offer any empirical data for his position but rather borrows from Plessner and his speculations on the living body and the human being as physical object.

It is often the case in analysis that different sources of universals are mixed together. It also remains unclear whether specifically named universals represent axioms, or whether they are deduced from theories or understood through empirical methods. I can offer an example from a work on cultural fragmentation and social inequality in U.S. society. In his book entitled *Culture of Intolerance*, the anthropologist Mark Nathan Cohen describes many universals within a section under the subheading "What Cultures Have in Common: Shared Content and Structure" (Cohen 1998: 74–105). The subtitles within this section of the text take on the form of twelve consecutively numbered statements, beginning with those that are considered established and empirically based remarks, such as the following: that all sociocultural systems develop principles of property and exchange that foster the movement of goods and that define social ties (Cohen 1998: 76). Most of the subtitles that follow then read as examples of universals, as in "Cultural Rules Organize Shared Communication" or "Cultures Represent a Shared and Conventional Definition of the Goals and Values of Groups and Individuals" (1998: 80, 87). These statements do not represent inductively and empirically determined universals but rather universals produced through deduction or abduction, the latter being a generalization of types based on systematic case comparisons. In this case, universals are obtained via inference from functionalistic assumptions about human needs and their consequences for societies. Deductions are made from a theoretical holistic anthropology that understands culture as a systematic means for organizing human groups.

Another case of deducing universals occurs when criteria explicitly generated by theory set perimeters governing whether or not a phenomenon is to be considered empirically universal. I can give an example of this that, unlike the information presented in this book, brings causal assumptions into the defining process of what makes something universal. Ellen Dissanayake, an anthropologist of art and a prehistorian, searches for universals in art, or aesthetics. With this as her background, she names certain conditions for determining whether behavioral patterns are universal or not: they must have already existed among protohumans, and they must be compatible with present-day art (Dissanayake 1992: 42). She continues: "in order to show that a behaviour of art is universal and undeniable, it is necessary to identify a core behavioural tendency upon which natural selection could act" (Dissanayake 1992: 42). Tenbruck offers an example of deducing universals that is especially relevant for this chapter, as it refers to cultural comparison. He claims that the intellectual comparison of cultures must be a universal, because societies did not develop in isolated forms but rather through intersocietal relationships. Since societies live fundamentally with or against each other, cultural comparison is then unavoidable and existentially necessary for each society (Tenbruck 1992: 14–17). What other possibilities do we have for finding candidate universals (Ochs 2004: 86) besides through deductive reasoning, as presented here briefly? There are in fact quite a few empirical approaches, as I will discuss below.

Case Studies: Testing Postulated Universals

Alleged Universals

If anthropologists want to put an alleged universal phenomenon to the test, they do not simply venture out into the world in order to show that it occurs everywhere. Instead they demonstrate that no known society is without it. The pervasiveness of something, or the pancultural occurrence of a phenomenon, is thus extrapolated from the evidence produced in many cultures, or from evidence that is pluricultural (D. Brown 1991: 51; van Damme 2000: 263). As such, isolated or individual items or occurrences, or lack thereof, become important as potential empirical evidence in criticizing the claims that universals exist. For example, if someone wants to doubt the universality of murder, one simply needs to find examples of culture where murder does not occur. A single or isolated case documenting that murder does not occur on a regular or consistent level would be enough to question the universality of murder everywhere. Examples would be the Semai in Malaysia with a yearly murder rate of 0.56 per 100,000 people and the Norwegians with 1.4 per 100.000 inhabitants (Fry 2006: 72–80).

Problems develop above all due to a lack of data, the poor quality of data, or data that are no longer relevant. Despite the existence of thousands of ethnographies and systematically produced cross-cultural databanks like the Human Relations Area Files (HRAF; see, e.g., Bourgignon and Greenbaum 1973 and www.yale.edu/hraf), our knowledge of cultures throughout the world is, as always, fragmentary and incomplete. In the example mentioned above, for instance, certain cases of murder might have not been reported. It could also be that the time frame selected for carrying out a study was not necessarily useful, or that it was too short for a particular phenomenon to occur. Another example would include competition or competitive games, which were long regarded as not universal but today are considered most likely so.

I would like to show with two further examples that individual case studies, or studies based on only a few societies, are important in revealing how certain universal claims turn out to be only alleged universals. In contrast to the statements made by Berlin and Kay (1969; also Brown 1991), we know today that in almost all languages, though not in every single one, there are words for "white" and "black" (Wierzbicka 2005: 280). It is constantly claimed that there are wars in all societies, which is documentary proof of the aggressive nature of human beings. War as collective and organized violence with the use of weapons must be differentiated from aggression that reveals an individual behavioral tendency. Empirically we find aggression and violence between individuals in all societies. War though, understood as organized and collective deathly violence beyond the level of revenge killing and feuding, does occur as a regular phenomenon in the vast majority of societies, but not in all of them. Not even blood vengeance and feuding are universal (Fry 2006: 90, 242–46), corroborating the cross-cultural finding that some societies are internally and regularly peaceful and that many societies have certain mechanisms at their disposal that explicitly serve to manage or regulate conflicts (Fry 2006: 62–65, 71–82, 200–16). We cannot consider war a part of human nature any more than we can claim peace and willingness are. One of the very few researchers involved in large-scale culturally comparative work has described this as follows:

> The evidence of a substantial number of peoples without warfare, or with mainly a defensive and/or low-level warfare (i.e. seldom exceeding the level of petty feuding or desultory skirmishes) does not support the view of universal belligerence. It does not support the equally erroneous view of universal peaceability either. Rather it supports Dentan's and my own view that peace as well as war are the results of illuminated and opportunistic self-interest in the political arena. (van der Dennen, pers. comm., 2006)

Individual case studies allow us to explain and examine accepted or assumed universals. All kinds of societies have disappeared over time, so studies involving the few relatively intact nonliterate societies are all the more important (D. Brown 2013: 413). By means of single or isolated cases, we can determine the legitimacy of claims concerning supposedly impossible phenomena. If someone were to say that there is no culture with such-and-such (i.e., a negative universal), then the proof of a single example of an extreme characteristic in human culture can become significant (Kroeber 1948a). In this respect, lists of extremely unusual phenomena take on particular relevance, with the one produced by Keiter as a case in point (Keiter 1956: 663–68; 1966: 252–61). The proof of one single, well-documented case of a culture with regularly occurring marriage between women (gynaegamia) is enough to crush the Eurocentric idea of the supposedly absolute universal of marriage and family forms. Things once considered "unnatural" can now be demonstrated—even in only very rare cases—as within the scope of cultural variance (Hildebrandt 1996: 175–77; 1978). Not finding evidence of certain societal features that were assumed to exist is another important contribution of case studies.

Another example includes cannibalism (anthropophagy). Until the 1970s it was assumed that cannibalism, though definitively not universal, was in fact widespread. Various explanations were given for this, but what is relevant here is William Arens's (1978) analysis of a large number of traditional observations on cannibalism. His results showed that there were no reliable reports among them, and that not one single truly reliable report from an actual eyewitness was available. Rather, frequent reports of neighboring groups engaging in cannibalism appear to be a cause of its reputation as a widespread practice, leading to the conclusion that it is not almost universal but rather something that occurs in extremely rare cases. What looks almost universal then is prohibiting cannibalism within groups while attributing cannibalism to other, often neighboring groups. Thus we discover that cannibalism has less to do with food or nourishment and more to do with the inclusion or exclusion of groups, or how different groups of people are classified. More recent discussion on the topic, however, has made Arens's conclusions more relative.

According to primarily archaeological findings, it appears cannibalism was more intensely widespread than assumed (Ehrlich 2002: 406).

Thus, as Donald Brown (2013) emphasizes, ethnographies oriented to particularist Heraclitean concerns are needed for the more Platonian interests in commonalities. Further examples that I will only touch upon here due to their abundance in the literature indicate the significance of case studies in discussing the topic of universals. One such example is the ongoing inconclusive search for societies in which women dominate the public political sphere; another is the failed attempt to prove that sensory perception is almost exclusively shaped by culture (Segall et al. 1966: 209). One needs to be careful with conclusions drawn from examples that are basically exceptions to the rule. A quotation taken from a work in behavioral ecology will illustrate this point. Here, exceptions lead to a change in causal assumptions because what is claimed to be universal is equated with being predetermined: "It appears that whenever someone uncovers so-called behavioural universals among human beings, someone else comes along and reveals an exception to the rule. We move quite quickly from the idea of 'universal' and 'pre-programmed' to 'probable' and 'predisposed'" (Markl 1986: 83).

Empirical Case Studies with Implied Comparison

In his attack on universalistic research, Geertz criticized the object of research, that is, the universal itself, as being void of content—"empty" or "bloodless" (1965: 105). According to him, universals are not in any way combinable with the truly interesting aspects of culture, whose variations are, for Geertz, the "essences of human existence" (Geertz 1965: 97). But this is only the case if universals are kept in abstract form. What is necessary is to look comparatively at variations while seeking general patterns in their occurrence.

The combination of comparative studies with individual case studies is important in researching universals. An example will illustrate my point. In all known societies, responsibility for child rearing and care is left primarily to the mother (Murdock 1967; Maryansky and Turner 1992; Lopreato and Crippen 2002: 187). In all societies studied thus far, fathers spend 2 to 3 percent of their time involved in direct care of small children, whereas for mothers it is 20 to 25 percent. Only in hunter-gatherer societies do we find fathers spending more time caring for children. Studies among the Aka in the Western Congo Basin, for instance, indicate that fathers there dedicate as much as 47 percent of their time to children (Hewlett 1991). Without these case studies we would have no empirical basis for even examining such alternatives or considering them possible. On the other hand, in the absence of the background material of comparative knowledge we would be unable to weigh the meaning or significance of case studies. Only the empirical and comparative data on the very limited amount of time men spend with children in almost all other societies make it possible to recognize the rarity of the Aka case and to search then for explanations (Munroe and Munroe 2001: 224).

In contrast to cross-cultural laboratory experiments, field-based experiments are seldom used. This is generally the case for anthropology as well as for psychology, but especially so for experiments that have to do with the explicit search for universals. It is very rare to find experiments in which studies done in mostly Western societies are replicated in other (e.g., nonindustrial) societies (Wassmann 1993, 2006; Levinson 1996). The numerous reasons for this include high costs, logistical problems, and above all methodological difficulties finding locally adapted methods in nonfamiliar cultural situations, as well as unresolved ethical issues. As one of the few researchers of religion who has performed such experiments in the field has written: "Replicating an experiment in different cultures involves more than just transporting a protocol to a different location" (Boyer 2001: 83).

Archaeological and Historical Documentation of Cultural Parallels

Individual case studies in the area of pre- and protohistory are also relevant to the study of universals. In the Old and New Worlds, archaeologists have found consistencies in the structure and development of complex societies that developed completely independent of each other. Universal historians, especially those interested in world history (or global history; see Christian 2005; Schissler 2005; R. Marks 2006; Bayly 2006), point to similar dynamics at work in complex, stratified societies, where parallels have been found especially with regard to economic structures and political institutions. In a type of historical experiment, independently but similarly formed structures have developed out of a Paleolithic cultural heritage. Clear parallels are revealed, for example, in the early agricultural societies of the Old World and of the Americas between AD 200 and 1000, especially relating to the functional need to store and protect agricultural resources in favorable areas (McNeill and McNeill 2003: 114–15; also see Spier 2002: 89–96). Separate and independent states developed during this time in at least seven regions of the world (Kidder 1940; see Holenstein 1997: 50–51; E. Wilson 1998: 149), where similar circumstances and demands produced then parallel solutions.

Parallels also occur in other areas of culture. Alongside examples of intense historical influence, historically independent counterparts have emerged in various religions' systems of philosophy and meaning as well. Elmar Holenstein has uncovered such "contextual independent counterparts" (*kontextunabhängige Entsprechungen*) between Europe, China, and India (Holenstein 1997: 64; also see G. Paul 2008a: 42–115; Pinxten 1976) and documented them in his *Atlas of Philosophy* through comparisons of the meaning of words, also demonstrating the parallels in detailed maps (Holenstein 2004). The explanations for these similarities are for the most part purely speculative. One could start with a systematic assumption similar to the concept of the modular human brain, as presented in evolutionary psychology (Carruthers 2005; Sperber 2005): "There are cultural phenomena and entire cultural areas that have a kind of autonomous nature separate from the general culture in which they develop" (Holenstein 1997: 65).

Concepts beyond Cultural Bias?

Anthropologists are extremely divided over the question of whether it is possible for concepts to develop in historically independent cultures. In the extreme case, terms such as religion or kinship can be considered problematic, as Rodney Needham (1975) has claimed. Following the same line of thought, Edmund Leach has written, "any anthropologist who selects a particular category word from his own mother tongue, e.g. incest, marriage … and then embarks on some kind of cross-cultural study of institutions which he lumps together under such headings, is begging all the questions which are of serious interest" (Leach 1982: 180).

In questions of concrete research, most anthropologists are downright conservative. They use terms such as "marriage," "religion," and "economy" despite their reservations (Saler 2000: 6). This is also the case, as mentioned above, in the way textbook chapters are divided and named, with the terminology remaining only vaguely defined. Culturally independent terms and concepts are most often used to structure or build theory. Moreover, they are necessary for cultural comparisons, such as when concepts of "property" are compared. Cross-cultural concepts are important even for purely descriptive purposes, as Goodenough (1970: 2) has declared: "We have to find some set of terms that will enable us to describe other cultures *with minimal distortion from ethnocentric cultural bias*. And we need some set of universally applicable concepts that will enable us to compare cultures and arrive at valid generalizations about them" (italics mine).

The more recent forms of cross-cultural psychology offer approaches to this problem area that could be helpful for cultural comparison in anthropology. In earlier forms of cross-cultural psychology, comparisons referred to studies with preset or predefined concepts to allow average values to be compared directly between countries. Such studies are important in identifying cultural differences. It remains unclear, though, whether similar-sounding concepts in cultures being compared share the same meaning. In more recent work, researchers have attempted a decentering approach (Smith et al. 2006: 23–24) to avoid the danger of using ethnocentric concepts. Instead of referring to a purely imposed etic terminology or indigenous or emic concepts—thus making comparisons impossible—they now work step-by-step to form a kind of derived etic (see Berry et al. 2011: 23). Correlates are initially sought within one and the same cultural context. Out of these correlates, researchers can derive a nomological net from which to obtain more correlates between a new concept and existing concepts, eventually developing into a theory on the meaning of the concept in question. When a concept proves to have similar correlates in different societies, subcultures, or contexts, it is likely that an equivalent kind of meaning exists among these correlates and concepts as well. A methodological maxim can thus be inferred, stating that universals are more likely to be found through parallel studies within several separate societies than through direct and intercultural comparison (Smith et al. 2006: 26).

Transcultural Definitions: The Example of Religion and Kinship

The problem of finding usable definitions that are both formal and general with regard to comparative research on kinship and religion has often been discussed (Saler 2000: 27–86). In general, anthropologists of religion who are particularist or constructivist in orientation are against using formal definitions. But even colleagues who are not against using explicit definitions for phenomena do not agree totally on the matter. Melford Spiro, for example, has argued for an explicit definition of religion but does not insist upon tying this definition to universal features. According to Spiro (1966: 86), this would only lead to constant modification of the definition based on new examples turning up due to diversity. Universals would not be found, but rather created through definition. In contrast, Robert Horton has argued for a "real" definition of religion, in light of widespread understanding of the term, and for an explicit emphasis on universal aspects within the definition in order to avoid culturally specific concepts. He defines religion as the broadening of social relationships to nonhuman partners (Horton 1960: 211).

To empirically test the universality of phenomena, we need concepts that are proven to be cross-cultural (Jensen 1999; Straub and Shimada 1999). And to obtain such reliable concepts, we need to be able to test them against material from as many different cultures as possible. These concepts must show that, for example, all the possible elements in concept X make observable phenomena understandable in the same way in all cultures under consideration. If concepts prove capable of making phenomena from different cultures understandable, then they have verified an existential hypothesis and are thus valuable for research purposes. Testing the value of concepts helps us decipher which concepts are useful on a universal level and which are more specific to certain societies: "The key to proving whether a concept is cross-cultural involves observing similar, recognizable and equally linked elements of phenomena that are otherwise marked by differences" (Jensen 1999: 60).

The concept "marriage" is a good example here. Many anthropologists think that kinship relationships that are not based on blood descent have an emic place in all societies. This would imply that marriage is a universal institution—a supposition that carries with it many problems. A few anthropologists argue that the institution of marriage demonstrates a *family resemblance* (Leach 1982: 226, 235). This concept, borrowed from Wittgenstein (1982), is not used precisely enough. One of the problems concerns the development of the terms marriage and family. Arguing for the universality of marriage is for the most part functionalist, involving the following steps (reconstructed from Leach 1982: 178–79):

1. Human offspring need parental care in order to survive as organisms.
2. Each society has to regulate how its members are to live together in units so that the adults are required to care for their young. Marriage is the mechanism that makes this requirement and care legitimate.
3. The unit used for the care of young is normally a household, formed by a core family of married adults and children.
4. If family in this sense has a reasonable function, it must then be necessary and therefore universal.

The counter argument is that the form of a societal institution is not determined through its functional adequacy. Contrary to Malinowski and Radcliffe-Brown, it is not specific forms of institutional arrangements that are determined, but rather "basic patterns within the structure of person-to-person relationships" (Leach 1982: 179). The debate rests upon the matter of whether the core family made up of biological parents and their children is universal. It definitively is not. In many regions of the world, like parts of the Caribbean and West Africa, we find female-headed households composed of mothers (and often their sisters) and children, with the fathers of the children living elsewhere as migratory workers and rarely being home. The critics' reasoning runs as follows: Marriage is not universal. Institutions that are described as "marriage" in various societies may have certain "family resemblances," but "there is no single cross-cultural matrix into which these several 'marriage' institutions can all be fitted," and they are "not strictly comparable from a sociological point of view" (Leach 1982: 180, 35). It remains often unclear whether the point of contention is merely a question of specifics within likenesses. The problem is often that the terms used to describe cultural phenomena are the ones we use in daily life. A general problem in anthropology, it appears more intensely in cultural comparisons. The use of everyday terms and their common meanings allows certain connotations from Western cultures to find their way into academic discussion. This is most striking when we use the words family and marriage. The problem also arises that even in "Western culture," these very common words are understood differently as well, as Leach has pointed out (Leach 1982: 181–83).

Approaches and Critical Cases

Any attempt to solve the problem of concepts in methodology involves maintaining the use of certain terms but qualifying them with precise, culturally independent definitions (Table 5.1). Though problematic as well, these more technical solutions further our research endeavors. An example of the use of more technical precision is found in the step-by-step approach Ward Hunt Goodenough (1970; see also Greenwood and Stini 1977: 337–41; Saler 2000: 119) described in establishing a definition for "marriage":

Step 1: Choose ad hoc a definition from, say, a dictionary, such as: "Marriage is a social institution in which men and women enter into a specific social relationship within a legal structure in order to start and maintain a family."
Step 2: Divide definitions up into components: (1) relationship of man and woman, (2) social and legal dependency, and (3) goal of creating a family.
Step 3: Expand and correct definition based on reports from other societies. Place information in tables, listing which features are present and which additional features could be necessary, such as (4) legitimate children, (5) preferential access to sex, and (6) mutual rights with regard to work.
Step 4: For individual cases, explain the specific functions, for example, in terms of the differences in certain features within the social organization or the economy. Functionalism is therefore key in researching universals.

According to this method, isolated cases take on significant meaning. The case of the Nayar, for example, refutes the universality of the family, while the case of the Nuer does the same for the universality of the bond between man and woman, since a union between a woman and another woman is possible among the Nuer. The result is that of the six features, only three—social and legal dependency, legitimate children, and mutual rights concerning work— are found in all known societies. Goodenough concludes that marriage has to be understood more as a means of regulating access to females who can have children and less as a response to universal nature, especially with regard to universal male dominance and competition for females.

Table 5.1. Extrapolating cross-cultural definitions through the example of marriage

Western Case (1)	Case 2	Case 3	Case 4	Case 5	Case 6
(a) Marriage is a union between a man and a woman	no	yes	yes	yes	yes
(b) Social and legal dependency	yes	yes	yes	yes	yes
(c) Establishing a partnership and maintaining a family	yes	no	yes	no	yes
(d) Only married people have legitimate children	yes	yes	yes	yes	yes
(e) Partners have preferential access to sexuality	yes	yes	yes	yes	yes
(f) Partners have mutual rights when it comes to work	yes	yes	yes	no	yes

Source: modified after Greenwood and Stini 1977: 338

On one level, the example described above shows the problems associated with cross-cultural concepts, thereby revealing the importance of finding concepts free of cultural associations. Furthermore, it highlights the individual case study's importance in researching universals. We can conclude then that in the discussion on universals, it is helpful to abandon the normal fixation on absolute universals. Despite the difficulties involved, constructing culturally independent concepts is still a useful challenge. They must not lose their empirical reference. Anna Wierzbicka, working with the diversity and universality of semantic concepts, has come up with an interesting, radical way of dealing with the problem. She maintains that we can only formulate cognitive or other types of cultural universals if linguistic universals are available to us in the form of a "universal language" (Wierzbicka 2005: 257–58). She therefore recommends using an empirically based language of universals—the conceptual "primes" described above—that are universal emic models of mind, of person, and of the human being, and using these primes as the basis for both studying other universals and understanding diversity.

Inventories of Universals

Lists of universals are one of the many tools used in universals research. Such lists are known beyond the field of anthropology because they were, among other things, important to the form of an empirical argument against Eurocentric claims of cultural deficits in other societies. Among the anthropological contributions to the topic of universals, lists or catalogs of universals are as prominent as they are contested. I want to emphasize, though, that the creation of such lists is only one of anthropology's many contributions to the study of universals. Furthermore, these lists are not to be seen as an end product of research. They form a step or phase in the overall process of research, and they have a heuristic function. Universal inventories form an empirical starting point, as they name all the phenomena on which any reasonable theory about human beings is based (Greenwood and Stini 1977: 312, 315; Opolka 1999: 4). These universal catalogs come with their own share of problems, which I explore in detail below. But crucially, they represent a clear alternative to other approaches in the research on human nature. Among the approaches that consider general human characteristics by way of features, one important distinction of forming lists is that the features this approach concentrates on are not associated with individuals, species, or all of humanity, but rather with societies. Social universals are the aim of research, in the sense of "man-in-society" (C. Berry 1986: 83).

Murdock's List

The various ways of creating lists of universals will be presented and analyzed by way of examples, and evaluated according to pros and cons. A classic example of list making, mentioned earlier, is the "partial list" of seventy-three absolute universals that Murdock created through a comparison of approximately one hundred societies (Murdock 1945). Though it is often referred to in either very positive or negative terms, this list is rarely discussed. Murdock has said that these universals "occur, as far as the author's knowledge goes, in every culture known to history or ethnography." He listed them alphabetically in the form of seventy-three universal "frame categories of culture," as he named them, revealing their diversity in units of data such as age grading, athletic sports, bodily adornment, calendar, cleanliness training, community organization, cooking, and so on (Murdock 1949: 124). According to Murdock, each of these seventy-three categories can be divided into universal subcategories.

Murdock's list is by far the most often cited. Murdock himself had certain—though not many—doubts about his methods and narrowed his list of universals later in life (Murdock 1957a). In 1981 he published a list in which only seventy-two of the original seventy-three categories appeared, without commenting on the change (Murdock 1981). His inventory, like any other such list, carries with it many unanswered questions:

- Are the universals in fact transculturally verifiable universals, or are they the result of pure speculation?
- Which of the given universals can be empirically verified?
- What is considered empirical proof?

- Is a substantial list of universals compiled solely on an empirical basis possible, or do we need deductively based universals as well?
- Is the list complete? According to the most recent data, do we need to add to or change the list in any way? (Schiefenhövel 1999: 4)
- What value do such inventories or lists have for research into human universals?
- Where do the boundaries of irreducible differences between cultures begin, or where do cultures begin to become separate? (Schiefenhövel 1999: 4)

Other Inventories

Besides the varied forms of Murdock's list appearing in the literature, we do come across alternative inventories as well. In the 1950s, Clyde Kluckhohn examined over ninety ethnographic monographs, looking for universals. He did not convert the information he perused into a detailed catalog, but rather derived general patterns and categories based on the necessary requirements of the human organism:

> Every society's patterns for loving *must provide* approved and sanctioned ways for dealing with such universal circumstances as the existence of two sexes; the helplessness of infants; the *need for* satisfaction of the *elementary biological requirements* such as food, warmth and sex; the presence of individuals of different ages and of differing physical and other capacities ... equally there are certain *necessities* in social life for this kind of animal regardless of where that life is carried on or in which culture. Cooperation to obtain subsistence or for other ends *requires* a certain minimum of reciprocal behaviour, of a standard system of communication, and indeed, of mutually accepted values. (Kluckhohn 1953: 520–21; italics mine)

Like Murdock, Charles F. Hockett presented an especially comprehensive catalog of universals, which are divided into many lists in his monumental work *Man's Place in Nature* (Hockett 1973: 154, 183, 276–79). He refers to Murdock, but in contrast to Murdock's "common denominator of cultures," he names his corresponding chapter "... common denominator of humanness" (Hockett 1973: 275–77). Although this step introduces a certain measure of nonclarity, Hockett's contribution is useful because in many ways he reaches beyond Murdock. First off, he distinguishes in his catalog between features that humans share with nonhuman species and features he considers to be aspects of a "human historical base line." Second, he notes that some items are universals that are "only" widespread and at best are near universals. Third, he also presents a list of non-universals, that is, features that are assumed to be universal but in fact are not (Table 5.2). Finally, Hockett emphasizes the practical importance of such lists, seen in the example of politics:

"The full realization that a human community simply doesn't have to have (for example) any political organization or behavior, comes very hard. But if we are ever to achieve a useful understanding of our fellow man, that is the sort of realization we must attain. Anything less is a pinchbeck" (Hockett 1973: 279). A comparison of Hockett's list with Murdock's catalog of universals reveals the following:

(1) Neither list is systematic. Murdock's list is explicitly so through its alphabetical ordering of items only.
(2) In both catalogs, similar things turn up in different places.
(3) Both lists are in many areas very different, in other places not.
(4) Murdock's list is much more comprehensive, with his seventy-three universals.
(5) Despite the scope of Murdock's list, some universals listed by Hockett do not correspond to any of Murdock's universals.
(6) In some cases, two items from Hockett's list correspond to one of Murdock's universals, for example, in items concerning "sexual restrictions." Hockett, despite creating a shorter list, distinguishes more carefully between items with regard to such things as social structure, forms of ownership, incest restraints, and especially political structures, whereas Murdock uses only the one term "government" for the latter item.
(7) Interestingly enough, the two catalogs of universals are especially different when it comes to what might at first appear to be more trivial universals. While Murdock lists items such as "housing," "grief," and "punishment," Hockett names such things as "boredom," "sleep," and "feelings." Hockett probably mentions this latter item because he was keenly interested in psychology and behavioral science. Hockett concludes that "perhaps the more important thing is for us to recognize how little we know." He also points out that we need to keep our distance from more holistic assumptions that tend to see correlations and connections between everything in one culture with everything else (1973: 276–77).

Even from the standpoint of cultural ecology and functionalism, researchers have argued by way of universals. An example comes from Robert Edgerton's critical remarks about romanticizing indigenous peoples. He emphasizes that in all societies there are practices that restrict or even threaten individual well-being (Edgerton 1992: 6). In the German-speaking world, the human ethologist Schiefenhövel has produced an interesting list in which he translates Murdock's universals into German and adds some of his own, primarily from the viewpoint of comparative behavioral science (Schiefenhövel 1999: 2–4). This list, like Murdock's, is in alphabetical order.

Table 5.2. Features (traits) that, contrary to Western notions, are not universal

1. Society as a unit over and beyond the individual
2. Political economic "establishment" as the result of conscious effort
3. Morality and justice as impersonal absolutes
4. Concept of a "best" in every category
5. Government and State
6. Political spheres
7. Justice (or law?)
8. Legalized and impersonal relationships to property
9. Land as possession
10. Demarcated and defended borders, inclusive national borders
11. Fictive (legal) entities as possessions
12. Religion
13. Philosophy
14. Science
15. Marriage and social paternity
16. Nuclear family as ideal household
17. Emphasis on "husband vs. wife"
18. Romantic love
19. Sexual frustration as source of emotional conflict
20. Sacredness of the home and motherhood
21. Marriage as the only acceptable framework for societal relationships
22. Work as a value and the assumption that humans are "naturally" lazy
23. Value placed on individual initiative
24. The unavoidability of change and eventual "progress"
25. The opinion that "you cannot change human nature"

Source: Hockett 1973: 278–79

The non-anthropological literature contains lists of universals independent of the Murdock catalog and the tradition behind it. The American social psychologist Fathali Moghaddam, for example, has written a textbook based on a comparative approach. The work describes three fundamental norms that Moghaddam considers to be strong universal candidates. He indentifies an additional thirteen "basic similarities across cultures" (Moghaddam 1998: 9–12), which I have listed in Table 5.3. This list proves interesting in that it was produced using methods that differ greatly from those used to create the lists grounded in the comparative tradition of anthropology. It is based mostly on experimental results and observations of so-called small groups. In practice, social psychological findings as a rule are generated on the basis of studies performed in Western countries and on or with students. Moghaddam, however, has examined these findings by way of cultural comparison in order to produce a textbook that is not Euro- or Americentric. The results reveal a clear contrast to the information presented in the lists by Murdock and Hockett.

Table 5.3. Universals according to findings from social psychology

1. Norm of reciprocal trust
2. Norm of assuming the truthfulness in our interactive partners
3. Norm of turn-taking in dialogue
4. Concept that within every human body there exists a self (even when terms such as "I" or "me" are lacking)
5. Qualifying the world in positive and negative concepts
6. Searching for causes (e.g., in social change)
7. Recognizing differences in status, with greater trust placed in those with higher status
8. Conforming to social norms or rules and obeying authority
9. Preference and love for persons who are similar (and spatially close) to us
10. Helpful behavior (social behavior) toward other (culturally different) people
11. Differentiating between "We" and "They," and favoring the "We" category
12. Conscious injury to others (aggression)
13. Less aggression and higher degree of empathy found in women (in most societies)
14. Social groups and leadership
15. Feelings of injustice as cause for conflict between groups
16. Concept of fairness and differentiating between just and unjust

Source: modified after Moghaddam 1998: 12–13

Evaluating Lists of Universals and Holistic Forms of Representation

Problems and Critiques

Lists of universals offer a phenomenological kind of descriptive inventory of likenesses at the cultural comparative level. The information presented above on universal cataloguing reveals certain problems associated with such a methodology. A fundamental problem is the reckless handling of these inventories, both in their use and in the criticism thereof. Almost consistently we find a lack of discussion about the lists in and of themselves. Even in D. Brown (1991), there are only suggestions of such. A well-known exception in the German-speaking world comes from Karl Eibl, who briefly but accurately discusses lists in a book's appendix (2004: 353–58). Those who support or produce such lists often do so without trying to keep a critical eye on the approach, so the number of universals may vary from one list to the next, or a list might later be changed without comment as to why the changes were necessary. A list produced by Scupin and deCorse is a more recent example of a catalog that varies only slightly from Murdock's list (2006: 65). They list only sixty-five, not seventy-three, universals, and the names of five items differ from those assigned by Murdock. The authors neither mention nor qualify either of these changes. The differences reveal themselves only upon careful comparison of the lists. Reduction and alteration of the items on the list can also be found in the work of Stephen King Sanderson, who, with reference to Brown and Pinker, produced a list of forty-three universals without discussing previous lists (Sanderson 2001: 125–26).

Lists of universals are popular in some circles and have become popularized in various forms. Murdock's list from 1945 and Pinker's tables, which are a reworking of D. Brown's data, are the representational forms found in more recent literature as well as on the Internet, and they have proven more accessible to a wider audience than Brown's empirically and conceptually more sophisticated text. Finally, there are the lists presented according to Pinker's reworking of the Brown models, translated into German and arranged in another order. Payer's application-oriented contribution offers an example of something similar, relative to her wish to use universals as a basis for global communication between cultures. She organizes Pinker's items in five categories without explaining or mentioning why, and completes the list with caricatures (Payer 2000). This runs the risk of producing arbitrary changes in content in the same manner as the children's game of musical chairs produces changes in seating arrangements.

Another problem with these kinds of inventories develops when an author's choice of words causes changes in content or other discrepancies. It remains unclear as to whether a change in vocabulary suggests meaningful changes to content motivated by the wish to find simpler forms of expression, or occurs through pure recklessness. This difficulty occurs most pointedly in translations, starting with lists originally arranged in alphabetical order. For example, the most accessible translation of Murdock's catalog in the German-speaking world, found in table form in a German atlas der Ethnologie (Haller and Rodekohr 2005: 28), is organized very differently from Murdock's original, revealing deviations from other German translations as well (see Hejl 2001: 57–59). In a corresponding manner, Steven Pinker's very long list of approximately 320 universals, which represents a restructuring of Donald Brown's textual descriptions, offers a completely different view depending on whether one reads it in the original or in the German translation. In Pinker's different original English-language inventories, word choice differs as well. There are especially broad discrepancies, depending on the translator, in the various German editions of Pinker's work. With respect to the scientific reception and the popularization of lists, another problem involves the tendency toward what botanists call "secondary growth in girth": the lists become longer and longer.

The fundamental argument against inventories of universals is that such lists lump together concepts that vary in terms of objective importance and basic quality (Opolka 1999: 4). Below I present criticisms of lists of universals that concern individuals but, with regard to content, have to do with universals involving societies as well. A key criticism is that many so-called cultural universals are in fact trivial (Leach 1981: 268; Hinde 1994: 189). Isolating certain features by removing them from their own context easily leads to their trivialization. We cannot speak of representing cultural content without knowing something about what is being represented (Bruner 1981: 262). Geertz's criticism of universals as banal and therefore uninteresting has already been mentioned above. Some say that universals are something like stating the obvious or representing a kind of meaningless chatter (or *flatus vocis*; see Rorty 1979: 43). And this criticism does not issue solely from anthropological and philosophical circles—from the viewpoint of primatology too, it has been said that features appearing in these lists represent nothing more than "loosely defined biological limitations" (Sussman 1995: 6).

Critics also emphasize that it is hardly possible to isolate specific features (Hinde 1994: 189; Bruner 1991: 262), as is evident in the comparison of items on similar topics in the lists of Murdock and Hockett, described above. Here we find a basis for further criticism, namely, that very different levels of abstraction are found within the universals in these inventories. Sussman speaks of a "grab-bag of universals" (1995: 6). Lists unite the almost trivial, such as the existence of social organization in societies, with the very specific, such as modesty concerning bodily functions. The number of universals corresponds to the chosen level of abstraction. An increase in the level of abstraction will generate a higher number of universals, whereas a thoroughly empirical consideration will allow constants to dilute into particularities (Masson 1980: 134).

As a behavioral scientist, Robert Hinde has objected to supposed universals that refer to individuals and not cultures, though he finds them altogether worth considering. He has argued that, strictly speaking, there are no such things as universals since no single attribute can be absolutely constant between individuals due to the fact that there are always inter-individual differences. At the most, a feature can be considered stable within the framework of culture or in the realm of variations within a typical environmental setting (Hinde 1994: 189). The same applies to attributes for species, but even more so for universals: high-quality data that would prove their existence are simply lacking. Hinde names, as an example, the plausible but unproven assumption that all babies in all cultures behave the same when searching for and suckling at their mother's breast (Hinde 1994: 189).

Lists of Universals as a Useful First Step

Criticism of universal inventories is to be taken as seriously as the lists themselves. Scientists who reject the prospect of finding universals per se are not the only ones to object to the listing of universals. A fundamental criticism of such lists argues that they present an ethnocentric viewpoint. The political scientist Christopher Berry, who is no stranger to the debate on universals, has succinctly determined with regard to private ownership that any supposed universal says more about the classifier than the classified (Berry 1986: 84).

In spite of the objections, it is important to keep in mind that these lists do not enumerate instincts, inborn psychic tendencies, or inevitabilities (Pinker 1994: 466). They do not serve as a means of defining possibilities or things simply wished for. Instead, universal inventories offer, as Pinker has remarked, a list of complex interactions "between a universal human nature and the conditions that correspond to human beings living on this planet" (Pinker 1994). The lists indicate that certain convergences in cultural patterns are not simply a random matter of diffusion but rather correspond to human nature or human societies, though they do not clarify just how this actually comes about. If there are concrete or formal universals then it is "improbable that all cultures should just happen to have hit upon these recurrent features" (Berry 1986: 85). This is important in formulating culturally theoretical explanations if we, contrary to Geertz, assume that what is universal is more explainable than what is particular or more specific in form (Berry 1986: 85–87). Fundamental elements of human life, such as an interest in status, a sense of justice, pride, honor, retribution, feelings of shame, gossip and the contents of gossip, and so forth, appear obvious.

From a less anthropocentric viewpoint, universals would not slide under the cloak of self-evident invisibility because they are anything but self-evident. Referring to the above elements, Wright (1994: 8) argues: "But things didn't have to be this way. We could live on a planet where social life featured none of the above. We could live on a planet where some ethnic groups felt some of the above and others felt others. But we don't." Moreover, a large share of these social characteristics have been deprived of introspection, as Sigmund Freud strongly suggested. It is not surprising that a research project coming out of, for example, literary anthropology, and therefore using sources very different from those in the Murdock approach, would end up formulating lists of fundamentals, even if these are not understood in the same way that universals are (SFB 511 2005: 54–56). In view of the criticisms, we should not forget that universals have yet to be properly studied. In terms of specifics, we can make the following assertions using Murdock as a case in point:

1. His list contains "absolute" universals that have not yet been empirically disproven.
2. The existence of many supposed universals is not empirically substantiated, and this concerns universals in both the area of cognition and matters of behavior and material culture.
3. The list deals with universals from the viewpoint of the outside observer; that is, they are etic universals. From the inner perspective of the respective groups being observed, they are often not seen as universal.

4. In terms of action-specific or behavioral universals, "behavior" means that which relates to norms or follows norms, and not deviant forms of behavior.
5. Universals often appear banal only as long as they are not examined, as in the case of why something might occur universally. Murdock's list contains some universals that at first appear self-evident but in fact define specific groups from the perspective of early discoverers, travelers, or missionaries (Murdock 1945: 24; Greenwood and Stini 1977: 312–13). So it has been claimed, for example, that some societies have no forms of government and law. Similarly, it is assumed that there are societies in which people live in "primitive promiscuity," that is, they do not place limitations on their sexual behavior.
6. Murdock's lists, and especially Brown's textual composition, contain some universals that at first appear trivial but are not necessarily so. Items that are not just far from trivial but downright surprising include, for example, rumors, concepts of lying, situation-specific forms of speech, poems with the common recitative form of ca. three-second lines, knowledge of dance, and music specifically for children (Cronk 1999: 25).

The use of lists is above all heuristic. We can take a suggested universal out of the lists and determine the diversity of its manifestations in some or even many cultures, ideally in all known human societies. In this way, the diversity culminating from these manifestations and the limitations of this diversity are made clear to us. It is again worth noting that exotic places and unusual cultural practices should not be mentioned merely to quench our thirst for the strange or the exotic. The over-emphasis on the exotic weakens the quality of any study on cultural likenesses (Bloch 1977: 285). In terms of specifics, these studies on extreme cultural forms are important for determining the scope and the limits of cultural variation (Bloch 2005: 1–2). Only in that context can a reference to a very specific cultural manifestation of a general variant be understood. And only then can we form meaningful explanations, not only for universals but for the particularities of cultural variation as well. One of the very few anthropology books to follow this methodology consistently is the bioculturally oriented textbook by Greenwood and Stini (1977).

An Alternative: Representing Universals Holistically

Lists of universals are well established and popular, but they are not the only possible way of compiling our most current knowledge on pancultural patterns. There are alternatives that respond to the criticism of the lack of order associated with the list form. D Brown, for example, has produced an important alternative to list making. In a chapter to his book, to which I have already referred, he describes an imaginary "universal people" (1991: 130–41) whose personal attributes are reduced to confirmed universals. His chapter title "Universal People" was inspired by Noam Chomsky's *Universal Grammar* (Chomsky 1995). Most readers would expect such a chapter to be particularly short (Cronk 1999: 25), but what Brown offers here, in the form of a mini-ethnography of a "universal folk," is a systematic, or holistic, representation of hundreds of ethnographically or historically documented universals covering more than ten pages of text. And not only does Brown describe many more universals than did Murdock: through his unique representational form, Brown also lends us certain insights that extend far beyond the possibilities offered by a pure inventory. By systematically linking separate universal characteristics, his work reveals that universals are not simply disconnected or trivial generalizations, as so many critics have claimed. Brown presents a second alternative to universal catalogs. His book is also unique for its extensive annotated bibliography, which represents both a reference list and universal catalog, as next to many entries he notes which universals are either postulated or proven within the given work. This amounts to a treasure trove of information on the state of research since the late 1980s (Brown 1991: 157–201).

The advantages of these representational forms—systematic ordering, functional or systematic linking, and theoretical referencing—come with their share of disadvantages. They are longer, less lucid, and more difficult to compare than lists. Brown's narrative representation of a "universal people," for instance, is not easy to compare with Murdock's list. His ingenious chapter on a "universal folk" and his annotated reference section are often reconfigured in catalog form by other authors in application-oriented work, in popular forms of literature, and especially on the Internet. Steven Pinker has taken Brown's "universal people" and reworked the idea in order to explicate it, returning it to the form of a catalog of universals and adding some of his own items. Two different versions of the Pinker catalog now exist (Pinker 1994: 464–65; 2002: 601–8). The more recent one of 320 universals is considerably longer than the first and includes an appendix of another 42 universals that have been added since 1989. John Sherry has reworked Brown's annotated bibliography into a list of 140 universals (Sherry 1995: 288–89).

Cross-Cultural Comparison

Comparison is central to the study of universals. The relevance of comparison as a method in universal research springs directly from the definition of universals as features that occur in all cultures or in almost all cultures. This definition implies the broadest possible comparison of societies. In contrast to the daily use of the word, "compare" does not mean here "equate." Comparisons have a more open-ended meaning depending on whether sameness, likenesses, or differences in cultures have been uncovered. But any type of comparison must be based on something, must be considered from a particular time or place.

Dangers of Nostrification

A comparison is never made in a vacuum without goals or criteria, originating from nowhere. Studies in cross-cultural psychology and in the field of intercultural communication tend to emphasize differences, even though finding or identifying likenesses can be just as useful or insightful (Georgas et al. 2006: 188, 222). From another perspective, comparisons made in the framework of research into universals tend to emphasize the general or universal and ignore the particular or more specific. Early on, Malinowski criticized a universalism based on semantic equivalents (Cappai 2007: 94). Two types of psychically motivated dangers lurk in such a semantic universalism: ignoring likenesses, and making disparities seem similar, especially by universalizing the particularities of our own societies. Projection remains a constant danger. Because I speak out against the obsession for "otherness" in anthropology, I must address the additional hazard that develops in cross-cultural comparison and the related search for universals: that of equating other cultures with our own in a form of assimilation and projection, or "nostrification" (Stagl 1992; Wenzel, pers. comm., 29 May 2007; also see Pohl 1999: 30).

Simply adding up the number of times a trait or phenomenon occurs in many societies is not enough to prove its universality, as there are still too many unstudied cultures and too many problems in the data. Declarations on the existence of universals should therefore be seen as only hypotheses. We need explicitly designed comparative studies. Comparisons are never simple, as they include many potential pitfalls (Matthes 1992a; Straub 1999: 331–42; also see Srubar et al. 2005). They often become implausible because their *tertium comparationis,* or the quality of what is being compared, is never neutral but is made up of elements that are already defined. This predefined quality remains implicit, as the act of comparison involves not only the things being compared but also the nondefined criteria by which comparisons are measured (Straub 1999: 333; Cappai 2007: 95ff). Criteria arising from this universalizing way of thinking already presuppose the existence of likenesses, as they are formed by concepts and standards for describing likenesses to begin with. For example, the term "family" appears everywhere as basically the same. The complicated act of comparison is hardly possible without an initial kind of nostrification, that is, without presupposing that norms elsewhere are equivalent to our own (Matthes 1992a: 83–84, 96).

Differences are too easily reduced to a variant of a pervasive pattern that is presumed without empirical evidence to back it up. What appears different is downgraded to a marginal difference. Our norms are too quickly equated with the norms of other cultures when we confirm one by recognizing the other, creating a problem in comparative methods that is equally as problematic as the polarizing effect of magnifying the differences in cultures. Without truly recognizing it, we project our own norms and behavior onto foreign cultures. We tend to do this especially in dualistic comparisons of our own culture with one other, usually non-Western culture. Projecting aspects of our own culture onto another as a way of officially recognizing the legitimacy of others is a danger that develops in such limited comparisons. Therefore we first need comparisons that are made between many cultures, and then comparisons that are made on an intra- as well as an intercultural level.

Comparative Strategies and a Complementary Perspective

Anthropology is not the only comparative discipline within the human sciences. Comparisons are also among the fundamental tools of sociology, linguistics, and literary studies, with linguists developing a particularly distinctive form of comparative studies. Language universals are sought according to two different approaches. The first involves interpreting or considering language universals in a very concrete form, searching for them on the basis of a large number of regionally widespread languages and trying to somehow explain them. The second approach describes universals more as abstract structures, attempting to prove them within tightly delimited samples through evolutionary causal assumptions (Comrie 1989: 15). Universals are determined in general by means of a so-called typological method, an approach developed by Greenberg in the 1960s that involves examining grammatical structures cross-culturally in order to arrive at generalizations, or universal implications (Croft 2003a: 49–86, 2003b: 434; Haase 2006). The method includes three steps. First, languages are divided into types (classification). In the second step, substantiated types are compared with plausible typologies, and universals are formulated that reduce the plausible typologies to forms that have actually been found (generalization). Finally, functional causes are sought to explain the universals (explanation) (Croft 2001, 2003b: 434–35). A prerequisite to the first step is to form both variety samples—samples that increase the probability of observing worldwide diversity in grammatical variables—and probability samples, which preferably include only historically independent languages. Comparative methods are common in such areas of comparative psychology as comparative animal psychology and especially cross-cultural psychology, with its sophisticated methods, as well as in history (Vogel and Eckensberger

1988; Osterhammel 2004). But anthropology offers particularly strong comparative possibilities with a wide comparative range.

Following Cappai (2007: 95), comparisons of societies can be divided into three fundamental methods, each dealing differently with cultural differences. The first, nomological strategy is applied in experimental approaches, primarily in cross-cultural psychology. Differences are considered exceptions and have the status of falsifying elements. The second strategy uses comparisons to establish particularities as a research goal, making any reference to universals seemingly unnecessary. The third strategy regards universalizing and particularizing as complementary approaches. Cultural difference remains a separate factor, recognizable only against the backdrop of cross-cultural likenesses. In the history of research, the nomological and universalistic approaches were dominant in the 1950s and 1960s. By the mid-1970s, though, research strategies had moved to the opposite extreme, focusing on idiographic comparisons and an emphasis on differences (Cappai 2007: 95; see Acham 2001).

My research strategy follows the third, complementary form, even in this book, where I argue for a focus on universals. It corresponds well with approaches based on a moderate relativism in the tradition of Boas and Kroeber. Even Geertz used it as a method in his more programmatic works, though in complete contrast to some of his more extreme and cultural-relativistic arguments. In cross-cultural studies, a phenomenon is considered across many, or at least quite a few, cultural units. Comparative studies are possible across several levels:

- within one culture (intracultural comparison),
- between specific cultural units (intercultural comparison, or systematic case study comparison), or
- between a large number of societies (systematic, intercultural, and hologeistic comparison).

A problem arising in many cross-cultural studies concerns their limited scope. This is especially the case in numerous studies from cross-cultural psychology and in organizational studies. In these areas of research, studies done on people from non-European or non-American societies are almost always carried out on members of the middle class in urban areas, or in industrial societies (India, Japan, Korea). In contrast, the general strengths of cross-cultural approaches in anthropology are as follows: (1) they expand the empirical base beyond Western societies, (2) they address the question of which phenomena found in isolated cultures are also found elsewhere, on a wider scale, and (3) they offer an empirical basis for generalizations on human beings (Munroe and Munroe 2001: 223–26). Together, they further the inductive search for universal "candidates." We can distinguish two approaches to typological cultural comparison (Holenstein 1985b: 139) that strongly influence the different variants found in the conceptualization of universals:

1. Cultures can be distinguished through attributes that they alone possess, that is, through discrete and even exclusive attributes. Cultures then have a discontinuous relationship to each other.
2. Cultures can be distinguished by ranking attributes that are basically found everywhere. Differences are gradual, and the relationship among cultures is continuous. Attributes are not exclusive to cultures; rather, they vary in terms of their rank or status. The more prominent attributes of a culture determine the ranking of all other attributes.

This book advances the argument that the latter comparative model is the more appropriate in cases of doubt. This approach recognizes a fundamental problem in every intercultural comparison, namely, the compared cultures' delimitation as separate units (see de Munck 2000b), but does not abandon the potential of the comparative process.

Intracultural Comparison and Comparison of Societal Types

A cultural comparison can be carried out within a single culture. Such within-culture studies (e.g., Munroe and Munroe 2001: 231) are rare among the forms of cultural comparison that will be described below. One basic insight in recent anthropology is that every individual society reveals internal, or intracultural, diversity. Holenstein demonstrates, through the example of sweeping comparisons such as Western vs. non-Western, why intracultural variation in the framework of research into universals is so relevant but at the same time so little understood: "In cultural comparison, denying the existence of intercultural *in*variants is coupled with the systematic disregard of intracultural variants" (Holenstein 1985b: 104; italics mine).

The intercultural and the intracultural dimensions are compared in Table 5.4. The two stand in an orthogonal relationship to each other, as intracultural diversity is not simply a more refined form of intercultural variation. The schematic design of the figure was developed from one that refers originally to subject-relevant issues in psychology (Jüttemann 1992: 103–4). Such a refined differentiation is more useful than a simple contrasting of idiographic vs. nomothetic knowledge. Cultural phenomena, like psychic phenomena (Jüttemann 1992: 102; see Maiers 1993: 53–55), can always appear in singular, differential, and universal form.

Universality as intercultural subject matter can only refer to entire societies as units. But universality can also refer to individuals. It can take on a personal perspective, or "intracultural dimension." This is, for example, the case if universals are being identified for *Homo sapiens,* since these are universals postulated for all human beings as individuals. The following restrictions should be kept in mind: the intercultural dimension is the only dimension that extends beyond separate cultures. The intra-individual dimension summarizes descriptive and explanatory subdivisions. It is a schema that is not meant to be a subject model but to serve as a means of classification (Jüttemann 1992: 104–107).

Delimiting intracultural from intercultural comparisons is difficult because it is difficult to analytically separate ethnic communities or societies. This is particularly the case for comparisons between groups in multiethnic countries. Jere Brophy and Janet Alleman (2005) have compared, as an example, the concepts that grade-school children in the United States have of basic components of society and human activities. They named nine broadly divided features—food, clothing, shelter, communication, transport, family life, environment, money, and politics—describing them as "cultural universals" (2005: 4–6, 421–23). Given the many ways or situation-specific means of identifying people in the United States, such as both American and at the same time Hispanic, we could pose the question of whether their comparative study should be characterized as intercultural or intracultural.

A second comparative form that could provide indications of universals involves comparing societal types, meaning types of political organization and economic units, as in comparing peasant with industrial societies. Universal implications would be indicated if a certain type of society is correlated with specific features. Examples of this can be found in the anthropology of kinship and the correlation of matrilineality and matrilocality. A specific example is the similarity of specific features of music in otherwise very different egalitarian societies, or the complex economies that develop in stratified societies (Lomax 1994; Wallin et al. 2000; also see Ferraro 2001a: 338). Studies in cross-cultural psychology indicate that several aspects of the psyche have less to do with belonging to a specific culture than with types of social organization (Diener and Suh 2003; Van Hemert 2003). Systematic variations exist in modern cities with a large diversity in social partners, as well as in older, denser cities like Bhaktapur in Nepal and country settlements with intensive face-to-face relationships such as in Tonga (R. Levy 1990: 28). A further form of cultural comparison concerns large regional cultural units or historical comparison of civilizations (Osterhammel 2004: 59–63). Finally, there are transculturally conceived comparisons of structures and processes (Schulin 1974; Matthes 1992a; Weber 2001: 88–91; Srubar et al. 2005).

Table 5.4. Two fundamental dimensions of cultural variation

```
                    Generality (e.g., attributes)
                              ▲
         ┌──────────────┐
         │ Intra-cultural│──┐
         │  Dimension    │  │
         │  (Gradient of │  ▶
         │ Generalization)│
         └──────────────┘
Universality ◀─────────────────┼─────────────────▶ Singularity
(Total                         │                    (individual
population                     │     ▲              person)
of all human                   │  ┌──┴───────────┐
beings)                        │  │ Inter-cultural│
                               │  │  Dimension    │
                               │  │  (Gradient of │
                               │  │  Universality)│
                               │  └──────────────┘
                              ▼
                    Specificity (e.g., Situation)
```

Source: adapted from Jüttemann 1992: 103

Pairwise Comparison and Systematic Worldwide Comparisons

A comparison of different cultures would involve a least a single pair of cultures. At most it would include all or many cultures from a worldwide sample (i.e., a holocultural, hologeistic, or worldwide study). Even in terms of pairwise comparisons, we can draw general conclusions, as Johansen has done in a comparative study of German and Turkish attitudes toward cleanliness (Johansen 1989). However, problems of interpretation might also develop for many possible reasons, as demonstrated in a comparison of Malinowski's assertions on dreams in Tobriand and Freud's findings in Vienna. Nonetheless, single case study analyses and especially systematic case study comparisons could lead to empirically based identification of types that would represent universals of varying scope and degree. In this sense, explicitly qualitative and interpretive research contains a fundamentally comparative approach, as more recent trends in sociology and cultural psychology have demonstrated (Glaser and Strauss 1967; Boesch and Straub 2007: 31–32; Shweder and Le Vine 1984). Such research uses abductive thinking, a process that works beyond the simple difference between inductive and deductive reasoning. The fundamental methods of finding empirical evidence for universals, however, are systematic and worldwide cross-cultural comparisons (see Rokkan 1970 for a summary, but also Kaelble and Schriewer 2003; see also Giesecke 2007). Anthropologists active in this area have accurately described anthropology's central contribution as follows: "The only feasible way to find out what is true for all humans [all cultures] is to look at a representative sample of them. That is exactly what worldwide cross-cultural research does and exactly what anthropology is uniquely good for, because only anthropology provides data on thousands of different human populations, past and present" (Ember and Ember 1999: 350).

A useful database for worldwide comparison is the Human Relations Area Files (HRAF) already mentioned above. It contains primary-source and full-text documents that are carefully indexed at the paragraph level using more than 700 categories (Peregrine 2013: 408). As of this writing the database includes over 1.3 million pages of information covering more than 400 cultures and is growing by 40,000 pages a year (Bernard 2002: 483–85). The search for universals can occur, for example, by way of a worldwide sample like the Standard Cross-Cultural Sample (SCCS; Murdock and White 1969), which includes 186 well-documented, mostly nonindustrial cultures that are physically and temporally far apart. To date, 1,100 variables have been recorded, with the average observational period being the year 1860 and the *median* year being 1910 (Schweizer 1989: 481–82). Besides this sample, the Human Relations Area Files offer a wealth of different cross-cultural samples (Ember and Ember 2009: 176–84; www.yale.edu/hraf), extending from the comprehensive and ever-expanding *Ethnographic Atlas,* which as of the year 2000 recorded 1,264 cultures, a number representing one-fifth of all human societies, to the HRAF Probability Sample with only sixty recorded cultures. Important samples and databases are listed below:

- The "World Ethnographic Sample" (Murdock 1957a; 565 case studies)
- The *Ethnographic Atlas* (Murdock 1967a) in installments in the journal *Cultural Anthropology* since 1962; 1,264 cases)
- A summary version of the *Ethnographic Atlas* (Murdock 1967b; 862 cases)
- The *Atlas of World Cultures* (Murdock 1981; 563 cases)
- The "Standard Ethnographic Sample" (Naroll and Sipes 1973; 273 cases)
- The "Standard Cross-Cultural Sample" (Murdock and White 1969; 186 case studies)
- The *HRAF Probability Sample* (also called the *HRAF Quality Control Sample*; Naroll 1967; 60 cases)
- The online database eHRAF WORLD CULTURES (formerly *Collection of Ethnography*; 260 cultures)
- The online database eHRAF ARCHAEOLOGY (formerly *Collection of Archaeology*; 85 archaeological traditions; on this see Peregrine 2013: 409).

How can a systematic intercultural comparison serve empirically to test a supposed universal? The following steps are useful for such a test:

1. Establish, by perusing the literature, whether any exceptions are known for the supposed universal. If none are known, then
2. Look for a logical or theoretical reason why a supposed universal cannot be a universal. If no reason is found, then
3. Examine whether the supposed universal is verifiable in intercultural comparison from the secondary data that have undergone cross-cultural content analysis. If so, then
4. Establish that the supposed universal is in fact a near universal, and
5. Examine the data in more detail and expand the sample. If the spread of the universal is in fact limited, then the universal is more regional, such as female-headed households in the Caribbean.
6. Examine the diachronic universality.

Table 5.5. Synchronic and diachronic cultural comparison in relation to universal concepts of varying breadth

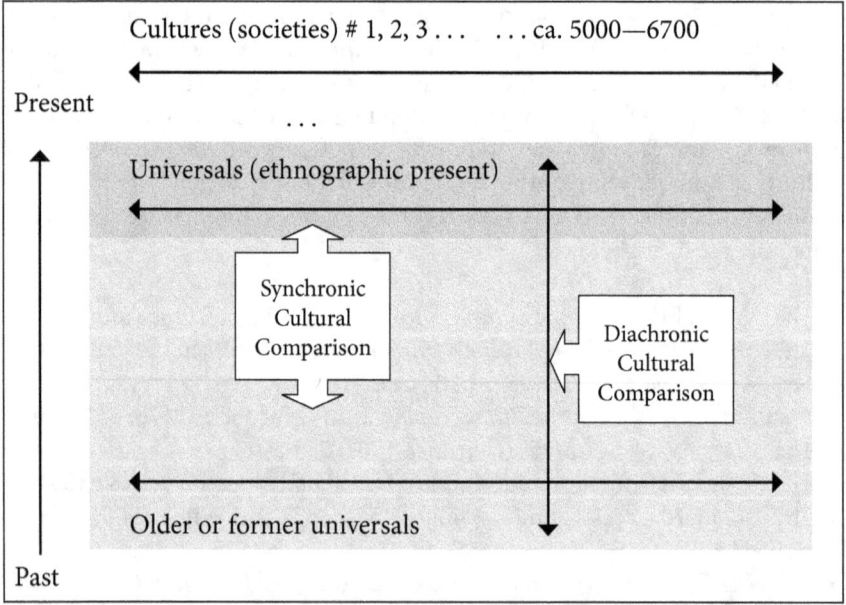

The concrete examination outlined above is problematic in three main aspects: delimiting cultural units, establishing the historical independence of the compared cases (Galton's Problem; Ember and Ember 2009: 89–81), and ascertaining the quality of the highly diverse, often sparse data. All three problems have often been discussed, but in my opinion, only the issue of useful data poses a serious problem here. Delimiting cultural units is notoriously difficult due to their nebulous borders. Societies, as collections of persons, are less amorphic than whole cultures when they are reduced to what is specifically shared among members. Pragmatic solutions to this problem are arrived at, for example, by way of languages, because not understanding a language is a clear social boundary (Ember and Ember 1999: 353–59). Quite a number of possible solutions to Galton's so-called problem are available in the process of sampling, so it represents only a slight problem for causal relationships (de Munck 2000; Ember, Ember and Peregrine 2015: 598–90).

Low data quality is mostly a factor in working with secondary data, or data collected by other researchers for other purposes. The circumstances behind the original collection of data often can no longer be examined at the time that the data is being evaluated for a more recent purpose. These difficulties increase considerably if we are searching, by means of diachronic cultural comparison, for phenomena that are not only universal in all recent cultures but in cultures from all time periods and all places (Table 5.5).

Frugal and Efficient Comparisons: The "Most Different Design"

Methodological reservations regarding empirical foundations and procedures have led the majority of researchers in anthropology to adopt more qualitative comparative approaches (Gingrich 2012) or to defy comparison altogether. All three problems seem less overwhelming when we are only dealing with a selection of a few societies in the same time period. This process or method allows us to collect primary data for a specific purpose instead of using secondary data. If we choose sample societies that are very far apart geographically and therefore unlikely to have influenced each other, or that have not been influenced by a common third party, then we might be able to find candidates for universals. The following steps make this approach simple:

1. Form a small sample of (e.g., five to ten) societies that are in every possible way different and historically independent. Galton's Problem is part of this step, though its relevance is disputed among anthropologists who work with cross-cultural studies (Schweizer 1978; Ember and Ember 2009: 89). A small, arbitrary selection makes it improbable that the cultures will, through geographic proximity, be affected by diffusion or have common historical roots.
2. Search the primary data for significant likenesses.
3. In cases of discovered likenesses, carefully draw conclusions about whether they are universals.
4. Identify or establish finely structured likenesses in order to make the universality more probable.

A classic example of the approach outlined above is a large-scale study on socialization, bonding, and child care in six societies published in 1975 ("six-culture study"; Whiting and Whiting 2014). Eibl-Eibesfeldt's human ethological studies, discussed above, were carried out using such an approach. A more recent example of the same method comes from Munroe and Munroe's (2001: 225–26) study on the effects of absent fathers. They compared 188 children in families with and without fathers present in four culturally different, spatially far-flung societies (Samoa, Belize, Kenia, and Nepal). A variant here is to mix a selection of modern and traditional societies (Ekman 1992; Walbott and Scherer 1986, 1989; Scherer et al. 2001: 81–82) or combine individuals in modern societies with other individuals from traditional societies. A recent example of this mixing strategy is the series of studies on cooperation and costly punishment by Joseph Henrich and colleagues. In this comparison of economic behavior in field experiments involving fifteen societies, the factors of environment, economic basis, and type of residence within the cultures under study were deliberately kept widespread (Henrich et al. 2006: 1768, Table 1).

Cross-Species Comparison

Diversity among the Great Apes and "Ape Universals"

Charles Darwin and Konrad Lorenz can be considered the founders of cross-species comparison. Interspecies comparisons are primarily undertaken in comparative psychology, or comparative animal psychology and behavioral science (Zuberbühler 2006). Most cultural anthropologists are very skeptical when it comes to species comparisons, but even Kroeber recommended making comparisons among animals once he became convinced of the need to search for universals (Degler 1991: 221–22). In all the subdisciplines of anthropology, there is strong resistance to working with species comparisons. This is even true for physical anthropology; primatologists in anthropology departments in the United States do not have it easy (Pavelka 2002: 27–28). While anthropologists look at cultural diversity and complexity, comparative primatologists, facing fifty primate genera and 250 very diverse species, consider more the common attributes of every single species. In general, we need to keep in mind that whereas the common attributes between species make comparison possible, the differences among species make comparison all the more interesting: "It is not in the categorical comparison of human beings with the 'animal' but in the species comparison with primates that leads to a more legitimate assertion of human uniqueness" (Kattmann 1974; similar to Bischof-Köhler 1991: 145).

With regard to the topic of universals, comparisons between human beings and other primates are of primary importance. Such comparisons are above all meaningful if the features being compared can be regarded as homologous, that is, if the causes of features are the same, occurring in a historical continuum. It must be possible to keep them separate from convergent developments, or similarities arising from different origins. In the study of features that are genetically determined, such as the characteristics of plants, and the study of culturally determined features like languages, this method has proven successful, as it also has for genealogies in comparative biology and for language families in comparative linguistics. The method is problematic for features that have a more complex origin, however (Markl 1986: 83, 2002).

In trying to understand what human beings have inherited from animals, comparisons between animals and humans must be drawn carefully regarding two points (Bischof-Köhler 1991: 145). First, analogies and homologies must be carefully distinguished from one another, as confusing them risks putting human beings on the level of the animal. Second, qualitatively different features can also be homologous if a common inheritance is concealed by species-specific modification: "We human beings and other species are both similar and dissimilar. The former is a reasonable framework for the formation of the latter" (de Waal 2001: 332). A psychologist adept in the field of biology has concluded: "The particular appeal here is in considering both possibilities in analysis when posing the question of what is specifically human, of what was qualitatively new and unique for human beings in their development out of an animal pre-form, leading them to be separate from them" (Bischof-Köhler 1991: 145).

The comparison of human beings to higher primates is the central methodological approach in all human and animal comparisons. The diversity and complexity found among the latter does pose a problem for comparison of human cultures with populations of higher primates. But all these primate groups have in common their highly complex character. Alongside the existence of ongoing conflicts, they reveal many cooperative social relationships as well in the form of alliances, common or joint hunting, cooperative efforts to defend food, food sharing, and strategies for avoiding predators (Henke and Rothe 2003: 102–3; Rothe and Henke 2005: 166–67; de Waal 2005). All societies of higher primates rely on networks of personal relationships and close ties. In all systems we find the personal knowledge of relationships with others and recognition of one's own position in the group, as well as general high social competence. Certain aspects shown in coalitions in primate societies are also found among coalitions of human groups (de Waal 2006).

The social systems of nonhuman primates are very different from each other (A. Paul 1998: 9–32, 2006: 72–78; Henke and Rothe 2003: 98–99, 2005: 168–69; Goldschmidt 2006: 16; see Boesch and Tomasello 1998; Boesch, Hohmann, and Merchant 2002; Geissmann 2003; Schlegel 2007: 228). Although both chimpanzees and bonobos live in groups with many males, their social structures differ drastically. Chimpanzees live in groups of many adult males and females that are often divided up in so-called fission-fusion groups, whereas bonobos typically live in long-lasting associations of many adult females and males with non-adult offspring, which have adult, nonrelated females and their children at their core. While cooperative male alliances are typical among chimpanzees, they are missing among bonobos. The basic unit of orangutan ties is, in contrast, the mother-child group, to which adult males do not belong on a long-term basis. Gorillas live in age-related groups with many males.

Here we face the problem of deciphering which attributes are shared among apes but not among monkeys and defining ape or great ape universals (Silverman 2002: 186; van Schaik and van Duijnhoven 2004: 169–74). Some primatologists consider it important to compare primates on a broad scale in order to be able to understand differences, for example between chimpanzees and bonobos (*Pan paniscus*), and the likenesses they both share with other apes (Strier 2001: 72; Byrne 2001: 170, Table 6.4; Pavelka 2002: 26–30; de Waal 2005; A. Paul 2006: 72–73). Other researchers go even further and regard the real Rubicon to be more between apes and monkeys than between primates and humans. They criticize the corresponding "primatocentrism." Some call for explicit comparisons to other animals, since nonprimates such as whales, birds, and rats show protocultural capacities (McGrew 2001: 232; also see contributions in de Waal and Tyack 2003). With regard to cooperative behavior, it is important to keep in mind that lions and wolves cooperate together when hunting. Homologies, or phyletic correlations, are not the only things that can be determined through interspecies comparisons. Species comparisons can explain analogies, or convergences, as due to similar environments or similar functional correlations. But in contrast to widespread assumptions, it is not only comparisons between closely related species that are useful, as Eibl-Eibesfeldt (2004: 203) has emphasized with regard to convergence research in human ethology: "The comparative study of certain phenomena in those animal groups, which are not closely related, provides information on the underlying functional aspects behind behavioural patterns."

Anthropomorphism, Embarrassing Relatives, and Ethics

Comparisons between animals and human beings always return us to the question of whether we are in fact comparing the same phenomena. This concerns not only questions of description but theoretical assumptions as well. There are risks here involving excessive anthropomorphism, on the one hand, and an exaggerated linguistic purism, on the other. As I will demonstrate more clearly in Chapter 7, there are many different levels of explanation for universals, primarily with regard to explanations involving actual mechanisms (proximate causes) and evolutionary explanations concerning adaptation (ultimate causes). The avoidance of inbreeding in animals such as insects and in humans can simultaneously have the same indirect causes (selection pressure hindering incest) but varying direct causes (scattering before mating among insects, incest taboos among humans). Incest avoidance among insects and among humans is the same phenomena and yet two different phenomena at the same time.

The question then arises of whether we should use the same term for a phenomenon occurring among both animals and humans (Sober 1993: 199–200). Incest is by definition a culturally prohibited behavior; therefore, incest among animals, in contrast to inbreeding, is a nonexistent phenomenon (Vivelo 1994: 214–19). According to the level of active behavior, one can clearly differentiate the avoidance of inbreeding as an observable individual behavior from the "incest taboo" as a social and symbolically based institution. More problematic is the choice of proper terms in more contested societal topics, such as rape. Rape can be defined social-scientifically as forced sexual violence. It can be conventionally explained by sexual urges, as an effect of the lust for power, or as injury or humiliation. There are, though, biologists who speak of rape among animals, since the term refers to forced reproduction (Barash 1979: 54–55, 69, 76). Social biologists and evolutionary psychologists point out that rape occurs in all cultures under similar conditions (Thornhill and Palmer 2000; Alcock 2006: 500). In the subsequent reassessment, many cases of forced sex among humans would not be considered rape, since rape, in general, does not lead to procreation. The ultimate social biological explanation for forced sex as a means of gaining a reproductive advantage—an explanation that has not remained uncontested among biologists (Smith, Borgerhoff Mulder, and Hill 2001: 132–33)—might be negotiated with different proximate explanations as well (Bischof 1985). The problem is mainly that choosing to describe the phenomenon as "rape" is not only a pragmatic act but one that carries with it certain ramifications. The choice of terminology, whatever the case, entails a certain danger of taking one aspect of the phenomenon, be it reproduction or power or control, and pulling it into the foreground while pushing something else into the background.

Figure 6. Banana transport in Kottayam, India. Photo by Maria Blechmann-Antweiler.

CHAPTER 6

Taxonomy
The Forms, Levels, and Depth of Universals

> *As such, universals are both
> constraining and generative.*
> —Donald E. Brown, "Human Universals"

One of the more significant problems in the search for universals is figuring out the level of abstraction at which to look for them (Greenfield 1997: 334–35). The extremely divergent points of view on whether there are only a handful or possibly hundreds of legitimate universals point to a problem connected not only with levels of abstraction but with the phenomenon of cultural diversity as well. Turning the general idea of universals into working propositions for comparative research requires that we clarify, classify, and extend the very notion of universals (D. Brown 2013: 411). In this chapter I will explore the methods used to record the manifestations and varieties of universals. How can we classify universals? What are the basic forms and the variants, and what sort of typology can we use to organize them?

Levels, Spheres, and Time Frames

Universals fall within larger cultural spheres, for example, individual behavior, social behavior, social control and upbringing, technology, and collective ideas or mindsets. John Berry (1989 with reference to Lonner 1980: 151), for example, subdivided Murdock's seventy-three universals into six preconceived categories in order to take them out of the nontheoretical alphabetical ordering of the original. From human ethology, Hinde has produced eight categories (Hinde 1994: 190). The cross-cultural psychologist Walter Lonner (1980: 150–51, Table 5-1, 167–77) has also carried out this kind of thematic subdividing or structuring. Even if most of these divisions and subdivisions are produced ad hoc, they generate some interesting questions. Why, for example, do so many universals have to do with kinship and social or sexual reproduction?

Furthermore, universals exist on varying levels and in different categories. They can be divided into levels of social complexity as individual attributes, group attributes, or attributes of social and cultural structures (Hinde 1994: 189). This book presents universals as attributes of societies (groups, communities, ethnicities, nations). Attributes that all healthy adult individuals of the species *Homo sapiens* have, that is, attributes related to species, are described here as species-specific features that are not to be equated with universals. Knowledge of these "universals of individualization" (Hejl 2001a: 51–52) is necessary for an understanding of universals. I have therefore devoted an entire chapter to this topic. But these species-specific features are not sufficient to be counted as universals. On the spectrum of universals related to individuals at one end and groups or societies at the other, the latter is the focus in anthropology. The reason for this is not that individuals do not create cultures, or that they are unimportant, but more that individuals take on culture more than they create it. Melvin Konner (2003: 440, also see 2002) drew useful distinctions among the levels described above that I have modified into the following:

(a) Attributes concerning all healthy adult *individuals* of the species *Homo sapiens*, as in upright posture or social smiling;
(b) Features of all healthy individuals in all societies from a particular age group, such as the sucking reflex in babies;
(c) Attributes in all healthy individuals in all societies and of the same sex, such as patterns of ejaculation in men;
(d) Features in all societies, but not in every individual, for example, differences between the sexes with regard to physical conflict (violence);
(e) Characteristics that occur in all societies, though sometimes rarely, such as murder, suicide, depression, incest, autism, and schizophrenia.

Universals are basically found in the final two levels.

Furthermore, the temporal continuity must be a consideration. With regard to society, Messelken (2002a: 647) has produced the following categories:

1. Features that are continually present (e.g., family)
2. Features that occur periodically (e.g., celebrations)
3. Occasional or episodic features (e.g., war)
4. Temporary features (e.g., rites or rituals)

On occasion, some authors have distinguished between universals of form and universals of function, as in what and how something is expressed (Leach 1982: 180). Also, potential universals are distinguished from actual universals, or inherent from developed universals (Redfield 1957). An important yet rarely made distinction is between emic and etic universals (see Pinxten 1976). *Emic* universals are likenesses that consist of universals from the inner perspective of cultures, while *etic* universals are likenesses that are visible from an outer perspective. For instance, religion falls under the cultural sphere and grammar is a feature of language, but they are not emically conceived. Many cultures have no word for religion. One other important distinction separates "essential universals" from "accidental universals." The former are also called "intrinsic universals" because they cannot be modified. An example of an accidental universal would probably include the Oedipus complex. It is considered a de facto universal or a near universal, but this, according to Spiro, might not be the case, since children are raised differently in different cultures. This is then an example of something likely or possible, but never proven to be fact.

Peter Hejl made a particularly important distinction in separating universals between the individual, microsocial, and macrosocial levels (Hejl 2001: 50–55). Of these three interconnected types, I will discuss the social universals only, as I have already dealt with the universals related to the individual, or as Hejl has put it, the "universals of individualization." Microsocial universals encompass, for instance, the potential for forming coalitions, and for deception and lying. The universals on this level primarily play a role in solving constantly reappearing social problems. Every kind of collective must have a means of dealing with issues of communication and coordination. The universals that belong to this group include those marking social differentiation, the creation of complex and abstract forms of communication, and systems of morality. Cognitive limitations in thinking about large collectives play a role here as features that are species-specific.

Macrosocial universals develop when new structural problems come about in societies due to changes in population size and density, or increasing complexity. New demands arise, primarily concerning procurement and coordination of resources, calling for new and specialized subsystems to be created. These systems must be autonomous yet in tune with the entire system as a whole. There are only a limited number of possible solutions to these problems of self-organization or self-regulation. The limited combinations of functional structures within complex social systems presuppose a kind of intrinsic logic, allowing for the existence of social-functional universals. The further division of systems into subsystems must be ensured through a "*Sozialsysteme zweiter Ordnung*" (secondary order social system) (Hejl 2001: 54). Prime examples of this are political institutions like those found in modern societies. Murdock has already identified general cross-cultural patterns in socially stratified systems (Murdock 1978: 157–58). Macrosocial universals are therefore "emerging" universals. Emerging, within historical processes, can mean a slow materialization or a sudden appearance of attributes on one systemic level that cannot yet be recognized on a lower level. In the social sciences, these have represented, at least since Durkheim, an important but less explored subject of study (Sawyer 2005: 63–99, 100–34). Macrosocial universals are called such because they only and always appear in large, complex societies, therefore making them universal implications. In the history of humankind their appearance coincides with the arrival of complex societies, a point that has led sociologists to describe them as evolutionary universals, a topic already discussed above. This leads on to a historically diachronic distinction of universals.

In longitudinal section, universals that occur in all cultures and in all time periods are distinct from discontinuous universals. There are also, historically understood, newly appearing universals. Fire or the use of fire did not exist in all societies known to cultural anthropology, though today its use is universal. Further examples include domestic dogs, plastic containers, and money. "The intercultural likenesses are increasing along with the global spread of technology" (Holenstein 1997: 61). This is what Eric Voegelin (2004: 178) described as "the route of experience known to all people in a commonly shared humanity" (den Erfahrungsgrund einer allen Menschen gemeinsamen Humanität). A more recent example is the basic value placed on common global knowledge and shared history, as reproduced through photography and spread across the planet via the mass media. Nowadays, (almost) all people can experience what only a few people could see in the past, such as the roundness of the earth from outer space. We can assume that deterritorialized media production—or more specifically, transcultural media markets (Hepp 2006: 129–31, 155)—will have an effect on the psyche of (almost) all human beings, even if only in specific ways. A collective consciousness shaped by images, or an "overview-effect," can thus arise in, for instance, experiencing the earth as a unique planet in the overall universe. This strengthens the universal consciousness of living in one world, a feeling that can be regarded, apart from global connectedness, as a core feature of globalization, something discussed today under the term of globality (Roland Robertson 1992: 132; Nederveen Pieterse 2015: 71; Binder 2005). Through these processes, human beings end up becoming "somehow more similar" (*etwas gleicher;* Schuster 2005: 175–77, 237; also see Goldberg 1993). The globalized world of images—as well as of technology, consumerism, tourism, and information—typically does not involve a developing universality of values (Baudrillard 2002: 155–57).

There are, though, universals that existed in an earlier time period but are no longer with us today. One of the more especially important universals of the past is high child mortality. It is relevant because it apparently helped form some basic psychic human tendencies. The same applies for the former universal of living in small groups, which shaped a great part of human evolution and is today considered in evolutionary psychology to be a core social feature in the "environment of evolutionary adaptedness" (EEA; Tooby and Cosmides

1992; Barrett, Dunbar and Lycett 2002: 12–14; Buss 2003: 72, 84; Workman and Reader 2014: 1). Inversely, knowledge of present-day universals could allow careful inferences to be made concerning the environment of evolved adaptation (Hagen 2005: 156).

Substance and Depth

A central problem in describing universals concerns matters of detail, depth, and therefore general relevance. We often simply know too little about certain widespread behavior and ideas. This problem is reflected in the characteristically cautious way sociologists and anthropologists talk about the topic, often using diffuse expressions like "somehow," "some sort of" or "some kind of" (*irgendwie,* in German). Alois Hahn (2002: 575; italics mine) reaffirms Frazer's earlier work on cross-cultural findings on concepts of death and an afterlife: "There are only a few societies known to us that do not have *some sort of* form of belief in an afterlife." Ulla Johansen (2005: 178–79), on the topic of friendliness, has determined that "there is some kind of means of greeting occurring in all societies, but smiling is more a specific type of behavior that occurs in a more limited form in human greetings."

Many authors distinguish so-called trivial from important universals as polarized forms. With regard to systems of meaning, Pascal Boyer has claimed in eloquent prose that there are such things as "rich universals." Murdock made one of the first distinctions between substance, or depth, and general relevance. He separated substantive universals, or those related to human action or behavior (Murdock 1945; similarly, see Mühlmann 1966: 20; Masson 1980: 134; Boyer 1994: 5; D. Brown 1991: 43, 2005b: 3) from formal, more profound, or processual universals. Substantial, or manifest, material universals are more empirically apparent, whereas formal universals can be comprehended only in an empirically indirect way, similar to deep grammar structure in linguistics.

Another distinction is that drawn between innate and manifest universals. The intention here is to differentiate between psychic processes on the one hand, and visible phenomena seen in behavior on the other. An example would be that the core family in the sense of a family with a mother, father, and children is, as an institution, not universal, even though it is extremely widespread. In practically all situations, it is the psychic bonding process between the social mother who in most cases is the biological mother—and the child that forms the basis of the core family and is highly universal (Bowlby 1953). Similar distinctions are made in the literature on anthropological constants. Wilhelm Emil Mühlmann (1966: 20) separates formal constants from substantive diversity: "These constants are not more than *formal* principles. Their *substance,* though, is culturally determined, or culturally specific, and therefore more strongly varied. But exactly in these variations we find the appearance of human cultural pluralism out of behavioural possibilities."

In the "Literature and Anthropology" research project at the University of Constance, Ruth Groh presents a similar point of view on formal universals within the framework of a "formal anthropology," which looks for "anthropological attributes that have a universal value, produced out of historical, cultural and social particularities" (SFB 511 2005: 44). These universals maintain a formal status, since only particularities are capable of being empirically comprehended. Boyer (1994: 12, italics mine), with his concept of rich universals, has contended from the perspective of cognitive anthropology or cultural anthropology and evolutionary psychology that "there are rich universals, *substantive or formal.*"

An almost identical distinction separating substantive universals from classificatory universals (Murdock 1945) is based on ideas in anthropology that go back to Clark Wissler or even further back to Lafitau. Substantive universals correspond with each other even in detail, whereas classificatory universals reveal only a general correspondence. Substantive universals are therefore also called specific content universals (Kluckhohn and Kroeber 1961). Murdock thought that most of the universals included in his list (Murdock 1945: 89) revealed similarities in classification but not "identities in specific cultural content." According to Murdock (1945: 90), these similarities are of a categorical type and are hardly "identities in habit" or a "specific element of behavior." According then to the present state of knowledge, the division of labor based on gender, for example, is a universal or at least a near universal. However, exactly how this division of labor is conceived or how it operates in practice is definitively not a universal. Emotional facial expression, such as in gestures of shyness, is very similar across the planet even in its details, but the occasions that evoke shyness vary greatly depending on the locality or region. In the sense of Murdock and his classificatory universals, however, it remains uncertain whether the phenomena in an *etic* classification from the side of anthropology resemble the *emic* classification of the people being studied.

Other authors separate abstract universals from concrete, or true, universals. An abstract universal, for instance the capacity to experience pain, is independent of time and space. Leach, though, speaks of abstract universals in terms of structural likenesses between societies (Leach 1982: 111). Precise distinctions among universals can be found in the empirically based naturalistic or experimental disciplines, particularly the behavioral sciences (ethology) and cross-cultural psychology. Behavioral research on humans (human ethology) has contributed to universals research by precisely distinguishing variants of universals. This is especially so in the work of Irenäus Eibl-Eibesfeldt and colleagues on explicitly cross-cultural universals. Eibl-Eibesfeldt distinguished between formal similarities and principal similarities. The former are similar even in detail. A well-known example is raising the eyebrows for approximately one-sixth of a second in greetings performed at a distance, an expression interpreted as a sign of friendliness. In contrast, principal similarities are a universal system of rules for nonverbal and verbal social interaction. An example would be greeting rituals, which Eibl-Eibesfeldt reterms as a "universal grammar" and equates with deep structures (1986: 88–89).

In transculturally cross-cultural psychology, more precise distinctions are made here and there, whereas hardly any distinction is made between universals on an individual level and universals on a cultural level. Walter J. Lonner, who as founder of the *Journal of Cross-Cultural Psychology* has strongly influenced the search for psychic universals, distinguishes between seven forms of universal in a well-known typology (Lonner 1980, 2005: 23):

1. Simple universals, such as the fact of sexuality in human groups;
2. Variform universals, which vary in scope, intensity, and frequency, such as aggression, which always occurs but not at the same time everywhere;
3. Functional universals, that is, phenomena that have similar social effects but are locally modified, such as the punishment of children;
4. Diachronic universals, which are temporally invariant but interpreted differently, such as the blacksmith of yesterday and the rocket engineer of today;
5. Ethologically oriented universals, which are evolutionarily based, such as facial expressions indicating emotion;
6. Systematic behavioral universals, that is, subcategories of the psyche; and last but not least, and nicely phrased by Lonner,
7. Cocktail-party universals—phenomena that humans share but that are impossible to measure, such as feeling similar things without knowing why.

Whereas Lonner's typology blends different criteria (e.g., causes or variance), Van de Vijver and colleagues (Van de Vijver and Poortinga 1982: 389–93; Van de Vijver and Leung 1997; Van de Vijver, Chasiotis, and Breugelmans 2011) differentiate types of universals according to a special feature—the degree of psychometric precision in comparability—and have come up with four levels of universals. According especially to the degree of possible empirical controls, they distinguish between (1) conceptual universals, (2) weak universals (or "functional equivalents"), (3) strong universals (or "metric equivalents"), and (4) strict universals (or "scalar equivalents") (Van de Vijver and Poortinga 1982: 388–91). Conceptual universals operate on an abstract level without measurability; examples include the "psychic unity of human beings" (Boas, Kroeber) or the modal personality. Consequently, conceptual universals cannot be falsified based on empirical information alone. Weak universals are functional equivalents to which measurable procedures apply and for which construct validity has been accepted to the extent that proof of validity is not considered necessary. This is the implicit acceptance that holds, for example, for the basic concepts in textbooks. Strong universals are scalar in that they have the same metric in all societies and are therefore metric equivalents, though they do not always have the same scalar origins. Strict universals have the same metric *and* the same scalar origins in all societies, and are therefore scalar equivalents. They require instruments that allow for full score equivalence. Berry et al. (2011: 289) has properly emphasized that this typology once more shows how absurd the dichotomy is between universals and cultural particularities.

Degree of Universality

A unicate (one case) and a full universal are separated by a continuum. Some universals are more widespread than others, with a distinction currently being made between true and near universals. True universals involve features occurring in all (known) societies, so they are also called absolute universals. I would refrain from using the latter term, since universals are phenomena with frequency and therefore cannot be equated with absolutes in the philosophical sense. The term near universal (or semi-universal; Welsch 2006: 144) delineates phenomena found in almost all cultures, such as keeping domestic dogs. These near universals are known to be such, whereas the formulation "x is universal or near universal" is used to cautiously hedge claims of universality, since it is often difficult to be certain that something exists in all known societies (D. Brown 2013: 412). Near universals can be described as highly probable cross-cultural invariants. An example of such usage appears in a widely used American college textbook on cultural anthropology, which states that "it is not just true that hunting is *universally* a male activity" and gives examples of hunting women. The authors argue that such cases do not prove the "Man the hunter" image entirely wrong, since "these patterns are not *universal* but they are *widespread* enough that many anthropologists believe that there must be some physical differences between men and women that are relevant to explaining them" (Peoples and Bailey 2015: 252, italics original).

Following D. Brown, and analogous to the significance in statistical tests, 95 percent prevalence indicates a near universal. The exact determination always contains a quantum of subjectivity. Boyer (1994: 5) speaks of recurring cross-cultural or synchronic patterns, and John Dupré (2003: 100) of "almost universal culturally evolved human universals," while Ehrlich (2002: 12, 72) describes them as "virtually universal" and "near-universal aspects." In Ehrlich (2002: 122) and in Charles Hockett's catalog of universals—which I analyze below—they are described as "widespread similarities" (Hockett 1973: 276–78; see Gaskell and Fraser 1990: 3). They are also described as "regularities" or "generalities" in some cases, as in Mühlmann's (1966: 19) discussion of abstracted constants "that can be found in practically all cultures" or, in the case of a cultural anthropologist of ethnocentrism, as follows: "virtually all human groups find it easy to consider other human social groups to be inferior or not quite human" (Dissanayake 1992: 16). The anthropologist Kottak (2008: 54, 284, 699) has defined near universals as "regularities that occur in different times and places, but not in all cultures ... cultural pattern of trait that exist in some but not in all societies ... common to several but not all human groups," and the cognitive cultural philosopher Boyer (1994: 9) refers to a "repertoire of salient ideas, which tend to be found in many different cultures yet are not necessarily present in any given cultural environment."

The tentative proof of absolute ubiquity—tentative, considering the fragmentary nature of our knowledge of all the cultures in the world—is important in the long term but not prerequisite for raising theoretically interesting questions or issues. Near universals are more than adequate: "a near universal is universal enough" (D. Brown 1991: 44). Domesticated dogs are not found in 5 percent of all known societies, but the other 95 percent can say quite a bit about human beings' general relationship to dogs. Fear of the "evil eye" occurs across the board in cultures throughout the world. Although some societies are known not to have a connection to this phenomenon, its pervasiveness is enough to make it an elucidatory fact (Hauschild 2005: 71–74). A phenomenon that occurs quite often, like the animal groom story with its 1,500 variations the world over (Burkert 1996: 69–71), is also enough to raise questions related to universals.

In this book, universals are not, as already argued in the first chapter, understood as absolutes but rather as features that are found in all known, or in many, societies. The term is used in a sense similar to that of the term statistical universal, which is a feature that falls short of near universality but occurs in unrelated societies at a frequency well above chance (Greenberg 1975, Greenberg, Ferguson, and Moravcsik 1978; Hogan 1997: 228–29; Brown 2005b: 2). An example would be the word used for the pupil of the human eye. Despite all the possibilities one could imagine in naming this part of the eye, in one-third of the languages of the world the pupil has a name that is similar to "small person." One-fifth of the world's languages describe the arm muscles with names of small animals (e.g., *muscle* in English comes from the Latin *mus* for small rodent; Brown and Witkowski 1981). This example shows that a very widespread feature can be important for research into universals, even if the feature are not, strictly speaking, a universal.

An inherent problem in research is that the degree of universality is dependent upon the content, or relevance, of the phenomenon in question as well as its definition. An example here would be incest as act and incest taboos or prohibitions in general. One must be very specific about what is meant by incest in order to examine exactly how universal it is. Determining how ubiquitous incest is as a form of deviant behavior depends upon the definition of incest, for example, on whether we are speaking of sexual intercourse, marriage, or reproduction. If incest is defined as close relatives producing offspring, then it occurs less often than it would if it were defined as sex between relatives (Sober 1993: 199; also see Turner and Maryanski 2005). Incest is still rarer if it means marriage between persons who are emically understood as closely related. These distinctions factor into determination of the universality of incest taboos, an area where the need to observe the perimeters carefully has led to the careful formulations currently used in research today: in all societies it is forbidden for "close kin" to be sexual partners. Or expressed differently: there is no known society where sexual intercourse is allowed with all persons (categories) who are considered to be close kin (similar to Lévi-Strauss on marriage; Lévi-Strauss 1949: 12–13). A second example is linguistic marking, mentioned earlier in the text. The process of marking is an absolute universal. In practice, though, it takes on several variants, one being the word or syllable complement, which is so widespread that we can speak here of a near universal. Accordingly, Bruner distinguishes between process universals and product universals (Bruner 1981: 256). It is to be expected that there are far fewer real process universals than product universals.

Conditional Universals and Other Specific Forms

Linguists are especially known for distinguishing between different kinds of universals using a specific terminology to name various forms (see Holenstein 1985b: 126–28 for a summary). Implicational universals (or universal implications) are if/then universals in the following form: if A occurs, then B will always exist. This implies a correlation but not necessarily causality. Here I can return to two examples mentioned earlier. If a society shows a preference for one hand, as many Western societies do, then it is always the right hand (D. Brown 2005a: 2). If cultures have rites of passage (which are very widespread but probably not an absolute universal), then boys are always more likely to undergo these rites than are girls (Sommer 1992). Universal implications are weaker than absolute universals, since their existence depends on the presence of other features with which they are causally linked. These kinds of universals are also called conditional universals (vs. unlimited universals), implicational universals, or constraints. They consist in a relationship between two similar characteristics, meaning that if one feature occurs in a society—a feature that itself is not a universal—then another will always be found in that society as well, but not vice versa; that is, they are unidirectional. If condition A exists, then B occurs regularly as well; meanwhile, A is not an individual, a society, a language, or even a universal.

Implications, another universal form, are bidirectional and are also known as "restricted equivalences." A language only has a form of *dual* (i.e, a specific plural of two) if it also has an inexact plural form, but the plural form also exists in languages that do not have a dual plural form, as in German. Quite often there are hierarchical chains of such implicative constraints, for example in terms of number in the series quadral > trial (paucal) > dual > plural > singular (Holenstein 1998a: 245; "Sprachuniversalien" 2008). Early on, Malinowski (1935: 625) described (though without using the term) another example of a universal implication with, in this case, two preconditions: the institution of gardening is widespread throughout the world, or everywhere where there is arable land and the social level is complex enough to permit its existence.

The emphasis in universal implications rests on the objective correlation of attributes (Holenstein 1985b: 127). To determine that centralized rule proves to exist in all societies with asphalt streets is to make a connection between a relative statement and a universal observation. A similar statement would be that agricultural societies are often associated with polygyny. It is important to note that we are speaking here of empirically observed implications, not those that are deductively or abductively determined. The causal link behind the association could be that women's contribution to farming and private property can be assured through the marriage of children to economically equal partners (Schweizer 1989: 471). Cross-cultural research is particularly useful in determining such links or correlations when the research looks into correlations between a small number of selected dimensions in a widely distributed sample of local communities (see Hunt 2007: 8; for an example, see Valdés-Pérez and Pericliev 1999).

A special form of universal implications combines a statistical universal and a universal implication: if a feature A occurs, then there is a tendency for feature B to develop. Many cross-cultural generalizations in anthropology take this form, such as statements on the presence of certain kinship terms in matrilineal societies. These statements are not often brought into association with the topic of universals because they are of a statistical nature. A further variant of universal implications is the "universal evolutionary sequence," which states that after a certain developmental phase A, a complex B will occur. Such statements are often made in theoretical or descriptive frameworks according to unilinear sequences, as in the following implication: if a society has C, then it also has B, and with B it also has A, though the reverse does not necessarily hold true . The trivial example of locomotives can illustrate this. Locomotives have existed everywhere since the invention of the wheel. One must be careful here, as this does not necessarily mean that the wheel had to have been invented in every society where we find locomotives. The possibility of diffusion means an invention can be created in one place and then borrowed. This works phylogenetically as well as ontogenetically. The plural form *dual*, mentioned above, indicating the existence of an imprecise plural form, and an imprecise plural indicating the existence of a singular form is another example (Holenstein 1985b: 126–27). Finally, there can also be special or unique forms of universals in a "universal pool of elements," as when, for example, many kinship terminologies can be described by way of very few elements, such as sex, generation, and collateral lines.

All these distinctions in universals are seldom made or maintained in the literature outside of the field of linguistics (but see, in contrast, Roughley 2000). They are, however, of prominent importance not only for scholars of universals but also for those who are critical of them. Failing to distinguish among levels (individuals, populations, cultures) often leads to an exaggerated dichotomy between relativistic and universalistic interpretations. To make this clear, I can name the example of cross-cultural research on conceptions of the self, an area of research empirically studied above all in cross-cultural psychology and ethnopsychology through two opposing interpretive approaches. The dominant, cultural relativistic approach is presented in the form of "outside" theories (de Munck 2000a: 59). Accordingly, societies are regarded as quasi agents that, through symbols, structures, and socialization practices, lead more or less to unified psychic configurations of individuals in a culture. By contrast, the alternative approach of "inside" theories argues that individual experiences form not only subjective experience but concepts of the self as well. These theories furthermore assume that these concepts of self vary according to context. One would then expect that individuals who have similar experiences also have similar concepts of self. This does not mean drawing a cultural relativistic conclusion, as Dorothy Holland (1997) has shown. She has plausibly argued that there could be commonalities between certain individuals that go beyond cultural and social boundaries, and that exactly these commonalities could indicate other universal features of the psyche. This example clearly shows how important it is to draw analytical distinctions between different basic forms and variants of universals, not only in matters of description but also in terms of interpretation. Universal implications are especially interesting in the way they open up so many questions about the causes behind them.

Relations between Basic Anthropological Orientations

Binary Systems and Distorted Isomorphisms

Scientific discussion concerning universals must confront two key obstacles: dualistic thinking, often formulated through simple dichotomies; and the tendency to draw parallels between varying dichotomies pertaining to different phenomena. Joining these obstacles in a two-step process produces cascades of vague or unclear formulations. Geertz offers a characteristic example of this in his argument against universals, objecting at one point to delineating aspects of human culture but at the same time referring to the problem of drawing a line "between what is natural, universal and constant in man and what is conventional, local and variable" (1965: 96). One would tend to agree with this initially, but understanding universals as embodied in nature and natural structures is not untenable, according to today's knowledge from evolutionary biology, biological philosophy, and philosophical anthropology.

Naturalistic assumptions about reality are often associated with natural scientific knowledge and practices or procedures, whereas culturally scientific ontic realities are equated with epistemic knowledge and methods. Here we find certain affinities, since the choice of methods is oriented (ideally) along assumptions about reality and perceptibility. But by no means is there a necessary relationship between the two (Thies 2004: 116; Lemke 2006: 27). This is similarly true when naturalism is equated with conservative or right-wing ideology and culturalism with left-wing politics. Finally, and crucially for the subject matter of this book, a universalistic perspective is not necessarily naturalistic, exactly as a culturalistic attitude must not be only particularistic in its search for specialities: "Human beings resemble one another not only through nature but also through culture, just as natural as well as cultural factors may determine the differences between human beings" (Thies 2004: 116).

Flawed isomorphisms between dualisms greatly hinder the discussion on universals. Tables 6.1 to 6.3 contrast ideal cases of polarities, including examples that expose the severe isomorphic assumption between them. Each of the three isomorphisms plays a role in the anthropological debate. Especially the third case is of particular relevance for cultural anthropology and the discussion on universals. In the debate currently underway in cultural anthropology, particularistic approaches are compared with generalizing approaches, while constructivist and realist approaches are contrasted. It is assumed that realism is isomorphic with generalization, and that particularism has a similar relationship to a constructivist approach. This neglects the point that constructiv-

Table 6.1. Critique of isomorphism 1: Missing parallels between ontics and epistemics, i.e., methodology (shaded = ideal-typical positions)

		Ontics (assumed existence of things)	
		Naturalism: Human as natural being (according to critics: "biologism")	Culturalism: Human as cultural being (according to critics: "culturalism")
Epistemics, Methodology	Natural scientific	Physicalistically oriented human geneticists	Cultural behaviorism, e.g., Watson
	Cultural scientific	Cultural and social scientists with naturalistic anthropology	Interactionist social scientists (hermeneutics)

Table 6.2. Critique of isomorphism 2: Missing parallels between ontic and political positions (shaded = typical-ideal positions)

		Ontics (Assumed existence of things)	
		Naturalism: Human as natural being ("biologism" ")	Culturalism: Human as cultural being ("culturalism")
Political position, ideology	Conservative, "right wing"	Racism, social Darwinism, e.g., Lorenz	Conservative culturalists, e.g., Gehlen; e.g., Skinner
	"left wing"	Leftist social Darwinism, leftist scholars, e.g., Chomsky (vs. Skinner); e.g., Gould	Leftist cultural critics, e.g., the Frankfurt School

ism can be universalistic as well. Instead of seeing construction as only social, or cultural, one could speak of heterogenic forms of construction (Hejl 2001; see also Griffiths 1997; Hacking 1999; Searle 2010: 19–24). Widespread flawed isomorphism intensifies the already deep chasms existing within cultural anthropology as well as between cultural anthropology and other academic fields. Forming parallels as such is incorrect, but at the same time both defenders and detractors of academic fields use parallels, as Strathern has demonstrated (1995: 175).

Since this confusion has broadened in both research into universals and criticism of this research, Table 6.4 illustrates that this uncertainty is based

Table 6.3. Critique of isomorphism 3: Missing parallels between ontics and perspectives relating to diversity (shaded = ideal-typical positions)

		Ontics (assumed existence of things)	
		Naturalism: human as natural being ("biologism ")	Culturalism: Human as cultural being ("culturism")
Methodology, Perspective	Universalist: equality, similarity	Genetic unity of humanity (genome, genetic code), e.g., one aspect of the Human Genome Project	Diffusion universals, e.g., cooking food Functional universals, e.g., short paths to goals
	Particularist: difference, particularities	Genetic uniqueness of each individual (with the exception of identical twins); population differences (clines)	Culturally and historically related particularities or diversities

on two independent dichotomies. To highlight this association, the figure is in many other respects greatly oversimplified. In fact, it is not concerned with polarities but with continuums. Cultural phenomena, like psychic material or matters, appear not only in the singular (in the form of "person" within a society) or in a universal form, but differentially as well (Jüttemann 1992: 21, 102, Chap 5 this volume).

Generalization and specification stand in an intrinsic relationship to each other (K. Müller 1997b: 28; also see Doise 1990: 144–46). In the same way that studies on specific cultures are used to form generalizations for many or all other cultures, so are studies on specific cultures generated from information from only a few persons or from a sample of persons and interpreted as representing persons not specifically studied or entire cultures (Rippl and Seipel 2008: 55). Cultural anthropologists who seek universals cannot ignore the use of the individual case study. At the same time, clearly articulated particularistic or perspectivistic approaches cannot avoid making generalized assumptions, since they are not designed simply to produce idiosyncratic work. Strathern demonstrates this in three examples (1995: 176–78). In Table 6.5, I have used arrows to mark these movements from a generalized to a particularistic perspective and vice versa. Melford Spiro has argued against Malinowski and for the universality of the Oedipus complex. However, he does this primarily through ethnographic descriptions in specific cases to show the invariants that make the Oedipus complex necessary.

At the other end of the theoretical spectrum, Michael Jackson, an anthropologist with a phenomenological orientation, has emphasized the sensual and physical dimension of culture. He attacks superorganic theories of culture and approaches his work through his own personal experiences with hatha yoga (Jackson 1989). He forms his arguments using phenomenological and therapeutic concepts that he considers to be universal, such as mimetic use of the body as a means of understanding (bodily empathy) as well as general categories such as initiation rituals for girls. Lila Abu-Lughod has argued against culturalistic and orientalizing texts that "freeze" and thereby solidify strangeness as immovable or nonretractable. She calls for a particularistic cultural anthropology through personal experience in order to represent the specific living conditions of human beings more concretely. But despite her critique of generic concepts, like Jackson, she tends to use general assumptions such as categories of "familiar" or concepts such as polygamous marriage (Abu-Lughod 1991: 149).

Universalism versus Relativism and Absolutism

The systematization described above places universals in a dichotomous format. The binary poles thus produced are completed differently, and the polarities form in some ways an orthogonal relationship to one another. From this viewpoint, the distinction between universalism and relativism as opposite poles is relatively simple. A ternary form, though, is more useful. In it, universalism is contrasted with relativism and also with absolutism (Berry ,Poortinga, and Pandey 1997; Adamopoulos and Lonner 1994: 130; Lonner 2005: 16). An absolutist position assumes that a phenomenon such as "honor" is in principle qualitatively the same in all cultures and can therefore be determined in a context-free manner. Such phenomena could then be understood

Table 6.4. Independent dimensions that are inaccurately discussed as isomorphic in cultural analysis (simplified polarized representation of continua).

	Realism, materialistic approach	
Universals, Universality – generalization – metanarratives – general knowledge – science	⬅ ➡	Particulars, Singular – perspectivism – contextualism – local knowledge – humanities
	Constructivism interpretative approach (ideational, idealist)	

Table 6.5. Localizing universals research with regard to constructivist approaches among cultural theorists and (in parentheses) anthropologists.

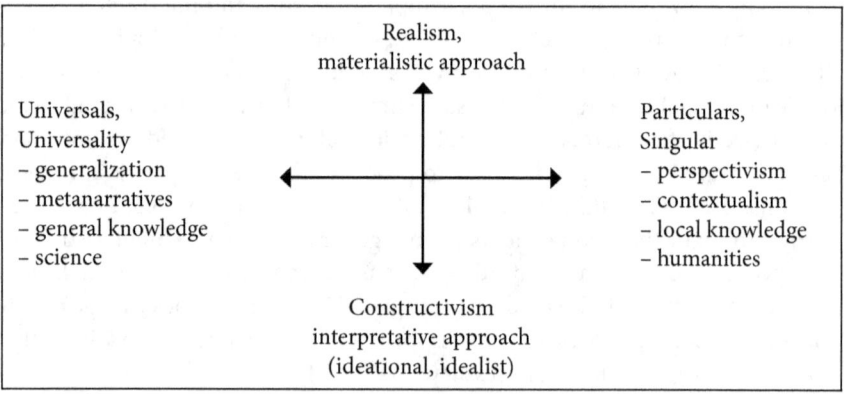

Source: inspired by text in Strathern 1995: 175–77, see text for details

through a simpler and empirically standardized approach, without the need for cultural-specific interpretations. Comparisons appear nonproblematic and produce quantitative differences. The relativist perspective holds that a culturally specific context is of central importance and tries to represent cultures in terms of their own concepts and values. As for the use of comparisons, they are generally feared to lead to ethnocentric distortions and therefore are best avoided.

Above all, the willingness to draw or make comparisons is what separates universalism from relativism. Meanwhile, due to its name alone and to the comparative approach involved, universalism is often falsely associated with absolutism. But counter to absolutism, it is principally open both to culture as the mechanism producing diversity and to the discovery of specific cultural features along with universals.

A universalistic position then lies between the two extremes. It assumes that there are fundamental phenomena and processes that are basically the same in all cultures and for all people, as members of the same species, but recognizes how these features vary according to cultures operating within separate societies. Metaphorically speaking, we are considering variations on the same human themes. Universalism thus defined rejects absolutism as a theoretically naïve form of universalism. The culturally specific context must be considered during the collection of data and their subsequent interpretation.

The differences between universalism, absolutism, and relativism are primarily discussed in transcultural psychology (Berry et al. 2011: 4–5, 429; Poortinga and Van Hemert 2001: 1003–5; Lonner 1993: v, 2005: 16–17; Straub and Layes 2002: 344–45; Berry and Poortinga 2006: 54–56; Chasiotis 2007: 204–5). Study results concerning Western cultures, when used in studies on non-Western cultures, could contribute to our knowledge of universals. And yet, when such replication fails, the failure, along with the understanding of methodological mistakes, can lead to the development of theories that communicate how variants can indicate universals that are not obvious or apparent (Smith and Bond 1993: 47). This would be a more productive attitude than that derived from a purely emic approach, which leaves cultural comparison and the search for universals by the wayside. As to methodology, instead of an imposed etics that incorporates an absolutist approach, the methods used should allow for comparisons and the possible determination of universals but at the same time consider and respect local circumstances and concepts (for "derived etic" see J. Berry 1989; Berry et al. 2011: 23–24; for the transfer and test approach see Lonner 2005: 17; also see Rippl and Seipel 2008: 45–46). This useful maxim is now being followed in some projects grounded in cultural comparative social psychology. Consequently, in ever more studies outside researchers are cooperating with those from within the cultures being studied as a means of "decentering" the conceptual field (Smith et al. 2006: 23–26).

Figure 7. Electrical engineer in Hong Kong, China. Photo by Maria Blechmann-Antweiler.

CHAPTER 7

Toward Explanation
Why Do Universals Exist?

> *Appearances are deceptive.*
> —Edmund Leach, *Social Anthropology*

The possible causes behind pancultural patterns are not limited to the two popular explanations of human nature or worldwide cultural contact and diffusion. Quite a few explanations can be given, though only a few might feasibly account for their existence. This chapter should make clear that obvious and less obvious features specific to the human species ("uniformities that come from being a single species": Boehm 1992: 743) represent one, and only one, important cause behind universals on the level of culture. The fundamental explanations discussed below are often regarded as alternative interpretations. In earlier chapters we have seen that universals occur in different realms. These phenomenal realms have significant bearing on how each universal is to be explained, that is, how it originated and is reproduced (D. Brown 2013: 413). Distinguishing amongst various levels of explanation allows us to better understand how these explanations actually complement one another. Before systematically discussing these interpretations—all the while asking which of them in fact compete with and which complement each other, and how—I will begin by examining various pitfalls that one comes across in universal research.

Ten Pitfalls in Research and in Anti-universalism

A problem already mentioned a number of times already concerns falsely equating universal features on the level of culture with universal characteristics on the level of the individual. This assumption often leads to a faulty conclusion that can then be used as an argument against the existence of universals. Some allege, for example, that to say religion is a cultural universal means that each and every human being must be a believer because each and every human being is a member of some particular culture (a "fallacy of division"; Lett 1997: 65). The faulty conclusions described below, in tabular and then in question-and-answer format, are found in more universalistic work as well as in work that is particularist, and occur more among biology-oriented authors than cultural scientists (Table 7.1) The same, I am sure, can be found in a few places in this book as well.

Table 7.1. Faulty assumptions and causal reasoning found in research on universals

1. To assume particularity and universality are exclusive and exhaustive dimensions of culture
2. To reason from the influence of context to universals or to triviality
3. To focus on total or absolute universalism
4. To attribute commonalities to biotic causes and differences to cultural causes
5. To equate universal processes with invariant results
6. To reason from universality to uniform causes
7. To reason from ubiquity to genetic causes
8. To reason from universality to functionality and from adaptation to genetic causes
9. To reason from evolutionary genesis to universality
10. To regard nature and nurture dichotomous as dichotomous causal factors

1 Particularism and Universalism: Does One Preclude the Other?

When social scientists want to explain the state of a culture at one particular place and time, they often see two causes at work: universal attributes associated with the human being, the mind, or the society; and specific historical or traditional attributes of the group being examined. Anthropologists concentrate almost exclusively on the latter causal framework. This duality of factors conceals two underlying, often implicit assumptions. First, it is often thought that each causal explanation rules the other out. Accordingly, no specific feature of culture can work in both frameworks. They form not only a duality or a polarity, but also a dichotomy. Second, both frameworks are exhaustive. They are assumed in themselves to be enough to explain all features of a culture (for a critical perspective, see Boyer 1994: 4–5). Consequently, the process of the passing on of culture is seen as completely specific to a given culture. Thus it remains unclear why some cultural patterns are diachronically more stable than others. If individuals have certain attitudes that their forebears also had, these attitudes could indicate traditional norms and values as well as universal cultural attributes. Boyer presents an interesting analogy. Giraffes are similar to whales in that they sexually reproduce. Otherwise, they are very different species. It is, however, the shared mechanism of sexual reproduction that creates new giraffes from existing giraffes and new whales from existing whales, while leaving both very different from each other.

2 Does the Influence of Context Imply Triviality in a Universal?

This faulty conclusion is based on a pre-theoretical relativism. If anthropologists identify, for example, the occurrence of similar ideas or practices, they often argue that the occurrence only at first appears to reveal similarities or likenesses, and that the differences, which are deeper and more relevant, are hidden behind superficial parallels. The ideas and practices are in fact different, because they are lived out in different cultural contexts. Therefore, any supposed universals are at best trivial. However, as the following example from Boyer (1994: 6–7) will show, this is indeed a faulty conclusion. The near universal religious concept of believing that a special medium is necessary in order to communicate with distant gods can, of course, have very different meanings in different cultural contexts, and can also imply completely different consequences, depending on whether or not one believes in something. But the fact remains that the concept of privileged individuals having special access to the gods is everywhere the same, and anything but banal. Although it is a plausible idea that each person could be a medium, or channel to the gods, but every day a different medium, an anthropologist would see it as extremely far-fetched. The important question here is why the idea of privileged media is so widespread, compared to other possible ideas. The explanation could be the same for all cultures. Too often we find the reverse, that is, the frequent mistake of attributing great difference to behavior that, upon closer inspection, turns out to reveal similarities among cultures. A well-known textbook example of this are the very different gestures for yes and no used by, for example, people in Mediterranean cultures and people in Western Europe, between whom the same gesture can have completely opposite meanings. Detail analyses in cultural ethology have shown, however, that the details of these differences are more superficial than are the underlying similarities found in the gestures (Holenstein 1985b: 142–43).

3 Does the Search for Universals Require Concentrating on Absolutes?

Absolutely not! Universality is often equated with absolute universality. In this book, I have elaborated an argument that universals are clearly not absolutes. Universal questions arise when a feature is found to occur frequently, or if variance comes about in a nonarbitrary manner. A few cases that in fact equate the two could be relevant to the search for universals. The many cultural similarities between complex cultures in the Old World before 1492 and pre-Columbian cultures such as the Maya, Aztecs, or Incas are too numerous to be random coincidences (Wissler 1965: 73–98; Goldenweiser 1922: 235–70; Harris 1999: 15–16). We could be looking in part at universal implications, such as the unavoidable consequences arising out of the growth of state territory or out of the increased complexity in societies—for example, the demand for a written language for purposes of both administration and the passing on of traditions.

4 Do Commonalities Arise from Biotic Causes and Differences from Culture?

When we discover the universal occurrence of a certain characteristic in human cultures, we often look at human nature to explain it (e.g., Izard 1994). This faulty use of parallelism appears not only in criticism of universal approaches but also in their defense. The widespread notion that we can separate human phenomena into universal and variable aspects and then explain the universal through biology and the variable through culture lies behind this problematic parallelism. In light of research on emotions, Griffiths has shown how wrong it is to associate each variation of a phenomenon with "culture" and thereby rule out the possibility of biotic causes (Griffiths 1997: 160–61). Conversely, not all universal behavior can be regarded as a manifestation of universal human nature: Many phenomena grow out of the interaction between general attributes of the mind, general attributes of the body, and general attributes of the world (Pinker 2002: 55).

Quite a number of widespread cultural phenomena refer to universal needs or functional correlations. Their ubiquity demands no explanation by way of natural selection. This does not mean that they should be exclusively identified with culture or cultures, but rather that they could be completely or partially explained through culture. Evolution requires genetic variation as material, and if genes can explain likenesses they can also explain differences, which shows how critically important the difference is between inborn variation and inborn universals (Pinker 2002: 145–46). Horgan (2001) points out that this equating of likenesses with biology and differences with culture could have a political basis among the evolutionary psychologists, who then could defend a liberal (i.e., European liberal) position in which observed differences between people and populations are considered solely environmental. A correlation between specific behavioral differences and certain genetic differences can be very difficult to prove, but that does not mean such a correlation is impossible.

5 Do Universal Mechanisms Imply Invariant Results, and Vice Versa?

A widespread argument contends that human nature can only be manifested in universal features associated with the species. Accordingly, everything not universal is to be distinguished from human nature. Here we are distinguishing between cultural invariants on the one hand, which cannot be explained by culture, and everything else that is variant on the other, meaning everything that is not universal or that can be explained by culture, that is, everything that is ecological, evolutionary, or psychological. The underlying basis here is a mixture of processes and their effects or outcomes. But what we need to remember is that universal processes do not and must not necessarily lead to the same results (Boyer 1994: 7). The mechanisms involved in organic evolution provide an appropriate example. Evolution can produce features that are highly reactive to environmental influences. An approach that could properly explain universals must then show how limitations in plausible diversity also refer to fully realized diversity in an interaction of general mechanisms under varying circumstances. This holds true for both synchronic universals and temporally stable patterns. Pancultural phenomena and stable cross-generational patterns can be sensitive to environmental influences. Such influences can be seen in individual human development, as humans inherit not only their genes but also their social environment. The stable development of individuals over generations is based on a "system of development" in which genes are integrated within structural contexts and passed on through parents and other social partners (Griffiths 1997: 61). Humans inherit genes and cultural traditions at the same time.

6 Can Universality Be Traced Back to a Single Uniform Cause?

This faulty conclusion is structurally similar to the one described directly above. A universal does not have to have a genetic cause. It need not have an underlying single cause at all. It must not be explained in a generative way because it does not have to be based on one single mechanism. This holds true particularly for widely recurrent universals, or near universals. The existence of the universally recognized fact among humans that organisms grow and then at some point die does not require explanation by way of any specific mechanism. It is simply based on the point that humans encounter conditions that could be different, that are contingent but are de facto similar, or, as Boyer states, are "contingently similar conditions of existence" (Boyer 1994: 13).

7 Do Pancultural Patterns Imply Genetic Causes?

Associating universal distribution with genetic causes is a widespread pitfall in universals research that is common among social biologists as well as other researchers (e.g., Burkert 1996; D. Brown 1991; Sanderson 2001: 125; for a critical perspective, see Degler 1991: 323; Hauser 2007: 164). Even biologists who are not oriented along social biological lines often assume that behavior apparent in all individuals of the same species could not have been learned or be a matter of culture. De Waal has critiqued this equating of species-specific with biologically determined in the field of primatology, providing a counterexample of learned matrilineality among the macaques (de Waal 2001: 267). Both proponents and critics of biotic factors (evolutionary or genetic) are likely to draw similarly false conclusions based on genetic causation. Wilson has tempered the existence of similarities between cultures by remarking that genes hold culture on a leash. In a manifesto against such positions that is a well-known attack on human social biology, Stephen Jay Gould makes the same faulty conclusion with regard to biotic universals: "We are not denying that there are genetic components to human behavior. But we suspect that human biological universals are to be discovered more in the generalities of eating, excreting, and sleeping than in such specific and highly variable habits as warfare, sexual exploitation of women and the use of money as a medium of exchange" (Gould 1976, quoted in Pinker 2002: 122).

Speaking about Devendra Singh's research project on notions of beauty, John Horgan has similarly argued that what matters is finding out whether men reveal certain universal *and therefore* inborn sexual preferences (Horgan 2001). But universality, or pervasiveness alone, is not sufficient proof that a feature, such as an ability, is inborn. Even with regard to nonhuman animals it is a mistake to infer that species-specific behavior is an indication of genetic wiring. Studies of birds have shown an entire population or species can adopt new singing behavior that through the learning process (Markl 1986: 80).

Proof that a feature is prevalent in cultures, or that it can be found almost everywhere, or that it occurs at least in many geographically distant cultures, does not necessarily mean that we are looking at a genetic disposition or a process of natural selection. Features can always come about and become selected due to matters of practical functionality. This must be clearly emphasized as a counterargument against the conclusions often implicitly drawn in social biology or evolutionary psychology (but explicitly in Tooby and Cosmides 1992). Horgan argues that in view of the close reciprocal interactions between cultures nowadays it would be possible to trace some of the universal instinctive attitudes and actions back to social adaptation. He maintains that many of our commonalities could be explained by culture and many of our differences by genetic variation. Horgan refers mainly to the extreme forms of contact and diffusion occurring in the global era. But the objection to the conclusion that ubiquity is genetically caused is more general, because it applies even without the factor of diffusion. Harris makes this point with the simple example of the use of tools, fire, and boiling water: "It may simply be so useful under a broad variety of conditions that it has been *culturally selected* for over and over again" (Harris 2001b: 156; italics mine). Human beings in all cultures would say that 2 + 3 = 5, but that has nothing to do with human beings developing out of hominid primates; rather, it is based on the internal principle of addition that was (repeatedly) invented and has spread throughout the world via diffusion. Rolston (1999: 156) has illustrated this with a computer metaphor: "These universals might well be due to their historical genesis in our evolutionary history, but they might be due to other causes.... To some extent this universal humanity will be hard-wired into genetics; to some extent it will rest on common plausibility for cultural softwares that can be run on the common biological endowment."

Daniel Dennett reveals that ubiquity does not have to be associated with genetic causes with the following example: in all the hunting cultures known to cultural anthropologists, arrows are shot with the pointed end first. By no means does this fact indicate the existence of a point-first throwing gene—rather, it is the result of practical and physical circumstances supplemented by learning processes. The explanation for such behavior remains linked to these learning processes. It can be reproduced or repeated by social partners without hindsight or discovered individually, even independently, by quite a number of individuals—an act Dennett describes as a "good trick" (Dennett 1995: 486–87). Other widespread cultural phenomena also refer to universal needs or to functional relationships. Similar social needs and cultures' universal ability to develop these features could explain such features and behaviors. Their ubiquity does not necessitate an explanation based on natural selection. This does not mean, however, that they are exclusively explained by culture, but rather that they could be completely or partially explained thusly.

This likewise applies to explaining universal thought patterns as evolved adaptation, as Scott Atran assumes for a universal folk biology. He has argued that all humans are good biologists because we all have the same species-specific hardwired brain structures. The similarities found in the classification of the living world (especially with the emphasis on the category of species) could also simply be based on the fact that although different cultures in the world are confronted with very different animal species, the natural order makes the hierarchical relationships of these species the same everywhere. The relationships and hierarchical levels between different life forms in the real world of comparable living environments are more similar than relationships between cultural units, or levels in social organization. However, this explanation involving experience in the actual natural order could be refuted by showing that human beings in the modern world emphasize species as a category above all other categorical levels, since humans in modern living situations have very little contact or experience with the natural living world (see Malik 2001: 258).

There is, however, strong evidence of a genetic basis for behavior based not on ubiquity but on the reoccurrence of something in all individuals in a number of historically independent societies that in other aspects, be they economic or political, are very different. The human ethologist Eibl-Eibesfeldt has therefore determined that certain behavioral features that appear in comparable situations in cultures geographically and otherwise very far apart are "inborn" (and accordingly part of human nature) (Eibl-Eibesfeldt 1993a, 2007; for critical comments, see Herbig 1988: 31–33). As was the case earlier for linguistic universals, we need to differentiate between direct and indirect inborn features. The universal fear of lions is most certainly not an inborn feature, but rather a general strategy that more or less says to us "don't get involved in a fight with someone who is stronger than you are" (R. Keller 2003: 153).

8 Does Universality Mean Functionality as Well, and Does Conformity Imply a Genetic Cause?

Features that are very widespread or even universal are often considered fundamental in the sense that they are functionally significant. This is a false conclusion that often threatens to materialize in comparative studies concerning both human-to-animal and intercultural comparisons. The false assumption follows that widespread features are fundamentally more important than new and therefore less widespread, or apomorphic, features. Yet features that are very widespread could actually be the outdated remains of features that have lost their functional meaning (Markl 1986: 83). This applies especially if only slight effort is needed to produce these features.

It is also incorrect to suppose that because a trait is adaptive, it is therefore genetic in origin (Distin 2011: 3). The assertion that a particular behavior is useful for the total biotic fitness of the organism says nothing about the behavior's causes. It is obvious that not only genetics but cultural traditions and individual experience as well can play a part in behavior, benefiting fitness altogether. This applies vice versa, in that a behavioral form that results from a supposedly genetic maladaptation, can in fact be based on a cultural maladaptation. Culture can copy nature—a phenomenon known in comparative ethology as *phenocopy* (Markl 1986: 80, 83).

9 Does Evolutive Genesis Imply Individual or Pancultural Universality?

It is often said that features that develop through evolution must be universal. There is also the particular argument that patterns developing through evolution must be "innate" and therefore universal. These statements are neither reliable nor clear when the words "universal" and "innate" remain vague (Griffiths 1997: 62–63). What is decisively adds clarity to these conclusions is distinguishing between, on the one hand, features that appear in all cultures, that is, features that are pancultural, and on the other hand, features that occur in all healthy individuals. It goes without saying that the evolutive development of a feature does not mean each and every individual must have this monomorphic feature. Some features occur in quite a number of various forms in one species and are therefore polymorphic. A simple example is the genetically determined but variable color of eyes. One should avoid drawing false conclusions of universality based on genetic determinism, as mixed strategies and behavior based on genetic polymorphism can produce adaptive advantages (Markl 1986: 80). Models of behavioral evolution often predict polymorphic results. The assumption of a monomorphic cognition, as held by evolutionary psychologists, is therefore problematic.

Can we at least say that an evolutive characteristic is pancultural? We could assume yes, since all human beings are members of a single species with the same evolutionary history and therefore the same evolutive attributes. But caution is warranted here as well, as this does not prove to be the case even on the level of bio-populations. First off, humanity reveals differences from population to population that are sometimes traceable to smaller original groups, so that due to matters of chance, certain very old evolutionary features may appear or be lacking to an unusual degree in some groups (Cavalli-Sforza, Menozzi and Piazza 1994). Secondly, groups defined as homologous include those descendants of an ancestor who are now missing certain features that have been lost through reverse evolution. A case in point would be snakes, which are tetrapods but have no legs. The same is true for the finding that although human beings share homologous behaviors with other primate species, those species' behaviors do not necessarily serve the same function and probably also are not clearly manifested (Griffiths 1997: 63–64).

The lack of distinction between universality on an individual level and on a cultural level is not the only cause of ambiguities. A second problem is the vague meaning of the word "innate," which even in biology does not have a single uniform meaning. It can mean either existing at birth or (decidedly, substantially) genetic. Outside of biology the confusion associated with the term increases. In philosophy, linguistics, and the cognitive sciences, innate is a dubious concept that can mean a number of things, such as "integrated," "genetically determined," "genetically paved," "canalized," developmentally limited," "uninfluenced by external factors," "with low norm of reaction," or "triggered" (vs. learned or acquired; Griffiths 1997: 61–62; Cowie 2003: 561–63; see the contributions in Carruthers, Laurence and Stich 2005). At this point we are confronted with the last problem, a fundamental issue that criss-crosses through most of the false conclusions described above.

10 Nature and Nurture: Does One Exclude the Other?

A further pitfall occurs within the empirically nebulous relationship between nature and environment or experience, that is, the nature versus nurture dilemma (D. Moore 2003). Here the diffuse nature of terms is set against the emotionalized and ideological use of certain words. The relationship should be separated analytically in the Cartesian sense, but such a task is empirically impossible due to the difficulty of untangling the causal components of the relationship. Scientifically it is a problem that is dealt with in a dualistic fashion, thereby shaping the many different so-called science wars. Edward Wilson established the image of the explanatory power of genetic and cultural factors in terms of values: "The genes hold culture on a leash. The leash is very long, but inevitably values will be constrained in accordance with their effects on the human gene pool" (Wilson 2004: 167; see Dennett 1995: chap. 16). This famous and contentious metaphor of the leash has often been interpreted as a claim of reducing culture to biology, leading to all sorts of misunderstandings as well as, and above all, exaggerated claims. For example, Rolston (1999: 148, italics mine) has suggestively and critically asked the following: "Can there be a lawlike science of human nature that explains *all the variety, diversity, and decision making that have characterized cultures?*" (see also Rolston 1999: 156). It can never, by definition, be the intent of generalized explanations or natural laws to explain specific situations.

In public debate, emotionally laden words are used that exaggerate the facts. In contrast to what is critically said about biology, very few biologists would claim that "biology is our destiny" or that genes *determine* behavior. Exposing certain inborn constructions does not mean that we are claiming a gene for every feature. The few cases where this may be assumed almost exclusively involve genes that lead to illness or disease. There is a big difference between deterministic or monocausal claims and claims such as the following, from a biophilospher who only describes influences: "I argue that Darwinian factors *inform and infuse* the whole of human experience, most particularly our cultural dimension ..." (Sober 1993: 140; italics mine). Metaphorically speaking, the question of predisposition or environment is as senseless as the question of whether the length or the width of a square covers more surface area.

In more recent work, the relationship of predisposition and environment, or learning, is often conceptualized in three ways (following Pinker 1997: 32): (1) inborn structures and learning processes act as opposing causal forces; (2) inborn structures and learning processes are components that complement each other in the formation of the psyche and in behavior; and (3) inborn structures and learning processes appear to be correlative forces, that is, integrated forms. The last two formulations are to be valued as progressive. By contrast, one-sided monocausal models such as genetic determinism on the one hand and extreme forms of social constructivism on the other, which, via an exaggerated emphasis of certain factors, present arguments from only one or the other extreme. All three positions, however, remain trapped by their own sense of dichotomy. Mechanical notions of a "mixing" of genes and learning, like metaphors delineating predisposition and environment as "ratios" or "shares," are completely inappropriate when considering the complicated processes involved in epigenesis. This applies even to the concept of "interaction." Hubert Markl (1986: 79) summed it up as follows: "The point here is not whether we have yet to find the appropriate method for disentangling nature from environmental influences. If we actually want to talk about real human beings, we must speak of them as constructors and creators of their own conceptual world, which represents an inextricable fabric made out of predispositions and experiences."

Systematics of Explanatory Approaches

A Broad Spectrum of Unexamined Explanations

Many universals refer to components of human nature or reflect human nature closely (D. Brown 2013: 412). But universals can have very different causes. Accordingly, the literature offers naturalistic explanations as well as diverse cultural, historical, and interactionist explanations, in a number of respective variants. And not all possible explanations are necessarily biological (or selectionist or genetic), a point that is important to emphasize in view of the oscillating assumptions of many anti-universalist researchers. Furthermore, and contrary to widespread assumptions, biological explanations are not linked per se with universality or variability. We see this when considering the history of biology in the last century. At the beginning of the twentieth century, variants were explained above all by biology. There were, for example, attempts to explain cultural differences with reference to varying levels of biological development. Nowadays, however, biologists more often explain the uniformity of human beings biologically.

Very few published explanations for universals in the literature can be regarded as detailed studies. The various explanations are rarely presented in any kind of relationship to each other or systematically compared (at best, see D. Brown 1991, 2005a). The question as to whether varying explanatory attempts compete with or complement one another almost always remains unanswered. In this respect, the explanations given below can best be described as approaches in the literal sense and as a real attempt at approaching the topic systematically. I am interested in explanations, but not in the sense of having, as Geertz put it, an "everything goes back to this" attitude (Geertz 1984). Explanations can illuminate various aspects of one and the same phenomenon.

Proximate and Ultimate Causes: The Example of Incest Avoidance

Explanations can describe the origin, the continued existence, the function, or the inconsistencies in universals. Frank Robert Vivelo has has described the varying ways incest is interpreted and prohibited (1994: 214–30; also see Wolf 1993: 165–67). Incest prohibitions are not the same as exogamic rules or regulations because sexual intercourse and marriage are not the same. Persons who cannot marry due to concerns of incest may possibly have sex with each other (J. Fox 1984: 4). In the case of incest prohibitions, we need to distinguish not only between (a) sexual intercourse, reproduction, and marriage, but also among (b) origin, continuity, and the systematic response to prohibiting incest with regard to (c) the form of the dyad of partners, that is, of mother-son, brother-sister, or father-daughter forms of incest, as well as whether (d) the social regulation of the tendency toward incest is done through prevention or prohibition. Consequently, it is not a contradiction to say that there are common functional causes in the behavioral tendencies to limit sexual activity but no universal explanation for all of the various bans on sexual behavior (Vivelo 1994: 225–26; also see Turner and Maryanski 2005: 27–52 and contributions in Wolf and Durham 2005).

Furthermore, not all explanations of universals provide the same specific information. Some interpretations want only to explain particular universals, as the example of incest has shown. Other explanations of universals look at certain cultural dimensions, such as art. Here it is also relevant to consider the different degrees of universality that are expounded in lists of universals. Various explanations do not necessarily have to exclude others, because there are different goals behind the explanations as regards the depth or profundity of the explaining. Useful distinctions in terminology in evolutionary biology have been drawn since the time of Ernst Mayr with his proximate and ultimate causes, and in behavioral biology with Nikolaas Tinbergen's distinction of four answers to questions of why (Tinbergen 1963; Mayr 1982; Alcock 2006: 9, 27–53). From the ultimate to the proximate poles, we can distinguish four kinds of explanations, from that of historical origin (phylogenesis), to adaptive value (function), individual development (ontogenesis), and finally direct physiological processes (e.g., Kappeler 2006: 5; A. Paul 2006: 72). Proximal explanations, such as those concerning actual function, answer different questions than do ultimate or distal (nonproximate) explanations like those concerning the historical origin of a universal. These distinctions can be traced back to Aristotle and are today best established in the field of biophilosophy (Mayr 2001; Krohs and Toepfer 2005).

Proximate and ultimate explanations can complement each other. The example of incest shows that different proximal explanations can correspond with one and the same ultimate explanation (Table 7.2 below; also see Sober

1993: 198–99). The standard argument is that the cultural prohibition of incest would not be necessary if there were a universally natural incest barrier. This argument, though, implies an unspoken contentious acceptance of culture versus nature, as Karl Eibl has correctly pointed out (Eibl 2007: 3). The argument implies that cultural regulations serve only to curb natural desires. Incest avoidance occurs among human beings as well as among other species, such as certain insects. Social biologists argue that the same causes exist here, namely that of selection pressures controlling incest avoidance in view of reduced diversity and poorer health and fitness due to the risk of homozygosity (or inbreeding depression). Such an explanation could be correct and does not have to mean that incest avoidance among humans is not attributable to special causes (see Wolf and Durham 2005; Silverman and Bevc 2006). Symbolic prohibitions of incest exist only among human beings. On the ultimate level of causal explanation, the same explanation of incest avoidance—that of the selection for outbreeding—applies for both humans and insects. Every closed social group, let it be said, can be equated with an inbred group. The exchange of members, exogamy, and incest avoidance are the rule among nonhuman primates (A. Paul 2006: 76). This ultimate (causal?) explanation must be formulated so as to clarify why reproduction between opposite-sex siblings occurs often in some animals and rarely in others (Sober 1993: 199).

This ultimate explanation is complemented by different proximal causes for insects and humans. In the case of insects, the move away from the nest before mating is an example of a proximal explanation. For human beings, the proximate cause of incest avoidance is the existence of incest taboos, or socially institutionalized value systems. The question of why humans avoid incest can be answered on different levels. The best empirically based explanation at the personal or individual level is the Westermarck effect, which posits sexual disinterest or aversion to sexual intercourse between individuals who know each other very well—either since childhood or through intensive parent-child bonds—independent of any genetic kinship correlation. This has to be explained on an even deeper level, though. The explanation of selection pressure does not conflict with an explanation pertaining to psychic mechanisms, such as conforming to societal taboos. On one level, human societies are unique with regard to incest; on another level they are not. Incest avoidance among human beings could be explained as the cultural reinforcement or re-forming of a natural predisposition.

A problem often occurs because certain scientists, or even entire disciplines, not only concentrate or specialize in just one of these levels of explanation, but also devalue or criticize all other possible ways of explaining universals. This applies in and beyond the cultural battle between the culturalists and the biologists. Something similar is also found within biology itself, between evolutionary psychology and social biology or even within specific schools of

Table 7.2. A look at more immediate and distant explanations, with incest as an example

	Human beings	Animal species X
Behavior	Incest avoidance	Incest avoidance
More immediate cause: proximate mechanism	Incest taboo	Spatial
More distant cause: evolutionary mechanism	selection pressure in incest avoidance (*outbreeding*)	

Source: modified after Sober 1993: 198

thought, such behavioral ecology. Most authors hardly even consider distinguishing between older universals that no longer exist (such as the high rate of infant mortality), and historically more recent universals (e.g., the use of fire). Hence, researchers concentrate on uniformist explanations for the phenomenon of universals.

Major Explanations and Generative versus Selective Interpretations

At the simplest level, we can distinguish between three basic types of explanations (Thies 2004: 117) for universals: (1) as the result of diffusion, or cultural expansion that leads to a form of horizontal learning across time and space, examples being the universal of money or the idea of democracy; (2) as an outcome of internal factors that have evolved in human beings, producing similar capabilities found in all people, such as the dichotomous structures in myths; and (3) as a response to similar living conditions, or by way of function. These distinctions among different explanations widely correspond to a means of classification elaborated by William Durham according to possibilities for the historical development of similarities between cultures. He distinguishes among the following factors: coincidence; convergence (independent invention); homology; divergent development arising out of the same descent, or a separation and emigration of subgroups; and diffusion or acculturation, or synology (Durham 1990: 191).

In another systematic approach, the so-called generative explanation is separated from selective explanations (Boyer 1994: 9–14). A generative model interprets a universal through a single and exhaustive mechanism. An example of this would be Lévi-Strauss's explanation of universal cultural patterns according to species-specific and therefore universal thought structures, or characteristics of a human brain. A selective model is an explanation of a universal through a (nonexhaustive) mechanism, with additional occurrences coming in play, influencing the outcome. One of many selective explanations includes the selectionist model: the explanation of a phenomenon or the spread of a phenomenon through fitness-maximizing selection (as a mechanism) plus mutation or innovation (as additionally necessary conditions). General features concerning ritual behavior, for example, should not be equated with general features in ritual situations. This is also the case with generative explanations. A selective model would separate ritual from the situation as a general behavior modality (Boyer 1994: 191).

Cultural Contact: Universals through Cultural Transfer and Diffusion

For anthropologists and historians, the most relevant explanation of cultural similarities involves either contact between societies or chance. This concerns mostly cultural transfer and diffusion, and independent invention (Kottak 2008: 55). Cultural transfer, or intercultural transfer, occurs in the movement of ideas, practices, or institutions from one societal system to another (Lüsebrink 2005: 129), leading either to one-sided acculturation or assimilation, or to forms of intensive and radical reciprocal influence—or transculturation, which also occurs frequently. In contrast, diffusion is the spreading of cultural patterns across space, with contact between cultures being often indirect, as when third cultures act as brokers. Artifacts and ideas originating in one culture as innovations are then spread across territories to other cultures, where they become selectively borrowed (Rogers 2003).

In a radical diffusionism, spatial diffusion explains all important human inventions. Under this assumption, an innovation occurs only in one particular place in the world and then is transported away from its place of origin across the planet, leading to convergence (Thies 2004: 117). More moderate diffusionists have explained at least some universals through diffusion (Herskovits 1966: 461). As a natural scientist, Horgan warns against hasty conclusions that tie ubiquity to human nature and argues against exaggerations in human social biology (Horgan 2001: 266). Runciman, an anthropologist, has stated: "Wilson is quite right to point out that cultures evolve major features in common as well as major differences. But the explanation of these major features in common lies in convergent cultural evolution, not reductionist socio-biology" (Runciman 2002: 11). Recent work on universals has focused on how useful inventions are borrowed and passed on from one human group to another, as suggested in the trend toward globalization and the worldwide distribution of products and ideas. Pasta, for example, can now be considered a "universal food" (Serventi and Sabban 2003). Earlier, Georg Forster posed the question of whether universals could have been manufactured only after the uniting of the world through Western influence (see Heintze 1990: 76).

Diffusion that is spatially very widespread is not, however, a privilege of recent globalization or of a global system. Knowledge of how to make fire, for example, spread about one hundred thousand years ago (Spier 2002: 66–70). In anthropologists' experience, very few groups have been found that did not already have fire or know how to produce fire before coming into contact with Western culture. With regard to diffusion in general, we can differentiate between fundamentally different degrees of human contact in global history. William Hardy McNeill, a leading figure in global history, distinguishes between different *webs* representing historical levels that are at times fused together (McNeill and McNeill 2003: 3–5, 7, 18, 162–78, 323–24; also see Bayly 2006: 55–111). An earlier form of worldwide communication and interaction network based on genetic exchange, language, and early technologies existed, though in a weak form due to sparse human populations. Only after 10,000 BC was this early World Wide Web supplemented, if not replaced, by the rise of states, which created a number of intensive human networks that allowed innovations such as writing, pack animals, and wheel-based transport to spread. Around 4000 BC new metropolitan networks developed out of the first two, but only around 500 years ago did there emerge a cosmopolitan network that in some ways incorporated the original three, bringing humanity into one great unit of diffusion. While agriculture developed independently ca. seven times between 10,000 and 3000 BC, spreading across the globe from its original places of origin, the steam engine had only to be invented once before it spread around the world (McNeill and McNeill 2003: 7). We can distinguish among different forms of universals that have developed through diffusion.

Universals formed through an archaic diffusion (Holenstein 1985b: 159) are those that existed for all humanity at a time when human beings possessed only one territory, that is, before they began their spread across the planet. Examples of these universals would be fire, family, incest avoidance, religion, and language—features that could be considered the traits originating in the "cradle of human culture" (Aginsky and Aginsky 1948: 168). Stone artifacts and domesticated animals could possibly be placed in this group of universals. A typical example is the domesticated dog as human companion, which is a near universal found across the planet (Wissler 1965: 111). Other examples involve totemic images of the world that are found on all the continents and could have spread across the planet as humans began to spread as well. One can speak here of the continuous differentiation between nature (represented in totemic objects) and culture, as well as their set affiliation in totemism, or even shamanism (Fernández-Armesto 2005: 39–40).

Modern diffusion universals, in contrast, are those that spread much later in human history, such as travel, discovery, conquest, and trade. Examples would include tobacco consumption, use of paper, alphabetic writing, and such things as the use of the terms factory and radio (Aginsky and Aginsky 1948: 168–70). Only some are of Western origin; many originated in other parts of the world. The compass, paper, and gunpowder, mentioned by Francis Bacon as chief factors in creating the modern world, were all, as we now know, invented in China (J. Needham 1986: 7). The horse is a prototypical example of a domesticated animal (Boas 1938: 167–68; Wissler 1965: 111). Finally, a third form of universal development through diffusion, termed archosis, has been suggested, according to which universals could have arisen via dissemination in the time when human beings were becoming human, even if these universals are dysfunctional. A very hypothetical example is the widely held notion that bone marrow and brain are the origin of sperm, known as the *muelos* belief complex (LaBarre 1947), which does not always appear everywhere as a complex, when it does in fact appear. Ruth Benedict wrote in 1934 about extremely early innovations that are not "biologically determined" but rather socially conditioned, like every other local custom (Benedict 1934). "Cross cultural similarities do not always mean historical one-sided or mutual dependence" (Holenstein 1997: 64). The most important insights coming out of diffusion research on universals suggest that universals do not necessarily have to point back to constants or be closely tied to a biotic human nature or even to a naturally determined human nature. "The most interesting universals in cultural philosophy are of a random nature and not vitally necessary" (Holenstein 1998a: 230).

If various cultures develop similar mechanically effective commodities, it could indicate similar but independent reactions to the same problems, as in convergent adaptation. Below I examine this as a third explanatory form. If, however, we find similarities in the area of symbolism, culture, or language, these would more likely indicate a common cultural origin, as they are not to be explained as functional adaptation but are instead based on convention (Lorenz 1970: 11). This does not eliminate the possibility of cross-cultural motifs in the visual arts, such as circles, faces, eyes, hands, and many more (examples in Eibl-Eibesfeldt and Sütterlin 2007: 212–17). Areas of research that examine explanations for diffusion as well as alternative explanations could be of particular interest here. An example includes finding an explanation for the fact that ethnic groups who do not speak related languages and are culturally very separate from each other have almost identical knowledge and selection criteria for medicinal plants. Ethnobiologists and ethnohistorians have been discussing, with regard to Latin America, whether this is based on a common knowledge conserved through time that goes back as far as the Paleolithic or whether this involves a development that occurs independently in separate ethnic groups due to similar circumstances and similar selection criteria (Waldstein and Adams 2006: 133–34).

Within the context of current globalization processes, new universals developing by way of diffusion include features that are present in all extant peoples, like the use of plastic or metal objects. Besides materials, examples include the concepts, perceptions, and emotions that are generated on a global level by the visual power of photographs, such as images of our planet from outer space or of the events of September 11, 2001. Current discussion asks to what extent not only Western commodities but also Western principles or standards have spread across the world. In his essay "World Polity," John W. Meyer (2005) discusses rational thought patterns and institutions, and their projected goals, such as individualism, justice, fairness, and world citizenry. These principles are spread throughout the world by international governmental and nongovernmental organizations, especially since the end of World War II. New universals could develop through the transnational spread of a cultural order, bringing a world culture into being. A new "cultural universalism," or world or global culture (Roland Robertson 1992: 108–14; Lechner and Boli 2005: 22–25, 44–46; Schlehe 2006: 54–55; see also Weiß 2005: 86) is not then a question of Euro-American homogeny but rather a concern with cultural diversity being globally organized in such a way that the world is regarded as a whole, for example, in the worldwide movement of nongovernmental organizations, in civil society, or in science. Key here are "universalistic elements," or elements presented as though they were universally relevant, for example, in the *Diagnostic and Statistical Manual of Mental Disorders* (DSM IV) and its classification of psychic illnesses. "The element is *presumed* to have universal (worldwide) scope; it is *presumed* to be interpretable in a largely uniform way and to *make sense* both cognitively and, often normatively, in any particular local culture or social framework" (Lechner and Boli 2005: 21–22; italics mine).

These attitudes emphasize the historical development of new universals, something especially important for Keith Hart, who has argued that since World War II, the world has for the first time formed one single interactive network. The emerging world community is not only an idea but rather an absolute fact. Increasing cosmopolitan ties now form "a new human universal" (Hart 2008: 1–2, 6–8), which leads us to a cause for universals that is often overlooked: globally similar circumstances or demands arising in individual lifeways and in social living conditions.

Function, Convergence, and Structural Implication: Universals Emerging through Real-Life Circumstances

Human beings everywhere in the world have the same kinds of experiences in everyday life. We learn not only through social contact but also, as individuals, through our interaction with similar material environments. The *conditio humana*, shared by all human beings, is not limited to life as organisms. All human beings observe time and again that the sun travels across the sky, night follows day, objects fall to the earth, and people walk upright (Hauser 2007: 164, 301–2). And they pass these experiences on through stories. Individuals and collective groups from very different cultures have experiences that result from the same practical circumstances everywhere, and ultimately result from the same physics everywhere. Human beings, completely independent of one another around the world, look at blood and see it is red. In almost all known cultures, the color red is the symbol of blood. A panhuman experiential universal (Yengoyan 1978, quoted by D. Brown 1991: 47) produces a nearly pancultural symbol.

Furthermore, human beings have psychic experiences that are generated by needs such as hunger or sexual desire (Trommsdorff 2007: 442). These experiences in turn stimulate analogous cultural responses that are similar across the globe (Eibl 2007: 2). An example would be the universal attempt to predict or even influence the weather. Similar individual behavioral practices would lead us to expect that independent invention (Kottak 2008: 55) would occur frequently. We could link this to the principle of minimal effort elaborated in 1949 by George Kingsley Zipf (1902–50), which follows the principles of mechanical physics. Zipf showed through empirical case studies that human beings generally tend to act in ways that require the minimal amount of time, energy, and material (Zipf 1965; also see Schelling 1978; Ball 2004: 305–6). Zipf's principle is often cited in linguistics to explain that the language universal of marking is a result of energy saving. Thus, words most often used in a language are those that are not marked (Greenberg 1963). A number of such emerging universals could be expected, for example, in a social system of language users who reciprocally influence one another. If all the vowels in a particular language sound alike, the vowels tend to drift apart over time, without the intentions or awareness of the speakers playing a part. Therefore, no language has only similar-sounding vowels, although such a thing is physiologically plausible.

Social actors' learning is everywhere based on similar situations and according to the same "recurrent structure of human life" (Tooby and Cosmides 1992: 50–51). Humans everywhere in the world daily come across phenomena that demand an explanation. Everywhere, then, there is a need or compulsory wish to explain things (Opolka 1999: 3–4). This variant of explanation is particularly interesting with regard to sub-universals, especially those that cannot be properly explained by general selective usefulness. Practical matters of daily life not only require explanation from the actors involved, but also produce concrete problems. Comparable problems occur in all cultures throughout all areas of the world, and human beings, regardless of the exact region, develop similar solutions to these problems, because these solutions either appear almost obvious or simply are available (Thies 2004: 117; Welsch 2006: 144; Appiah 2007: 124). Many widespread cultural phenomena refer to universal needs or functional relationships, such as the existence of hygienic standards. Another example is the division of labor, which exists due to awareness of different interindividual capabilities, knowledge, differences in power, and surpluses that could exempt certain people from work. Calendars refer back to objective regularities in the world, to the capability of humans as organisms to perceive these regularities, and to the social need to understand them (Malik 2001: 260). The sameness of social needs and the universal capability of cultures to evolve or develop these needs, or features, could be a way of explaining such features and behavior. Their ubiquity does not require an explanation by way of natural selection. This does not, however, mean that they must only be explained as cultural, but rather that they could be thus explained, partially or entirely.

A well-known prehistoric example of cultural parallels on the macro level of societal learning is the existence of irrigated agriculture, already mentioned above, in independent cultures along the Nile, Euphrates, Tigris, Indus, and Huang Ho Rivers. Others include the later development of writing, cities, and states. Such historically independent innovations moved through diffusion to other societies. Cultures are not closed language games. They exist in a living environment because humans' physical constitution do not allow them to step out of the biosphere. At the micro level, universals arise through daily practical experiences in the material world, especially as regards the production of material goods and the area of reproduction. This is evident in similar ways in terms of building materials, tools, and technologies, and leads to empirical, intersubjective knowledge (Bloch 1977). Over generations, symbolic forms are also not completely variable. Symbols have to be formed a way that allows goal-directed activities to correspond properly to a given environment (Kather 2008: 52, 61–62).

One example of a cognitive universal is the conceptual equivalent of the passage of time as an "arrow of time" or mental time line. The time arrow or time line concept is found everywhere, even in societies that tend toward cyclical notions of time, or static concepts, or noncontinual concepts of time. Though modified by every respective culture, this concept basically reflects the human experiences that each and every individual has with his or her own inner clock. Another example is kinship terminology that does not refer to an evolution-based psychological model but instead to a kinship-oriented cognitive model that could be explained as reflecting daily experience with sexual reproduction, though sexual reproduction itself is something to be explained separately. Meanwhile, the (widespread) exaggerated symbolic importance of the right hand might not be related to certain cognitive preferences but rather might simply reflect the, on average, greater abilities of the right hand.

Current living environments might explain universal practices that cannot be traced to biological adaptations but are due to the brain's response to particularly human practices, which are themselves contingent. These practices can be quite different in effect but in general are often carried out in a certain way, with universal and physiologically contingent results. Quite a few religious experiences could be examples of this, as they reflect knowledge of human physiology and the human psyche that is independently found in many cultures. Near universal experiences, such as those related to ecstasy, could indicate physical reactions to certain practices that are widespread yet not somehow biotically determined and therefore can, in theory, be quite different. Examples here would be spiritual possession, dancing in a trance, percussion music played during rituals, sleep deprivation, and use of drugs. Emotions of love could be similarly explained. From the emic perspective of many cultures, being in love is described as a sickness. This could be simply because the symptoms of stress are the same as those associated with love. This in turn can be explained by the fact that both conditions stimulate the medial amygdala of the brain, where sexual receptors and stress receptors are located (G. Roth 2003: 370).

Cross-cultural social psychologists and organization specialists, employing a functional approach, seek out "social axioms"—empirically based expectations about how issues or processes are created, independent of the space, time, context, or acting agent (individual) involved. Functionally understood, they encompass widespread and elementary beliefs that allow the functioning of organizations to be possible in the first place (Gaskell and Fraser 1990; Bierbrauer and Klinger 2001; Leung et al. 2002; Oerter 2007: 506–8). Altogether, social axioms refer to the "homogeneity in the daily practical demands occurring in different places within the historical continuum of time" (Maiers 1993: 68) that is often overlooked when fundamental causes are postulated for universals. Holenstein, addressing the meaning of current living conditions as a means of explaining universals, comes to the following conclusion: "The prevailing as well as most important aspect of cultural universals is of a contingent nature and in a conventional way explainable through the structure and function of cultural phenomena" (Holenstein 1998c: 326).

Universals can also originate via a combinational logic, that is, in preset formal structures within the descriptive tools or phenomena of the world. Hans Lenk uses the example of networks to explain such "structural implications." Observations in all societies have shown that small social networks often take the form of cliques. Sociograms show that if the number of choices of preferred or rejected partners is pre-given, cliques with weak ties necessarily emerge due to structural reasons. In these small networks, the formation of a ring network is not an empirical fact but an unavoidable result of logical premises, if each member (of the clique) is allowed to choose at least one other contact partner (Lenk 1975: 353–54, 1978). Presenting a contrast to other causal explanations for universals are the explanations for what might be called strict universals, that is, the analytical conclusions of formal, logical, or conceptual structures. In such instances empirical data are not needed, and a formal analysis shows that it is not even necessary to conduct observations and experiments in search of exceptions here (Brandtstädter 1998: 73; 2006: 532–33). Still, empirical data can be useful even when they do not offer new information. They confirm that the model chosen can be applied in studying real-life phenomena. When working with structural implications, we can distinguish between two types of situations. The implication is either tied to concepts and descriptive tools used in analysis, such as in the example of cliques, or the implication involves rules from within the subject matter, as within a social institution like sporting matches (Lenk 1975: 358). Structural implications should always be considered when choosing among means of explaining universals. With regard to more complicated social issues, we often have no idea of what is formally possible and impossible in terms of causal links. This is particularly true for cross-generational change in societies and especially for phenomena concerning ultrasociality in large and complex societies, something I discuss below.

Some universals even have been explained purely on cultural grounds. Problematically, though, a given complexity of a phenomenon in question, e.g. a complicated behavior pattern, and the lack of a direct practical functionality any culture worldwide direct us to a noncultural explanation. Universals on the individual level, such as worldwide behavioral differences based on sex, do not *necessarily* stem from behavioral tendencies arising out of evolution. In principle, these universals could be culturally determined through an ubiquitous form of differential socialization. But this proximal sameness would also then need to be explained. In any case, a random pancultural independent development is highly improbable in such cases (Cronk 1999; Schmitt et al. 2005: 101). Are there then more elementary commonalities lying much deeper beneath the surface that influence or cause the subsequent cultural universals (Welsch 2006: 122)? At this point I want to introduce another explanatory approach, which is neither a matter of diffusion nor of cultural convergence but an approach based on a deeper biotic structure.

Evolution: Universals Based on Adaptation

A third possible way of explaining universals is based on an evolutionary approach. Evolutionary explanations are a variant of naturalistic interpretation. Universals showing likenesses or commonalities on the level of societies are interpreted with reference to universal capabilities or behavioral tendencies in humans as organisms who are members or parts of these societies. A candidate that is understandable by way of an ultimate explanation would be an ability found in children, specifically their relative resistance to cultural influences. This ability is also something that occurs for only a very short period of time (Hauser 2007: 164, 303). Ultimate evolutionistic explanations show that universals can be explained through biotic adaptation, or more concretely, through natural selection. Peoples and Bailey have determined that there are biological needs and desires that occur in all societies and that this simple fact has historically led anthropologists to discover cultural universals (Peoples and Bailey 2015: 44). Rather than obvious features that are related to species and survival, what is meant here are the less obvious features without obvious causal correlations.

Adaptive explanations for universals vary depending on whether supposed selective pressures, which produce universal similarities, are thought to currently exist or existed in the past. This question produces various responses (see Laland, Odling-Smee, and Feldman 2000; Kronfeldner 2007; Kronfeldner, Roughley and Toepfer 2014; Shennan 2009; Hodgson and Knudsen 2010; Rossano 2010; Distin 2011; Mesoudi 2011; Pagel 2012; Sterelny 2012; Read 2012; Sanderson 2014). Human social biology, evolutionary ecology, and Darwinian psychology use assumptions based on current selection in their explanations. Evolutionary psychologists apply assumptions stemming from environmental challenges that arise from the past and subsequently appear time and again (e.g., Tooby and Cosmides 1992; also see Hinde 1994). They are not interested in creating lists of adaptations, but rather in looking for and examining common fundamental principles within various adaptations in light of basic societal problems.

A more current, dynamic form of evolutionary psychology compares various social types and distinguishes the core problem areas in social life, otherwise called social problem domains. The basic domains articulated thus far are coalition building, status, self-protection against loss and robbery, choice of sexual partners, partner relations, and care of offspring. Depending on the circumstances, different problems and different decisions pertain to certain social types, such as freeloaders. Core problems are examined for commonalities, and correlations between similar behaviors and universal challenges are analyzed. The universal principles used in finding solutions that have so far been determined are inclusive fitness, sexual selection, reciprocal altruism, and differential parental investment. Observations and computer simulations have both shown that the different fundamental societal domains occurring in different types of environments lead too often to different "social geometries" and dynamics (Kenrick, Li and Butner 2003: 6–10, 23).

How are we to discover which evolutionary adaptations pertain to which cultural universals? Selection-based explanations arise out of specific conditions that Ellen Dissanayake discusses using the example of art as a potential universal: "In order to show that a behavior of art is universal and indelible, *it is necessary to identify a core behavioral tendency upon which natural selection could act*" (Dissanayake 1992: 42; italics mine). As an example, we can examine the question of universal psychic mechanisms as the basis for behavior. A quasi-programmatic methodological recommendation would be as follows: Look for behaviors that are, with regard to their function or efficiency, arbitrary or irrational. Look then for behavior that leads regularly to certain problems. The strategy would be different if applied to animal behavior. Here one would look for "highly designed" or perfectly functional behavior (Malik 2001: 262–63). With humans, we would look for behavior that might be universally described as quirky, bizarre, inexplicable, or irrational. In view of the incredible variety found in human cultures, it is highly improbable that all societies would arrive at the same possible behavioral patterns. An example would be fear of insects, or the mimic involved in expressing so-called basic emotions (Ekman 1970; Ekman et al. 1969).

A second potential candidate for an adaptational explanation would be behaviors that could not have been learned. An example can be drawn from language skills and the preexisting principles of transformation grammar in language learning among small children, along with their natural history intelligence, with its intuitive assumption that they and their social partners have separate intentions, as in the theory of mind (Premack and Woodruff 1978; Whiten 2003; Förstl 2006; Whiten et al. 2012). These are characteristics, or features, that cannot be individually or socially learned (or not as yet) because the environment does not provide opportunities for such or offer the necessary information.

We need to be aware of certain limitations involved here. Organisms in populations, and their features, do not have to be adaptive in every respect (Markl 1986: 782–83). They do not have to be found in all features, always present at all times, or found in every single member of a population. Deviations in optimal adaptation, as variability (or diversity), have direct significance for adaptive potential. A minimum of level of fault tolerance is important in considering uncertain environmental change and the corresponding adaptation demands. Long-term and average adaptive behavior does not exclude short-term nonadaptive behavior. This is particularly true for the human species, which is strongly individualistic with high intraspecies diversity (or strong interindividual differences). The interpretation of maladaptations in an environment based on civilizations, which only exist at all because of the biological past of human beings, does not correspond with an approach based on pan-adaptation (Markl 1986: 74; Pigliucci and Kaplan 2000; J. Marks 2004: 185). It does, however, correspond quite well with the assumption of average and long-term adaptation. Strictly speaking, an adaptive disadvantage would be proven only if the overall fitness of a feature is quantitatively lower than a competing allele (Markl 1986: 74).

Altogether, clear evidence of a universal based on evolutionary adaptation would be that (1) many possibilities for doing something are not only generally plausible but functionally plausible as well, and that (2) many of these possibilities actually exist, but that (3) only a few variants or a single variant occurs often. An example is the fact that throughout all cultures, human social relationships are organized on the basis of kinship lines more often than any other relationship form or any other, non-kinship networks, even when we grant that kinship can be understood quite variously at times. Any other kind of organization, such as that practiced on a kibbutz, will eventually be just as rational and functional (Malik 2001: 261). An adaptation in hunter-gatherer groups, seen from the perspective of evolutionary history, can be understood as a mechanism of kinship selection. This does not mean that kinship relationships play the same role in all present-day societies.

Possible universals that can be explained by adaptation are those associated with reproduction, or biotic kinship. All the possible meanings of kinship, such as nepotism or incest, fall within this category. The continuity of the significance of kinship as an organizational principle of social relationships in complex societies can also be explained by selection. The causes, though, could be other than adaptive, something social biologists too often overlook. Concerning human activity, there are means other than the either-or construct of God or natural selection (Tooby and Cosmides 1992) to describe why humans act the way they do, such as other functionally reasonable designs. Social and biological adaptations are both plausible; indeed, both are so interwoven together that we would find it almost impossible to separate them analytically (Malik 2001: 262). To determine whether a universally widespread feature has developed as a solution to real-life problems, we could use the following cognitive experiment: Could an extremely well-functioning and well-informed computer, having simulated the cumulative experience that occurs over many generations, generate this feature as a solution? If the answer were yes, the feature could just as likely have emerged for cultural reasons. If such a computer could not find this exact solution, we can assume that evolutionary powers were at work (Malik 2001: 262).

Classic examples of universals that have been understood through adaptive explanations are the worldwide likenesses in emotions and in the area of cognition, especially with regard to classification strategies of the living world. In both areas, cross-cultural psychologists have postulated universals and to some extent documented them. In this way, they have determined that human beings who live in very different cultures lying far apart from another have similar emotional reactions. The fear of snakes is just as widespread as the symbolic meaning associated with snakes. In all, or almost all, cultures we also find spinning games, carousels, percussion rhythms, and other forms of physical movement that bring on modified states of consciousness. In many cultures, poetry recited orally is often unknowingly created in units lasting three seconds.

In this case as well, a selectionist explanation is only one of several that could be relevant. With regard to the similar means of classifying the living environment, we could argue as follows: If the actual environment (1) offers enough information by way of clear regularities, and if (2) there is enough selection pressure for (3) brain structures to develop taxonomic markers that enable classification, then conditions 1 and 2 could signify that human groups have enough information available to them to classify the world without necessarily having a particular type of brain structure. Kenan Malik has described this informally as follows: "You don't need natural selection to be able to tell your ash from your elm" (Malik 2001: 257).

Further universals suggest a selectionist interpretation but demand alternative explanations as well. In cultures all over the world, we find that great value is bestowed on perfection, or artistry. The ideal of creating things that go beyond functional worth—things that are considered "really special"—seems to be found everywhere. Both archaeological and ethnographic evidence indicate that the notion of a sphere of life beyond the ordinary is widespread. Within such a construct, art can be seen as the universal response to the link between symbols, classification, order, tool manufacture, and emotion, all of critical importance in ritual and play (Dissanayake 1992). The key mechanism could simply be that similar behavior or activity arises out of universally occurring positive feelings: "In fact there are two sides of a coin: people universally do something because it feels good; and because something feels good, people do it. ... A corollary of this view is that what feels good is also a clue concerning what we need" (Dissanayake 1992: 32). This is demonstrated in the positive emotions experienced or created by artists when their work, be it physical art such as dance, musical performance, or figurative art, is made consciously to be beautiful, or aesthetically "special." These inherently rewarding emotions correspond with the higher values found the world over. Examples are the value placed on agility, stamina, endurance, and grace in dance; liveliness, rhythm, and echo in language; and resonance and strength in percussion (Dissanayake 1992: 54, 130).

As mentioned above, there are of course variants among the possible evolutionary explanations for universals. Only from a cultural perspective do evolutionary explanations appear too constricted by adaptation, or too selectionist, or simply too monomaniacal. Some authors, writing from an evolutionary perspective, have speculated, for example, that emulation learning is a cause for universals—that is, learning that is tied to registering that changes in the environment generated by social partners, without knowing what strategies stand behind these changes. Such emulation learning can contribute to the forming of cognitive constraints, or universal cognitive processes (Boyer 1994: 5, 111–12). Charles J. Lumsden and Edward Wilson (1981) have introduced another evolutionary explanation into the debate. They ascribe universals to the effects produced by so-called "epigenetic rules," which are regularities that limit the reaction norms in ontogenesis. More concretely, they are physiologically established, genetically determined preferences and predispositions, such as inductively guided heuristics and phobias. Epigenetic rules are neurobiological features that mediate between developmental needs and the social environment. They limit the cultural playing field through cognitive preferences, preparedness, and inclinations. These rules channel (or predetermine) culture in a particular direction, as demonstrated by the fact that some thoughts call up certain intensive emotions more than others. Groups of these genetically determined channels create predispositions in human beings toward specific or certain ways of thinking, kinds of behavior, and social conventions. These tendencies are found in societies that are otherwise very different. The more consequential of these epigenetic rules then produce cultural universals. The rules that allow for a wider range of reactive norms are those that create cultural diversity (on predispositions see Dissanayake 1992: 229; Boyer 1994: 269–70).

In my opinion, the problem behind selective explanations is not that they are naturalistic. The problem lies in finding which is the right or proper naturalistic explanation. We should also consider what proximate explanations would complement them. Explanations that interpret everything as naturalistic do not say too little, but rather too much. This problem appears in the work of quite a few social biologists and Darwinian anthropologists. Lumsden and Wilson, for example, argue as social biologists with the implicit help of an assumed methodological individualism. They assume that group behavior is merely the sum of activities or behavior of separate individuals. However, there are both theoretical arguments (Ball 2004: 145–163) and empirical studies (e.g., Schelling 1978) that show that even this assumption is not reasonable. Laura Betzig (1997) has published a volume including classical contributions from the field of social biology and other Darwin-oriented areas in anthropology. The authors were invited to write an epilogue to their original publications describing the current state of research. One noted that the anthropological contributions stressed the enormous changes that occurred in the behavior of those originally studied. Steven Rose, in his critical commentary on the volume, poses the sarcastic question, "Why have these assumed human universals suddenly failed to operate?" (Rose 2006: 263).

It is also necessary to mention that not every biological explanation is argued from an evolutionary point of view. An example of a non-evolutionary biological explanation would be one in which universals are explained by assumed brain structures, or cognitive capabilities, though these would not in themselves be understood as ultimate explanations. An example includes the explanation presented by Lévi-Strauss for universal binary, or dualistic, structures in thinking and behaving through universal "mental structures" (Lévi-Strauss 1949). In a theoretical debate currently taking place in the cultural sciences, Wolfgang Welsch's concept of "transculturation" (for the revised variant, see Welsch 2006 and 2012) comes closest to an approach for researching universals. Welsch argues that commonalities in cultures emerge through cultural exchange and reciprocal interpenetration, and through the increasingly intercultural character of people. According to Welsch, commonalities underlie all cultural differences because, in evolutionary terms, they came first. Human cultures shared these commonalities before cultural diversification caused these cultures to drift apart. The universals in question are primary "proto-cultural" universals joined only by secondary cultural differences (Welsch 2006: 113, 132, 144). The possibility of cross-cultural understanding arises through this basic constitution of all cultures. Another approach that could be used to explain universals in the same sense is Bruno Latour's concept of an "actor network" (Latour 2001, 2015), which I explore in the closing chapter.

Complex Causes

Interaction: The Interplay of Several Factors

We can assume that universals emerge through the combined effect of multiple factors. These factors can work either against each other or through a kind of cumulative effect to produce universals. White (1980: 776) has postulated that universal forms in speaking that develop around interpersonal relationships, or rather, concepts of personality, are based on a combination of (inborn) psycholinguistic structures and panhuman conditions existing within human societies. Comparatively few authors are so explicit in describing interaction. Yet vagueness proves problematic, as developing interactional explanations of universals involves risks, the first being the danger of going against the principle of parsimony by trying to argue by way of unexamined claims. This includes not being concrete enough when using the terms multiple or reciprocal. The second risk here, with regard to universals, is falling victim to the same pitfalls described above due to the use of even more assumed determinants when discussing interaction. Stephen Mithen, a prehistorian with interests in cognitive and evolutionary psychology, discusses, for instance, genetic and cultural factors at the same time. He equates universality with genes and diversity with culture *en passant* in the following: "The need to reconcile genetic similarity and cultural diversity requires a cognitive anthropology, one that is concerned with how observed behaviour is a product of the interaction between universal properties of the human mind and the unique environmental, cultural, and historical settings within which individuals are located" (Mithen 2006: 59).

An example of an interactionist explanation for a universal would be cultural exaggeration of physiological or material facts, such as in the similar way differences in gender are described on a worldwide basis. The biotic difference in sex as tied to reproduction is perceived in all cultures, is culturally marked, and is—most of the time—exaggerated through an emphasis on contrasts. Those proposing ontogenetic explanations for universals tend also to produce interactionist arguments. An example of such an interpretive argument, with a consideration for both ontogenesis and socialization, is Melford Spiro's discussion of the Oedipus complex (Spiro 1982; see also Bischof 1985; Johnson and Price-Williams 1996). Spiro argues that this complex arises in a specific social environment at a critical psychosexual phase of development. The Oedipus complex is almost universal because the constellation of persons represented in the complex correlate to a basic form found in all cultures. Language universals are also understandable from an interactionist approach. Steven Pinker has explained them as an effect of interaction corresponding to genetic presets for language learning in a particular age group or stage of life (proven among deaf-mutes as well) with specific environmental cues, and not, as earlier authors have described, a result of associative learning. Children learning to speak their mother tongue do so at a remarkable speed, especially the complexity of language forms. Pinker describes language basically as an organ (Pinker 1994).

More recent, convergent findings in developmental psychology show that there are certain age-based tasks that each child in every culture must perform in order to develop an independent as well as interdependent self. Three central "developmental tasks" include close bonding with social partners, resolution of the tension between autonomy and dependency with other people, and the learning of social knowledge (Greenfield et al. 2003: 468–80; Grossmann and Grossmann 2007: 265–70). Since simple determinisms do not apply, Greenfield et al. speak appropriately of cultural practices through universal developmental tasks (similar to Chasiotis 2007: 197). The psychic working through of these universal tasks is a good example of how universals can form ontogenetically through interaction or phylogenetically through coevolution.

Universals as the Result of Other Universals

Universals can also be explained as the result of other universals. One single universal, to start with, can be an outcome of a broad number of universals. Examples would be the universal consequences arising out of the needs Malinowski described in his basic needs theory (Malinowski 1944). Concrete indications of possible candidates for this type of explanation arise when a strong correlation is found between two universals or between near universal phenomena. Matrilineal descent or parentage, for example, is empirically very often tied to high rates of divorce. When such a co-variation, or concomitant variation, is determined, one can assume a causal link is involved. The direction of causality remains unclear, though, as does the answer to whether both universals could actually have been determined by a third universal. In addition, this creates a shift in the explanation altogether.

An example of a universal that can be explained thusly is the dominance of men in the public or political sphere, a phenomenon found in all societies known to history and anthropology. Patriarchy seems inevitable in larger social systems. Even matrilineal and matrilocal societies and societies where women are accorded respect and veneration reveal a system of social organization in which an overwhelming number of higher positions in the social hierarchy are occupied by males (S. Goldberg 1993: 14). Pure social scientific explanations, like those concerning cultural ideals and the worldwide assertion of patriarchal relationships of power, can explain certain aspects of this. But they cannot explain the universality, given that it seems highly improbable that male-dominated structures have spread across the globe, even in societies showing none of the similarities that indicate patriarchal systems. The initial emergence of male dominance spreading by diffusion throughout the world would have to be explained (Lopreato and Crippen 2002: 136). Sherry Ortner postulated such an explanation in 1974, arguing in terms of another universal that divides the world into two spheres, that of culture and that of nature. The natural sphere is valued less than the cultural, and women have been assigned to the natural world due to their role in reproduction (Ortner 1996). The evidence supports these statements somewhat, even though there are no cross-cultural studies to provide empirical support to her claims. There are also exceptions. A classic image has the female represented as the one who "civilizes" the male, with the man in Western countries often characterized as more like an animal.

Figure 8. Building worker in Madurai, India. Photo by Maria Blechmann-Antweiler.

CHAPTER 8

Critical Positions
Arguments against Universalism

> *Careful anthropologists do not usually go around making global, universalist statements.*
> —Nigel Rapport and Joanna Overing,
> Social and Cultural Anthropology

Having already dealt with the particular criticism against the creation of lists of universals, below I discuss the fundamental objections to the existence of universals and the positions against even dealing at all with universals as subject matter. We need to be cautious in assuming we can understand human beings independently of their specific biography, living situation, or form of being. In the academic world, however, this assumption, unexamined and unexpressed, remains implicitly widespread. Universalizing premises are often not based on scientific knowledge, but rather on preset images of human beings arising from the philosophical undertones of a folk psychology (Carrithers 1992: 169). From the vantage point of relativism, all critics of generalization or science as an intersubjective project explicitly confront universalistic directions in research. The criticism was stated most explicitly by Geertz, who argued via a hermeneutic approach to epistemology. Other symbolic anthropologists, such as Sahlins, Schneider, Turner, and Douglas, did not relate explicitly to epistemological assumptions. Their objections departed from the anthropological movement countering the imposition of Western categories (Boghossian 2006; Lewis 2014; Schnegg 2015: 35). Before I begin with the specific lines of argument presented by the critics, I respond by way of examples to some of the logical problems involved in the study of universals.

Reification, Hidden Syllogisms, and Implicit Primitivity

There are many works that postulate a specific universal with wide-ranging implications. They are often problematic in that they produce general statements that are then coupled with fundamental questions. In the previous chapter, I discussed the pitfalls in conceptualizing and explaining universals. The information presented there is relevant because universal postulating is often linked with explanations for universals. Too often universals are seen as answering fundamental questions, such as "why do human beings have celebrations?" or "why do all folk groups have or make music?" Such questions imply universal assumptions that lead to a mistake often found in the literature concerning isolated universals: the implied syllogism.

Books about dance in human culture, for instance, are often based on extreme cosmological remarks, such as that the world is filled with never-ending movement. The authors of such books then pose the question of "why do humans (or folk groups) dance?" In the anthropology of dance, some argue that dance is universal because movement is in itself universal. Movement functions everywhere as a medium for communicating and expressing emotion. This is the thrust of work by Judith Lynne Hanna (1987: 5, 13, 31, 231), for example. Every human institution, action, and emotion is linked to movement, as languages too seem to be. Such arguments conceal conclusions (Williams 2004: 34) like the one drawn in two different ways below:

1. All human beings move.
2. Every kind of dance is a form of movement.
3. Conclusion: every movement made by human beings is dance.

1. Every dance is movement.
2. All human beings move.
3. Conclusion: every movement made by human beings is dance.

Drid Williams has convincingly shown that these arguments lead nowhere because we simply do not know what we are supposed to do with them. She brings up the case of kinship. Even when social relationships are found everywhere, anthropologists would not likely begin studies on kinship relationships with remarks on the universality of kinship or human relationships, nor would they conclude from the ubiquity of relationships that all kinship systems are the same (Williams 2004: 34). Williams, through the example of dance, shows how making claims of universality can entail the additional problem of their connection to implicitly made causal assumptions. Both popular scientific and anthropological representations of dance often try to show parallels between certain documented forms of dance (often among non-Western peoples) and specific movements made by animals. These representations combine an implicitly biological explanation with the assumption that primitivism is equated with unspoiled human origins. The assumption of a primordium supposedly explains everything. Accordingly, parallels are postulated between any and every (!) animal movement and all (!) human dance (Williams 2004: 53; see examples in Williams 2000). There is, however, a great difference between understanding the expression "dance of cultures" or "primitive dance" as all dance among all people (or, all dance with a simple structure) and a monolithic primordium (Williams 2004: 98, 118).

Monolithic claims of "somehow the same everywhere" or "always the same" easily emerge out of the combination of such conclusions, even in the opposing movements of left and right in dance as having the "same meaning everywhere." These are exactly the conclusions that appear in the literature as universals, especially in the field of evolutionary psychology. Reifications, which emerge from such conclusions and fulfill the wish for simple explanations, form a basic problem in research on universals, already discussed above in the instances of describing specific or separate or certain universals. This is one of the reasons why universals in this book are not defined with respect to any causal assumptions. Comparisons made in universal research often become problematic when different things are too quickly identified as being somehow equivalent and especially in likening the foreign too quickly with the familiar (nostrification). If critics regard this problem as great and irresolvable, it implies then a fundamental criticism of universal research. Since I have already dealt with this problem in Chapter 6, I do not explore it further here.

Relativist and Empirical Criticisms

Clifford Geertz has discussed universals especially in connection with our understanding or the idea of human beings (in particular Geertz 1965). In his early writings he quite clearly presented universalistic assumptions. In later works, however, he turned vehemently against determining or defining human nature by way of universals. According to Geertz, we should not try to separate human nature from culture, as human beings are fundamentally cultural creatures. Human beings are "cultural artifacts" because they only become complete through culturation. We first become people when we become individuals. This individualization is specific to context or culture and determined through historically contingent systems of meaning. Geertz (1965: 102–5) concludes that the essence of human beings does not rest in their unity ("transcultural consensus") but in their differences, or diversity, within the framework of cultural distinction. This remained his opinion until his death in 2006. His last statement on the topic formulated his thoughts in his usual eloquent style:

> My own view, merely to give it, because in a short compass I can hardly defend it, it is that either: (a) most (conceivably all) universals are so general as to be without intellectual force or interest, are large banalities lacking either circumstantially or surprise, precision or revelation, and thus are of pretty little use ... or (b) if universals do have a degree of non-triviality, circumstantiality, and originality, if they actually assert something interesting enough to be wrong ... they are ill-based. (Geertz 2000: 134–35)

Geertz accepts universals in the form of general existential problems, which are found in all societies. He sees the solutions as unique solutions to be understood only within their specific context, through a circumscriptual understanding. Human behavior is exceptionally malleable and, except for the trivial, lacking in constancy. In one publication alone, Geertz characterized supposed universals in harsh terms like "trivial," "pseudo-universal," "bloodless," "powerless," "banal," "vague," and "tautological," or as mere "clichés" (Geertz 1965: 105). Universals appear trivial because they are empty abstractions said about "everyone, everywhere" and are "... vague tautologies and forceless banalities" (Geertz 1965: 103; see "fake universals" in Lonner 1980). Even anthropologists who cannot be placed among the symbolists hold similar opinions. Edmund Leach, for one, although he makes universalistic statements in his own structuralist work, regards anthropology as an endeavor producing insights but not as a science producing refutable knowledge. In one of his late works he writes: "During the hundred years of their existence academic anthropologists have not discovered a single universally valid truth concerning either human culture or human society other that those which are treated as axioms: e.g., that all men have a language" (Leach 1982: 52)

Geertz postulates beyond this that human nature is a chimera, as there is no human nature independent of culture. Anthropological studies have shown this to be the result of human evolution. Culture did not arise sequentially in a cultural evolution that occurred after physical evolution, in a quasi-temporal "stratigraphic model" or as a later addition to a finished animal; rather, it played a deciding role in the development of the human animal. The cerebral cortex, as the most important human organ, emerged with culture. Human beings are then cultural artifacts (Geertz 1965: 110–13). Like Ernst Cassirer, Geertz maintains that the human being is an *animal symbolicum*, existing in a cultural web of meaning. And like Peter Berger and Thomas Luckmann, he considered humans to be *Homo socius*. Geertz backed his position with the example of Balinese culture. But Maurice Bloch, in his lecture on Malinowski (Bloch 1977), used Geertz's data on Bali in order to show the opposite, namely, that practical (instead of only ritual) concerns and contact with a natural environment led to cognitive universals, and in this particular case in a form of linear (in addition to cyclical) temporal concepts.

The classical argument against the existence of universals links the argument against universals to the argument against using biotic factors to understand societies. It follows, briefly put, that the sheer diversity existing within human culture reveals the uniqueness of the human being and represents the only human universal. This line of argument was advanced by Clifford Geertz and has been in use ever since. We can reconstruct the argumentation involved here as follows (see Carrithers 1992: 6–7):

1. The empirically documented diversity in human culture is vast.
2. This diversity is set down in ethnographic monographs, which act as an archive of human possibilities, showing how malleable human beings are.
3. The malleability results from the ability of each individual to be formed specific to a respective culture.
4. This ability of diversity separates human beings from other animals.
5. The diversity in cultures is the sum of effects of local cultural influences.
6. This malleability, understood as the ability to be different, is the only human universal.
7. Anthropologists do not need to consider biology and evolution.

A well-known argument against universals is based on the assertion that many societies do not have a word for a certain phenomenon such as "religion" or "art." However, that a society gets along, so to speak, without a word for a phenomenon does not mean that the phenomenon is not within that society or that it represents a trivial component of the culture (on art, see Anderson 2004: 282). The limits of our language are not simply a reflection of the limits of our world. This faulty conclusion is known to evolutionary biologists as "Sahlins's fallacy" (Irons and Cronk 2000: 6–10). Sahlins had criticized human sociobiology by arguing that many societies have no word for mathematical fractions, and therefore people from these societies would not be able to perform the calculations a socio-biologist requires to reason through "genetic interests" and kinship ratios (Sahlins 1976: 45). Richard Dawkins has responded by remarking that the implied conclusion here is like saying a snail must be able to understand mathematics because the form of a snail shell is a logarithmic spiral (Dawkins 1996: 310).

Fundamental Criticism: Charges of Eurocentrism and Hegemony

Some critics consider universals the result of a Eurocentric construct. The moderate, more methodologically based variants of this criticism were discussed in this volume's chapter on methods. At the level of empirical research, the problem of centrism is already apparent in the language. As already discussed, culturally centric or Eurocentric terminology can lead to claims of alleged universals. I find the fundamental criticisms to be exaggerated for the most part, but they need to be addressed. They could be useful as a corrective measure in dealing with overstated and hastily drawn universalizing conclusions. The search for universals, according to the critics, is often equated with normative projects of universalism. Claiming something is universal is thus seen as suspicious, absolutist, totalitarian, Eurocentric, ethnocentric, colonialist, imperialist, Orientalist, cultural imperialist, patriarchal, or in some way repressive, hegemonic, or simply arrogant (see the classic example of Said 2003). This is often the opinion in times of forced globalization: "The illusion of a cultural universalism is fed by an extrinsic egalitarianism, but must be regarded as a staged masking of globalization that arises out of the striving to usurp the strange" (Steixner 2008: 1).

It is therefore always necessary to ask whether claims of general or universal characteristics of people or cultures do not merely represent a generalizing of their uniqueness. Such an improper or illegitimate ethnocentric generalization occurs only through the marginalization of the other or in ignorance of difference (see Rüsen 1998: 28). It is important to separate the scientific discussion of universals—what this book is all about—from the normatively directed postulation of certain values as supposedly universal concepts.

The fundamental criticisms from this direction can be found in Geertz, who was one of the more profound critics of universal research. He ties universalism to fear of diversity and depicts it as a defensive reaction to relativization and rejection of everything that could lead to relativism (Geertz 1965). In particular, he criticizes a kind of universalism that was a form of anti-relativism, which he considered as morality beyond culture and knowledge beyond both. Geertz argues that universalistic statements and assumptions of human nature—whether as common sense, yearning ecumenicalism, or aggressive scientism—would try to ban the danger of relativism at the cost of truth (Geertz 1984: 263–66).

This criticism concerns many of the explicit and implicit universalistic positions presented in this book's introduction with regard to the debate on human rights and other normative universals. The normative interest in universals exists in the grand story of universalism and the "notion that all human beings are equal. Their different histories *should* flow together in the common current of one *single*, true and just order" (Wimmer 1997: 123, italics mine). The introduction dealt with current examples of such postulates with universalistic claims of validity, these being the right to equality, self-determination, solidarity, identity, or the right to be different, and the talk of a "new world order." Contrary to their claims of universalism, these normative postulates are often accompanied by ethnocentrism. Every culture can appear as a comprehensive worldly construct, as a possible human order, and therefore as a model with the claim of universality (Fuchs 1997: 142). If universalism is propagated as such a project, then it should be regarded as a goal and an effort to be produced in general agreement. Universalism understood as such is revealed only in a contextual form. It has to invoke a number of traditions and must be worked out interactively (Fuchs 1997: 149).

As already remarked several times in this text, many anthropologists are skeptical even of less challenging projects like the systematic comparison of several cultures. Many anthropologists find the comparison of monogamy between two cultures as problematic, mainly because of the difficulty in finding comparable units, a point already made by Edward Evan Evans-Pritchard (1902–73). This point, then, leads to a fundamental rejection of ever seriously conducting research in the area of universals. Authors who are more oriented toward a cultural relativism doubt the existence of even trivial universals, such as that human beings eat everywhere, and thereby question the basic translatability of cultures. Mark Hobart (1987: 39), for example, asks: "Everywhere animals and people eat. Is this not a universal which underwrites all translation?" His question is suggestive, and his answer negative. In Bali, he argues, there are at least eight words for "eating." Terms and concepts vary according to the depth of the speakers' acquaintance, forms of politeness, health [of the speakers], and caste affiliation. The supposed universal, on closer inspection, ends up revealing cultural uniqueness or peculiarity.

From the perspective of several critics, such as Geertz, every universal or universal position indicates in realistic terms a kind of absolutism or even cultural imperialism. Post-colonialists attack the assumption of universal features and phenomena under the catchword "universalism." Universalism is interpreted as an assumption that proceeds from an irreducibly common or universal feature found in the human being, in "common humanity," or in culture. This interpretation necessarily leads to the neglect of socially constructed influences, that is, the constitutive effects of local culture or local environment. As such, universalism is Eurocentric and serves only to support hegemonic dominance (Ashcroft, Griffiths, and Tiffin 1998: 235).

A prime example of this is the way English literature is used to teach Western values, leading to social control in the colonies. India is a striking or marked example. In the colonial British past, those writers who described the "universal human condition" were valued as truly great. Through this ideology, English people were characterized as both attractive and universal, or transcendental. This defined the entire colonial discussion in India in the nineteenth century and in other colonies in the twentieth. Homi Bhabha has said that a particularly perverse aspect of this universalistic-style hegemony is that the reader is made into a universally culturated reader through the literary canon. His or her cultural or social uniqueness and material condition are thereby denied (Bhabha 2000: 125–27). The Indian Gauri Viswanathan (1989: 22–23) has described this in sharp terms as "refraction of the rapacious, exploitative and ruthless actor of history into the reflexive subject of literature."

Charles Larsen brings up an example of these kinds of implicit, universalistic, naturalistic assumptions from his personal experience. During discussion of a novel by Thomas Hardy, his African students did not know what to make of the line "disappointed kisses" in the text. They localized, or subverted, his assumptions by simply asking, "What is a kiss?" (Larsen 1973). Postcolonial critics bring up another example, saying that mathematics, though supposedly universal, is anything but free of culture because it is constructed by human beings with a cultural history. Mathematics includes certain Western assumptions arising out of rationalism, atomism, and objectivism (Bishop 1990: 52; cf. Lakoff and Nunez 2000; G. Paul 2008b). David Suzuki has similarly been criticized for looking for epistemic parallels between the cosmology of American Indians and Western science, namely because he does not reflect on the use or necessity of such a comparison. It implies that two things are equivalent, or even worse, that Western science is "the 'real' ground of comparison" (Ashcroft et al. 1998: 237).

The claim of universality in Western culture is looked upon with suspicion when it sets borders around itself against "lesser" cultures through a false form of exclusion. Eagleton argues that if universality means that the Tungus people of Siberia will find themselves reflected in the work of Noel Coward, then it should be rejected, but if it means that these peoples feel pain just as Germans do, then it should be accepted (Eagleton 2000). The claim of wanting to make the rest of the world more "open" or "ready" for modern communication is also criticized. It seems universal but follows very specific Western interests, and serves, through specific means, an attitude that is Eurocentric and logocentric, for instance by debasing or devaluating non-European "nature" and non-European human beings or cultures (Kozlarek 2000: 86–88, 132–37, 238–40; also see J. Meyer 2005). This has book dealt with universals in a systematic way. The fascination and meandering history of universalistic and anti-universalistic thinking awaits a major study, but that would be another book (for an overview see Antweiler 2012a: 55–124). Still, in this chapter on critical positions a short remark on the history of thinking in American and British anthropology seems necessary.

Not until the student movement of the late 1960s was the search for universals seen as futile, wrong-headed, or even arrogant. At this time Clifford Geertz's writings became popular. Ever since, there has been a tendency to indiscriminately attack anthropology as a whole. The three main accusations are that anthropology is othering, is ahistorical, and treats other cultures as isolated units (e.g., Abu-Lughod 1991: 143; Fabian 1983; Keesing 1994a: 301, 306;

Said 2003). According to the primary charge, anthropology treats the peoples it studies as radically "alter." This "othering" is allegedly due to its culture concept and done through anthropological fieldwork and the writing of ethnographies. As Lewis critically comments on this attack: "The extraordinary idea has been put forth that choosing an object to study that is far from home is a way of distancing and alienating oneself from the object" (Lewis 2014: 13). The postmodern and postcolonial critiques had tremendous effects, especially in the teaching of U.S.-American departments. Till that time there had been two general types of courses. First, topically oriented courses taught students about broad "universals" such as kinship or culture and ecology. These courses often were comparative and considered both generalities and differences. Second, there were courses in ethnography or areas. Nowadays the majority of courses at the perhaps 550 colleges and universities teaching anthropology are on problematic aspects in human affairs, such as misery, inequality, and racism (Lewis 2014: 63–64).

Beyond that, in an ingenious paradox, anthropology since then has been accused of both exoticizing others and universalizing them (Lewis 2014: 12). The politicization of anthropology and the suspicion of established ways reached its extreme during the meetings of the American Anthropological Association in the early 1970s. During the AAA conference in 1972, Pierre Maranda opened the program with a message of welcome titled "Universals or Imperialism?" and asked whether our endeavor to find universals is an act of "covert intellectual imperialism" (quoted in Lewis 2014: 44). Instead of Geertz's harsh but at least arguably justified censure against the search for universals (Geertz 1965) being read as a constructive critique, his positions were canonized in radicalized ways. Lewis (2014: esp. 1–26, 73–105) convincingly demonstrates through a careful reading of classics of twentieth-century anthropology that large parts of the anthropological enterprise are simply dismissed by critics like Fabian, Abu-Lughod, and Keesing. Portrayals of anthropological theories and fieldwork in these widely used texts should not be regarded as reasonable characterizations of the storehouse of knowledge about the peoples of the world established in twentieth-century anthropology. Like Lewis (2014: 21), I would argue that the broad heritage of literature of concern for both differences among cultures and universals has been reduced to a handful of convenient stereotypes. This misrepresentation and the accompanying loss of anthropological knowledge have too easily have led students, younger professionals, and scientists in other disciplines to ignore this body of ideas, problems, and data.

Figure 9. Traveling in South Asia. Photo by Maria Blechmann-Antweiler.

CHAPTER 9

Synthesis
Human Universals and Human Sciences

> *Given the diversity of human forms of life,*
> *what must be true of humans in general?*
> —Michael Carrithers, *Why Humans Have Cultures*

Human universals challenge researchers in the human and cultural sciences with a simple empirical fact: Considering all the possibilities we might be able to come up with, there exist only a limited number of diverse cultural forms and variants. One might then ask why the actual spectrum of human diversity might be vast yet is still much narrower than all the plausible variations in "ethnographic hyperspace." Once we find a cultural pattern in only a few cultures that are historically (almost) unrelated, we are faced with having to try to explain it. We do not need to be completely fixated on the general universality of a cultural phenomenon in order to come across pertinent questions that are important in the human sciences. Where do the limits of randomness end, and what factors restrain plausible diversity? In Table 9.1 I have outlined some of these factors, ordered by way of proximate to ultimate poles.

Many diverse and specific observations concerning universals have been not backed with substantial evidence that would make their alleged existence empirically certain. Both theoretically and methodologically, universals represent a problematic field in research. This book is therefore in many respects no more than a preliminary study toward a theoretically oriented but empirically based project known of universals research. We need more knowledge on the topic, as universals are more than just a challenge for researchers: they are also relevant as a topic in current political and societal debate, especially because of their global component with regard to human rights, racism, the "conflict of cultures," and cultural globalization. If we look carefully at the discussion of these issues involving universal human features or human culture, we find constant assumptions. They mostly remain only implicitly understood and are therefore left unexamined. But they are potent nevertheless.

Table 9.1. Factors limiting the potential diversity in "ethnographic hyperspace" to realized or actual diversity

Dimension	Factors involved in limiting diversity (ordered from proximate to ultimate)
Ratio, individual goals and values	– Nondesirable options (e.g., due to anticipation)
Everyday life and degree of activity in the physical world	– Options that are not practiced, are inefficient, or are deemed too risky (see Zipf's Law)
Individual limitations in perception and intelligence (interindividual, extremely variable)	– Unrecognized potential (e.g., options in daily activities that remain unseen)
Individual limitations in memory	– Options that are forgotten or remembered too late (e.g., forgotten possibilities)
Cultural standards: goals and values specific to a particular culture	– Options that are not desired, not pursued, or not found acceptable (e.g., individual innovations that have not been socially accepted)
Cultural standards: norms specific to a particular culture	– Not socially expected (e.g., negative) sanctioned behavior
Standardized goods, services, procedures (policies)	– Deviations specifically prevented (e.g., process of work, as in "McDonaldization")
Diffusion of artifacts	– Variants that do not reach recipients (e.g., through loss or dispersal)
Diffusion of ideas ("stimulus diffusion")	– Options that are unrecognized or misunderstood (e.g., within intercultural communication)
Diffusion of innovations	– Inventions or discoveries that are not wanted or desired by the recipient (e.g., non-adopters)
Globalization	– Reduction of existing diversity (e.g., languages)
Intragenerational structural limitations to the passing on of nongenetic material/information	– Information that cannot be passed on by oral communication alone (e.g., complex visual data through oral transmission)
Transgenerational structural limitations to the passing on of nongenetic material/information:	– Inadequate transmission of cross-generational information without external media (e.g., comprehensive language information)
Structural demands within sociality	– Nonviable transgenerational options in societies (e.g., constant discharge conflicts)
Functional demands of complex societies (ultrasociality)	– Options that are unfeasible in large societies (e.g., collective decisions made through face-to-face communication)

Biotic behavioral tendencies (inclinations)	– Potential that is forgotten or not considered, rationalized, or verbalized (e.g., in body language and in quick reactions)
Biotic limitations to capabilities	– Behavior that is not psychologically possible (e.g., extreme multitasking, absolute memory)
Needs related to the organism (survival, metabolism, nourishment)	– Behavior that is damaging to the organism (e.g., options that cause illness or death)
Evolutionary demands (reproduction)	– Fitness-reducing options (e.g., total celibacy)

The topic of universals corresponds to the question of the nature of human beings and is relevant to any questions posed on human nature as well. But these two points are not in fact the same. Research into universals offers an empirical approach to the topic of being human that avoids pure speculation. Anthropological research into universals provides a particular cultural theoretical perspective with cross-cultural data. With such tools at their disposal, researchers into universals can make a useful contribution by examining ideas or images of human beings that are all too often ideologically tainted or marked by pure wishful thinking in the end. Universal research can also be useful in limiting or preventing rashly made normative, idealistic, or extreme sociobiological assumptions, as well as nonbiological images or concepts of the world. An important quality of anthropological universal research—one that contrasts with other ways of studying universal human characteristics—is that here, universal features do not refer to individuals, human beings as members of a species, or humanity in general, but to societies.

Universals as Pancultural Patterns

Universals are phenomena that occur regularly in all or almost all known societies. In this book universals are defined with conscious avoidance of attempts to make causal assumptions. This is not only advisable when dealing with descriptive definitions— I can name two more reasons for avoiding causalities exactly here, in a discussion on universals. Firstly, universals are not simply conjectured out of a void but rather are discussed with a certain degree of assumed obviousness. Here as well we see that universals are often equated per se with human nature or explained through human biology. It is a fact that many universals are connected in some way or another with biotic factors. The connection is indirect, though, and not all universals have biotic causes. They could, for example, be traced back to worldwide diffusion or simply to having been formed under similar circumstances in the practice of daily life.

Reflections on universals swing between the two poles of the trivial and the insightful. Lists of supposed universals do not present real results, but their use offers a critical treatment of the topic. They also represent an important step in generating empirical questions and constructive explanations. Universals can be either very general or very specific. The more general they appear, the more obvious and trivial they become in our understanding of them. Specific universals, in contrast, are more surprising but tend to be classified as "mere speculation" or doubtful. Research into universals fundamentally includes both invariance and variation. It is important to keep in mind that the many possible modes of variation are also subject to rules governing invariance. Not only claims of universals but also each and every established universal should be considered at best a hypothesis or, even more cautiously, a suggestion. Research into universals means not just postulating or proving universals, but also exposing supposed universals as false!

Universalization and Universalism: A Necessary Debate

In this study, two issues that have come up over and over need to be addressed for the sake of further debate on the political implications of universals, which have not been the focus of this book. The first issue concerns the problem of projecting cultural views onto others, which can also be a form of wishful thinking. The second issue involves the notorious polarity—and not necessarily the contradiction—between cultural universals and the specifics or particularities of culture. Both issues show that the discussion on universals is tightly intertwined with the worldwide debate on cultural uniqueness, difference, and diversity. If this discussion is to remain useful from within a polarized context, then it is important to remember that universality does not stand in opposition to difference, and must not be a universalism pitted against a particularism. Following the lead of Étienne Balibar, we can accept that in their core forms, concepts of diversity represent universalism. The notoriously incipient dichotomies are a clear indication "that every speaker (and every statement) of the universal is located *within* and not *outside* the field of discourse and ideologies that is or are being examined" (Balibar 2008: 3; italics mine). This becomes particularly clear in programmatic versions of multiculturalism, when the right to be different is purported together with universal or universalized values.

In this respect, a fundamental discussion on the different forms of universalism becomes more appropriate than a debate on universalism vs. particularism. We must take a systematic look at the different forms of universalisms and their relationship to each other. According to Balibar (2008: 2), an "intensive universalism" fabricates sameness or oneness and thereby suppresses differences, whereas an "extensive universalism" wants to remove the limitations of recognition with the final goal of creating a cosmopolitan order. In contrast, Michael Walzer (1996) distinguishes between an all encompassing law of universalism with coherent or consistent legal claims or entitlements, and a "repeating universalism" with an inherent principle of differentiating recognition. Alain Badiou (2009: 193) separates a "true universalism" of equality, a form that goes back to St. Paul, from a "false universalism" of the liberal world economy that is based on equivalence and formal homogeneity rather than equality. Ideas about universalism as a project of expansion are now considered antiquated. Comparable oppositions are found in the work of Rousseau and Marx, and in current positions from, for example, Chakrabarty's "two models for translation" (2007). Remarkably, all these typologies concerning universalisms—whether from Rousseau, Marx, Balibar, Walzer, Badiou, or Chakrabarty—are once again dichotomous.

Anthropology and Cross-Cultural Comparison

In cooperation with many other disciplines, anthropology can make a major contribution to exploring the topic of universalism. Classic studies of specific ethnic groups can be important in rebutting the claim that a certain type of behavior is not found in any single culture. The documentation of widespread cultural patterns through systematic cultural comparison is a central contribution of anthropology. Moreover, in collaboration with historians anthropologists can describe the specifically local and temporally conditioned forms of universals. Anthropologists are also, due to their holistic and functionally oriented concept of culture, capable of determining universal implications by exposing their functional qualities. But they must guard against the pitfalls of seeing likenesses too quickly where a more careful analysis would reveal the finer differential structures, on the one hand; and emphasizing differences too quickly on the other. Despite the many methodological problems, however, there exist anthropological procedures that enable us to approach the topic empirically and systematically rather than only speculatively.

So far, studies of universals have been dominated by explanations based on evolutionary biological theories. I see here the importance of a contribution from anthropology in that the field, in contrast to sociobiology and evolutionary psychology, belongs more in the humanities than the natural sciences. The evolutionary biological perspective is important for understanding universals. As opposed to many of my colleagues in anthropology, I find behavioral ecology, sociobiology, and evolutionary psychology to be of central importance when we are trying to formulate a scientific idea of who human beings are. An anthropological perspective is therefore even more useful, as its healthy skepticism is of service in confronting biological explanations for everything.

Thus I would like to conclude this topic with a quote from a book on the anthropology of religion by Brian Morris: "Anthropology, despite its diversity, has a certain unity of purpose and vision. It is unique among the human sciences in both putting an emphasis and value on cultural difference, thus offering a cultural critique of Western capitalism and its culture, and in emphasizing people's shared humanity, thus enlarging our sense of moral community and placing humans squarely 'within nature'" (Morris 2006: 2).

Culture and Bios

The theoretical and methodological problem of the fusion of culture and bios is included under the topic of universals. Culture, in the sense of nongenetic factors in the creation of the self, forms a biotic existential necessity for human beings, which means there can be no empirical version of what human beings are, in any "natural" sense, without considering the role of culture. The question of innate vs. environmental—as always a dominant dichotomy, be it as contrast, complement, or interaction—presents one of the more important obstacles in the research into universals. Culture and nature as phenomena are factors to be decoupled into likenesses and differences. In theory, genes could explain likenesses and differences, and culture can as well.

But organizing universals in two categories as related either to the organism, or to the cultural "veneer" between the nonvariable biotic level and the variable cultural level, does not offer a reasonable solution to our debate on universals. Universals do not have to be partially genetic. More than one combination of causes is always possible. If the human being is the subject matter, then we need to use knowledge from both the cultural and the living sciences to gain an understanding of the human being in his or her entirety. This would produce a naturalistic worldview that is not reduced to biology but is, by necessity, oriented along biocultural lines. Many ways of doing this are possible. A naturalistic worldview is not to be simply equated with a sociobiological or evolutionary psychological view (see Slingerland and Collard 2012). This is evident in, for example, a comparison of Bidney's (1947) concept of culture as self-cultivation of human nature, Rensch's (1991) "universal worldview," and Edward Wilson's (1998) "consilience."

Research Outlook: Ultrasociality and Latour's Hybrids

Current human communities, whether in ethnic groups or organized states, are demographically and spatially much larger than anything we know from primates or anthropogenesis. They represent highly complex societies or parts of such societies. These societies, being larger and more complex than the human groups existing in the evolutionary history of human beings, as far back to the Holocene with groups comprising ca. 150 individuals, are characterized as "ultrasocial" (Dunbar 1993, 2004: 59–94; also see D. Campbell 1983: 12–

13). Beyond this, almost all human groups have at their disposal an incredible supply of material objects. These are often artifacts that extend over generations. In addition, human groups make intensive and at the same time often transgenerational changes to the physical environment. Almost everywhere on earth, human beings live together as members of ultrasocial collectives, not only socially close together but also together in anthropogenically transformed landscapes that are physical environments decisively determined by culture.

According to an evolutionary or historical perspective, human beings have only recently begun to live in large, complex community structures. The greater part of the history of *Homo sapiens* is marked by life in small groups. This fact has generally been considered relevant only by evolutionary psychologists, who, as opposed to sociobiologists, focus less on the commonalities between humans and other animals than on the unique particularities of human beings (Eibl 2007: 2). Evolutionary psychologists are concerned with how the human psyche was formed through "recurrent environmental problems" (Kenrick, Li and Butner 2003: 4), an issue of great significance for an understanding of universals. Early human groups were not only small; they also used comparatively few artifacts and modified their physical environment very little. The earlier societies in which most of human history was played out had very few material or nonphysical transporters of information. Writing or monuments as cross-generational transporters of social memory did not yet exist.

The phenomenon of ultrasociality, and the requirements of living in large and complex societies, played a part in the formation of universals. On a functional level, these complex societies require complex institutions that extend beyond the level of kinship organizations (Richerson and Boyd 1999, 2001: 201–2). Spatially large, demographically dense, socioeconomically complex societies need a division of labor and subsystems such as bureaucracy. Along with the domestication of plants and animals and the development of cities and translocal polities, social divisions emerged over time along the following lines: occupation (peasant, pastoralist, craftsman, or merchant), haves vs. have-nots, educated vs. illiterate people, military personnel vs. civilians, urban vs. rural life, and center vs. periphery. Once these divisions came into being, we do not know of any larger society that has been able to permanently remove the resulting inequalities beyond small subgroups (Holenstein, pers. comm., 2009). They are not biotically determined, but the biotic divisions the groups share, such as those between ages and sexes, prove to be pancultural.

Such societies must develop particular adaptations to the problems of their own complexities as well as their environment, with its complex neighboring societies. Accordingly, we can expect that human groups, regardless of culture, begin to develop particular similarities after reaching a certain degree of expansion, population size, population density, and complexity. The beginning and formation of writing in complex societies is then to be expected, as it is the only way of passing on the information necessary for continuing certain complex traditions. Features of writing systems include calculated practices that strongly resemble each other. Architecture and art are likewise nonphysical media significant for the transfer of cultural information in complex societies (Welsch 2006: 144). One of the conditions of industrial societies is the development of mass media, representing, historically, a new kind of near universal. In mass media products such as films, we can search further for specific universals (Uhl and Kumar 2000; Hejl 2005).

We can postulate universals that are in fact universal implications, tied to the preconditions that create ultrasociality. Since in today's world almost all societies have crossed over Dunbar's threshold to ultrasociality (Dunbar 1993, 2004: 75–84), we can expect to find at least near universals. Thus a reflection of ultrasociality can complement the "tribal" perspective of the fields of sociobiology and evolutionary psychology as a way of explaining evolved psychic universals. It offers a more comprehensive dimension to the understanding of long-term social development in larger societies. I would like to use a long-standing topic in sociology and anthropology—the nexus of kinship, altruism, and sexuality—to speculate on how certain scenarios are plausible in ultrasocial societies:

> Altruism among kin (or among familiar persons) as a bio-evolutionary universal becomes stabilized through cultural norms of kinship solidarity, functioning as a (universal) binding agent of culturally *variable* social structures. The functional easing of kinship relationships and their elimination from evolving functional subsystems is a *universal of development* in modern types of society. In the process of this development, the gratification of undoubtedly universal sexual needs is no longer constrained by societal considerations, and can develop more informally. (Hejl and Antweiler 2004: 11)

This suggests that (1) universals produce generally systemic correlations and are useful in understanding cultures as social systems, that (2) biotic universals can be integrated with nonbiotic universals, and finally that (3) universals are able to exist not only in particular conditions but also in sequences, or dynamic relationships. Such universals of development at the level of social systems, which are not to be confused with ontogenetic universals of development, could be an especially interesting topic for future research into universals.

These considerations could correspond to work in other fields, such as sociological research into functional conditions or demands in societies. With regard to correlations between social complexity and ubiquitous patterns, we find indications of parallels between the development of different early, historically independent states. In the past, the sociologists who dealt with these concepts, such as Talcott Parsons (1964), described them as "evolutionary universals." Yet their work has remained almost untouched in the research on universals. Bourdieu also touched on these issues with his formulation of "structural dominants" at the level of system integration that delimits the developmental corridors of societies (see D. Groh 1992a: 19–20). Recently some universal historians and global historians have produced contributions that make it possible to search for universals in ultrasociality. The work coming out of civilization studies—when compared to earlier world system studies—is especially interesting for its expanded empirical approach along with its concentration of society over longer periods of time. Working on a quantitative and longitudinal level, these studies explore the spatial extent, internal dynamic, and regional effects of larger civilizations.

On a theoretical level, the historically directed French sociology of knowledge holds potential, as in the work of Serge Moscovici and of Michel Callon especially, and some of the work of Bruno Latour. Long before the work of cultural evolutionists and their co-evolutionary concepts, Moscovici had already made clear that human beings have drastically changed their environment through work and technology to the extent that nature—including human nature—has become intensely domesticated. Nature therefore has a "human history" (Moscovici 1990: 52–53, 447–504). We then have to look deeper at the new composites coming out of a cultivated nature and a natural culture. A useful maxim would be to ease up on all a priori distinctions between what is natural and what social, something Michael Callon has postulated as principle of free association (Callon 1986: 196–201).

Latour has offered us a good starting point with his concept of "hybrids," which combines the supposedly purely social with the supposedly purely natural. We can assume that those societies that are ultrasocial are especially capable of producing hybrids through co-production or coevolution. These hybrids, which basically are physical objects, have to be regarded together with Latour's model of actor networks, which in contrast to social networks unite persons and objects from different times and places (Latour 2001: 35–36, 2015; Degele and Dries 2006: 136–38; for a critique see Schulz-Schaeffer 2000: 202–7). An example of this can be found in Callon and his studies on a cross-generational network of fishermen, mussel populations, and even scientists (Callon 1986: 204–6). A central point here is that societies are held together not only by social ties but also through objects. This distinguishes them from the societies of other primates (Strum and Latour 1987: 785–7). A more precise analysis of the role of objects (whether natural objects or artifacts) in the sense of hybrid fusion, would give us a proper, concrete tool for the empirical study of universals through ultrasociality.

Table 9.2. Basic orientations found in the human sciences: Universal approach vs. absolutism and relativism

		Is the specific context of a particular culture a fundamental factor in the forming of human groups?	
		no	yes
Are the commonalities within human experience a fundamental factor in the forming of human life?	no	(Limited possibilities in an intersubjective and generalizing science of human beings)	Radical relativism
	yes	Absolutism: e.g., "human nature" in the sense of "anthropological constants," "psychic unity"	Universal approach

Source: modified after Adamopoulos and Lonner 1994: 130 and Lonner 2005: 16

Conclusion

Research into universals implies the general problem of methodologically driven abstraction. Universals are to be understood as features that potentially occur in all human groups, that exist in most or almost all cultures, and that vary between individuals. Human groups show universal features that manifest themselves in different ways and at the same time to varying degrees as they are modified, exaggerated, or reduced. Simply put, all cultures are the same, and all cultures are different. On of this book's fundamental points is that when it comes to universals, the status of humans differs from that of animals. With animals, universal statements emerge in terms of ethograms for species that we expect to find in any population of thet species. Thus we can examine a single population of a certain species with consideration of environmental parameters and then make universal statements as concerns this particular species. Even among some other primates this is true only within limits: for example, behavioral differences do occur between various open-landscape populations among chimpanzees and orangutans. This kind of generalization cannot be made for human populations.

Universals are simply not to be equated with the *conditio humana* or with "anthropological constants" as discussed in philosophy. If understood in absolute terms, universalism remains as untenable as a one-sided, mutated form of particularism coming out of relativism. In a dogmatic form of universalism, one's own and not one's own, or the "other," become exclusive instances of the same, or become identical (Acham 2001: 121). On the other hand, a one-sided insistence on cultural difference leads into a scientific cul-de-sac. Both the one-sided celebration of difference and the obsession regarding otherness give "culture" an impenetrable stature, thereby making it politically dangerous (J. Fox 1971; Pohl 1999: 28; van der Walt 2006: 237–39; Malik 2014).

Going a step further in emphasizing this point, Table 9.2 presents, in a somewhat simplistic manner, the position of the universal approach in comparison to absolutist and extreme relativist positions. I have avoided using the term "universalism" because it too often represents an ideological perspective. Likenesses and particularities are both theoretically meaningful. In this book I have discussed universals, not cultural universals. Doing so has allowed me to define the phenomenon of "universal" free of any explanation, or in this case, cultural explanation. Keeping the *definition* free of causes allows us to look precisely for causality. Universals are nevertheless called cultural universals because they are found empirically by comparing cultures, not individuals. More precisely formulated, the term would be "pancultural universals," but this seems inconvenient. These pancultural universals are not to be equated with biopsychic universals. Some, but only some, universals are based on direct or indirect effects of biopsychic universals.

The fundamental challenge of universals is based in empirical findings of nontrivial likenesses among the peoples of this planet, despite tremendous cultural diversity. Perhaps Donald Brown, the doyen of an anthropology of universals, said it best in his recent summation of the current anthropological relevance of universals and the central role of ethnographic research: "Given the present assumptions and conditions impinging upon and shaping anthropological theory, the study of human universals is assuming a larger role to play than was possible during much of the last century. That role extends well beyond anthropology yet remains centrally dependent on ethnographic reporting" (Brown 2013: 412).

Figure 10. A German woman selects postcards. Photo by Maria Blechmann-Antweiler.

Bibliography

Abu-Lughod, Lila. 1991. Writing Against Culture. In Richard G. Fox (ed.), *Recapturing Anthropology. Working in the Present*. Santa Fe: School of American Research Press, 137–62.
Acham, Karl. 2001. "Soziale Universalien und sozialwissenschaftliche Anthropologie." In Peter M. Hejl (ed.), *Universalien und Konstruktivismus*. Frankfurt am Main: Suhrkamp Verlag, 95–125.
Adamopoulos, John and Walter J. Lonner. 1994. "Absolutism, Relativism and Universalism in the Study of Human Behavior." In Walter J. Lonner and Roy S. Malpass (eds.), *Psychology and Culture*. Boston: Allyn and Bacon, 129–34.
Adams, William Yewdale. 1998. *The Philosophical Roots of Anthropology*. CSLI Lecture Notes, 86. Stanford, CA: Center for the Study of Language and Information, CSLI Publications.
Aginsky, Burt W. and Ethel G. Aginsky. 1948. The Importance of Language Universals. *Word* 4: 168–72.
Aiken, Nancy E. 1998. *The Biological Origins of Art*. Human Evolution, Behavior, and Intelligence. Westport, CT, and London: Praeger Publishers.
Aitchison, Jean. 1996. *The Seeds of Speech. Language Origin and Evolution*. Cambridge Approaches to Linguistics. Cambridge: Cambridge University Press.
Alcock, John. 2006. *Animal Behavior. An Evolutionary Approach*. Munich: Elsevier, Spektrum Akademischer Verlag.
Aleksandrowicz, Dariusz. 2011. *Kultur statt Wissenschaft? Gegen eine kulturalistisch reformierte Epistemologie*. Kulturwissenschaften 10. Berlin: Frank and Timme Verlag für Wissenschaftliche Literatur.
Alland, Alexander. 1970. *Evolution und menschliches Verhalten*. Conditio Humana. Ergebnisse aus den Wissenschaften vom Menschen. Frankfurt am Main: S. Fischer Verlag. Originally *Evolution and Human Behavior*, Garden City, NY: Natural History Press, 1967.
Alverson, Hoyt. 1994. *Semantics and Experience. Universal Metaphors of Time in English, Mandarin, Hindi, and Sesotho*. Baltimore, MD: Johns Hopkins University Press.
Amborn, Hermann. 1993. "Handlungsfähiger Diskurs: Reflexionen zur Aktionsethnologie." In Wolfdietrich Schmied-Kowarzik and Justin Stagl (eds.), *Grundfragen der Ethnologie. Beiträge zur gegenwärtigen Theorie-Diskussion*. Berlin: Dietrich Reimer Verlag, 129–52.
Ambos, Claus, Stephan Hotz, Gerald Schwedler, and Stefan Weinfurter (eds.). 2005. *Die Welt der Rituale. Von der Antike bis heute*. Darmstadt: Wissenschaftliche Buchgesellschaft.
American Anthropological Association. 1947. Statement on Human Rights. Submitted to the United Nations Commission on Human Rights. *American Anthropologist* 49: 539–43.

Anderson, Richard L. 2004: *Calliope's Sisters. A Comparative Study of Philosophies of Art*. 2nd ed. Englewood Cliffs, NJ: Prentice Hall, Pearson Education.
Annan, Kofi A. 2002. "Die Nobelpreisrede." *Vereinte Nationen* (Spring): 21–27.
Antweiler, Christoph. 1988. *Kulturevolution als transgenerationaler Wandel. Probleme des neueren Evolutionismus und Lösungsansätze dargestellt unter besonderer Berücksichtigung der angloamerikanischen Diskussion um sogenannte kulturelle Selektion*. Kölner Ethnologische Studien 13. Berlin: Dietrich Reimer Verlag.
———. 1989. "Eibl-Eibesfeldts Thesen zu einer multiethnischen Gesellschaft: Ein Kommentar." *Zeitschrift für Ethnologie* 114(1): 21–26.
———. 1993. "Universelle Erhebungsmethoden und lokale Kognition am Beispiel urbaner Umweltkognition in Süd-Sulawesi/Indonesien." *Zeitschrift für Ethnologie* 118(2): 251–87.
———. 1994. "Bios-Kultur-Geschichte: Anthropos. Neue Literatur zu einer integrierten Humanwissenschaft." *Anthropos* 90(1–3): 228–34.
———. 1998. "Local Knowledge and Local Knowing. An Anthropological Analysis of Contested 'Cultural Products' in the Context of Development." *Anthropos* 93(4–6): 469–94.
———. 2000. *Urbane Rationalität. Eine stadtethnologische Studie zu Ujung Pandang (Makassar), Indonesien*. Kölner Ethnologische Mitteilungen, 12. Berlin: Dietrich Reimer Verlag.
———. 2003. "Kulturelle Vielfalt. Ein ethnologischer Forschungsüberblick zu inter- und intrakultureller Diversität." In Helmut Wächter, Günther Vedder, and Meik Führing (eds.), *Personelle Vielfalt in Organisationen*. Trierer Beiträge zum Diversity Management 1. Munich and Mering: Rainer Hampp Verlag, 45–69.
———. 2004a. "Ethnozentrismus. Konzentrischer Dualismus als ubiquitäres Toleranzhindernis." In Hamid Reza Yousefi and Klaus Fischer (eds.), *Interkulturelle Orientierung. Grundlegung des Toleranz-Dialogs, Teil I: Methoden und Konzeptionen*. Nordhausen: Verlag Traugott Bautz, 261–87.
———. 2004b. "Local Knowledge Theory and Methods. An Urban Model from Indonesia." In Alan Bicker, Paul Sillitoe, and Johan Pottier (eds.), *Investigating Local Knowledge. New Directions, New Approaches*. Aldershot and Burlington: Ashgate Publishing, 1–34.
———. 2005a. *Ethnologie. Ein Führer zu populären Medien*. Ethnologische Paperbacks. Berlin: Dietrich Reimer Verlag.
———. 2005b. "Analogisierung als spezielle Form von Vergleich: eine nützliche Methode der interdisziplinären Evolutionsforschung." In *Erwägen, Wissen, Ethik, Deliberation, Knowledge, Ethics* 16(3): 370–71.
———. 2007. *Grundpositionen interkultureller Ethnologie*. Interkulturelle Bibliothek 79. Nordhausen: Verlag Traugott Bautz.
———. 2008a. "Evolutionstheorien in den Sozial- und Kulturwissenschaften. Zusammenhangs- und Analogiemodelle." In Christoph Antweiler, Nicole Thies, and Christoph Lammers (eds.), *Die unerschöpfte Theorie. Evolution und Kreationismus in den Wissenschaften*. Aschaffenburg: Alibri Verlag, 115–41.
———. 2008b. "Universalien – Muster im Meer kultureller Vielfalt." In "Universalismus," special issue, *Polylog. Zeitschrift für Interkulturelles Philosophieren* 20: 103–5.
———. 2012a. *Was ist den Menschen gemeinsam? Über Kultur und Kulturen*. 2nd ed., special edition (WBG Bibliothek, BoD). Darmstadt: Wissenschaftliche Buchgesellschaft.
———. 2012b. *Inclusive Humanism. Anthropological Basics for a Realistic Cosmopolitanism*. Reflections on (in) Humanity 4. Göttingen: V+R Unipress and Taipeh: National Taiwan University Press.
———. 2012c. "On Cultural Evolution. A Review of Current Research toward a Unified Theory of Societal Change." *Anthropos* 107(1): 217–27.

———. 2013. "Kulturen sind keine Flüsse oder Landschaften, sondern Systeme." *Zeitschrift für Kulturwissenschaft* 1: 177–82.
———. forthcoming. "On the Human Addiction to Norms. Social Norms and Cultural Universals of Normativity." In Neil Roughley and Kurt Bayertz (eds.), *The Normative Animal? On the Anthropological Significance of Social, Moral, and Linguistic Norms.* Oxford: Oxford University Press.
Antweiler, Christoph and Richard Newbold Adams (eds.). 1991. *Social Reproduction, Cultural Selection, and the Evolution of Social Evolution.* Cultural Dynamics. Leiden: E.J. Brill.
Apel, Karl-Otto. 1995. "Anderssein, ein Menschenrecht?" In Hilmar Hoffmann and Dieter Kramer (eds.), *Anderssein, ein Menschenrecht. Über die Vereinbarkeit universaler Normen mit kultureller und ethnischer Vielfalt. Römerberg-Gespräche 1994.* Weinheim and Basel: Beltz-Athenäum, 9–20.
Appiah, Kwame Anthony. 2007. *Der Kosmopolit. Philosophie des Weltbürgertums.* Munich: Verlag C. H. Beck. Originally *Cosmopolitanism. Ethics in a World of Strangers,* New York and London: Norton, 2006.
Arendt, Hannah. 1994. *Zwischen Vergangenheit und Zukunft. Übungen im politischen Denken I.* Munich and Zürich: Piper Verlag.
Arens, William. 1978. *The Man-Eating Myth. Anthropology and Anthropophagy.* Oxford: Oxford University Press.
Argyrou, Vassos. 2005. *The Logic of Environmentalism. Anthropology, Ecology and Postcoloniality.* Studies in Environmental Anthropology and Ethnobiology 1. New York and Oxford: Berghahn Books.
Arlt, Gerhard. 2001. *Philosophische Anthropologie.* Sammlung Metzler 334. Stuttgart and Weimar: Verlag J. B. Metzler.
Armstrong, David Malet. 1989. *Universals. An Opinionated Introduction.* Boulder, CO: Westview Press.
Armstrong, Karen. 2006. *Die Achsenzeit. Vom Ursprung der Weltreligionen.* Frankfurt am Main Siedler Verlag. Originally *The Great Transformation. The Beginning of Our Religious Traditions,* New York: Alfred A. Knopf, 2006.
Arnhart, Larry. 1998. *Darwinian Natural Right. The Biological Ethics of Human Nature.* SUNY Series in Philosophy and Biology. Albany, NY: State University of New York Press.
———. 2005. *Darwinian Conservatism.* Societas: Essays in Political and Cultural Criticism 18. Exeter and Charlottesville, VA: Imprint Academic.
Ashcroft, Bill, Gareth Griffiths, and Helen Tiffin (eds.). 1998. *Key Concepts in Post-Colonial Studies.* Key Concepts. London and New York: Routledge.
Assiter, Alison. 2003. *Revisiting Universalism.* Basingstoke and New York: Palgrave Macmillan.
Assmann, Aleida. 2004a. "Einleitung." In Aleida Assmann, Ulrich Gaier, and Gisela Trommsdorff (eds.), *Positionen der Kulturanthropologie.* With Karolina Jeftic. Frankfurt am Main: Suhrkamp Verlag, 9–18.
———. 2004b. "Neuerfindungen des Menschen. Literarische Anthropologien im 20. Jahrhundert." In Aleida Assmann, Ulrich Gaier, and Gisela Trommsdorff (eds.), *Positionen der Kulturanthropologie.* With Karolina Jeftic. Frankfurt am Main: Suhrkamp Verlag, 90–117.
Assmann, Aleida, Ulrich Gaier, and Gisela Trommsdorff (eds.). 2004. *Positionen der Kulturanthropologie.* With Karolina Jeftic. Frankfurt am Main: Suhrkamp Verlag.
——— (eds.). 2005. *Zwischen Literatur und Anthropologie.* Tübingen: Gunter Narr Verlag.
Astuti, Rita, Gregg Solomon, and Susan Carey. 2004. *Constraints on Conceptual Development. A Case Study of the Acquisition of Folkbiological and Folksociological Knowledge*

in Madagascar. Monographs for the Society for the Research in Child Development 277. London: Blackwell.
Atran, Scott. 1990. *Cognitive Foundations of Natural History. Towards an Anthropology of Science.* Cambridge: Cambridge University Press.
———. 1998. "Folk Biology and the Anthropology of Science. Cognitive Universals and Cultural Particulars." *Behavioral and Brain Sciences* 21: 547–609.
———. 2002. *In Gods We Trust. The Evolutionary Landscape of Religion.* Evolution and Cognition. Oxford: Oxford University Press.
Atran, Scott and Douglas L. Medin. 2008. *The Native Mind and the Cultural Construction of Nature.* Life and Mind: Philosophical Issues in Biology and Psychology. Cambridge, MA, and London: The MIT Press.
Averson, Hoyt. 1994. *The Semantics of Experience. Universal Metaphors of Time in English, Mandarin, Hindi, and Sesotho.* Baltimore: Johns Hopkins University Press.
Avital, Eytan and Eva Jablonka. 2000. *Animal Traditions. Behavioral Inheritance in Evolution.* Cambridge: Cambridge University Press.
Bachmann-Medick, Doris. 2006. *Cultural Turns. Neuorientierungen in den Kulturwissenschaften.* Rowohlts Enzyklopädie. Reinbek bei hamburg: Rowohlt Taschenbuch Verlag.
Back, Jean and Gabriel Bauret (eds.). 1994. *The Family of Man. Témoignages et documents.* Luxembourg: Editions artsevents, Ministère des Affaires culturelles, Centre national de l'audiovisuel.
Back, Jean and Victoria Schmidt-Linsenhoff (eds.). 2004. *The Family of Man 1955–2000. Humanismus und Postmoderne. Eine Revision von Edward Steichens Fotoausstellung. Humanism and Postmodernism. A Reappraisal of the Photo Exhibiton by Edward Steichen.* Marburg: Jonas Verlag für Kunst und Literatur.
Badiou, Alain. 2009. *Paulus. Die Begründung des Universalismus.* Transpositionen. 2nd ed. Munich and Berlin: Diaphanes, Sequenzia. Originally *Saint Paul. La fondation de l'universalisme.* Paris: Presses Universitaires de la France, 1998.
Bahn, Paul. 2005. *Uniformitarianism.* In Colin Renfrew and Paul Bahn (eds.), *Archaeology. The Key Concepts.* London and New York: Routledge, 274–78.
Baker, Mark. 2001. *The Atoms of Language. The Mind's Hidden Rules of Grammar.* New York: Basic Books.
Balibar, Étienne. 2008. "Universalismus. Diskussion mit Alain Badiou." (Introductory statement of "Koehn Vorlesungen in kritischer Theorie 2007," University of California at Irvine, 2 February 2007). Retrieved 21 November 2014 from http://translate. eipcp.net /transversal /0607/balibar/de/print.
Ball, Philip. 2004. *Critical Mass: How One Thing Leads to Another. Being an Inquiry into the Interplay of Chance and Necessity in the Way That Human Culture, Customs, Institutions, Cooperation and Conflct Arise.* London: William Heinemann, Arrow Books.
Bammé, Arno. 2004. *Science Wars. Von der akademischen zur postakademischen Wissenschaft.* Frankfurt am Main and New York: Campus Verlag.
Barash, David P. 1979. *The Whisperings Within. Evolution and the Origin of Human Nature.* New York: Harper and Row.
Barash, David P. and Nanelle R. Barash. 2005. *Madame Bovary's Ovaries. A Darwinian Look at Literature.* New York: Delacorte Press.
Bargatzky, Thomas. 2000. "Menschliche Natur und Kulturkritik. Anmerkungen zur Universalität der Religion." *Universitas* 55(645): 266–74.
Barker Chris 2012. *Cultural Studies. Theory and Practice.* 4th ed. London: Sage Publications.
Barkhaus, Annette, Matthias Mayer, Neil Roughley, and Donatus Thürnau (eds.). 1996. *Identität, Leiblichkeit, Normativität. Neue Horizonte anthropologischen Denkens.* Frankfurt am Main: Suhrkamp Verlag.

Barkow, Jerome H. 1975. "Prestige and Culture. A Biosocial Interpretation." *Current Anthropology* 16: 553–55.

———. 2001. "Universalien und evolutionäre Psychologie." In Peter M. Hejl (ed.), *Universalien und Konstruktivismus*. Frankfurt am Main: Suhrkamp Verlag, 126–38.

———. 2005. "Some Remarks on the Paper of the Reporter." Lecture, Transcultural Universals I, Co-Operation and Competition Conference, 13 April 2005, Hanse-Wissenschaftskolleg, Delmenhorst.

Barkow, Jerome H., Leda Cosmides, and John Tooby (eds.). 2001. *The Adapted Mind. Evolutionary Psychology and the Generation of Culture*. New York and Oxford: Oxford University Press.

Barrett, Louise, Robin I. M. Dunbar and John Lycett. 2002. *Human Evolutionary Psychology*. Basingstoke: Palgrave, Macmillan.

Barrett, Robert and Mary Katsikis. 2003. "Foreign Faces: A Voyage to the Land of Eepica." In Mary Katsikis (ed.), *The Human Face. Measurement and Meaning*. Boston: Kluwer Academic Publishers, 1–28.

Barsch, Achim and Peter M. Hejl (eds.). 2000. *Menschenbilder. Zur Pluralisierung der Vorstellung von der menschlichen Natur (1850–1914)*. Frankfurt am Main: Suhrkamp Verlag.

Barth, Fredrik. 1995. "Other Knowledge and Other Ways of Knowing." *Journal of Anthropological Research* 51: 65–68.

Barthes, Roland. 1981. *Das Reich der Zeichen*. Frankfurt am Main: Suhrkamp Verlag. Originally *L'empire des signes*, Paris: Éditions Seuil, 1970.

———. 2013. *Mythologies*. New York: Simon and Schuster. Originally *Mythologies*, Paris: Éditions du Seuil, 1957.

Bastian, Adolf. 1881. *Der Völkergedanke im Aufbau einer Wissenschaft vom Menschen und seine Begründung auf ethnologische Sammlungen*. Berlin: F. Dümmler.

———. 1895. *Ethnische Elementargedanken in der Lehre von Menschen*. Berlin: Weidmann'sche Buchhandlung.

Batson, C. Daniel, David A. Lishner, and E. L. Stocks. 2003. "Human Altruism." In Lynn Nadel (ed.), *Encyclopedia of Cognitive Science*, vol. 2: *Epilepsy—Mental Imagery, Philosophical Issues*. London: Nature Publishing Group, Macmillan, 374–77.

Baudrillard, Jean. 2002. "The Global and the Universal." In Jean Baudrillard, *Screened Out*. London and New York: Verso. Originally *Ecran Total*, Paris: Editions Galilée, 2000: 155–59.

Baumgartner, Hans Michael, Winfried Böhm, and Martin Lindauer (eds.). 1999. *Streitsache Mensch—Zur Auseinandersetzung zwischen Natur und Geisteswissenschaften*. Neuntes Würzburger Symposium der Universität Würzburg. Stuttgart: Ernst Klett Verlag.

Davin, Edith L. 1995. Language Aquisition on Crosslinguistic Perspective. *Annual Review of Anthropology* 24: 373–96.

Bayertz, Kurt. 1987. *GenEthik. Probleme der Technisierung menschlicher Fortpflanzung*. Rowohlts Enzyklopädie 450. Reinbek bei Hamburg: Rowohlt Taschenbuch Verlag.

Bayly, Christopher Alan. 2006. "Die Geburt der modernen Welt. Eine Globalgeschichte 1780–1914." Frankfurt am Main: Campus Verlag. Originally *The Birth of the Modern World, 1780–1914. Global Connections and Comparisions*, Blackwell History of the World, London: Blackwell.

Beck, Ulrich. 2004. *Der kosmopolitische Blick oder: Krieg ist Frieden*. Edition Zweite Moderne. Frankfurt am Main: Suhrkamp Verlag.

Beckermann, Stephen and Paul Valentine. 2002. *Cultures of Multiple Fathers. The Theory and Practice of Partible Paternity in Lowland South America*. Gainsville: University Press of Florida.

Beer, Bettina. 1999. "Universalien." In Wolfgang Müller (ed.), *Wörterbuch der Völkerkunde*. Founded by Walter Hirschberg. Berlin: Dietrich Reimer Verlag, 391.
Benedict, Ruth Fulton. 1934. *Patterns of Culture*. Boston: Houghton Mifflin.
Benhabib, Seyla. 2008. *Die Rechte der Anderen*. Frankfurt am Main: Suhrkamp Verlag. Originally *The Rights of Others. Aliens, Residents, and Citizens*, John Robert Seeley Lectures, Cambridge: Cambridge University Press.
Bennardo, Giovanni and Victor C. De Munck. 2014. *Cultural Models. Genesis, Methods, and Experiences*. Oxford and New York: Oxford University Press.
Bennison, Amira K. 2002. "Muslim Universalism and Western Globalization." In A. G. Hopkins (ed.), *Globalization in World History*. A Pimlico Original 494. London: Pimlico, 74–97.
Berger, Peter L. and Thomas Luckmann. 1997. *Die gesellschaftliche Konstruktion der Wirklichkeit. Eine Theorie der Wissenssoziologie*. Fischer Wissenschaft. Frankfurt am Main: Fischer Taschenbuch Verlag. Originally *The Social Construction of Reality*, Garden City, NY: Doubleday, 1966.
Berg-Schlosser, Dirk. 1997. "Menschenrechte und Demokratie—universelle Kategorien oder eurozentrische Betrachtungsweise?" In Manfred Brocker and Heino Heinrich Nau (eds.), *Ethnozentrismus. Möglichkeiten und Grenzen des interkulturellen Dialogs*. Darmstadt: Wissenschaftliche Buchgesellschaft, 289–306.
Berlin, Brent. 1970. "A Universalist-Evolutionary Approach to Ethnographic Semantics." In Ann Fisher (ed.), *Current Directions in Anthropology*. Washington, DC: American Anthropological Association, 3–18.
———. 1992. *Ethnobiological Classification. Principles of Categorization of Plants in Traditional Societies*. Princeton, NJ: Princeton University Press.
Berlin, Brent, D. Breedlove, and Paul Raven. 1973. "General Principles of Classification and Nomenclature in Folk-Biology." *American Anthropologist* 75: 214–42.
Berlin, Brent and Paul Kay. 1969. *Basic Color Terms. Their Universality and Evolution*. Berkeley: University of California Press.
Bernard, Harvey Russel 2002. *Research Methods in Anthropology. Qualitative and Quantitative Approaches*. 3rd ed. Walnut Creek, CA: Altamira Press.Bernstein, Leonard. 1991. *Musik—die offene Frage. Vorlesungen an der Harvard-Universität*. Munich: Wilhelm Goldmann Verlag. Originally *Unanswered Question: Six Talks at Harvard*, Charles Eliot Norton Lectures.
Berry, Christopher J. 1986. *Human Nature*. Issues in Political Theory. London: Macmillan.
Berry, John W. 1989. "Imposed Etics, Emics, Derived Etics." *International Journal of Psychology* 24: 721–35.
Berry, John W., Pierre R. Dasen, and T. S. Saraswathi (eds.). 1997. *Handbook of Cross-Cultural Psychology*, vol. 2: *Basic Processes and Human Development*. Boston: Allyn and Bacon.
Berry, John W. and Ype H. Poortinga. 2006. "Cross–Cultural Theory and Methodology." In James Georgas, John W. Berry, Fons J. R. de Vijver, Cigdem Kagitcibasi, and Ype H. Poortinga (eds.), *Families Across Cultures. A 30-Nation Psychological Study*. Cambridge: Cambridge University Press, 51–71.
Berry, John W., Ype H. Poortinga, Seger M. Breugelmanns, Athanasios Chasiotis, and David L. Slam. 2011. *Cross-Cultural Psychology. Research and Applications*. 2nd ed. Cambridge: Cambridge University Press.
Berry, John W., Ype H. Poortinga, and Janak Pandey (eds.). 1997. *Handbook of Cross-Cultural Psychology*, vol. 1: *Theory and Method*. 2nd ed. Boston: Allyn and Bacon.
Bertelsen, Preben. 2005. *Free Will, Consciousness, and Self. Anthropological Perspectives on General Psychology*. Studies in the Understanding of the Human Condition. New York and Oxford: Berghahn Books.

Betzig, Laura L. (ed.). 1997. *Human Nature. A Critical Reader*. New York and Oxford: Oxford University Press.

Bhabha, Homi K. 2000. *Die Verortung der Kultur*. Stauffenburg discussion 5. Tübingen: Stauffenburg Verlag Brigitte Narr. Originally *The Location of Culture*, London: Routledge, 1995.

Bialas, Wolfgang. 2004. "Lebensführung in exzentrischer Positionalität. Hellmut (sic!) Plessners Grundlegung philosophischer Anthropologie." In Friedrich Jaeger and Jürgen Straub (eds.), *Was ist der Mensch, was ist Geschichte? Annäherungen an eine kulturwissenschaftliche Anthropologie. Jörn Rüsen zum 65. Geburtstag*. Bielefeld: Transcript, 103–21.

Bickerton, Derek. 2014. *More than nature needs. Language, Mind and Evolution*. Cambridge, MA and London: Harvard University Press.

Bidney, David. 1947. "Human Nature and the Cultural Process." *American Anthropologist* 49: 375–99.

Bielefeldt, Heiner. 1994. "Menschenrechtliche Universalität und Entwicklungszusammenarbeit." In André Habisch and Ulrich Pöner (eds.), *Signale der Solidarität. Wege christlicher Nord-Süd-Ethik*. Paderborn: Schöningh, 31–47

———. 2004. Rechte kultureller Minderheiten als Freiheitsanspruch. Zur menschenrechtlichen Begründung des Minderheitenschutzes. In Heiner Bielefeld and Luer (eds.), *Rechte nationaler Minderheiten. Ethische Begründung, rechtliche Verankerung, historische Erfahrung*. Bielefeld: Transcript, 27–56.

Bierbrauer, Günter and Edgar W. Klinger. 2001. "Soziale Axiome. Gibt es universale Überzeugungen über das Funktionieren der Welt?" *Wirtschaftspsychologie* 8(3): 80–83.

Binder, Jana. 2005. *Globality. Eine Ethnographie über Backpacker*. Forum Europäische Ethnologie 7. Münster: Lit Verlag.

Birdwhistell, Ray L. 1963. "The Kinesic Level in the Investigation of Emotions." In Peter H. Knapp (ed.), *Expression of the Emotions in Man*. New York: International Universities Press.

Bischof, Norbert. 1985. *Das Rätsel Ödipus. Die biologischen Wurzeln des Urkonflikts zwischen Intimität und Autonomie*. Munich: Piper Verlag.

———. 1996. *Das Kraftfeld der Mythen. Signale aus der Zeit, in der wir die Welt erschaffen haben*. Munich: Piper Verlag.

Bischof-Köhler, Doris. 1991. "Jenseits des Rubikon. Die Entstehung spezifisch menschlicher Erkenntnisformen und ihre Auswirkung auf das Sozialverhalten." In Ernst Peter Fischer (ed.), *Mannheimer Forum 90/91. Ein Panorama der Naturwissenschaften*. Serie Piper. Munich and Zürich: Piper Verlag, 143–93.

———. 2006. *Von Natur aus anders. Die Psychologie der Geschlechtsunterschiede*. 3rd ed. Stuttgart: W. Kohlhammer Verlag.

Bishop, Alan. 1990. "Western Mathematics: The Secret Weapon of Cultural Imperialism." *Race and Class* 32(2): 51–65.

Bloch, Maurice. 1977. "The Past and the Present in the Present." Malinowski Lecture. *Man, N.S.* 12: 278–92.

———. 2005. *Essays on Cultural Transmission*. London School of Economics Monographs on Social Anthropology 75. Oxford and New York: Berg.

Bloom, Harold. 1998. *Shakespeare. The Invention of the Human*. New York: Riverhead Books.

Blute, Marion. 2010. *Darwinian Sociocultural Evolution. Solutions to Dilemmas in Cultural and Social Theory*. Cambridge: Cambridge University Press.

Boas, Franz. 1938. "The Universality of Culture Traits." In Franz Boas, *The Mind of Primitive Man*, rev. ed. Originally 1911, New York: Macmillan.

Bochenski, Innocentius M. 1956. "The Problem of Universals." In *The Problem of Universals. A Symposium.* Notre Dame, IN: University of Notre Dame Press, 35–54.
Bock, Kenneth. 1980. *Human Nature and History. A Response to Sociobiology.* New York: Columbia University Press.
Boehm, Christopher. 1989. "Ambivalence and Compromise in Human Nature." *American Anthropologist* 91: 921–39.
———. 1992. "Review of Brown 1991." *American Anthropologist* 94: 742–43.
———. 1997. "Egalitarianism and Political Intelligence." In David Whiten and Richard W. Byrne (eds.), *Machiavellian Intelligence II: Evaluations and Extensions.* Cambridge: Cambridge University Press, 341–46.
Boehnigk, Volker. 1999. *Weltversionen. Wissenschaft zwischen Relativismus und Pluralismus.* Vienna: Passagen.
Boesch, Christophe, Gottfried Hohmann, and Linda F. Merchant (eds.). 2002. *Behavioral Diversity in Chimpanzees and Bonobos.* Cambridge: Cambridge University Press.
Boesch, Christophe and Michael Tomasello. 1998. "Chimpanzee and Human Cultures." *Current Anthropology* 39: 591–614.
Boesch, Ernst Eduard and Jürgen Straub. 2007. "Kulturpsychologie—Prinzipien, Orientierungen, Konzeptionen." In Gisela Trommsdorff and Hans-Joachim Kornadt (eds.), *Enzyklopädie der Psychologie,* Themenbereich C: Theorie und Forschung 7, *Kultur-vergleichende Psychologie,* vol. 1: *Theorien und Methoden.* Göttingen: Hogrefe Verlag.
Boghossian, Paul A. 2006. *Fear of Knowledge. Against Relativism and Constructivism.* Oxford: Clarendon Press.
Bohannan, Laura. 1966. "Shakespeare in the Bush." *Natural History* 75: 28–33.
Bohlken, Eike and Christian Thies (eds.). 2009. *Handbuch Anthropologie. Der Mensch zwischen Natur, Kultur und Technik.* Weimar: J. B. Metzler.
Böhme, Gernot. 1999. "Kant und die Family of Man. Wie begründet sich die Universalität der Menschenrechte?" *Lettre Internationale* 25: 23–26.
Böhme, Hartmut, Peter Matussek, and Lothar Müller. 2000. *Orientierung Kulturwissenschaft. Was sie kann, was sie will.* Rowohlts Enzyklopädie. Reinbek bei Hamburg: Rowohlt Taschenbuch Verlag.
Bolz, Norbert and Andreas Münkel (eds.). 2003. "Was ist der *Mensch*?" Forum, Heinz Nixdorf Museumsforum. Munich: Wilhelm Fink Verlag.
Boster, James Shilts. 1996. "Human Cognition as a Product and Agent of Evolution." In Roy F. Ellen and Katsuyoshi Fukui (eds.), *Redefining Nature. Ecology, Culture and Domestication.* Explorations in Anthropology. Oxford and Washington, DC: Berg, 268–89.
———. 1999. "Cultural Variation." In Robert Anton Wilson and Frank C. Keil (eds.), *The MIT Encyclopedia of the Cognitive Sciences.* London: The MIT Press, 217.
Boster, James Shilts and Roy D'Andrade. 1989. "Natural and Human Sources of Cross-Cultural Agreement in Ornithological Classification." *American Anthropologist* 91: 132–42.
Boucher, Jerry D. 1979. "Culture and Emotion." In A. J. Marsella R. Tharp and T. Ciborowski (eds.), *Perspectives on Cross-Cultural Psychology.* New York: Academic Press, 159–78.
Bourgignon, Erika and Lenora Greenbaum. 1973. *Diversity and Homogeneity in World Societies.* New Haven: Human Relations Area Files, HRAF Press.
Bowlby, John. 1953. *Child Care and the Growth of Love.* Harmondsworth: Penguin Books.
Boyd, Brian. 2005. "Evolutionary Theories of Art." In Jonathan Gottschall and David Sloan Wilson (eds.), *The Literary Animal. Evolution and the Nature of Narrative.* Rethinking Theory. Evanston, IL: Northwestern University Press.

———. 2009. *On the Origin of Stories. Evolution, Cognition, and Fiction.* Cambridge, MA, and London: The Belknap Press of Harvard University Press.
Boyd, Robert and Peter J. Richerson. 1985. *Culture and the Evolutionary Process.* Chicago: Chicago University Press.
Boyd, Robert and Joan B. Silk. 2003. *How Humans Evolved.* New York and London: W. W. Norton and Company.
Boyer, Pascal. 1994. *The Naturalness of Religious Ideas. A Cognitive Theory of Religious Ideas.* Berkeley: University of California Press.
———. 2001. *Religion Explained. The Evolutionary Origins of Religious Thought.* New York: Basic Books. Originally *Et l'homme créa Dieu*, Paris: Éditions Laffont, 2001.
Bracht, Elke. 1994. *Multikulturell leben lernen. Psychologische Bedingungen universalen Denkens und Handelns.* Heidelberg: Ronald Asanger Verlag.
Brady, F. Neil (ed.). 1996. *Ethical Universals in International Business.* Studies in Economic Ethics and Philosophy. Berlin: Springer Verlag.
Brandom, Robert B. 2004. *Begründen und Begreifen. Eine Einführung in den Inferentialismus.* Frankfurt am Main: Suhrkamp Verlag. Originally *Articulating Reasons. An Introduction to Inferentialism,* Cambridge, MA: Harvard University Press, 2000.
Brandtstädter, Jochen. 1998. "On Certainty and Universality in Human Development: Developmental Psychology Between Apriorism and Empiricism." In Michael Chapman and Roger A. Dixon (eds.), *Meaning and the Growth of Understanding. Wittgenstein's Significance For Developmental Psychology.* Berlin: Springer, 69–84.
———. 2006. "Action Perspectives on Human Development." In Richard M. Lerner (ed.), *Handbook of Child Psychology,* vol. 1: *Theoretical Models of Development.* Hoboken, NJ: John Wiley and Sons, 516–68.
Bredow, Udo and Annemarie C. Mayer (eds.). 2001. *Der Mensch—das Maß aller Dinge. 14 Antworten der großen Denker.* Darmstadt: Primus Verlag, Wissenschaftliche Buchgesellschaft.
Brieskorn, Norbert (ed.). 1997. *Globale Solidarität. Die verschiedenen Kulturen und die eine Welt.* Globale Solidarität – Schritte zu einer neuen Weltkultur 1. Stuttgart: Verlag W. Kohlhammer.
Briggs, Jean L. 1978. *Inuit Morality Play. The Emotional Education of a Three-Year-Old.* New Haven, CT: Yale University Press.
British Museum. 2006. *Living and Dying.* Information plates photographed by author in the Wellcome Trust Gallery, London, January 2006.
Brocker, Manfred and Heino Heinrich Nau (eds.). 1997. *Ethnozentrismus. Möglichkeiten und Grenzen des interkulturellen Dialogs.* Darmstadt: Wissenschaftliche Buchgesellschaft.
Bröckling, Ulrich. 2004. "Um Leib und Leben. Zeitgenössische Positionen Philosophischer Anthropologie." In Aleida Assmann, Ulrich Gaier, and Gisela Trommsdorff (eds.), *Positionen der Kulturanthropologie.* With Karolina Jeftic. Frankfurt am Main: Suhrkamp Verlag, 172–95.
Brockman, John. 1996. *Die dritte Kultur. Das Weltbild der modernen Naturwissenschaft.* Munich: Wilhelm Goldmann Verlag. Originally *The Third Culture,* New York: Simon and Schuster, 1995.
Brophy, Jere and Janet Alleman. 2005. *Children's Thinking About Cultural Universals.* Mahwah, NJ, and London: Lawrence Earlbaum Associates.
Brown, Cecil H. 1984. *Language and Living Things. Uniformities in Folk Classification and Naming.* New Brunswick, NJ: Rutgers University Press.
Brown, Cecil H. and Stanley R. Witkowsky. 1980. "Language Universals." In David Levinson and Martin J. Malone, *Toward Explaining Human Culture. A Critical Review of the*

Findings of Worldwide Cross-Cultural Research. New Haven, CT: HRAF Press, Appendix B, 359–84.

———. 1981. "Figurative Language in a Universalist Perspective." *American Ethnologist* 8: 596–615.

Brown, Donald E. 1988. *Hierarchy, History, and Human Nature. The Social Origins of Historical Consciousness.* Tucson: University of Arizona Press.

———. 1991. *Human Universals.* New York: McGraw Hill and Temple University Press.

———. 1996. "Human Universals." In David Levinson and Melvin Ember (eds.), *Encyclopedia of Cultural Anthropology,* vol. 1. New York: Henry Holt and Company, 607–13.

———. 1999a. "Human Universals." In Robert Anton Wilson and Frank C. Keil (eds.), *The MIT Encyclopedia of the Cognitive Sciences.* London: The MIT Press, 382–84.

———. 1999b. "The Return of Science: Evolutionary Ideas and History." In "Studies in the Philosophy of History," special issue, *History and Theory* 38: 138–57.

———. 2000. "Human Universals and Their Implications." In Neil Roughley (ed.), *Being Humans. Anthropological Universality and Particularity in Transdisciplinary Perspectives.* Berlin and New York: Walter de Gruyter, 156–74.

———. 2004. "Human Universals, Human Nature and Human Culture." *Daedalus* (Fall): 47–54.

———. 2005a. "Opening Lecture, Conference on Co-Operation and Competition," 13 April 2005, Hanse-Wissenschaftskolleg, Delmenhorst.

———. 2005b. "Human Universals and the Ethnocentric Syndrome," Lecture, Conference on Transcultural Universals I, December 2005, Hanse-Wissenschaftskolleg Delmenhorst.

———. 2012. "Ethnicity and Ethnocentrism: Are They Natural?" (revised). In Raymond Scupin (ed.), *Race and Ethnicity. The United States and the World,* 2nd ed. Boston: Pearson, 81–94.

———. 2013. "Human Universals." In R. Jon McGee and Richard L. Warms (eds.), *Theory in Social and Cultural Anthropology. An Encyclopedia.* Thousand Oaks, CA: Sage Publications, 410–13.

Brown, Penelope. 2002. "Language as a Model for Culture: Lessons From the Cogitive Sciences." In Robert G. Fox and Barbara J. King (eds.), *Anthropology Beyond Culture.* Wenner-Gren International Symposium Series. Oxford and New York: Berg Publishers, 169–92.

Brown, Penelope and Stephen C. Levinson. 1978. "Universals in Language Usage." In Esther N. Goody (ed.), *Questions and Politeness. Strategies of Social Interaction.* Cambridge: Cambridge University Press, 56–289.

———. 1987. *Politeness: Some Universals in Language Use.* Cambridge: Cambridge University Press.

Bruck, Andreas. 1985. *Funktionalität beim Menschen. Ein konstruktuiv-systematischer Überblick.* Europäische Hochschulschriften, Series 22, Soziologie 112. Frankfurt am Main: Peter Lang.

Bruck, Andreas. 1997. *Lebensfragen. Eine praktische Anthropologie.* Opladen: Westdeutscher Verlag.

Bruner, Jerome. 1981. "Review and Prospectus." In Barbara Lloyd and Peter Gay (eds.), *Universals of Human Thought. Some African Evidence.* Cambridge: Cambridge University Press, 256–62.

Buller, David J. 2006. *Adapting Minds. Evolutionary Psychology and the Persistent Quest For Human Nature.* Cambridge, MA: The MIT Press (A Bradford Book)

Burkert, Walter. 1987. *Anthropologie des religiösen Opfers. Die Sakralisierung der Gewalt.* Munich: C.H. Beck Verlag.

———. 1996. *Creation of the Sacred. Tracks of Biology in Early Religions.* Cambridge, MA, and London: Harvard University Press.
———. 2000. "Wozu braucht der Mensch Religion? Die Mensch-Gott-Beziehung in den alten Religionen." In Sigurd Martin Daecke and Jürgen Schnakenberg (eds.), *Gottesglaube—ein Selektionsvorteil. Religion in der Evolution—Natur- und Geisteswissenschaftler im Gespräch.* Gütersloh: Chr. Kaiser, Gütersloher Verlagshaus, 103–24.
Busch, Dominic 2007. *Interkulturelle Mediation. Eine theoretische Grundlegung triadischer-Konfliktbearbeitung in interkulturell bedingten Kontexten.* 2nd ed. Studien zur Interkulturellen Mediation 1. Frankfurt: Peter Lang Verlag der Wissenschaften.
Buss, David. 1989. "Sex Differences in Human Mate Preferences. Evolutionary Hypotheses Tested in 37 Cultures." *Behavioral and Brain Sciences* 12: 1–49.
———. 1997. "Sex Differences in Human Mate Preferences. Evolutionary Hypotheses Tested in 37 Cultures." In Laura L. Betzig (ed.), *Human Nature. A Critical Reader.* New York and Oxford: Oxford University Press, 175–90. Originally in *Behavioral and Brain Sciences* 12: 1–12, plus comments 13–49, 1997.
———. 2003. *The Evolution of Desire. Strategies of Human Mating.* 2nd ed. New York: Basic Books.
———. 2004. *Evolutionäre Psychologie.* Munich: Person Studium, Pearson Education.
——— (ed.). 2005. *Handbook of Evolutionary Psychology.* Hoboken, NJ: John Wiley and Sons.
Butler, Judith P. 2000. "Competing Universality." In Judith P. Butler, Ernesto Laclau, and Slavoj Žižek, *Contingency, Hegemony, Universality. Contemporary Dialogues of the Left.* Phronesis. New York and London: Verso, 136–81.
Butler, Judith P., Ernesto Laclau, and Slavoj Žižek. 2000. *Contingency, Hegemony, Universality. Contemporary Dialogues of the Left.* Phronesis. New York and London: Verso.
Bybee, Joan. 2006. "Language Change and Universals." In Ricardo Uson Mairal and Juana Gil (eds.), *Linguistic Universals.* Cambridge: Cambridge University Press, 179–94.
Byrne, Richard W. 1995. *The Thinking Ape. Evolutionary Origins of Intelligence.* Oxford: Oxford University Press.
———. 2001. "Social and Technical Forms of Primate Intelligence." In Frans B. M. de Waal (ed.), *Tree of Origin. What Primate Behavior Can Tell Us about Human Social Evolution.* Cambridge, MA, and London: Harvard University Press, 145–72.
Callon, Michel. 1986. "Some Elements of a Sociology of Translation: Domestication of the Scallops and the Fisherman of St Brieuc Bay." In John Law (ed.), *Power. Action and Belief. A New Sociology of Knowledge?* London: Routledge and Kegan Paul (Sociological Review Monograph 32), 196–233.
Calloway-Thomas, Carolyn. 2010. *Empathy in the Global World. An Intercultural Perspective.* Los Angeles: Sage Publications.
Campbell, Anne. 2013. *A Mind of her Own. The Evolutionary Psychology of Women.* 2nd ed. Oxford: Oxford University Press.
Campbell, Donald T. 1967. "Stereotypes and the Perception of Group Differences." *American Psychologist* 22: 817–29.
———. 1983. "The Two Distinct Routes Beyond Kin Selection to Ultrasociality: Implications for the Humanities and Social Sciences." In Diane L. Bridgeman (ed.), *The Nature of Prosocial Developoment. Interdisciplinary Theories and Stratgies.* New York: Academic Press, 11–41.
Campbell, Joseph. 1953. *Der Heros in tausend Gestalten.* Frankfurt am Main: S. Fischer Verlag. Originally *The Hero With a Thousand Faces,* New York: Pantheon Books, 1949.
Cappai, Gabriele. 2007. "Vergleichen." In Jürgen Straub, Arne Weidemann, and Doris

Weideman (eds.), *Handbuch interkulturelle Kommunikation und Kompetenz. Grundbegriffe—Theorien—Anwendungsfelder.* Stuttgart and Weimar: Verlag J. B. Metzler, 94–101.

Carneiro, Robert Leonard. 1995. "Godzilla Meets New Age Anthropology: Facing the Post-Modern Challenge to a Science of Culture." *Europaea* 1(1): 3–22.

Carrithers, Michael. 1992. *Why Humans Have Cultures. Explaining Anthropology and Social Diversity.* Oxford and New York: Oxford University Press.

———. 2000. "Hedgehogs, Foxes and Persons: Resistance and Moral Creativity in East Germany and South India." In Neil Roughley (ed.), *Being Humans. Anthropological Universality and Particularity in Transdisciplinary Perspectives.* Berlin and New York: Walter de Gruyter, 356–78.

Carroll, Joseph. 1995. *Evolution and Literary Theory.* Columbia and London: University of Missouri Press.

———. 2001. "Universalien in der Literaturwissenschaft." In Peter M. Hejl (ed.), *Universalien und Konstruktivismus.* Frankfurt am Main: Suhrkamp Verlag, 235–56.

———. 2005. "Literature and Evolutionary Psychology." In David Buss (ed.), *Handbook of Evolutionary Psychology.* Hoboken, NJ: John Wiley and Sons, 931–52.

Carruthers, Peter. 2005. "Distinctively Human Thinking: Modular Precursors and Components." In Peter Carruthers, Stephen Laurence, and Stephen P. Stich (eds.), *The Innate Mind. Structure and Contents.* Oxford: Oxford University Press, 69–88.

Carruthers, Peter, Stephen Laurence, and Stephen P. Stich (eds.). 2005. *The Innate Mind. Structure and Contents.* Oxford: Oxford University Press.

Cartmill, Matt. 1990. "Human Uniqueness and Theoretical Content in Paleoanthropology." *International Journalö of Primatology* 11(3): 173–92.

Cartwright, John H. 2000. *Evolution and Human Behaviour. Darwinian Perspectives on Human Nature.* Houndmills and London: Macmillan.

Casimir, Michael Jan and Michael Schnegg. 1999. "Shame Across Cultures: The Evolution, Ontogeny and Function of a 'Moral Emotion.'" In Heidi Keller (ed.), *Between Culture and Biology: Perspectives on Ontogenetic Development Cambridge Studies in Cognitive and Perceptual Development 8.* Cambridge: Cambridge University Press, 270–300.

Cassara, Ernst. 1968. "Universalism." *Encyclopedia Brittannica,* vol. 22: 744–45.

Cassirer, Ernst. (1940) 1990. *Versuch über den Menschen. Einführung in eine Philosophie der Kultur.* Frankfurt am Main: Suhrkamp.

Cavalli-Sforza, Luigi, Paolo Menozzi and Alberto Piazza. 1994. *The History and Geography of Human Genes.* Princeton, NJ: Princeton University Press.

Chakrabarty, Dipesh. 2007. *Provincializing Europe. Postcolonial Thought and Historical Difference.* 2nd ed. Princeton Studies in Culture/Power/History. Princeton: Princeton University Press.

Chapais, Bernard. 2014. "Complex Kinship Patterns as Evolutionary Constructions, and the Origins of Sociocultural Universals." *Current Anthropology* 55: 751–83.

Chasiotis, Athanasios. 2007. "Evolutionstheoretische Ansätze im kulturvergleich." In Gisela Trommsdorff and Hans-Joachim Kornath (eds.), *Theorien und Methoden der kulturvergleichenden Psychologie.* Enzyklopädie der Psychologie, Theme section C, series VII, vol. 1: Kulturvergleichende Psychologie. Göttingen: Hogrefe, 179–219.

Cheney, Dorothy L. and Robert M. Seyfarth. 1994. *Wie Affen die Welt sehen.* Frankfurt am Main: Hanser Verlag. Originally *How Monkeys See the World,* Chicago: Chicago University Press, 1990.

Chevron, Marie-France. 1998. "Man's Special Position in Nature. The Relationship Between Biological and Cultural Development." *Evolution and Cognition* 4(2): 173–84.

———. 2004. *Anpassung und Entwicklung in Evolution und Kulturwandel. Erkenntnisse aus der Wissenschaftsgeschichte für die Forschung der Gegenwart und eine Erinnerung an das Werk A. Bastians.* Ethnologie 14. Münster: Lit Verlag.
Chevron, Marie-France and Karl R. Wernhart. 2000–2001. "Ethnologische Reflexion über die universellen Grundlagen gesellschaftlicher Phänomene. Der kultur- und sozialwissenschaftliche Forschungszugang." *Archaeologica Austriaca. Beiträge zur Paläanthropologie, Ur- und Frühgeschichte Österreichs,* 84–85: 15–22.
Child, Alice B. and Irvin L. Child. 1993. *Religion and Magic in the Life of Traditional Peoples.* Englewood Cliffs, NJ: Prentice-Hall.
Choi, Sang-Chin, Gyuseog Han, and Chung-Woon Kim. 2007. "Analysis of Cultural Emotion. Understanding Indigenous Psychology for Universal Implications." In Jaan Valsiner and Alberto Rosa (eds.), *The Cambridge Handbook of Sociocultural Psychology.* Cambridge: Cambridge University Press, 318–42.
Chomsky, Noam. 1995. "Language and Nature." *Mind* 104(413): 120–35.
Christian, David. 2005. *Maps of Time. An Introduction to Big History.* The California World History Library 2. Berkeley: University of California Press.
Claessens, Dieter and Rainer Mackensen (eds.). 1992. *Universalism Today. Contributions at the IInd International Symposium for Universalism, Berlin, August 22nd to 26th, 1990.* Soziologische Forschungen, 19. Berlin: Technische Universität Berlin.
Cleveland, Alice Ann, Jean Craven, and Maryanne Danfelser. 1979. "What Are Universals of Culture?" *Global Perspectives in Education* (May): 92–93.
Cohen, Mark Nathan. 1998. *Culture of Intolerance. Chauvinism, Class, and Racism in the United States.* New Haven and London: Yale University Press.
Cole, Michael and Sheila R. Cole. 1993. *The Development of Children.* 2nd ed. New York: Scientific American Books.
Collins, Elizabeth Fuller and Ernaldi Bahar. 2000. "To Know Shame. Malu and Its Uses in Malay Society." *Crossroads. An Interdisciplinary Journal of South East Asian Studies* 14(1): 35–62.
Collins, Samuel Gerald. 2002. "Review of Herzfeld 2001." *Anthropological Quarterly* 75(2): 441–45.
Colpe, Carsten. 1997. "Wie universal ist das Heilige?" In Hans-Joachim Klimkeit (ed.), *Vergleichen und Verstehen in der Religionswissenschaft. Vorträge der Jahrestagung Deutschen Vereinigung für Religionsgeschichte.* Wiesbaden: Otto Harrassowitz, 1–12.
Comrie, Bernard 1989. *Language Universals and Linguistic Typology. Syntax and Morphology.* 2nd ed. Oxford: Basil Blackwell.
Cooke, Brett and Frederick Turner (eds.). 1999. *Biopoetics. Evolutionary Explorations in the Arts.* Lexington, KY: ICUS Book (International Conference on the Unity of Sciences).
Coon, Charleton S. 1946. "The Universality of Natural Groupings in Human Societies." *Journal of Educational Sociology* 20: 163–68.
Corning, Peter Andrew. 2003. *Nature's Magic. Synergy in Evolution and the Fate of Humankind.* Cambridge: Cambridge University Press.
———. 2011. *The Fair Society. The Science of Nature and the Pursuit of Social Justice.* Chicago and London: The University of Chicago Press.
Cowan, Jane K., Marie Bénédicte Dembour, and Richard Wilson (eds.). 2001. *Culture and Rights. Anthropological Perspectives.* Cambridge: Cambridge University Press.
Cowie, Fiona. 2003. "Innatenes, Philosophical Issues about." In Lynn Nadel (ed.), *Encyclopedia of Cognitive Science,* vol. 2: *Epilepsy: Mental Imagery, Philosophical Issues.* London: Nature Publishing Group, Macmillan, 559–65.
Cramer, Friedrich and Klaus Mollenhauer. 1998. "Dialog." *Zeitschrift für Erziehungswissenschaft* 1(1): 119–25.

Croft, William. 2003a. *Typology and Universals*. 2nd ed. Cambridge: Cambridge University Press.
———. 2003b. "Typology." In Lynn Nadel (ed.), *Encyclopedia of Cognitive Science*, vol. 3. London: Nature Publishing Group, Macmillan, 434–40.
Cronk, Lee. 1993. "Review of Brown 1991." *Zygon* 2883: 386.
———. 1999. *That Complex Whole. Culture and the Evolution of Human Behavior*. Boulder, CO: Westview Press.
Cronk, Lee, Napoleon A. Chagnon, and William Irons (eds.). 2000. *Adaptation and Human Behavior. An Anthropological Perspective*. Evolutionary Foundations of Human Behavior. New York: Aldine De Gruyter.
Crook, John H. 1985. *The Evolution of Human Consciousness*. Oxford: Clarendon Press.
Cuche, Denys. 1996. *La Notion de culture dans les sciences sociales*. Repères 205. Paris: Édition la Découverte.
"Cultural Universal." 2008. Retrieved 19 September 2008 from http://en.wikipedia.org/wiki/Cultral_Universals.
Cunningham, Michael R., Alan R. Roberts, Anita P. Barbee, Perri B. Druen, and Cheng-Huan Wu. 1995. "'Their Ideas of Beauty Are, on the Whole, the Same as Ours': Consistency and Variability in the Cross-Cultural Perception of Female Attractiveness." *Journal of Personality and Social Psychology* 68: 261–79.
Cyran, Wolfgang (ed.). 1990. *Die Sonderstellung des Menschen in der Evolution*. Kirche und Welt. Schriftenreihe der Katholischen Akademikerarbeit Deutschlands 3. Melle: Verlag Ernst Knoth.
Cziko, Gary. 1995. *Without Miracles. Universal Selection Theory and The Second Darwinian Revolution*. Cambridge, MA, and London: The MIT Press (A Bradford Book).
Dahrendorf, Ralf 2006. *Homo sociologicus. Ein Versuch zur Geschichte, Bedeutung und Kritik der Kategorie der sozialen Rolle*. Wiesbaden: Verlag für Sozialwissenschaften. Originally published in *Kölner Zeitschrift für Soziologie und Sozialpsychologie* 10(2): 178–208 and 10(3): 345–78, 1958.
Daly, Martin and Margo Wilson. 1988. *Homicide*. New York: Aldine de Gruyter.
D'Andrade, Roy. 1995. "Moral Models in Anthropology." *Current Anthropology* 36(3): 399–408.
Danziger, Eve. 2001. "Cross-Cultural Studies in Language and Thought: Is There a Metalanguage?" In Carmella C. Moore and Holly F. Mathews (eds.), *The Psychology of Cultural Experience*. Publications of the Society for Psychological Anthropology. Cambridge: Cambridge University Press, 199–222.
Darwin, Charles Robert. 2000. *Der Ausdruck der Gemütsbewegungen bei den Menschen und den Tieren*. Critical Edition. Die Andere Bibliothek 188. Frankfurt am Main Eichborn Verlag. Originally Stuttgart: Schweitzerbarth'sche Verlagsbuchhandlung, 1871.
———. (1871) 2005. *Die Abstammung des Menschen*. Frankfurt am Main: Fischer Taschenbuch Verlag.
Dasen, Pierre R. 1977. "Are Cognitive Processes Universal? A Contribution to Cross-Cultural Piagetian Psychology." In Neill Warren (ed.), *Studies in Cross-Cultural Psychology*, vol. 1. London: Academic Press, 155–201.
———. 1981. "'Strong' and 'Weak' Universals: Sensori-Motor Intelligence and Concrete Operations." In Barbara Lloyd and Peter Gay (eds.), *Universals of Human Thought. Some African Evidence*. Cambridge: Cambridge University Press, 137–56.
Davies, Tony 2007. *Humanism*. 2nd ed. New Critical Idiom. London and New York: Routledge.
Dawkins, Richard. 1996. *Das Egoistische Gen*. Reinbek bei Hamburg: Rowohlt Taschenbuch Verlag. Originally *The Egoistic Gene*, Oxford: Oxford University Press, 1976.

Deacon, Terrence W. 1998. *The Symbolic Species. The Co-Evolution of Language and the Human Brain*. Harmondsworth: Penguin.

De Coppet, Daniel. 1992. "Comparison, A Universal for Anthropology: From 'Re-Presentation' to the Comparison of Values." In Adam Kuper (ed.), *Conceptualizing Society*. European Association of Social Anthropologists. London and New York: Routledge, 59–74.

Degele, Nina and Christian Dries. 2006. *Modernisierungstheorie. Eine Einführung*. Munich: Wilhelm Fink.

Degler, Carl N. 1991. *In Search of Human Nature. The Decline and Revival of Darwinism in American Social Thought*. New York and Oxford: Oxford University Press.

2.De Lannoy, Jacques-Dominique and Pierre Feyereisen. 1995. *L'inceste*. Collection Que sais-je? 2645. Paris: Presses Universitaires de France.

———. 1996. *L'inceste. Un siècle d'interprétations*. Paris and Lausanne: Delachaux et Niestlé.

DeLoache, Judy and Alma Gottlieb (eds.). 2000. *A World of Babies. Imagined Childcare Guides for Seven Societies*. Cambridge etc.: Cambridge University Press.

De Munck, Victor C. 2000a. *Culture, Self, and Meaning*. Prospect Heights, IL: Waveland Press.

———. 2000b. "Introduction: Units for Describing and Analyzing Culture and Society." In Victor De Munck (ed.), "Comparative Research and Cultural Units," special issue, *Cultural Anthropology* 39(4): 279–92.

——— (ed.). 2000c. "Comparative Research and Cultural Units" special issue, *Cultural Anthropology* 39(4): 279–408.

Dennett, Daniel C. 1987. *The Intentional Stance*. Cambridge, MA: The MIT Press

———. 1995. *Darwin's Dangerous Idea. Evolution and the Meanings of Life*. London: Allen Lane; New York: Simon and Schuster.

———. 2001. *Spielarten des Geistes. Wie erkennen wir die Welt? Ein neues Verständnis des Bewusstseins*. Science Masters. Munich: Wilhelm Goldmann Verlag Originally *Kinds of Minds*, New York: Basic Books, 1996.

Derichs, Claudia. 1998. "Universalität und Kulturspezifik. Das Modell westlicher Demokratie in der Defensive?" In Michael Th. Greven (ed.), *Demokratie—eine Kultur des Westens? 20. Wissenschaftlicher Kongreß der Deutschen Vereinigung für Politische Wissenschaft*. Opladen: Leske + Budrich, 107–21.

Descola, Philippe. 1992. "Societies of Nature and the Nature of Society." In Adam Kuper (ed.), *Conceptualizing Society*. European Association of Social Anthropologists. London and New York: Routledge, 107–26.

De Waal, Frans B. M. 1996. *Good Natured. The Origins of Wright and Wrong in Humans and Other Animals*. Cambridge, MA: Harvard University Press.

———. 1999. "Cultural Primatology Comes of Age." *Nature* 399: 635–36.

———. 2001. *The Ape and the Sushi Master. Cultural Reflections by a Primatologist*. New York: Basic Books.

———. 2005. "A Century of Getting to Know the Chimpanzee." *Nature* 437(September): 56–59.

———. 2006. *Our Inner Ape. A Leading Primatologist Explains Why We Are Who We Are*. New York: Riverhead Books.

De Waal, Frans B. M. and Peter L. Tyack (eds.). 2003. *Animal Social Complexity. Intelligence, Culture, and Individualized Societies*. Cambridge, MA, and London: Harvard University Press.

Dickens, Peter. 2002. *Social Darwinism. Linking Evolutionary Thought to Social Theory*. Concepts in the Social Sciences. New Delhi: Viva Books Pivate Limited.

Diener, Ed and Eunkook E. Suh (eds.). 2003. *Culture and Subjective Well-Being*. Cambridge, MA: The MIT Press.

Dissanayake, Ellen. 1992. *Homo Aestheticus. Where Art Comes From and Why*. New York: The Free Press, Macmillan.
———. 1995. "Chimera, Spandrel, or Adaptation. Conceptualizing Art In Human Evolution." *Human Nature* 6(2): 99–117.
———. 1999. "'Making Special': An Undescribed Human Universal and the Core of a Behavior of Art." In Brett Cooke and Frederick Turner (eds.), *Biopoetics. Evolutionary Explorations in the Arts*. Lexington, KY: Paragon House (ICUS Book; International Conference on the Unity of Sciences), 27–46.
———. 2001: "Kunst als menschliche Universalie. Eine adaptionistische Betrachtung." In Peter M. Hejl (ed.), *Universalien und Konstruktivismus*. Frankfurt am Main: Suhrkamp Verlag, 206–34.
———. 2008. "The Arts after Darwin. Does Art Have an Original and Adaptive Function?" In Kitty Zijlmans and Wilfried A. van Damme (eds.), *World Art Studies. Exploring Concepts and Approaches*. Amsterdam: Valiz Publishers, 241–63.
Distin, Kate. 2011. *Cultural Evolution*. Cambridge: Cambridge University Press
Dobzhansky, Theodosius Grigorievich. 1972. "On the Evolutionary Uniqueness of Man." In Theodosius Grigorievich Dobzhansky, Michael K. Hecht, and W. Steer (eds.), *Evolutionary Biology* 6. New York: Plenum Press and Appleton Century Crofts, 415–30.
Doise, Willem. 1990. "Social Beliefs and Integroup Relations: The Relevence of Some Sociological Perspectives." In Colin Fraser and George Gaskell (eds.), *The Social Psychological Study of Widespread Beliefs*. Oxford: Clarendon Press, 142–59.
Donald, Merlin. 2008. *Triumph des Bewusstseins. Die Evoltion des menschlichen Geistes*. Stuttgart: Klett-Cotta. Originally *A Mind So Rare. The Evolution of Human Consciousness*, New York and London: W. W. Norton and Company, 2001.
Donnelly, Jack. 2005. "Human Rights as an Issue in World Politics." In Bruce Mazlish and Akira Iriye (eds.), *The Global History Reader*. London and New York: Routledge, 158–68. Originally in Jack Donelly, *International Human Rights*, Boulder, CO: Westview Press, 1998, 2–17.
Douglas, Mary. 1970. *Natural Symbols. Explorations in Cosmology*. London: Barrie and Rockliff.
———. 2002. *Purity and Danger. An Analysis of Concepts of Pollution and Taboo*. Routledge Classics. London and New York: Routledge.
Draper, Patricia and Henry Harpending. 1988. "A Sociobiological Perspective on the Development of Human Reproductive Strategies." In Kevin B. MacDonald (ed.), *Sociobiological Perspectives on Human Development*. New York: Springer, 341–72.
Drechsel, Paul. 1984. "Vorschläge zur Konstruktion einer 'Kulturtheorie' oder was man unter einer 'Kulturinterpretation' verstehen könnte." In Ernst Wilhelm Müller, René König, Klaus-Peter Koepping, and Paul Drechsel (eds.), *Ethnologie als Sozialwissenschaft*. Cologne: Westdeutscher Verlag, 44–83.
Dubos, René. 1968. *So Human an Animal*. New York: Scribner's and Sons.
Duerr, Hans-Peter. 1988. *Nacktheit und Scham*. Frankfurt am Main Suhrkamp Verlag.
———. 1999–2003. *Der Mythos vom Zivilisationsprozeß* (5 vols.). Frankfurt: Suhrkamp Verlag.
Dunbar, Robin I. M. 1993. "Coevolution of Neocortical Size, Group Size, and Language in Humans." *Behavioral and Brain Sciences* 16: 681–94.
———. 2004. *The Human Story. A New History of Mankind's Evolution*. London: Faber and Faber.
Dupré, John. 2003. *Human Nature and the Limits of Science*. Oxford: Oxford University Press.

Durand, Gilbert. 1993. *Les Structures anthropologices de L'Imaginaire.* 11th ed. Paris: Bordas.
Durham, William H. 1990. "Advances in Evolutionary Culture Theory." *Annual Reviews of Anthropology* 19: 187–210.
———. 1991. *Coevolution. Genes, Culture and Human Diversity.* Stanford, CA: Stanford University Press.
During, Simon. 2005. *Cultural Studies. A Critical Introduction.* London and New York: Routledge.
Durkheim, Emile. (1895) 2013. *The Rules of Sociological Method and Selected Texts on Sociology and Its Method.* Ed. Steven Lukes. Houndmills: Palgrave Macmillan.
Dutton, Denis. 2000. But They Don't Have Our Concept of Art. In Noel Caroll (ed.), *Theories of Art Today.* Madison: University of Wisconsin Press, 217–38.
———. 2005. Aesthetic Universals. In Berys Gaut and Dominic McIver Lopez (eds.), *The Routledge Companion to Aesthetics.* 2nd ed. London and New York: Routledge, 279–93.
———. 2009. *The Art Instinct. Beauty, Pleasure and Human Evolution.* New York: Bloomsbury Press and Oxford: Oxford University Press.
Eagleton, Terry. 2000. *The Idea of Culture.* London: Blackwell (Blackwell Manifestos).
Eckensberger, Lutz H. 1996. "Auf der Suche nach den (verlorenen?) Universalien hinter den Kulturstandards." In Alexander Thomas (ed.), *Psychologie interkulturellen Handelns.* Göttingen: Hogrefe, 165–97.
Eco, Umberto. 2002. *Die Suche nach der vollkommenen Sprache.* Munich: C.H. Beck Verlag. Originally *The Search for a Perfect Language,* London, Fontana Press, 1997.
Edgerton, Robert B. 1992. *Sick Societies. Challenging the Myth of Primitive Harmony.* New York: The Free Press.
Eggan, Fred. 1954. "Social Anthropology and the Method of Controlled Comparison." *American Anthropologist* 56(4): 743–63.
Ehlers, Eckart. 2008: *Das Anthropozän. Die Erde im Zeitalter des Menschen.* Darmstadt: Wissenschaftliche Buchgesellschaft.
Ehrlich, Paul R. 2002. *Human Natures. Genes, Cultures, and the Human Prospect.* Harmondsworth: Penguin Books.
Ehrlich, Paul R., Anne H. Ehrlich, and Gretchen C. Daily. 1995. *The Stork and the Plow. The Equity Answer to the Human Dilemma.* New York: Grosset/Putnam.
Eibl, Karl. 2004. *Animal Poeta. Bausteine der biologischen Kultur- und Literaturtheorie.* Poetogenesis. Studien und Texte zur empirischen Anthropologie der Literatur. Paderborn: Mentis-Verlag.
———. 2007. "Warum der Mensch etwas Besonderes ist. Einige evolutionsbiologische Aspekte." *Literaturkritik.de* 2. Retrieved 26 September 2014 from www.literaturkritik.de/public/ rezension.php?rez_id=10428.
———. 2009. *Kultur als Zwischenwelt. Eine evolutionsbiologische Perspektive.* Edition Unseld 20. Frankfurt am Main Suhrkamp Verlag.
Eibl-Eibesfeldt, Irenäus. 1976. *Menschenforschung auf neuen Wegen. Die naturwissenschaftliche Betrachtung kultureller Verhaltensweisen.* Vienna und Munich: MTV-Molden-Taschenbuch-Verlag.
———. 1986. "Universalien im menschlichen Sozialverhalten." In Hans Rössner (ed.), *Der ganze Mensch. Aspekte einer pragmatischen Anthropologie.* Munich: Deutscher Taschenbuchverlag, 80–91.
———. 1987. *Liebe und Haß. Zur Naturgeschichte elementarer Verhaltensweisen.* Munich and Zürich: Piper.
———. 1990. "Zur Problematik einer multiethnischen Immigrationsgesellschaft: Anmerkungen zu Christoph Antweilers Kommentar." *Zeitschrift für Ethnologie* 115: 261–67.

———. 1993a. "Universalien. Mit altsteinzeitlichem Erbe in der modernen Welt." In Wulf Schiefenhövel, Johanna Uher, and Renate Krell (eds.), *Eibl-Eibesfeldt. Sein Schlüssel zur Verhaltensforschung*. Munich: Langen Müller Verlag, 128–33.

———. 1993b. *Das verbindende Erbe. Expeditionen zu den Wurzeln unseres Verhaltens*. Munich: Wilhelm Heyne Verlag.

———. 2007. *Human Ethology*. Chicago: Aldine de Gruyter. Originally *Die Biologie des menschlichen Verhaltens. Grundriß der Humanethologie*. Weyarn: Seehamer, Blank, 5th ed. 2004.

Eibl-Eibesfeldt, Irenäus and Christa Sütterlin. 2007. *Weltsprache Kunst. Zur Natur- und Kunstgeschichte bildlicher Kommunikation*. Vienna: Christian Brandstätter Verlag.

Eichinger Ferro-Luzzi, Gabriella. 1996. "Review of Boyer 1994." *Anthropos* 91(4–6): 581–82.

Eisenstadt, Shmuel Noah. 2006. *Die großen Revolutionen und die Kultuen der Moderne*. Wiesbaden: VS Verlag für Sozialwissenschaften.

Ekman, Paul. 1970. "Universal Facial Expressions of Emotion." *California Mental Health Digest* 8: 151–58.

———. 1992. "Facial Expression of Emotion: New Findings, New Questions." *Psychological Science* 3: 34–38.

———. 1993. "Facial Expression and Emotion." *American Psychologist* 48(4): 384–92.

———. 2003. *Emotions Revealed. Understanding Faces and Feelings*. London: Weidenfeld and Nicolson.

Ekman, Paul and Wallace V. Friesen. 1971. "Constants across Cultures in the Face and Emotion." *Journal of Personality and Social Psychology* 17(2): 124–29.

Ekman, Paul and Erika L. Rosenberg (eds.). 1997. *What the Face Reveals. Basic and Applied Studies of Spontaneous Expression Using the Facial Action Coding System (FACS)*. New York: Oxford University Press.

Ekman, Paul, E. R. Sorensen, and Wallace V. Friesen. 1969. "Pan-Cultural Elements in Facial Displays of Emotion." *Science* 164: 86–88.

Elfenbein, Hillary Anger and Nalini Ambady. 2002. "On the Universality and Cultural Specifity of Emotion Recognition. A Metaanalysis." *Psychological Bulletin* 128(2): 203–35.

Ellen, Roy. 2003. "Variation and Uniformity in the Construction of Biological Kowledge Across Cultures." In Helaine Selin (ed.) and Arne Kalland (adv. ed.), *Nature Across Cultures. Views of Nature and the Environment in Non-Western Cultures*. Science across Cultures: The History of Non-Western Science 4. Dordrecht: Kluwer Academic Publishers, 47–74.

———. 2006a. "Introduction." In Roy Ellen (ed.), *Ethnobiology and the Science of Humankind*. Malden, MA: Blackwell Publishing and Royal Anthropological Institute (*Journal of the Royal Anthropological Institute*, Special Issue 1: 1–27.

———. 2006b. *The Categorial Impulse. Essays in the Anthropology of Classifying Behaviour*. Oxford and New York: Berghahn Books.

Ellsworth, Phoebe C. 1994. "Sense, Culture, and Sensibility." In Shinobu Kitayama and Hazel Rose Markus (eds.), *Emotion and Culture. Empirical Studies and Mutual Influences*. Washington, DC: American Psychological Association, 23–50.

Elsner, Norbert and Hans-Ludwig Schreiber (eds.). 2002. *Was ist der Mensch?* Göttingen: Wallstein Verlag.

Elworthy, Charles. 1993. *Homo Biologicus. An Evolutionary Model For the Human Sciences*. Sozialwissenschaftliche Schriften 25. Berlin: Duncker and Humblot.

Ember, Carol R. and Melvin Ember. 1997. *Anthropology*. Englewood Cliffs, NJ: Prentice-Hall.

———. 1999. "Testing Theory and Why the "Unit of Analysis" Problem Is Not a Problem." In Victor de Munck (ed.), "Comparative Research and Cultural Units," special issue, *Cultural Anthropology* 39(4): 349–63.

———. 2009. *Cross-Cultural Research Methods*. 2nd ed. Lanham, MD: Altamira Press.
Ember, Carol R., Melvin Ember, and Peter N. Peregrine. 2015. "Cross-Cultural Research." In Harvey Russel Bernard and Clarence C. Gravlee (eds.), *Handbook of Methods in Cultural Anthropology*. Lanham, MD: Rowman and Littlefield, 561–99.
Endruweit, Günter. 1999. "Soziologische Menschenbilder." In Rolf Oerter (ed.), *Menschenbilder in der modernen Gesellschaft. Konzeptionen des Menschen in Wissenschaft, Bildung, Kunst, Wirtschaft und Politik. Der Mensch als soziales und personales Wesen* 15). Stuttgart: Enke Verlag, 5–21.
Enfield, Nicholas J. and Stephen C. Levinson (eds.). 2006. *Roots of Human Sociality. Culture, Cognition and Interaction*. Wenner-Gren International Symposium Series. Oxford and New York: Berg Publishers.
Erdal, David and Andrew Whiten. 1996. "Egalitarianism and Machiavellian Intelligence in Human Evolution." In Peter Mellars and Kathleen Gibson (eds.), *Modeling the Early Human Mind*. McDonald Institute Monographs. Cambridge: McDonald Institute for Archaeological Research: 139–160.
Erickson, Paul A. and Liam Donat Murphy. 2003. *A History of Anthropological Theory*. 2nd ed. Calgary, Alberta and Peterborough, Ontario: Broadview Press.
Eriksen, Thomas Hylland. 2001. "Between Universalism and Relativism. A Critique of the UNESCO Concept of Culture." In Jane K. Cowan, Marie Bénédicte Dembour, and Richard Wilson (eds.), *Culture and Rights. Anthropological Perspectives*. Cambridge: Cambridge University Press, 127–48.
———. 2015. *Small Places, Large Issues. An Introduction to Social and Cultural Anthropology*. 4th ed. Anthropology, Culture and Society. London and East Haven, CT: Pluto Press.
Ernst, Heiko and Madlen Ottenschläger (Interview). 2003. "Abkürzung zu Erfolg, Ruhm, Geld." *Stern* 28(3 July): 142.
Errington, Shelly. 1998. *The Death of Authentic Primitive Art and Other Tales of Progress*. Berkeley: University of California Press.
Esfeld, Michael. 2002. *Einführung in die Naturphilosophie*. Einführungen Philosophie. Darmstadt: Wissenschaftliche Buchgesellschaft.
Etcoff, Nancy. 1999. *Survival of the Prettiest. The Science of Beauty*. New York: Doubleday/Random House.
Fabian, Johannes. 1983. *Time and the Other. How Anthropology Makes Its Object*. New York: Columbia University Press.
Fahrenberg, Jochen. 2004. *Annahmen über den Menschen. Menschenbilder aus psychologischer, biologischer, religiöser und interkultureller Sicht. Texte und Kommentare zur Psychologischen Anthropologie*. Heidelberg and Kröning: Asanger Verlag.
Feest, Christian F. and Karl-Heinz Kohl (eds.). 2001. *Hauptwerke der Ethnologie*. Kröner Taschenausgabe 380. Stuttgart: Alfred Kröner Verlag.
Fehr, Ernst and Suzann-Viola Renninger. 2004. Das Samariter-Paradox. *Gehirn and Geist* 1: 34–41.
Fernández-Armesto, Felipe. 2005. *So You Think You're Human? A Brief History of Humankind*. Oxford: Oxford University Press.
Ferraro, Gary P. 2001. *The Cultural Dimension of International Business*. Upper Saddle River, NJ: Prentice-Hall.
Ferraro, Gary P. and Susan Andreatta. 2014. *Cultural Anthropology. An Applied Perspective*. 10th ed. Stamfort, CT: Cengage Learning.
Fessler, Daniel M. T. 1999. "Towards an Understanding of the Universality of Second Order Emotions." In Alexander Laban Hinton (ed.), *Biocultural Approaches to the Emotions*. Publications of the Society for Psychological Anthropology. Cambridge: Cambridge University Press, 75–116.

———. 2004. "Shame in Two Cultures: Implications for Evolutionary Approaches." *Journal of Cognition and Culture* 4(2): 207–62.
Fetchenhauer, Detlef and Hans-Werner Bierhoff. 2004. "Altruismus aus evolutionstheoretischer Perspektive." *Zeitschrift für Sozialpsychologie* 35(3): 131–42.
Field, Alexander J. 2004. *Altruistically Inclined? The Behavioral Sciences, Evolutionary Theory, and the Origins of Reciprocity.* Economics, Cognition and Society. Ann Arbor: The University of Michigan Press.
Figl, Johann. 1993. *Die Mitte der Religionen. Idee und Praxis universalreligiöser Bewegungen.* Darmstadt: Wissenschaftliche Buchgesellschaft.
Fikentscher, Wolfgang. 1995. *Modes of Thought. A Study in the Anthropology of Law and Religion.* Tübingen: J. C. B. Mohr (Paul Siebeck).
Finkielkraut, Alain. 1989. *Die Niederlage des Denkens.* Reinbek bei Hamburg: Rowohlt Verlag.
Finnegan, Ruth. 1998. *Tales of the City. A Study of Narrative and Urban Life.* Cambridge: Cambridge University Press.
Fischer, Hans 1998. "Feldforschung." In Hans Fischer and Bettina Beer (eds.), *Ethnologie. Einführung und Überblick.* 4th ed. Ethnologische Paperbacks. Berlin: Dietrich Reimer Verlag, 73–92.
———. 2012. "Ethnologie als wissenschaftliche Disziplin." In Bettina Beer and Hans Fischer (eds.), *Ethnologie. Einführung und Überblick.* 7th ed. Ethnologische Paperbacks. Berlin: Dietrich Reimer Verlag, 13–31.
Fiske, Andrew P. 1991. *Structures of Social Life. The Four Elementary Forms of Human Relations.* New York: The Free Press.
Flohr, Heiner. 1989. "The Anthropology of Human Social Behavior. Towards a Biocultural Reorientation in the Social Sciences." In Tuomi Paastela (ed.), *Democracy in the Modern World. Essays for Tatu Vanhanan.* Tampere: Tampereen Pikakopio Oy, 25–40.
Florence, Penny. 2004. *Sexed Universals in Contemporary Art.* Aesthetics Today. New York: Allworth Press.
Foley, Robert. 1987. *Another Unique Species. Patterns in Human Evolutionary Ecology.* Harlow and Essex: Longman Scientific and Technical.
Förstl, Hans (ed.). 2006. *Theory of Mind. Neurobiologie und Psychologie sozialen Verhaltens.* Berlin: Springer Verlag.
Foster, George M. and Barbara Gallatin Anderson. 1978. *Medical Anthropology.* New York: John Wiley and Sons.
Foucault, Michel. 191997. *Die Ordnung der Dinge. Eine Archäologie der Humanwissenschaften.* 14th. ed. Frankfurt am Main: Suhrkamp. Originally *Les mots et les choses,* Paris, 1966.
Fox, J. Robin. 1971. "The Cultural Animal." In John F. Eisenberg and Wilton S. Dillon (eds.), *Man and Beast. Comparative Social Behavior.* Washington, DC: Smithsonian Press, 273–96.
———. 1984. *The Red Lamp of Incest. An Enquiry into the Origins of Mind and Society.* Notre Dame, IN: University of Notre Dame Press (1980).
Fox, Katie. 2014. *Watching the English. The Hidden Rules of English Behaviour.* 2nd ed. London: Hodder and Staughton.
Frank, Mark G. 2003. "Getting to Know Your Patient: How Facial Expression Can Help to Reveal True Emotion." In Mary Katsikis (ed.), *The Human Face. Measurement and Meaning.* Boston: Kluwer Academic Publishers, 255–83.
Frayser, Suzanne G. 1985. *Varieties of Sexual Experience. An Anthropological Perspective on Human Sexuality.* New Haven, CT: HRAF Files.
Frenzel, Elisabeth. 1999. *Motive der Weltliteratur. Ein Lexikon dichtungsgeschichtlicher Längsschnitte.* Kröners Taschenausgabe 301. Stuttgart: Kröner Verlag.

———. 2005. *Stoffe der Weltliteratur. Ein Lexikon dichtungsgeschichtlicher Längsschnitte*. Kröners Taschenausgabe, 300. Stuttgart: Kröner Verlag.
Freud, Sigismund Schlomo. (1939) 1956. *Totem und Tabu. Einige Übereinstimmungen im Seelenleben der Wilden und der Neurotiker*. Frankfurt am Main and Hamburg: Fischer Bücherei.
———. (1917) 1969. *Vorlesungen zur Einführung in die Pschoanalyse*, vol. 11 of Sigmund Freud, *Gesammelte Werke*. Frankfurt am Main: S. Fischer Verlag.
Friedl, Ernestine. 1994. "Sex the Invincible." *American Anthropologist* 96: 833–44.
Friedlmeier, Wolfgang. 2005. "Kultur und Emotion. Zur Sozialisation menschlicher Gefühle." In Bernhard Kleeberg, Tilman Walter, and Fabio Crivellari (eds.), *Urmensch und Wissenschaften. Eine Bestandsaufnahme*. Darmstadt: Wissenschaftliche Buchgesellschaft, 137–60.
Friedlmeier, Wolfgang, Pradeep Chakkarath, and Beate Schwarz (eds.). 2005. *Culture and Human Development. The Importance of Cross-Cultural Research to the Social Sciences*. Hove and New York: Psychology Press.
Fritzsche, Andreas and Manfred Kwiran (eds.). 1998. *Der Mensch*. Ökumenische Sozialethik 1. Munich: Bernward bei Don Bosco.
Frobenius, Leo. 1921. *Paideuma. Umrisse einer Kultur- und Seelenlehre*. Munich: C.H. Beck'sche Verlagsbuchhandlung Oskar Beck.
Frühwald, Wolfgang. 2004. "Das 'Sprachtier' verabschiedet sich oder Über den Rückzug der Sprache aus der Existenzdeutung des Menschen." In Wolfgang Frühwald, Konrad Beyreuther, Johannes Dichgans, Durs Grünbein, Karl Kardinal Lehmann, and Wolf Singer, *Das Design des Menschen. Der Wandel des Menschenbildes unter dem Einfluss der modernen Naturwissenschaft*. Cologne: DuMont Literatur and Kunst Verlag, 232–59.
Frühwald, Wolfgang, Konrad Beyreuther, Johannes Dichgans, Durs Grünbein, Karl Kardinal Lehmann and Wolf Singer. 2004. *Das Design des Menschen. Der Wandel des Menschenbildes unter dem Einfluss der modernen Naturwissenschaft*. Cologne: DuMont Literatur und Kunst Verlag.
Fry, Douglas P. 2006. *The Human Potential for Peace. An Anthropological Challenge to Assumptions about War and Violence*. New York and Oxford: Oxford University Press.
Fuchs, Martin. 1997. "Universalität der Kultur. Reflexion, Interaktion und das Identitätsdenken—eine ethnologische Perspektive." In Manfred Brocker and Heino Heinrich Nau (eds.), *Ethnozentrismus. Möglichkeiten und Grenzen des interkulturellen Dialogs*. Darmstadt: Wissenschaftliche Buchgesellschaft, 141–52.
Fukuyama, Francis 2002. *Das Ende des Menschen*. Stuttgart and Munich: Deutsche Verlags-Anstalt. Originally *Our Posthuman Future. Consequences of the Biotechnology Revolution*, New York: Farrar, Straus and Giroux, 2002.
Gächter, Simon and Christian Thöni. 2004. "Rationalität, Eigennutz und Fairness: Ökonomisches Entscheidungsverhalten aus verhaltenswissenschaftlicher Sicht." In Heinrich Schmidinger and Clemens Sedmak (eds.), *Der Mensch—ein „animal rationale"? Vernunft—Kognition—Intelligenz*. Topologien des Menschlichen 1. Darmstadt: Wissenschaftliche Buchgesellschaft, 256–74.
Gagneux, Pascal, D. S. Woodruff, and Christophe Boesch. 1997. "Furtive Mating in Female Chimpanzees." *Nature* 387: 358–59.
Gairdner, William Douglas. 2008. *The Book of Absolutes. A Critique of Relativism and a Defense of Universals*. Montreal and Kingston: McGill-Queen's University Press.
Gangestad, Steven W. and Glenn J. Scheyd. 2005. "The Evolution of Human Physical Attractiveness." *Annual Review of Anthropology* 34: 523–48.
Ganten, Detlev, Thomas Deichmann, and Thilo Spahl. 2005. *Naturwissenschaft. Alles, was man wissen muss*. Munich: Deutscher Taschenbuch Verlag.

Gärdenfors, Peter. 2003. *How Homo became sapiens. On the Evolution of Thinking.* Oxford: Oxford University Press.
Gardner, Gerald T. and Paul C. Stern. 1995. *Environmental Problems and Human Behavior.* Boston: Allyn and Bacon.
Gaskell, George and Colin Fraser. 1990. "The Social Psychological Study of Widespread Beliefs." In Colin Fraser and George Gaskell (eds.), *The Social Psychological Study of Widespread Beliefs.* Oxford: Clarendon Press, 3–24.
Gaulin, Steven J. C. 1997. "Cross-Cultural Patterns and the Search for Evolved Psychological Mechanisms." In Martin Daly (ed.). *Characterizing Human Psychological Adaptations.* CIBA Foundation Symposium, 208. Chichester: John Wiley and Sons, 195–211.
Gaulin, Steven J. C. and Donald H. McBurney. 2004. *Evolutionary Psychology.* 2nd ed. Upper Saddle River, NJ: Pearson, Prentice-Hall.
Geertz, Clifford J. 1965. "The Impact of the Concept of Culture on the Concept of Man." In John R. Platt (ed.), *New Views of the Nature of Man.* The Monday Lectures. The University of Chicago. Chicago and London: The University of Chicago Press, 93–118.
———. 1984. "Distinguished Lecture: Anti-Anti-Relativism." *American Anthropologist* 86: 263–78.
———. 1986. "The Uses of Diversity." *Michigan Quarterly Review* (Winter): 105–25.
———. 2000. *Available Light. Anthropological Reflections on Philosophical Topics.* Princeton, NJ: Princeton University Press.
———. 2007. *Welt in Stücken. Kultur und Politik am Ende des 20. Jahrhunderts.* 2nd ed. Passagen Forum. Vienna: Passagen Verlag.
Gehlen, Arnold. (1940) 2004. *Der Mensch. Seine Natur und Stellung in der Welt.* Wiebelsheim: Aula Verlag.
Geissmann, Thomas. 2003. *Vergleichende Primatologie.* Berlin: Springer Verlag.
Gelman, Susan A. 2005. *The Essential Child. Origins of Essentialism in Everyday Thought.* Oxford Series in Cognitive Development. Oxford: Oxford University Press.
Gell-Mann, Murray. 1994. *The Quark and the Jaguar. Adventures in the Simple and the Complex.* New York: Little Brown.
Gellner, Ernest. 1985. *Relativism in the Social Sciences.* Cambridge: Cambridge University Press.
Genkova, Petia. 2012. *Kulturvergleichende Psychologie. Ein Forschungsleitfaden.* Berlin: Springer VS.
Gentner, Dedre and Susan Goldin-Meadow (eds.). 2003. *Language in Mind. Advances in the Study of Language and Cognition.* Cambridge, MA, and London: The MIT Press (A Bradford Book).
Girard, René. 2011. *Das Heilige und die Gewalt.* Ostfildern: Patmos Verlag. Originally *La Violence et le sacré*, Paris: Grasset et Fasquelle, 1972.
Georgas, James. 2011. "Differences and Universals in Families across Cultures." In Van de Vijver et al. (eds.), 341–75.
Georgas, James, John W. Berry and Cigdem Kagitcibasi. 2006. "Synthesis: How Similar and How Different Are Families Across Cultures?" In Georgas et al. (eds.), 186–240.
Georgas, James, John W. Berry, Fons J. R. de Vijver, Cigdem Kagitcibasi, and Ype H. Poortinga (eds.). 2006. *Families Across Cultures. A 30-Nation Psychological Study.* Cambridge: Cambridge University Press.
Gesellschaft für Völkerkunde zur Förderung des Rautenstrauch-Joest-Museums. [2005]. *Das neue Rautenstrauch-Joest-Museum für Völkerunde im Zentrum von Köln* (Flyer). Cologne: Gesellschaft für Völkerkunde zur Förderung des Rautenstrauch-Joest-Museums.
Giesecke, Michael. 2007. *Die Entdeckung der kommunikativen Welt. Studien zur kulturvergleichenden Medioiengeschichte.* Frankfurt am Main: Suhrkamp Verlag.

Gingrich, Andre. 1999. *Erkundungen. Themen der ethnologischen Forschung.* Vienna: Böhlau.

———. 2002. "When Ethnic Majorities are 'Dethroned.' Towards A Methodology of Self-reflexive, Controlled Macrocomparison." In Gingrich and Fox (eds.), *Anthropology, by Comparison.* London and New York: Routledge, 225–48.

———. 2012. "Comparative Methods in Socio-Cultural Anthropology Today." In Richard Fardon, Olivia Harris, Trevor H. Marchand, Mark Nuttall, Cris Shore, Veronica Strang, and Richard A. Wilson (eds.), *The Sage Handbook of Social Anthropology,* vol. 2. Los Angeles: Sage Publications, 201–14.

Gingrich, Andre and Richard G. Fox (eds.). 2002. *Anthropology, by Comparison.* London: Routledge.

Giri, Ananta Kumar. 2006. *Cosmopolitism.* Lecture, Universität Trier, Zentrum für Ostasien- und Pazifikstudien (ZOPS), 27 June 2006.

Gladigow, Burkhard. 2004. "Homines hominem causa. Kultur und Menschenbild: Zur Logik der Deutungsebenen." In Friedrich Jaeger and Jürgen Straub (eds.), *Was ist der Mensch, was ist Geschichte? Annäherungen an eine kulturwissenschaftliche Anthropologie. Jörn Rüsen zum 65. Geburtstag.* Bielefeld: Transcript, 73–88.

Glaser, Barney G. and Anselm L. Strauss. 1967. *The Discovery of Grounded Theory. Strategies For Qualitative Research.* Chicago: Aldine de Gruyter.

Goddard, Cliff. 1996. "The 'Social Emotions' of Malay (Bahasa Melayu)." *Ethos* 24(3): 426–64.

———. 2001. "Lexico-Semantic Universals. A Critical Overview." *Linguistic Typology* 5: 1–65.

———. 2003. "Whorf Meets Wierzbicka: Variation and Universals in Language and Thinking." *Langage Sciences* 25: 393–432.

Goddard, Cliff and Anna Wierzbicka (eds.). 1994. *Semantic and Lexical Universals. Theory and Empirical Findings.* Amsterdam and Philadelphia: John Benjamins (Studies in Language Companion, SLCS).

Godelier, Maurice. 1994. "'Mirror, Mirror on the Wall…' The Once and Future Role of Anthropology: A Tentative Assessment." In Robert Borowsky (ed.), *Assessing Cultural Anthropology.* New York: McGraw-Hill, 97–118.

Goldberg, Steven. 1993. *Why Men Rule. A Theory of Male Dominance.* Peru, IL: Open Court.

Goldberg, Vicki. 1993. *The Power of Photography. How Photographs Changed Our Lives.* New York: Abbeville Publishing Group.

Goldenweiser, Alexander A. 1922. *Early Civilization. An Introduction to Anthropology.* New York: Alfred A. Knopf.

Goldschmidt, Walter R. 2006. *The Bridge to Humanity. How Affect Hunger Trumps the Selfish Gene.* New York and Oxford: Oxford University Press.

Goldstein-Sepinwall, Alyssa. 2005. *The Abbé Grégoire and the French Revolution. The Making of Modern Universalism.* Berkeley: University of California Press.

Goodenough, Ward Hunt. 1956. "Residence Rules." *Southwestern Journal of Anthropology* 12: 24–37.

———. 1970. *Description and Comparison in Cultural Anthropology.* Chicago: Aldine (The Lewis Henry Morgan Lectures, 1968).

Goodwin, Robin. 1999. *Personal Relationships across Cultures.* London and New York: Routledge.

Goody, Esther N. 1997. "Social Intelligence and Language: Another Rubicon?" In Andrew Whiten and Richard W. Byrne (eds.), *Machiavellian Intelligence II: Evaluations and Extensions.* Cambridge: Cambridge University Press, 365–96.

Goody, Jack. 1977. *The Domestication of the Savage Mind.* Themes in the Social Sciences. Cambridge: Cambridge University Press.

Gordon, Raymond G. (ed.). 2005. *Ethnologue.* Vol. 1: *Languages of the World.* Vol. 2: *Maps and Indexes.* 15th ed. Dallas: Summer Institute of Linguistics.

Görgens, Siegrid, Annette Scheunpflug, and Krassimir Stojanov (eds.). 2001. *Universalistische Moral und weltbürgerliche Erziehung. Die Herausforderung der Globalisierung im Horizont der modernen Evolutionsforschung.* Frankfurt am Main: IKO Verlag für Interkulturelle Kommunikation.

Gottschall, Jonathan and David Sloan Wilson (eds.).2005. *The Literary Animal. Evolution and the Nature of Narrative.* Rethinking Theory. Evanston, IL: Northwestern University Press.

Gough, Kathleen E. 1968. Is the Family Universal? The Nayar Case. In Norman Bell and Ezra F. Vogel (eds.), *A Modern Introduction to the Family.* New York: The Free Press, 80–96.

Gould, Stephen J. 1985. "Human Equality Is a Contingent Fact of History." In Stephen J, Gould, *The Flamingo's Smile.* New York: W. W. Norton, 185–222.

———. 1986. "Evolution and the Triumph of Homology, or Why History Matters." *American Scientist* 74: 60–69.

———. 1996. *The Mismeasure of Man.* New York: W. W. Norton.

Gould, Stephen J. and Richard C. Lewontin. 1979. "The Spandrels of San Marco and the Panglossian Paradigm: A Critique of the Adaptationist Programme." *Proceedings of the Royal Society London B* 205: 581–98.

Gould, Stephen J. and Elizabeth S. Vrba. 1982. "Exaptation: A Missing Term in the Science of Form." *Paleobiology* 8: 4–15.

Graf, Friedrich Wilhelm. 2004. *Die Wiederkehr der Götter. Religion in der modernen Kultur.* Munich. Verlag C.H. Beck.

Grammer, Karl. 2005. *Signale der Liebe. Die biologischen Gesetze der Partnerschaft.* Munich: Deutscher Taschenbuch Verlag.

Grammer, Karl and Elisabeth Oberzaucher. 2006. "The Reconstruction of Facial Expressions in Embodied Systems. New Approaches to an Old Problem." *ZIF Mitteilungen* 2: 14–31.

Greenberg, Joseph H. (ed.). 1963. *Universals of Language.* Cambridge, MA: The MIT Press.

———. 1975. "Research in Language Universals." *Annual Review of Anthropology* 4: 75–94.

Greenberg, Joseph H., Charles A. Ferguson, and Edith A. Moravcsik, (eds.). 1978. *Universals of Human Language.* 4 Vols. Stanford, CA: Stanford University Press.

Greenfield, Patricia M. 1997. "Culture as Process. Empirical Methods for Cultural Psychology." In John W. Berry, Ype H. Poortinga, and Janak Pandey (eds.), *Handbook of Cross-Cultural Psychology.* Vol 1: *Theory and Method.* Boston: Allyn and Baco, 301–46.

Greenfield, Patricia M., Heidi Keller, Andrew Fuligni, and Ashley Maynard. 2003. "Cultural Pathways Through Universal Development." *Annual Review of Psychology* 54: 461–90.

Greenwood, Davyd J. and William A. Stini (eds.). 1977. *Nature, Culture and Human History. A Bio-cultural Introduction to Anthropology.* New York: Harper and Row.

Gregor, Paul, Thomas Göller, Hans Lenk, and Guido Rappe (eds.). 2001. *Humanität, Interkulturalität und Menschenrecht.* Schriften zur Humanitäts- und Glücksforschung 1). Frankfurt am Main: Peter Lang Verlag.

Gregor, Thomas A. and Donald F. Tuzin. 2001. "Comparing Gender in Amazonia and Melanesia: A Theoretical Orientation." In Dies (ed.), *Gender in Amazonia and Melanesia. An Exploration of Comparative Methdod.* Berkeley: University of California Press, 1–16.

Griese, Hartmut M. 2008. Review of first ed. of Antweiler 2012a. http://www.socialnet.de/rezensionen/5247.php, Retrieved 28 July 2012.

Griese, Hartmut M. 2014. "Rolle." In Günter Endruweit, Gisela Trommsdorff and Nicole Burzan (eds.), *Wörterbuch der Soziologie*. 2nd ed. Konstanz and Munich: UVK verlagsgesellschaft, 411–15.

Griffith, Jeremy. 2004. *The Human Condition Documentary Proposal*. Sydney: FHA Publishing and Communications. Retrieved 10 October 2015 from www.fhapublishing.com.

Griffiths, Paul E. 1997. *What Emotions Really Are: The Problem of Psychological Categories*. Science and Its Conceptual Foundations. Chicago: The University of Chicago Press.

Groh, Dieter. 1992a. "Pierre Bourdieus 'allgemeine Wissenschaft der Ökonomie praktischer Handlungen.'" In Dieter Groh, *Anthropologische Dimensionen der Geschichte*. Frankfurt am Main: Suhrkamp Verlag, 15–34.

———. 1992b. "Ethnologie als Universalwissenschaft." In Dieter Groh, *Anthropologische Dimensionen der Geschichte*. Frankfurt am Main: Suhrkamp Verlag, 42–53.

Groh, Ruth. 2004. "Negative Anthropologie und kulturelle Konstruktion." In Aleida Assmann, Ulrich Gaier, and Gisela Trommsdorff (eds.), *Positionen der Kulturanthropologie*. With Karolina Jeftic. Frankfurt: Suhrkamp, 318–57.

———. 2005. "Das Vertikale und das Horizontale. Zur soziobiologischen Begründung von Gesellschaftsmodellen." In Bernhard Kleeberg, Tilman Walter, and Fabio Crivellari (eds.), *Urmensch und Wissenschaften. Eine Bestandsaufnahme*. Darmstadt: Wissenschaftliche Buchgesellschaft, 214–25.

Grossmann, Klaus E. and Karin Grossmann. 2007. "Universale Bedingungen für die Entwicklung kultureller Vielfalt: Eine verhaltensbiologische Perspektive." In Gisela Trommsdorff and Hans-Joachim Kornath (eds.), *Theorien und Methoden der kulturvergleichenden Psychologie*. Enzyklopädie der Psychologie, Theme section C, Theorie und Forschung, Series VII, Kulturvergleichende Psychologie 1. Göttingen: Hogrefe, 221–85.

Grunwald, Armin, Mathias Gutmann, and Eva M. Neumann-Held (eds.). 2002. *On Human Nature. Anthropological, Biological and Philosophical Foundations*. Wissenschaftsethik und Technikfolgenbeurteilung 15. Berlin: Springer-Verlag.

Grupe, Gisela, Kerrin Christiansen, Inge Schröder, and Ursula Wittwer-Backofen. 2012. *Anthropologie. Einführendes Lehrbuch*. 2nd ed. Berlin: Springer-Verlag.

Gumpertz, John J. and Stephen C. Levinson (eds.). 1996. *Rethinking Linguistic Relativity*. Cambridge: Cambridge University Press.

Gutmann, Amy. 1995. "Das Problem des Multikulturalismus in der politischen Ethik." *Deutsche Zeitschrift für Philosophie* 43(2): 273–305.

Haase, Martin. 2006. *Sprachtypologie. Eie Einführung in die Erforschung der Vielfalt menschlicher Sprachen*. Wiesbden: Verlag für Sozialwissenschaften.

Habermas, Jürgen. 1973. "Philosophische Anthropologie. Ein Lexikonartikel." In Jürgen Habermas: *Kultur und Kritik. Verstreute Aufsätze*. Frankfurt am Main: Suhrkamp Verlag, 89–111.

———. 1997. "Der interkulturelle Diskurs über die Menschenrechte. Vermeintliche und tatsächliche Probleme." *Entwicklung und Zusammenarbeit* 38(7): 164–66.

———. 2005. *Die Zukunft der menschlichen Natur. Auf dem Weg zu einer liberalen Eugenik? Erweiterte Ausgabe*. 5th ed. Frankfurt am Main: Suhrkamp Verlag.

Hacking, Ian. 1999. *The Social Construction of What?* Cambridge, MA, and London: Harvard University Press.

Hagège, Claude. 1987. *Der dialogische Mensch. Sprache—Weltbild—Gesellschaft*. Reinbek bei Hamburg: Rowohlt Taschenbuch Verlag. Rowohlts Enzyklopädie 442. Originally *L'homme des paroles. Contribution linguistique aux sciences humaines,* Paris: Librairie Arthème Fayard, 1975.

Hagen, Edward H. 2005. "Controversial Issues in Evolutionary Psychology." In David Buss (ed.), *Handbook of Evolutionary Psychology.* Hoboken, NJ: John Wiley and Sons, 145–73.
Hahn, Alois. 2002. "Tod und Weiterleben in vergleichend soziologischer Sicht." In Jan Assmann and Rolf Trauzettel (eds.), *Tod, Jenseits und Identität. Perspektiven einer kulturwissenschaftlichen Thanatologie.* Freiburg and Munich: Verlag Karl Alber, 575–86.
Haiman, John. 1983. "Iconic and Economic Motivation." *Language* 59: 781–819.
Haller, Dieter and Bernhard Rodekohr. 2005. *Dtv-Atlas Ethnologie.* Munich: Deutscher Taschenbuch Verlag.
Haller, Dieter and Cris Shore (eds.). 2005. *Corruption. Anthropological Perspectives.* Anthropology, Culture, Society. London: Pluto Press.
Hamill, James F. 1990. *Ethno-Logic. The Anthropology of Human Reasoning.* Urbana, IL, and Chicago: University of Illinois Press.
———. 1998. "Rational Culture. Universals of Meaning in First-Ascending-Generation Kin Terms." *Anthropos* 93(4–6): 455–68.
Hanna, Judith Lynne. (1979) 1987. *To Dance Is Human. A Theory of Nonverbal Communication.* Chicago and London: The University of Chicago Press.
Handwerker, W. Penn. 2015. *Our Story. How Cultures Shaped People to get Things Done.* Walnut Creek, CAL.: Left Coast Press.
Hanse Wissenschaftskolleg Delmenhorst. 1993. *Arbeitsgruppe Transkulturelle Universalien.* Retrieved 10 January 2016 from (https://www.tatup-journal.de/tadn992_opol99a.php)
Hansen, Klaus P. 2003. *Kultur und Kulturwissenschaft. Eine Einführung.* Tübingen und Basel: A. Francke Verlag.
Hardin, C. L. and Luisa Maffi (eds.). 1997. *Color Categories in Thought and Language.* Cambridge: Cambridge University Press.
Hardonk, Marius M. and F. A. J. Boselie. 1998. "Cross-Cultural Universals of Aesthetic Appreciation." In *Proceedings of the XV International Association of Empirical Aesthetics.* Rome: Institute for Cognition and Information, 87–99.
Harkness, Janet A., Fons J. R. de Vijver, and Peter Ph. Mohler (eds.). 2003. *Cross-Cultural Survey Methods.* Wiley Series in Survey Methodology. Hoboken, NJ: John Wiley and Sons.
Harré, Rom. 1993. *Social Being.* London: Blackwell Publishers
———. 2006. "Universals and the Psychology of Music: An Exemplar For Cultural Studies." In Jürgen Straub, Doris Weidemann, Carlos Kölbl, and Barbara Zielke (eds.), *Pursuit of Meaning. Advances in Cultural and Cross-Cultural Psychology.* Bielefeld: Transcript Verlag, 153–62.
Harris, Marvin. 1980. *Cultural Materialism. The Struggle for A Science of Culture.* New York: Vintage Books.
———. 1999. *Theories of Culture in Postmodern Times.* Walnut Creek, CA: Altamira Press.
———. (1968) 2001a. *The Rise of Anthropological Theory. A History of Theories of Culture,* rev. ed. Walnut Creek, CA: Altamira Press.
———. (1979) 2001b. *Cultural Materialism. The Struggle for A Science of Culture,* rev. ed. Walnut Creek: Altamira Press.
Hart, John P. and John Edward Terrell (eds.). 2002. *Darwin and Archaeology. A Handbook of Key Concepts.* Westport, CT, and London: Bergin and Garvey.
Hart, Keith. 2008. *Toward A New Human Universal.* University of Wisconsin-Milwaukee, lecture Series "Disciplinary Dialogs: Past Knowing", 7 September 2007 (The Memory Bank. A New Commonwealth, Vers. 4.0). Retrieved 12 February 2013 from http://www.thememorybank.co.uk/2007/09/01/toward-a-new-human-universal.

Haspelmath, Martin. 1997. *From Space to Time. Temporal Adverbials in the World's Languages.* Lincom Studies in Theoretical Linguistics 2. Munich: Lincom Europa Academic Publishers.
Haspelmath, Martin, Matthew S. Dryer, David Gil, and Bernhard Comrie (eds.). 2005. *The World Atlas of Language Structures.* Oxford Linguistics. Oxford: Oxford University Press (incl. CD-ROM).
Hasse, Jürgen and Ilse Helbrecht (eds.). 2003. *Menschenbilder in der Humangeographie.* Wahrnehmungsgeographische Studien 21. Oldenbourg: Bibliotheks- und Informationssystem der Carl von Ossietzky Universität Oldenburg (BIS).
Hauck, Gerhard. 2003. *Die Gesellschaftstheorie und ihr anderes. Wider den Eurozentrismus in den Sozialwissenschaften.* Münster: Westfälisches Dampfboot.
———. 2006. *Kultur. Zur Karriere eines sozialwissenschaftlichen Begriffs.* Einstiege. Grundbegriffe der Sozialphilosophie und Gesellschaftstheorie 16/17. Münster: Westfälisches Dampfboot.
Hauschild, Thomas (ed.). 1995. *Lebenslust und Fremdenfurcht. Ethnologie im Dritten Reich.* Frankfurt am Main: Suhrkamp.
———. 2000. Bimbes statt Bimbos. Ob in Neuguinea, Italien oder in der CDU – überall entdecken Ethnologen die gleichen Rituale. *Die Zeit,* No. 6, 3.2.2000, p. 42.
———. 2004. "Kultureller Relativsmus und anthropologische Nationen. Der Fall der deutschen Völkerkunde." In Aleida Assmann, Ulrich Gaier, and Gisela Trommsdorff (eds.), *Positionen der Kulturanthropologie.* With Karolina Jeftic. Frankfurt am Main: Suhrkamp, 121–47.
———. 2005. "Ethnologie als Kulturwissenschaft." In Klaus Stierstorfer and Laurenz Volkmann (eds.), *Kulturwissenschaft interdisziplinär.* Tübingen: Gunter Narr Verlag (Narr Studienbücher), 59–79.
Hauser, Marc D. 2007. *Moral Minds. The Nature of Right and Wrong.* New York: Harper Perennial.
Hauser, Marc D., Noam Chomsky, and William Tecumseh Fitch. 2002. "The Faculty of Language: What Is It, Who Has It, and How Did It Evolve?" *Science* 298: 1,569–79.
Hawkins, John A. (ed.). 2002. *Explaining Language Universals.* Cambridge, MA: Blackwell.
Heider, Eleanor Rosch. 1972. "Universals in Color Naming and Memory." Journal of Experimental Psychology 93(1): 10–20.
Heider, Karl G. 1991. Landscapes of Emotion. Mapping Three Cultures in Indonesia. Cambridge Cambridge University Press.
Heine, Steven J., Derrin R. Lehman, Kaiping Peng, and Joe Greenholtz. 2002. "What's Wrong with Crosscultural Comparison of Subjective Likert Scales? The Reference-Group Effect." *Journal of Personality and Social Psychology* 82(6): 903–18.
Heinrichs, Hans-Jürgen. 1993. "Über Ethnopsychoanalyse, Ethnopsychiatrie und Ethno-Hermeneutik." In Wolfdietrich Schmied-Kowarzik and Justin Stagl (eds.), *Grundfragen der Ethnologie. Beiträge zur gegenwärtigen Theorie-Diskussion.* Ethnologische Paperbacks. Berlin: Dietrich Reimer Verlag, 359–80.
Heintze, Dieter. 1990. Georg Forster (1754–1794). In Wolfgang Marschall (ed.), *Klassiker der Kulturanthropologie. Von Montaigne bis Margaret Mead.* Munich: Verlag C.H. Beck, 69–87.
Hejl, Peter M. 1999. "Konstruktivismus, Beliebigkeit, Universalien." In Gebhard Rusch (ed.), *Wissen und Wirklichkeit. Beiträge zum Konstruktivismus. Eine Hommage an Ernst Glasersfeld.* Heidelberg: Carl Auer-Systeme Verlag, 163–97.
———. 2001a. "Konstruktivismus und Universalien—eine Verbindung contre Nature?" In Peter Hejl (ed.), *Universalien und Konstruktivismus.* Frankfurt am Main: Suhrkamp Verlag, 7–67.

——— (ed.). 2001b. *Universalien und Konstruktivismus*. Frankfurt am Main: Suhrkamp Verlag.

———. 2005. "Introduction—Culture: Universals and Particulars." Lecture, Conference *Media and Universals 2005, Focus on Film and Print*. SFB/FK 615, Media Transitions, Project A 3: Social and Anthropological Factors of Media Use, Siegen: University of Siegen.

Hejl, Peter M. and Christoph Antweiler. 2004. "Kooperation und Konkurrenz." In Gerhard Roth (comp.), *Antrag auf eine internationale Konferenz Transkulturelle Universalien am Hanse-Wissenschaftskolleg in Delmenhorst*, o.O. (Delmenhorst). Unpublished manuscript, 11–13.

Helfrich, Hede. 2003. "Methodologie kulturvergleichender Forschung." In Alexander Thomas (ed.), *Kulturvergleichende Psychologie*. Göttingen: Hogrefe, 111–38.

———. 2013. *Kulturvergleichende Psychologie*. Basiswissen Psychologie. Berlin: Springer VS.

Henke, Winfried. 2005. "Human Biological Evolution." In Franz M. Wuketits and Francisco J. Ayala (eds.), *Handbook of Human Evolution*. Vol. 2: *The Evolution of Living Systems (Including Hominids)*. Weinheim: Wiley-VCH, 117–222.

———. 2006. "Ursprung und Verbreitung des Genus Homo—paläobiologische Anmerkungen zum evolutiven Erfolg unsrere Gattung." In Gabriele Uelsberg and Stefan Lötters (eds.), *Roots. Wurzeln der Menschheit*. Bonn: Rheinisches Landesmuseum and Mainz: Verlag Philipp von Zabern, 33–52.

Henke, Winfried and Hartmut Rothe. 2003. *Menschwerdung*. Fischer Kompakt. Frankfurt am Main: Fischer Taschenbuch Verlag.

———. 2005. "Ursprung, Adaptation und Verbreitung der Gattung Homo. Marginalien zur Evolution eines global player." In Bernhard Kleeberg, Tilman Walter, and Fabio Crivellari (eds.), *Urmensch und Wissenschaften. Eine Bestandsaufnahme*. Darmstadt: Wissenschaftliche Buchgesellschaft, 89–123.

Hennig, Christoph. 1999. *Reiselust. Touristen, Tourismus und Urlaubskultur*. Frankfurt am Main: Suhrkamp.

Henrich, Joseph. 2002. "Decision Making, Cultural Transmission, and Adaptation in Economic Anthropology." In Jean Ensminger (ed.), *Theory in Economic Anthropology*. Society for Economic Anthropology Monographs 18. Walnut Creek, CA: Altamira Press, 251–95.

Henrich, Joseph, Steven Heine, and Ara Norenzayan. 2010. "The Weirdest People in the World." *The Behavioral and Brain Sciences* 33: 61–135 (plus commentary).

Henrich, Joseph, Richard McElreath, Abigail Barr, Jean Ensminger, Clark Barrett, Alexander Bolyanatz, Juam Camilo Cardenas, Michael Gurven, Edwins Gwako, Natalie Henrich, Carolyn Lesorogol, Frank Marlowe, David Tracer, and John Ziker. 2006. "Costly Punishment Across Human Societies." *Science* 312: 1767–70.

Henss, Ronald. 1998. *Gesicht und Persönlichkeitseindruck*. Lehr- und Forschungstexte Psychologie. Göttingen: Hogrefe.

Hepp, Andreas. 2006. *Transkulturelle Kommunikation*. Konstanz: UVK Verlagsgesellschaft.

Herbig, Jost. 1988. *Nahrung für die Götter. Die kulturelle Neuerschaffung der Welt durch den Menschen*. Munich: Carl Hanser Verlag.

Herder, Johann Gottfried. (1774) 2003. *Auch eine Philosophie der Geschichte zur Bildung der Menschheit*. Stuttgart: Philipp Reclam.

Héritier, Françoise. 1982. "The Symbolics of Incest and Its Prohibition." In Michel Izard and Pierre Smith (eds.), *Between Belief and Transgression. Structuralist Essays in Religion, History and Myth*. Chicago Originals. Chicago: University of Chicago Press, 152–79.

———. 1994. *De l'inceste*. Opus. Paris: Éditions Odile Jacob.

———. 1999. *Two Sisters and Their Mother. The Anthropology of Incest.* New York: Zone Books and Cambridge, MA: The MIT Press. Originally *Les deux soeurs et leur mère. Anthropologie de l'inceste*, Paris: Éditions Odile Jacob, 1994.
Héritier-Augé, Françoise. 1991. *L'exercise de la parenté.* Paris: Hautes Etudes, Gallimard-Le Seuil.
Herskovits, Melville J. (1948) 1966. *Man and His Works. The Science of Cultural Anthropology.* New York: Alfred Knopf.
Hertz, Robert. (1909) 2006. *Death and the Right Hand.* Routledge Library Editions. London and New York: Routledge.
Herzfeld, Michael. 2001. *Anthropology. Theoretical Practice in Culture and Society.* Malden, MA, and Oxford: Blackwell Publishers and UNESCO.
Herzog-Schröder, Gabriele. 2001. "Eine kulturelle Universalie." In Christa Sütterlin and Frank K. Salter (eds.), *Irenäus Eibl-Eibesfeldt. Zu Person und Werk.* Frankfurt: Peter Lang Europäischer Verlag der Wissenschaften, 154–56.
Hewlett, Barry S. 1991. *Intimate Fathers.* Ann Arbor: University of Michigan Press.
Heyer, Paul. 1982. *Nature, Human Nature, and Society. Marx, Darwin, Biology, and the Human Sciences.* Contributions in Philosophy 21. Westport, CT: Greenwood Press.
Heymer, Armin. 1977. *Ethologisches Wörterbuch.* Berlin and Hamburg: Verlag Paul Parey.
Hildebrandt, Hans-Jürgen. 1978. "Kritische Bemerkungen zum Kulturrelativismus und seiner Rezeption in der deutschen Ethnologie." *Kölner Zeitschrift für Soziologie und Sozialpsychologie* 30: 136–57.
———. 1996. *Selbstwahrnehmung und Fremdwahrnehmung. Ethnologisch-soziologische Beiträge zur Wissenschaftsgeschichte und Theorienbildung.* Mammendorf: Septem Artes Verlag.
Hinde, Robert P. 1994. "Individuals and Culture." In Jean-Pierre Changeaux and Jean Cavallion (eds.), *Origins of the Brain.* Oxford: Clarendon Press, 186–99.
———. 1999. *Why Gods Persist. A Scientific Approach to Religion.* London and New York: Routledge.
———. 2003. *Why Good Is Good. The Sources of Morality.* London and New York: Routledge.
Hinkmann, Jens. 1996. *Philosophische Argumente für und wider die Universalität der Menschenrechte.* Marburg: Tectum Verlag.
Hinton, Alexander Laban (ed.). 1999. *Biocultural Approaches to the Emotions.* Publications of the Society for Psychological Anthropology. Cambridge: Cambridge University Press.
Hockett, Charles F. 1966. "The Problems of Universals in Language." In Joseph H. Greenberg (ed.), *Universals of Language.* 2nd ed. Cambridge, MA: The MIT Press, 1–22.
———. 1973. *Man's Place in Nature.* New York: McGraw-Hill.
Hodgson, Geoffrey M. and Thorbjörn Knudsen. 2010. *Darwin's Conjecture. The Search for General Principles of Social and Economic Evolution.* Chicago: The University of Chicago Press.
Hofer, Helmut and Günter Altner (eds.). 1998. *Die Sonderstellung des Menschen. Naturwissenschaftliche Aspekte.* Munich: Urban and Fischer.
Hoffmann, Johannes (ed.). 1991. *Begründung von Menschenrechten aus der Sicht unterschiedlicher Kulturen.* Frankfurt am Main: IKO, Verlag für interkulturelle Kommunikation.
——— (ed.). 1994. *Universale Menschenrechte im Widerspruch der Kulturen.* Symposium "Das eine Menschenrecht für alle und die vielen Lebensformen" 2. Frankfurt am Main: IKO, Verlag für interkulturelle Kommunikation.
Hofmann, Martin Ludwig, Tobias F. Korta, and Sibylle Niekisch (eds.). 2004. *Culture Club. Klassiker der Kulturteorie.* Frankfurt am Main: Suhrkamp Verlag.

——— (eds.). 2006. *Culture Club II. Klassiker der Kulturteorie*. Frankfurt am Main: Suhrkamp Verlag.
Hofstede, Geert and Jan Gert Hofstede. 2005. *Cultures and Organizations. Software of the Mind. Cooperation and Its Importance for Survival*. New York: McGraw-Hill.
Hogan, Patrick Colm. 1997. "Literary Universals." *Poetics Today* 18 (2): 223–49.
———. 2003a. *The Mind and Its Stories. Narrative Universals and Human Emotion*. Studies in Emotion and Social Interaction. Cambridge: Cambridge University Press and Paris: Éditions de la Maison des Sciences de l'Homme.
———. 2003b. *Cognitive Science, Literature, and the Arts. A Guide For Humanists*. New York and London: Routledge.
Holenstein, Elmar. 1979. *Zur Begrifflichkeit der Universalienforschung in Linguistik und Anthropologie*. Akup. Arbeiten des Kölner Universalien-Projekts 35. Cologne: University of Cologne.
———. 1981. "Sprache und Gehirn. Phänomenologische Perspektiven." In Helmut Schnelle (ed.), *Sprache und Gehirn. Roman Jacobsen zu Ehren*. Frankfurt am Main: Suhrkamp Verlag, 197–216.
———. 1985a. *Sprachliche Universalien. Eine Untersuchung zur Natur des menschliches Geistes*. Bochumer Beiträge zur Semiotik 1. Bochum: Studienverlag Dr. Norbert Brockmeyer.
———. 1985b. *Menschliches Selbstverständnis. Ichbewußtsein—Intersubjektive Verantwortung—Interkulturelle Verständigung*. Frankfurt am Main: Suhrkamp.
———. 1995. "Human Equality and Intra- as Well as Intercultural Diversity." *The Monist. An International Quarterly Journal of General Philosophical Inquiry* 78(1): 65–79.
———. 1997. "Wo verlaufen Europas Grenzen? Europäische Identität und Universalität auf dem Prüfstand." In Manfred Brocker and Heino Heinrich Nau (eds.), *Ethnozentrismus. Möglichkeiten und Grenzen des interkulturellen Dialogs*. Darmstadt: Wissenschaftliche Buchgesellschaft, 46–68.
———. 1998a. "'Europa und die Menschheit'. Zu Husserls kulturphilosophischen Meditationen." In Elmar Holenstein, *Kulturphilosophische Perspektiven. Schulbeispiel Schweiz, Europäische Identität auf dem Prüfstand, Globale Verständigungsmöglichkeiten*. Frankfurt am Main: Suhrkamp, 230–53.
———. 1998b. "Intra- und Interkulturelle Hermeneutik." In Elmar Holenstein, *Kulturphilosophische Perspektiven. Schulbeispiel Schweiz, Europäische Identität auf dem Prüfstand, Globale Verständigungsmöglichkeiten*. Frankfurt am Main: Suhrkamp, 257–87.
———. 1998c. "'Kulturnation'. Eine systematisch in die Irre führende Idee." In Elmar Holenstein, *Kulturphilosophische Perspektiven. Schulbeispiel Schweiz, Europäische Identität auf dem Prüfstand, Globale Verständigungsmöglichkeiten*. Frankfurt am Main: Suhrkamp, 313–45.
———. 1998d. "Ein Dutzend Daumenregeln zur Vermeidung interkultureller Missverständnisse." In Elmar Holenstein, *Kulturphilosophische Perspektiven. Schulbeispiel Schweiz, Europäische Identität auf dem Prüfstand, Globale Verständigungsmöglichkeiten*. Frankfurt am Main: Suhrkamp, 288–312.
———. 1998e. *Kulturphilosophische Perspektiven. Schulbeispiel Schweiz, Europäische Perspektiven, Globale Verständigungsmöglichkeiten*. Frankfurt am Main: Suhrkamp.
———. 2004. *Philosophie-Atlas. Orte und Wege des Denkens*. Zürich: Amman Verlag.
———. 2013. "Intrakulturelle Variationen unterscheiden sich nicht selten weder der Art nach noch dem Grad nach von interkulturellen Variationen." *Zeitschrift für Kulturwissenschaft* 1(13): 167–76.
Hollan, Douglas. 1992. "Cross-Cultural Differences in the Self." *Journal of Anthropological Research* 48: 283–300.

Holland, Dorothy. 1997. "Selves as Cultured: As Told by an Anthropologist Who Lacks a Soul." In Richard D. Ashmore and Lee Jussim (eds.), *Self and Identity. Fundamental Issues.* New York: Oxford University Press, 160–90.
Hollis, Martin. 1974. "The Limits of Irrationality." In Bryan R. Wilson (ed.), *Rationality. Key Concepts in the Social Sciences.* London: Blackwell; Oxford and New York: Harper and Row, 214–20.
Holy, Ladislav (ed.). 1987. *Comparative Anthropology.* London: Basil Blackwell.
Honneth, Axel. 1992. *Kampf um Anerkennung. Zur moralischen Grammatik sozialer Konflikte.* Frankfurt am Main: Suhrkamp Verlag.
Honneth, Axel and Hans Joas. 1980. *Soziales Handeln und menschliche Natur. Anthropologische Grundlagen der Sozialwissenschaften.* Campus Studium, Kritische Sozialwissenschaft 545. Frankfurt am Main and New York: Campus Verlag.
Hoppe, Thomas. 1998. "Menschenrechte: international verpflichtende Minimalstandards oder Manifestation säkularer Religiösität? Zum Spannungsverhältnis zwischen universalem Geltungsanspruch der Menschenrechte und der Partikularität seiner Begründungen." In Andreas Fritzsche and Manfred Kwiran (eds.), *Der Mensch.* Ökumenische Sozialethik 1. Munich: Bernward bei Don Bosco, 26–36.
Horgan, John. 2001. *Der menschliche Geist. Wie die Wissenschaften versuchen, die Psyche zu verstehen.* Frankfurt am Main: Fischer Taschenbuch Verlag. Originally *The Undiscovered Mind. How the Human Brain Defies Replication, Medication and Explanation,* New York: The Free Press, 1999.
Horton, Robin. 1960. "A Definition of Religion, and Its Uses." *Journal of the Royal Anthropological Institute* 90(2): 210–26.
———. 1982. "Tradition and Modernity Revisited." In Martin Hollis and Steven Lukes (eds.), *Rationality and Relativism.* Oxford: Basil Blackwell and Cambridge, MA: MIT Press, 201–60.
Hruschka, Daniel J. 2010. *Friendship. Development, Ecology and Evolution of a Relationship.* Origins of Human Behavior and Culture 5. Berkeley: University of California Press.
Huinink, Johannes. 2001. *Orientierung Soziologie. Was sie kann, was sie will.* Rowohlts Enzyklopädie. Reinbek bei Hamburg: Rowohlt Taschenbuch Verlag.
Huizinga, Johan. 1956. *Homo Ludens,. Der Ursprung der Kultur im Spiel.* Rowohlts Deutsche Enzyklopädie. Reinbek bei Hamburg: Rowohlt Taschenbuch Verlag.
Hull, David. 1998. "On Human Nature." In David Hull and Michael Ruse (eds.), *The Philosophy of Biology.* New York: Oxford University Press, 383–396.
Hultkrantz, Åke. 1960. "General Ethnological Concepts." In *International Dictionary of Regional European Cultural Anthropology and Folklore,* vol. 1. Copenhagen: Rosenkilde and Bagger.
Hume, David. (1739–40) 1888. *A Treatise of Human Nature.* Oxford: Clarendon Press.
Hunn, Eugene. 2006. "Meeting of Minds: How Do We Share Our Appreciation of Traditional Environmental Knowledge?" In Roy Ellen (ed.), *Ethnobiology and the Science of Humankind.* Malden, MA: Blackwell and Royal Anthropological Institute (*Journal of the Royal Anthropological Institute,* special issue, 1: 177–96.
Hunt, Robert C. 2007. *Beyond Relativism. Rethinking Comparability in Cultural Anthropology.* Lanham, MD: Altamira Press.
Huntington, Samuel Phillips. 1996. "The West. Unique, to Universal." *Foreign Affairs* 75(6), 28–46.
Hutchins, Edwin. 1995. *Cognition in the Wild.* Cambridge, MA: The MIT Press.
———. 2006. "The Distributed Cogition Cognition Perspective on Human Interaction." In Nicholas J. Enfield and Stephen C. Levinson (eds.), *Roots of Human Sociality. Culture,*

Cognition and Interaction. Wenner-Gren International Symposium Series. Oxford and New York: Berg, 375–98.
Huxley, Julian. 1941. *The Uniqueness of Man*. London: Chatto and Windus.
Huxley, Thomas H. (1863) 2003. *Man's Place in Nature*. London: New York: Dover Publications.
Iltis, Hugh, Orie Louks, and Peter Andrews. 1970. "Criteria for an Optimum Human Environment." *Bulletin of the Atomic Scientists* 25: 2–6.
Imai, Mutsumi and Dedre Gentner. 1997. "A Cross-Linguistic Study of Early Word Meaning: Universal Ontology and Linguistic Influence." *Cognition* 62: 169–200.
Immelmann, Klaus, Klaus R. Scherer, and Christian Vogel (eds.). 1986–87. *Funkkolleg Psychobiologie. Verhalten bei Mensch und Tier. Studienbegleitbriefe 1–10*. Weinheim and Basel: Beltz Verlag, Deutsches Institut für Fernstudien an der Universität Tübingen (DIFF).
Ingham, John M. 1996. *Psychological Anthropology Reconsidered*. Publications of the Society for Psychological Anthropology 8. Cambridge: Cambridge University Press.
Ingold, Tim. 2002. "Between Evolution and History: Biology, Culture, and the Myth of Human Origins." In Michael Wheeler, John Ziman, and Margaret A. Boden (eds.), *The Evolution of Cultural Entities*. Proceedings of the British Academy 112. Oxford: Oxford University Press for the British Academy, 9–25.
Irons, William and Lee Cronk. 2000. "Two Decades of A New Paradigm." In Lee Cronk, Napoleon A. Chagnon, and William Irons (eds.). *Adaptation and Human Behavior. An Anthropological Perspective*. Evolutionary Foundations of Human Behavior. Hawthorne, NJ and New York: Aldine De Gruyter, 3–26.
Iser, Wolfgang. 2001. *Das Fiktive und das Imaginäre. Perspektiven literarischer Anthropologie*. Frankfurt: Suhrkamp Verlag.
———. 2004. "Fingieren als anthropologische Dimension der Literatur." In Aleida Assmann, Ulrich Gaier, and Gisela Trommsdorff (eds.), *Positionen der Kulturanthropologie*. With Karolina Jeftic. Frankfurt am Main: Suhrkamp, 21–43.
Izard, Carroll E. 1994. "Innate and Universal Facial Expressions. Evidence From Developmental and Cross-Cultural Research." *Psychological Bulletin* 115: 288–99.
Jablonka, Eva. 2002. "Between Development and Evolution: How to Model Cultural Change." In Michael Wheeler, John Ziman, and Margaret A. Boden (eds.), *The Evolution of Cultural Entities*. Proceedings of the British Academy 112. Oxford: Oxford University Press for the British Academy, 27–41.
Jablonka, Eva and Marion J. Lamb. 2005. *Evolution in Four Dimensions. Genetic, Epigenetic, Behavioral and Symbolic Variation in the History of Life*. Cambridge, MA: The MIT Press.
Jack, Rachel E., Oliver G.B. Garroud, Hui Yu, Roberto Caldara, and Philippe G. Schyns. 2012. "Why Facial Expressions of Emotion Are Not Culturally Universal." *Proceedings of the National Academy of Sciences*. Retrieved 25 October 2015 from http://www.pnas.org/content/early/ 2012/04/10/1200155109.full.pdf+html.
Jackendorff, Ray. 2003. *Foundations of Language. Brain, Meaning, Grammar, Evolution*. Oxford: Oxford University Press.
Jackson, Michael. 1989. *Paths Toward Clearing. Radical Empiricism and Ethnographic Enquiry*. Bloomington: Indiana University Press.
Jacob, François. 1977. "Evolution and Tinkering." *Science* 196 (June): 1,161–66.
Jaeger, Friedrich and Burkhard Liebsch (eds.). 2004. *Handbuch der Kulturwissenschaften. Grundlagen und Schlüsselbegriffe*. Stuttgart and Weimar: Verlag J. B. Metzler.
Jaeger, Friedrich and Jürgen Straub (eds.). 2005. *Was ist der Mensch, was Geschichte? Annäherungen an eine kulturwissenschaftliche Anthropologie. Jörn Rüsen zum 65. Geburtstag*. Bielefeld: Transcript Verlag.

James, Wendy. 2003. *The Ceremonial Animal. A New Portrait of Anthropology*. Oxford: Oxford University Press.
Jankowiak, William R. (ed.). 1995. *Romantic Passion. A Universal Experience?* New York and Chichester: Columbia University Press.
———. 2008. "Appendix: The Ethnographic Evidence for the Universality of Romantic Love." In William R. Jankowiak (ed.), *Intimacies. Love and Sex Across Cultures*. New York: Columbia University Press: 267–79.
———. (ed.). 2008b. *Intimacies. Love and Sex Across Cultures*. New York: Columbia University Press.
Jankowiak, William R. and Edward F. Fisher. 1992. "A Cross-Cultural Perspective on Romantic Love." *Cultural Anthropology* 31(2): 149–55.
Jankowiak, William R. and Thomas Paladino. 2008. "Desiring Sex, Longing For Love. A Tripartite Conundrum." In William R. Jankowiak (ed.), *Intimacies. Love and Sex Across Cultures*. New York: Columbia University Press, 1–36.
Jarvie, Ian C. 1984. *In Search of A Philosophy and History of Anthropology*. London: Routledge and Kegan Paul.
Jaspers, Karl. 1955. *Vom Ursprung und Ziel der Geschichte*. Frankfurt am Main: Fischer Taschenbuch Verlag.
Jaynes, J. and M. Bressler. 1971. "Evolutionary Universals, Continuities, Alternatives." In J. F. Eisenberg and W. S. Dillon (eds.), *Man and Beast. Comparative Social Behaviour*. Washington, DC: Smithsonian Institution Press.
Jenkins, Lyle (ed.). 2004. *Variation and Universals in Biolinguistics*. North-Holland Linguistic Series. Linguistic Variations 62. Amsterdam: Elsevier Science Publishing.
Jensen, Jürgen. 1999. "Probleme und Möglichkeiten bei der Bildung kulturenübergreifender Begriffe im Vergleich kultureller Phänomene. Ein Beitrag zu Aspekten des Prozesses ethnologischer Theoriebildung." In Waltraud Kokot and Dorle Dracklé (eds.), *Wozu Ethnologie? Festschrift für Hans Fischer*. Kulturanalysen 1. Berlin: Dietrich Reimer Verlag, 53–73.
Joas, Hans and Axel Honneth. 1980. *Soziales Handeln und menschliche Natur. Anthropologische Grundlagen der Sozialwissenschaften*. Campus Studium. Frankfurt am Main: Campus.
Job, Sebastian. 2006. "Humankind, Psychic Unity of." In H. James Birx (ed.), *Encyclopedia of Anthropology*. Thousand Oaks, CA: Sage Publications, vol. 3, 1252–54.
Johansen, Ulla. 1989. "Der Reinheitsbegriff: Ein exemplarischer Vergleich zwischen türkischer und deutscher Kultur." In *Akademie der Wissenschaften zu Berlin; Jahrbuch 1988*. Berlin and New York: Walter de Gruyter: 296–305.
———. 2005. "Die Lächelgrenze." In Anett C. Oelschlägel, Ingo Nentwig, and Jakob Taube (eds.), *"Roter Altai, gib dein Echo!". Festschrift für Erika Taube zum 65. Geburtstag*. Leipzig: Leipziger Universitätsverlag, 175–82.
Johnson, Allen and Orna Johnson. 2001. "Introduction to the Updated Edition." In Marvin Harris, *Cultural Materialism. The Struggle for a Science of Culture. Updated Edition*. Walnut Creek, CA: Altamira Press, vi–xiv.
Johnson, Allen and Douglass Price-Williams. 1996. *Oedipus Ubiquitous. The Family Complex in World Folk Literature*. Stanford, CA: Stanford University Press.
Jörke, Dirk. 2005. *Politische Anthropologie. Eine Einführung*. Studienbücher für Politische Theorie und Ideengeschichte. Wiesbaden: VS Verlag für Sozialwissenschaften.
Jüttemann, Gerd. 1992. *Psyche und Subjekt. Für eine Psychologie jenseits von Dogma und Mythos*. Rowohlts Enzyklopädie. Reinbek bei Hamburg: Rowohlt Taschenbuch Verlag.
Jullien, François. 2014. *On the Universal, the Uniform, the Common and Dialogue between Cultures*. Cambridge and Malden, MA: Polity Press. Originally *De l'universel, de l'uni-*

forme, du commun et du dialogue entre les cultures, Paris: Librairie Arthème Fayard, 2008.
Junker, Thomas. 2006. *Die Evolution des Menschen.* C. H. Beck Wissen. Munich: Verlag C. H. Beck.
Kaelble, Helmut and Jürgen Schriewer (eds.). 2003. *Vergleich und Transfer. Komparatistik in den Sozial-, Geschichts- und Kulturwissenschaften.* Frankfurt am Main and New York: Campus Verlag.
Kahle, Gerd. 1981. "Nachwort." In Gerd Kahle (ed.), *Logik des Herzens. Die soziale Dimension der Gefühle.* Frankfurt am Main: Suhrkamp Verlag, 283–313.
Kahn, Joel S. 1995. *Culture, Multiculture, Postculture.* London: Sage Publications.
Kamper, Dietmar. 1973. *Geschichte und menschliche Natur. Die Tragweite gegenwärtiger Anthropologie-Kritik.* Munich: Carl Hanser Verlag.
Kapp, K. William. 1983. *Erneuerung der Sozialwissenschaften. Ein Versuch zur Integration und Humanisierung.* Fischer Alternativ-Perspektiven. Frankfurt: Fischer Taschenbuch Verlag. Originally *Toward A Science of Man in Society: A Positive Approach to the Integration of Social Knowledge,* The Hague: Marinus Nijhoff, 1961.
Kappeler, Peter M. 2006. *Verhaltensbiologie.* Berlin and Heidelberg: Springer-Verlag.
Kappeler, Peter M. and Joan B. Silk (eds.). 2010. *Mind the Gap. Tracing the Origins of Human Universals.* Heidelberg: Spinger-Verlag.
Kaschuba, Wolfgang. 2003. "Anmerkungen zm Gesellschaftsvergleich aus ethnologischer Perspektive." In Helmut Kaelble and Jürgen Schriewer (eds.), *Vergleich und Transfer. Komparatistik in den Sozial-, Geschichts- und Kulturwissenschaften.* Frankfurt am Main and New York: Campus Verlag, 341–50.
Kasper, Gabriele. 2004. "Linguistic Etiquette." In Scott F. Kiesling and Christina Bratt Paulston (eds.), *Intercultural Discourse and Communication. The Essential Readings.* Linguistics. The Essential Readings 5. Oxford and Malden, MA: Blackwell, 58–77. Originally in Florian Coulmas, ed. *The Handbook of Sociolinguistics,* Oxford: Blackwell, 1997.
Kasten, Erich. 2001. "Franz Boas." In Christian F. Feest and Karl-Heinz Kohl (eds.), *Hauptwerke der Ethnologie.* Kröner Taschenausgabe 380. Stuttgart, 47–52.
Kather, Regine. 2008. "Von der Vielfalt der Kulturen und der Verbundenheit der Menschen. Aufgaben und Methoden einer interkulturellen Philosophie." In Hamid Reza Yousefi, Klaus Fischer, Rudolph Lüthe, and Peter Gerdsen (eds.), *Wege zur Wissenschaft. Eine interkulturelle Perspektive. Grundlagen, Differenzen, Interdisziplinäre Dimensionen.* Nordhausen: Traugott Bautz, 47–66.
Kattmann, Ulrich. 1974. "Sonderstellung oder Eigenart? Zur Stellung des Menschen innerhalb der Lebewesen." *Praxis der Naturwissenschaften: Biologie* 23(10): 253–64.
Kay, Paul and Terry Regier. 2007. "Color Naming Universals: The Case of Berinmo." *Cognition* 102(2): 51–54.
Kay, Paul, Brent Berlin, Luisa Maffi, and W. Merrifield. 1997. "Color Naming Across Languages." In Clyde L. Hardin and Luisa Maffi (eds.), *Color Categories in Thought and Language.* Cambridge: Cambridge University Press, 21–56.
Kearney, Michael. 1984. *World-View.* Chandler and Sharp Publications in Anthropology and Related Fields. Novato, CA: Chandler and Sharp.
———. 1996. "World-View." In David Levinson and Melvin Ember (eds.), *Encyclopedia of Cultural Anthropology,* vol 4. New York: Henry Holt and Company, 1,380–84.
Keeley, Lawrence H. 1996. *War before Civilization. The Myth of the Peaceful Savage.* Oxford and New York: Oxford University Press.
Keesing, Roger M. 1994a. "Theories of Culture Revisited." In Robert Borowsky (ed.), *Assessing Cultural Anthropology.* New York: McGraw-Hill, 301–10.

———. 1994b. "Radical Cultural Difference: Anthropology's Myth." In Martin Pütz (ed.), *Language Contact and Language Conflict*. Amsterdam: John Benjamins, 3–24.
Keesing, Roger M. and Felix M. Keesing. 1971. *New Perspectives in Cultural Anthropology*. New York: Holt, Rinehart and Winston.
Keesing, Roger M. and Andrew J. Strathern. 1998. *Cultural Anthropology. A Contemporary Perspective*. 3rd ed. Fort Worth: Harcourt Brace College Publishers.
Keil, Frank C. 1981. "Constraints on Knowledge and Cognitive Development." *Psychological Review* 8881): 197–227.
———. 1986. "The Acquisition of Natural Kind and Artefact Terms." In A. Marrar and W. Demopoulos (eds.), *Conceptual Change*. Norwood, NJ: Ablex Publishers.
Keiter, Friedrich. 1956. "Die Naturvölker." In Werner Ziegenfuss (ed.), *Handbuch der Soziologie*. Stuttgart: Ferdinand Enke Verlag, 641–715.
———. 1966. *Verhaltensbiologie des Menschen auf kulturanthropologischer Grundlage*. Monographien und Studien zur Konflikt-Psychologie, Abt. I: Konflikt-Analyse 4. Munich and Basel: Ernst Reinhart Verlag.
Keller, Heidi. 2007. "Die soziokulturelle Konstuktion impliziten Wissens in der Kindheit." In Gisela Trommsdorff and Hans-Joachim Kornath (eds.), *Theorien und Methoden der kulturvergleichenden Psychologie*. Enzyklopädie der Psychologie, Themenbereich C, Theorie und Forschung, Serie VII, Kulturvergleichende Psychologie 1. Göttingen: Hogrefe, 703–34.
Keller, Heidi, Ype H. Poortinga, and Axel Schölmerich (eds.). 2002. *Between Biology and Culture. Perspectives on Ontogenetic Development*. Cambridge Studies in Cognitive and Perceptual Development. Cambridge: Cambridge University Press.
Keller, Rudi. 2003. *Sprachwandel. Von der unsichtbaren Hand in der Sprache*. Tübingen und Basel: A. Francke Verlag.
Kellert, Stephen R. 1993. "Introduction." In Stephen R. Kellert and Edward Osborne Wilson (eds.), *The Biophilia Hypothesis*. Washington, DC: Island Press/Shearwater Books, 20–27.
Kellert, Stephen R. 2003. *Kinship to Mastery. Biophilia in Human Evolution and Development*. Washington, DC: Island Press, Shearwater Books.
Kennedy, John Stodart. 1992. *The New Anthropomorphism*. Cambridge: Cambridge University Press.
Kenrick, Douglas T., Norman P. Li and Jonathan Butner. 2003. "Dynamic Evolutionary Psychology: Individual Decision Rules and Emergent Social Norms." *Psychological Review* 110(1): 3–28.
Kephart, Ronald. 2006. Universals in Language. In H. James Birx (ed.), *Encyclopedia of Anthropology*. Thousand Oaks, CA: Sage Publications, vol. 5, 2247–48.
Kidder, Alfred V. 1940. "Looking Backward." *Proceedings of the American Philosophical Society* 83(4): 527–37.
Kirby, Simon. 1999. *Function, Selection, and Innateness. The Emergence of Language Universals*. Oxford: Oxford University Press.
Kissler, Alexander. 2000. "Tanzt, Kinder, tanzt, die Nacht ist lang. Diese Hand der ganzen Welt. Eine Tagung in Trier über 'The Family of Man', die größte Fotoausstellung aller Zeiten." *Frankfurter Allgemeine Zeitung* 243 (19 October 2000), 52.
Klass, Morton. 1995. *Ordered Universes: Approaches to the Study of Religion*. Boulder, CO: Westview Press.
———. 2003. *Mind over Mind. The Anthropology and Psychology of it Possession*. Lanham, MD: Rowman and Littlefield Publishers.
Kleeberg, Bernhard, Stefan Metzger, Wolfgang Rapp, and Tilmann Walter (eds.). 2001. *Die List der Gene. Strategeme eines neuen Menschen*. Literatur und Anthropologie 11. Tübingen: Gunter Narr Verlag.

Kleeberg, Bernhard and Tilmann Walter. 2001. "Der mehrdimensionale Mensch. Zum Verhältnis von Biologie und kultureller Entwicklung." In Bernhard Kleeberg, Stefan Metzger, Wolfgang Rapp, and Tilmann Walter (eds.), *Die List der Gene. Strategeme eines neuen Menschen*. Literatur und Anthropologie 11. Tübingen: Gunter Narr Verlag, 19-72.

Kleeberg, Bernhard, Tilman Walter, and Fabio Crivellari (eds.). 2004. *Urmensch und Wissenschaften. Eine Bestandsaufnahme*. Darmstadt: Wissenschaftliche Buchgesellschaft.

Kluckhohn, Clyde K. M. 1950. "The Special Character of Integration in an Individual Culture." In Foundation of Integrated Education (ed.). *The Nature of Concepts. Their Inter-Relation and Role in Social Structure, Proceedings of the Stillwater Conference*. New York, 1950.

———. 1951. "Values and Value-Orientations in the Theory of Action: An Exploration in Definition and Classification." In Talcott Parsons and Edward Shils (eds.), *Toward A General Theory of Action*. New York: Harper and Row.

———. 1953. "Universal Categories of Culture." In Alfred L. Kroeber (ed.), *Anthropology Today: An Encyclopedic Inventory*. Chicago: The University of Chicago Press, 507-23.

———. 1959. "Common Humanity and Diverse Cultures." In Daniel Lerner (ed.), *The Human Meaning of the Social Sciences*. New York: Meridian, 245-84.

Kluckhohn, Clyde K. M. and Alfred L. Kroeber. 1961. "Notes on Some Anthropological Aspects of Communication." *American Anthropologist* 63: 895-909.

Kluckhohn, Clyde K. M. and W. Morgan. 1951. "Some Notes on Navaho Dreams." In George B. Wilbur and Warner Muensterberger (eds.), *Psychoanalysis and Culture. Essays in Honor of Géza Róheim*. New York: International Universities Press, 120-131.

Kluckhohn, Clyde K. M. and Henry A. Murray. 1953. "Personality Formation: The Determinants." In Clyde K. M. Kluckhohn and Henry A. Murray Dies. (eds.), *Personality in Nature, Society and Culture*. New York: Alfred A. Knopf, 53-70.

Knight, Chris D. 1991. *Blood Relations. Menstruation and the Origins of Culture*. New Haven, CT, and London: Yale University Press.

Kocka, Jürgen. 2002. "Multiple Modernities and Negotiated Universals." In Dominic Sachsenmaier and Jens Riedel (eds.), *Reflections on Multiple Modernities. European, Chinese and Other Interpretations*. With Shmuel Noah Eisenstadt. Leiden: E. J. Brill, 119-28.

Koenig, Otto. 1970. *Kultur und Verhaltensforschung. Einführung in die Kulturethologie*. Munich: Deutscher Taschenbuch Verlag.

Koepl, Regina. 1995. "Das Subjekt ist tot—es lebe das Subjekt. Zum Ende des Universalismus in der feministisch-postmodernen Diskussion." *Österreichische Zeitschrift für Politikwissenschaft* 24(2): 169-81.

Kohl, Karl-Heinz. 2006. "Die Syntax von Ritualen." In Helwig Schmidt-Glintzer (ed.), *Liturgie, Ritual, Frömmigkeit und die Dynamik symbolischer Ordnungen*. Wolfenbütteler Hefte 19. Wiesbaden: Harrassowitz Verlag, 103-26.

———. 2008. "Erstbegegnungen. Über den Umgang mit Neuem in indigenen Kulturen." *Merkur* 712-713 (September–October) : 848-58.

Kokot, Waltraud and Dorle Dracklé (eds.). 1999. *Wozu Ethnologie? Festschrift für Hans Fischer*. Kulturanalysen 1. Berlin: Dietrich Reimer Verlag.

Kolakowski, Leszek. 1980. "Wo sind die Barbaren? Ein Lob des Eurozentrismus oder: Die Illusion des kulturellen Universalismus." *Der Monat* 277: 70-83.

Komatsu, Yukio and Eiko Komatsu. 2006. *Humankind. An Emotional Journey*. Salt Lake City and Layton, UT: Gibbs Smith.

Konersmann, Ralf. 2003. *Kulturphilosophie zur Einführung*. Hamburg: Junius.

———. 2006. *Kulturelle Tatsachen*. Frankfurt am Main: Suhrkamp Verlag.

König, René. (1958) 1975. "Biosoziologie." In Rene König (ed.), *Soziologie. Das Fischer Lexikon*. Neuausgabe. Frankfurt: Fischer Taschenbuch Verlag, 48–53.
Konner, Melvin. 2002. "Seeking Universals." *Nature* 415 (10 January), 121
———. 2003. *The Tangled Wing. Biological Constraints on the Human It*. 2nd ed. New York: Henry Holt and Company.
Köpping, Klaus-Peter. 1993. "Ethik in ethnographischer Praxis: Zwischen Universalismus und pluralistischer Autonomie." In Wolfdietrich Schmied-Kowarzik and Justin Stagl (eds.), *Grundfragen der Ethnologie: Beiträge zur gegenwärtigen Theorie-Diskussion*, Ethnologische Paperbacks. Berlin: Dietrich Reimer Verlag: 107–28.
Köpping, Klaus-Peter, Michael Welker, and Reiner Wiehl (eds.). 2002. *Die autonome Person. Eine europäische Erfindung?* Munich: Wilhelm Fink Verlag.
Kottak, Conrad Philip. 1990. *Prime Time Society. An Anthropological Analysis of Television and Culture*. Belmont, CA: Wadsworth Publishing.
———. 2008. *Cultural Anthropology*. Boston, MA: McGraw-Hill College Division.
Kövecses, Zoltán. 2010. *Metaphor in Culture. Universality and Variation*. 2nd ed. Cambridge: Cambridge University Press.
Kozlarek, Oliver. 2000. *Universalien, Eurozentrismus, Logozentrismus. Kritik des disjunktiven Denkens der Moderne*. Frankfurt am Main: IKO Verlag für interkulturelle Kommunikation.
Kramer, Jürgen. 2000. "Geertz im Kontext. Anmerkungen zur interpretativen Anthropologie eines *Merchant of Astonishment*." *Anglistik* 11(1): 97–127.
Kroeber, Alfred L. 1948a. *Anthropology. Race, Language, Culture, Psychology, Prehistory*. New York: Harcourt.
——— (ed.). 1948b. *Anthropology Today: An Encyclopaedic Inventory*. Chicago: University of Chicago Press.
Kroeber, Alfred L. and Clyde M. Kluckhohn. 1952. *Culture. A Critical Review of Concepts and Definitions*. Papers of the Peabody Museum of American Archaeology and Cultural Anthropology 47, 1. Cambridge, MA: Harvard University Press.
Kroger, Rolf O. and L. A. Wood. 1992. "Are the Rules of Address Universal? IV: Comparison of Chinese, Korean, Greek, and German Usage." *Journal of Cross-Cultural Psychology* 23: 148–62.
Krohs, Ulrich and Georg Toepfer (eds.). 2005. *Philosophie der Biologie. Eine Einführung*. Frankfurt am Main: Suhrkamp Verlag.
Kronenfeld, David B. 1996. *Plastic Glasses and Church Fathers. Semantic Extension from the Ethnoscience Tradition*. Oxford: Oxford University Press.
Kronfeldner, Maria E. 2007. Is Cultural Evolution Lamarckian? *Biology and Philosophy* 22: 493–512.
Kronfeldner, Maria E., Neil Roughley and Georg Toepfer. 2014. "Recent Work on Human Nature: Beyond Traditional Essences." *Philosophy Compass* 9(9): 642–652.
Kühnhardt, Ludger. 1987. *Die Universalität der Menschenrechte*. Schriftenreihe, Studien zur Geschichte und Politik 256. Bonn: Bundeszentrale für politische Bildung.
Kull, Ulrich 1996. *Evolution des Menschen. Biologische, soziale und kulturelle Evolution*. 2nd ed. Studienreihe Biologie 6. Hannover: Schroedel.
Kulturwissenschaftliches Institut Essen. 2006. "Graduiertenkolleg 'Der Humanismus in der Epoche der Globalisierung'. Ein interkultureller Dialog über Kultur, Menschheit und Werte". *Die Zeit* 52 (21 December 2005: 83.
Küng, Hans. 2008. *Projekt Weltethos*. Munich: Piper Taschenbuch Verlag.
Küng, Hans and Karl-Josef Kuschel (eds.). 2000. *Erklärung zum Weltethos. Die Deklaration des Parlamentes der Weltreligionen*. Munich and Zürich: R. Piper Verlag.

Kuper, Adam (ed.). 1992. *Conceptualizing Society*. European Association of Social Anthropologists. London and New York: Routledge.
———. 1994. *The Chosen Primate. Human Nature and Cultural Diversity*. Cambridge, MA, and London: Harvard University Press.
———. 2000. *Culture. The Anthropologists' Account*. Cambridge, MA, and London: Harvard University Press.
———. 2005. *The Reinvention of Primitive Society. Transformations of A Myth*. London and New York: Routledge. Originally *The Invention of Primitive Society. Transformations of an Illusion,* London and New York: Routledge, 1998.
LaBarre, Weston. 1947. "The Cultural Basis Emotions and Gestures." *Journal of Personality* 16: 49–68.
Laclau, Ernesto. 2000. "Identity and Hegemony. The Role of Universality in the Construction of Political Logic." In Judith P. Butler, Ernesto Laclau, and Slavoj Žižek, *Contingency, Hegemony, Universality. Contemporary Dialogues of the Left*. Phronesis. New York and London: Verso, 44–89.
Lafitau, Joseph François. 1974. *Moeurs des sauvages Amériquains, compareés aux moeurs des premiers temps*. Paris: Saugrin l'âiné.
Lakoff, George. 1987. *Women, Fire, and Dangerous Things. What Categories Reveal About the Mind*. Chicago: University of Chicago Press.
Lakoff, George and Mark Johnson. 2003. *Leben in Metaphern. Konstruktion und Gebrauch von Sprachbildern*. Heidelberg: Carl-Auer-Systeme Verlag. Originally *Metaphors We Live By,* Chicago: The University of Chicago Press, 1980.
Lakoff, George and Rafael E. Núnez. 2000. "Where Mathematics Comes From. How the Embodied Mind Brings Mathematics into Being." New York: Basic Books.
Laland, Kevin N. and Gillian R. Brown. 2002. *Sense and Nonsense. Evolutionary Perspectives on Human Behaviour*. Oxford: Oxford University Press.
Laland, Kevin N., John Odling-Smee, and Marcus Feldman. 2000. "Niche Construction, Biological Evolution, and Cultural Change." *The Behavioural and Brain Sciences* 23: 131–75.
Lancy, David F. 2015. *The Anthropology of Childhood. Cherubs, Chattel, Changelings*. 2nd ed. Cambridge: Cambridge University Press.
Landmann, Michael 1969. *Philosophische Anthropologie. Menschliche Selbstdeutung in Geschichte und Gegenwart*. Berlin: de Gruyter.
Langdon, John Howard. 2005. *The Human Strategy. An Evolutionary Perspective on Human Anatomy*. Oxford: Oxford University Press.
Langlois, Judith H., et al. 2000. "Maxims or Myths of Beauty? A Meta-Analytic and Theoretical Review." *Psychological Bulletin* 126: 390–423.
Larsen, Charles. 1973. "Heroic Ethnocentrism: The Idea of Universality in Literature." *The American Scholar* 42(3): 463–75.
Latour, Bruno. 2001. "Eine Soziologie ohne Objekt? Anmerkungen zur Interobjektivität." *Berliner Journal für Soziologie* 2: 237–52.
———. 2015. *We Have Never been Modern*. Harvard University Press. Originally *Nous n'avons jamais été modernes. Essai d'anthropologie symétrique,* Paris: Édition de la Découverte, 1991.
Laubichler, Manfred D. 2005. "Systemtheoretische Orgnismuskonzeptionen." In Ulrich Krohs and Georg Toepfer (eds.), *Philosophie der Biologie. Eine Einführung*. Frankfurt am Main: Suhrkamp Verlag, 109–24.
Laughlin, Jr., Charles D. and Eugene G. d'Aquili. 1974. *Biogenetic Structuralism*. New York and London: Columbia University Press.
Lautmann, Rüdiger. 2002. "Sexualität." In Günter Endruweit and Gisela Trommsdorff (eds.), *Wörterbuch der Soziologie*. 2nd ed. Stuttgart: Lucius and Lucius, 473–75.

Leach, Edmund R. 1958. "Magical Hair." *Proceedings of the Royal Anthropological Institute of Great Britain and Ireland* 88(2): 147–64.
———. 1967. "Virgin Birth." *Proceedings of the Royal Anthropological Institute of Great Britain and Ireland* 97(1): 3–49.
———. 1981. "Biology and Social Science: Wedding or Rape?" *Nature* 291: 267–68.
———. 1982. *Social Anthropology*. Fontana Master Guides. London: Fontana.
Leavitt, John. 1996. "Meaning and Feeling in the Anthropology of Emotions." *American Ethnologist* 23(3): 514–39.
Lechner, Frank J. and John Boli. 2005. *World Culture. Origins and Consequences*. Oxford: Blackwell.
Lecointre, Guillaume and Hervé le Guyader. 2006. *Biosystematik*. Berlin and Heidelberg: Springer Verlag. Originally *Classification phylogénetique du vivant*, Paris: Éditions Belin, 2001.
Legerstee, Maria. 2005. *Infants' Sense of People. Precursors to A Theory of Mind*. Cambridge: Cambridge University Press.
Lehmann, Walter. 1994. *Anthropology 109: Human Universals*. Lecture notes. Santa Barbara: University of California, Department of Anthropology.
Leininger, Madelaine M. (ed.). 1991. *Culture Care Diversity and Universality. A Theory of Nursing*. New York: National League for Nursing Press. (Publication No. 15–2402).
Lemke, Thomas. 2006. "Der dritte Weg. Abschied vom anzthropozentrischen Paradigma. Die Soziologie muss ein neues disziplinäres Verständnis jenseits von Naturalismus und Konstruktivismus entwickeln." *Frankfurter Rundschau* 283 (5 December 2006), 27.
Lenk, Hans. 1974. *Wozu Philosophie? Eine Einführung in Frage und Antwort*. Munich: Piper Verlag.
———. 1975. "Über strukturelle Implikationen." *Zeitschrift für Soziologie* 4(4): 350–58.
———. 1978. "Strukturelle und empirische Implikationen: Über einige strukturinduzierte Implikatonen und deren Umkehrungen in der Soziometrie und Sozialpsychologie." In Jochen Brandtstädter (ed.), *Struktur und Erfahrung in der psychologischen Forschung*. Berlin: Walter de Gruyter, 14–34.
———. 1995. "Das metainterpretierende Wesen." *Allgemeine Zeitschrift für Philosophie* 20(1): 39–47.
———. 2008. *Humanitätsforschung als interdisziplinäre Anthropologie. Zur philosophischen Anthropologie zwischen Stammesgeschichte und Kulturdeutung*. Schriften zur Humanitäts- und Glücksforschung 3. Frankfurt am Main: Peter Lang.
———. 2010. *Das flexible Vielfachwesen. Einführung in die moderne philosophische Anthropologie zwischen Bio-, Techno- und Kulturwissenschaften*. Weilerswist: Velbrück Wissenschaft.
Lenk, Hans and Gregor Paul. 2014. *Transkulturelle Logik. Universalität und Vielfalt*. Kultur and Philosophie 9). Bochum and Freiburg: Projekte Verlag.
Lenzen, Manuela. 2003. *Evolutionstheorien in den Natur- und Sozialwissenschaften*. Campus Einführungen. Frankfurt am Main and New York: Campus Verlag.
Lepenies, Wolf (ed.). 2003. *Entangled Histories and Negotiated Universals. Centers and Peripheries in Changing World*. Frankfurt am Main: Campus Verlag.
Lepenies, Wolf and Helmut Nolte. 1972. *Kritik der Anthropologie. Marx und Freud. Gehlen und Habermas. Über Aggression*. Munich: Carl Hanser Verlag.
Lesser, Alexander. 1985. *History, Evolution, and the Concept of Culture: Selected Papers*. Cambridge: Cambridge University Press.
Lethmate, Jürgen. 1992. "Vom Affen zum Halbgott. Die Besonderheiten des Menschen." In *Funkkolleg Der Mensch. Anthropologie heute*. Tübingen: Deutsches Institut für Fernstudien an der Universität Tübingen (DIFF), 1–77.

Lett, James William. 1997. *Science, Reason and Anthropology. The Principles of Rational Inquiry.* Lanham, MD, and Oxford: Rowman and Littlefield Publishers.

Leung, Kwok, Michael Harris Bond, Sharon Reimel de Carrasquel, Carlos Munoz, Marisela Hernández, Fumio Murakami, Susumo Yamaguchi, Günter Bierbrauer, and Theodore M. Singelis. 2002. "Social Axioms. The Search For Universal Dimensions of General Beliefs About How the World Functions." *Journal of Cross-Cultural Psychology* 33(3): 286–302.

Le Vine, Robert A. and Donald T. Campbell. 1971. *Ethnocentrism. Theories of Conflict, Ethnic Attuitudes, and Group Behavior.* New York: John Wiley and Sons.

Levinson, David and Melvin Ember (eds.). 1996. *Encyclopedia of Cultural Anthropology,* vol. 4. New York: Henry Holt and Company.

Levinson, David and Martin J. Malone. 1980. *Toward Explaining Human Culture. A Critical Review of the Findings of Worldwide Cross-Cultural Research.* New Haven: HRAF Press.

Levinson, Stephen C. 1996. "Language and Space." *Annual Review of Anthropology* 25: 353–82.

———. 2003. *Space in Language and Cognition. Explorations in Cognitive Diversity.* Cambridge: Cambridge University Press.

Lévi-Strauss, Claude. 1949. *Les Structures Élémentaires de la parenté.* Paris: Presses Universitaires de France (PUF).

———. 1958. *Anthropologie structurale.* Paris: Librairie Plon.

———. 1962. *Le pensée sauvage.* Paris: Librairie Plon.

Levy, Marion J., Jr. 1989. *Maternal Influence. The Search for Social Universals.* Berkeley: University of California Press.

Levy, Robert I. 1990. *Mesocosm. Hinduism and the Organization of a Traditional Newar City in Nepal.* Berkeley, CA: University of California Press.

Lewis, Herbert S. 2001. "Boas, Darwin, Science and Anthropology." *Current Anthropology* 42(3): 381–406.

———. 2014. *In Defense of Anthropology. An Investigation of the Critique of Anthropology.* New Brunswick, NJ and London: Transcation Publishers.

Lewis, M. Paul, Charles D. Fennig and Gary F. Simons (eds.). 2015. *Ethnologue.* 18th ed. 3 Vols. Dallas: Summer Institute of Linguistics International Publishing.

Lewontin, Richard Charles. 1986. *Menschen. Genetische, kulturelle und soziale Gemeinsamkeiten.* Spektrum-Bibliothek 10. Heidelberg: Spektrum der Wissenschaft Verlagsgesellschaft. Originally *Human Diversity,* New York: Scientific American Books, 1982.

Light, Timothy and Brian C. Wilson (eds.). 2004. *Religion as A Human Capacity. A Festschrift in Honour of E. Thomas Lawson.* Numen. Studies in the History of Religions 99. Leiden and Boston: Koninklijke Brill.

Lillard, Angeline. 1998. "Ethnopsychologies: Cultural Variations in Theories of Mind." *Psychological Bulletin* 123(1): 3–22.

Linton, Ralph. 1936. *The Study of Man.* New York: Appleton-Century Crofts.

Lloyd, Barbara and John Gay (eds.). 1981. *Universals in Human Thought. Some African Evidence.* Cambridge: Cambridge University Press.

Loflin, Marvin D. and James Silverberg (eds.). *Discourse and Inference in Cognitive Anthropology. An Approach to Psychic Unity and Enculturation.* World Anthropology. The Hague and Paris: Mouton Publishers.

Loizos, Peter and Patrick Heady (eds.). 1999. *Conceiving Persons. Ethnographies of Procreation, Fertility and Growth.* London School of Economics Monographs on Social Anthropology. London: Athlone Press.

Lomax, Alan. (1968) 1994. *Folk Song Style and Culture.* New York: Transaction Publishers.

Lonely Planet (ed.). 2005. *One People. Many Journeys*. Foostcray, Victoria: Lonely Planet Publications.
Lonner, Walter J. 1980. "The Search for Psychological Universals." In Harry Chralambos Triandis and William Wilson Lambert (eds.), *Handbook of Cross-Cultural Psychology*, vol. 1: *Perspectives*. Boston: Allyn and Bacon, 143–204.
———. 1993. "Foreword." In Jeanette Altarriba (ed.) *Cognition and Culture. A Cross-Cultural Approach to Cognitive Psychology*. Advances in Psychology 103. Amsterdam: North-Holland, v–vii.
———. 1994. "Review of Brown 1991." *American Ethnologist* 21(4): 920–21.
———. 2005. "The Psychological Study of Culture: Issues and Questions of Enduring Importance." In Wolfgang Friedlmeier, Pradeep Chakkarath, and Beate Schwarz (eds.), *Culture and Human Development. The Importance of Cross-Cultural Research to the Social Sciences*. Hove and New York: Psychology Press, 10–29.
López, Austin A., Scott Atran, J. Coley, Douglas Medin, and E. Smith. 1997. "The Tree of Life. Universals of Folk-Biological Taxonomies and Inductions." *Cognitive Psychology* 32: 251–95.
Lopreato, Joseph. 1984. *Human Nature and Biocultural Evolution*. Boston: Allen and Unwin.
Lopreato, Joseph and Timothy Crippen. (1999) 2002. *Crisis in Sociology. The Need for Darwin*. New Brunswick, NJ, and London: Transaction Publishers.
Lorenz, Konrad Zacharias. 1970. "Vorwort." In Otto Koenig, *Kultur und Verhaltensforschung. Einführung in die Kulturethologie*. Munich: Deutscher Taschenbuch Verlag, 7–13.
Lossau, Julia. 2002. *Die Politik der Verortung. Eine postkoloniale Reise zu einer 'anderen' Geographie der Welt*. Bielefeld: Transcript Verlag.
Lounsbury, Floyd G. 1964. "A Formal Account of Crow-Omaha-Type Kinship Terminologies." In Ward Hunt Goodenough (ed.), *Explorations in Cultural Anthropology*. New York: McGraw-Hill, 351–93.
Low, Bobbi S. 2015. *Why Sex Matters. A Darwinian Look at Human Behavior*. Princeton, NJ, and Oxford: Princeton University Press.
Lucy, John A. 1996. *Grammatical Categories and Cognition. A Case Study of the Linguistic Relativity Hypothesis*. Cambridge: Cambridge University Press.
Lueptow, L. B. L. Garovich and M. B. Lueptow. 1995. "The Persistence of Gender Stereotypes in the Face of Changing Sex Roles: Evidence Contrary to the Sociocultural Model." *Ethology and Sociobiology* 15: 509–30.
Lull, James. 1991. *China Turned On: Television, Reform and Resistance*. London and New York: Routledge.
———. 2000. *Media, Communication, Culture. A Global Approach*. 2nd ed. London: Polity Press.
Lumsden, Charles J. and Edward O. Wilson. 1981. *Genes, Mind, and Culture. The Coevolutionary Process*. Cambridge, MA: Harvard University Press.
Lurker, Manfred. 1992. *Die Botschaft der Symbole in Mythen, Kulturen und Religionen*. Munich: Kösel Verlag.
Lüsebrink, Hans Jürgen. 2005. *Interkulturelle Kommunikation. Interaktion, Fremdwahrnehmung, Kulturtransfer*. Weimar: J. B. Metzlersche Verlagsbuchhandlung.
Lutz, Catherine A. 1988. *Unnatural Emotions. Everyday Sentients on a Micronesian Atoll and Their Challenge to Western Theory*. Chicago: The University of Chicago Press.
Lyon, Margot L. 1995. "Missing Emotion: The Limitations of Cultural Constructivism in the Study of Emotion." *Current Anthropoogy* 10: 244–63.
Lyotard, Jean-François. 1987. *Der Widerstreit*. Supplemente. Munich: Wilhelm Fink.

Macklin, Ruth. 1999. *Against Relativism. Cultural Diversity and the Search for Ethical Universals in Medicine.* Oxford: Oxford University Press.

Maddieson, Ian. 2006. "In Search of Universals." In Ricardo Uson Mairal and Juana Gil (eds.), *Linguistic Universals.* Cambridge: Cambridge University Press, 80–100.

Maier, Hans. 1997. *Wie universal sind die Menschenrechte?* Freiburg im Breisgau: Herder Verlag.

Maiers, Wolfgang. 1993. "Historische Psychologie und das Problem der menschlichen Natur: Kommt eine psychologische Subjektwissenschaft ohne Naturgeschichte aus?" In Michael Sonntag and Gerd Jüttemann (eds.), *Individuum und Geschichte. Beiträge zur Diskussion um eine "Historische Psychologie."* Heidelberg: Roland Asanger Verlag, 49–72.

Mairal, Ricardo Uson and Juana Gil. 2006a. "A First Look at Universals." In Dies. (eds.), *Linguistic Universals.* Cambridge: Cambridge University Press, 1–45.

—— (eds.). 2006b. *Linguistic Universals.* Cambridge: Cambridge University Press.

Malik, Kenan. 2001. *Man, Beast and Zombie. What Science Can and Cannot Tell Us About Human Nature.* London: Phoenix.

——. 2008. *Strange Fruit. Why Both Sides Are Wrong in the Race Debate.* Oxford: Oneworld Publications.

——. 2014. *Multiculturalism and Its Discontents. Rethinking Diversity after 9/11.* Manifestos for the 21st Century. New York: Seagull Books.

Malinowski, Bronislaw K. 1924: "Mutterrechtliche Familie und Ödipuskomplex." *Imago* 10: 228–77.

——. 1935. "Culture." In Edwin R. Seligman (ed.), *The Encyclopedia of the Social Sciences*, vol. 4. New York: Macmillan, 625

——. 1944. *Scientific Theory of Culture and Other Essays.* Chapel Hill, NC: The University of North Carolina Press.

Mallon, Ron and Stephen P. Stich. 2000. "The Odd Couple: The Compatibility of Social Construction and Evolutionary Psychology." *Philosophy of Science* 67: 133–54.

Malotki, Ekkehart. 1983. *Hopi Time. A Linguistic Analysis of Temporal Concepts in the Hopi Language.* Berlin: Mouton Publishers.

Manganaro, Marc (ed.). (1990). *Modernist Anthropology. From Fieldwork to Text.* Princeton and New Jersey: Princeton University Press.

Marcus, George E. 2002. "Intimate Strangers: The (Non) Relationship Between the Natural and Human Sciences in the Contemporary U.S. University." *Anthropological Quarterly* 75(3): 519–26.

Markl, Hubert. 1986. *Evolution, Genetik und menschliches Verhalten. Zur Frage wissenschaftlicher Verantwortung.* Munich und Zürich: R. Piper.

——. 2002. "Einführung: Was ist der Mensch?" In Hubert Markl, *Schöner neuer Mensch?* Munich and Zürich: Piper Verlag, 11–37.

Marks, Jonathan. 2004. "What, If Anything, Is a Darwinian Anthropology?" *Social Anthropology* 12(2): 181–93.

Marks, Robert B. 2006. *The Origins of the Modern World. A Global and Ecological Narrative.* Lanham, MD: Rowman and Littlefield Publishers.

Marschall, Wolfgang. 1990a. "Einleitung." In Wolfgang Marschall (ed.), *Klassiker der Kulturanthropologie. Von Montaigne bis Margaret Mead.* Munich: Verlag C.H. Beck, 7–18.

—— (ed.). 1990b. *Klassiker der Kulturanthropologie. Von Montaigne bis Margaret Mead.* Munich: Verlag C.H. Beck.

Marsella, Anthony J., Joan Dubanoski, Walter C. Hamada, and Heather Morse. 2000. "The Measurement of Personality across Cultures. Historical, Conceptual, and Methodological Issues and Considerations." *American Behavioral Scientist* 44(1): 41–62.

Maryansky, Alexander and Jonathan H. Turner. 1992. *The Social Cage: Human Nature and the Evolution of Society*. Stanford, CA: Stanford University Press.

Masson, Peter. 1980. "Interpretative Probleme in Prozessen interkultureller Verständigung." In Wolfdietrich Schmied-Kowarzik and Justin Stagl (eds.), *Grundfragen der Ethnologie: Beiträge zur gegenwärtigen Theorie-Diskussion*. Ethnologische Paperbacks. Berl: Dietrich Reimer Verlag, 125–49.

Masters, Roger D. 1989. *The Nature of Politics*. New Haven: Yale University Press.

———. 1996. "Human Nature." In Adam Kuper and Jessica Kuper (eds.), *The Social Science Encyclopaedia*. London and New York: Routledge, 381–82.

Mathews, Holly F. and Carmella C. Moore. 2001. "Introduction. The Psychology of Cultural Experience." In Carmella C. Moore and Holly F. Mathews (eds.), *The Psychology of Cultural Experience*. Publications of the Society for Psychological Anthropology. Cambridge: Cambridge University Press, 1–18.

Matjan, Gregor. 1995. "Von der Dekonstruktion zur Rekonstruktion. Kommunitarismus als Herausforderung von liberalem Universalismus und Kulturrelativismus." *Österreichische Zeitschrift für Politikwissenschaft* 24(2): 183–97.

Matsumoto, David R. and Linda Juang. 2008. *Culture and Psychology*. Stanford, Ct.: Thomson Wadsworth Learning.

Matthes, Joachim. 1992a. "The Operation Called 'Vergleichen.'" In Joachim Matthes (ed.), *Zwischen den Kulturen? Die Sozialwissenschaften vor dem Problem des Kulturvergleichs*. Soziale Welt, Sonderband 8. Göttingen: Vandenhoeck and Ruprecht, 75–99.

———. (ed.). 1992b. *Zwischen den Kulturen? Die Sozialwissenschaften vor dem Problem des Kulturvergleichs*. Soziale Welt, Sonderband 8. Göttingen: Vandenhoeck and Ruprecht.

Mauss, Marcel 1990. *Die Gabe. Form und Funktion des Austauschs in archaischen Gesellschaften*. Originally *Le Don*, Paris: Seuil, 1923/24.

Mayr, Ernst. 1982. *The Growth of Biological Thought. Diversity, Evolution, and Inheritance*. Cambridge, MA, and London: Harvard University Press.

———. 2001. *What Evolution Is*. New York: Basic Books.

McCauley, Robert N. and E. Thomas Lawson. 2002. *Bringing Ritual to Mind. Psychological Foundations of Natural Forms*. Cambridge: Cambridge University Press.

McCrae, Robert R. and Paul T. Costa, Jr. 1997. "Personality Trait Structure as a Human Universal." *American Psychologist* 52(5): 509–16.

McGee, R. Jon and Richard L. Warms (eds.). 2003. *Anthropological Theory. An Introductory History*. 3rd ed. New York: McGraw-Hill Education.

McGrew, William C. 1992. *Chimpanzee Material Culture. Implications for Human Evolution*. Cambridge: Cambridge University Press.

———. 1998. "Culture in Non-Human Primates?" *Annual Review of Anthropology* 27: 301–28.

———. 2001. "The Nature of Culture. Prospects and Pitfalls of Cultural Primatology." In Frans B. M. de Waal (ed.), *Tree of Origin. What Primate Behavior Can Tell Us about Human Social Evolution*. Cambridge, MA, and London: Harvard University Press, 229–54.

———. 2003. "Ten Dispatches From the Chimpanzee Culture Wars." In Frans B. M. de Waal and Peter L. Tyack (eds.), *Animal Social Complexity. Intelligence, Culture, and Individualized Societies*. Cambridge, MA, and London: Harvard University Press, 419–39.

———. 2004. *The Cultured Chimpanzee. Reflections on Cultural Primatology*. Cambridge: Cambridge University Press.

McNeill, David. 2007. *Gesture and Thought*. Chicago and London: University of Chicago Press.

McNeill, John R. and William Hardy McNeill. 2003. *The Human Web. A Bird's-Eye View of World History*. New York and London: W. W. Norton and Company.
Mead, Margaret. 1928. *Coming of Age in Samoa*. New York: William Morrow.
Mecklenburg, Norbert. 2009. *Das Mädchen in der Fremde. Germanistik als interkulturelle Literaturwissenschaft*. Munich: Iudicium Verlag.
Medicus, Gerhard. 2012. *Was uns Menschen verbindet. Humanethologische Angebote zur Verständigung zwischen Leib- und Seelenwissenschaften. Am Zügel der Evolution 9*. Berlin: Verlag für Wissenschaft und Bildung.
Medin, Douglas L., Norbert Ross, Scott Atran, Russel C. Burnett, and Sergey V. Blok. 2002. Categorization and Reasoning in Relation to Culture and Expertise. *The Psychology of Learning and Motivation* 41: 1–41.
Meier-Seethaler, Carola. 1997. *Gefühl und Urteilskraft. Ein Plädoyer für emotionale Vernunft*. Munich: Verlag C. H. Beck.
Meier-Walser, Reinhard C. and Anton Rauscher (eds.). 2005. *Die Universalität der Menschenrechte*. Materialien zum Zeitgeschehen 44. Munich: Hanns-Seidel-Stiftung.
Meinberg, Eckard. 1988. *Das Menschenbild in der modernen Erziehungswissenschaft*. Darmstadt: Wissenschaftliche Buchgesellschaft.
Menninghaus, Winfried. 2003. *Das Versprechen der Schönheit*. Frankfurt am Main: Suhrkamp Verlag.
Menzel, Peter and Faith D'Aluisio. 2004. *So lebt der Mensch. Familien aus aller Welt zeigen, was sie haben*. Hamburg: Gruner and Jahr. Originally *The GeoSphere Project: Material World; A Global Family Portrait*, Santa Monica, CA: The GeoSphere Project, 1994.
———. 2005. *So isst der Mensch. Familien in aller Welt zeigen. Was sie ernährt*. Hamburg: Gruner and Jahr. (Geo-Buch) Originally *Hungry Planet. What the World Eats*, Napa, CA: Material World and Ten Speed Publications.
Merten, Jörg. 2003. *Einführung in die Emotionspsychologie*. Stuttgart: Verlag. W. Kohlhammer.
Mesoudi, Alex. 2011. *Cultural Evolution. How Darwinian Theory Can Explain Human Culture and Synthesize the Social Sciences*. Chicago and London: The University of Chicago Press.
Mesoudi, Alex, Andrew Whiten and Kevin N. Laland. 2006. "Towards a Unified Science of Cultural Evolution." *The Bevioral and Brain Sciences* 29: 329–83.
Mesquita, Batja and Nico H. Frijda. 1993. "Cultural Variations in Emotions: A Review." *Psychological Buetin* 112(2): 179–204.
Messelken, Karlheinz. 2002a. Universalien. In Günter Endruweit and Gisela Trommsdorff (eds.), *Wörterbuch der Soziologie*. 2nd ed. Stuttgart: Lucius and Lucius, 647–48.
———. 2002b. "Konstante, anthropologische." In Günter Endruweit and Gisela Trommsdorff (eds.), *Wörterbuch der Soziologie*. 2nd ed. Stuttgart: Lucius and Lucius, 287. 1999)
Meuter, Norbert. 2006. *Anthropologie des Ausdrucks. Die Expressivität des Menschen zwischen Natur und Kultur*. Munich: Wilhelm Fink Verlag.
Meyer, John W. 2005. *Weltkultur. Wie die westlichen Prinzipien die Welt durchdringen*. Ed. Georg Krücken. Edition Zweite Moderne. Frankfurt am Main: Suhrkamp Verlag.
Meyer, Peter. 1990. "Universale Muster sozialen Verhaltens: Wie entstehen aus genetischer Variabilität strukturell ähnliche Lösungen?" *Homo. Journal of Comparative Biology* 38(3–4): 133–44.
———. 1998. "Universale soziale Institutionen. Einführung in naturale Grundlagen menschlicher Gesellschaft." In Armin Günther, Rolf Haubl, Peter Meyer, Martin Stengel, and Kerstin Wüstner (eds.), *Sozialwissenschaftliche Ökologie. Eine Einführung*. Berlin: Springer Verlag, 8–60.

Meyer, Wulf-Uwe 2002. *Zur Geschichte der Evolutionären Psychologie.* Bielefeld: Universität Bielefeld, Abteilung für Psychologie. Retrieved 25 June 2005 from http://www.uni-bielefeld.de/psychologie/ae/AE02/Lehre/EvolutionaerePsychologie.html.

Midgley, Mary. 1996. *The Ethical Primate. Humans, Freedom, and Morality.* London: Routledge.

Miner, Horace. 1974. "Das Körperritual der Renakirema." In Leon E. Stover and Harry Harrison (eds.), 4. *Anthropofiction. Eine Anthologie.* Frankfurt am Main: Fischer Taschenbuch Verlag. (Fischer Orbit, 21) Originally "Body Ritual among the Renacirema," *American Anthropologist* 58(3): 504–20.

Mithen, Steven. 1996. *The Prehistory of the Mind: A Search for the Origins of Art, Religion and Science.* London: Thames and Hudson.

———. 2006. "Ethnobiology and the Evolution of the Human Mind." In Roy Ellen (ed.), *Ethnobiology and the Science of Humankind.* Malden, MA: Blackwell Publishing and Royal Anthropological Institute (*Journal of the Royal Anthropological Institute,* special issue, 1), 55–75.

Mittelstraß, Jürgen. 2004. "Das 'nicht festgestellte Wesen'. Der Mensch zwischen Endlichkeit und Vollkommenheit." In Heinrich Schmidinger and Clemens Sedmak (eds.), *Der Mensch – ein „animal rationale"? Vernunft – Kognition – Intelligenz.* Topologien des Menschlichen 1. Darmstadt: Wissenschaftliche Buchgesellschaft, 20–31.

Moebius, Stephan and Christian Papilloud (eds.). 2006. *Gift – Marcel Mauss' Kulturtheorie der Gabe.* Wiesbaden: Verlag für Sozialwissenschaften.

Moghaddam, Fathali M. 2002. *Social Psychology. Exploring Universals Across Cultures.* 2nd ed. New York: W. H. Freeman and Company.

Momin, A. R. 1994. "Islamic Sociology in Perspective. A Rejoinder to Professor Tapper." *Journal of Objective Studies* 6(2): 101–16.

Mommsen, Wolfgang. (1961) 1974. "Universalgeschichte." In Waldemar Besson (ed.), *Geschichte. Das Fischer Lexikon.* Frankfurt am Main: Fischer Taschenbuch Verlag, 322–32.

Monod, Jacques. 1975. *Zufall und Notwendigkeit. Philosophische Fragen der Biologie.* Munich: Deutscher Taschenbuch Verlag.

Moore, Carmella C., A. Kimball Romney, Ti Lien-Hsia, and Craig D. Rusch. 1999. "The Universality of the Semantic Structure of Emotion Terms: Methods for the Study of Inter- and Intracultural Variability." *American Anthropologist* 101: 529–46.

Moore, Carmella C. and Holly F. Mathews (eds.). 2001. *The Psychology of Cultural Experience.* Publications of the Society for Psychological Anthropology. Cambridge: Cambridge University Press.

Moore, David Scott. 2003. *The Dependent Gene. The Fallacy of "Nature vs. Nurture."* New York: W. H. Freeman.

Moore, George Edward. (1903) 1993. "Naturalistische Ethik." In Kurt Bayertz (ed.), *Evolution und Ethik.* Stuttgart: Philipp Reclam, 84–101.

Moore, Henrietta L. (ed.). 1999. *Anthropological Theory Today.* Cambridge: Polity Press

Moreland, James Porter. 2001. *Universalien. Eine philosophische Einführung.* Frankfurt am Main: Ontos Verlag. Originally *Universals,* Central Problems in Philosophy, Chesham: Acumen Publishing.

Morin, Edgar and Massimo Piattelli-Palmarini (eds.). 1974. *L 'Unite de l'Homme. Invariants biologiques et universaux culturels.* Paris: Editions du Seuil.

Morris, Brian. 1987. *Anthropological Studies of Religion. An Introductory Text.* Cambridge: Cambridge University Press.

———. 2006. *Religion and Anthropology: A Critical Introduction.* Cambridge: Cambridge University Press.

———. 2014. *Anthropology and the Human Subject*. London: Trafford Publishing.
Moscovici, Serge. 1990. *Versuch über die menschliche Geschichte der Natur*. Frankfurt am Main: Suhrkamp Verlag. Originally *Essais sur l'histoire humaine de la nature*, Paris: Flammarion, 1968.
Mühlmann, Wilhelm E. 1962. *Homo Creator. Abhandlungen zur Soziologie, Anthropologie und Ethnologie*. Wiesbaden: Otto Harrassowitz.
———. 1966. "Umrisse und Probleme einer Kulturanthropologie." In Wilhelm Emil Mühlmann and Ernst W. Müller (eds.), *Kulturanthropologie*. Neue Wissenschaftliche Bibliothek 9. Cologne and Berlin: Kiepenheuer and Witsch, 15–49.
———. 1984. *Geschichte der Anthropologie*. Wiesbaden: Aula-Verlag. Sammlung Aula Originally Bonn: Universitätsverlag, 1948.
Müller, Johannes. 1997. *Entwicklungspolitik als globale Herausf.orderung. Methodische und ethische Grundlegung*. Kon-Texte 5. Stuttgart: Verlag W. Kohlhammer
———. 2002. "Ethische Grundsatzprobleme in der Entwicklungspolitik: Der Imperativ menschlicher Solidarität und die Entwicklungsethnologie." In Frank Bliss, Michael Schönhuth, and Petra Zucker (eds.), *Welche Ethik braucht die Entwicklungszusammenarbeit? Beiträge zur Kulturkunde* 22. Bonn: Politischer Arbeitskreis Schulen, 50–64.
Müller, Johannes and Michael Reder (eds.). 2003. *Der Mensch vor der Herausforderung nachhaltiger Solidarität*. Globale Solidarität –Schritte zu einer neuen Weltkultur 9. Stuttgart: Verlag W. Kohlhammer.
Müller, Klaus E. 1997a. *Geschichte der antiken Ethnologie*. Rowohlts Enzyklopädie. Reinbek bei Hamburg: Rowohlt Taschenbuch Verlag.
Müller, Klaus E. 1997b. "Obicere—von den Balken im Auge der euklidischen Ethnologie." *Zeitschrift für Ethnologie* 122: 19–31.
———. 1998. *Geschichte der antiken Ethnographie und ethnologischen Theoriebildung von den Anfängen bis auf die byzantinischen Historiographien*. 2 vols. Wiesbaden: Franz Steiner Verlag.
———. 2003a. "Vorwort." In Klaus E. Müller (ed.), *Phänomen Kultur. Perspektiven und Aufgaben der Kulturwissenschaften*. Kultur und soziale Praxis. Bielefeld: Transcript Verlag, 7–12.
———. 2003b. "Das Unbehagen mit der Kultur." In Klaus E. Müller (ed.), *Phänomen Kultur. Perspektiven und Aufgaben der Kulturwissenschaften*. Kultur und soziale Praxis. Bielefeld: Transcript Verlag, 13–47.
Müller-Funk, Wolfgang. 2006. *Kulturtheorie. Einführung in die Schlüsseltexte der Kulturwissenschaften*. Tübingen: A. Francke Verlag.
Mundkur, Balaji. 1983. *The Cult of the Serpent. An Interdisciplinary Survey of Its Manifestations and Origins*. Albany, NY: State University of New York Press.
Munroe, Robert L. and Ruth H. Munroe. 2001. Comparative Approaches to Psychological Anthropology. In Carmella C. Moore and Holly F. Mathews (eds.), *The Psychology of Cultural Experience*. Publications of the Society for Psychological Anthropology. Cambridge: Cambridge University Press, 223–37.
Munroe, Ruth H., Robert L. Munroe, and Beatrice Blyth Whiting (eds.). 1981. *Handbook of Cross-Cultural Development*. New York: Garland.
Murdock, George Peter. 1932. "The Science of Culture." *American Anthropologist*, 34, 200–15.
———. 1945. "The Common Denominator of Cultures." In Ralph Linton (ed.), *The Science of Man in the World Crisis*. New York: Columbia University Press, 123–40. Also in George Peter Murdock (ed.), *Culture and Society: Twenty-Four Essays*. Pittsburgh: The University of Pittsburgh Press, 1964, 88–110.

———. 1949. *Social Structure*. New York: The Free Press, Macmillan
———. 1955. "Universals of Culture." In Edward Adamson Hoebel, Jesse D. Jennings, and Elmer R. Smith (eds.), *Readings in Anthropology*, 4–5. New York: McGraw-Hill.
———. 1957a. "World Ethnographic Sample." *American Anthropologist* 59: 664–87.
———. 1957b. "Anthropology as a Comparative Science." *Behavioral Science* 2: 249–54.
———. 1967a. *Ethnographic Atlas*. New Haven: Human Relations Area Files, HRAF Press.
———. 1967b. "Ethnographic Atlas. A Summary." *Ethnology* 6: 109–232.
———. (1958) 1975. *Outline of World Cultures*. New Haven, CT: Human Relations Area Files, HRAF Press.
———. 1978. "Social Classes in the State: An Essay in Correlation." In G. L. Ulmen (ed.), *Society and History. Essays in Honor of Karl August Wittfogel*. The Hague: Mouton: 157–58.
———. 1981. *Atlas of World Cultures*. Pittsburgh: University of Pittsburgh Press.
Murdock, George P., Clellan S. Ford and A. E. Hudson, Raymond Kennedy, L. W. Simmons, and John W. M. Whiting. 2008. *Outline of Cultural Materials*. New Haven, CT: HRAF Press.
Murdock, George P. and Douglas R. White. 1969. "Standard Cross-Cultural Sample." *Cultural Anthropology* 8: 329–69.
Murphy, Robert F. 1971. *The Dialectics of Social Life. Alarms and Excursions in Anthropological Theory*. New York and London: Basic Books.
Myers, David G. 2002. *Social Psychology*. 7th ed. Boston: McGraw-Hill Higher Education.
Nader, Laura. 1994. "Comparative Consciousness." In Robert Borowsky (ed.), *Assessing Cultural Anthropology*. New York McGraw-Hill, 84–94.
Naroll, Raoul. 1967. "The Proposed HRAF Probability Sample." *Behavior Science Notes* 2: 70–80.
———. 1973. "Holocultural Theory Tests." In Raoul Naroll and Frada Naroll (eds.), *Main Curents in Cultural Anthropology*. New York: Appleton-Century-Crofts, Educational Division, Meredith Corporation, 309–84.
———. 1983. *The Moral Order. An Introduction to the Human Situation*. Beverly Hills, CA: Sage Publications.
Naroll, Raoul and Richard G. Sipes. 1973. "Standard Ethnographic Sample." *Current Anthropology* 14: 111–40.
Nederveen Pieterse, Jan. 2015. *Globalization and Culture. Global Mélange*. 3rd ed. Globalization. Lanham, MD: Rowman and Littlefield.
Needham, Joseph. 1986. "Introduction." In Robert K. G. Temple, *China. Land of Discovery and Invention*. Wellingborough: Patrick Stephens, 7–10.
Needham, Rodney. 1975. "Polythetic Classification. Convergence and Consequences." *Man* 10(3): 349–69.
Nettl, Bruno. 1983. *The Study of Ethnomusicology. Twenty-Nine Issues and Concepts*. Urbana: University of Illinois Press.
Nettle, Daniel. 2006. "The Evolution of Personality Variation in Humans and Other Animals." *American Psychologist* 61: 622–31.
Newman, Graeme. 1976. *Comparative Deviance. Perception and Law in Six Cultures*. New York: Elsevier Scientific.
Neyer, Franz J. and Frieder R. Lang. 2007. "Psychologie der Verwandtschaft und der Kooperation." In Johannes F. K. Schmidt, Martine Guichard, Peter Schuster, and Fritz Trillmich (eds.), *Freundschaft und Verwandtschaft. Zur Unterscheidung und Verflechtung zweier Beziehungssysteme*. Constance: UVK Verlagsgesellschaft, 45–64.
Niehoff, Arthur H. 1998. *On Being A Conceptual Animal*. Bonsall, CA: The Hominid Press.
Nieke, Wolfgang. 2000. *Interkulturelle Erziehung und Bildung. Wertorientierungen im Alltag*. 2nd ed. Opladen: Leske und Budrich.

Niemitz, Carsten. 2004. "Spiel, Erotik, List und Tücke – stammesgeschichtliche Wurzeln menschlicher Kulturfähigkeit." In Heinrich Schmidinger and Clemens Sedmak (eds.), *Der Mensch – ein „animal rationale"? Vernunft – Kognition – Intelligenz.* Topologien des Menschlichen 1. Darmstadt: Wissenschaftliche Buchgesellschaft, 161–78.

Nietzsche, Friedrich. (1886) 1968. "Jenseits von Gut und Böse." In *Werke. Kritische Gesamtausgabe,* vol. VI, 2. Berlin: De Gruyter.

Nisbett, Richard E. 2003. *The Geography of Thought. How Asians and Westerners Think Different ... and Why.* New York: The Free Press and London: Nicholas Brealy.

Nisbett, Richard E., K. Peng, I. Choi, and Ara Norenzayan. 2001. "Culture and Systems of Thought: Holistic versus Analytic Cognition." *Psychological Review* 108(2): 291–310.

Nordenstam, Tore. 2001. "Der Mensch ist in vielen Kulturen zu Hause (Interview mit Florian Krebs)." *Humboldt Kosmos* 78: 11–13.

Norenzayan, Ara. 2013. *Big Gods. How Religion Transformed Cooperation and Conflict.* Princeton and Oxford: Princeton University Press.

Norenzayan, Ara and Steven J. Heine. 2005. "Psychological Universals: What Are They and How Can We Know?" *Psychological Bulletin* 131(5): 763–84.

Norenzayan, Ara, Mark Schaller, and Steven J. Heine. 2006. "Evolution and Culture." In Mark Schaller, Jeffery A. Simpson, and Douglas T. Kenrick (eds.), *Evolution and Social Psychology.* Frontiers of Psychology. London: Psychology Press, 343–66.

Nozick, Robert. 2001. *Invariances. The Structure of the Objective World.* Cambridge, MA, and London: The Belknap Press of Harvard University Press.

Oatley, Keith, Dacher Keltner, and Jennifer M. Jenkins. 2013. *Understanding Emotions.* 3rd ed. Oxford: Blackwell Publishing.

Obeyasekere, Gannanath. 1990. *The Work of Culture. Symbolic Transformation in Psychoanalysis and Anthropology (Lewis Henry Morgan Lectures).* Chicago: The University of Chicago Press.

Ochs, Elinor. 2004. "Constructing Social Identity: A Language Socialization Perspective." In Scott F. Kiesling and Christina Bratt Paulston (eds.), *Intercultural Discourse and Communication. The Essential Readings.* Linguistics: The Essential Readings 5. Oxford and Malden, MA: Blackwell Publishing, 78–91.

Ochs, Elinor and Bambi Schieffelin. 1984. "Language Acquisition and Socialization: Three Developmental Stories." In Richard Shweder and Robert A. LeVine (eds.), *Culture Theory. Essays on Mind, Self and Emotion.* Cambridge: Cambridge University Press, 276–320.

Oerter, Rolf. 1999a. "Das Menschenbild im Kulturvergleich." In Rolf Oerter (ed.), *Menschenbilder in der modernen Gesellschaft. Konzeptionen des Menschen in Wissenschaft, Bildung, Kunst, Wirtschaft und Politik.* Der Mensch als soziales und personales Wesen 15. Stuttgart: Enke Verlag, 185–98.

———. (ed.). 1999b. *Menschenbilder in der modernen Gesellschaft. Konzeptionen des Menschen in Wissenschaft, Bildung, Kunst, Wirtschaft und Politik.* Der Mensch als soziales und personales Wesen 15. Stuttgart: Enke Verlag.

———. 2007. "Menschenbilder im Kulturvergleich." In Gisela Trommsdorff and Hans-Joachim Kornath (eds.), *Theorien und Methoden der kulturvergleichenden Psychologie.* Enzyklopädie der Psychologie, Themenbereich C, Theorie und Forschung, Series 7, Kulturvergleichende Psychologie, Vol. 1. Göttingen: Hogrefe, 487–530.

Ogawa, Tadashi and Barry Smith (eds.). 1995. "Editorial Preface." In "Cultural Universals," special issue, *The Monist. An International Quarterly Journal of General Philosophical Inquiry* 78(1): 3–4.

O'Hear, Anthony. 2001. *Beyond Evolution. Human Nature and the Limits of Evolutionary Explanation.* Oxford: Clarendon Press.

Ohler, Peter and Gerhild Nieding. 1997. "Sind menschliche Denkformen universell? Ein kognitionspsychologischer Beitrag zur Globalisierungsdiskussion." In Peter Schimany and Manfred Seifert (eds.), *Globale Gesellschaft? Perspektiven der Kultur- und Sozialwissenschaften*. Frankfurt am Main: Peter Lang, 21–38.

Ohlig, Karl-Heinz. 2012. *Religion in der Geschichte der Menschheit. Die Entwicklung des religiösen Bewusstseins*. 2nd ed. WBG-Bibliothek BoD. Darmstadt: Wissenschaftliche Buchgesellschaft.

Olson, David R. and Nancy Torrance (eds.). 1996. *Modes of Thought. Explorations in Culture and Cognition*. Cambridge: Cambridge University Press.

Ommer, Uwe. 2000. *1000 Families. Das Familienalbum des Planeten Erde. The Family Album of Planet Earth. L'album de famille de la planète Terre*. Cologne: Taschen Verlag.

Opolka, Uwe. 1999. *Versuch eines Ergebnisprotokolls*. Delmenhorst: Hanse-Wissenschaftskolleg. Unpublished manuscript, 4 pp.

Ortega y Gasset, José. 1943. *Geschichte als System und über das römische Imperium*. Stuttgart and Berlin: Deutsche Verlags-Anstalt.

———. (1943) 1961. *Der Aufstand der Massen*. Berlin: Deutsche Verlags-Anstalt.

Orth, Ernst W. 1994. "Universalität und Individualität der Kultur." In Ram Adhar Mall and Notker Schneider (eds.), *Ethik und Politik aus interkultureller Sicht*. Amsterdam: Rodopi B. V., 183–97.

Ortner, Sherry B. 1974. "Is Female to Male as Nature is to Nurture?" In Louise Lamphere and Michelle Zimbalist Rossaldo (eds.), *Women, Culture, and Society*. Stanford: Stanford University Press, 67–88.

———. 1996. *Making Gender. The Politics and Erotics of Culture*. Boston, MA: Beacon Press.

Osche, Günther. 1983. "Die Sonderstellung des Menschen in evolutionsökologischer Perspektive." *Nova Avta Leopoldina* NF 55(253): 57–72.

———. 1987. "Die Sonderstellung des Menschen aus biologischer Sicht. Biologische Bedingungen und kulturelle Evolution." In Rolf Siewing (ed.), *Evolution. Bedingungen – Resultate – Konsequenzen*. Stuttgart and New York: Gustav Fischer Verlag, 499–523.

Osgood, Charles E., William H. May, and Murray S. Miron. 1975. *Cross-Cultural Universals of Affective Meaning*. Urbana: University of Illinois Press.

Osterhammel, Jürgen. 2004. "Die Vielfalt der Kulturen und die Methoden des Kulturvergleichs." In Friedrich Jaeger and Jürgen Straub (eds.), *Handbuch der Kulturwissenschaften. Band 2. Paradigmen und Disziplinen*. Stuttgart and Weimar: Verlag J. B. Metzler, 50–65.

Oswalt, Wendell H. 1972. *Other Peoples, Other Customs. World Ethnography and Its History*. New York: Holt, Rinehart and Winston.

Otto, Hiltrud and Heidi Keller (eds.). 2014. *Different Faces of Attachment. Cultural Variations on a Universal Human Need*. Cambridge: Cambridge University Press.

Ottomeyer, Klaus. 1976. *Anthropologieproblem und marxistische Handlungstheorie. Kritisches und Systematisches zu Sève, Duhm, Schneider und zur Interaktionstheorie im Kapitalismus*. Argumentationen 29. Gießen: Focus Verlag.

Over, David E. (ed.). 2003. *Evolution and the Psychology of Thinking. Current Issues in Thinking and Reasoning*. Howe and New York: Psychology Press.

Pagel, Mark. 2012. *Wired for Culture. Origins of the Human Social Mind*. New York and London: W. W. Norton.

Palmer, Craig T. 1989. "Is Rape A Cultural Universal? A Re-Examinantion of the Ethnographic Data." *Cultural Anthropology* 28(1): 1–16.

Palmer, Douglas. 2006. *Seven Million Years. The Story of Human Evolution*. London: Phoenix Press.

Parsons, Talcott. 1964. "Evolutionary Universals in Society." *American Sociological Review* 29: 339–57.
Patman, Robert G. 2004. *Universal Human Rights*. Houndmills: Palgrave Macmillan.
Paul, Andreas W. 1998. *Von Affen und Menschen. Verhaltensbiologie der Primaten*. Darmstadt: Wissenschaftliche Buchgesellschaft.
———. 2006. "Von der Natur der menschlichen Geselligkeit." In Heinrich Schmidinger and Clemens Sedmak (eds.), *Der Mensch – ein „zôon politikón"? Gemeinschaft – Öffentlichkeit – Macht*. Topologien des Menschlichen. Darmstadt: Wissenschaftliche Buchgesellschaft, 71–84.
Paul, Gregor. 2008a. *Einführung in die interkulturelle Philosophie*. Darmstadt: Wissenschaftliche Buchgesellschaft.
———. 2008b. "Logik und Kultur. Allgemeingültige und nicht-allgemeingültige Prinzipien logischer Form." In "Universalismus," special issue, *Polylog. Zeitschrift für Interkulturelles Philosophieren* 20: 53–68.
Paul, Gregor, Thomas Göller, Hans Lenk, and Guido Rappe (eds.). 2001. *Humanität, Interkulturalität und Menschenrecht*. Schriften zur Humanitäts- und Glücksforschung 1. Frankfurt am Main: Peter Lang Verlag.
Payer, Margarete. 2000. *Internationale Kommunikationskulturen. Kulturelle Universalien als Voraussetzung für interkulturelle Kommunikation*. Retrieved 6 May 2015 from www.payer.de/kommulturen/ kultur02.htm.
Payne, Harris and Susan Gray. 1997. "Exploring Cultural Universals." *Journal of Geography* 96: 220–23.
Pavelka, Mary M. 2002. "Resistance to Cross-Species Perspective in Anthropology." In Agustín Fuentes and Linda D. Wolfe (eds.), *Primates Face to Face. Conservation Implications of Human-Nonhuman Primate Interconnections*. Cambridge: Cambridge University Press, 25–44.
Peacock, James L. 1995. "Challenges Facing the Discipline." *Anthropology Newsletter* 35(9): 1–5.
———. 2001. *The Anthropological Lens. Harsh Light, Soft Focus*. 2nd ed. Cambridge: Cambridge University Press.
Peacock, James L. and A. Thomas Hirsch. 1980. *The Human Direction. An Evolutionary Approach to Social and Cultural Anthropology*. 3rd ed. Englewood Cliffs, NJ: Prentice-Hall.
Pears, David Francis. 1968. "Universal." In *Encyclopedia Brittanica*, vol. 22, 744.
Peoples, James G. and Garrick Alan Bailey. 2015. *Humanity. An Introduction to Cultural Anthropology*. 14th. ed. Stamford, CT: Cengage Learning.
Peregrine, Peter N. 2013. "Human Relations Area Files, Cross-Cultural Studies." In R. Jon McGee and Richard L. Warms (eds.), *Theory in Social and Cultural Anthropology. An Encyclopedia*. Thousand Oaks, CA: Sage Publications, 408–10.
Perler, Dominik and Markus Wild. 2005. "Der Geist der Tiere – eine Einführung." In Dominik Perler and Markus Wild (eds.), *Der Geist der Tiere. Philosophische Texte zu einer aktuellen Diskussion*. Frankfurt am Main: Suhrkamp Verlag, 10–74.
Petermann, Franz, Kay Niebank, and Herbert Scheitauer. 2004. *Entwicklungswissenschaft. Entwicklungspsychologie – Genetik – Neuropsychologie*. Berlin and Heidelberg: Springer Verlag.
Philipp, Claudia Gabriele. 1987. "Die Ausstellung 'The Family of Man' (1955). Fotographie als Weltsprache." *Fotogeschichte* 23: 45–61.
Phillips, Anne. 2007. *Multiculturalism without Culture*. Princeton, NJ: Princeton University Press.

Pigliucci, Massimo and Jonathan Kaplan. 2000. "The Fall and Rise of Dr. Pangloss: Adaptationism and the Spandrels Paper 20 Years Later." *Trends in Ecology and Evolution* 15: 66–70.
Pike, Kenneth L. 1954. "Emic and Etic Standpoints for the Description of Behavior." In Kenneth L. Pike (ed.), *Language in Relation to a Unified Theory of the Structure of Human Behavior.* Glendale, IL: Summer Institute of Linguistics, 8–28.
———. 1993. *Talk, Thought, and Thing. The Emic Road toward Conscious Knowledge.* Dallas: Summer Institute of Linguistics.
Pinker, Steven. 1994. *The Language Instinct. How the Mind Creates Language.* New York: William Morrow.
———. 1997. *How the Mind Works.* New York: W. W. Norton.
———. 1999. *Words and Rules. The Ingredients of Language.* London: Weidenfeld and Nicolson. New York: Basic Books.
———. 2002. *The Blank Slate. The Modern Denial of Human Nature.* New York: Viking.
———. 2008. *The Stuff of Thought. Language as a Window into Human Nature.* London: Penguin.
Pinxten, Rik. 1976. "Epistemic Universals." In Rik Pinxten (ed.), *Universalism versus Relativism in Language and Thought. Proceedings of a Colloquium on the Sapir-Whorf Hypotheses.* Contributions to the Sociology of Language 11. The Hague and Paris: Mouton, 117–75.
Plachetka, Uwe C. 1997. "Multikulturalität und Kannibalismus am Beispiel der Tupí- Guaraní. Zur Frage der 'humana et cultura.'" *Mitteilungen der Anthropologischen Gesellschaft in Vienna* 127: 111–19.
Plamper, Jan. 2012. *Geschichte und Gefühl. Grundlagen der Emotionsgeschichte.* Munich: Siedler Verlag.
———. 2013. "Vergangene Gefühle. Emotionen als historische Quellen." *Aus Politik und Zeitgeschichte* 63(32–33): 12–19.
Platenkamp, Josephus D. M. 1999. "Natur als Gegenbild der Gesellschaft. Einige Betrachtungen zu einer paradoxen Idee." In Ruth-Elisabeth Mohrmann (ed.), *Argument Natur – Was ist natürlich? Worte – Werke – Utopien.* Thesen und Texte Münsterscher Gelehrter 7. Münster: Lit Verlag, 5–16.
Plessner, Hellmuth. 1976. *Die Frage nach der Conditio Humana. Aufsätze zur philosophischen Anthropologie.* Frankfurt am Main: Suhrkamp Verlag.
———. (1928) 1981. *Die Stufen des Organischen und der Mensch. Einleitung in die philosophische Anthropologie.* Gesammelte Schriften 4. Frankfurt am Main: Suhrkamp Verlag.
Pluciennik, Mark. 2005. *Social Evolution.* Duckworth Debates in Archaeology. London: Gerald Duckworth.
Podach, Erich Friedrich. 1951. *Das Aktualitätsprinzip in der Völkerkunde.* Heidelberg: Vowinckel.
Pohl, Karl-Heinz. 1999. "Zwischen Universalismus und Relativismus—Gedanken zum interkulturellen Dialog mit China." In Alois Hahn and Norbert Platz (eds.), *Interkulturalität als neues Paradigma. Öffentliche Ringvorlesung WS 1996/1997.* Trierer Beiträge. Aus Forschung und Lehre an der Universität Trier 27. Trier: Universität Trier, 21–34.
Polhemus, Ted (ed.). 1978. *Social Aspects of the Human Body. A Reader of Key Texts.* Harmondsworth: Penguin Books.
Pollnac, Richard B. 1978. "Problems in Determining Universality of Inference-Making." In Marvin D. Loflin and James Silverberg (eds.), *Discourse and Inference in Cogitive Anthropology. An Approach to Psychic Unity and Enculturation.* World Anthropology. The Hague and Pars: Mouton Publishers, 229–37.

Polti, Georges. (1921) 1977. *The Thirty-Six Dramatic Situations*. Boston: The Writer.
Poortinga, Ype H. and Dianne D. A. Van Hemert. 2001. "Personality and Culture: Demarcating Between the Common and the Unique." *Journal of Personality* 69(6): 1,033–60.
Poortinga, Ype H. and James Georgas. 2006. "Family Portraits From 30 Countries: An Overview." In Georgas et al., 90–99.
Pope, Geoffrey Grant. 2000. *The Biological Bases of Human Behavior*. Boston, MA: Allyn and Bacon.
Portmann, Adolf. 1956. *Zoologie und das neue Bild vom Menschen. Biologische Fragmente zu einer Lehre vom Menschen*. Rowohlts Deutsche Enzyklopädie 20. Reinbek bei Hamburg: Rowohlt Taschenbuch Verlag.
Pospíšil, Leopold. 1986. *Belief Systems, Ritual and Magic.* unpublished ms., Yale University.
Potthast, Ulrich. 1999. *Die Evolution und der Naturschutz. Zum Verhältnis von Evolutionsbiologie, Ökologie und Naturethik*. Campus Forschung. Frankfurt am Main: Campus Verlag.
Premack, David and Guy Woodruff. 1978. "Does the Chimpanzee Have A Theory of Mind?" *Behavioral and Brain Sciences* 1: 515–26.
Pullum, Geoffrey K. 1991. *The Great Eskimo Vocabulary Hoax and Other Irreverent Essays on the Study of Language*. Chicago and London: University of Chicago Press.
Quant, Sylvia A. 1992. "Review of Brown 1991." *Choice. Current Reviews for Academic Libraries* 29(5): 2782.
Quinn, Naomi. 2005. "Universals of Child Rearing." *Anthropological Theory* 5(4): 477–516.
Quinn, Naomi and Jeannette M. Mageo (eds.). 2013. *Attachment Reconsidered. Cultural Perspectives on a Western Theory*. New York: Palgrave Macmillan.
Radcliffe-Brown, Alfred R. 1952. "On the Concept of Function in Social Science." In Alfred R. Radcliffe-Brown, *Structure and Function in Primitive Society. Essays and Addresses*. Glencoe, IL: The Free Press, 178–87.
Randall, Robert A. and Eugene S. Hunn. 1984. "Do Life-Forms Evolve or Do Uses for Life? Some Doubts about Brown's Universals Hypotheses." *American Ethnologist* 11: 329–49.
Rappaport, Roy A. 1999. *Ritual and Religion in the Making of Humanity*. Cambridge Studies in Social and Cultural Anthropology. Cambridge: Cambridge University Press.
Rapport, Nigel. 2014. *Social and Cultural Anthropology. The Key Concepts*. 3rd ed. Routledge Key Guides. London: Routledge.
Rapport, Nigel and Joanna Overing. 2007. *Social and Cultural Anthropology. The Key Concepts*. 2nd ed. Routledge Key Guides. London: Routledge.
Read, Dwight W. 2012. *How Culture makes us Human. Primate Social Evolution and the Formation of Human Societies*. Key Questions in Anthropology: Little Books on Big Ideas 3. Walnut Creek, CA: Left Coast Press.
Reck, Hans Ulrich. 1992. "Gibt es ästhetische Universalien?" In Wolfgang Marschall, Meinhard Schuster, and Theres Gähwiler-Walder (eds.), *Die fremde Form. L 'esthetique des autres*. Ethnologica Helvetica 16. Bern: Schweizerische Ethnologische Gesellschaft, 91–106.
Redfield, Robert. 1953. *The Primitive World and Its Transformations*. Ithaca, NJ: Cornell University Press.
———. 1957. "The Universally Human and the Culturally Variable." *General Education* 10: 150–60.
———. 1962. *Human Nature and the Study of Society*. Chicago: The University of Chicago Press.
Reichardt, Anna Katharina and Eric Kubli (eds.). 1999. *Menschenbilder*. Bern: Peter Lang Europäischer Verlag der Wissenschaften.

Reichelt, Gregor. 2002. *Universalien*. Sonderforschungsbereich 511, Literatur und Anthropologie, Universität Konstanz. With Bernhard Metz. Retrieved 6 May 2014 from http://www.uni-konstanz.de/FuF/ueberfak/sfb511/publikationen/universalien.html.
Rein, Anette. 2008. "Menschen sind anders und gleich! Menschenrechte zwischen Partikularität und Universalität." In Günter Nooke, Georg Lohmann, and Gerhard Wahlers (eds.), *Gelten Menschenrechte universal? Begründungen und Infragestellungen*. Freiburg im Breisgau: Herder Verlag, 236–51.
Relethford, John H. 2012. *The Human Species. An Introduction to Biological Anthropology*. 9th ed. Mountain View, CA, and London: Mayfield Publishing.
Renn, Jürgen. 2002. "In der Kirche der Wissenschaft." *Frankfurt am Mainer Allgemeine Sonntagszeitung* 51 (22 December 2002), 57–58.
Rensch, Bernhard 1991. *Das universale Weltbild. Evolution und Naturphilosophie*. Darmstadt: Wissenschaftliche Buchgesellschaft.
Renteln, Alison D. 1988. "Relativism and the Search for Human Rights." *American Anthropologist* 90(19): 56–72.
———. 1990. *International Human Rights. Universalism versus Relativism*. Newbury Park, CA: Sage Publications.
Renz, Ulrich. 2006. *Schönheit. Eine Wissenschaft für sich*. Berlin: Berlin Verlag.
Rhodes, Gillian. 2006. "The Evolutionary Psychology of Facial Beauty." *Annual Review of Psychology* 57: 199–226.
Richards, Janet Radcliffe. 2000. *Human Nature after Darwin. A Philosophical Introduction*. London and New York: Routledge.
Richerson, Peter J. and Robert Boyd. 1998. "The Evolution of Human Ultrasociality." In Irenäus Eibl-Eibesfeldt and Frank K. Salter (eds.), *Indoctrinability, Ideology and Warfare. Evolutionary Perspectives*. New York: Berghahn Books, 71–95.
———. 1999. "Complex Societies: The Evolutionary Origins of a Crude Superorganism." *Human Nature* 10: 253–90.
———. 2001. "Institutional Evolution in the Holocene: The Rise of Complex Societies." In Walter Garrison Runciman (ed.), *The Origin of Human Social Institutions*. Proceedings of the British Academy 110. Oxford: Oxford University Press, 197–234.
———. 2005. *Not by Genes Alone. How Human Culture Transformed Human Evolution*. Chicago and London: The University of Chicago Press.
Ricken, Norbert. 2004. "Menschen – Zur Struktur anthropologischer Reflexionen als einer unverzichtbaren kulturwissenschaftlichen Dimension." In Friedrich Jaeger and Burkhard Liebsch (eds.), *Handbuch der Kulturwisssenschaften. Band 1. Grundlagen und Schlüsselbegriffe*. Stuttgart and Weimar: J. B. Metzler, 152–72.
Riedel, Jens. 2002. "The Multiple Modernities Perspective: Enriching Business Strategy." In Dominic Sachsenmaier and Jens Riedel (eds.), *Reflections on Multiple Modernities. European, Chinese and Other Interpretations*. With Shmuel N. Eisenstadt. Leiden: E.J. Brill, 271–92.
Rippe, Klaus Peter. 1999. "Brauchen wir ein Menschenbild?" In Anna Katharina Reichardt and Eric Kubli (eds.), *Menschenbilder*. Bern: Peter Lang Europäischer Verlag der Wissenschaften, 9–33.
Rippl, Susanne and Christian Seipel. 2008. *Methoden kulturvergleichender Sozialforschung. Eine Einführung*. Wiesbaden: VS Verlag für Sozialwissenschaften.
Roberson, Debi, Ian Davies, and Jules Davidoff. 2000. "Color Categories are Not Universal: Replications and New Evidence From a Stone-Age Culture." *Journal of Experimental Pschology: General* 129(3): 369–98.
Robertson, Robbie. 2003. *The Three Waves of Globalization. A History of a Developing Global Consciousness*. London: Zed Books.

Robertson, Roland. 1992. *Globalization. Social Theory and Global Culture*. Theory, Culture and Society. London: Sage Publications.
Rodseth, Lars, Richard W. Wrangham, Alisa M. Harrigan, and Barbara B. Smuts. 1991. "The Human Community as a Primate Society." *Current Anthropology* 32(3): 221–54.
Rogers, Everett M. 2003. *Diffusion of Innovations*. 5th ed. New York: Simon and Schuster.
Rogoff, Barbara. 2003. *The Cultural Nature of Human Development*. New York: Oxford University Press.
Róheim, Géza. 1977. *Psychoanalyse und Ethnologie Drei Studien über die Kultur und das Unbewußte*. Frankfurt: Suhrkamp Verlag. Originally *Psychoanalysis and Anthropology*, New York: International Universities Press, 1950.
Rokkan, Stein. 1970. "Cross-Cultural, Cross-Societal and Cross-National Research." In R. Maheu for UNESCO (ed.), *Main Trends in the Social and Human Sciences*, Part 1: *Social Sciences*. New Babylon Studies in the Social Sciences. Paris and The Hague: Mouton Publishers, 645–89.
Rolston III, Holmes. 1999. *Genes, Genesis and God. Values and Their Origins in Natural and Human History*. Cambridge: Cambridge University Press.
Romney, A. Kimball, Carmella C. Moore, and Craig D. Rusch. 1997. "Cultural Universals: Measuring the Semantic Structure of Emotion Terms in English and Japanese." *Proceedings of the National Academy of Sciences* 94(5): 489–94.
Rorarius, Winfried. 2006. *Was macht uns einzigartig? Zur Sonderstellung des Menschen*. Darmstadt: Wissenschaftliche Buchgesellschaft.
Rorty, Richard. 1979. *Philosophy and the Mirror of Nature*. Princeton: Princeton University Press.
Rosaldo, Renato. 1976. "The Story of Tukbaw: 'They Listen as He Orates.'" In Frank E. Reynolds and Donald Capps (eds.), *The Biographical Process. Studies in the History and Psychology of Religion*. The Hague: Mouton Publishers, 121–51.
Rose, Hilary and Steven Rose (eds.). 2001. *Alas Poor Darwin. Arguments Against Evolutionary Psychology*. London: Vintage.
Rose, Steven. 2006. *Lifelines. Biology Beyond Determinism*. 2nd ed. New York and Oxford: Vintage.
Ross, Andrew (ed.). 1989. *Universal Abandon. The Politics of Postmodernism*. Cultural Politics. Minneapolis: University of Minnesota Press. Also published in *Social Text* 7(3), 1989.
Ross, Norbert. 2004. *Culture and Cognition Implications for Theory and Method*. Thousand Oaks, CA: Sage Publications.
Rossano, Matthew J. 2010. *Supernatural Selection. How Religion Evolved*. Oxford: Oxford University Press.
Rossi, Ino. 1978. "Toward the Unification of Scientific Explanation: Evidence from Biological, Psychic, Linguistic, Cultural Universals." In Marvin D. Loflin and James Silverberg (eds.), *Discourse and Inference in Cogitive Anthropology. An Approach to Psychic Unity and Enculturation*. World Anthropology. The Hague and Pars: Mouton Publishers, 201–28.
Rössner, Hans (ed.). 1986. *Der ganze Mensch. Aspekte einer pragmatischen Anthropologie*. Munich: Deutscher Taschenbuch Verlag.
Roth, Eric Abella. 2004. *Culture, Biology, and Anthropological Demography*. Cambridge: Cambridge University Press.
Roth, Gerhard. 2003. *Fühlen, Denken, Handeln. Wie das Gehirn unser Verhalten steuert*. 2nd ed. Frankfurt am Main: Suhrkamp Verlag.
Rothbum, Fred and Gianna Morelli. 2005. "Attachment and Culture: Bridging Relativism and Universalism." In Wolfgang Friedlmeier, Pradeep Chakkarath, and Beate Schwarz

(eds.), *Culture and Human Development. The Importance of Cross-Cultural Research to the Social Sciences*. Hove and New York: Psychology Press, 99–123.

Rothe, Hartmut and Winfried Henke. 2005. "Machiavellistische Intelligenz bei Primaten. Sind Sozialsysteme der Menschenaffen ein Modell für frühmenschliche Gesellschaften?" In Bernhard Kleeberg, Tilman Walter, and Fabio Crivellari (eds.), *Urmensch und Wissenschaften. Eine Bestandsaufnahme*. Darmstadt: Wissenschaftliche Buchgesellschaft, 161–94.

Rothfuchs-Schulz, Cornelia. 1980. *Aspekte der Kunstethnologie. Beiträge zum Problem der Universalität von Kunst*. Berlin: Dietrich Reimer Verlag.

Röttger-Rössler, Birgitt. 2004. *Die kulturelle Modellierung des Gefühls. Ein Beitrag zur Theorie und Methodik ethnologischer Emotionsforschung anhand indonesischer Fallstudien*. Göttinger Studien zu Ethnologie 13. Münster: Lit Verlag.

Röttger-Rössler, Birgitt and Eva-Maria Engelen (eds.). 2006. *"'Tell Me About Love'. Kultur und Natur der Liebe*. Paderborn: Mentis Verlag.

Röttger-Rössler, Birgitt and Hans J. Markowitsch. 2006. "Emotionen als biokulturelle Prozesse." Bericht über Abschlusstagung der ZIF- Forschungsgruppe, 1–3 September 2005. *ZIF-Mitteilungen* 1: 30–32.

Röttger-Rössler, Gabriel Scheidecker, Susanne Jung, and Manfred Holodynski. 2013. "Socializing Emotions in Childhood: A Cross-Cultural Comparison between the Bara in Madagascar and the Minangkabau in Indonesia." *Mind, Culture, and Activity*, doi: 10.1080/10749039.2013.806551 (retrieved 8 June 2014).

Roughley, Neil (ed.). 2000. *Being Humans. Anthropological Universality and Particularity in Transdisciplinary Perspectives*. Berlin and New York: Walter de Gruyter.

———. 2005. "Was heisst „menschliche Natur"? Begriffliche Differenzierungen und normative Ansatzpunkte." In Kurt Bayertz (eds.), *Die menschliche Natur. Welchen und wieveil (sic!) Wert hat sie?* Ethica, 10. Paderborn: Mentis Verlag, 133–56.

———. 2011. "Human Natures." In Sebastian Schleidgen, Michael Jungert, Robert Bauer, and Verena Sandow (eds.), *Human Nature and Self Design*. Paderborn: Mentis, 11–33.

Rowe, David C. 1997. *Genetik und Sozialisation. Die Grenzen der Erziehung*. Weinheim: Beltz, Psychologie Verlags-Union. Originally *The Limits of Family Influence. Genes, Experience, and Behavior*, New York: Guilford Press, 1994.

Rückriem, Georg. 1978a. "Einleitung." In Georg Rückriem (ed.), *Historischer Materialismus und menschliche Natur*. Sudien zur Dialektik, Kleine Bibliothek 109. Cologne: Pahl-Rugenstein Verlag, 9–17.

———. (ed.). 1978b. *Historischer Materialismus und menschliche Natur*. Sudien zur Dialektik, Kleine Bibliothek, 109. Cologne: Pahl-Rugenstein Verlag.

Rudolph, Wolfgang. 1968. *Der kulturelle Relativismus. Kritische Analyse einer Grundsatzfragendiskussion in der amerikanischen Ethnologie*. Forschungen zur Ethnologie und Sozialpsychologie 6. Berlin: Duncker and Humblot.

———. 1973. "Kultur, Psyche, Weltbild." In Wolfgang Rudolph: *Ethnologie. Zur Standortbestimmung einer Wissenschaft*. Das wissenschaftliche Arbeitsbuch 8/21. Tübingen: Verlag Elly Huth, 143–67.

Rudolph, Wolfgang and Peter Tschohl. 1977. *Systematische Anthropologie*. Munich: Wilhelm Fink Verlag.

Runciman, Walter G. 2000. *The Social Animal*. Ann Arbor: The University of Michigan Press.

———. 2002. "Heritable Variation and Competitive Selection as the Mechanism of Sociocultural Variation." In Michael Wheeler, John Ziman, and Margaret A. Boden (eds.), *The Evolution of Cultural Entities*. Proceedings of the British Academy 112. Oxford: Oxford University Press for the British Academy, 9–25.

Ruse, Michael. 1986. *Taking Darwin Seriously*. Oxford: Basil Blackwell.
Rüsen, Jörn. 1998. "Einleitung: Für eine interkulturelle Kommunikation in der Geschichte. Die Herausforderungen des Ethnozentrismus in der Moderne und die Antwort der Kulturwissenschaften." In Jörn Rüsen et al. (eds.), *Die Vielfalt der Kulturen*. Frankfurt am Main: Suhrkamp Verlag, 12–36.
Russell, Edmund. 2011. *Evolutionary History. Uniting History and Biology to Understand Life on Earth*. Studies in Environment and History. Cambridge: Cambridge University Press.
Russell, James A. 1991. "Culture and the Categorization of Emotions." *Psychological Bulletin* 110(3): 426–50.
———. 1995. "Facial Expressions of Emotion: What Lies Behind Minimal Universality?" *Psychological Bulletin* 118(3): 379–91.
———. 2003. "Core Affect and the Psychological Construction of Emotion." *Psychological Review* 110: 145–72.
Rust, Alois. 1999. "Abschied von Menschenbildern?" In Anna Katharina Reichardt and Eric Kubli (eds.), *Menschenbilder*. Bern: Peter Lang Europäischer Verlag der Wissenschaften, 153–75.
Rusterholz, Peter and Rupert Moser (eds.). 2003. *Wie verstehen wir Fremdes?* Collegium Generale Universität Bern, Kulturhistorische Vorlesungen 2002/2003. Bern: Peter Lang Verlag.
Ryn, Claes G. 2003. *A Common Human Ground. Universality and Particularity in a Multicultural World*. Columbia and London: University of Missouri Press.
Saalmann, Gernot. 2005. *Fremdes Verstehen. Das Problem des Fremdverstehens vom Standpunkt einer "metadisziplinären" Kulturanthropologie*. Aachen: Shaker Verlag.
Said, Edward W. 2003. *Orientalism. Western Concepts of the Orient*. Penguin Modern Classics. London: Penguin.
Sahlins, Marshall D. 1976. *The Use and Abuse of Biology. An Anthropological Critique of Sociobiology*. Ann Arbor: University of Michigan Press.
Salat, Jana. 2003. "Das Eigene im Fremden, das Fremde im Eigenen: Die Entdeckung von Gemeinsamkeiten." In Peter Rusterholz and Rupert Moser (eds.), *Wie verstehen wir Fremdes?* Collegium Generale Universität Bern, Kulturhistorische Vorlesungen 2002/2003. Bern: Peter Lang Verlag, 127–36.
Saler, Benson. 2000. *Conceptualizing Religion. Immanent Anthropologists, Transcendent Natives, and Unbounded Categories*. New York and Oxford: Berghahn Books.
Salmon, Catherine and Donald Symons. 2001. *Warrior Lovers. Erotic Fiction, Evolution and Female Sexuality*. London: Weidenfeld and Nicolson.
Salter, Frank K. 2001. "Resolving the Paradox of Human Universals in Political Diversity. Irenäus Eibl-Eibesfeldt and Political Ethology." In Christa Sütterlin and Frank K. Salter (eds.), *Irenäus Eibl-Eibesfeldt. Zu Person und Werk*. Frankfurt: Peter Lang Europäischer Verlag der Wissenschaften, 172–78.
Sanderson, Stephen K. 2001. *The Evolution of Human Sociality. A Darwinian Conflict Perspective*. Lanham, MD: Rowman and Littlefield.
———. 2014. *Human Nature and the Evolution of Society*. Boulder, CO: Westview Press.
Sandler, Wendy and Diane Lillo-Martin. 2006. *Sign Language and Linguistic Universals*. Cambridge: Cambridge University Press.
Sarasin, Philipp and Marianne Sommer (eds.). 2010. *Evolution. Ein interdisziplinäres Handbuch*. Stuttgart and Weimar: Verlag J.B. Metzler.
Saunders, Barbara A. C. 2000. "Revisiting Basic Color Terms." *Journal of the Royal Anthropological Institute*, n.s. 6: 81–99.
Sawyer, Robert Keith. 2005. *Social Emergence*. Cambridge: Cambridge University Press.

Scalise Sugiyama, Michelle. 2003. "Cultural Variation Is Part of Human Nature. Literary Universals, Context-Sensitivity, and 'Shakespeare in the Bush." *Human Nature* 14(4): 383–96.
———. 2006. "Lions and Tigers and Bears. Predators as a Folklore Universal." In Uta Klein, Katja Mellmann, and Steffanie Metzger (eds.), *Heuristiken der Literaturwissenschaft. Disziplinexterne Perspektiven auf Literatur.* Poetogenesis 3. Paderborn: Mentis, 319–31.
Scarre, Chris (ed.). 2005. *The Human Past. World Prehistory and the Development of Human Societies.* London: Thames and Hudson.
Schaeffler, Richard. 2005. "Universalien religiöser Erfahrung in der Vielfalt religiöser Überlieferung. Ein notwendiger, aber problematischer Begriff." In Torsten Larbig and Siegfried Wiedenhofer (eds.), *Kulturelle und religiöse Traditionen. Beiträge zu einer interdisziplinären Traditionstheorie und Traditionsanalyse.* Studien zur Traditionstheorie (Studies in Tradition Theory). Münster: Lit Verlag, 212–52.
Scharfstein, Ben-Ami. 2008. "The Common Humanity Evident in European, African, Indian, Chinese and Japanese Aesthetic Theory." In Kitty Zijlmans and Wilfried A. van Damme (eds.), *World Art Studies. Exploring Concepts and Approaches.* Amsterdam: Valiz Publishers, 343–67.
———. 2009. *Art Without Borders. A Philosophical Exploration of Art and Humanity.* Chicago and London: The University of Chicago Press.
Scheler, Max. (1947) 2005. *Die Stellung des Menschen im Kosmos.* Bonn: Bouvier Verlag.
Schelling, Thomas C. 1978. *Micromotives and Macrobehavior.* New York: W. W. Norton.
Schenker, Heinrich. (1954) 1980. *Harmony.* Chicago: The University of Chicago Press.
Scherer, Klaus R., Rainer Banse, and Harald G. Wallbott. 2001. "Emotion Inferences From Vocal Expression Correlate Across Languages and Cultures." *Journal of Cross-Cultural Psychology* 32(1): 76–92.
Schiefenhövel, Wulf. 1997. "Universals in Interpersonal Interactions." In Ullica Segerstråle and Peter Molnár (eds.), *Nonverbal Communication. Where Nature Meets Culture.* Mahwah, NJ: Lawrence Erlbaum Associates, 61–79.
———. 1999. "Exposé für die konstituierende Sitzung am 22./23.Juni 1999 im HWK." Delmenhorst: Hanse-Wissenschaftskolleg. Unpublished manuscript, 4 pp.
———. 2003. "Mängelwesen Homo sapiens? Vom Menschenbild in Anthropologie und Medizin." In Hartmann Hinterhuber, Manfred P. Heuser, and Ullrich Meise (eds.), *Bilder des Menschen. Das Menschenbild der Psychiatrie und der Medizin, der Religionen und Künste, der Kultu- und Sozialwissenschaften.* Innsbruck: VIP Verlag Integrative Psychiatrie, 141–47.
———. 2004. "Kognitions- und Entscheidungsmuster in Melanesien." In Heinrich Schmidinger and Clemens Sedmak (eds.), *Der Mensch - ein „animal rationale"? Vernunft - Kognition - Intelligenz.* Topologien des Menschlichen 1. Darmstadt: Wissenschaftliche Buchgesellschaft, 275–92.
Schiffauer, Werner. 1997. "Kulturalismus vs. Universalismus. Ethnologische Anmerkungen zu einer Debatte." In Werner Schiffauer, *Fremde in der Stadt. Zehn Essays über Kultur und Differenz.* Frankfurt am Main: Suhrkamp Verlag, 144–56.
Schimmel, Annemarie. 1996. *Wie universal ist die Mystik? Die Seelenreise in den großen Religionen der Welt.* Herder Spektrum. Freiburg: Herder Verlag.
Schissler, Hanna. 2005. "Weltgeschichte als Geschichte der sich globalisierenden Welt." *Aus Politik und Zeitgeschichte* 1: 33–39.
Schlegel, Alice. 2007. "Cross-Cultural Gender Differences in Adolescent Socialization." In Uwe Krebs and Johanna Forster (eds.), *„Sie und Er" interdisziplinär. Aktuelle Themen interdisziplinär* 1. Münster: Lit Verlag, 227–38.

Schlehe, Judith. 2006. "Kultur, Universalität und Diversität." In Ernestine Wolfart and Manfred Zaumseil (eds.), *Transkulturelle Psychiatrie – Interkulturelle Psychotherapie. Interdisziplinäre Theorie und Praxis.* Heidelberg: Springer Medizun Verlag.

Schmidinger, Heinrich. 2004. "Topologien des Menschlichen." In Heinrich Schmidinger and Clemens Sedmak (eds.), *Der Mensch – ein „animal rationale"? Vernunft – Kognition – Intelligenz.* Topologien des Menschlichen. Darmstadt: Wissenschaftliche Buchgesellschaft, 7–15.

Schmidinger, Heinrich and Clemens Sedmak (eds.). 2004. *Der Mensch – ein „animal rationale"? Vernunft – Kognition – Intelligenz.* Topologien des Menschlichen. Darmstadt: Wissenschaftliche Buchgesellschaft.

———. (eds.). 2007. *Der Mensch – ein „animal symbolicum "? Sprache – Dialog – Ritual.* Topologien des Menschlichen. Darmstadt: Wissenschaftliche Buchgesellschaft.

Schmidt, Julia. 1996. "Edward Steichens' 'The Family of Man.'" *Kunstchronik* 8: 365–70.

Schmidt, Johannes F. K. 2007. "Soziologe der Verwandtschaft: Forschung und Begriff." In Johannes F. K. Schmidt, Martine Guichard, Peter Schuster, and Fritz Trillmich (eds.), *Freundschaft und Verwandtschaft. Zur Unterscheidung und Verflechtung zweier Beziehungssysteme.* Constance: UVK Verlagsgesellschaft, 15–43.

Schmidt, Ulrich (Red.). 1987. *Kulturelle Identität und Universalität. Interkulturelles Lernen als Bildungsprinzip.* Frankfurt am Main: IKO Verlag für Interkulturelle Kommunikation. (Pädagogik, Jahrbuch Dritte Welt 1986).

Schmied, Gerhard. 2007. *Das Rätsel Mensch – Antworten der Soziologie.* Opladen and Farmington Hills: Verlag Barbara Budrich.

Schmitt, David P. et al. (118 co-authors). 2005. "Universal Sex Differences in the Desire For Sexual Variety: Tests From 52 Nations, 6 Continents, and 13 Islands." *Journal of Personality and Social Psychology* 85(1): 85–104.

Schnegg, Michael. 2015. "Epistemology. The Nature and Validation of Knowledge." In H. Russel Bernard and Clarence C. Gravlee (eds.), *Handbook of Methods in Cultural Anthropology.* Lanham, MD: Rowman and Littlefield, 21–53.

Schneider, David M. 1984. *A Critique of the Study of Kinship.* Ann Arbor: University of Michigan Press.

Schöfthaler, Traugott. 1983. "Kultur in der Zwickmühle. Zur Aktualität des Streits zwischen kulturrelativistischer und universalistischer Sozialwissenschaft." *Das Argument* 139: 333–47.

Scholte, Bob. 1984. "Reason and Culture: The Universal and the Particular Revisited (Review of Hollis and Lukes, eds. 1982)." *American Anthropologist* 86: 960–65.

Schönhuth, Michael. 2005. "Authentizität und Inszenierung. Eine Reise durch populäre deutschsprachige Ethnoliteratur." In Christoph Antweiler, *Ethnologie. Ein Führer zu populären Medien.* Ethnologische Paperbacks. Berlin: Dietrich Reimer Verlag, 65–99.

Schramkowski, Barbara. 2001. *Interkulturelle Mediation. Mediation als eine Methode des konstruktiven Umgangs mit interkulturellen Konflikten in Städten mit hohem interkulturellen Bevölkerungsanteil.* MenschenArbeit, Freiburger Studien 13. Constance: Hartung-Gorre Verlag.

Schröder, Inge. 2000. *Wege zum Menschen. Theoretische Beiträge zur evolutionären Anthropoogie.* Göttingen: Cuvillier Verlag.

Schulin, Ernst (ed.). 1974. *Universalgeschichte.* Neue Wissenschaftliche Bibliothek 72. Cologne: Verlag Kiepenheuer and Witsch.

Schulz-Schaeffer. 2000. "Akteur-Netzwerk-Theorie. Zur Koevolution von Gesellschaft, Natur und Technik." In Johnnes Weyer (ed.), *Soziale Netzwerke. Konzepte und Methoden der sozialwissenschaftlicheh Netzwerkforschung.* Munich and Vienna: R. Oldenbourg, 187–209.

Schuster, Martin. 2005. *Fotos sehen, verstehen, gestalten. Eine Psychologie der Photographie.* 2nd ed. Berlin: Springer Verlag.
Schwartz, Shalom H. 1994. "Are There Universal Aspects in the Structure and Contents of Human Nature?" *Journal of Social Issues* 50(4): 19–45.
Schwartz, Shalom H. and Anat Bardi. 2001. "Value Hierarchies Across Cultures. Taking a Similarities Perspective." *Journal of Cross-Cultural Psychology* 32(3): 268–90.
Schwartz, Shalom H. and Wolfgang Bilsky. 1987. "Toward a Universal Psychological Structure of Human Values." *Journal of Personality and Social Psychology* 53(3): 550–62.
———. 1994. "Toward a Theory of the Universal Content and Structure of Values: Extensions and Cross-Cultural Replications." *Journal of Personality and Social Psychology* 58(5): 878–91.
Schweizer, Thomas. 1978. *Methodenprobleme des interkulturellen Vergleichs. Probleme, Lösungsversuche, exemplarische Anwendung.* Kölner ethnologische Mitteilungen 6. Cologne and Vienna: Böhlau Verlag.
———. 1989. "Perspektivenwandel in der ethnologischen Primär- und Sekundäranalyse. Die frühere und die heutige Methode interkulturellen Vergleichs." *Kölner Zeitschrift für Soziologie und Sozialpsychologie* 41: 465–82.
Scupin, Raymond. 2006. *Cultural Anthropology. A Global Perspective.* 6th ed. Upper Saddle River, NJ: Pearson Prentice Hall.
Scupin, Raymond and Christopher R. DeCorse. 2015. *Anthropology. A Global Perspective.* 8th ed. Upper Saddle River NJ: Pearson.
Searle, John R. 2010. *Making the Social World. The Structure of Human Civilization.* Oxford: Oxford University Press.
Sedmak, Clemens. 2004. "Homo est animal rationale." In Heinrich Schmidinger and Clemens Sedmak (eds.), *Der Mensch – ein „animal rationale"? Vernunft – Kognition – Intelligenz. Topologien des Menschlichen.* Darmstadt: Wissenschaftliche Buchgesellschaft, 12–15.
Seel, Martin. 1998. "Philosophie nach der Postmoderne." In "Postmoderne. Eine Bilanz," special issue. *Merkur* 52(9–10): 890–97.
———. 2005. "Vom Nutzen und Nachteil einer evolutionären Ästhetik." In Bernhard Kleeberg, Tilman Walter, and Fabio Crivellari (eds.), *Urmensch und Wissenschaften. Eine Bestandsaufnahme.* Darmstadt: Wissenschaftliche Buchgesellschaft, 323–34.
Segalen, Martine. 1994. "The Family of Man ou la Grande Illusion." In Jean Back and Gabriel Bauret (eds.), *The Family of Man. Témoignages et documents.* Luxembourg: Editions artsevents, Ministère des Affaires culturelles, Centre national de l'audiovisuel, 117–28.
Segall, Marshall H. et al. 1966. *The Influence of Culture on Visual Perception.* New York: Bobbs-Merrill.
Segall, Marshall H., Pierre R. Dasen, John W. Berry, and Ype H. Poortinga. 1999. *Human Behavior in Global Perspective. An Introduction to Cross-Cultural Psychology.* 2nd ed. Boston: Allyn and Bacon. Pergamon General Psychology Series 160. New York: Pergamon Press.
Segerstråle, Ullica. 2003. "Sociobiology." In Lynn Nadel (ed.), *Encyclopedia of Cognitive Science*, vol. 4: *Similarity – Zombies.* London: Nature Publishing Group, Macmillan, 85–91.
Segerstråle, Ullica and Peter Molnár. 1997a. "Nonverbal Communication: Crossing the Boundary Between Nature and Culture." In Ullica Segerstråle and Peter Molnár (eds.), 1–21.
———. (eds.). 1997b. *Nonverbal Communication. Where Nature Meets Culture.* Mahwah, NJ: Lawrence Earlbaum Associates.
Seiler, Hansjacob (ed.). 1973/74. *Linguistic Workshop I/II. Vorarbeiten zu einem Universalienprojekt.* Munich: Wilhelm Fink Verlag.

———. 2000. *Language Universals Research. A Synthesis*. Language Universals Series 8. Tübingen: Gunter Narr Verlag.
Serventi, Silvano and François Sabban. 2001. *Pasta. The Story of a Universal Food*. New York: Columbia University Press. Arts and Traditions of the Table: Perspectives of Culinary History. Originally *La pasta: Storia e cultura di un cibo universale*, Bari, Rome: Laterza, 2000.
Servier, Jean. 1991. "Histoire des Idéologies." In Jean Poirier (ed.), *Histoire des Moeurs, Tome II: Moeurs et Modèles*. Encyclopédie de la Pleiade. Paris: Éditions Gallimard, 1,419–27.
SFB 511. 2005. "Erster Verlängerungsantrag" (1998): In Aleida Assmann, Ulrich Gaier, and Gisela Trommsdorff (eds.), *Zwischen Literatur und Anthropologie*. Tübingen: Gunter Narr Verlag, 29–66.
Shennan, Stephen. 2002. *Genes, Memes and Human History. Darwinian Archaeology and Cultural Evolution*. London: Thames and Hudson.
———. (ed.). 2009. *Pattern and Process in Cultural Evolution*. Origins of Human Behavior and Culture. Berkeley: University of California Press.
Sheper-Hughes, Nancy. 1995. "The Primacy of the Ethical Propositions For a Militant Anthropology." *Current Anthropology* 36: 409–20.
Sherry, John F. Jr. 1995. *Contemporary Marketing and Consumer Behavior. An Anthropological Sourcebook*. Thousand Oaks, CA: Sage Publications.
Shim, HyunJu. 2004. *Die Herausforderung der koreanischen Kultur durch die hegemoniale Globalisierung. Ein Beitrag zur Bestimmung des Verhältnisses intra-, supra- und transkultureller Werte*. Ethik – Wissen – Gesellschaft 18. Frankfurt am Main: IKO – Verlag für Interkulturelle Kommunikation.
Shiraev, Eric B. and David A. Levy. 2013. *Cross-Cultural Psychology. Critical Thinking and Contemporary Applications*. 5th ed. Boston: Pearson Allyn and Bacon.
Shore, Bradd. 1996. *Culture in Mind. Cognition, Culture, and the Problem of Meaning*. New York and Oxford: Oxford University Press.
———. 2000. "Human Diversity and Human Nature. The Life and Times of A False Dichotomy." In Neil Roughley (ed.), *Being Humans. Anthropological Universality and Particularity in Transdisciplinary Perspectives*. Berlin and New York: Walter de Gruyter, 81–103.
Shweder, Richard A. and Edmund J. Bourne. 1984. "Does the Concept of the Person Vary Cross-Culturally?" In Richard A. Shweder & Robert A. Levine (eds.), *Culture Theory. Essays in Mind, Self, and Emotion*. Cambridge: Cambridge University Press, 158–199.
Shweder, Richard and Robert A. LeVine (eds.). 1984. *Culture Theory. Essays on Mind, Self and Emotion*. Cambridge: Cambridge University Press.
Sidky, Homayun. 2003. *A Critique of Postmodern Anthropology. In Defense of Disciplinary Origins and Traditions*. Mellen Studies in Anthropology 10. Edwin Mellen Press.
———. 2004. *Perspectives on Culture. A Critical Introduction to Theory in Cultural Anthropology*. Upper Saddle River, NJ: Pearson Prentice Hall.
Sieferle, Rolf Peter. 1989. *Die Krise der menschlichen Natur. Zur Geschichte eines Konzepts*. Frankfurt: Suhrkamp Verlag.
Silverberg, James. 1978. "The Scientific Discovery of Logic: The Anthropological Significance of Empirical Research on Psychic Unity (Inference-Making)." In Marvin D. Loflin and James Silverberg (eds.), *Discourse and Inference in Cognitive Anthropology*. The Hague: Mouton, 280–95.
Silverman, Irwin and Irene Bevc. 2006. "Evolutionary Origins and Ontogenetic Development of Incest Avoidance." In Bruce F. Ellis and David F. Bjorklund (eds.), *The Origins of the Social Mind. Evolutionary Psychology and Child Development*. New York: The Guilford Press, 292–313.

Silverman, Sydel. 2002. *The Beast on the Desk. Conferencing with Anthropologists.* Walnut Creek, CA: Altamira Press.
Simon, Herbert A. 1990a. "A Mechanism for Social Selection and Successful Altruism." *Science* 250: 1, 665–68.
———. 1990b. "Invariants of Human Behavior." *Annual Review of Psychology* 41(1): 1–19.
Simpson, George G. 1969. *Biology and Man.* New York: Harcourt, Brace and World.
Simpson, Jeffrey A. and T. Douglas Kenrick (eds.). 1997. *Evolutionary Social Psychology.* Mahwah, NJ: Lawrence Earlbaum Associates.
Sitter-Liver, Beat. 2009. *Universality: From Theory to Practice. An Intercultural and Interdisciplinary Debate about Facts, Possibilities, Lies and Myths.* Ed. assistance by Thomas Hiltbrunner. 25th Colloquium (2007) of the Swiss Academy of Humanities and Social Sciences. Freiburg, Schweiz: Academic Press Fribourg.
Slingerland, Edward and Mark Collard (eds.). 2012. *Creating Consilience. Integrating the Sciences and the Humanities.* New Directions in Cognitive Science. New York: Oxford University Press.
Slobin, Dan I. 1982. "Universal and Particular in the Acquisition of Language." In E. Wanner and L.R. Gleitman (eds.), *Language Acquisition.* Cambridge: Cambridge Universoity Press, 128–70.
Sloboda, John A. 2003. *The Musical Mind. The Cogitive Psychology of Music.* Oxford: Oxford University Press.
Smith, Eric A., Monique Borgerhoff Mulder, and Kim Hill. 2001. "Controversies in the Evolutionary Social Sciences: A Guide For the Perplexed." *Trends in Ecology and Evolution* 16(3): 128–35.
Smith, Eric Alden and Bruce Winterhalder. 2003. "Human Behavioural Ecology." In Lynn Nadel (ed.), *Encyclopedia of Cognitive Science,* vol. 2: *Epilepsy: Mental Imagery.* London: Nature Publishing Group, Macmillan, 377–85.
Smith, Peter B. and Michael Harris Bond. 1993. *Social Psychology Across Cultures. Analysis and Perspectives.* New York: Harvester Wheatsheaf.
Smith, Peter B., Michael Harris Bond, and Cigdem Kagitcibasi. 2006. *Understanding Social Psychology Across Cultures. Living and Working in A Changing World.* London: Sage Publications.
Snow, Charles Percy. (1959) 1967. *Die zwei Kulturen.* Stuttgart: Ernst Klett Verlag.
Sober, Elliott. 1993. *Philosophy of Biology.* Dimensions of Philosophy. Oxford: Oxford University Press.
Sober, Elliott and David Sloan Wilson. 1998. *Unto Others. The Evolution and Psychology of Unselfish Behavior.* Cambridge, MA: Harvard University Press.
Sobo, Elisa J. 2013. *Dynamics of Human Biocultural Diversity. A Unified Approach.* Walnut Creek, CA: Left Coast Press.
Somit, Albert. 1992. "Darwinism Redux: An Alternative Explanation." *Politics and the Life Sciences* 1: 281–82.
Sommer, Volker. 1992. *Feste, Mythen, Rituale. Warum die Völker feiern.* Hamburg: Geo, Gruner und Jahr.
Spencer, Herbert. 1873-1934. *Descriptive Sociology,* 13 vols. New York: Apple-Century-Crofts.
———. 1986. *The Principles of Sociology.* New York: Appleton.
Sperber, Dan. 1989. *Das Wissen des Ethnologen.* Frankfurt am Main and New York: Edition Qumran im Campus Verlag and Paris: Editions de la Maison des Sciences de l'Homme. Originally *Le savoir des anthropologues,* Collection Savoir, Paris: Hermann, 1982.
———. 2005. "Modularity and Relevance: How Can a Massively Modular Mind be Flexible and Context-Sensitive?" In Peter Carruthers, Stephen Laurence, and Stephen P.

Stich (eds.), *The Innate Mind. Structure and Contents*. Oxford: Oxford University Press, 53–68.

———. 2006. "Why a Deep Understanding of Cultural Evolution in Incompatible With Shallow Psychology." In Nicholas J. Enfield and Stephen C. Levinson (eds.), *Roots of Human Sociality. Culture, Cognition and Interaction*. Wenner-Gren International Symposium Series. Oxford and New York: Berg Publishers, 431–49.

Sperber, Dan and Lawrence Hirschfeld. 2004. "The Cognitive Foundations of Cultural Stability and Diversity." *Trends in Cognitive Sciences* 8(1): 40–46.

Spier, Fred. 2002. *Big History. Was die Geschichte im Innersten zusammenhält*. Darmstadt: Primus Verlag. Originally *The Structure of Big History. From the Big Bang until Today*, Amsterdam: Amsterdam University Press, 1996.

Spindler, Paul. 1984. "Universalia Humana. Gedanken über einige arttypische Verhaltensweisen des Menschen." *Mitteilungen der Anthropologischen Gesellschaft in Vienna* 114: 13–19.

Spiro, Melford E. 1966. "Religion: Problems of Definition and Explanation." In Michael Banton (ed.), *Anthropological Approaches to the Study of Religion*. London: Tavistock Publications, 85–126.

———. 1982. *Oedipus in the Trobriands*. Chicago: University of Chicago Press.

———. 1994. *Culture and Human Nature. Theoretical Papers of Melford E. Spiro*. Ed. Benjamin Kilbourne and L. L. Langness. 2nd ed. New Brunswick, NJ and London: Transaction Publishers.

Splett, Jörg. 1990. "Die Sonderstellung des Menschen." In Wolfgang Cyran (ed.), *Die Sonderstellung des Menschen in der Evolution*. Kirche und Welt. Schriftenreihe der Katholischen Akademikerarbeit Deutschlands 3. Melle: Verlag Ernst Knoth, 59–73.

"Sprachuniversalien". 2008. Retrieved 19 September 2008 from http://de.wikipedia.org/wiki/Sprachuniversalien.

Spradley, James P. 1997. *Participant Observation*. New York: Holt, Rinehart and Winston.

Srubar, Ilja, Joachim Renn, and Ulrich Wenzel (eds.). 2005. *Kulturen vergleichen. Sozial- und kulturwissenschaftliche Grundlagen und Kontroversen*. Wiesbaden: Verlag für Sozialwissenschaften.

Staal, Frits. 1988. *Universals. Studies in Indian Logic and Linguistics*. Chicago: The University of Chicago Press.

Stagl, Justin. 1985. "Die Beschreibung des Fremden in der Wissenschaft." In Hans-Peter Duerr (ed.), *Der Wissenschaftler und das Irrationale*, vol. 2: *Beiträge aus Ethnologie und Anthropologie II*. Taschenbücher Syndikat/VA, 56, 57. Frankfurt am MaSyndikat Autoren- und Verlagsgesellschaft, 96–118.

———. 1992. "Eine Widerlegung des kulturellen Relativismus." In Joachim Matthes (ed.), Zwischen den Kulturen? Die Sozialwissenschaften vor dem Problem des Kulturvergleichs. Soziale Welt, Sonderband 8. Göttingen: Vandenhoeck and Ruprecht, 145–66.

———. 1993. "Der Kreislauf der Kultur." *Anthropos* 88: 477–88.

———. 2000. "Anthropological Universality. On the Validity of Generalizations about Human Nature." In Neil Roughley (ed.), *Being Humans. Anthropological Universality and Particularity in Transdisciplinary Perspectives*. Berlin and New York: Walter de Gruyter, 25–46.

———. 2002. "Tabu." In Günter Endruweit and Gisela Trommsdorff (eds.), *Wörterbuch der Soziologie*. 2nd ed. Stuttgart: Lucius and Lucius, 592.

———. 2004. "Kulturalismus." In Clemens Albrecht (ed.), *Die bürgerliche Kultur und ihre Avantgarden. Kultur, Geschichte, Theorie. Studien zur Kultursoziologie* 1. Würzburg: Ergon Verlag, 65–68.

Stagl, Justin and Wolfgang Reinhardt (eds.). 2005. *Grenzen des Menschseins. Probleme einer Definition des Menschlichen*. Veröffentlichungen des Instituts für Historische Anthropologie 8. Bonn: Böhlau.
Stanford, Craig B. 2001. *Significant Others. The Ape-Human Continuum and the Quest for Human Nature*. New York: Basic Books.
Stea, David, James M. Blaut, and Jennifer Stephens. 1996. "Mapping as a Cultural Universal." In Juval Portugali (ed.), *The Construction of Cognitive Maps*. The GeoJournal Library 32. Dordrecht: Kluwer Academic Publishers, 345–60.
Steadman, Lyle B., Craig T. Palmer, and Christopher F. Tilley. 1996. "The Universality of Ancestor Worship." *Cultural Anthropology* 35(1): 63–76.
Stegmüller, Wolfgang. 1974. *Glauben, Wissen und Erkennen. Das Universalien-Problem einst und jetzt*. Reihe Libelli 94. Darmstadt: Wissenschaftliche Buchgesellschaft.
———. (ed.). 1978. *Das Universalienproblem*. Wege der Forschung 83. Darmstadt: Wissenschaftliche Buchgesellschaft.
———. 1986. *Rationale Rekonstruktion von Wissenschaft und ihrem Wandel*. Stuttgart: Philipp Reclam, Jun.
———. 1955. *Theory of Culture Change*. Urbana: University of Illinois Press.
Steichen, Edward. 1955. *The Family of Man. The Greatest Photographic Exhibition of All Time—503 Pictures From 68 Countries*. New York: Maco Magazine Corporation, for the Museum of Modern Art.
Steiner, Franz B. 1999. *Taboo, Truth, and Religion. Selected Writings*, vol. 1. Ed. Jeremy Adler and Richard Fardon. Methodology and History in Anthropology 2. New York and Oxford: Berghahn Books.
Steinmann, Horst and Andreas Georg Scherer (eds.). 1998. *Zwischen Universalismus und Relativismus. Philosophische Grundlagenprobleme des interkulturellen Managemants*. Frankfurt am Main: Suhrkamp Verlag.
Steixner, Margret. 2008. *Lernraum Interkultur. Von interkukultureller Erfahrung zu interkultureller Kompetenz. Potentiale und Relevanz des interkulturellen Coachings am Beispiel von Fachkräften der Entwicklungszusammenarbeit*. ÖFSE Forum 34. Vienna: Südwind-Verlag.
Stephens, William N. 1963. *The Family in Cross-Cultural Perspective*. New York: Holt, Rinehart and Winston.
Sterelny, Kim. 2003. *Thought in a Hostile World. The Evolution of Human Cognition*. Malden, MA: Blackwell Publishing.
———. 2012. *The Evolved Apprentice. How Evolution Made Humans Unique*. Cambridge, MA and London: The MIT Press.
Stevenson, Leslie and David L. Haberman. 1998. *Ten Theories of Human Nature*. New York and Oxford: Oxford University Press.
Steward, Julian H. 1950. *Area Research. Theory and Practice*. Social Science Research Council Bulletin 63. Washington, DC: Social Science Research Council.
Stocking, George W. Jr. 1987. *Victorian Anthropology*. New York: The Free Press and London: Collier Macmillan.
Storey, Robert F. 1996. *Mimesis and the Human Animal. On The Biogenetic Foundations of Literary Representation*. Rethinking Theory. Evanston, IL: Northwestern University Press.
Stout, David B. 1971. "Aesthetics in 'Primitive Societies.'" In Carol F. Jopling (ed.), *Art and Aesthetics in Primitive Societies. A Critical Anthology*. New York, E.P. Dutton, 30–34.
Strachan, Tom and Andrew P. Read. 2005. *Molekulare Humangenetik*. Heidelberg: Elsevier Spektrum Akademischer Verlag. Originally *Human Molecular Genetics*. New York: Garland Science, 2004.

Strathern, Andrew. 1995. "Universals and Particulars: Some Current Contests in Anthropology." *Ethos* 23(2): 173–86.
Strathern, Andrew J. and Pamela J. Stewart (eds.). 2000. *Identity Work. Constructing Pacific Lives*. Association of Social Anthropologists of Oceania Monograph. Pittsburgh: University of Pittsburgh Press.
Straub, Jürgen. 1999. *Handlung, Interpretation, Kritik. Grundzüge einer textwissenschaftlichen Handlungs- und Kulturpsychologie*. Perspektiven der Humanwissenschaften, Phänomenologisch-psychologische Forschungen 18. Berlin and New York: Walter de Gruyter.
———. 2003. "Was hat die Psychologie bei den Kulturwissenschaften verloren?" In Klaus E. Müller (ed.), *Phänomen Kultur. Perspektiven und Aufgaben der Kulturwissenschaften*. Kultur und soziale Praxis. Bielefeld: Transcript Verlag, 131–56.
———. 2007. "Historische Positionen und Entwicklungslinien einer Kultur integrierenden Psychologie." In Gisela Trommsdorff and Hans-Joachim Kornadt (eds.), *Theorien und Methoden der kulturvergleichenden Psychologie*. Enzyklopädie der Psychologie, Themenbereich C, Theorie und Forschung, Serie 7, Kulturvergleichende Psychologie, vol. 1. Göttingen: Hogrefe, 119–78.
Straub, Jürgen and Gabriel Layes. 2002. "Kulturpsychologie, Kulturvergleichende Psychologie und Interkulturelle Psychologie: Aktuelle Ansätze und Perspektiven." *Handlung, Kultur, Interpretation* 11(2): 334–81.
Straub, Jürgen and Shingo Shimada. 1999. "Relationale Hermeneutik im Kontext interkulturellen Verstehens. Probleme universalistischer Begriffsbildung in den Sozial- und Kulturwissenschaften – erörtert am Beispiel Religion." *Deutsche Zeitschrift für Philosophie* 47: 449–77.
Streeter, Simon A. and Donald H. McBurney. 2003. "Waist-Hip Ratio and Attractiveness: New Evidence and a Critique of a 'Critical Test.'" *Evolution and Human Behavior* 24: 89–98.
Strier, Karen B. 2000. *Primate Behavioral Ecology*. Boston: Allyn and Bacon.
———. 2001. "Beyond the Apes: Reasons to Consider the Entire Primate Order." In Frans B. M. de Waal (ed.), *Tree of Origin. What Primate Behavior Can Tell Us about Human Social Evolution*. Cambridge, MA, and London: Harvard University Press, 69–93.
Strum, Shirley S. and Bruno Latour. 1987. "Redefining the Social Link: From Baboons to Humans." *Informations sur les Sciences Sociales, Social Science Information* 26: 783–802.
Sumner, William G.(1906) 1959. *Folkways. A Study of the Sociological Importance of Usages, Manners, Customs, Mores, and Morals*. New York; Dover Publications.
Sumner, William G. and Albert G. Keller. 1927. *The Science of Society*. 4 vols. New Haven, CT: Yale University Press.
Sussman, Robert W. 1999. "The Nature of Human Universals." In Robert W. Sussman (ed.), *The Biological Basis of Human Behavior. A Critical Review*. Advances in Human Evolution Series. Upper Saddle River, NJ: Prentice Hall, 246–52. Originally "Review of Brown 1991 and Degler 1991", *Reviews in Anthropology* 24: 1–11, 1995.
Sütterlin, Christa. 1992. "Was uns gefällt. Kunst und Ästhetik." *Funkkolleg Der Mensch. Anthropologie heute*. Tübingen: Deutsches Institut für Fernstudien an der Universität Tübingen, 3–57.
Sütterlin, Christa and Frank K. Salter (eds.). 2001. *Irenäus Eibl-Eibesfeldt. Zu Person und Werk*. Frankfurt: Peter Lang Europäischer Verlag der Wissenschaften.
Swanson, Guy E. 1964. *The Birth of the Gods. The Origin of Primitive Beliefs*. Ann Arbor: University of Michigan Press.
Symons, Donald. 1979. *The Evolution of Human Sexuality*. New York: Harper and Row.
Szalay, Miklós. 1999. "Objektwelt und Gesellschaft. Der Kunstbegriff im Kulturvergleich." *Sociologia Internationalis* 37(1): 115–29.

Taylor, Charles. 1997. *Multikulturalismus und die Politik der Anerkennung*. Frankfurt am Main: Fischer Taschenbuch Verlag. In German, Frankfurt: S. Fischer Verlag, 1993. Originally *Multiculturalism and the Politics of Recognition. An Essay*, Princeton, NJ: Princeton University Press, 1992.
Tenbruck, Friedrich H. 1992. "Was war der Kulturvergleich, ehe es den Kulturvergleich gab?" In Joachim Matthes (ed.), *Zwischen den Kulturen? Die Sozialwissenschaften vor dem Problem des Kulturvergleichs*. Soziale Welt, Sonderband 8. Göttingen: Vandenhoeck and Ruprecht, 13–36.
Terkessidis, Mark. 1998. *Psychologie des Rassismus*. Opladen: Westdeutscher Verlag
Thies, Christian. 2004. *Einführung in die philosophische Anthropologie*. Einführungen Philosophie. Darmstadt: Wissenschaftliche Buchgesellschaft.
Thiessen, Del and Yoko Umezawa. 1998. "The Sociobiology of Everyday Life. A New Look at a Very Old Novel." *Human Nature* 9(3): 293–320.
Thomas, Alexander (ed.). 2003. *Kulturvergleichende Psychologie*. 2nd ed. Göttingen: Hogrefe.
Thornhill, Randy and Craig T. Palmer. 2000. *A Natural History of Rape. Biological Bases of Sexual Coercion*. Cambridge, MA: The MIT Press.
Thornhill, Randy and Nancy W. Thornhill. 1983. "Human Rape. An Evolutionary Analysis." *Ethology and Sociobiology* 4: 137–73.
Thurnherr, Urs (ed.). 2005. *Menschenbilder und Menschenbildung. Interdisziplinäre Vortragsreihe zu Grundfragen der modernen Anthropologie*. Hodos – Wege bildungsbezogener Ethikforschung in Philosophie und Theologie 3. Frankfurt am Main: Peter Lang Verlag.
Tinbergen, Nikolaas. 1963. "On Aims and Methods of Ethology." *Zeitschrift für Tierpsychologie* 20: 410–33.
Todorov, Tzvetan. 1993. *On Human Diversity. Nationalism, Racism and Exoticism in French Thought*. Cambridge, MA: Harvard University Press. (Convergences. Inventories of the Present) Originally *Nous et les autres. La réflexion Francaise sur la diversité humaine*, Paris: Éditions du Seuil, 1989.
Tomasello, Michael. 1999. *The Cultural Origins of Human Cognition*. Cambridge, MA, and London: Harvard University Press.
———. 2004. "The Human Adaptation for Culture." In Franz M. Wuketits and Christoph Antweiler (eds.), *Handbook of Evolution*, vol. 1: *The Evolution of Human Societies and Cultures*. Weinheim: Wiley-VCH, 1–23.
———. 2006. "Why Don't Apes Point?" In Nicholas J. Enfield and Stephen C. Levinson (eds.), *Roots of Human Sociality. Culture, Cognition and Interaction*. Wenner-Gren International Symposium Series. Oxford and New York: Berg Publishers, 506–24.
Tomberg, Friedrich. 1978. "Menschliche Natur in historisch-materialistischer Definition." In Georg Rückriem (ed.), *Historischer Materialismus und menschliche Natur*. Sudien zur Dialektik, Kleine Bibliothek 109. Cologne: Pahl-Rugenstein Verlag, 42–79.
Tönnies, Sibylle. 2001. *Der westliche Universalismus. Die Denkwelt der Menschenrechte*. 3rd ed. Opladen: Westdeutscher Verlag.
Tooby, John and Leda Cosmides. 1992. "The Psychological Foundations of Culture." In Jerome H. Barkow, Leda Cosmides, and John Tooby (eds.), *The Adapted Mind. Evolutionary Psychology and the Generation of Culture*. New York and Oxford: Oxford University Press, 19–136.
———. 2001. "Does Beauty Build Adapted Minds? Toward an Evolutionary Theory of Aesthetics, Fiction and the Arts." *Substance. A Review of Theory and Literary Criticism* 30(1-2): 6–27.
Tooten, Ralf. 2002. *Augen der Weisheit. Das ituelle Gesicht der Religionen*. Freiburg: Herder Verlag.

Trabant, Jürgen. 2003. *Mithridates im Paradies. Kleine Geschichte des Sprachdenkens.* Munich: C. H. Beck.

Triandis, Harry C. 1978. "Some Universals of Social Behavior." *Personality and Social Psychology Bulletin* 4: 1–16.

Trommsdorff, Gisela. 2007. "Entwicklung im kulturellen Kontext." In Gisela Trommsdorff, and Hans-Joachim Kornadt (eds.), *Enzyklopädie der Psychologie.* Themenbereich C, Theorie und Forschung, Serie 7, Kulturvergleichende Psychologie, vol. 2: *Erleben und Handeln im kulturellen Kontext.* Göttingen: Hogrefe, 435–519.

Tschohl, Peter. 1984. "Interkultureller Umgang." Cologne: Universität zu Köln, Institut für Völkerkunde. Sommersemester 1984 (seminar transcript by author CA).

Türk, Hans J. 1994. "Zwischen Universalismus und Partikularismus: Zur politischen Ethik des Kommunitarismus." *Stimmen der Zeit* 212(107): 537–45.

Turke, Paul. 1996. "Nepotism." In David Levinson and Melvin Ember (eds.), *Encyclopedia of Cultural Anthropology.* New York: Henry Holt and Company, 853–55.

Turner, Jonathan H. and Alexandra Maryansky. 2005. *Incest. Origins of the Taboo.* Boulder, CO, and London: Paradigm Publishers.

Turner, Victor Witter. 1974. *Dramas, Fields, and Metaphors. Symbolic Action in Human Society.* Ithaca, NJ: Cornell University Press.

Tylor, Andrea B. and Michele L. Goldsmith. 2003. "Introduction: Gorilla Biology: Multiple Perspectives on Variation within A Genus." In Tylor, Andrea B. and Michele L. Goldsmith (eds.), *Gorilla Biology. A Multidisciplinary Perspective.* Cambridge: Cambridge University Press, 1–8. Tyler, Edward B. 1871. Culture

Uhl, Matthias. 2009. *Medien, Gehirn, Evolution. Mensch und Medienkultur verstehen. Eine transdisziplinäre Medienanthropologie.* Medienumbrüche, 43. Bielefeld: Transcript Verlag.

Uhl, Matthias and Keval J. Kumar. 2004. *Indischer Film. Eine Einführung.* Bielefeld: Transkript Verlag.

Ulrich, Roger. 1993. "Biophilia, Biophobia, and Natural Landscapes." In Stephen R. Kellert and Edward Osborne Wilson (eds.), *The Biophilia Hypothesis.* Washington, DC: Island Press/Shearwater Books."Universalien der Musikwahrnehmung." 2008. Retrieved 19 September 2008 from http://de.wikipedia.org/wiki/ Universalien der Musikwahrnehmung.

Valdés-Pérez, Raúl E. and Vladimir Pericliev. 1999. "Computer Enumeration of Significant Implicational Universals of Kinship Terminology." *Cross-Cultural Research* 33(2): 162–74.

Valjavec, Friedrich Alexander. 2003. *Diversitätsstudien. Ethno-ökologische Argumente.* Schriften zur Ethno-Anthropologie 4. Montella: Vivarium Novum and Munich: Akademischer Verlag.

Van Damme, Wilfried A. 1996. *Beauty in Context. Towards an Anthropological Approach to Aesthetics.* Philosophy of History and Culture 17. Leiden: E. J. Brill.

———. 2000. "Universality and Particularity in Visual Aesthetics." In Neil Roughley (ed.), *Being Humans. Anthropological Universality and Particularity in Transdisciplinary Perspectives.* Berlin and New York: Walter de Gruyter, 258–83.

Van der Dennen, Johan M. G. 2006. "A Critical Appraisal of Sanderson's Social Evolution of Human Warfare." Lecture, Conference "The Evolution of Human Sociality," Innsbruck, 8–10 June 2006.

Van der Walt, Sibylle. 2006. "Die Last der Vergangenheit und die kulturrelativistische Kritik an den Menschenrechten. Ursprung und Folgen der westlichen Alteritätsobsession." *Saeculum* 57(2): 231–53.

Van de Vijver, J. R. Fons, and Ype H. Poortinga. 1982. "Cross-Cultural Generalization and Universality." *Journal of Cross-Cultural Psychology* 13(4): 387–408.

Van de Vijver, J. R. Fons, and Kwok Leung. 1997. *Methods and Data Analysis for Cross-Cultural Research*. Cross-Cultural Psychology Series. Thousand Oaks, CA: Sage Publications.

Van de Vijver, J. R. Fons, Athanasios Chasiotis, and Seger M. Breugelmans (eds.). 2011. *Fundamental Questions in Cross-Cultural Psychology*. Cambridge: Cambridge University Press.

Van Gennep, Arnold. (1909) 1960. *The Rites of Passage*. London: Routledge and Kegan Paul.

Van Hemert, Dianne D. A. 2003. *Patterns of Cross-Cultural Differences in Psychology. A Meta-Analytic Approach*. Amsterdam: Dutch University Press.

Van Ijzendoorn, Marinus and A. Sagi. 2002. "Cross-Cultural Patterns of Attachment: Universal and Contextual Determinants." In Jude Cassidy and Phillip R. Shaver (eds.), *Handbook of Attachment. Theory, Research and Clinical Applications*. New York: The Guilford Press, 713–34.

Van Schaik, Carel, Marc Ancrenaz, Gwendolyn Borgen, Birute Galdikas, Cheryl D. Knott, Ian Singleton, Akira Suzuki, Sri Suci Utami, and Michelle Merrill. 2003. "Orangutan Cultures and the Evolution of Material Culture." *Science* 299: 102–5.

Van Schaik, Carel and Robert O. Deaner. 2003. "Life History and Cognitive Evolution in Primates." In Frans B. M. De Waal and Peter L. Tyack (eds.), *Animal Social Complexity. Intelligence, Culture, and Individualized Societies*. Cambridge, MA, and London: Harvard University Press, 5–25.

Van Schaik, Carel and Perry van Duijnhoven. 2004. *Among Orangutans. Red Apes and the Rise of Human Culture*. Cambridge, MA: The Belknap Press of Harvard University Press.

v. d. Pfordten, Dietmar. 1996. *Ökologische Ethik. Zur Rechtfertigung menschlichen Verhaltens gegenüber der Natur*. Rowohlts Enzyklopädie 567. Reinbek bei Hamburg: Rowohlt Taschenbuch Verlag.

Vico, Giovanni Battista. (1725) 1990. *Prinzipien einer Neuen Wissenschaft über die gemeinsame Natur der Völker*. Hamburg: Felix Meiner Verlag.

Viswanathan, Gauri. 1989. *Masks of Conquest: Literary Study and British Rule in India*. New York: Columbia University Press.

Vivelo, Frank Robert. 1994. *Cultural Anthropology. A Basic Introduction*. New York: McGraw-Hill. Reprint. Originally *Cultural Anthropology Handbook. A Basic Introduction*. Lanham, MD.: University Press of America, 1978.

Voegelin, Eric. 2004. *Das ökonomische Zeitalter. Weltherrschaft und Philosophie*. Munich: Wilhelm Fink.

Vogel, Christian. 1986. "Von der Natur des Menschen in der Kultur." In Hans Rössner (ed.), *Der ganze Mensch. Aspekte einer pragmatischen* Anthropologie. Munich: Deutscher Taschenbuch Verlag, 29–46.

———. *Anthropologische Spuren. Zur Natur des Menschen*. Ed. Volker Sommer. Edition Universitas. Stuttgart: Hirzel Verlag.

Vogel, Christian and Lutz Eckensberger. 1988. "Arten und Kulturen – Der vergleichende Ansatz." In Klaus Immelmann, Klaus R. Scherer, Christian Vogel, and Peter Scxhmoock (eds.), *Psychobiologie. Grundlagen des Verlhaltens*. Stuttgart: Gustav Fischer Verlag and Weinheim and Munich: Psychologie Verlags-Union, 563–606.

Vogler, Christopher. 1998. *The Writer's Journey. Mythic Structures for Writers*. Studio City: Michael Wiese Productions and London: Macmillan.

Voland, Eckart. 2000. "Natur oder Kultur? Eine wissenschaftliche Jahrhundertdiskussion entspannt sich." In Siegfried Fröhlich (ed.), *Kultur – ein interdisziplinäres Kolloquium zur Begrifflichkeit.* Halle (Saale), 18–21 February 1999. Halle, Saale: Landesamt für Archäologie – Landesmuseum für Vorgeschichte – Sachsen-Anhalt, 41–53.

———. 2001. "Ziele, Chancen und Grenzen weltbürgerlicher Erziehung. Kritische Zwischenrufe eines Soziobiologen in eine pädagogische Debatte." In Siegrid Görgens, Annette Scheunpflug, and Krassimir Stojanov (eds.), *Universalistische Moral und weltbürgerliche Erziehung – Die Herausforderung der Globalisierung im Horizont der modernen Evolutionsforschung.* Frankfurt am Main: Verlag für Interkulturelle Kommunikation, 326–40.

———. 2003. "Aesthetic Preferences in the World of Artifacts. Adaptations For the Evaluation of 'Honest Signals'?" In Eckart Voland and Karl Grammer (eds.), *Evolutionary Asthetics.* Berlin: Springer Verlag, 239–59.

Voland, Eckart, Athanasios Chasiotis, and Wulf Schiefenhövel (eds.). 2005. *Grandmotherhood. The Evolutionary Significance of the Second Half of Female Life.* New Brunswick, NJ: Rutgers University Press.

Voland, Eckart and Karl Grammer (eds.). 2003. *Evolutionary Aesthetics.* Berlin: Springer Verlag.

Voland, Eckart and Wulf Schiefenhövel (eds.). 2009. *The Biological Evolution of Religious Mind and Behavior.* The Frontiers Collection. Heidelberg: Springer Verlag.

Volkswagenstiftung. 2014. Retrieved 12 February 2014 from http://www.volkswagenstiftung.de/service/presse.html?datum=20080731).

Wahl, Klaus. 2000. *Kritik der soziologischen Vernunft. Sondierungen zu einer Tiefensoziologie.* Weilerswist: Velbrück Wissenschaft.

Waldstein, Anna and Cameron Adams. 2006. "The Interface between Medical Anthropology and Medical Ethnobiology." In Roy Ellen (ed.), *Ethnobiology and the Science of Humankind.* Malden, MA: Blackwell Publishing and Royal Anthropological Institute (*Journal of the Royal Anthropological Institute,* Special Issue, 1), 117–45.

Wallace, Anthony F. C. 1961. "The Psychic Unity of Human Groups." In Bert Kaplan (ed.), *Studying Personality Cross-Culturally.* New York: Harper and Row, 129–63.

Wallbott, Harald G. 2003. "Nonverbale Kommunikation im Kulturvergleich." In Alexander Thomas (ed.), *Kulturvergleichende Psychologie.* Göttingen: Hogrefe, 415–32.

Wallbott, Harald G. and Klaus R. Scherer. 1986. "How Universal and Specific Is Emotional Experience? Evidence From 27 Countries on Five Continents." *Social Science Information* 25: 763–95.

———. 1989. "Gefühle ohne Grenzen." *Psychologie Heute* 16(4): 42–47.

Wallerstein, Immanuel Maurice. 2007. *Die Barberei der anderen. Europäischer Universalismus.* Taschenbücher 554. Berlin: Wagenbach Verlag. Originally *European Universalism. The Rhetoric of Power,* New York and London: The New Press, 2006.

Wallin, Nils L., Björn Merker, and Steven Brown (eds.). 2000. *The Origins of Music.* Cambridge, MA, and London: The MIT Press.

Walzer, Michael. 1996. *Lokale Kritik – globale Standards. Zwei Formen moralischer Auseinandersetzung.* Rotbuch Rationen. Berlin: Rotbuch Verlag.

Warburg, Aby Moritz. (1929) 2008. *Der Bilderatlas Mnemosyne.* 3rd ed. Ed. Martin Warnke, with Claudia Brink. Gesammelte Schriften. Berlin Akademie Verlag.

Wassmann, Jürg. 1993. *Das Ideal des leicht gebeugten Menschen. Eine ethno-kognitive Analyse der Yupno in Papua-New Guinea.* Berlin: Dietrich Reimer Verlag.

———. 2006. "Kognitive Ethnologie." In Hans Fischer and Bettina Beer (eds.), *Ethnologie. Einführung und Überblick.* Berlin: Dietrich Reimer Verlag, 323–40.

Watts, Ian. 2005. "'Time, Too, Grows on the Moon': Some Evidence For Knight's Theory of a Human Universal." In Wendy James and David Mills (eds.), *The Qualities of Time. Anthropological Approaches.* Oxford and New York: Berg Publishers, 95–118.

Wax, Murray. 1984. "Religion as Universal: Tribulations of An Anthropological Enterprise." *Zygon* 19(1): 5-20.
Weber, Wolfgang E. J. 2001. "Universalgeschichte." In Michael Maurer (ed.), *Aufriß der historischen Wissenschaften*, vol. 2: *Räume*. Stuttgart: Philipp Reclam Jr., 15-98.
Weber-Schäfer, Peter. 1997. "'Eurozentrismus' contra 'Universalismus'. Über die Möglichkeit, nicht-europäische Kulturen zu verstehen." In Manfred Brocker and Heino Heinrich Nau (eds.), *Ethnozentrismus. Möglichkeiten und Grenzen des interkulturellen Dialogs*. Darmstadt: Wissenschaftliche Buchgesellschaft, 241-55.
———. 1998. "Wie verschieden sind Kulturen wirklich? Über die Universalität des Spiels." In Stanca Scholz-Cionca (ed.), *Japan, Reich der Spiele*. Munich: Iudicium Verlag, 33-46.
Wehler, Joachim. 1990. *Grundriß eines rationalen Weltbildes*. Stuttgart: Philip Reclam jun. Jr.
Weiner, James F., Howard Morphy, Joanna Overing, Jeremy Coote, and Peter Gow. 1996. "1993 Debate: Aesthetics Is a Cross-Cultural Category." In Tim Ingold (ed.), *Key Debates in Anthropology*. London and New York: Routledge, 249-93.
Weingart, Peter, Sandra D. Mitchell, Peter J. Richerson, and Sabine Maasen. 1997. *Human by Nature. Between Biology and the Social Sciences*. Mahwah, NJ, and London: Lawrence Earlbaum Associates.
Weinke, Kurt and Anton Grabner-Haider (eds.). 1993. *Menschenbilder im Diskurs. Orientierungen für die Zukunft*. Graz: Leykam Buchverlagsgesellschaft.
Weinrich, Harald. 1986. "Das erste Gesetz des guten Tones. Gibt es Universalien der Höflichkeit." *Frankfurter Allgemeine Zeitung* (11 June), S. N5.
Weiss, Dieter 2002. "Kultur und Entwicklung. Entwicklung ist das, was geschieht, wenn Kreativität sich entfalten kann." In Reinhold E. Thiel (ed.), *Neue Ansätze der Entwicklungstheorie*. Bonn: Deutsche Stiftung für internationale Entwicklung, 366-78.
Weiß, Johannes. 2005. "Universalismus der Gleichheit, Universalismus der Differenz." In Ilja Srubar, Joachim Renn, and Ulrich Wenzel (eds.), *Kulturen vergleichen. Sozial- und kulturwissenschaftliche Grundlagen und Kontroversen*. Wiesbaden: Verlag für Sozialwissenschaften, 79-89.
Welker, Lorenz. 2007. "Kategorien musikVlischen verhaltens in evolutionärer Perspektive. Geschlechtsdifferenzen, Universalien und ein Schichtenmodell musikalischer Wahrnehmung." In Karl Eibl, Katja Mellmann, and Rüdiger Zymner (eds.), *Im Rücken der Kulturen*. Poetogenesis, 5. Frankfurt am Main: Mentis-Verlag, 271-90.
Welsch, Wolfgang. 1992. "Transkulturalität. Lebensformen nach der Auflösung der Kulturen." *Information Philosophie* 2: 5-20.
———. 2004. "Wandlungen im humanen Selbstverständnis." In Heinrich Schmidinger and Clemens Sedmak (eds.), *Der Mensch - ein „animal rationale"? Vernunft - Kognition - Intelligenz*. Topologien des Menschlichen 1. Darmstadt: Wissenschaftliche Buchgesellschaft, 48-70.
———. 2006. "Über den Besitz und Erwerb von Gemeinsamkeiten." In Claudia Brinkmann, Hermann Josef Scheidgen, Tobias Voßhenrich, and Markus Wirtz (eds.), *Tradition und Traditionsbruch zwischen Skepsis und Dogmatik. Interkulturelle philosophische Perspektiven*. Studien zur Interkulturellen Philosophie 16. Amsterdam and New York: Rodopi, 113-45.
———. 2012. *Homo mundanus. Jenseits der anthropischen Denkform der Moderne*. Weilerswist: Velbrück Wissenschaft.
Welzer, Harald. 2004. "Die fünfte Dimension: Intersubjektivität." In Friedrich Jaeger and Jürgen Straub (eds.), *Was ist der Mensch, was ist Geschichte? Annäherungen an eine kulturwissenschaftliche Anthropologie. Jörn Rüsen zum 65. Geburtstag*. Bielefeld: Transcript, 363-70.

Wenker, Marie-Claude. 2001. *So leben sie. Familien aus 16 Ländern zeigen, wie sie wohnen.* Mühlheim: Verlag an der Ruhr.
Wenzel, Ulrich. 2005. "Die ontogenetische Menschwerdung." In Justin Stagl and Wolfgang Reinhardt (eds.), *Grenzen des Menschseins. Probleme einer Definition des Menschlichen.* Veröffentlichungen des Instituts für Historische Anthropologie 8. Bonn: Böhlau, 53–77.
Werlen, Iwar. 2002. *Sprachliche Relativität. Eine problemorientierte Einführung.* Tübingen und Basel: A. Francke Verlag.
Werner, Oswald and G. Mark Schoepfle. 1987a. *Systematic Fieldwork,* vol. 1: *Foundations of Ethnography and Interviewing.* Newbury Park, CA: Sage Publications.
———. 1987b. *Systematic Fieldwork,* vol. 2. *Ethnography and Data Management.* Newbury Park, CA: Sage Publications.
Wernhart, Karl R. 1986. "Religious Beliefs per se: A Human Universality." *Anthropos* 81: 648–52.
———. 1987. "Universalia humana et cultura. Zur Frage von Mensch, Kultur und Umwelt." *Mitteilungen der Anthropologischen Gesellschaft in Vienna* 117: 17–25.
———. 2001. "Von der Strukturgeschichte zum transkulturellen Forschungsansatz. Ethnohistorie und Kulturgeschichte im neuen Selbstverständnis." In Karl R. Wernhart and Werner Zips (eds.), *Ethnohistorie. Rekonstruktion und Kulturkritik: Eine Einführung.* 2nd ed. Promedia Forschung. Vienna: Promedia Druck- und Verlagsgesellschaft, 41–54.
———. 2004. *Ethnische Religionen. Universale Elemente des Religiösen.* Grundwissen Religion, Topos Plus Taschenbücher 545. Kevelaer: Verlagsgemeinschaft Topos Plus.
Wescott, Roger W. 1970. "Of Guilt and Gratitude. Further Reflections on Human Uniqueness." *The Dialogist. A Journal of Dialogue in Theory and Practice* 2(3): 69–85.
Whaley, Lindsay J. 1997. *An Introduction to Typology. The Unity and Diversity of Language.* Thousand Oaks, CA: Sage Publications.
Wheeler, Michael, John Ziman, and Margaret A. Boden (eds.). 2002. *The Evolution of Cultural Entities.* Proceedings of the British Academy 112. Oxford: Oxford University Press for the British Academy.
White, Geoffrey M. 1980. "Conceptual Universals in Interpersonal Language." *American Anthropologist* 82(4): 759–81.
White, Leslie A. 1949. *The Science of Culture. A Study of Man and Civilization.* New York: Farrar and Strauss.
Whitehead, Harriet. 2000. *Food Rules. Hunting, Sharing, and Tabooing Game in Papua New Guinea.* Ann Arbor: The University of Michigan Press.
Whiten, Andrew. 2003. "Theory of Mind." In Lynn Nadel (ed.), *Encyclopedia of Cognitive Science,* vol. 4: *Similarity – Zombies.* London: Nature Publishing Group, Macmillan, 376–79.
Whiten, Andrew and Richard W. Byrne (eds.). 1997. *Machiavellian Intelligence II: Evaluations and Extensions.* Cambridge: Cambridge University Press.
Whiten, Andrew, Robert A. Hinde, Christopher B. Stringer, and Kevin N. Laland (eds.). 2012. *Culture Evolves.* Oxford Oxford University Press.
Whiting, Beatrice B. and Carolyn P. Edwards. 1988. *Children of Different Worlds. The Formation of Social Behavior.* Cambridge, MA: Harvard University Press.
Whiting, Beatrice B. and John W. M. Whiting. (1975) 2014. *Children in Six Cultures. A Psycho-Cultural Analysis.* With Richard Longabaugh. Cambridge, MA: Harvard University Press.
Whorf, Benjamin Lee. 1956. *Thought and Reality.* Cambridge, MA: The MIT Press.
Wiegand, Wilfried. 1999. "Warum muß die Politik viele Kulturen verstehen, Herr von Barloewen?" Interview. *Frankfurt am Mainer Allgemeine Magazin* (May): 42–43.

Wierzbicka, Anna. 1986. "Human Emotions: Universal or Culture-Specific?" *American Anthropologist* 88: 584–94.
———. 1992. *Semantics, Culture, and Cognition. Universal Human Concepts in Culture-Specific Configurations*. New York and Oxford: Oxford University Press.
———. 1995. "Kisses, Handshakes, Bows: The Semantics of Nonverbal Communication." *Semiotica* 103(3–4): 207–52.
———. 1999. *Emotions across Languages and Cultures. Diversity and Universals*. Studies in Emotion and Social Interaction. Cambridge: Cambridge University Press.
———. 2002. "The Conceptual System in the Human Mind. Lingua Mentalis." *Humboldt Kosmos* 78: 20–21.
———. 2005. "Empirical Universals of Language as a Basis for the Study of Other Human Universals and as a Tool for Exploring Cross-Cultural Differences." *Ethos* 33(2): 256–91.
Wieviorka. Michel. 2003. *Kulturelle Differenzen und kollektive Identitäten*. Hamburg: Hamburger Edition HIS.
Wilk, Richard R. 2007. *Economies and Culture. Foundations of Economic Anthropology*. 2nd ed. Boulder, CO: Westview Press.
Wilk, Stan. 1985. "Universals of Culture." In Roger Pearson (ed.), *Anthropological Glossary*. Malabar, FL: Robert E. Krieger, 396.
Williams, Drid (ed.). 2000. *Anthropology and Movement. Searching for Origins*. Readings in the Anthropology of Movement 1. Lanham, MD and London: The Scarecrow Press.
———. 2004. *Anthropology and the Dance. Ten Lectures*. Urbana, IL, and Chicago: University of Illinois Press. Originally *Ten Lectures on Theories of the Dance*, Methuen, NJ: The Scarecrow Press, 1991.
Williams, John E., R. C. Satterwhite, and D. L. Best. 1999. "Pancultural Gender Stereotypes Revisited: The Five Factor Model." *Sex Roles* 40: 513–25.
Wills, Christopher. 1996. *Das vorauseilende Gehirn. Die Evolution der menschlichen Sonderstellung*. Frankfurt am Main: S. Fischer Verlag. Originally *Children of Prometheus. The Accelerating Pace of Human Evolution*, New York: Perseus Books, 1999 and London: Allen Lane, 1999.
Wilson, David S. 2002. *Darwin's Cathedrals. Evolution, Religion and the Nature of Society*. Chicago: The University of Chicago Press.
Wilson, David S. and Elliott Sober. 1998. *Unto Others. The Evolution and Psychology of Unselfish Behavior*. Cambridge, MA, and London: Harvard University Press.
Wilson, Edward O. 1975. *Sociobiology. The New Synthesis*. Cambridge, MA, and London: The Belknap Press of Harvard University Press.
———. 1984. *Biophilia. The Human Bond with Other Species*. Cambridge, MA: Harvard University Press.
———. 1998. *Consilience. The Unity of Knowledge*. New York: Alfred A. Knopf.
———. 1999. *Des Lebens ganze Fülle. Eine Liebeserklärung an die Wunder der Natur*. Munich: Claassen Verlag. Originally *Naturalist,* Washington, DC: Island Press, 1994.
———. 2004. *On Human Nature*. 2nd ed. Cambridge, MA: Harvard University Press.
Wimmer, Andreas. 1997. "Die Pragmatik der kulturellen Produktion. Anmerkungen zur Ethnozentrismusproblematik aus ethnologischer Sicht." In Manfred Brocker and Heino Heinrich Nau (eds.), *Ethnozentrismus. Möglichkeiten und Grenzen des interkulturellen Dialogs*. Darmstadt: Wissenschaftliche Buchgesellschaft, 121–40.
Winch, Peter. 1958. *The Idea of Social Science and Its Relation to Philosophy*. London: Routledge and Kegan Paul.
Winkelman, Michael. 2000. "Review of Klass and Weissgrau und zu Cunningham." *American Ethnologist* 102(2): 380–82.

Winkler, Eike and Joseph Schweikadt. 1982. *Expedition Mensch. Streifzüge durch die Anthropologie*. Vienna and Heidelberg: Ueberreuter.
Winston, Robert. 2004. *Human. The Definitive Visual Guide*. London: Dorling Kindersley
Wiredu, Kwasi. 1996. *Cultural Universals and Particulars. An African Perspective*. African Systems of Thought. Bloomington and Indianapolis: Indiana University Press.
———. 2001. "Gibt es kulturelle Universalien?" In Peter M. Hejl (ed.), *Universalien und Konstruktivismus*. Frankfurt am Main: Suhrkamp Verlag, 76–94. Originally in *The Monist* 78(1), 1995.
Wissler, Clark. (1923) 1965. *Man and Culture*. New York: Johnson.
Witkowski, Stanley R. 1996. "Color Terminology." In David Levinson and Melvin Ember (eds.), *Encyclopedia of Cultural Anthropology*. New York: Henry Holt, 218–22.
Witkowski, Stanley R. and Cecil H. Brown. 1982. "Whorf and Universals of Color Nomenclature." *Journal of Anthropological Research* 38: 411–20.
Wittgenstein, Ludwig (1958) 1982. *Philosophische Untersuchungen*. Frankfurt am Main: Suhrkamp Verlag.
Wolf, Arthur P. 1993. "Westermarck Redivivus." *Annual Reviews of Anthropology* 22: 157–75.
Wolf, Arthur P. and William H. Durham (eds.). 2005. *Inbreeding, Incest and the Incest Taboo. The State of Knowledge at the Turn of the Century*. 2nd ed. Stanford, CA: Stanford University Press.
Wolters, Gereon. 1999. "Darwinistische Menschenbilder." In Anna Katharina Reichardt and Eric Kubli (eds.), *Menschenbilder*. Bern: Peter Lang Europäischer Verlag der Wissenschaften, 95–115.
Wood, Bernard. 2006. *Human Evolution. A Very Short Introduction*. Very Short Introductions. Oxford: Oxford University Univesity Press.
Workman, Lance and Will Reader. 2014. *Evolutionary Psychology. An Introduction*. 3rd ed. Cambridge: Cambridge University Press.
World Commission on Culture and Development. 1995. *Our Creative Diversity*. Paris: UNESCO.
Worsley, Peter. 1997. *Knowledges. Culture, Counterculture, Subculture*. London: Profile Books and New York: The New Press.
Wrangham, Richard W., William C. McGrew, Frans B. M. De Waal, and Paul G. Heltne (eds.). 1994. *Chimpanzee Cultures*. Cambridge, MA: Harvard University Press.
Wright, Robert. 1994. *The Moral Animal. Why We Are the Way We Are. The New Science of Evolutionary Psychology*. New York: Pantheon Books.
Wrightsman, Lawrence S. 1975. *Assumptions about Human Nature. A Social-Psychological Approach*. Monterrey, CA: Brooks/Cole Publishing.
Wrong, Dennis H. 1999. *The Oversocialized Conception of Man*. New Brunswick, NJ, and London: Transaction Publishers.
Wuketits, Franz Manfred. 2003. "Die Grenzen der Moral. Moralischer Universalismus im Lichte der Evolutionären Ethik." In Susanne Popp and Johanna Forster (eds.), *Curriculim Weltgeschichte. Globale Zugänge für den Geschichtsunterricht*. Forum Historisches Lernen. Schwalbach/Taunus: Wochenschau Verlag, 122–33.
Wuketits, Franz Manfred and Christoph Antweiler (eds.). 2004. *Handbook of Evolution*, vol. 1: *The Evolution of Cultures and Societies*. Weinheim: Wiley-VCH.
Wulf, Christoph (ed.). 1997. *Vom Menschen. Handbuch Historische Anthropologie*. Beltz Handbuch. Weinheim and Basel: Beltz Verlag.
———. 2013. *Anthropology. A Continental Perspective*. Chicago and London: The University of Chicago Press. Originally *Anthropologie. Geschichte – Kultur – Philosophie*. Reinbek bei Hamburg: Rowohlt Taschenbuch Verlag.

Xanthopoulos, John A. 2006. "Universals in Cultures." In H. James Birx (ed.), *Encyclopedia of Anthropology*, vol. 5. Thousand Oaks, CA: Sage Publications, 2,244–47.
Zahavi, Amotz. 1975. "Mate Selection: A Selection for Handicap." *Journal of Theoretical Biology* 53: 205–14.
Zahavi, Amotz and Avishag Zahavi. 1997. *The Handicap Principle. A Missing Piece of Darwin's Puzzle*. New York and Oxford: Oxford University Press.
Zeier, Hans. 1980. "Zur Evolution von Gehirn und Geist." In John Eccles and Hans Zeier, *Gehirn und Geist. Biologische Erkenntnisse über Vorgeschichte, Wesen und Zukunft des Menschen*. Munich: Kindler, 15–124.
Zijlmans, Kitty and Wilfried A. van Damme (eds.). 2008. *World Art Studies. Exploring Concepts and Approaches*. Amsterdam: Valiz Publishers.
Zipf, George Kingsley. (1948) 1965. *Human Behavior and the Principle of Least Effort*. New York: Hafner.
Žižek, Slavoj. 2008. *In Defense of Lost Causes*. London and New York: Verso.
Zuberbühler, Klaus. 2006. "Kulturvergleichende Psychologie." In Kurt Pawlik (ed.), *Handbuch Psychologie*. Heidelberg: Springer Medizin Verlag, 369–83.

Index

A

absolutism, vs. universalism, 207–210, 262
Abu-Lughod, Lila 60, 207–8, 251
Acculturation, 224–25
actor concepts, 120, 130
Adams, William Y., 62, 121
adaptation, 35, 63, 102, 259. *See also* explanations: adaptionistic, evolutionary
    biotic, 235
    cognitive, 87
    culturally caused maladaptation, 235
    pan–adaptionism, 235
    relation to genetic causes, 212
    universality as a clue, to 233
Adorno, Theodor W., 80
address, forms of, 115
aesthetics, 103–7. *See also* art
age, categories of, 115
aggression, 92
    male involvement, 147–48
    violence between individuals within societies, 160
Aginsky, Burt W., 226–7
Aginsky, Ethel S., 226–7
agriculture, origins and diffusion of, 226, 230
alliance, 92, 111, 189–90
alterity, 51. *See also* othering, difference
Althusser, Louis, 74
altriciality, secondary, 87, 90
altruism, 149, 234, 260
    among kin, 260
    extending beyond relatives, 111
    reciprocal, 111
analogy, 115, 212

Anderson, Richard L., 104–5, 247
animal behavior, study of indicating universals, 234
animal symbolicum, 246
Annan, Kofi, 11
Anthropika, list of binary human designations, 79
Anthropocene, epoch of, 1
anthropocentrism, 20, 176
anthropogenically modified landscapes, 72, 259. *See also* niche construction
anthropological constants, vs. universals, 12, 43–48. *See also* biotic universal
anthropology. *See also* cultural anthropology
    biological anthropology, 54, 71
    cognitive, 27, 112, 198, 239
    contribution in identifying universals, 6
    cultural (*see under* cultural anthropology)
    Darwinian, 237
    historical, 59
    as humanistic science, 3, 17, 52, 56
    negative, 79–80
    philosophical, 73–75, 80, 158, 205
    postmodern, 76, 251
    psychological, 57. *See* also cognition, emotion
    of the senses, 105
anthropomorphism, 78, 90, 190–1
anthropophagy, 161
apomorphic features, 93, 218
Appadurai, Arjun, 208
    arbitrariness, 60
    as key of culture, 60, 69, 95, 213
    of cultural phenomena vs. limited or patterned diversity, 213

archetype, 22, 102
archosis, 227. *See also* diffusion
Arens, William, 161
art, 103–6. *See also* aesthetics
artifacts, 71–72, 87, 226
    cognitive, 87. *See also* ratchet effect
assimilationism, 85
Assmann, Aleida, 63, 80
Atran, Scott, 5, 134, 217
axial age, 171

B
Badiou, Alain, 257
Bailey, Garrick A., 13, 40
Barash, David, 34, 102, 191
Barash, Nanelle R., 102
Barkow, Jerome, 58, 103, 115
Barthes, Roland, 15, 18
Bastian, Adolf, 3
Beck, Ulrich, 24
Benedict, Ruth F., 227
Berger, Peter, 246
Berlin, Brent, 133–4, 140, 160
Berry, Christopher J., 169, 175
Berry, John W., 40, 47, 59, 209
Betzig, Laura, 238
Bhabha, Homi K., 249–50
Bidney, David, 258
Biocultural, 1, 36, 72, 177, 258
biodiversity, 135. *See also* diversity
biology, 65–96
    behavioral, 37
    as (one) cause of universals (*see under* factors causing universals)
    critique of by relativists, 51
    evolutionary, 135, 205, 222
    human, comparative, 31, 89
biophilia, 133–135
biopoetics, 102
biopolitics, 21, 32, 146
biotic universals. *See under* universals: biotic; *see also under* human nature
Blaffer Hrdy, Sarah, 59
Bloch, Maurice, 56, 59, 177, 230, 246
Boas, Franz, 45, 59, 84, 103, 181, 199, 227
body, 83, 93, 214
    body language, 255
    human, 86–87
    mimetic use for understanding, 207
    vs. mind, 71

Boehm, Christopher, 32, 82–83, 114, 120, 211
Bohannan Laura, 100–101
bonding (emotional bonding), 188, 197, 240
Bowlby, John, 197
Boyd, Robert, 259
Boyer, Pascal, 5, 60, 124–28, 201, 212, 225, 237
Brecht, Berthold, 79
Broca's area, 89
Bröckling, Ulrich, 21, 48, 65
Brown, Cecil H., 133
Brown, Donald E., 28–32
    definition of universals, 35
    on grand theory of universals, 32
    holistic representation of universals (*see also* Universal People, The), 32, 177–8
    Human Universals, 31
    on importance of ethnographies, 162
    on near universals, 201
    on sub-universals within ethnocentrism, 32, 118
    slant toward evolutionary biology, 32
    as trained in relativistic tradition, 31
    Universal People, The (chapter) as holistic narrative of universals 32, 177–8
    work apprehended in Europe mostly through Pinker, 32
Brown, Roger, 115
Bruck, Andreas, 4, 44, 47, 153
Burke, Kenneth, 80
Burkert, Walter, 44, 128, 201, 216
Buss, David, 152, 197
Butler, Judith P., 24, 208
    rejecting human nature, 24

C
Campbell, Joseph, 23, 101–2
cannibalism. *See under* anthropophagy
capacities of humans, 72, 80, 190
Carrithers, Michael, 44, 55, 77, 84, 89, 247, 253
    on unacknowledged search for universals in Firth's work on Tikopia, 54–55
    on variation and human nature, 77, 247

Carroll, Joseph, 102–3
cases, 161, 207
    case study, 29, 159–163
    importance of individual cases, 161, 167–68, 185
    relevance of extreme and exotic cases or places, 177
    Western cases, 168 (see also WEIRD people)
Cassirer, Ernst, 246
categorization, 132. See also binary categories, thinking
causes, causation, causal reasoning, 6, 40, 214–18, 232. See also explanation
    faulty causal assumptions, 212, 214–18
Chevron, Marie-France, 4, 41–42
children
    childrearing, 54, 109–14, 162
    natural-history intelligence, 234
    six-cultures study, 188
Chomsky, Noam, 138, 178, 206
Christian, David, on parallels in world history, 163
classification. See under categorization
code-switching, code-mixing in talk, 139
coevolution, 45, 75, 240, 245, 261
    as argument against a fixed human nature, 75
    as complex cause for universals, 238–9
    as Latour's co-production, 261
cognition
    cognitive domains, 132–3
    developmental, stages, 63, 83
    essentialist, 129–33
Cohen, Mark N., 158
colonialist thinking, universalism as, 248–50
color terms, 140
Common Denominator of Cultures, The (Murdock, G.P.), 29
communication functions, 88
communitarian social model, 21
comparison, 180–2. See also method
    and anthropology, 49–51, 56, 257–78
    cross-cultural, intercultural, 3, 178–82, 257
    cross-species, 188
    diachronic, 186
    danger of nostrification, 179
    Galton's problem, 186–7
    implicit, in ethnographies, 57
    intracultural, 94, 181–3
    most-different design, 171, 187–88
    synchronic, 186
    typological, two approaches of, 180–2
    worldwide and systematic, 184–87 (see also Human Relations Area Files)
complexity, societal, 149, 259. See also ultrasociality
concealed ovulation, 90
concept of time and space, 122
conditional universals. See under universals
conflict regulation, 115–7
conformity and nonconformity, 67, 114
Consilience (Wilson, E.O.), 258
constructivism, vs. realism, 36, 55–58, 80, 208, 221
contextualism, 208
contingency, 79, 130. See also history
convergence, 176, 190, 229–33
Coon, Charleton S., 108
cooperation, 81, 88, 108
Cosmides, Leda, 41, 43, 235
cosmogony, 119
cosmology, 119, 122, 250
cosmopolitanism, 21–25
creole languages, 139
criticism on universals research, 243–251. See also universals, universalism
Cronk, Lee, 61, 178
Crook, John H., 38, 42, 84
cross-cultural comparison. See under comparison
cross-species comparison. See under comparison
cultural anthropology, 3–5
    British Social Anthropology, 63, 250–1
    cognitive, 27, 58, 87
    comparative (See under comparison and Murdock)
    ecological, cultural ecology, 28, 171
    economic, 148–150
    focus on difference, 4, 53, 55–58
    German-language, 4
    monographs (see under monograph, anthropological and ethnography)
    national traditions, 51

politicization, 251
psychological, 63, 106
reluctance to study universals, 3
research trends, 3
symbolic, semantic, 56, 77, 243 (*see also* Geertz, Clifford)
textbooks, 12, 40, 57, 147, 200
US-American, 63, 250-1
cultural boundaries, of collectives, ethnic units, 4, 34, 44, 170. *See also* ethnic groups
cultural determinism. *See under* relativism
cultural diversity. *See under* diversity
cultural imperialism, 8, 19, 251
cultural materialism, 56, 120
cultural psychology, 62, 184. *See also* psychology: cultural
cultural relativism, cultural relativity, 58
   as atheoretical, 53, 58-61
   as cultural determinism, 76
   as another reductionism, 76
   as strength of cultural anthropology, 58 (*see also* Geertz)
cultural theory, 22, 42, 66 (*see also* universals)
cultural transfer (intercultural transfer), 225-9
cultural universals. *See under* universals
culturalism, culturalist, vs. naturalism, 205-6
culturalization, 50-52 (*see also* ethnicization)
culture
   ability for biotic capacity, for, 44, 73, 88, 119, 137
   as autonomous phenomenon or level, 72, 75
   cultural reductionism (*see under* cultural relativism)
   culture core (core culture), 28
   culture sciences relative to humanities, 32, 56, 59
   meta-culture, 43
   monadic concept, of 66
   pancultural, 6, 7, 37, 40-43, 65, 215
   popular, 13 (*see also* Family of Man, the)
   as self-cultivation of human nature, 258
   transcultural, transculturation, 238
culturism, 58, 206. *See also* relativism

D

Daly, Martin, 146-148
Darwin, Charles R., 5, 28, 188
Darwinian approaches, 237-8
data collection and analysis. *See also* method
   primary fieldwork data, 187
   quality of, and alleged universals, 159-161, 185-6
   secondary, 186-7
de Waal Frans B., 90, 114, 216
decision making, 120, 220
DeCorse, Christopher R., 34, 62, 173
definition, 32-36
   cross-culturally valid, comparative, transcultural, 165
   of universals (*see under* universals)
Dennett, Daniel C., 37, 287
developmental psychology, 76, 239
Dickens, Peter, 82
difference, 74, 214, 256
   as anthropological orientation, 4, 53, 55-58
   cultural (*see under* ethnicity)
   as "ethnographic dazzle", 1-3
   seen as only environmentally caused, 214
   ignorance of, 248 (*see also* comparison, nostrification)
differentia specifica, 78. *See also* genus proximum
diffusion, 28, 203, 211. *See also* archosis
disciplines, 5, 61, 98, 251
display rules, 144
Dissanayake, Ellen, 39, 84, 104-6, 159, 236, 247
diversity, cultural diversity, 1-3, 193, 206, 256. *See also* difference, ethnographic hyperspace
   as challenged by commonalities among cultures, 263
   between cultures, cross-cultural, inter-cultural, 6
   factors limiting potential diversity, 253-4
   intra-cultural, 65-68, 182-4
   in non-human primates, vs. humans, 93

not to be outplayed by search for universals, 1–3, 6–7
patterns in, 28–32
relation to universality as seen in antiquity and the modern era, 69
division of labor, 13, 34, 95, 198, 230, 259
domestic dog, 196, 200
dualism, binarism, 58
conceptions of humans, 78
concepts in thinking, 130
dichotomic anthropological orientations, 204
good vs. evil polarity and ambivalence, 81–83
Lévi-Strauss on, 238
terminology, 58
Duerr, Hans-Peter, 36, 142
Dupré, John, 36–37, 45
Durham, William H., 60, 222–5
Durkheim, Emile, 78, 81, 126, 196

E
ecstasy, 23, 126, 231
Edgerton, Robert B., 171
Eibl, Karl, 11, 29–30, 88, 9, 107, 173, 223, 229, 259
Eibl-Eibesfeldt, Irenäus, 37, 40, 44, 83, 146, 198. *See also* biotic universals, ethology
Ekman, Paul (and associates), 142–145
Elias, Norbert, 142
Ellen, Roy, 133–35
Ember, Carol, 29, 57, 110, 185–187
Ember, Melvin, 29, 57, 110, 185–187
emic (see also etic), 116, 176, 195
emotions, 142–7, 199
basic, 142, 234
facial expression and recognition, 143
empathy, 51, 91, 109–111
emulation learning, 95, 237
enlightenment, 3, 17, 53, 70
enphronesis, 91, 95
environment, 28, 72, 94, 259–262. *See also* niche construction, anthropocene
epigenetics, 77, 221
epistemics, 70, 133, 205, 250
Eriksen, Thomas Hylland, 36, 42, 70
essentialism, 66, 129–33
ethics, 20–25. *See also* morality

ethical dualism, 118
medical, 21
ethnic groups. *See also* indigenous peoples
ethnicity, 66, 117–8, 123
ethnicization, and nationalism, 50–52
ethnobiology, 133–5, 141
ethnocentrism, ethnocentricity, sociocentrism, 32, 48–51, 117–8, 200–1
ethnography. *See also* monograph
ethnographic hyperspace, 254
fieldwork as important for understanding universals, 263 (*see also* cases)
imaginative, 49
primate (cultural primatology), 89
person–centered, 147
presentation of universals as, 177–8
ethnonym, 117–8
ethnosemantics, 130, 133. *See also* ethnobiology
ethogram, 145, 262
ethology, 37, 190
cognitive, 89
cultural ethology, 37, 89, 117, 213
etic, 116, 176, 195. *See also* emic
derived vs. imposed, 165, 209
etiquette, 110. *See also* politeness
Eurocentrism, 7, 17, 48–9, 115, 161, 168, 247–251. *See also* WEIRD people
Evans-Pritchard, Edward E., 124, 249
everyday discourse and experiences, 108, 137, 167, 229
evolution, 65–96
Marxist-oriented evolutionism, 74, 82
multi-linear (in neoevolutionism), 28
evolutionary biology. *See under* biology
evolutionary ecology, 233
evolutionary psychology, 259–60
examples of universals, 97–155
exogamy rules, 223
experiment. *See under* method
explanations, 211–41. *See also* factors causing universals
adaptionistic, 191
evolutionary, 237
functionalist, 56, 167, 171
generative, 224–5
interactionist, 238–240
naturalistic, 221, 237, 233–238, 258

nonevolutionary, in biology, 238
ontogenetic, 239
proximate and ultimate, four why-
questions, 191, 222–224
selectionist, 225, 236
extrinsic universals. *See under* universals:
extrinsic

F
face. *See* emotions
factors causing universals, 211–42
adaptation and common problem
domains, 233–38
complex causation, 238–40
convergent development, 189
cultural transfer and diffusion,
226–229
function, 229–33
independent invention or innovation,
224–5, 229 (*see also* historical
independence)
other universals (*see under* types of
universals: implicational)
structural implication, 229–33
fairness, 149, 173, 228
family
core family, as widespread, 197
human family as metaphor, 15 (*see
also* Family of Man, The)
unique features of human, 109–10
universal functions, 109
Family of Man, The (exhibition, and
critiques thereof), 14–15
family resemblance, 44–5, 166
female-headed households, 166, 188
Fernández-Armesto, Felipe, 21, 70–1,
85–6, 88, 157, 227
Finnegan, Ruth, 99
fire, use of, 196
Firth, Raymond, 55
folk biology, 123–4, 217
formal universals. *See* universals: formal
forms of address, 115. *See also* etiquette,
and politeness
Forster, Georg Heinrich, 226
Forster, Johann Georg Adam, 2
Foucault, Michel, 59, 79
Fox, J. Robin, 33, 42, 72, 163
Fox, Katie, 2, 4, 41, 107
Frazer, James George, 101, 126, 197

Freud, Sigismund S., 12, 119, 147, 176, 184
Friesen, Wallace V., 44, 142–3
Fuchs, Martin, 52, 249
Fukuyama, Francis, 21, 32, 86
functional social requirements. *See
under* needs: functional; *see under*
ultrasociality
functionalism, 56, 167, 171. *See also*
explanation: functional

G
Galton, Francis, 48, 186–7
Geertz, Clifford J., 53–54
on banal or trivial universals, 246
on empty, tautological and fake
universals, 246
contra notion of human nature, 77
moderate critique on universals, 8,
53–54, 245–7
pro anthropologists as traders of
diversity, 54
radicalized reception, 251
gender, 150–55
and aggression and violence, 147
categories, 150–51
division of labor, 198
ideas and roles, 95
language, 138
generative model, 126, 225
genetics, 19, 36, 217–18
genome, 71, 78, 206
genus proximum vs. differentia specifica, 78
gifts giving, 30, 110, 151–52
Gingrich, Andre, 51, 60, 187
Girard, René, 127
Giri, Ananta Kumar, 24
global history, 163, 226
Godelier, Maurice, 1–2
Goldschmidt, Walter R., 93, 189
Goodenough, Ward H., 27, 164, 167
Gottschall, Jonathan, 102
Gould, Stephen J., 76, 105, 206, 216
grammar, 83, 138, 195, 234. *See also*
Universal Grammar
Greenberg, Joseph H., 118, 180, 201, 229
Greenblatt, Stephen, 59
Greenwood, J. Davyd, 32, 48, 72, 167–69,
177
Gregorian creatures, 87
Griese, Hartmut, 114

H

Habermas, Jürgen, 18, 22, 59, 67–68, 94, 158, 208
handicap principle, 105
Harris, Marvin, 39–40, 54, 214, 217
Hauschild, Thomas, 2, 4, 17, 25, 55, 58–59, 201
hegemonic dominance, 248–49
Hejl, Peter M., 6, 57–58, 78, 103, 174, 194–95, 206, 260
Herder, Johann Gottfried von, 20, 57, 66
Héritier, Françoise, 33
hermeneutics, 205
Herskovits, Melville J., 59, 225
Heymer, Armin, 37
Hinde, Robert P., 43, 175, 193, 233
historical independence, 163–4, 180, 186–87, 218, 230, 261. *See also* factors causing universals
historical materialism, 74, 121
historically new universals. *See under* universals: historically new
historicity, 74–75
Hobart, Mark, 249
Hobbes, Thomas, 81, 149
Hockett, Charles F., 142, 171–75, 200
Hogan, Patrick Colm, 60, 102, 201
Holenstein, Elmar, 182, 202–3, 213, 226–27, 231–32, 259
holism, 66. *See also* Brown, D.: holistic representation of universals
homo absconditus, 80
homo duplex, 78
homo mundanus, 78
homo sapiens, 78–79, 84–95
homology, 115, 189, 224
homosexuality, 34, 50
Hopi time, 32, 122
Horgan, John, 214–16, 225,
Horton, Robin, 125–26, 165
humankind, mankind, 11–25
human nature, 65–96, 2, 6, 8, 12
    conceptions, as deterministic or reactionary, 74, 83
    as dynamic and fundamentally biocultural, 72
    human condition, universal conditions of human existence, 2, 13, 73, 107, 239, 249
    positions rejecting human nature, 36–37
Human Relations Area Files (HRAF), 29, 160, 185–86
human rights, 17–21, 253
human sciences, 5, 76, 180. *See also* humanities
    basic orientations, 205–6, 208, 262
    related to humanities, 253–262
human uniqueness, 92. *See also homo sapiens*, humans
human universals. *See under* universals
Human Universals (Brown, D.), 31. *See also* Brown, Donald E.
humanistic anthropology. *See under* anthropology
humanities, 2, 208, 257
    dichotomy vs. sciences, 61, 76, 208
    as focused on particulars, 2
    as focused on WEIRD people, 2
    and lack of research on universals, 7
humans, 65–96. *See also* human nature
    essence of, 22, 76, 80, 162, 245
    genus proximum vs. differentia specifica, 78
    human commonalities caused by biology, 51 (*see also* biotic universals)
    species traits, 65–96, 233–238 (*see also* human uniqueness, and biotic universals)
hunter-gatherer societies (foragers), 73, 81, 162, 235
Huxley, Julian, 93

I

identity
    collective, 110, 117, 131, 141 (*see also* ethnicity)
    identity politics, 1 (*see also* ethnicization)
    personal, 120
implicational universals. *See under* types of universals universals: implicational
incest, 30, 164, 200–2, 222–225
    avoidance, 110, 224, 226
    competing and complementing explanations, 222–224
    as prohibition not existing among animals, 191

taboo, 12, 30, 99, 191
inclusive fitness, 225, 255. *See also* evolutionary explanation
indigenous peoples, 171. *See also* ethnic groups, ethnicity
individualism, 67, 81-83, 235
Ingold, Tim, 75
innateness, 218-9, 258
innovation, 72, 94, 225
instinct, 151, 176
institutions, 34, 38, 40, 111-4, 132, 149
instruction, 90-91, 95, 114
intentionality, first-order and second-order, 90-93, 95, 119
intrinsic universals, *See* universals: intrinsic
Inuit, 113, 140
invariance, 68, 147, 247, 256
invention, 93, 203, 224-5, 229. *See also* historical independence
Iser, Wolfgang, 80
isomorphisms, critique of, 205-8
Izard, Caroll E., 142, 214

J
Jackson, Michael, 207-8
Jacob, François, 66
Jaspers, Karl, 71
Jensen, Jürgen, 4, 48, 133, 165-6
joking, humor, 30
Jüttemann, Gerd, 182-4, 207
Jung, Carl G., 101

K
Kahn, Joel S., 51
Kant, Immanuel, 19, 75
Kay, Paul, 140, 160
Kearney, Michael, 120
Keesing, Felix, 42, 122
Keiter, Friedrich, 161
Keller, Albert G., 28-29
Keller, Rudi, 58, 87, 137, 218
Kellert, Stephen R., 135
Kidder, Alfred V., 28, 163
kinship, 108-11
Kluckhohn, Clyde K. M., 30-31, 35, 42, 45, 116, 170, 198
Kohlberg, Lawrence, 22, 115
Konner, Melvin, 34, 45, 194
Kottak, Conrad Philip, 40, 101, 109, 201, 225

Kroeber, Alfred L., 62, 161, 181, 188, 199
Küng, Hans, 24
Kuper, Adam, 46, 58-60

L
LaBarre, Weston, 227
marking, 118, 202
Lakoff, George, 129, 140, 250
landscapes, fondness for, 123, 135
language capacity, for, exemplifying relativism, 139
language universals. *See* universals: language
Lara Croft theories of history (assuming humans without culture), 72
Larsen, Charles, 250
Latour, Bruno, 5, 56, 72, 238, 258-261
Lautmann, Rüdiger, 42, 45, 150
Leach, Edmund R., 54, 71, 83-86, 110, 117, 119, 122, 164, 166, 194, 198, 211, 246
Lenk, Hans, 78-79, 85, 87, 129-30, 232
Lévi-Strauss, Claude, 17, 66-67, 117, 202, 225, 238
Lewis, Herbert, 251
  on canonization and radicalization of Geertz's views, 251
  on misrepresentation of anthropology within the discipline, 63, 251
  on universals at core of cultural anthropology, 63
Lickert scale, 147
linguistic universals. *See under* universals: linguistic
linguistics, comparative, 140-42, 197, 229
Linné, Carl von, 68, 78
Linton, Ralph, 42
lists of universals, catalogs, inventories, 30-31, 169-71, 173-178
  compared to narratives (*see under* Brown: Universal People, The)
  as only first step in research, 255-6
literature, 100-103, 152
living world, classification of (*bios*), 134, 136. *See also* ethnobiology
local knowledge
  as indigenous knowledge, 133-35, 208
  as a universal mode of knowledge, 136

logic, 129–30, 133, 232 (*see also* mathematics)
Lonner, Walter J., 32, 41, 191, 193, 199, 208–209, 246, 262
Lopreato, Joseph, 94, 123, 148, 150–52, 240
Lorenz, Konrad Z., 188, 206, 227
Lumsden, Charles J., 237
Lyotard, Jean-François, 17, 208

M
Machiavellian intelligence, 81, 92
magic, 30, 102, 121, 124, 151
making special, 103–4
male paternal investment, 95
Malik, Kenan, 1, 51, 70, 72, 134, 230, 234–6
Malinowski, Bronislaw K., 12–13, 31, 39, 55, 124, 168, 179, 184, 203, 207, 240, 246
Man. *See under* human, humankind, *homo sapiens*
marking, 118, 202
Markl, Hubert, 39, 47, 77, 84, 120, 162, 216–9
marriage, 166–8, 172, 202–3, 207, 222
Marx, Karl, 74, 82, 120, 257
mass media, 11–12, 143, 196, 260
mathematics, 87, 240, 250. *See also* logic
matrilocality, 183, 240
matrilineality, 183, 216
Maya, 68, 123, 214
Mayr, Ernst W., 222
McGrew, William, 86, 190
McNeill, William H., 146, 163, 226
Mead, Margaret, 144, 154
memory, 122, 128
    collective, 106, 259
    individual, as limited, 254–55
Mencius, 7
metaphor, 32–33, 44, 108, 120, 122, 140–41, 145
methods, 157–191. *See also* ethnography
    abduction, 159
    case study (*see under* cases: case study)
    comparative (*see under* comparison)
    deduction, philosophical arguments to find universals, 158–59, 184
    experiment, 105, 132, 144, 149, 163, 172, 181, 198, 232, 235
    induction, 68, 184
    retrodiction, 35
Miner, Horace, 53–4
modularity, 92
Moghaddam, Fathali M., 45, 107–8, 114, 144, 172–73
monograph, anthropological (ethnography), 55, 97, 170, 247. *See also* ethnography
morality, 108, 118, 124, 172, 195, 248. *See also* norms: education of social norms
Morris, Brian, 65, 125, 257
Moscovici, Serge, 261
muelos belief, 227
Müller, Johannes, 16
Müller, Klaus E., 4, 35, 42, 49–50, 87, 118, 207
Munroe, Robert L., 33, 56–57, 84, 131, 163, 182, 188
Munroe, Ruth H., 33, 56–57, 84, 131, 163, 182, 188
murder, homicide, 95, 116, 142, 147–48, 160
Murdock, George P., 28–32
    aiming at cultural diversity, 28–29 (*see also* Human Relations Area Files)
    catalog of universals, 30–31, 169–70, 174, 177
    Common Denominator, The, 29
    on cross-cultural similarities as one core of anthropology, 63
    definition of universals, 35, 40
    early relativist phase, 29
Murphy, Robert, 76
music, 106–7
Myers, David G., 45, 114–15, 146, 151–52
myth, mythology, 101, 102, 122

N
Nader, Laura, 56, 116
Naroll, Raoul, 22, 185
narrative structures, 99–100
natural history intelligence, 234
natural law, 115, 121
naturalism (ontology, epistemology), 205, 221, 233–38, 250
nature. *See also* human nature
    nature vs. culture antinomy, 61. (*see also* dualism)

nature vs. nurture, 48, 212, 220–21
near universal. *See* universals: near
Needham, Rodney, 164, 227
needs, 38–40
 basic, primary, biotic, 31, 159, 170, 229–30, 233, 240
 developmental, 237
 functional, 217
 in relation to universals, 39–40
 as societal prerequisites, 38, 217, 258–59 (*see also* ultrasociality)
negative universals. *See* universals: negative
nepotism, 148–49, 235
Nettl, Bruno, 106, 147
niche construction, 133
noesphere, related to ratchet effect, 93
norms, social
 education of social norms, using violence, 112–113
 normative ideas influencing research on universals, 16–18, 22–23, 54
nostrification, as danger of universalism, 179, 245

O
Obeyasekere, Gannanath, 149
Ochs, Elinor, 45, 48, 151, 159
Oedipus complex, 12–13, 32, 195, 207, 239
Opolka, Uwe, 33–34, 41–42, 47, 169, 174, 230
Ortega y Gasset, José, 74–75
Ortner, Sherry B., 240–41
Oswalt, Wendell H., 30
Othering, 48–49, 56, 250–51
Otto, Rudolf, 23
Overing, Joanna, 243
overview-effect, (view of the whole planet earth), 196

P
pancultural phenomena or patterns, 6–7, 37, 40–43, 65, 74, 105, 117, 219
pancultural universals. *See under* universals: pancultural
parallels cultural, 163–4
Parsons, Talcott, 124, 260–61
particularism, in relation to universalism, 54–55, 61–63, 212–13, 256, 262
patriarchal structures, power, 15, 240, 248
Paul, Gregor, 129

Payer, Margarete, 32, 174
performance, 106–7
Peoples, James G., 13, 40
Pinker, Steven, 12, 22, 32, 58–59, 81, 138, 148–49, 174, 220, 239
 catalog of universals, different versions of, 174, 178
 equating of likenesses with biology and differences with culture, 214
play, games playing, role-playing, 104, 106, 113, 236
political succession, 115
politeness, 31, 115, 146, 249
pornographic literature, 152
postcolonial and postmodern criticism, 6, 24, 52, 250–51
power, 46, 114–16, 124, 230, 240
prefrontal cortex, and language faculty, 88
primates
 cultural primatology, 89
 higher primates, 13, 20, 87
 nonhuman, 87–88, 90, 93, 148, 261–62
 primate characters in humans, 85–86
primitive people, deficit models of, 48–50. *See also* othering
principle of minimal effort, 229
product universals. *See under* universals: product
psychic unity of mankind, 22
psychology, 76, 239
 cross-cultural, 64, 180–84, 198–200, 204
 cultural, 62, 184
 social, 173
public societal debates, 8, 11–25

Q
questions, identity-related, 10
Quinn, Naomi, 54, 97, 111–14, 132

R
racism, 3, 70, 206, 251, 253
Rapport, Nigel, 243
ratchet effect, 93. *See also* tools, technologies: cognitive
rationality, 130, 133, 148–150
reasoning, 68, 159. *See also* cognition
reciprocity, 108, 110, 149
religion, 194, 199, 207, 225, 231, 236, 246

residence rules, 30
Richerson, Peter J., 5, 259
right hand, 123, 129, 202, 231
ritual, 128–29, 194, 199, 207, 225, 231, 236, 246
rule-making, 107. *See also* social norms

S

Sapir-Whorf hypothesis, 122
Sanderson, Stephen K., 174
Sartre, Jean-Paul, 79
Schiefenhövel, Wulf, 13, 23, 34, 46, 55, 91, 133, 145, 170–71
Scupin, Raymond, 34, 62, 173
selective model, 225. *See also* explanation: selectionist
semantic categories, 28. *See also* categorization
sex partners, 110, 153
sexual attractiveness, 142
sexual jealousy, 45, 153
shame, 36, 113–14, 142–45, 176
Sober, Elliott, 149, 191, 202, 220, 224
social axioms, 231
social complexity, 104, 121, 194–95, 214, 239, 259–60. *See also* ultrasociality
social constructivism, 58, 81, 208
social Darwinism, 74, 206
social exclusion, 100, 116, 161, 250
social exchange, 34, 99, 110–11, 151, 159, 216, 223, 238. *See also* reciprocity
social norms. *See under* norms, social
social role, 108–9, 114–15. *See also* family, and gender
social smiling, 37, 112, 145–46, 194, 107
social status, 30–31, 114–15, 176
social universals. *See under* universals: social
sociality, 3, 81–82, 86, 107–18. *See also* ultrasociality
space concepts, classification, 88, 122–23, 130
spandrels, 105. *See also* arbitrariness
species-typical vs. species-specific characteristics, 86, 90, 92–94
Spiro, Melford, 125, 165, 207–8, 239
Stagl, Justin, 5, 51, 58, 87, 179
statistical universals. *See* universals: statistical

Stegmüller, Wolfgang, 38
Stini, William A., 32, 48, 72, 167–69, 177
strangers, perception of and behavior towards, 10, 16, 146. *See also* ethnocentrism, *see also* xenophobia
Strathern, Andrew, 42, 122, 206–208
substantive universals. *See under* universals: substantial
political succession, 115
surface universals. *See* universals: surface
symbols, 56, 80. *See also* animal symbolicum, *see also* cultural anthropology: symbolic
  arbitrary vs. constrained, 88, 95, 230
  meta-symbols, 68
  widespread, 95, 129

T

taboos, 7, 30, 202, 223. *See also* incest: taboo
taxonomy of universals, 193–209. *See also* types of universals
terms and synonyms for universals. *See* universals: terms of, synonyms for
time concepts, 32, 122–23
Tooby, John, 41, 43, 235
tools, technologies, 13, 34, 87, 230
  cognitive, tools for thinking, 87
  as Gregorian creatures, 287 (*see also* ratchet effect)
Turner, Victor W., 244
turn taking, 107
types of universals (according to degrees of universality)
  absolute, vs. widespread, 60, 168–69, 176
  implicational, conditional, if-then universals, 260
  near, semi-universals, 35, 200, 260
  true, 200
  statistical, 201, 203
  widespread, vs. absolute, 45, 170

U

ubiquity, as not to be equated with genetic causes, 217
ultrasociality, 258–61
UNESCO man, concept of, 70–71
Universal Grammar (Chomsky N.), 178

universal history, 163, 261
universalism
    vs. absolutism, 207, 262
    anti-universalism, 53–54, 211
    criticism against, 243–52
    ethical, moral (deliberative, relative and others), 19
    fallacies of, 179, 212
    implicitly normative, 16–25 (see also norms, social)
    vs. particularism, 62
    relative, 18–19 (see also universals: negotiated)
    vs. relativism, 207
universalistic hegemony, 17, 247–251
universality, degree of, 200–2 (see also universals: absolute, near, statistical)
universals, human universals. See also factors causing universals, See also types of universals
    according to social psychology, 173
    alleged, 160
    application-oriented, 174
    biotic, 33 (see also ethological universals, human species traits)
    causes (see under factors causing universals)
    classification of (see taxonomy of universals)
    conditional (see under types of universals: implicational)
    deducted, 158
    deep, 232
    as defined in this book, 34
    definitions of, 32–35
    diachronic, as defined by Brown, 34
    by diffusion, 226
    emic, 176, 195
    essential, intrinsic, 195
    etic, 176, 195
    examples, 97–155
    exceptions to, 148, 162
    experiential, 229
    extrinsic, accidental, 195
    evolutionary (in T. Parsons' sense), 260–1
    fake, 103
    fallacies in research on, 212
    as family resemblance, 166
    formal, 24, 126, 176, 198 (see also Common Denominator, the in Murdock's sense)
    great ape universals, 188–90
    historically new, 228
    implicational (see under types of universals: implicational)
    in human ethology, vs. in anthropology, 36–37
    lists of, catalogues of, inventories of, 30–31, 169–71, 173–178, 255–6
    in narrative form vs. lists, 102–3
    negative, non-universals, 50, 172 (see also universals: alleged)
    negotiated, 18–19
    normative aspects in the search for, 7, 16–18, 22–23
    pancultural, 263
    as pool of elements, 204
    product, 202
    relevance for culture theory, 46, 66
    relevance for ethnographic research, 263
    as rich, 126
    social, micro- and macro-, 169, 195
    substantive, 31
    surface, 54
    taxonomy (kinds of universals), 193–210 (see also types of universals)
    terms of, synonyms for, 40–45
    transcultural, 34–35
    trivial, banal, 6–7, 12, 24, 38, 175, 212–13, 246
    vague, 246
    weak, 132
    as universal pattern, 30

V

variability, intracultural and interindividual, 94 184. See also diversity
violence and rape, as forced sexual violence, and condemnation of, 116, 148, 160, 191, 194
virgin birth, 127
Voland, Eckhart, 23, 48, 105

W

weather control, 30

WEIRD (Western, Educated, Industrial, Rich, Democratic) people, 2, 50
Welsch, Wolfgang, 5, 38, 46, 85, 91, 94, 200, 232, 238
Wernhart, Karl, 4, 41–42
Westermarck, Edward, 223. *See also* incest: explanations
Whorf, Benjamin Lee, 122
widely spread cultural traits. *See under* types of universals: widespread vs. absolute
Wierzbicka, Anna, 120, 122, 137, 141, 146, 149, 160, 168
Wilson, Edward O., 163, 216, 220, 225, 237, 258

Wissler, Clark, 30, 198, 214
word order, 137, 139
worldview, 119–123

X

xenophobia, 3. *See also* ethnocentrism, and strangers, perception of and behavior towards

Y

Yengoyan, Aram, 229

Z

Zipf, George K., 229, 254
Žižek, Slavoj, 59

www.ingramcontent.com/pod-product-compliance
Lightning Source LLC
Chambersburg PA
CBHW072143100526
44589CB00015B/2057